FUNDAMENTALS OF CRIMINOLOGY

2nd edition

FUNDAMENTALS OF CRIMINOLOGY

Henry W. Mannle

J. David Hirschel

PRENTICE HALL, Englewood Cliffs, NJ 07632

Library of Congress Cataloging-in-Publication Data

MANNLE, HENRY W.
    Fundamentals of criminology.

    Includes index.
    1. Crime and criminals. I. Hirschel, J. David.
II. Title.
HV6024.M36 1988   364   87–12786
ISBN 0–13–332552–0

Editorial/production supervision: Merrill Peterson
Manufacturing buyer: Lorraine Fumoso

© 1988, 1982 by Prentice Hall
A Division of Simon & Schuster
Englewood Cliffs, New Jersey 07632

Printed in the United States of America
10 9 8 7 6 5 4 3 2 1

ISBN 0-13-332552-0 025

Prentice-Hall International (UK) Limited, *London*
Prentice-Hall of Australia Pty. Limited, *Sydney*
Prentice-Hall Canada Inc., *Toronto*
Prentice-Hall Hispanoamericana, S.A., *Mexico*
Prentice-Hall of India Private Limited, *New Delhi*
Prentice-Hall of Japan, Inc., *Tokyo*
Simon & Schuster Asia Pte. Ltd., *Singapore*
Editora Prentice-Hall do Brasil, Ltda., *Rio de Janeiro*

To all of our parents . . .

Charlotte and Walter Mannle
and
John and Harriet Gentry

And

Antoinette and Saul Hirschel
and
Phenie and Mike Dreher

Contents

section 7   THE POLICE

Preface

Crime is a complex, multifaceted problem with seemingly more issues than answers. Acquiring a mastery of the subject requires a firm grasp of statistical procedures, research methodology, and theoretical constructs. Because of time restraints or insufficient preparation, this presents a formidable task for the beginning student or interested layperson. Unfortunately, many current textbooks confuse rather than clarify the issues by attempting to cover all of the bases.

This text is not designed to provide a complete exploration of criminology. It is, as the title indicates, an attempt to present the fundamentals. Statistics are used to illustrate relatively stable and broad trends, not as narrow or immutable facts in and of themselves. Research findings are sparingly selected for their capacity to enrich a given topic rather than to supply the introductory student with a working bibliography. Theoretical discussions are geared to providing readers with a general overview of past and present explanations of crime with a minimal use of abstract jargon. Finally, substantive areas dealing with offenses, offenders, the law, police, courts, corrections, and crime control are written to be informative through a concise, not exhaustive, coverage of subjects.

The book's format is also intended to facilitate comprehension. Each chapter outlines learning objectives, subdivides material at appropriate points, and provides learning checks. Instructors should encourage students to complete the chapter quizzes and reread troublesome material before advancing to the next chapter.

ACKNOWLEDGMENTS

The authors wish to acknowledge those who have assisted the project in one way or another. Heartfelt gratitude goes to our wives, Beth and Fran, for many long and frenzied hours of critiquing, inspiring and cajoling. And to Fran Hirschel, who undertook prime responsibility for much of the learning materials in this book, the authors are much indebted.

The scheduled completion of the manuscript would not have been possible without the skills and talents provided by Robin Greenwood. Recognition is also accorded to Cheryl Scott Brumley for her contributions to the project as well as the exemplary service given to the local judicial system by her and her mother, the late Mrs. Polly Scott. Our special thanks to Julia Horner, Betty Winters and the late Ted Winters and Edith Mannle for their timeless interest and encouragement. To our good friends, Professors Dennis Dorin and Peter Lewis, we extend our appreciation for their comments and suggestions. Likewise, acknowledgment is also due the reviewers, Gary R. Perlstein and Phillip Quinn, for their necessary and constructive input.

Finally, we wish to express sincere appreciation to our editor, Matt McNearney, and the staff at Prentice-Hall for their professional advice and guidance in the production of this manuscript.

Henry W. Mannle
and
J. David Hirschel

ABOUT THE AUTHORS

Henry W. Mannle is presently Professor of Criminology and Director of the Criminal Justice Program at Tennessee Technological University. J. David Hirschel is currently an Associate Professor of Criminal Justice at the University of North Carolina at Charlotte.

FUNDAMENTALS OF CRIMINOLOGY

1

Definition of Crime, Criminals, and Criminology

OBJECTIVES

After studying this chapter, the student should be able to:

- State a social definition, a strict legal definition, and a less rigid legal definition of crime.
- Define *corpus delicti* as well as the two major elements that form the *corpus delicti* of a crime.
- Compare common law and statutory law.
- Distinguish between crimes which are felonies or misdemeanors and crimes which are *mala in se* or *mala prohibita*.
- Define crime, criminal, and criminology according to the concepts that will be used in this book.

On a Friday evening, a man enters a "singles bar" and introduces himself to an attractive woman who has just seated herself at an adjoining table. After some drinks, an occasional dance, and much small talk, the conversation assumes sexual overtones. Both parties seem to be mutually interested in one another, and both appear to be free to discontinue their interaction at will. Responding to perceived cues, the man propositions the woman. The woman smiles and they leave, hand in hand, for the man's apartment.

During the same evening, another man walks into a lounge and strikes up a conversation with a woman seated next to him at the bar. After some drinks, occasional dances, and much small talk, the man's remarks begin to have sexual implications. As in the first instance, both individuals seem to be mutually interested in one another, and both appear to be free to part company at will. Responding to perceived cues, the man propositions the woman. The woman, however, frowns, announces that she is a vice officer, and that he is under arrest for soliciting for purposes of prostitution. This couple leaves, "hand in hand," for the nearest police precinct station.

In both cases we have two parties who are not acting under duress or force. In both cases we have an exchange of favors (dancing, buying of drinks, and so on). In both cases there is an apparent mutual interest in a potential sexual encounter. Nevertheless, in the latter case we might assume that the proposition included a more direct financial condition. This second episode also included an exchange involving a party with sworn arrest powers whose intention, unbeknownst to the man, was not to generate a sexual relationship.

Why is one situation possibly considered part of the "dating game" while the other may be dealt with as criminal behavior? Is it simply because the latter case involved money in exchange for sexual favors? If sex for money is the distinguishing feature, one could conceivably argue that some marriages between rich elderly men and young women should be classified as crimes.

Frequently what seems to be very clear and straightforward is, in fact, quite complicated. Arriving at a definition of crime is a difficult task. Defining a criminal act is much easier on an impersonal or abstract level than on a personal, case-by-case basis. For example, most of us would agree that the unjustifiable or inexcusable killing of a human being is a crime, that is, criminal homicide. Suppose, however, that the following circumstances have occurred:

> A recently divorced man meets his former wife who is pregnant by another man with whom she is currently living. The ex-husband says, "I hear you're pregnant. If you are, you had better stay away from the girls [their children] and from here." Upon a closer look at his wife, the former husband becomes angry and says, "You sure are [pregnant]. I'm going to stomp it out of you." He then kicks her in the abdomen and strikes her face several times. The unborn child is delivered by Caesarian section and is dead.
>
> Physicians later testify that the fetus [a girl]: (1) weighed 5 pounds and was 18 inches in length, (2) was 31½ to 36 weeks old [the average full-term pregnancy is approximately 40 weeks], (3) would have had a 75 percent to 96 percent chance of survival had it been prematurely born under normal conditions at the time of the alleged offense, and (4) died of a skull fracture with consequent cerebral hemorrhaging likely as a result of force applied to the mother's abdomen by her ex-husband.[1]

Given the circumstances described, has a criminal homicide taken place? What do you think?

This incident actually occurred some years ago in California. The prosecutor filed a charge of murder against the defendant, stating that the defendant did "unlawfully kill a human being . . . with malice aforethought." However, based on a writ of prohibition,[2] the California court subsequently ruled that the petitioner could not be charged with murder because he had not killed a human being. At the time of the alleged offense, California law stated that a fetus must be in the process of being born before it is considered a human being and is thus subject to the homicide statute. In this case, the fetus was not in the process of being born when attacked by the ex-husband.

DEFINITION OF CRIME

Before any problem can be systematically studied, it must be adequately defined. The criminologist's major concern over the definition of "crime" is the extent to which that definition affects the specific field of inquiry. If "crime" is too narrowly defined, then one's research will omit much of what should be studied. On the other hand, if "crime" is too broadly defined, then the term may become meaningless and lost in a sea of conflicting or overlapping concepts.

The Relative Nature of Crime

Crime is not absolute. Crime is relative. That is, what is a crime varies with time and place. There was a period when crime was not officially defined and criminal acts were handled through private vengeance. Justice was left to the concerned individuals. Punishment was intended to satisfy revenge. No outside parties acted as referees. Reactions to crime eventually passed from those of private vengeance to the kinship or blood revenge.

Blood feuds involved the administration of unspecified punishments by the victim's family or tribe against the offender's kinship group. Crimes as well as punishments were not typically codified under this system. The concept of crime and criminal law developed with the beginning of the state or monarchy.

At first, only acts against the monarch were considered crimes by the state. In the due course of events, the notion of collective state responsibility and financial compensation acted to eliminate private vengeance and blood feuds. Consequently, the state through the ruler's authority assumed the administration of justice by defining crimes, codifying laws, establishing fines, and implementing the jury system. The development of law in Western society is more fully explored in Section 6.

Today we have specific laws that pertain to income tax evasion and skyjacking. At the turn of the century such laws were nonexistent because there was no federal income tax and air piracy was not a problem for a nation that lacked a commercial airline industry. Likewise, our drug laws that make the possession or sale of certain substances a crime were unheard of prior to World War I.

In the past there have been laws making it a crime to teach blacks to read, to sell firearms to American Indians, and to teach the biological theory of evolution. Some rather curious, outdated laws still remain on the books in some states even though they are rarely enforced. According to Hyman's investigation, it is illegal (or was so until recently) to hunt or shoot camels in Arizona, to use a beanshooter in Arkansas, to slap a man on the back in Georgia, to whistle underwater in Vermont, to use a mule to hunt ducks in Kansas, to slurp soup in New Jersey, to lasso fish in Knoxville, Tennessee, and to race turtles within the city limits of Key West, Florida.[3]

Crime is also relative to place. What is against the law in one jurisdiction may be perfectly legal in another. Gambling, *per se*, is legal in Nevada, while other states permit only specific kinds of wagering (dog races, horse races, state lotteries) or none at all. Interestingly enough, even states which criminalize all forms of gambling do not prohibit playing the stock market.

Most jurisdictions consider the possession of marijuana in small amounts to be a minor misdemeanor. Some states classify possession of more than a few ounces as a felony (serious crime). On the other hand, Alaska permits cultivation of the drug for personal use.

Certain forms of sexual behavior are defined as crimes in some places but simply as private matters elsewhere. Prostitution, for example, is generally illegal except in Nevada, where it is permitted on a county-option basis. Though public attitudes toward homosexuality between consenting adults have become more liberal in recent years, some states continue to criminalize this behavior. Some jurisdictions label premarital sex, adultery and oral-genital sex as crimes, whereas other states view such conduct as simply a matter of personal discretion.

The Legal Definition of Crime

Behavior can be dealt with as criminal only when it violates a criminal law. Without a law, there can be no officially recognized crime. This is not to suggest that only acts prohibited by law are "wrong." Many individuals feel that some acts currently labeled as crimes should be legalized or that certain legal acts should be criminalized. The issue of what should or should not be a crime is different from that of what is a crime according to law. The political and social implications of lawmaking are more fully discussed in Section 6.

From a strict legal point of view, "a crime is an act or omission to act that endangers the public, is prohibited by the law, and is prosecuted and punished by the state." Criminal wrongs refer to those prohibited acts that harm the public. Civil wrongs (torts) refer to private injuries (e.g., slander, libel, injury caused by negligent driving) whereby the injured party (plaintiff) seeks protection of his or her civil rights or compensation for their violation.

The criminal law originates from two major sources: (1) common law, and (2) statutory law. The common law is that body of customs, precedents, and traditions that developed over time without formal legislative action. Following the Norman Invasion of 1066, the king's messengers began to communicate the results of criminal prosecutions occurring throughout England. As various cases were decided, certain legal principles emerged and became common to all jurisdictions. It is these principles that make up the common law. Criminal law in the United States has been greatly influenced by the English common law.

Statutory law includes those acts or omissions defined as crimes through the legislative process. The vast majority of states have criminal laws that are derived from both the English common law and statutory law. Some jurisdictions have incorporated the entire common law into statutory law. In others, the common law remains as a guide for interpreting the provision of certain statutes.

According to common law, some crimes were viewed as serious enough to merit such sanctions as the forfeiture of property or loss of life. Common law crimes considered grave enough to warrant such punishments were termed "felonies." Included among felonies were the crimes of murder, manslaughter, rape, robbery, burglary, larceny, arson, mayhem (dismemberment), and sodomy. The common law also specified less serious offenses known as misdemeanors. It further designated treason to be a crime apart from felonies and misdemeanors.

Today, several felonies have been added to the common law list by way of statutory law. The current major distinction between felonies and misdemeanors is the degree of punishment that the state specifies for the offense. For example, felonies are crimes that may result in a death penalty or imprisonment for more than one year. Misdemeanors typically provide for a maximum period of incarceration that does not exceed one year.

Crimes may be classified in a way other than as felonies versus misdemeanors. Acts which are "believed to be wrong in themselves, or naturally evil, or inherently dangerous to the public welfare" are termed *mala in se*. On the other hand, "acts prohibited by statute but not necessarily inherently wrong" are referred to as *mala prohibita*. Consequently, some statutory felonies may be classified as *mala in se* if they are considered to be wrong in themselves. Statutory misdemeanors are *mala prohibita*.

Before an alleged crime becomes a legal fact, the state must present a *prima facie* (at first view) case that a crime has, indeed, been committed. The "essential ingredients of a *prima facie* case" are known as the *corpus delicti*. The *corpus delicti* of an actual crime includes (1) *mens rea*, and (2) *actus reus*. *Mens rea* refers to "a criminal state of mind." The kind of *mens rea* that is necessary, however, varies with the nature of the offense. General *mens rea* is required for those crimes which list no specific state of mind and exists whenever the defendant did whatever he or she intended to do. Some crimes require a particular state of mind other than general *mens rea*. Some examples of specific *mens rea* are intent, knowledge, recklessness, and negligence.

Actus reus, the second major element of the *corpus delicti*, "refers to the actual occurrence of a criminal act." One may not be punished merely for thinking about committing a crime. The criminal act may be one of commission, or the criminal act may be one of omission to do something, where possible, when a legal duty to act exists. For example, X, a superior swimmer, accidentally rams his boat into Y's boat causing it to sink. If X makes no rescue attempt, X may be criminally liable for Y's drowning even though X had no intention of causing harm to Y.

Regarding the association between *mens rea* and *actus reus*, the law requires that the criminal act (*actus reus*) must have resulted from the criminal state of mind (*mens rea*). Basically, this means that there is no true crime where an innocently committed act occurs prior to the criminal state of mind. Finally, the *actus reus* must have legally caused the injurious results that led to the criminal charge. Essentially this means that the relationship between the act and the resulting consequences must have been reasonably direct.

The Social Definition of Crime

When crime is defined socially rather than legally, the term usually takes on a much broader meaning. A social definition of crime, rather than a legal definition, is more likely to allow for ethical considerations of what should or should not be criminal behavior. One example of a social concept of crime is a definition stating that crime is "antisocial behavior that is injurious to those social interests which rules of behavior (including legal codes) are designed to support." [4] Under such a definition it would be possible to include present drug marketing practices that are legal but, according to some people, injurious to the public and thus criminal in nature.

Shaw notes, for example, that large drug companies take advantage of patent laws through a technique known as *molecular manipulation*. This practice involves juggling the chemical structure of a medicine just enough to qualify for a patent on a "new" drug. The more recent drug may, in fact, have essentially the same healing properties as the original compound. By using molecular manipulation, however, one parent company may get a monopoly and price-fixing advantage on a large grouping of related medicines. [5]

Social definitions of crime may also serve to emphasize its political nature. Pursuing this approach, some people have proposed that crime should be defined on the basis of social morality rather than legalistic criterion. Accordingly, it has been observed that the use of legal definitions of crime has resulted in criminologists overlooking injurious acts that are not specifically prohibited by criminal law. Quinney and Wildeman advocate this position in stating that:

> Criminal behavior, according to critical analysis, is best conceptualized not as simply that behavior that the law so defines; for this is far too simplistic an interpretation of our social experience. Criminal behavior is formulated as behavior that results in social injury, social injury arising, for example, from the denial of the right to racial, sexual, and economic equality. [6]

Consequently, a broad sociopolitical definition of crime would categorize as criminal behavior such "immoral" acts as racial injustice, sexual discrimination and international aggression. [7]

The social definition of crime also raises the question of the imperfect nature of our legal system. Suppose an individual commits a crime but is not caught. Would we still have a crime? Or, if caught, suppose the guilty defendant "beats the rap." Has a crime still taken place? In these instances, we would not have a criminal according to a strict legal definition because the violator has not been prosecuted and convicted. However, using a social definition, one could correctly assume both that a crime has been committed and that a criminal exists regardless of the legal outcome.

Strict legal definitions confine crime to those acts (*acta rea*) which are all of the following (1) harmful, (2) forbidden by criminal law, (3) committed by an offender possessing the necessary state of mind (*mens rea*), (4) causally related to the resulting harm, and (5) prosecuted and punished by the state. If a criminologist's study were limited to acts meeting these criteria, his or her knowledge about crime would indeed be slight. Other legal definitions of crime are less narrow in not insisting on the requirement of formal legal processing. Sutherland has thus defined crime as "behavior which is prohibited by the State as an injury to the State and against which the State may react, at least as a last resort, by punishment." [8]

As indicated in our discussion, various social definitions of crime provide for even broader possible meanings of the concept. According to Sellin, a definition of crime should be based upon those acts which violate basic rules or "conduct norms" that "arouse(s) a group reaction." [9] Expressed in terms of conduct norms, crime may be defined as

> an act by a member of a given social group, which by the rest of the members of that group is regarded as so injurious or as showing such a degree of antisocial attitude in the actor that the group publicly, overtly and collectively reacts by trying to abrogate (abolish) some of his rights. [10]

Regardless of the range of actions encompassed (narrow or broad) by legal or social definitions, both perspectives dwell on the notion of behavior as a focal point. Hartjen has sought a compromise between these two positions by observing that behavior, *per se*, does not determine criminality. [11] Rather, it is the process of attaching a criminal label to someone that is crucial to the criminologist. For purposes of counting, classifying, and analyzing crime officially recognized by the state, some variant of a legal definition is appropriate. However, for purposes of studying the complex phenomenon that we call crime, the following definition is appropriate:

> Crime is a socially recognized status constructed by societal members or their representatives in the course of labeling someone as a criminal. [12]

DEFINITION OF THE CRIMINAL

A strict legal definition would limit the "criminal" label to those who have been convicted of a crime. As noted previously, however, many crimes go undetected, and many criminals go unapprehended and unconvicted. On the other hand, a broad social definition could result in the criminal label being assigned to anyone who does anything felt to be offensive to the subjective observer.

Behavior itself does not constitute crime. Actions taken by authorized others against the individual determine who becomes a criminal. Rather than relying upon the legal or social boundaries of criminal behavior, the examination of crime as social status should be our starting point. Thus, crime viewed as a social status directs us to explore the process of being labeled a criminal.

The crime-as-status approach encourages the criminologist to consider those forces that operate when assigning the criminal label to certain acts and actors while overlooking the actions of others that may merit, legally or socially, similar treatment. The notion of crime as a status also beckons the criminologist to study those forces that lead to the creation of new classes of criminals. That is, behavior of special interest groups that sponsor legislation making certain previously legal activities a crime (e.g., prohibition) becomes a key interest to one who interprets crime as a label. Consequently, this book will adopt the following definition:

> A criminal is one who is given his or her status by those in society that have the legal or political power to establish the label as a social fact.

DEFINITION OF CRIMINOLOGY

The study of crime includes many related areas. Quite often, the layperson thinks of a criminologist as one who appears at a crime scene with a magnifying glass in one hand and a solution of ninhydrin powder and acetone in the other (a chemical that is commonly used to pick up latent fingerprints). That part of criminology which focuses upon the analysis of physical evidence is known as criminalistics. It is simply one subarea of criminology; it is not criminology *per se*.

Criminology also includes the study of etiological (causal) variables related to criminal behavior. In this sense, the traditional approach has been that of attempting to identify those factors which cause individuals to commit crime. Consequently, sociologists and criminologists have devoted much of their energy to the study of criminals and the methods of correcting or treating such behavior (penology). Unfortunately, sufficient answers to questions regarding cause and solution have not been forthcoming.

Within the past decade, criminology has enlarged its field of inquiry to include an analysis of the process of creating and applying criminal definitions to selected members of society. In this respect, criminology has become more meaningful by redirecting its focus to the "why, where, when, and how" of crime rather than simply the criminal who is the product of this process. Moreover, in a very real sense, criminology is no longer primarily the scientific study of crime and criminals but a humanistic discipline as well. By being humanistic, it is meant that criminologists should also concern themselves with (1) the advancement of basic human rights, (2) the study of crime at all social and institutional levels, and (3) the search for responsible solutions that are neither repressive nor motivated by self-serving interests. Criminology may thus be defined as the scientific and humanistic study of the social process of identifying crime, criminals, and compatible solutions.

SUMMARY

Establishing an acceptable definition of crime, criminals, and criminology is a difficult task. The foremost concern of the criminologist is that of arriving at a definition of crime that will give meaning to his or her research efforts. Concepts which are too narrow critically restrict the study of crime. Conceptualizations which are too broad may result in confusion and ambiguous research. No definition of crime is completely satisfactory to all who are concerned with this particular social problem.

This chapter has attempted to point out the shortcomings of various suggested legal and social definitions of crime. As a compromise, a definition of crime was adopted based upon the notion of crime as a status resulting from a social process involving the actions of authorized agents against selected individuals. Further, the definition established for crime formed the basis of a definition of criminals and criminology.

SUGGESTED ACTIVITIES

- Using different criminology textbooks, compare and contrast three definitions for each of the following: (1) crime, (2) criminals, and (3) criminology.
- Obtain a copy of your state's criminal code (prosecutors and other practicing attorneys usually have copies available). Determine (1) whether your state has incorporated the common law into statutory law, and (2) the number of additional felonies and misdemeanors, if any, since the code's last revision.
- Identify three of the more troublesome types of illegal activities in your area and discuss the advantages and disadvantages of basing research on legal and social definitions of crime.
- Carefully read your local newspaper for one week. Cut out all articles relating to illegal activities (or alleged illegal behavior) and group them according to crimes which you feel are felonies or misdemeanors. Compare your selections with other students' and your state's criminal code.

REVIEW

A. Define crime using a strict legal definition.

B. Define the terms *mala in se* and *mala prohibita*.

C. Define the terms *corpus delicti*, *mens rea*, and *actus reus*.

D. Define crime using a social definition.

E. Define crime, criminal, and criminology using the preferred definitions given in this chapter.

F. Discuss the importance of selecting a definition of crime for purposes of criminological research.

G. Multiple Choice. Select the best answer.

1. The notion of private vengeance involved:
   a. only the concerned parties
   b. specific punishments
   c. prosecution by the state
   d. trial by a jury of peers

2. In a strict legal sense, behavior can become criminal only when:
   a. reported to the police
   b. a suspect is arrested
   c. a defendant is convicted
   d. it violates a provision of the criminal law

3. All crimes that result from formal legislative definition are said to be part of:
    a. constitutional law
    b. common law
    c. tort law
    d. statutory law

4. The English common law did not include which of the following crimes?
    a. mayhem
    b. sodomy
    c. vagrancy
    d. arson

5. Acts considered to be "naturally evil" or "wrong in themselves" are typically termed:
    a. *mala prohibita*
    b. *mala in se*
    c. *actus reus*
    d. *corpus delicti*

6. Criminal state of mind is termed:
    a. *mala in se*
    b. *actus reus*
    c. *mala prohibita*
    d. *mens rea*

7. A particular state of mind required in addition to general intent for some crimes is termed:
    a. general *mens rea*
    b. specific *mens rea*
    c. volitional *mens rea*
    d. *actus reus*

8. This chapter proposes that crime should be viewed or defined:
    a. as a social status arising from the actions of authorized others against the individual
    b. in strict legal terms
    c. in social terms
    d. as having no legal basis

9. Crime is:
    a. absolute
    b. unchanging
    c. free from politics
    d. relative to time and place

REFERENCES

1. Keeler v. Superior Court, 2 Cal. 3d. 619, 87 Cal. Rptr. 481, 470 P.2d. 617 (1970).
2. An order from a superior court to prevent an inferior court from determining an issue that is not in its jurisdiction. In this case the petitioner (Mr. Keeler) contended that he did not kill a human being according to California law and "that the courts of the state did not have the power to broaden the definition of murder so as to include the killing of an unborn but viable fetus." See Wayne R. LeFave and Austin W. Scott, Jr., *Criminal Law* (St. Paul: West, 1972), 68. It should be noted that California now defines the "unlawful killing of a human being, or a fetus (except in cases of abortion), with malice aforethought" as murder. Most states, however, follow the common law rule that the killing of an unborn baby (fetus) is not homicide. See Thomas J. Gardner, *Criminal Law: Principles and Cases* (St. Paul: West, 1985), 258–259.
3. Dick Hyman, "It's Against the Law," *Readers Digest,* 1971 (reprint).
4. Elmer H. Johnson, *Crime Correction and Society* (Homewood, Ill.: Dorsey Press, 1968), 13, cited from George L. Wilber, "The Scientific Adequacy of Criminological Concepts," *Social Forces*, 28 (1949), 170.

5. Philip Shaw, ''The Privileges of Monopoly Capitalism: Market Power in the Ethical Drug Industry,'' *The Review of Radical Political Economics*, 2 (1970) in Warner Modular Publications, 105.
6. Richard Quinney and John Wildeman, *The Problem of Crime* (New York: Harper and Row, 1977), 8.
7. Raymond J. Michalowski, *Order, Law, and Crime* (New York: Random House, 1985), 314–318.
8. Edwin H. Sutherland, *White Collar Crime* (New York: Holt, Rinehart and Winston, 1949), 31.
9. Thorsten Sellin, ''A Sociological Approach to the Study of Crime Causation,'' in Marvin E. Wolfgang, Leonard Savitz, and Norman Johnson (eds.), *The Sociology of Crime and Delinquency* (New York: John Wiley, 1962), 7.
10. J. Makarewicz, *Einfuhrung in die Philosophie des Strafrechts*. (Stuttgart: Enke, 1906), 79–80.
11. Clayton A. Hartjen, *Crime and Criminalization* (New York: Holt, Rinehart and Winston/Praeger, 1978), 225.
12. *Ibid.*, 9.

2

Significance
of the Crime Problem

After studying this chapter, the student should be able to:

- Identify five major categories of crime and give examples of each.
- Discuss the extent or impact of the five major types of crime in general terms.
- Discuss crime as a social issue and as a public policy issue.
- Discuss the relationship between crime and the media.

People today are very much aware of a crime problem. Crime is one of the few issues that holds a lingering grip on the public's consciousness. Recent opinion polls and media stories even suggest that ours is a crime-prone society. The problem not only is sizable but also covers a broad range of behavior.

NATURE OF CRIME

A crime typology represents an attempt to organize the many different kinds of offenses into meaningful categories. Criminologists have developed several typologies. A large number of these typologies have been of criminals rather than of crimes. Obviously, one cannot separate completely the concept of crime from that of the criminal. A particular actor (criminal) is required for the commission of a particular offense (crime). Typologies of criminals may be very complex. They are commonly based on legal, individualistic, or social characteristics. For example, Gibbons and Clinard and Quinney have developed rather elaborate criminal typologies based on behavior systems.[1]

A fundamental typology of crime would be one that groups offenses according to broad characteristics of the illegal acts. This, necessarily, means that some of the categories will overlap. However, no typology will find completeness. No single typology is likely to emerge as being uniformly accepted by criminologists. As Clinard and Quinney note, "Since there will continue to be a multitude of purposes, including levels of analysis and degrees of generality, there will be a number of typologies." [2]

One major purpose of this chapter is to classify crimes as they are commonly referred to by criminologists, the media, and/or in the professional literature. The following typology is simply a guideline designed to give some structure to the wide array of criminal activity. Thus, the five general categories (types) of crime are: *street crime*, *victimless crime*, *organized crime*, *occupational and career-oriented crime*, and *politically oriented crime*.

Street Crime

Crimes commonly committed against persons or property and labeled by the Federal Bureau of Investigation (FBI) as Index offenses are generally termed "street crimes." This does not mean that they are always actually committed on some street. Many occur in commercial or private buildings. The term simply refers to the fact that these crimes are routine, everyday occurrences often, although not always, involving unsophisticated offenders from the "streets" rather than from corporate boardrooms and crime syndicates. Crimes against the person involve violence or an immediate potential for violence. Classified as violent (against the person) street crimes are criminal homicide, aggravated assault, forcible rape, and robbery. Property offenses comprise the remainder of street crimes. Included in this area are the crimes of burglary, larceny, motor vehicle theft, and arson. Street crimes, directed against persons or property, are widely feared by the public. There is strong community agreement that street crimes are a significant threat to the social order. Federal, state, and local governments devote much of their law enforcement time and budget to street crime matters.

Victimless Crimes

Transactions between two or more willing parties concerning the sale or purchase of desired, but illegal, goods or services are referred to as victimless crimes or consensual crimes. The question as to whether any crime is actually victimless remains unanswered. Taking a broad view, all crime produces some form of direct or indirect social harm. That is, society is the victim. Gambling, for example, may result in the siphoning of funds from more worthy causes (food for the hungry, housing, and education). The real question is whether behavior involving willing individuals who often "do not see themselves as victims" should be treated as crime.[3] Unlike street crime, victimless crimes (gambling, prostitution, illicit drug usage and distribution, homosexuality, vagrancy, drunkenness, and so on) are not, as a group, widely and uniformly feared by the public. The law enforcement response to victimless crimes has not been consistent. In general, the illicit drug trade has been subject to more severe and sustained police activity than has illegal gambling, or prostitution, for that matter.

Organized Crime

Several definitions of organized crime have appeared in the literature of criminology.[4] Because of its operational and economic features, the concept of organized crime overlaps considerably with that of white-collar crime. Nevertheless, criminologists have tended to treat organized crime and white-collar crime as separate types.[5] This distinction is appropriate provided that one (1) adopts the notion that white-collar crime exclusively includes the whole range of business-related crimes (phony automobile repair bills to corporate price fixing), and (2) views organized crime as principally the work of criminal societies such as the Mafia. However, if one focuses upon the economic and structural dimensions of organized crime, it becomes clear that much of white-collar crime is organized crime. Accordingly, one definition of organized crime that reflects this approach is the following:

> Organized crime consists of illegal acts, executed by five or more producers with varying degrees of participation, to directly or indirectly secure a system of recurring financial rewards through the provision of goods and services for consumer groups differing in size and knowledge of involvement.[6]

This definition would include white-collar crime at its most sophisticated level, illegal corporate behavior, as a major part of organized crime. The definition also includes criminal societies. Because several of the activities of organized crime societies (e.g., gambling) receive at least unofficial public support, prolonged, severe sanctions against them are uncommon. Due to their influence and respectable image, corporate criminal alliances have largely escaped the "strong arm of the law."

Occupational and Career-Oriented Crime

Occupational and career-oriented crime refers to illegal acts committed in the course of one's legitimate occupation (some of which are commonly termed "white-collar crimes") or sustained involvement in specialized forms of conventional crime. Generally speaking, shady business practices, crimes of the professions (medicine and law), and "career-oriented" criminal behavior (con games, pickpocketing, counterfeiting, shoplifting, and the like) fall within the range of this fourth type of crime. In addition, some kinds of street crime may fit into the career-oriented crime category (e.g., "professional" robbers, burglars) depending upon the degree of expertise and professionalization characteristic of the offenders.

Social reaction to this type of crime has been mixed. Low visibility combined with the victim's embarrassment (as in the case of con games) and minimal penetration by law enforcement have produced public apathy. Occasionally, however, such episodes as large-scale bank embezzlements or highly publicized health care rip-offs by physicians arouse demands for legal action.

Political Crime

One of the more difficult concepts in criminology is that of political crime. In the 1960s and early 1970s, several offenders were termed "political prisoners." The law, however, does not specify offenses that are political versus those that are nonpolitical. It is not a crime to desire money for a particular political movement. It is a crime to commit an armed robbery for the movement as it would be to rob a bank in order to send your kid brother to medical school. Thus, in a legal sense, so-called political prisoners find themselves in prison not for their radical political beliefs but because of their conviction for a felony regardless of any political motivation.

Since the law prohibits attacks on those values officially held by politically dominant groups (private property, heterosexuality, sobriety, etc.), violations of such values (theft, homosexuality, drunkenness, etc.) may be broadly viewed as political crimes. Further, as citizens become more removed from the lawmaking process, as legislation becomes a function of powerful interest groups, then crime (in general) begins to assume a more distinct political overtone.[7]

Basically, then, all crimes are relatively political in nature in that they represent a challenge to dominant values expressed politically in the law. However, when the criminal's attack (be it in the form of murder, hijacking, or terrorism) is directed toward a society's total value system or a basic institution (e.g., capitalism) then it may be termed an "absolute" political crime.[8] As noted by Clinard and Quinney, political crimes may include illegal acts by the government (violations of such values as "due process") as well as illegal acts against the government.[9]

COST OF CRIME

The social and economic costs of crime are quite high. Over two decades ago, the President's Commission estimated the cost of street crime to be about $1.5 billion.[10] Considering the effects of inflation over the years, the Commission's estimate is obviously far short of today's costs. Losses due to robbery, burglary, larceny, auto theft, and arson are now estimated to be $11 billion.[11] This figure, of course, does not include the psychological toll extracted from the victims of predatory crime and serious property offenses. Crime has other costs, such as those required to foster public safety and offender-related services. Thus, according to a recent analysis, federal, state, and local governments spend almost $25 billion annually on police and correctional services.[12]

These expenses also include the high costs of processing victimless crimes such as public drunkenness, narcotics investigations, and illegal gambling operations. Much of the latter categories, of course, overlap with organized crime syndicate activities. To this must be added the losses sustained by victims of crime, be it Index offenses, computer fraud, con games or inflated health insurance premiums resulting from fraudulent medical care. Here, estimates represent only the tip of the iceberg [13] since victim surveys reveal that so much crime goes unreported and undetected. [14]

Finally, there are substantial costs related to technological and security innovations required to combat crime. As Quinney notes, crime fighting has become a growth industry. Over $15 billion are spent annually on private police services. [15] On an international level, the alarming rise in the number of politically motivated skyjackings has produced dramatic, though unfortunately sometimes insufficient, restructuring of airport security systems. The endless possibilities for acts of piracy, as evidenced by the takeover of an Italian cruise ship in the fall of 1985, suggest further spiraling costs in terms both of dollar amounts and of a restriction of the sense of freedom of movement that we have taken for granted.

CRIME AS A SOCIAL AND PUBLIC POLICY ISSUE

The social consequences of crime have long been recognized. Scholars and public figures alike have commented on the problem and have suggested responses to it. Almost three centuries ago one historian described seventeenth century London in the following terms:

> When the evening closed in, the difficulty and danger of walking about London became serious indeed. . . . Thieves and robbers plied their trade with impunity; yet they were hardly as terrible for peaceful citizens as another class of ruffians. It was a favorite amusement of dissolute young gentlemen to swagger by night about the town, breaking windows, upsetting sedans, beating quiet men, and offering rude caresses to pretty women. [16]

Similar accounts exist regarding American cities of the eighteenth and nineteenth centuries. More recently, a book by a former attorney general of the United States includes this introductory statement:

> The crucial test of American character will be our reaction to the vastness of crime and turbulence in which we live. It will not be an easy test. The obvious instinctive reaction is repressiveness. It will not work. You cannot discipline this turbulent, independent, young mass society as if it were a child. Repression is the one clear course toward irreconcilable division and revolution in America. The essential action is to create a wholesome environment. Healthy people in a just and concerned society will not commit significant crime. [17]

Throughout history and around the world, societies have feared the threat of internal destructive forces. Thus, at the core of statements about the crime problem is the notion that it attacks the basic foundations of society. By the same token, the deeper political meanings of this social problem have not gone unnoticed. Authoritarian governments have outwardly identified crime as a direct challenge to the ruling political regime. On the other hand, democratic governments tend to link crime to attacks against individual freedoms such as the "right to life, liberty and the pursuit of happiness." Although a dominant social issue for some time, crime did not become a major public policy issue in the United States until the 1960s.

In the 1960s, several of the nation's main streets erupted in the wake of intense civil disorders. During this period, a president had been assassinated; student activism surfaced on campuses; an unpopular war (Vietnam) was on the horizon; and the civil rights movement was gaining increased national attention. In 1964, for the first time, "law and order" became a prime issue in a presidential election. Barry Goldwater introduced the issue but lost the election. However, renewed urban riots, alarming increases in street crime, and juvenile delinquency acted to reinforce Goldwater's campaign issue. The incumbent, Lyndon Johnson, realized that Goldwater had touched a sensitive nerve in the public. By way of an executive order, Johnson created the President's Commission on Law Enforcement and the Administration of Justice in the summer of 1965.

The Commission transferred its findings into public policy with the enactment of the Omnibus Crime Control and Safe Streets Act of 1968. One of its provisions called for the creation of the Law Enforcement Assistance Administration (LEAA). Between 1969 and 1980, LEAA spent almost $8 billion on action projects aimed at reducing street crime through prevention and control. LEAA has been dismantled and the level of federal funding for such projects has been cut to a trickle. Still, as already noted, governments continue to spend billions of dollars sustaining the criminal justice system each year.

CRIME AND THE MEDIA

One of the more powerful influences on our attitudes about crime is the news media. A few years ago, newspapers in New York City focused upon the plight of senior citizens at the hands of young thugs. Incensed over this rising tide of violence against the elderly, the public pressured city officials for remedial action. Soon, the national media seized upon the story. In fact, there was no such crime epidemic, although many people believed there was one. Violent crimes against the elderly that year had increased no more than had those against other age groupings.[18]

Television and the newspapers frequently cite official crime statistics with few explanations as to how the data are gathered and what the nature of possible errors is. Further, the relationship between the amount of crime and important social variables (age, sex, race, income level, etc.) of the population are absent from reports. Of equal concern is the point that the news media tend to portray crime in narrow terms. Except for occasional special reports, the media concentrate their attention primarily on street crime.

The coverage of street crime is often dependent upon this type of crime's sensationalistic value. As with any story, some crimes are more interesting than others are. Roshier has concluded that there are four factors which influence the decision to select certain offenses for media reporting: the crime's seriousness, its humor or irony content, the dramatic circumstances regarding the victim, and the involvement of prominent individuals.[19]

Crime is also a central topic of the entertainment media. Each season, the television industry trots out a new lineup of "good guys" who do battle against the forces of evil. Some programs attempt to imitate day-to-day law enforcement by emphasizing police patrol functions. By and large, however, the public is more likely to be exposed to the feats of fictional heroes or heroines than to the daily routine of police activity.

Much like news accounts, the entertainment media often misrepresent the diverse nature of crime. Dominick analyzed prime-time programming in one northeastern city and found that (1) television shows depict mostly crimes of violence; that is, few programs devoted attention to corporate crime or "garden variety" property offenses; (2) television "bad guys" tended to be white, middle class, and young adults; that is, few crimes were committed by young blacks or those with political motivations; (3) television crime episodes tended to support the myth that "crime doesn't pay"; that is, the criminals always got caught during the last five minutes of the show; and (4) television justice usually ended with the suspect's apprehension; that is, rarely were viewers taken through the machinery of justice (initial appearance, preliminary hearing, arraignments, and so forth).[20]

A final note about crime and the entertainment media centers around the nature of law enforcement tactics. In his study of police programs, Dominick discovered that only 11 percent of the television police officers used illegal or quasi-legal crime fighting methods. On the other hand, Katsh and Arons noted that many television police officers solve crime by: (1) committing crimes themselves (breaking and entering, theft, assault, and fraud), and (2) ignoring constitutional guarantees of due process (failing to present search warrants when required, coercing confessions, and failing to give *Miranda* warnings when necessary).[21] According to Katsh and Arons, such shows may lead viewers to subconsciously support the proposition that the ends (crime fighting) justify the means (police crime and constitutional abuses).

SUMMARY

Crime represents a broad cross section of human behavior. It is difficult to categorize crime into meaningful general types. Different kinds of offenses share similar characteristics. Nevertheless, there are five types of crime based on references among criminologists, in the professional literature, and the media. Offenses may be grouped into the five categories of street crime, victimless crime, organized crime, occupational and career-oriented crime, and politically oriented crime.

Crimes of various types have an enormous impact on our daily lives. The volume of street crime has risen dramatically in the past decade. Law enforcement personnel expend a significant amount of time and energy pursuing victimless crimes. Organized crime (at all levels) draws large sums of money from the legitimate marketplace each year. Occupational and career-oriented crime is on the increase as society becomes more impersonal and technological thus creating indifference and criminal opportunities. Crimes that spring from political motivations have altered our life-styles through increased security measures and decreased freedom of movement. Thus, crime generates considerable social and economic costs in any given year.

Academics and politicians alike have stated the social significance of crime, past and present. However, crime did not become a public policy issue until the 1960s. Due to intense civil unrest and shocking increases in street crime and juvenile delinquency, Lyndon Johnson created the President's Commission on Law Enforcement and the Administration of Justice in 1965. Now-defunct federal agencies, such as LEAA, pumped large sums of money into state and local crime fighting projects through action grants.

In recent years, the media have focused a great deal of attention on crime. While much of the content is informative and revealing, there is a tendency for news coverage to be superficial, narrow, or sensational. Further, the theme of crime has become a major source of entertainment. In an effort to reach the mass audience, television crime shows frequently depart from the broad reality of crime.

SUGGESTED ACTIVITIES

- Read the "Crime" or "Justice" sections of *Newsweek* or *Time* magazine for one month. Categorize the crimes discussed as street crime, victimless crime, organized crime, occupational and career-oriented crime, or politically oriented crime.
- Watch five crime-related television shows and analyze their content in terms of: (1) type of crime(s) committed, (2) characteristics of the criminals, (3) outcome, and (4) police behavior.
- Arrange an appointment with a representative of your local Chamber of Commerce to discuss the nature and extent of organized or business-related crime in the community. You may also wish to contact your local Better Business Bureau.
- Check your local newspaper for movie advertisements. What percentage of the motion pictures currently playing deal primarily with crime and/or violence?
- Contact your state's crime commission or law enforcement planning agency (usually located in a state's capital city). Identify and discuss five crime prevention or control programs presently under way in your state or local community.

REVIEW

A. List five major categories (types) of crime.
B. Discuss what is meant by a criminal typology.
C. Give a definition of organized crime.
D. Define the term victimless crime.
E. List four content characteristics of television police shows as cited in a study by Dominick.
F. Multiple Choice. Select the best answer.
1. Which of the following would not be classified as a street crime according to the typology discussed in this section?
        a. forcible rape
        b. aggravated assault

      c. murder

      d. prostitution

2. Organized crime:

      a. does not resemble forms of white-collar crime

      b. is carried out only by ''crime societies''

      c. resembles some forms of white-collar crime

      d. is decreasing in volume

3. Social reaction has been strongest regarding which types of crime?

      a. occupational crime

      b. street crime

      c. organized crime

      d. victimless crime

4. Which of the following would best be considered an example of organized crime?

      a. corporate price-fixing

      b. auto repair swindles

      c. computer crimes

      d. health care frauds

5. An ''absolute'' political crime is one that:

      a. involves public officials

      b. includes both theft and violence

      c. is directed toward a society's total value system or basic institutions

      d. is never prosecuted

6. Federal legislation drafted to support the President's Commission on Law Enforcement and the Administration of Justice:

      a. Wayne-Falkner Act

      b. Law Enforcement Bill

      c. Graham Bill

      d. Omnibus Crime Control and Safe Streets Act

7. LEAA:

      a. was proposed by Goldwater

      b. is no longer in existence

      c. was never approved by Congress despite public pressure

      d. still operates, but with substantially reduced funding

8. Media reporting of crime statistics frequently omits:

      a. *Uniform Crime Reports*

      b. sensational stories

      c. social variables that affect crime rates

      d. accounts of street crime

9. According to Katsh and Arons, television crime shows:

      a. are too realistic

      b. display crimes committed by the police

      c. are actually not popular with the police

      d. are infrequently viewed by the public

REFERENCES

1. Don C. Gibbons, *Society, Crime, and Criminal Careers*, 2nd ed. (Englewood Cliffs, N.J.: Prentice-Hall, 1977); Marshall B. Clinard and Richard Quinney, *Criminal Behavior Systems* (New York: Holt, Rinehart and Winston, 1973).
2. *Ibid.*, 14.

3. Gilbert Geis, "The Criminal Justice System without Victimless Crimes," in Peter Wickman and Phillip Whitten (eds.) *Readings in Criminology* (Lexington, Mass.: D. C. Heath, 1978).

4. Peter Reuter, *Disorganized Crime* (Cambridge, Mass.: MIT Press, 1983), 175.

5. See, for example, Joseph F. Sheley, *America's "Crime Problem"* (Belmont, Calif.: Wadsworth, 1985), 123–131.

6. Henry W. Mannle, "Organized Crime: Business as Usual," in Jack Wright and Peter Lewis (eds.) *Modern Criminal Justice* (New York: McGraw-Hill, 1977), 57. The number "five" was chosen to reflect legal boundaries established by the Crime Control Act of 1970.

7. Stephen Schafer, "The Relativity of Political Crimes," in Stephen Schafer (ed.) *Readings in Contemporary Criminology* (Reston, Va.: Reston, 1976), 75.

8. *Ibid.*, 77.

9. Clinard and Quinney, *op. cit.*, 155–166.

10. President's Commission on Law Enforcement and the Administration of Justice, *The Challenge of Crime in a Free Society* (Washington, D.C.: U.S. Government Printing Office, 1967), 33.

11. Federal Bureau of Investigation, *Uniform Crime Reports, 1984* (Washington, D.C.: U.S. Government Printing Office, 1985), 16–35.

12. Bureau of Justice Statistics, *Report to the Nation on Crime and Justice* (Washington, D.C.: U.S. Government Printing Office, 1983), 99.

13. Marshall B. Clinard and Peter C. Yeager, *Corporate Crime* (New York: Free Press, 1980); James W. Coleman, *The Criminal Elite* (New York: St. Martin's, 1985).

14. Bureau of Justice Statistics, *Households Touched by Crime, 1984* (Washington, D.C.: U.S. Government Printing Office, 1985).

15. Richard Quinney, *Class, State and Crime* (New York: David McKay, 1977), 123.

16. Thomas B. Macauley, *History of England*, Vol. 2 (Boston: Houghton Mifflin, 1899), 81, as cited in Hans Sebald, *Adolescence* (New York: Appleton-Century-Crofts, 1968), 17.

17. Ramsey Clark, *Crime in America* (New York: Pocket Books, 1971), 6.

18. Mark Fishman, "Crime Waves as Ideology," *Social Problems*, 25 (1978), 531–543.

19. Bruce Roshier, "The Selection of Crime News by the Press," in Cohen and Young (eds.) *The Manufacture of News* (Beverly Hills, Calif.: Sage Publications, Inc., 1973).

20. Joseph R. Dominick, "Crime and Law Enforcement on Prime-Time Television," *Public Opinion Quarterly*, 37 (1973), 241–250.

21. Ethan Katsh and Stephen Arons, "Television, the Law and the Police," *Wall Street Journal*, July 22, 1975, 16.

3

Scope
of the Study

After studying this chapter, the student should be able to:

- List three major areas that concern criminologists.
- Relate the contributions of theologians, philosophers, and social analysts to the study of crime causation.
- Describe the relationship between the law and being identified as a criminal.
- Understand how the law is applied at the discretion of officials and that this discretion is based on legal, illegal, and extralegal considerations.
- Define social control and how it relates to a consensus and a conflict view of society.
- Discuss recent developments in criminology and the relationship between criminology and criminal justice.

The word "crime" comes from the Latin term *crimen*, meaning a charge of wrongdoing. The Greek word *logos* means the "study of." Criminology translates simply to mean the study of crime. The use of the term criminology is thought to have originated in the late 1800s. Some writers claim that it was first used by a leading criminologist of the day named Garofalo.[1] Others have noted anthropology's (the study of human beings' physical and cultural development) early interest in bodily characteristics thought to be associated with criminals. They have credited Topinard, a French anthropologist, as the first to use the term criminology.[2]

Criminology includes three major areas of study. First, criminologists attempt to locate the causes of crime. This area is known as criminal etiology (etiology meaning the study of causes). Second, criminologists are concerned with an analysis of the development and application of law. Third, criminology is the academic study of the problems and issues having to do with the social control of crime.

CRIMINAL ETIOLOGY

Why is it that some individuals seem to lead a law-abiding life while others frequently violate the law? People have questioned the causes of crime for centuries. Explanations of crime may be found in the beliefs of theologians (those who study about God and the universe), the writings of philosophers, and the theories of social analysts.

Theologians Look at Crime

St. Augustine expressed the early Church's position on crime in his famous work *The City of God*. The church thought of an individual as a creature who constantly struggled with the forces of evil and the wishes of God. When one (a basically corrupt being in the eyes of Augustine) surrendered to the devil, the result was often crime. So, early theologians located the cause of crime in the relationship between humankind and the devil. Crime was seen as a problem of spiritual weakness and immorality. St. Thomas Aquinas stated that people, by nature, tried to perform good acts. Sin (or crime) took place when their power to reason failed. Both Augustine and Thomas Aquinas felt that crime equaled sin. They differed in that Augustine thought of individuals as prone to do evil, while Thomas Aquinas pictured them as prone to do good.

The idea that crime was caused by evil forces continued through the Middle Ages (1100 to 1500) and beyond. Colonial Massachusetts carried out witch hunts well into the seventeenth century.[3] While modern theologians tend to cite social forces (e.g., poverty, inequality, racism, and the like) as leading causes of crime, some religious groups still believe in a good-versus-evil concept of crime.

Philosophers' Thoughts on Crime

Philosophers have also searched for answers to the causes of crime. Centuries before Christ, Greek (and Roman) philosophers felt that human behavior could be explained in terms of natural (earthly) causes. Since these thinkers emphasized an earthly explanation of social acts, they have been called naturalist philosophers. For example, Plato stated that certain social and political factors encourage crime. In his writing, *The Republic*, Plato stated that the law could reduce crime-causing conditions in society.[4] Plato proposed that a government of philosophers should draft laws and rule in the best interests of the people. Within such a society, Plato argued that some people should have more rights and privileges than others. Nevertheless, all individuals would give complete obedience to the state. In this perfect society, no one would have cause to oppose the government. Aristotle also stressed the ability of law to improve social conditions, the distribution of rights, and the requirement for strict obedience to the state.[5]

In the eighteenth century (known as the Enlightenment period), philosophers such as Voltaire and Rousseau argued that all people have equal rights. Behavior (crime or otherwise) was thought to be based on one's ability to reason. Philosophers of this period stated that an unjust legal system encourages crime. When the government begins to take away natural rights, it is committing a crime and revolution is justified. Enlightenment philosophers greatly influenced the leaders of the American Revolution.

Social Analysts Search for Causes

A variety of social analysts have also contributed to ideas concerning the causes of crime. Beccaria, a mathematician with interests in economics and the administration of justice, established the Classical School of criminology. The Classical School was the first systematic attempt to explain crime. It was based upon the philosophy of the Enlightenment. In his *Essay on Crimes and Punishments*, Beccaria outlined the Classical School's position on the nature and prevention of crime. The Classicists argued that humankind reasons in such a way as to gain pleasure and avoid pain. In order to outweigh any pleasure gained from crime, punishment must be sufficiently severe, certain, and swift. Equally important was the Classicist principle that the law should be specific, well known, and uniformly applied. In keeping with the major ideas of the Enlightenment philosophers, Beccaria placed great importance upon the state's duty to ensure the protection of civil liberties.

About a century after the birth of the Classical School, a physician named Lombroso established the Positivist School of criminology. The Positivist School was less tied to philosophy than was the Classical School. In his book entitled *The Criminal Man*, Lombroso stressed the biological sources of crime. The Positivist School represented the first scientific approach to the study of criminals. The use of statistics and the physical examination of offenders was the cornerstone of the Positivist method. Unlike the Classicists, the Positivists denied the existence of free will and believed that crime was determined by biological forces. Also unlike the Classicists, the Positivists ignored the possibility that crime was related to a corrupt, unfair, and inefficient legal system.

Most of the current theories of crime can be traced to the ideas of the early Positivists. Modern Positivists continue to assume that criminal behavior is more or less determined. The Classical notion of free will is either denied or downplayed. The chief difference between early and modern Positivism is that most modern Positivists are concerned with sociological or psychological causes of crime rather than biological factors. Today, some central ideas of the Classicists are reappearing in criminological theory. In addition, modern criminology includes an approach called "critical criminology," which will be briefly identified later in this chapter.

The previous discussion is merely a sketch of criminal etiology. A more detailed treatment of this subject is presented in Section 3. Sections 4 and 5 include some remarks on the causes of crime as they relate to types of offenses and types of offenders.

DEVELOPMENT AND APPLICATION OF LAW

Nullum crimen sine poena (no crime without punishment) and *nulla poena sine lege* (no punishment without law) are phrases that make up the foundation of a criminal label in our society. In order to be dealt with as a criminal, one must commit an act that is punishable by law. Without a law there can be no crime. Evidence appears to indicate that there are no clear-cut individual differences between those who commit crimes and those who do not. In a very fundamental sense, the differences between criminals and noncriminals are not sociological or psychological but legal. Therefore, one primary objective of criminology should be a study of the development and application of the law.

Attention to the relationship between crime and the legal process declined as the Classical School was replaced by the Positivist School. Men such as Lombroso, Ferri, and Garofalo shifted attention to offenders in the hope of finding what it was that caused them to commit crimes. By the end of the nineteenth century, American criminology no longer dealt with the study of jurisprudence (the philosophy of law). For the most part, however, European criminology continued to include jurisprudence as a topic of discussion.

It was not until the early 1960s that American criminological research began to show a growing interest in the process of legal administration. Criminology's shift of attention to the legal system's impact on the crime problem has not been complete. Positivism is still present in criminology. That is, criminologists still continue to devote much of their energies to the sociological and psychological factors thought to cause crime. There even appears to be a rebirth of interest among some criminologists regarding biological factors associated with crime.[6]

Criminologists are interested in two key questions about crime and the law. First, why and how do some types of conduct become illegal? Second, why and how is the law differently enforced? The first question has to do with the development of law. Remember that without a law there can be no crime. The second question refers to the application of the law. Keep in mind that some groups (e.g., street criminals) are more likely to be officially labeled as criminals than are others (e.g., corporation criminals). Both questions have to do with the distribution of social and political power or influence.

The Development of the Law

Laws often arise as a product of interest group activity. By this it is meant that some groups in society may reap special benefits from certain laws. To support their interests, these groups attempt to influence legislation. According to Hartjen, the degree of interest group influence may vary in that:[7]

1. the interest group may take an active part instigating the legislative process, or
2. the interest group may play an active part in shaping the law's content but not be directly involved in the actual lawmaking process, or
3. a law may be passed that recognizes or reflects the wishes of an influential interest group.

Current federal drug laws stem from the Comprehensive Drug Abuse Prevention and Control Act of 1970. Prior to this Act's passage, there was much debate in the House and Senate over the need to control amphetamines ("uppers") and commonly abused tranquilizers such as Valium. Because these drugs represented annual sales of several million dollars, the pharmaceutical industry opposed tight controls that would restrict profits.

The Senate's version of the Act, calling for strict regulation, generated much drug industry lobbying in the House for reduced controls. When the weakened House version went back to the Senate, more debate and influence peddling occurred. In the end, a Senate-House compromise was reached whereby only liquid injectable methamphetamines ("speed") would be strictly controlled.

Other amphetamines (more than 99% of all amphetamines produced) would have significantly less regulation. The tranquilizers Librium and Valium were omitted from the compromise legislation. When asked about the public danger of easily available amphetamines, one senator remarked: "When the chips were down, the power of the drug companies was simply more compelling." [8]

The Classical School of criminology arose as a protest against the unequal administration of justice. The student should recall that the Classicists gave top priority to the principle of uniformity in the application of the law. Since the Classical School's emergence over two centuries ago, justice is still too frequently dispensed on an uneven basis.

The Application of the Law

The law is the work of human hands. The meaning and interpretation of the law depends on human decisions. The decision-making process, in turn, is the product of discretion (the ability to act according to one's judgment). The decision to arrest, to prosecute, to offer bail, to grant probation, to incarcerate, to grant appeals, to parole, or to pardon fully is based on the discretion of officials of the criminal justice system. Discretion is exercised on the basis of legal, illegal, and extralegal considerations.

Legal factors allowing for discretion refer to undefined areas of criminal procedure which permit (*legally*) a wide range of behavior on the part of criminal justice personnel, who are quite often the police. Perhaps the area of juvenile justice, as compared with adult proceedings, represents one of the more significant examples of discretion based upon legally permissible options. Even today, juveniles are not guaranteed the right to trial by the federal constitution. Just over twenty years ago, the rights of juveniles were much less defined than they are today.

In 1964, Gerald Gault (age fifteen years) was arrested and taken into custody on a charge of making obscene phone calls to a neighbor. No notice of the charges were provided for Gerald or his parents. During the juvenile court proceedings, Gault did not have legal counsel nor the right to confront and cross-examine witnesses. His privilege against self-incrimination (Fifth Amendment) was apparently abused. Finally, there was no transcript of the proceedings, and no right to appeal the court's decision. Following the hearing, the judge committed Gault to a state juvenile institution for a possible six-year term (until Gault reached the age of twenty-one). Had an adult been convicted of the same offense (making obscene telephone calls) the maximum penalty would have been a fine of $50 and two months in jail.

The United States Supreme Court eventually heard the case. The Court ruled that a juvenile who is charged with an offense that may result in institutionalization and denial of liberty is entitled to: [9]

1. a notice of the charges against him,
2. the right to be represented by counsel,
3. the right to confront and cross-examine, and
4. the privilege against self-incrimination.

Other issues in the case (right to a transcript and the right to appellate review) were not decided by the Court in the *Gault* case. Some jurisdictions may, however, extend these rights to juveniles as a result of the state's own legal provisions.

Discretionary justice administration may also be based upon illegal practices. The FBI and other federal enforcement agencies have recently come under fire for using illegal evidence-gathering methods against certain groups. There have also been instances in local police departments where legal procedures are violated for purposes of harassment. The so-called exclusionary rule forbids the introduction of evidence in a criminal trial that was obtained as the result of an illegal search and seizure. A search or seizure is typically illegal when "no probable cause" for a search exists or, in some cases, no warrant is obtained by the police where one would be required. Instances have occurred wherein the police intentionally conduct illegal searches and seizures knowing quite well that the evidence will not be admissible in court. The major purpose is to harass certain suspects so that they "get the message" and move on. [10]

By the same token, corrupt police officers who are taking bribes from organized crime may purposefully violate the exclusionary rule to insure continued payoffs. If, for example, a large gambling operation is receiving public exposure through the mass media, corrupt police will sometimes make illegal searches and seizures with the knowledge that the cases will be thrown out of court. Once the cases are dismissed (for violation of the exclusionary rule) and public pressure dies down, then it is "business as usual." [11]

Extralegal considerations are factors that exist in addition to factual legal issues. Some studies have shown, for example, that criminal sentences vary according to the offender's race and social class. [12] For juveniles, the likelihood of being arrested may also be related to extralegal variables. Such things as attitude, dress, and overall demeanor have been found to affect a youth's chances of being detained by the police. In general, adolescents who appear to be timid or respectful are less likely to be arrested than are those who are "streetwise" or hostile.[13]

The study of the development and application of the law is one of the more interesting areas of criminology. As mentioned previously, criminologists are now redirecting their attention to this important topic. Sections 6 and 8 of this textbook will deal more specifically with these matters.

SOCIAL CONTROL OF CRIME

In modern society, social control can be defined as "the forces and processes that encourage conformity, including internalization, informal social control, and formal social control."[14] This definition is appropriate as it relates to the social control of crime.

The nature of crime control differs according to time and place. What is considered socially acceptable punishment in one age may be viewed as quite barbaric by future generations. Savitz has recounted the execution of the murderer of Henry IV (king of France).

> He was drawn to his place of execution in a tumbrel (dung cart) "to convert all bloody-minded traytors from the like enterprise," and laid out on a St. Andrew's cross; and then his hand (which slew the king) was put into a brimstone fire until hand and arm were consumed. Next, red-hot pincers were used to pinch and burn his breasts, arms, thighs, legs and other parts of the body; after this, a mixture of scalding oil, rosin, pitch, and brimstone were poured into his open wounds. A rundle of clay with a hole in its middle was placed upon his navel, and into this molten lead was poured. Finally, four strong horses were tied to his four limbs, so as to tear his body into quarters.[15]

The cruelty of this execution did not end with the victim's death. What was left of the body was gathered, burned, and thrown away "as being thought to be unworthy of the earthly burial."[16]

Within the United States today, the approach to crime control varies from state to state. Although prostitution is illegal in all states except Nevada, it is controlled or managed in a variety of ways. Some jurisdictions set aside certain areas of a city wherein prostitution flourishes. Examples include Boston's notorious "Combat Zone" and New York's infamous "Minnesota Strip." Prostitutes who venture outside of these areas are more likely to be arrested. Other cities actively enforce laws against publicly displayed prostitution (streetwalkers) but do little to discourage call girl operations that are less visible. During the seventies, many cities experienced the growth of "massage" parlors offering a full range of sexual services. Today, many prostitution operations masquerade as so-called escort services. These unofficial brothels are usually known to the public and police alike.

A very important question has to do with the need for social control. Why is it that societies have formal (e.g., the law) and informal (e.g., group disapproval) methods to produce social order? The answer to this question depends upon how one views the nature of society.

Society Based on Consensus

Some criminologists feel that society is made up of people who widely agree on basic values. That is, most people are thought to be law abiding and to willingly act according to society's essential rules. It is further believed that these common values are learned through socialization. Socialization is that process whereby individuals learn society's values, traditions, customs, and approved behavior patterns as they mature. In this view, it is a minority of the population who are thought to be criminal or deviant. Crime or deviance is believed to result from incomplete or improper socialization. For these individuals, society has established formal and informal methods of control. This image of society and social control is known as the consensus view. It is termed a "consensus view" since it maintains that most people conform to rules because they agree on certain basic values learned through socialization.

Society Based on Conflict

There is another view of society. Criminologists have recently begun to examine the relationship between social power and social control. Society is thought to be very complicated and to be made up of people who live in different circumstances. People and groups are also believed to differ in the kinds of values and ideas that are taught in the socialization process. This other view also emphasizes that there is an unequal distribution of social power and influence in society. The law is thought to be controlled, as it is written and applied, by those groups having the most power and influence. So, as the argument goes, the law (formal control) tends to protect the interests of some groups (the powerful) at the expense of others (the powerless or less powerful). This view is used to explain the fact that crime is committed by all sorts of people but that our prisons are populated by lower-class people. This view is also used to explain unfair tax laws, the favored treatment of white-collar criminals, and drug laws that criminalize marijuana but lightly control the abuse of household amphetamines ("uppers") and tranquilizers ("downers"). This image of society and social control is known as the conflict view. It is termed a conflict view since it maintains that social control (particularly the law) is used to support the interests of influential groups and restrict the activities of less powerful opponents.

CRIME CONTROL AGENCIES

The foundation of formal social control is the law as it is written and applied. The agencies that directly attempt to control crime are the police and the correctional system. The police have several missions as the primary source of contact between the public and the criminal justice system. The police are most likely to be recognized in their role of crime control. However, the police are also a major social control agency charged with preserving social order. Correctional agencies are less visible than the police. Nevertheless, community and institutional correctional programs are responsible for isolating those officially identified (convicted) as threats to social order. Correctional agencies also assume the difficult task of attempting to change behavior that is labeled as socially harmful. Criminology includes the study of the police and corrections as agencies of social control. Sections 7, 9, and 10 of this text explore the subject of crime control.

CRIMINOLOGY TODAY AND CRIMINAL JUSTICE

Since the 1960s, criminology has undergone several important changes. Perhaps the most significant change has been a return to an interest in the daily operations of the legal system and how it affects crime. Many of us occasionally commit acts that violate the criminal law. Rather than search for individual (personal) factors that cause person X to commit a crime, criminologists should begin to examine crime more broadly. In other words, criminology should pay closer attention to the relationship between life experiences and situational factors that operate to make the commission of crime more probable. Situational factors include the opportunities for committing a crime and the opportunities for (likelihood of) being caught and prosecuted. For the most part, the criminology that arose in the 1960s is termed "critical criminology." Major themes in critical criminology include the notions that [17]

1. The study of why some people are singled out as criminals and others are not is at least as important as the study of individual causes of crime.
2. Social power and conflict influence the nature and volume of crime.
3. Voluntarism, or "free will," should at least compete with the idea that behavior is essentially determined by biological, psychological, or sociological forces.
4. The criminal law is written and applied to support the values of interest groups.

Criminology is a well-established part of sociology. But during the last ten to twenty years, criminology has begun to achieve its own independent identity. Some universities currently have separate departments of criminology. Florida State University, for example, now has a School of Criminology. For the most part, though, criminology courses are taught within sociology departments. As an area of study, criminology still receives a great deal of input from the more established disciplines of sociology, psychology, political science, and law. So, criminology is associated with the traditional matters of theory building, basic research, and the social dynamics of crime.

Criminal justice is sometimes viewed as the discipline which integrates theory and practice. Criminal justice programs began to mushroom in the late 1960s as crime became an important national issue. The problems of program planning, public policy analysis, cost-effectiveness research, administrative and management principles, and the delivery of system services are the chief concerns of criminal justice practitioners. But, as Gibbons and Blake warn, "what the sophisticated criminal justice practitioner needs to acquire from his educational experience, more than anything else, is theoretical wisdom." [18] Criminology, then, is an important link between the basic social sciences and the practice of criminal justice administration.

SUMMARY

The term "criminology" was coined in the late 1800s. Today criminologists are interested in the three principal areas of etiology, legal administration, and social control.

The causes of crime have been debated by theologians, philosophers, and social analysts for some time. Early theologians generally thought of crime as the work of the devil. Philosophers have tended to interpret crime as the result of earthly forces. The first systematic explanation of crime was put forth by the Classical School of criminology. The Classicists stressed the concept of "free will" based upon the principle of pleasure versus pain. The Classical School was highly influenced by the philosophy of the Enlightenment period. The Positivist School followed the Classicists and emphasized that behavior was determined. Rather than focus on the philosophy and application of law, the early Positivists studied the biological characteristics of offenders. Present-day theories of crime largely represent the viewpoints of modern Positivists, latter-day Classicists, or critical criminologists.

The basis of a criminal identity is the law. Following the Classical period of criminology, the Positivists turned their attention toward the offender and away from the offense. Criminology's emphasis upon the dynamics of law and its enforcement did not reappear until the early 1960s. Since then, criminologists have increasingly explored the significance of lawmaking and law enforcing.

Social control refers to the efforts of society to promote law-abiding behavior. The methods of social control vary with time and place. The role of social control may be understood as being dependent upon one's view of the nature of society. If society is seen as being held together by agreement (consensus), then social control exists to contain the minority who commit crime. If society is viewed as made up of different interests and values (conflict), then social control becomes a means of enforcing the interests and values of those with power and influence.

Criminology has experienced several changes in recent years. It has become more doubtful of its past concerns over theories of individual causes. It has become more aware of its past neglect of the social and legal process of being identified as a criminal. The developing focus on broader theories of crime and the political aspects of criminal justice administration is known as "critical criminology." Criminal justice is essentially criminology with a more applied focus. The creative application of criminal justice administration depends upon sound, basic research and theory. Criminology is a fundamental source of theory and research that may lead to problem solving in the criminal justice system.

SUGGESTED ACTIVITIES

- Obtain a copy of a criminology textbook that was written before 1960. Briefly discuss what this book says or does not say about the relationship between law and crime. Compare this book with the principal themes of critical criminology.
- Examine your community's (or city's) attitude toward behavior that is illegal but tolerated (prostitution, gambling, liquor sales, and so on). Discuss in class.

- Take a poll among your classmates. Ask the following questions: (1) How many would voluntarily pay taxes if they didn't have to? (2) For what purposes, if any, would they not want their tax money spent? (3) Do they feel that current tax laws are unfair? (4) Do they feel that tax laws represent social control based on a consensus or conflict view of society?

- If your school has a criminal justice department, determine the following information: (1) the year that it was founded, (2) the background of its instructors, (3) the kinds of courses that are offered, and (4) the objectives of the program. What role does a course in criminology have to play as a part of criminal justice education in your school? Discuss these matters in class.

REVIEW

A. Briefly discuss the three major areas of criminology.

B. Discuss the most basic, fundamental difference between criminals and noncriminals.

C. Give one example of how interest groups shape the law to benefit themselves.

D. Distinguish between legal, illegal, and extralegal types of discretion.

E. Distinguish between a consensus and a conflict view of society.

F. Multiple Choice. Select the best answer.

1. The Latin word *crimen* means:
    a. to punish
    b. a charge of wrongdoing
    c. to commit
    d. to attack

2. Famous early theologian who believed that man was, by nature, prone to sin:
    a. St. Thomas Aquinas
    b. St. Benedict
    c. St. Augustine
    d. St. Phillip

3. The title of Plato's writing in which he outlined a "perfect" society ruled by philosophers:
    a. *The Republic*
    b. *The City of God*
    c. *God and Utopia*
    d. *The Iliad*

4. The first scientific approach to the study of crime:
    a. Critical criminology
    b. Classical School
    c. Neoclassical School
    d. Positivist School

5. The law:
    a. is absolute; that is, it never changes
    b. has little relationship to crime and criminology
    c. is sometimes the direct product of interest group activity
    d. has nothing to do with politics

6. An example of discretion based upon legal (lawful) factors is:
    a. the provision of legal counsel to juveniles before the Gault decision
    b. arresting disrespectful juveniles more often than respectful juveniles
    c. using the exclusionary rule as a means of extending corrupt law enforcement practices
    d. none of these

7. An example of discretion based upon illegal (unlawful) practices is:
   a. arresting disrespectful juveniles more often than respectful juveniles
   b. using the exclusionary rule as a means of extending corrupt law enforcement practices
   c. the provision of legal counsel for juveniles before the Gault decision
   d. none of these
8. Which of the following supports a consensus view of society?
   a. different values are taught in the socialization process
   b. unequal distribution of social influence and power
   c. common values learned through socialization
   d. social control used to support interests of powerful members of society
9. Which of the following supports a conflict view of society?
   a. social control operates to support values and interests of powerful or influential societal members
   b. common values learned through socialization
   c. only a small minority of the population commit crime
   d. inadequate socialization causes crime
10. Group that opposed strict controls of amphetamines and tranquilizers in the drafting of the Comprehensive Drug Abuse Prevention and Control Act of 1970:
    a. U.S. Senate
    b. U.S. House of Representatives
    c. pharmaceutical industry
    d. none of these

REFERENCES

1. Thorsten Sellin, "Criminology," in David Sill (ed.) *International Encyclopedia of the Social Sciences*, Vol. 3 (New York: Free Press, 1968), 505.
2. Gilbert Geis, "Sociology, Criminology and Criminal Law," *Social Problems*, 7 (1959), 40–47.
3. Paul C. Higgins and Richard R. Butler, *Understanding Deviance* (New York: McGraw-Hill, 1982), 18.
4. See F. M. Conford (trans.), *The Republic of Plato* (New York: Oxford University Press, 1941).
5. Phillip Jenkins, *Crime and Justice: Issues and Ideas* (Monterey, Calif.: Brooks/Cole, 1984), 103, 105.
6. James Q. Wilson and Richard J. Herrnstein, *Crime and Human Nature* (New York: Simon and Schuster, 1985).
7. Clayton A. Hartjen, *Crime and Criminalization* (New York: Holt, Rinehart and Winston/Praeger, 1978), 29–30.
8. James M. Graham, "Amphetamine Politics on Capitol Hill," *Transaction*, 9 (1972), 14–22, 53.
9. *In re Gault*, 387 U.S. 1 (1967).
10. John Kaplan, *Criminal Justice* (Mineola, N.Y.: Foundation Press, 1973), 222.
11. *Ibid.*
12. Randall J. Thompson and Matthew T. Zingraff, "Detecting Sentencing Disparity: Some Problems and Evidence," *American Journal of Sociology*, 86 (1982), 869–880; Alan J. Lizotte, "Extra-Legal Factors in Chicago's Criminal Courts: Testing the Conflict Model of Criminal Justice," *Social Problems*, 25 (1978), 564–580.
13. Richard J. Lundman, "Routine Police Arrest Practices: A Commonwealth Perspective," *Social Problems*, 22 (1974), 127–141.
14. David B. Brinkerhoff and Lynn K. White, *Sociology* (St. Paul: West, 1985), 583.
15. Leonard Savitz, *Dilemmas in Criminology* (New York: McGraw-Hill, 1967), 108.
16. *Ibid.*
17. See Raymond J. Michalowski, *Order, Law, and Crime* (New York: Random House, 1985), 13–17.
18. Don C. Gibbons and Gerald F. Blake, "Perspectives in Criminology and Criminal Justice: The Implications for Higher Education Programs," (Paper presented at the Conference on Key Issues in Criminal Justice Doctoral Education, Omaha, Nebraska, October, 1975), 4.

4

Sources and Criticisms of Existing Crime Statistics

OBJECTIVES

After studying this chapter, the student should be able to:

- List three principal sources of crime statistics.
- Distinguish between Index and non-Index offenses.
- Compute a crime rate given the total population and crime volume of a locality.
- Discuss problems associated with the principal sources of crime data.
- Summarize the crime problem in terms of its nature, extent and current trends.

Crime statistics have been gathered by various state, local, and federal jurisdictions for over 150 years. New York state initiated a rather modest program in 1829 when it began cataloging the results of criminal court dispositions. Over time, several other states sought to develop and to maintain statistical records.

Today, there are three principal sources of crime statistics. They include *official data*, *victim surveys*, and *self-reports*. This chapter discusses these sources and examines what they tell us regarding the extent and trends of crime in the United States.

SOURCES OF DATA

Throughout the 1920s, crime and lawlessness were major public concerns. Prohibition had introduced Americans to colorful, gun-toting gangsters. The so-called Mafia had exploded as a national issue out of events that arose in New Orleans in 1890. The public also turned inward in search of foreign-born radicals believed to be responsible for the worldwide communist movement. In 1921, the National Police Conference called for the development of a federal program for criminal identification.[1]

In 1924, J. Edgar Hoover assumed the directorship of the Bureau of Investigation and began a campaign to make the Bureau a center of scientific criminology. He received support from the American Bar Association (ABA) and the International Association of Chiefs of Police (IACP). On January 20, 1930, the House unanimously passed the Graham Bill authorizing the Bureau (renamed the Federal Bureau of Investigation in 1935) to be in charge of gathering national crime statistics.

Official Data

The *Uniform Crime Reports* (UCR) are now the major source of official crime data. Over 15,000 law enforcement agencies currently submit statistics to the FBI for the annual preparation of the UCR,[2] which presents information on twenty-nine different offenses split into two major categories.

Part I offenses include the eight crimes of criminal homicide, forcible rape, robbery, aggravated assault, burglary, larceny-theft, motor vehicle theft, and arson. Part I crimes are also referred to as Index offenses because they are used to gauge the extent of the crime problem. They are considered to be serious acts which occur frequently and are typically reported.

Index crimes are further subdivided into crimes of violence (predatory offenses) and crimes against property. The former include criminal homicide, forcible rape, robbery, and aggravated assault. The latter refer to burglary, larceny-theft, motor vehicle theft, and arson. For Index offenses, two major levels of information are gathered: (1) crimes known (reported) to the police, and (2) crimes cleared through an arrest, formal charge, or prosecution.

The remaining twenty-one crimes recorded in the UCR are termed Part II offenses (non-Index) and include the following: [3]

Other assaults	Gambling
Forgery and counterfeiting	Offenses against the family and
Fraud	children
Embezzlement	Driving while under the
Stolen property; buying,	influence
receiving, possessing	Liquor laws
Vandalism	Drunkenness
Weapons; carrying, possessing,	Disorderly conduct
and so on	Vagrancy
Prostitution and commercialized vice	All other offenses
Sex offenses (except forcible	Suspicion
rape, prostitution, and	Curfew and loitering laws
commercialized vice)	(juveniles)
Narcotic drug laws	Runaway (juveniles)

While Index offense information contains the volume of crimes known—that is, those which are reported—Part II data are limited to the number of offenses cleared by arrest.

One of the most often-quoted UCR statistics is the crime rate. It may be used for a group of crimes, such as an Index offense rate, or for one specific offense (e.g., homicide). When a rate is given, say 9.6 for homicide, it means that there were that many (9.6) homicides for every 100,000 inhabitants in the population being considered. Rates are computed using the following formula:

$$\text{Crime Rate} = \frac{\text{Number of Crimes}}{\text{Total Population}} \times \frac{100,000}{1}$$

Besides the UCR, there are other sources of official data. The Bureau of Justice Statistics releases data on prison population size and distribution, types of admissions, prisoner rates (per 100,000 in the civilian population), and types of prison releases. Data on delinquency are gathered by the National Center for Juvenile Justice. The Center reports the number and rates of delinquency cases disposed of by juvenile courts. In addition, various federal agencies collect data relative to the objectives of their agencies. For example, the Bureau of Alcohol, Tobacco, and Firearms (Treasury Department) keeps a statistical count of the contraband that it seizes (distilleries, illegal weapons, etc.) each fiscal year. Still, the main source of official data on crime is the UCR.

Victim Surveys

The systematic surveying of crime victims began over two decades ago when the National Opinion Research Center polled 10,000 home units. These early surveys were largely a response to the need for probing the extent of ''hidden crime.'' [4] Among their findings was that the number of crimes reported by victims far exceeded the number recorded by the UCR. For a report now known as the *National Crime Survey* (NCS), victim accounts are regularly gathered by the Census Bureau under the sponsorship of the Department of Justice's Bureau of Justice Statistics.

NCS data are based upon a random sample of U.S. households. The sampling technique involves a face-to-face interview in which a family member is asked questions regarding victimization within his or her home unit during a recent annual period. Offenses surveyed are limited to serious crimes such as rape, robbery, assault, and various forms of theft. In addition, victims under the age of twelve years are not included in the surveys. NCS statistics are therefore more helpful in ascertaining the size of a segment of the hidden crime problem rather than that problem's diverse character.

To the extent that a victim's perceptions over time are accurate, NCS data may also shed light on the characteristics of offenders. However, one of the more important contributions of these surveys is that they help to establish which portions of the population are at high risk of becoming victims of serious crime.

Self-Reports

One method of determining the extent and nature of crime is simply to ask a sample of respondents for an admission of criminal behavior. There are essentially three procedures for administering self-reports. First, individuals can be asked to complete an anonymous questionnaire with no check on the honesty of responses (validity). Second, researchers can employ a structured or semistructured interview schedule for a sample of respondents. Third, completed questionnaires can be checked for accuracy by comparing them with police records, lie detector tests, or follow-up interviews.[5]

The interview approach is more favorable to gathering comprehensive and detailed information. However, it is time consuming and costly, and its one-on-one character may hinder honest responses. The questionnaire technique takes less time, is less expensive, and is anonymous. On the other hand, it reduces the amount of information that can be collected. Furthermore, the questionnaire may be administered in such a way that subjects do not receive sufficient assistance with interpreting difficult questions.

A major limitation of self-reports is that they have dealt almost exclusively with juvenile delinquency rather than adult criminality. Thus, at the present time, systematic self-report data regarding criminal behavior which spans all age categories are unavailable. Nevertheless, such data have some usefulness for checking validity and trend analysis concerning young offenders.

WEAKNESSES OF CRIME STATISTICS

In the final analysis, the collection and distribution of crime data is a human enterprise. Sophisticated computers and elaborate surveys are no guarantee of accuracy. Each of the sources of crime information discussed in the previous section has shortcomings. What follows is a brief summary of these limitations.

Problems with the UCR

Crime statistics are only as accurate as those who report, record, or transmit the information. A basic flaw in the UCR is that a substantially large number of crimes are not reported, even by victims. Depending upon the type of crime, as much as 50 to 75 percent of the annual incidents may go unrecorded.[6] Reasons why victims do not report crime vary from ignorance of reporting procedures to feelings that the police are incapable of doing much to solve the problem.

The visibility of the offense also affects whether crimes are likely to be underreported. Murder, for example, is usually reported because it is a highly visible and serious crime. Auto theft is also usually reported because of insurance considerations. A well-executed commercial burglary, however, may go unnoticed if the scene is undisturbed and only low-profile items are stolen.

Some crimes, such as assault, often involve individuals who are closely related. When victims refuse to file a complaint against spouses, neighbors, or friends, the police may take no action. In many such incidents, the police choose to dispense informal "curbside justice" and thus channel reports of offenses away from official statistics.

Besides victim failure to report or refusal to file a complaint, offense visibility, and police discretionary practices, there are additional recording difficulties associated with the UCR. Some of these shortcomings, as outlined by Chilton[7] and Savitz,[8] are as follows.

1. Police departments vary as to the regularity of their involvement in the UCR as well as the accuracy and precision of their reporting procedures.
2. The UCR omit broad categories of crime such as white-collar offenses (corporate violations) and all federal cases.
3. Though Part II (non-Index) offenses form the bulk of annual arrests, the UCR distorts the crime picture by focusing upon Index crimes. Furthermore, it is difficult to compare trends since only arrests, not reported offense data, are gathered for these Part II crimes.
4. When several offenses stem from one incident, only the more serious crime is entered into the UCR.
5. For some crimes, the use of rates may be misleading since this calculation is based upon 100,000 persons in the population. Rape rates, for example, would appear to be more meaningful if they were based upon 100,000 *females* in the population.
6. The UCR data lack refinement in that the crime Index total is obtained by simply adding the number of all known Index offenses. Perhaps a better measure of the extent and nature of crime would be one that weighs crimes according to their seriousness, such as resulting physical harm to victims, number of victims, medical and property costs to victims, and so on.

Shortcomings of Victim Surveys

Like other data sources, victim surveys present problems which are difficult to overcome. The most obvious are those directly related to the technique itself. A face-to-face interview may be intimidating. The interview may occur sometime after an event, thus making recall difficult. Victims may also purposefully distort the data by exaggerating or omitting incidents.[9]

There are, in addition, serious measurement problems with victim surveys. For example:

1. Victim surveys are limited to the common street crimes of rape, robbery, assault, and various forms of theft. No data are collected on many of the Part II offenses of the UCR, or on white-collar crimes.
2. Since the surveys concentrate on victims, one crime incident involving three victims is recorded as three crimes.
3. Victim surveys, until recently, have provided only imprecise measures of the risk of being randomly victimized since rates include multiple victimizations of the same individual rather than the number of separate persons victimized in a given year.
4. Like the UCR, multiple offenses result in only the more serious crime against a victim being recorded.

For these (and other) reasons, victim surveys have their drawbacks as well as their distinctive features. Furthermore, many of these specific characteristics make comparisons between victim surveys and the UCR quite difficult.[10] To cite just a few examples, victim surveys of rape include both male and female victims, whereas the UCR limits its coverage to females. Furthermore, as previously noted, victim surveys exclude those under the age of twelve years, whereas the UCR include such victims.

Flaws in Self-Reports

Self-reports, like victim surveys, have been used to gauge the extent of hidden crime. However, as already noted, they have been largely directed at the behavior of juveniles rather than at that of adults. There are several other grounds for criticism, among which are the following:

1. Self-report studies lack continuity and are often not representative. Many do not follow up initial research which, in most cases, was based on a sample drawn from a particular city or region. This makes it difficult to verify behavior over time and to make generalizations about the total youth population.
2. There are lingering concerns as to the accuracy of self-reports. Because of the nature of self-reports, there is the real potential for falsehood or for inaccuracy due to poor recall.
3. Validity is also at issue since self-reports are often restricted to acts which are petty and are not representative of the full range of offenses that juveniles are capable of committing.
4. It is difficult to compare the results of different studies since some call for admissions of "never," "sometimes," or "frequently," while others ask for "once," "twice," or "three or more times."
5. Self-report studies frequently refer to different time frames for recall. Some ask for the frequency of violations occurring in the last three months; others request such information in relation to the past year or even one's lifetime experiences.

Some of the flaws associated with self-reports have been minimized in a recent series of studies known as the *National Youth Survey* (NYS). The result of the NYS will be used when introducing the contributions of self-reports to our profile of crime and criminals in this section.

AN OVERVIEW OF CRIME STATISTICS

The limitations of crime statistics mean that one must be cautious when interpreting their meaning. In summarizing our three data sources, it would be easy to become lost in a sea of confusing statistics. Such might be the case if we attempted an exhaustive review of what each may imply about the direction and extent of crime.

Our focus, therefore, will be on those relatively few points for which the data appear to be in essential agreement. In this respect, clarity guided by caution will take priority over comprehensiveness.

Table 4-1 reveals that almost 12 million Index offenses were reported to the

Table 4-1   Offenses Reported: *Uniform Crime Reports—1984*

INDEX OFFENSES	VOLUME		PERCENTAGE OF TOTAL*
Total	11,881,755		100
Violent	1,273,282		11
		*Percent of Violent Offenses**	
Homicide	18,692	1	0.2
Forcible rape	84,233	7	0.7
Robbery	485,008	38	4
Aggravated assault	685,349	54	6
Property	10,608,473		89
		*Percent of Property Offenses**	
Burglary	2,984,434	28	25
Larceny-theft	6,591,874	62	55
Motor vehicle theft	1,032,165	10	9
Arson**			

* Percentages are rounded off.

** Data unavailable for arson.

Source: Federal Bureau of Investigation, *Uniform Crime Reports—1984* (Washington, D.C.: U.S. Government Printing Office, 1985), pp. 44–45.

FBI in 1984. The data also show that especially heinous crimes—violent offenses—represent a small proportion (11 percent) of the total. Furthermore, robbery and aggravated assault account for over 90 percent of all reported violent crimes. Thus, murder and rape may be the most feared street crimes but they constitute less than 10 percent of known violent crime and not quite 1 percent of all Index crimes reported in 1984. Although percentages may differ from year to year, the variation is usually relatively slight.

Approximately nine out of ten serious crimes reported to the FBI in 1984 involved a property offense. The most common was larceny-theft, which comprised over one-half of all Index crimes and nearly two-thirds of the crimes against property. Data from victimization studies lend additional support to these generalizations.

Table 4-2 indicates that victims report far more incidents of property crime than of violent encounters with offenders. In a recent survey, only about 9 percent of the victimizations resulted from a predatory offense. Furthermore, as in the case of UCR data, the bulk had to do with robbery and aggravated assault. Property offenses, 91 percent of the total in the survey, were characterized chiefly by larceny-theft. This crime, again similar to UCR data, made up over two-thirds of the total and 75 percent of all property crimes revealed by the survey.

Table 4-2 Victim Responses: *National Crime Survey—1984*

COMPARABLE INDEX OFFENSES	VOLUME	Percent of Violent Offenses* / Percent of Property Offenses*	PERCENTAGE OF TOTAL*
Total	32,492,000		100
Violent	2,970,000		9
		*Percent of Violent Offenses**	
Homicide**			
Forcible rape	180,000	6	0.6
Robbery	1,117,000	38	3
Aggravated assault	1,673,000	56	5
Property	29,522,000		91
		*Percent of Property Offenses**	
Burglary	5,643,000	19	18
Larceny-theft	22,539,000	76	69
Motor vehicle theft	1,340,000	5	4
Arson**			

* Percentages are rounded off.

** Data not gathered for homicide and arson.

Source: Bureau of Justice Statistics, *Criminal Victimization 1984* (Washington, D.C.: U.S. Government Printing Office, 1985), p. 4.

Statistics from the NCS tell another story as well. Many crimes do not find their way into the official count of the UCR. In 1984, victims reported almost three times as many crimes as were found in that year's UCR. Though there is much opportunity for victim surveys to inflate the crime count,[11] the fact remains that a substantial number of crimes go unreported to the police.[12] This is referred to as the "dark side" of the crime problem, or "hidden crime."

In 1980, the last year of the NYS, 1,500 respondents reported having committed 80,000 offenses. This amounted to an average of approximately fifty-three offenses per individual. Furthermore, the average number of admitted Index offense violations was less than one (0.6) per person.[13] The vast majority of these delinquent acts did not result in official processing and, thus, did not appear in official statistics.

Other self-reports have consistently found that delinquent behavior is quite prevalent among the young.[14] All of them, including the NYS (cited previously) appear to agree on three major points. First, most youths violate the juvenile code or criminal law during adolescence. Second, the bulk of these offenses are of a petty nature and typically center around such matters as curfew violations, running away from home, underage drinking, vandalism, shoplifting, and other forms of minor property offenses. Third, a substantial portion of law violating goes unreported and, if discovered, is handled unofficially.

Trends

The amount and rates of crime soared throughout the 1960s and early 1970s, lending support to fears of an epidemic. Some of the rapid inflation was due to improved, more comprehensive reporting procedures. Still, the volume of crime did in fact increase during this time.

Beginning in 1980, Index offenses started to decline and appear to have leveled off by 1984. This trend is presented in Figure 4-1. A more detailed, offense-specific analysis is provided in Table 4-3 as well as rate changes over long- and short-term periods.

For the long run (1975 to 1984), Index offenses decreased by 5 percent. The decline would have been greater had there not been overall increases in the numbers of reports of forcible rape and aggravated assault. However, between 1980 and 1984—the short run—rates for these two crimes declined modestly. This, coupled with further decreases in homicide and robbery—plus a continued slide in reported property offenses—produced a total Index decline amounting to three times that of the long-term period.

Data gathered by the NCS also suggest decreases in or a leveling off of the number of street crimes. Table 4-4 indicates notable declines in reported victimizations between 1974 and 1984. These rate reductions are especially evident for certain property offenses.

Concern about victimization understandably tends to focus on violent crime. The difficulty with determining one's vulnerabilities is that rates have traditionally reflected the number of *instances* in which victimization has occurred. Consequently, any given rate (rape, robbery, or assault) may include multiple victimizations of the *same individual* rather than the number of separate persons victimized.

Researchers have recently constructed a Crime Risk Index which measures the proportion of the population, the number of *distinct individuals*, victimized annually.[15] As Table 4-5 reveals, the proportion of the population victimized by violent crime remained relatively stable between 1978 and 1982. Except in the case of robbery, this general trend held for all of the offenses examined.

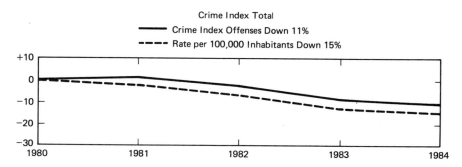

Figure 4-1   Crime Volume and Rates, 1980 to 1984: *Uniform Crime Reports—1984.*

Source: Federal Bureau of Investigation, *Uniform Crime Reports—1984* (Washington, D.C.: U.S. Government Printing Office, 1985), p. 43.

Table 4-3   Index Crime Rates (per 100,000) and Percentage Changes over Recent Time Periods: *Uniform Crime Reports—1979* and *1984*

INDEX OFFENSES	RATES*			PERCENTAGE CHANGE*		
	1975	1980	1984	1975–1979	1980–1984	1975–1984
Total	5299	5950	5031	+ 5	−15	− 5
Violent	488	597	539	+11	−10	+11
Homicide	10	10	8	+ 1	−23	−18
Forcible rape	26	37	36	+31	− 3	+36
Robbery	221	251	205	− 3	−18	− 7
Aggravated assault	231	299	290	+23	− 3	+26
Property	4811	5353	4492	+ 4	−16	− 7
Burglary	1532	1684	1264	− 2	−25	−18
Larceny-theft	2805	3167	2791	+ 7	−12	− 1
Motor vehicle theft	474	502	437	+ 6	−13	− 8
Arson**						

* Rates and percentages are rounded off.

** Data unavailable for arson.

Sources: Federal Bureau of Investigation, *Uniform Crime Reports—1984* (Washington, D.C.: U.S. Government Printing Office, 1985), p. 41; Federal Bureau of Investigation, *Uniform Crime Reports—1979* (Washington, D.C.: U.S. Government Printing Office, 1980), p. 37.

Table 4-4   Victim Responses, Selected Crimes, 1974 to 1984

OFFENSE	PERCENT* CHANGE IN VICTIMIZATION RATES, 1974–1984
Forcible rape	− 4
Robbery	−19
Aggravated assault	−16
Household burglary	−31
Larceny	
Household	−20
Personal with contact (purse snatching, pocket picking)	−11
Personal without contact	−25
Motor vehicle theft	−19

* Percentages are rounded off.

Source: Bureau of Justice Statistics, *Criminal Victimization 1984* (Washington, D.C.: U.S. Government Printing Office, 1985), p. 3.

Table 4-5 Percentage of U.S. Population Victimized by Violent Crime, 1978 to 1982

COMPARABLE INDEX OFFENSE	YEAR				
	1978	1979	1980	1981	1982
Violent (total)	2.94	3.23	3.00	3.21	3.15
Homicide*					
Forcible rape	0.09	0.11	0.09	0.09	0.07
Robbery	0.53	0.62	0.60	0.70	0.72
Aggravated assault	0.89	1.01	0.91	0.96	0.89

* Data not gathered for homicide.

Source: Bureau of Justice Statistics, *The Risk of Violent Crime* (Washington, D.C.: U.S. Government Printing Office, 1985), p. 4.

Unfortunately, self-report data are of little assistance in analyzing trends for the general population. They are based on either a local sample drawn at one point in time or, as regarding the NYS, a repeated surveying of the same respondents at different intervals. Trend data, using self-reports, would require standardized questionnaires or interviews to be administered to different representative samples on a regular basis.

SUMMARY

There are three major sources of crime statistics: official data, victim surveys, and self-reports. The best-known data are from official sources, principally the UCR. The UCR gathers information on twenty-nine offenses with a focus on the eight Index (Part I) crimes.

Each of these sources has drawbacks. Regarding the UCR, for example, much crime goes unreported to the police or FBI. Furthermore, only incidents, not the number of victims involved, are recorded. Consequently, there's the real possibility of data shrinkage. Victim surveys, on the other hand, may suffer from tendencies to exaggerate the volume of serious crime. Self-reports, too, have their limitations. They are confined to juveniles, plus the findings from different studies are difficult to compare due to a lack of standardization.

Despite these and other problems, it is possible to identify some generalizations concerning the extent and trends of street crime. The most feared acts, violent crimes, account for a small portion of offenses revealed by the UCR, victim surveys, and self-reports. Rather, the vast majority of offenses are property crimes—typically some form of theft. Victim surveys and self-reports also confirm other indicators that much crime is "hidden" and, therefore, escapes official statistical counts.

Finally, several sources suggest that the volume of crime began to decline or to stabilize in the 1980s. Though we lack concrete evidence that this pattern will continue over the long haul, there is little justification for fears of a dramatic upsurge that characterized much of the 1960s and early 1970s.

SUGGESTED ACTIVITIES

- Obtain a copy of the UCR from the Department of Justice or the nearest FBI office (your college library may have a copy) and familiarize yourself with it.
- Find out the current estimated population of your city (consult your Chamber of Commerce) and the number of burglaries known to the police since the first of the year. Compute your city's current burglary rate.
- Visit a data-processing or records division of your local police department and observe the computerized procedures.
- See if your state has established a Uniform Crime Reporting program. If so, what are the guidelines set up by the FBI, and what are the continuing problems, if any?
- With your instructor's assistance, construct a brief questionnaire in which you attempt to find out how many (and how often) students at your college or university have been victims of crime. Administer the questionnaire and discuss the results.

REVIEW

A. List the three principal sources of crime data.

B. List the eight Index offenses of the UCR.

C. Discuss the nature of victim surveys and self-reports.

D. Give at least three specific shortcomings of each of the major sources of crime data.

E. Discuss the general nature of known crime and recent trends in the United States.

F. Multiple Choice. Select the best answer.

1. Which of the following was an act or bill authorizing the FBI to gather nationwide crime statistics?
    a. Walker Act
    b. Davis Bill
    c. Wright-Patterson Act
    d. Graham Bill
    e. Smith-McCarren Act

2. Which of the following is not an Index offense as designated by the UCR?
    a. motor vehicle theft
    b. arson
    c. embezzlement
    d. larceny-theft
    e. forcible rape

3. Which of the following are not routinely gathered by the Bureau of Justice Statistics?
    a. self-reported crime data
    b. prison population statistics
    c. victim survey data
    d. all of the above
    e. self-report data are gathered by the Bureau, but only when requested by the FBI

4. A major weakness of the UCR is that:
   a. it includes all Index crimes arising out of the same incident
   b. it is too comprehensive
   c. rates are computed on the basis of different qualifiers depending upon the type of Index offense
   d. it distorts the crime picture by stressing the role of Index offenses
   e. crimes are assigned weights according to their degree of seriousness

5. One of the problems with most self-reports is that they:
   a. are too standardized for purposes of flexibility
   b. make comparisons among studies easy but are not administered on a frequent basis
   c. lack standardization and are not representative
   d. omit juvenile and other young offenders
   e. all of the above

6. Victim surveys have disadvantages in that they:
   a. are too comprehensive
   b. record only the most serious crime in an incident involving multiple offenses
   c. would count a crime incident involving three victims as only one crime
   d. were not begun until the late 1970s
   e. depend upon mailed questionnaires, which causes the response rate to fluctuate from year to year

7. Murder and rape collectively account for what percentage of all reported Index offenses?
   a. 10 percent
   b. 5 percent
   c. 15 percent
   d. 1 percent or less
   e. 20 percent

8. Based upon the UCR data, violent offenses amount to approximately what percentage of all index offenses?
   a. 25 percent
   b. 50 percent
   c. 30 percent
   d. 10 percent
   e. 35 percent

9. According to the data presented in this unit:
   a. crime rates are accelerating quickly
   b. crime rates decreased during the 1960s, increased during the 1970s, and are now declining
   c. crime rates escalated during the 1960s and early 1970s and are now somewhat declining and stabilizing
   d. violent crime is decreasing, but property crime is on the increase
   e. crime rates have been relatively stable since the 1950s

REFERENCES

1. *New York Times*, November 16, 1921, 13.
2. Federal Bureau of Investigation, *Uniform Crime Reports*, 1984 (Washington, D.C.: U.S. Government Printing Office, 1985), 1.
3. *Ibid.*, 166.

4. Phillip H. Ennis, *Criminalization in the United States: A Report of a National Survey*. President's Commission on Law Enforcement and the Administration of Justice, Field Survey II (Washington, D.C.: U.S. Government Printing Office, 1967).

5. Gwynn Nettler, *Explaining Crime*, 2nd ed. (New York: McGraw-Hill, 1978), 97.

6. U.S. Department of Justice, *Criminal Victimization in the United States, 1980* (Washington, D.C.: U.S. Government Printing Office, 1982), 76.

7. Roland Chilton, "Criminal Sanctions in the United States," *Journal of Criminal Law and Criminology*, 71 (1980), 56–67.

8. Leonard Savitz, "Official Statistics," in L. D. Savitz and N. Johnston (eds.) *Contemporary Criminology* (New York: John Wiley, 1982).

9. Wesley G. Skogan, *Issues in the Measurement of Victimization* (Washington, D.C.: U.S. Government Printing Office, 1981).

10. Robert Lehnen and Wesley Skogan (eds.), *The National Crime Survey: Working Papers*, Vol. I (Washington, D.C.: U.S. Government Printing Office, 1981), and Lehnen and Skogan (eds.), *The National Crime Survey: Working Papers*, Vol. II (Washington, D.C.: U.S. Government Printing Office, 1984).

11. Lehnen and Skogan (eds.), Vol. II, *op. cit.*

12. Larry J. Cohen and Mark I. Lichbach, "Alternative Measures of Crime: A Statistical Evaluation," *Sociological Quarterly*, 23 (1982), 253–266.

13. Delbert S. Elliott, et al., *The Prevalence and Incidence of Delinquent Behavior: 1976–1980* (Boulder, Colo.: Behavior Research Institute, 1983), 55–57.

14. Suzanne S. Ageton and Delbert S. Elliott, *The Incidence of Delinquent Behavior in a National Probability Sample of Adolescents* (Boulder, Colo.: Behavior Research Institute, 1978); Leroy Gould, "Discrepancies between Self-Reported and Official Measures of Delinquency," *American Sociological Review*, 46 (1981), 367–368.

15. Bureau of Justice Statistics, *The Risk of Violent Crime* (Washington, D.C.: U.S. Government Printing Office, 1985).

5

Crime and Population Characteristics

OBJECTIVES

After studying this chapter, the student should be able to:

- Discuss the relationship between crime and both region and place of residence.
- List some factors which affect the distribution of crime from place to place.
- Analyze the relationship between crime and the variables of age, sex, race, and social class.

Crime patterns of population groupings should be viewed with a cautious eye. As noted in Chapter 4, there are many problems that affect the accuracy and completeness of our data sources. The subsequent picture of crime as it relates to demographic (population) characteristics is similar to the construction of a jigsaw puzzle. Unfortunately, the composite is often ''fuzzy'' because the data do not fit neatly into place. Despite these shortcomings, we do possess sufficient data to allow us to draw some tentative conclusions.

CRIME AND RESIDENCE

The bulk of our data about crime and residence comes from the UCR. Though the UCR includes arrest data, we will focus upon Index crimes reported to the police by region and according to city, suburban, and rural areas. We will also make some guarded observations about recent trends.

By Region

The UCR divides the country into four major regions: the Northeast, Midwest, South, and West. In 1984, the West led the nation with the highest total Index rate (See Table 5-1). This region also had the highest rate for both violent and property crime categories. Except for the crimes of homicide (South), robbery, and motor vehicle theft (Northeast), the West surpassed other regions for specific offense rates.

This pattern appears to be rather stable. Over a recent five-year period, the same picture emerges. In 1979, the West's rates outdistanced those of other regions in all major categories. The specific exceptions were also the same as those in 1984, with the South having the highest homicide rate and the Northeast topping out for both robbery and motor vehicle theft.

Regarding trends, all four regions, particularly the Northeast and West, witnessed notable declines for combined Index offense rates between 1979 and 1984. The same trend prevailed for property offenses as a group. Violent crimes, however, declined less dramatically, with one region, the Midwest, reporting over a 10 percent increase for this period. Whether these trends will continue over the long run is open to question.

By Place of Residence

Places of residence are cities, suburbs, and rural areas. In 1984, cities recorded the highest rate of Index offenses, followed by suburban and rural areas; the latter with

Table 5-1   Index Crime Rates (per 100,000), by Region: *Uniform Crime Reports—1979* and *1984*

INDEX OFFENSES	RATES* (% CHANGE)							
	NORTHEAST		MIDWEST		SOUTH		WEST	
	1979	1984	1979	1984	1979	1984	1979	1984
Total	5349(−15)	4561	4988(−6)	4675	5203(−6)	4899	7039(−16)	6210
Violent	590(−1)	583	409(+11)	458	529(−.3)	527	661(−7)	616
Homicide	8	6	8	6	13	10	10	8
Forcible rape	26	28	30	33	36	38	49	44
Robbery	304	289	159	171	174	163	245	233
Aggravated assault	252	260	214	249	306	316	356	330
Property	4758(−16)	3979	4579(−8)	4217	4674(−6)	4371	6378(−12)	5595
Burglary	1473	1056	1220	1104	1486	1298	1949	1629
Larceny-theft	2625	2376	2926	2683	2808	2729	3823	3477
Motor vehicle theft	660	548	433	430	379	344	606	489
Arson**								

* Rates are rounded off.

** Data unavailable for arson.

Source: Federal Bureau of Investigation, *Uniform Crime Reports—1979* (Washington, D.C.: U.S. Government Printing Office, 1980), pp. 42–46; Federal Bureau of Investigation, *Uniform Crime Reports—1984* (Washington, D.C.: U.S. Government Printing Office, 1985), pp. 44–50.

a rate of less than one-third that of cities (see Table 5-2). Cities also had the highest rates for every Index offense. Rates were particularly disproportionate in favor of cities for violent offenses, most notably robbery. A strikingly similar breakdown is evident from UCR data gathered in 1979.

Trend analyses indicate overall decreases for Index offenses, especially in suburban and rural areas. Though crimes of violence fluctuated somewhat, more consistent, across-the-board declines occurred for property crime between 1979 and 1984. Cities, suburbs, and rural areas either approached or well exceeded 10 percent reductions for these offenses. As with regional trends, it would be premature to predict future patterns. Several things influence the amount and nature of crime from place to place. The FBI, for example, lists the following factors: [1]

Population density and size of locality and its surrounding area

Variations in composition of the population, particularly age structure

Stability of population with respect to residents' mobility and transient factors

Economic conditions, including job availability

Cultural conditions, such as educational, recreational, and religious characteristics

Climate

Effective strength of law enforcement agencies

Administrative and investigative emphases of law enforcement

Table 5-2 Index Crime Rates (per 100,000), by Place of Residence: *Uniform Crime Reports—1979 and 1984*

INDEX OFFENSES	RATES* (% CHANGE)					
	CITY		SUBURBAN		RURAL	
	1979	*1984*	*1979*	*1984*	*1979*	*1984*
Total	6622(−6)	6220	4833(−16)	4036	2270(−16)	1900
Violent	668(+1)	676	356(−7)	330	194(−18)	160
Homicide	11	9	6	5	8	5
Forcible rape	41	42	25	25	16	18
Robbery	294	285	99	85	23	15
Aggravated assault	323	340	225	215	148	122
Property	5954(−7)	5544	4477(−17)	3706	2076(−16)	1741
Burglary	1725	1486	1303	1022	803	651
Larceny-theft	3601	3493	2794	2391	1130	987
Motor vehicle theft	627	565	381	294	143	102
Arson**						

* Rates are rounded off.

** Data unavailable for arson.

Source: Federal Bureau of Investigation, *Uniform Crime Reports—1979* (Washington, D.C.: U.S. Government Printing Office, 1980), pp. 170–171; Federal Bureau of Investigation, *Uniform Crime Reports—1984* (Washington, D.C.: U.S. Government Printing Office, 1985), pp. 145–146.

Policies of other components of the criminal justice system (i.e., prosecutorial, judicial, correctional, and probational)

Attitudes of citizenry toward crime

Crime-reporting practices of citizenry

CRIME AND AGE

The relationship between crime and age is found chiefly in UCR arrest data. For juvenile offenders, additional information is provided by self-report studies. Victim surveys also supply clues regarding the relationship between age and the likelihood of becoming a victim of crime.

Offenders and Offenses

Crime is clearly a young person's domain. In a given year, more than one-half of all arrests are of individuals under the age of twenty-five years. As Table 5-3 reveals, this figure is nearly two-thirds for Index crimes. Arrest percentages for age categories beyond age thirty years begin to decline markedly and trail off to 1 percent or less after age fifty-nine.

It is also noteworthy that juveniles (people under eighteen) account for approximately one-third of the arrests for Index crimes as well as for those crimes within the property offense category. The vast majority of juveniles arrested each year are between the ages of thirteen and seventeen. What is alarming is the fact that this age group constitutes only 8 percent of the population.[2]

Juveniles ages thirteen to seventeen are disproportionately arrested for all violent crimes except murder. However, as Figure 5-1 indicates, the imbalance is rather modest until robbery is considered. Here, the percentage of juvenile arrests outnumber the portion of the population juveniles constitute by about three to one. For specific property offense, juveniles claim a particularly disproportionate share of burglary and auto theft

Table 5-3 Percentage of Arrests, by Age: *Uniform Crime Reports—1984*

AGE (YEARS)	PERCENTAGE ALL ARRESTS	INDEX CRIMES	VIOLENT CRIMES	PROPERTY CRIMES
Under 18	17	31	17	35
18–24	33	32	34	31
25–29	17	14	18	13
30–34	12	9	12	8
35–39	7	5	7	4
40–44	5	3	5	6

Source: Federal Bureau of Investigation, *Uniform Crime Reports—1984* (Washington, D.C.: U.S. Government Printing Office, 1985), pp. 172–173.

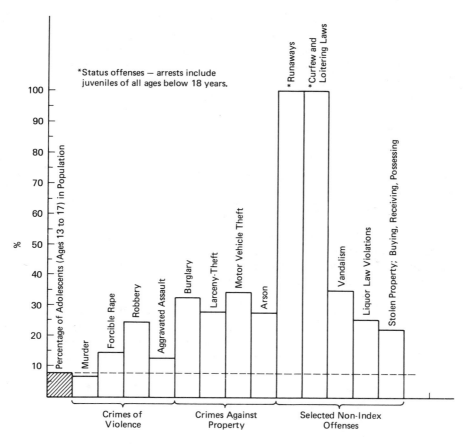

Figure 5-1 Percentage of Juvenile Arrests, by Crime, Relative to their Proportion of the U.S. Population, 1984.

Source: Federal Bureau of Investigation, *Uniform Crime Reports—1984* (Washington, D.C.: U.S. Government Printing Office, 1985), pp. 172–173; Bureau of the Census, *Estimates of the Population of the U.S., by Age, Sex and Race: 1980–1984* (Washington, D.C.: U.S. Government Printing Office, 1985), p. 17.

arrests. Since running away and curfew violations are status offenses—that is, they pertain only to minors—juveniles constitute 100 percent of all such arrests. However, there are other non-Index offenses, such as vandalism, that have a pronounced juvenile character.

Despite these data, one needs to keep in mind certain qualifications. First, two-thirds of all juvenile arrests are for the less serious, non-Index offenses. Second, self-report studies also indicate that an overwhelming proportion of juvenile offenses are nonserious in nature. The bulk typically include such violations as underage drinking, truancy, shoplifting and simple assault.[3] Third, additional evidence suggests that a very large portion of juvenile arrests for serious property and violent crime are due to a relatively small group of chronic offenders.[4] Fourth, many of these offenders are older adolescents or young adults between the ages of eighteen and twenty-one.[5]

Though most adolescent offenders commit minor violations and appear to reform with age, the fact remains that crime is highly associated with youth and young adulthood. So, too, is the likelihood of becoming a victim.

Victims of Offenses

According to data in Table 5-4, the chance of becoming a victim of crime is greatest for older juveniles and young adults. These remarkable rates do not begin to significantly decline until the potential victim reaches the age of twenty-five. The only exemption to this pattern is for victims of theft with contact (purse snatchings and pocket pickings). In this instance, the rates remain somewhat uniform throughout life.

Table 5-5 presents the percentage of the population by age, sex, race, and class—distinct individuals—that are victimized annually. It shows that the peak years are ages sixteen to nineteen and twenty to twenty-four for all types of predatory offenses surveyed. Over 6 percent of these juveniles and young adults fell victim to violent crime.

There are many interesting relationships between victimization risks and sex, race, and social class—both within and across age categories. However, the essential point to be made here is that crime victims are concentrated among the young. Furthermore, as you can observe from the data in Table 5-5, victims are likely to be males who are poor or working class. Race also seems to play a role in victimization risk depending upon the particular type of violent crime (e.g., robbery) being analyzed. For now, let us return to offenders and consider the variable of sex.

Table 5-4   Age and Rates of Victimization (per 100,000), by Crime, 1980

VIOLENT CRIME	AGE (YEARS)						
	12–15	16–19	20–24	25–34	35–49	50–64	65+
Rape	74	256	229	121	42	0	11
Robbery	840	1,053	1,022	700	458	425	331
Assault	3,709	5,104	5,324	2,955	1,504	725	317
Aggravated	1,190	1,962	2,041	1,025	541	293	124
Simple	2,519	3,142	3,283	1,930	963	432	193
Theft							
With contact*	291	347	301	267	258	251	355
Without contact	10,453	11,128	12,644	9,090	6,633	4,382	2,028

* Includes purse snatching, attempted purse snatching and pocket picking.

Source: Timothy J. Flanagan and Maureen McLeod (eds.) *Sourcebook of Criminal Justice Statistics—1982* (Washington, D.C.: U.S. Government Printing Office, 1983), p. 313.

Table 5-5 Percentage of U.S. Population Victimized by Violent Crime, 1982

| | | | | TYPE OF CRIME | | |
| | | | | | ASSAULT | |
CHARACTERISTIC	ALL** CRIMES	RAPE	ROBBERY	ALL	AGGRAVATED	SIMPLE
Age (years)						
12–15	4.83	0.13	1.08	3.87	1.08	2.97
16–19	6.51	0.19	1.18	5.35	2.14	3.51
20–24	6.22	0.14	1.41	4.92	1.92	3.29
25–34	4.03	0.12	0.84	3.23	1.19	2.21
35–49	2.09	0.03*	0.52	1.59	0.53	1.12
50–64	1.03	0.01*	0.37	0.66	0.21	0.44
65 and older	0.60	0.01*	0.27	0.33	0.11	0.22
Race, sex, and age summary						
White males, ages (years)						
12–15	5.85	0.00*	1.38	4.77	1.41	3.60
16–19	8.45	0.00*	1.19	7.45	3.12	4.79
20–24	8.13	0.01*	1.85	6.54	2.85	4.13
25–34	4.88	0.01*	0.96	4.04	1.63	2.63
35–49	2.45	0.00*	0.58	1.94	0.67	1.37
50–64	1.24	0.00*	0.38	0.86	0.29	0.56
65 and older	0.65	0.00*	0.23	0.43	0.14*	0.30
White females, ages (years)						
12–15	3.59	0.20*	0.50	3.04	0.65	2.53
16–19	4.58	0.43	0.72	3.62	1.09	2.64
20–24	4.52	0.26	0.83	3.64	0.91	2.89
25–34	3.12	0.22	0.48	2.56	0.73	1.96
35–49	1.53	0.06*	0.33	1.16	0.27	0.93
50–64	0.71	0.01*	0.24	0.46	0.14	0.32
65 and older	0.43	0.01*	0.19	0.22	0.07*	0.15
Black males, ages (years)						
12–15	7.05	0.15*	2.76	4.88	1.86	3.32
16–19	8.26	0.00*	3.67	5.29	3.45	2.43
20–24	7.30	0.00*	2.38	5.07	3.47	1.91
25–34	5.99	0.00*	1.97	4.37	2.29	2.46
35–49	3.60	0.00*	1.07	2.52	1.49	1.03
50–64	2.37	0.00*	1.40	0.96*	0.36*	0.60*
65 and older	1.54*	0.00*	0.72*	0.82*	0.29*	0.53*
Black females, ages (years)						
12–15	4.46	0.52*	1.04*	3.02	0.88*	2.14
16–19	5.03	0.14*	1.11*	3.77	1.67	2.34
20–24	4.38	0.29*	1.22	3.17	1.38	1.91
25–34	3.49	0.34*	1.51	1.93	0.80	1.18
35–49	2.45	0.00*	0.78	1.73	0.68	1.12
50–64	1.38	0.00*	0.61*	0.76*	0.16*	0.59*
65 and older	1.21	0.09*	0.74*	0.37*	0.26*	0.11*

Table 5-5 (Cont.)

CHARACTERISTIC	ALL** CRIMES	RAPE	ROBBERY	ASSAULT ALL	AGGRAVATED	SIMPLE
Family income						
White, victims with:						
Less than $3,000	6.26	0.20*	1.43	4.87	1.75	3.48
$3,000–$7,499	4.12	0.17	0.92	3.18	1.18	2.14
$7,500–$9,999	3.67	0.03*	0.91	2.86	1.25	1.90
$10,000–$14,999	3.53	0.11	0.69	2.86	1.06	1.94
$15,000–$24,999	2.87	0.05	0.58	2.32	0.77	1.64
$25,000 and over	2.50	0.03	0.45	2.10	0.63	1.56
Black, victims with:						
Less than $3,000	5.57	0.21*	2.13	3.49	1.59	1.98
$3,000–$7,499	5.18	0.11*	2.06	3.25	1.90	1.59
$7,500–$9,999	4.06	0.08*	1.32	2.72	1.48	1.35
$10,000–$14,999	4.12	0.12*	1.47	2.77	1.28	1.57
$15,000–$24,999	3.04	0.15*	1.24	1.84	0.62	1.29
$25,000 and over	2.74	0.00*	0.68	2.17	0.91	1.51

The column group heading "TYPE OF CRIME" spans RAPE, ROBBERY, and ASSAULT; "ASSAULT" spans ALL, AGGRAVATED, SIMPLE.

* Estimate, based on about ten or fewer sample cases, is statistically unreliable.

** Detail may not add to total shown because of rounding.

Source: Bureau of Justice Statistics, *The Risk of Violent Crime* (Washington, D.C.: U.S. Government Printing Office, 1985), p. 3.

CRIME AND SEX

Crime at all levels and among all major variables (age, race, and social class) is overwhelmingly a male phenomenon. Both the UCR and self-report studies attest to this fact.

Table 5-6 shows that, except for prostitution, significantly more males than females are arrested each year. The overall ratio (Index and non-Index offenses combined) is 5 : 1. For serious Index offenses, it remains a substantial 4 : 1, and for violent Index crimes the ratio climbs to a sizable 8 : 1 margin in favor of males. Even for non-Index offenses that have an unusually high degree of female involvement (e.g., embezzlement, forgery and counterfeiting, fraud, and stolen property), males still dominate arrest statistics. The ratios for 1984 are almost identical to those of 1979.[6]

Self-report studies agree with UCR data regarding the male character of law-violating behavior among juveniles. Hindelang's research showed boys to be far more involved in all but a few of the delinquent acts that were surveyed.[7] Data from the NYS also contribute to existing evidence that many more boys than girls are delinquent [8] and, furthermore, that they are delinquent with much greater frequency.[9]

Table 5-6 Arrests, by Sex: *Uniform Crime Reports—1984*

OFFENSES	PERCENT* MALE	PERCENT* FEMALE	APPROXIMATE MALE-TO-FEMALE RATIO
Total	83	17	5 : 1
Index	79	21	4 : 1
Violent	89	11	8 : 1
Property	77	23	3 : 1
Non-Index			
Embezzlement	60	40	1.5 : 1
Forgery and counterfeiting	66	37	1.7 : 1
Fraud	60	40	1.5 : 1
Prostitution	30	70	1.0 : 2.3
Stolen property	63	37	1.7 : 1

* Percentages are rounded off.

Source: Federal Bureau of Investigation, *Uniform Crime Reports—1984* (Washington, D.C.: U.S. Government Printing Office, 1985), p. 179.

Recent long-term statistics indicate that adult female arrests, while much lower in volume than arrests of adult males, have increased at a greater rate. Table 5-7 depicts this trend. Compared to males (+19%), total arrests for females were up 26 percent between 1975 and 1984. Whereas male arrests for Index offenses dropped by 4 percent during this period, female arrests increased by 7 percent. These patterns are also evident for serious violent and property crimes as well as for non-Index offenses.

Explanations for rising rates of female crime vary. Some criminologists think that, until recently, much female crime has gone undetected. Or they believe that, when discovered, female criminality and delinquency has tended to be handled with minimum sanctions. According to this line of reasoning, female crime, *per se*, is not

Table 5-7 Arrest Trends, by Sex, 1975 to 1984: *Uniform Crime Reports—1984*

OFFENSES	MALES			FEMALES		
	1975	1984	Percent* Change	1975	1984	Percent* Change
Total	4,633,166	5,492,628	+19	888,650	1,116,695	+26
Index	1,098,631	1,056,620	− 4	269,913	287,719	+ 7
Violent	231,065	237,878	+ 3	25,941	28,651	+10
Property	867,566	818,742	− 6	243,972	259,068	+ 6
Non-Index	3,534,535	4,436,008	+20	618,737	828,976	+25

* Percentages are rounded off.

Source: Federal Bureau of Investigation, *Uniform Crime Reports—1984* (Washington, D.C.: U.S. Government Printing Office, 1985), p. 167.

Table 5-8 Arrests, by Race: *Uniform Crime Reports—1984*

OFFENSES	NUMBER	PERCENT* WHITE	PERCENT* BLACK	PERCENT* OTHER**
Total	8,890,662	73	25	2
Index	1,831,683	65	33	2
Violent	381,890	53	46	1
Homicide	13,656	54	45	1
Forcible rape	28,297	53	46	1
Robbery	108,534	38	61	1
Aggravated assault	231,403	61	38	1
Property	1,449,793	68	30	2
Burglary	333,854	70	29	1
Larceny-theft	1,008,105	68	30	2
Motor vehicle theft	93,187	68	30	2
Arson	14,647	78	21	1

* Percentages are rounded off.

** "Other" includes American Indian, Alaskan Native, and Asian or Pacific Islander.

Source: Federal Bureau of Investigation, *Uniform Crime Reports—1984* (Washington, D.C.: U.S. Government Printing Office, 1985), p. 180.

increasing; rather, the criminal justice system is becoming more apt to recognize its presence officially. Other people argue, however, that increasing female crime, especially in traditionally male-dominated areas, is related to more pronounced female assertiveness that spills over into criminal behavior.[10] Still others view changes in female crime patterns as expressions of increased opportunities, primarily in the area of property crimes.[11]

CRIME AND RACE

Each year, about three-fourths of those arrested are white (see Table 5-8). For Index offenses, the ratio is 3 : 1 in favor of whites. In fact, whites make up the majority of arrests for all serious crimes except robbery. This should be kept in mind as we discuss the relationship between crime and race.

If whites dominate arrest statistics for the most part, why is there so much concern over black involvement in serious street crime?

The concern arises from the fact that blacks constitute only 12 percent of the population.[12] When the data are adjusted, blacks are overrepresented in arrest statistics for all major offenses. Regarding violent crimes, black arrest percentages outnumber the black population percentage by almost a 4 : 1 ratio. When robbery is considered, 61 percent of the arrests are derived from 12 percent of the population, an offense-to-population ratio of 5 : 1. Blacks also have a disproportionate, though less dramatic in size, ratio of arrests for property offenses that approaches a 2.5 : 1 margin.

Criminologists have debated the meaning of these data for some time. A common explanation has been that official statistics actually reflect a bias against blacks by the criminal justice system. However, there is mounting evidence to support the argument that racial discrepancies highlighted by the UCR are not artificial. Hindelang's analysis of victim surveys, where victims could recall the offender's race, found blacks to be disproportionately identified as offenders for the violent crimes of rape, robbery, and assault.[13]

Self-report studies generally indicate that routine juvenile offenses appear to be about equally prevalent among black and white youths.[14] However, when the frequency of serious law-violating behavior is measured, racial disparities exist: black adolescents report a much higher incidence of Index offenses, especially violent crimes, than do their white peers.[15]

There is no evidence that blacks, by virtue of race alone, are more crime-prone than are other members of the population. What does appear to make a difference is the social environment in which most blacks find themselves. Poverty, unemployment, and family strain have a long history in the black community. These negative forces have had a greater effect on blacks, as a group, than on other people. More specifically, the amount and nature of crime found among blacks can best be understood as a function of class position, wherein the vast majority of blacks are located on the lower rungs of the ladder.

CRIME AND SOCIAL CLASS

We have already noted that the victims of street crime tend to be lower class as well as young, male, and of minority status (see Table 5-5). Though the UCR does not specify arrest data by social class, the volume and content of reported crime in inner cities suggest that members of the lower class are affected heavily, both as offenders and as victims, by serious crime.

Much as in debates about the race issue, however, many people argue that official data paint a biased class picture of the crime problem. They believe that the criminal justice system discriminates against the lower class in several ways. Some people argue that the police, courts, and correctional agencies focus their attention on lower-class-oriented street crime while giving scant attention to the business-related and corporate crime of the middle class. Others point out that crime suspects are treated differently based on their class position, with the lower class being singled out for closer scrutiny and harsher punishments. Though limited to juveniles, self-reports provide some insights into the debate over the class nature of law-violating behavior.

Past studies have tended to produce little or no evidence of a relationship between delinquency and social class.[16] Hindelang and colleagues noted, however, that the instruments employed in these studies often failed to capture the range of behavior tapped by official data.[17] Furthermore, these instruments often have not been sufficiently attuned to the differentials of offense seriousness or frequency. Consequently, any existing class distinctions are likely to be blurred.[18]

In contrast, the more refined instruments of the NYS reveal consistent class differences, especially for males, throughout the Survey's five-year period, 1976 to

1980.[19] These differentials are evident in terms of both prevalence (the percentage of offending individuals within a social class) and incidence (the frequency of offenses) of serious violations.

Table 5-9 indicates that the proportion of boys reporting status offenses and routine delinquency differs little along class lines. However, there are marked differences when it comes to serious offenses. A significantly larger percentage of working- and lower-class males than of middle-class males report having committed Index offenses. Differences persist, both in size and direction, when the specific categories of crimes against the person and serious property offenses (felony theft) are considered.

The survey's findings on incidence present even more of a contrast. Working- and lower-class boys report greater delinquent involvement, overall, than do their middle-class peers. Table 5-10 further highlights the comprehensive span of offenses for which working- and lower-class boys appear to outdo middle-class ones. Significant and substantially greater frequencies prevail for working- and lower-class males regarding infractions ranging from status offenses to crimes of violence. The incidence ratio of working- or lower-class to middle-class boys varies from 2.5 : 1 to 11 : 1.

Thus far, we've observed that the probability of frequent and serious offending is associated with minority and lower-class status among youths. This seems to suggest an interactive effect [20] and raises the question as to which factor—race or class—is a more powerful influence on this dimension of the crime and delinquency problem. As previously stated, common sense points to the dynamics of social class, not the biology of race, as being more instrumental.

One of the more recent assessments of this issue again comes from the NYS. Using NYS data, Elliott and Huizinga [21] controlled for race and found that this variable has little effect on the class differentials regarding the prevalence and incidence of delinquency. Thus, serious and chronic delinquency seems to be more a matter of class than of race.

Table 5-9 Prevalence of Male Delinquent Behavior, by Class: According to *National Youth Survey*, 1979.

	CLASS (%)		
Crimes	*Middle*	*Working*	*Lower*
Index offenses	11.4	22.3	24.5
Crimes against persons	31.3	45.1	47.8
Felony theft	7.4	15.9	16.7
Status offenses*	53.9	62.0	67.2
General delinquency*	79.4	87.5	86.6

* Not statistically significant.

Source: Delbert S. Elliott and David Huizinga, "Social Class and Delinquent Behavior in a National Youth Panel," *Criminology*, 21 (1983), p. 162.

Table 5-10 Incidence (Rate per 100 Youth) of Male Delinquent Behavior, by Class: According to the *National Youth Survey*, 1979.

Crimes	CLASS (%)		
	Middle	Working	Lower
Index offenses	39	180	200
Crimes against persons	147	567	406
Felony theft	15	99	169
Status offenses	728	1897	1930
General delinquency	4155	6881	6097

Source: Delbert S. Elliott and David Huizinga, "Social Class and Delinquent Behavior in a National Youth Panel," *Criminology*, 21 (1983), p. 166.

SUMMARY

This chapter focused upon the relationship between crime and the key population variables of region, residence, age, sex, race, and social class. Profiles were presented based mainly on the UCR and, where appropriate, supplementary data from victim surveys and self-reports.

The West leads the nation in the number of Index crimes reported annually as well as in rates for violent and property offense categories. There are, however, some exceptions when specific crimes are taken into account. For example, the South continues to record the highest homicide rate, while the Northeast reports the highest rates for both robbery and motor vehicle theft. Regional trends show an overall, general decline in the rates of serious crime, especially property offenses.

As to place of residence, cities contribute the highest Index offense rates each year, and rural areas contribute the lowest. This pattern is particularly evident for violent crimes, most notably robbery. In most cases, rates have declined in cities, suburbs, and rural areas, primarily in the property offenses category. Though these trends now appear stable, we are not prepared to make long-term predictions.

Crime is characteristically a product of youth. Over one-half of all arrests, for nonserious as well as Index offenses, are attributed to individuals under the age of twenty-five. Furthermore, about one-third of the arrests for serious violent and property crimes involve juveniles who comprise less than 10 percent of the population. Despite these figures, it should be remembered that the vast majority of delinquent behavior is nonserious. What may be more alarming is the evidence that victims are also heavily represented among the young—especially those who are poor, working class, of minority status, and male.

Besides being a youthful activity, crime is also predominantly a male phenomenon. In general, the male-to-female arrest ratio stands at about 5 : 1. For violent Index offenses, the ratio escalates to a margin of 8 : 1. Although females, both adult and juvenile, have much less involvement in crime, their arrest rates have shown a greater percentage of increase than have those for males. There are a number of possible explanations for this fact, some of which have been presented in this chapter.

Though whites make up a clear majority of arrests for Index crimes except robbery, blacks are *disproportionately* arrested for all serious crimes by as much as 5 : 1 (robbery). Self-reports show that while delinquency in general is equally prevalent among both races, black youngsters report a much higher incidence of serious offenses, especially violent crimes, than do their white cohorts. Much of this disparity may be explained by social class differences between whites and blacks in general.

Survey data, for example, reveal consistent class differences regarding involvement in delinquent activities. Though routine delinquency differs little along class lines, a significantly larger proportion of lower-class males than of middle-class males report having committed Index crimes. These distinctions prevail for violent offenses and crimes against property. Data also indicate that lower-class males commit serious offenses with greater frequency than do their middle-class peers. Since blacks are overly represented among the poor and lower class, it seems reasonable to believe that this social fact is significantly related to their disproportionate involvement in serious crime and delinquency.

SUGGESTED ACTIVITIES

- Using the most recent UCR, compare Index offense statistics between your state and a neighboring jurisdiction for cities, suburbs, and rural areas. Discuss any significant differences.
- Develop a profile of arrested offenders by age, race, and sex for your state. Compare this profile with that of a state in another region and discuss possible reasons for differences, if any, between the two.
- Interview a representative of your local police department regarding that department's profile of offenders for Index crime in general, and for specific Index offenses. Compare this profile with ones based on the UCR nationwide.

REVIEW

A. List five factors which affect the distribution of amount and nature of crime from place to place.

B. Discuss why youthful crime may not be as alarming as Index offense arrest data seem to suggest.

C. What is the relationship between victims and offenders regarding serious crime and the variables of age, sex, race, and social class?

D. Multiple Choice. Select the best answer.

1. Which of the following regions reports the highest overall crime rate?
   - a. South
   - b. Northeast
   - c. West
   - d. Midwest

2. The highest rate of Index crime, by place of residence, tends to occur in:
   a. cities
   b. rural areas
   c. suburbs
   d. places with small police departments
3. Arrests for individuals under the age of twenty-five account for approximately what percentage of Index offense arrests?
   a. 35 percent
   b. 45 percent
   c. 55 percent
   d. 65 percent
4. Juveniles account for about what percentage of annual Index offense arrests?
   a. 50 percent
   b. 25 percent
   c. 33 percent
   d. 75 percent
5. A member of which of the following age groups is most likely to be a victim of crime?
   a. 35–49 years
   b. 25–34 years
   c. 16–19 years
   d. 12–15 years
6. The ratio of male to female arrests for Index offenses is approximately:
   a. 4 : 1
   b. 5 : 1
   c. 8 : 1
   d. 6 : 1
7. Regarding Index crime and race, which of the following statements is true?
   a. most of those arrested are black
   b. most blacks arrested are charged with a property offense
   c. blacks are disproportionately arrested for all serious crimes except robbery
   d. blacks are disproportionately arrested for all serious crimes, especially robbery
8. Regarding the relationship between crime and social class, which of the following statements is true?
   a. the lower class dominate as offenders for all forms of crime
   b. the lower class are more likely to be arrested for Index offenses
   c. members of the lower class, though more likely to be arrested, are less frequent offenders than are members of the middle class regarding Index crimes
   d. although there is a relationship between race and crime, there is none between social class and crime

REFERENCES

1. Federal Bureau of Investigation, *Uniform Crime Reports, 1984* (Washington, D.C.: U.S. Government Printing Office, 1985), v.
2. Bureau of the Census, *Estimates of the Population of the U.S., by Age, Sex and Race: 1980–1984* (Washington, D.C.: U.S. Government Printing Office, 1985), 17.
3. See, for example, John W. C. Johnstone, "Social Class, Social Areas and Delinquency," *Sociology and Social Research*, 63 (1978), 49–72.
4. Marvin Wolfgang, Robert Figlio, and Thorsten Selling, *Delinquency in a Birth Cohort* (Chicago: University of Chicago Press, 1972).
5. Michael Hindelang, "Variation in Sex-Race-Age–Specific Incidence Rates of Offending," *American Sociological Review*, 45 (1981), 461–474.

6. Federal Bureau of Investigation, *Uniform Crime Reports, 1979* (Washington, D.C.: U.S. Government Printing Office, 1980), 199.
7. Michael Hindelang, "Age, Sex and the Versatility of Delinquent Involvement," *Social Problems*, 18 (1971), 522–535.
8. Delbert S. Elliott, et al., *The Prevlance and Incidence of Delinquent Behavior: 1976–1980* (Boulder, Colo.: Behavior Research Institute, 1983).
9. Stephen Cernovich and Peggy Giordano, "A Comparative Analysis of Male and Female Delinquency," *Sociological Quarterly*, 20 (1979), 131–145.
10. Freda Adler, *Sisters in Crime: The Rise of the New Female Criminal* (New York: McGraw-Hill, 1975), 19–20; Nanci Koser Wilson, "The Masculinity of Violent Crime—Some Second Thoughts," *Journal of Criminal Justice*, 9 (1981), 111–123.
11. Rita James Simon, *Women and Crime* (Lexington, Mass.: D. C. Heath, 1975).
12. Bureau of the Census, *op. cit.*
13. Michael Hindelang, et al., "Correlates of Delinquency: The Illusion of Discrepancy between Self-Report and Official Measures," *American Sociological Review*, 44 (1979), 995–1014.
14. Delbert Elliott and Harwin Voss, *Delinquency and Dropout* (Lexington, Mass.: Lexington Books, 1974).
15. Delbert Elliott and Suzanne Ageton, "Reconciling Race and Class Differences in Self-Reported and Official Estimates of Delinquency," *American Sociological Review*, 45 (1980), 95–110; Elliott, et al., *op. cit.*
16. Charles Tittle, Wayne Villemez and Douglas Smith, "The Myth of Social Class and Community; An Empirical Assessment of the Empirical Evidence," *American Sociological Review*, 43 (1978), 643–656.
17. Hindelang (1979), *op. cit.*
18. *Ibid.*
19. Delbert Elliott and David Huizinga, "Social Class and Delinquent Behavior in a National Youth Panel," *Criminology*, 21 (1983), 149–177.
20. Elliott and Ageton, *op. cit.*
21. Elliott and Huizinga, *op. cit.*

6

The Classical School

OBJECTIVES

After studying this chapter, the student should be able to:

- Discuss the contributions of Enlightenment philosophers to ideas about humankind, the law, and government.
- State suggestions by Enlightenment philosophers regarding reforms in the administration of justice.
- List the primary features of the Classical School of criminology.
- Describe the major points of the Neoclassical School and compare or contrast them with those of the Classical School.

Ancient Hebrews interpreted the law as an expression of God's commands and crime as sinful conduct. Greek philosophers, in contrast, recognized law to be a human enterprise and its violation an offense against society or the state. Medieval Christian theologians, on the other hand, stressed the religious basis of law and the moral implications of crime. Most human misbehavior was explained as being the work of the devil or demons. The Middle Ages was a period when the events of life were often directly linked to the powers of the supernatural. This chapter examines that time frame when rational explanations of behavior began to replace those grounded upon the supernatural. Our starting point is the Enlightenment period. Although the origins of this period occurred in the 1600s, Enlightenment influence did not peak until a century later.

THE DEVIL, CRIME, AND THE LAW

The early Church condemned the use of pagan magic and certain notions about the devil's ability to control nature. In A.D. 563, for example, Church leaders attacked a common belief that the devil had the power to change the weather. Nonetheless, the Church continuously reaffirmed the devil's existence. Augustine (354–430) claimed that evil spirits could appear as humans or animals. Aquinas (1225–1274) stated that all magical acts resulted from the magician's agreement with the devil. Local superstitions made the devil appear to take a very active role in the daily misfortunes of life. Witches were believed to have the power to sink ships, cause the earth to tremble, destroy crops, and sour wine.[1]

Since crime was equated with sin, little effort was required to detect the devil's hand in such acts as murder, theft, and assault. Like witches, criminals and insane people were frequently accused of having a pact with the devil. Those believed to be possessed sometimes underwent the Church rite of exorcism. Exorcism, a ceremony involving prescribed prayers and actions by a priest specially trained in the rite, was intended to drive the demons or devil from the afflicted party. That failing, the Church would usually turn the offender over to civil authorities for execution. Needless to say, capital punishments of the day were as cruel as the law was vague.

Jurisdiction over criminal matters was often unclear since several bodies of law operated side by side. In addition to local customary law, Roman law and Church law could apply. Originally, the Church held jurisdiction only in matters of faith and morals (heresy or blasphemy) and family life (marriage and divorce). However, as the social and political power of the Church increased during the Middle Ages, its law (Canon law) intruded into civil matters. The result was often conflict between the clergy and lay rulers.

As early as 1066, William the Conqueror ruled that the bishops' courts in England could judge only offenses against the Church.[2] By the 1500s, the power of the Church was waning. Kings and princes increasingly resisted the interference of the Church in their political affairs. Still, legal codes were confusing, procedures haphazard, and punishments cruel. In the 1600s, one judge who boasted of having read the Bible fifty-three times had also condemned 20,000 people to death for witchcraft.[3] The dawning of the Enlightenment would, as we will see, do much to alter ideas about human behavior, law, and the administration of justice.

THE ENLIGHTENMENT PHILOSOPHERS

Thomas Hobbes (1588–1679) stressed humankind's power to reason as well as our natural desire for power. Our constant craving for status and control cannot be contained solely by natural law or eternal law from a higher being. Only human-made law, sometimes referred to as positive law, can prevent individuals from destroying one another in an unending struggle for power, wealth, and rank. Therefore, citizens must pledge obedience to the government. It is the power of the government, through law, that upholds justice and protects individuals from their own self-destruction. It is the threat of punishment that leads us to obey the law.[4]

John Locke (1632–1704) differed from Hobbes in two major respects. First, Locke did not believe that individuals were involved in a constant struggle for dominance over one another. Second, Locke emphasized the importance of the law being based upon an agreement, not a blind pledge, between subjects and the government. That is, the subjects agree to obey the laws so long as the government uses its power to uphold the public good. When laws no longer promote or protect the community welfare, they (and the government) no longer merit obedience.[5]

Francois Voltaire (1694–1778) first supported but later rejected the idea of democracy. As he grew older, he became more critical of established governments and the law. Still, Voltaire preferred progressive reform to revolution. He felt that meaningful change could not come from the unenlightened (ignorant) lower ranks of society. In principle, Voltaire wrote of the power of human reason and free will. In practice, he specified that only a small portion of humanity was capable of intelligence and reason. Voltaire thus advocated that change should begin at the top of the social ladder with reform-minded rulers. He assumed that the good example set by a just ruler would be imitated by the subjects. A particular incident, to be discussed, led Voltaire to the conclusion that reform should begin with a revision of the law.[6]

Jean Jacques Rousseau (1712–1778) insisted that people are basically good and are guided by the power to reason. But they also have instincts that could be destructive. So law and government were needed to insure social and legal equality. In 1762, Rousseau published his monumental work, *The Social Contract*. It served as a document that would eventually influence the French and American Revolutions.

To Rousseau, the social contract was an agreement between citizens and the government. The people agree to give up some of their selfish interests for the benefit of the group. The government, in turn, agrees to protect the public good by enforcing laws which control those actions (e.g., crime) that threaten society. The state must have the power to punish those who unjustly violate the contract. Likewise, the people have the right to destroy the contract when the state abuses basic human rights. Rousseau, at this point, went much further than Locke and Voltaire on methods by which the people can correct an unjust society. Rousseau believed that revolution is justified when a government becomes tyrannical.[7]

The Beginning of Legal Reform

In 1761, one year before Rousseau published *The Social Contract*, an event took place that would mobilize the forces of legal reform in France. Jean Calas, a French Huguenot (Protestant), was accused of murdering his eldest son. The government charged that Calas had killed the young man because of his intention to become a Catholic. The entire Calas family was arrested and confined in jail. They were denied legal counsel, forbidden to cross-examine witnesses, and not allowed to produce witnesses on their own behalf. At this time, only witnesses approved by the state could testify. Furthermore, trials were customarily held in secrecy. Though there was very little evidence against Calas, the court decreed that:

> the said Calas shall be broken alive and afterwards left to expire on a wheel which shall be set up quite near the said scaffold, his face turned to the sky, to live in pain

and repentance of his said crimes and misdeeds, as long as it pleases God to give him life, and his dead body to be thrown afterwards on a burning pyre prepared for this purpose in the said place, for it to be consumed and afterwards the ashes to be scattered to the wind.[8]

Upon his confession, which the court fully expected under these torturous conditions, Calas was to receive:

a fine of a hundred sous for the Crown, . . . his goods confiscated and acquired by those whom it may concern, subtraction made of the third part of them for his wife and children, if he has any, and for the expenses of those who exposed him.[9]

Calas did not confess and died protesting his innocence. In fact, evidence later revealed that the son had committed suicide by hanging himself. The father did not reveal this because French law then stipulated that the remains of a suicide victim were to be publicly abused and the surviving family shamed forever. To spare his dead son and the family this disgrace, Calas destroyed the evidence and stated that he had simply found his son dead. The prosecution claimed that the marks on the boy's neck had been inflicted by Calas while strangling his son.[10]

When Voltaire heard of the Calas incident, he immediately began to muster public opinion against the injustice. Dignitaries from throughout Europe made financial contributions to the cause. Famous lawyers who were drawn into the case petitioned the king's council for a retrial. The original verdict and sentence were struck down and a new trial ordered. Three years after his death, Calas was exonerated by the high French court. The king granted a sizable sum of money to the Calas family as compensation for their suffering.

Shortly after the reversal of the Calas conviction, French law underwent considerable reform. The defense was to have the right to cross-examine witnesses and to present evidence on its own behalf. Torture and secret trials were outlawed. Only socially harmful conduct was to be considered a crime.[11] Under the leadership of Voltaire, human reason had won out over superstition and prejudice in the administration of justice. It was the dawning of a new day. The Classical School of criminology was on the horizon.

THE CLASSICAL SCHOOL OF CRIMINOLOGY

As in France and other parts of Europe, Italian justice was inquisitorial in nature. Inquisitorial systems featured secret investigations and torture. Judges had unlimited powers to call for mildly painful "ordinary torture" and more severe "extraordinary torture." There was "preparatory torture" for purposes of getting a confession and "preliminary torture" used to determine the identity of the partners in crime. Laws were numerous and unclear. Legal counsel was denied to the defendant. Criminal procedures were not uniform and punishments were severe.[12] One could be executed for blasphemy, stealing small items, and insulting the clergy. People were sometimes given a life sentence to the galleys for the slightest display of public "immorality."

Beccaria (1738–1794) is credited with having founded the Classical School of criminology. He was born in Milan, Italy, and studied mathematics as a university student. He later became interested in legal reform and was influenced by Locke and Rousseau. In particular, Beccaria accepted the social contract theory that outlined the relationship between citizens and the government. This led him to question the cruel and barbaric legal practices that his government applied against citizens. Beccaria had also read the works of Helvetius (1715–1771). Helvetius is noted for his philosophy of utilitarianism and the principle of hedonism. Utilitarianism is the belief that the law should be used to promote the greatest amount of happiness for the greatest number of people. Hedonism is the notion that man is a pleasure-seeking creature who chooses to do those things that give him the greatest amount of pleasure while avoiding those things that are painful. Even though Helvetius was one of the first people to write about utilitarianism and hedonism, these two concepts are most often associated with the English philosopher, Jeremy Bentham (1748–1832).

The Classical School was first and foremost founded upon philosophy. It stressed the importance of a rational administration of justice based upon the social contract, utilitarianism, and hedonism. It represented the first systematic statement on criminal behavior and legal reform. In 1764, Beccaria published his famous book entitled *Essay on Crimes and Punishments*. The ideas contained within the following major topics form the basis of Beccaria's principles for a system of criminal justice.

Humanity, Society, and the State

The Classical School subscribed to the following points regarding individuals and their relationship to society and the state:

1. Humans have free will and choose courses of action that give them pleasure and avoid activities that are painful (the principle of hedonism).
2. People have a tendency to be guided by passions. If these passions are not regulated, humankind may destroy itself and society.
3. Citizens should agree to give up some of their personal interests and grant the state power to enforce laws and punish offenders in order to preserve domestic tranquility. In return, the state must not abuse the people's fundamental rights (the social contract).

The Nature of Law

Beccaria had much to say about the basis of law. He also listed several specific ways in which the law could be reformed. For example, he stated that:

1. Since human-made law varies with the needs of a particular society, it should be separated from divine law.
2. The purpose of the law is to provide the greatest amount of happiness for the greatest number of people (philosophy of utilitarianism).
3. The law must come from the legislature and not from judges. It is the legislature that represents the people.

4. The law must be specific, clear, well known, and equally applied to all citizens.
5. Guilt must be based on factual certainty rather than speculation. Trials and verdicts should be public.
6. Juries are more effective than judges or judicial tribunals for insuring impartial verdicts.
7. Torture should be absolutely forbidden. It benefits only the guilty who may be sturdy and condemns the innocent who may be weak.

The Nature of Punishment

In response to the horrible cruelties of his time, Beccaria spoke out against unreasonable and excessive punishment. It is on the subject of punishment that Beccaria emphasized the rational and hedonistic nature of humans. He proposed that:

1. Punishment will prevent crime if it is just painful enough to cancel out any pleasure derived from the crime. One will choose (by reason) to obey the law because the pain of punishment will outweigh the pleasure of crime (hedonism).
2. It is more important for punishment to be certain and swift than severe. If punishment is either uncertain or delayed, the impact of possible severe penalties has little meaning.
3. Punishment should be specific and fixed by the legislature.
4. Capital punishment should be abolished except for very exceptional cases.

The Classical School was a reaction to a corrupt and cruel legal system. Beccaria recognized that a poorly managed criminal justice system can provoke crime when he stated that "The [excessive] severity of punishment of itself [encourages] men to commit the very wrongs it is supposed to prevent." [13] The Classicists stressed the significance of the crime, not the characteristics of the criminal in determining the punishment. Of equal importance was the Classical School's concern for deterrence. If given reasonable, swift, and certain punishment, the Classicists believed, the criminal would not commit future crimes. Punishment administered in this way would also prevent others, through example, from committing crimes. Finally, the Classicists emphasized the necessity of making the state accountable (through a social contract) to the people as a means of insuring the protection of civil rights and liberties.

Essay on Crimes and Punishments was widely received throughout Europe. In a little over a year, the book had been printed in twenty-two different languages. Voltaire praised Beccaria's writing on several occasions.[14] Many European governments remodeled their criminal code and procedures in light of Beccaria's principles. Legal systems were reformed in various degrees in Italy, Prussia, Austria, Sweden, and Russia. The leaders of the American Revolution were also influenced by Beccaria. By 1791, the French penal code had undergone a significant revision. The following objectives of the French code were based on the writings of Beccaria and Voltaire: [15]

1. Equal treatment by the legal system and a reduction in the severity of punishments.
2. Reduction of the discretionary powers of judges regarding the definition of crimes and the determination of punishment. The law would define each crime and provide a specific, fixed punishment.

3. Introduction of the jury system.
4. Abolition of secret criminal procedures and crimes against religion.
5. Establishment of the right to have legal counsel and other defendant safeguards.

THE NEOCLASSICAL SCHOOL OF CRIMINOLOGY

One of the chief weaknesses of the Classical School was its focus upon the criminal act. Classical criminologists said that the seriousness (degree of harm done to society) of the crime should determine the punishment. The criminal's intention or personal characteristics should have nothing to do with the punishment.

It was difficult to put classical legal codes into practice. In actuality, the punishments were frequently very severe. Fixed, unchangeable sentences did not allow for differences in the offenders' environment, their prior criminal record, or even their mental abilities. The strict Classicists also failed to recognize that punishment affects different people in different ways.[16]

So countries began to modify their Classicist legal codes. In 1810, France changed its penal code by allowing judges to alter a sentence based on the circumstances of the case. Children and mentally retarded offenders were seen as less responsible for their actions than were normal adults. There was also some consideration of insanity as a defense to a criminal charge. Notice of the offender's characteristics began to play a greater role in the French Code of 1810. This slight shift in attention from the crime to the criminal is the essential feature of the Neoclassical School of criminology.

The Neoclassical School still held that individuals are accountable for their actions. It continued to assume that an individual chooses acts through free will. But the Neoclassicists argued that some individuals (children, the aged, mentally retarded, and insane) are less capable of free choice than are others. Nonlawyer experts were permitted to testify as to the accused's degree of responsibility. In addition, the social backgrounds and prior records of offenders were considered in sentencing and punishment. Finally, the Neoclassicists began to hint at the idea that punishment should play a part in character reformation (rehabilitation). As we shall see in the next chapter, the idea of free will was eventually replaced by the notion of determinism. During the 1800s, human behavior was beginning to be viewed as something determined by biological or other forces beyond a person's control.

SUMMARY

As the Church declined in power, much of the medieval thinking about human behavior, the law, and government began to change. The naturalistic philosophy of the ancient Greeks was reborn in the philosophy of the Enlightenment period (1700s). The essential feature of the Enlightenment was its humanistic concern for the happenings of this world. Enlightenment thinkers turned away from the supernatural (heaven and hell) concerns of the Middle Ages. Influential philosophers of the Enlightenment included Hobbes, Locke, Voltaire, and Rousseau.

The Enlightenment was a time when existing legal systems came under attack. A notable case occurred in 1761. It involved the execution of an innocent man (Jean Calas) through unjust, but legally approved, methods. The victim's cause was taken up by a leading French philosopher. Voltaire and his associates challenged the government for a posthumous (after death) reversal of Calas' conviction. In the process of this appeal being won, France's barbaric legal system was publicly exposed. More important, the Calas case dramatically pointed out the need for broad legal reform.

In Italy, Beccaria responded to similar conditions by writing *Essay on Crimes and Punishments*. Beccaria was influenced by such Enlightenment philosophers as Hobbes, Locke, Rousseau, and Helvetius. In particular, Beccaria's work contains elements of social contract theory, utilitarian philosophy, and the principle of hedonism—all products of the Enlightenment. Beccaria is credited with having founded the Classical School of criminology.

The Classical School was based on a philosophical approach to man and the law that stressed free will and rationality. The Classicists focused upon the significance of the crime's damage to society, not the criminal's characteristics, in determining punishment. Also, Beccaria and his followers felt that deterrence through swift, certain, and reasonable punishment should be a goal of the criminal justice system. Finally, the Classical School emphasized the state's obligation to promote justice and human rights through laws which were well known, uniform, and applied on an equal basis.

Criminal codes that were modeled after Classical principles were difficult to apply. They called for specific, fixed punishments regardless of individual differences. No allowances were made for the offender's age, mental condition, or social background. The Neoclassical School attempted to correct these inadequacies of the Classicists. The essential quality of the Neoclassical School was its focus upon the criminal (actor) and away from the crime (act). The Neoclassicists still acknowledged the existence of free will but argued that some individuals have less free will (mentally retarded, children, etc.) than others do. Therefore, they concluded, the law should take this into account. The legal system of the United States is based on a Neoclassical model. It assumes that individuals are responsible for what they do, but that there are circumstances that may reduce their responsibility.

SUGGESTED ACTIVITIES

- Obtain a copy of the Constitution of the United States. Familiarize yourself with the Bill of Rights section. What is its relationship to Rousseau's version of the social contract as described in this chapter? Write a brief essay on this topic and discuss in class.

- Thomas Hobbes argued that man is essentially greedy and hungry for power, wealth, and prestige. Other philosophers have stated that man is basically good. If man is basically good, what would explain crime? Would laws be necessary? If so, what would be the role of the law? Write an essay on this subject and discuss in class.

- Record your daily activities for one week. Relate your behavior to the principle of hedonism as discussed in this chapter. Does hedonism always apply to your behavior, or do you choose to do some things that are not pleasurable? Why do you choose to do some of these unpleasurable things?

● This chapter stated that our legal system is based upon Neoclassical principles. When sentencing convicted criminals, judges often consider the criminal's personal background. Does this create any inequalities or unfairness? If so, in what way? Write a brief essay on this topic and discuss in class.

REVIEW

A. Discuss, in general, the major contributions of the Enlightenment philosophers to ideas concerning man, the law, and government.

B. Discuss the importance of the Jean Calas case.

C. Define the terms: social contract, hedonism, and utilitarianism.

D. Compare and contrast the major points of the Classical and Neoclassical Schools of criminology.

E. Multiple Choice. Select the best answer.

1. Which of the following Enlightenment philosophers took the most negative (unfavorable) view of humankind's basic nature?
- a. Rousseau
- b. Locke
- c. Hobbes
- d. Voltaire

2. The social contract:
- a. justifies revolution under certain conditions
- b. forbids revolution under any conditions
- c. had little influence on the governments of the time
- d. was not developed until after the French and American Revolutions

3. The Enlightenment period refers to the:
- a. 1300s
- b. 1400s
- c. 1500s
- d. 1700s

4. Jean Calas was:
- a. an Enlightenment philosopher
- b. an influential theologian of the Protestant religion
- c. wrongfully executed and served as a cause for legal reform
- d. saved from execution through the efforts of Voltaire

5. Inquisitorial justice:
- a. relied upon secrecy and torture
- b. is found only in ancient societies
- c. is the model for the legal system of the United States
- d. condemns the use of torture and secret accusations

6. The Classical School of criminology:
- a. accepted the notion of free will
- b. adopted the social contract
- c. included the philosophy of utilitarianism and the principle of hedonism
- d. all of these

7. According to the Classicists, the law:
- a. must come from judges
- b. must be specific, clearly written, and well known
- c. may include torture only under specified legal conditions
- d. all of these

8. Beccaria stated that to be effective, punishment must be:
   a. very severe
   b. fixed by judges
   c. reasonably severe, swift, and certain
   d. none of these
9. The Neoclassicists:
   a. accepted the idea of people having free will
   b. stated that freedom of choice varies with different individuals
   c. considered the offender's background to be important in sentencing and punishment
   d. all of these
10. The Neoclassicists differed from the Classicists by hinting at the idea that punishment should:
   a. deter future crime
   b. act to rehabilitate offenders
   c. include torture
   d. have no place in societies based on a social contract

REFERENCES

1. H. C. Erik Midelfort, *Witch Hunting in Southwestern Germany, 1562–1684* (Stanford, Calif.: Stanford University Press, 1972), 12–18.
2. Rene A. Wormser, *The Law* (New York: Simon and Schuster, 1949), 193.
3. Stephen Schafer, *Theories of Criminology* (New York: Random House, 1969), 104.
4. S. P. Lamprecht, ''Hobbes and Hobbism,'' *American Political Science Review*, 8 (1966), 31–53.
5. Morris Ginsberg, *On Justice and Society* (Ithaca, N.Y.: Cornell University Press, 1965), 132–133.
6. Will and Ariel Durant, *Rousseau and Revolution* (New York: Simon and Schuster, 1967), 140–147.
7. *Ibid.*, 171–176; Ronald Grimsley, *The Philosophy of Rousseau* (New York: Oxford University Press, 1973); Jean-Jacques Rousseau, *The Social Contract*, C. M. Sherover (ed.) (New York: New American Library, 1974).
8. Edna Nixon, *Voltaire and the Calas Case* (New York: Vanguard Press, 1961), 99.
9. *Ibid.*, 100.
10. *Ibid.*, 34–47. See also, F. H. Maugham, *The Case of Jean Calas* (London: Heinemann, 1928).
11. *Ibid.*, 216–217.
12. Marcello T. Maestro, *Voltaire and Beccaria as Reformers of Criminal Law* (New York: Octagon Books, 1972), 9–10.
13. David J. Rothman, *The Discovery of the Asylum* (Boston: Little, Brown, 1971), 59.
14. Durants, *op. cit.*, 321.
15. Maestro, *op. cit.*, 144–145.
16. George B. Vold, *Theoretical Criminology*, 2nd ed., Thomas J. Bernard (ed.) (New York: Oxford University Press, 1979), 26–33.

7

Biological and Psychological Theories of Crime

OBJECTIVES

After studying this chapter, the student should be able to:

- Compare and contrast the major ideas of the Classical and Positivist Schools of criminology.
- Name and discuss three early Positivist criminologists and their theories.
- Explain four primary biological theories of crime.
- Discuss three major psychological approaches to the explanation of crime.
- List some of the major criticisms of early Positivism, biological, and psychological theories of crime.

The Classical School of criminology concentrated on the offense and how to prevent future crimes through reasonable, swift, and certain punishments. The Neoclassical School allowed for offender characteristics in sentencing and punishment. This recognition of differences among offenders opened up the issue of "free will." If some factors determined that certain individuals were more responsible for their crimes than others were, then a much broader question existed. What, then, determines (or causes) some to become criminals while others remain law-abiding? The Positivist School of criminology made a complete break with the Classical School's concept of free will. The Positivists were committed to finding out what it was that determined or caused criminal behavior.

Before the Positivist School arose, there were some people who claimed that criminals looked different than noncriminals. Johan Lavater (1741–1801) stated that criminals had a peculiar facial appearance such as a dishonest smile, sneaky eyes, curious eyebrows, and the like. Lavater's approach is known as "physiognomy" (the determination of personality characteristics from one's facial features). Franz Gall (1758–1828), John Spurtzheim (1776–1832), and Charles Caldwell (1772–1853) developed the study of "phrenology" (the theory that one's skull shape indicates mental characteristics). Phrenologists proposed that bumps and indentations of the skull revealed emotional and behavioral traits. Offenders were believed to possess certain crime-prone parts of the brain (identified by examining the skull) that could not be controlled by one's willpower. Physiognomy and phrenology did not survive as leading theories of the 1700s. They conflicted with the popular belief that man could control his behavior though free will.[1]

THE POSITIVIST SCHOOL OF CRIMINOLOGY

By the time that Charles Darwin had written the *Descent of Man* in 1871, science had become increasingly influential. According to the theory of evolution, humans developed from lower forms of life and had "evolved" to the highest level. Though humans were similar to other primates, they were the most capable of creatures.

Cesare Lombroso (1835–1909) was an Italian physician who became interested in the relationship between bodily characteristics and the brain. Having examined the body of a notorious thief, Lombroso noted that the deceased's unusual skull formations matched those found among some apes and monkeys. No doubt influenced by Darwin's work, Lombroso concluded that at least one-third of all criminals were humans who had not evolved to a civilized state. Such criminals were biological throwbacks who were not capable of adjusting to the laws of society. To Lombroso, these offenders were born criminals. Their biological inferiority determined their antisocial, criminal behavior.

Lombroso also examined many living convicts in a search for identifiable physical markings. His resulting criminal stigmata (characteristic traits) included long arms, large lips and ears, extended jaw, unusual mouth structure, stooped posture, and so on. In his later writings, Lombroso categorized two other kinds of criminals besides the born criminal. Insane criminals were those whose behavior resulted from mental disease. Criminaloids, the largest group, was a category composed of offenders who were sane and normal in appearance but emotionally inclined to commit crime under certain conditions. Lombroso is credited with having founded the Positivist School of criminology.[2] Lombroso's efforts to discover the causes of criminal behavior, although overly simplified by today's standards, resulted in his being referred to as the "father of scientific criminology."

Raffaele Garofalo (1852–1934) agreed with Lombroso that the Classical concepts of free will and hedonism must be abandoned. He also stated that crime and criminals must be scientifically analyzed. Garofalo replaced Lombroso's theory of the criminal's physical inferiority with that of moral inferiority. That is, according to Garofalo all true criminals lacked some degree of moral sensitivity. His theory was basically biological, however, since he assumed that the moral deficiency was inherited. Garofalo recommended that the seriousness of punishment (from death to victim compensation) be based upon a criminal's degree of moral inferiority.[3]

Enrico Ferri (1856–1929) studied under Lombroso. Like his teacher and Garofalo, Ferri also denied the existence of free will and the principle of hedonism. But he downplayed the importance of Lombroso's concept of the born criminal. Ferri believed that some criminals were born with a psychological tendency to commit crime. However, he emphasized that environmental factors (social, economic, and political conditions) operate to cause crime. Ferri's *Law of Saturation* stated that "in a given social environment with definite individual and physical conditions, a fixed number of [crimes], no more and no less, can be committed."[4] He agreed with Garofalo that improved environments can reduce crime. However, he went further than Garofalo in two major respects. First, Ferri advocated that the state should sponsor wide-scale social reforms to prevent crime. Second, he proposed that the legal system be based upon scientific principles. Ferri believed that scientists should draft laws (instead of legislatures) and that judges should be social scientists because they would know what was best for society and offenders.

Summary of Early Positivism

The early Positivists, beginning with Lombroso, were the first to call for a scientific study of crime and criminals. They believed that there were basic differences between criminals and noncriminals. Some emphasized physical differences (Lombroso), others stressed "inherited immorality" (Garofalo), or environmental factors (Ferri). Regardless of the differences, all rejected free will in favor of determinism. Something about criminals "caused them to do it." This line of reasoning led the early Positivists to concentrate on the offender rather than on the offense. The Positivists felt that sentencing should fit the criminal rather than the crime.

So, Classicists relied on law and philosophy, the concept of free will, the nature of the crime, and fixed sentences according to the offense. In contrast, the Positivists relied on science, the concept of determinism, the nature of the criminal, and flexible sentences according to the offender. While the Classicists emphasized deterrence before the act, the Positivists introduced the notion of rehabilitation after the act.

The Positivists had another less obvious quality. They generally held that scientific criminology was best prepared to defend society and the state. Armed with a belief in their superior knowledge, Positivists supported broad criminal codes and procedures that would allow them to remove, study, and treat those thought to pose a threat to the state. The possible connection between Positivism and dictatorial governments:

> is centered on the core idea of the superior knowledge and wisdom of the scientific expert, who, on the basis of his studies, decides what kind of human beings his fellow men are who commit crime, and who, on the basis of this knowledge and scientific

insight, prescribes appropriate treatment without concern for public opinion and without consent from the person so diagnosed (i.e., the criminal).[5]

Positivism continues to be a major approach to the study of crime. Since the days of the early Positivists, several causes of crime have been proposed. Modern Positivists include criminologists who hold that crime is more or less determined by biological, psychological (or psychiatric), or sociological causes. The remainder of this chapter is a brief survey of biological and psychological (and psychiatric) Positivism. Sociological theories, many of which have Positivistic assumptions, will be considered in Chapter 8.

BIOLOGICAL THEORIES OF CRIME

The early Positivists left their mark on the next generation of criminologists. Although Lombroso, Garofalo, and Ferri allowed for environmental factors, the lure of biology (especially the idea of inherited criminal traits) attracted the attention of their immediate successors. Biological explanations hinge upon theories involving body types, glandular dysfunctions, chromosome irregularities, and abnormal brain or nervous system activity.

Body Types and Crime

Using several physical characteristics, Charles Goring compared about 3,000 English convicts with soldiers, students, and hospital patients. After years of intensive study, he concluded that criminals, as a group, are physically the same as noncriminals. Ernest Hooton reacted to Goring's attack on Lombroso's theory of a criminal stigmata. He conducted a study involving a comparison of a large sample of prisoners and nonprisoners in the United States. Hooton concluded that criminals are biologically inferior. Further, he listed specific physical traits that were related to criminals and the types of crimes (homicide, theft, sex offenses, etc.) that they committed.

Eventually, body types were associated with certain personality dispositions. William Sheldon claimed that there were three body types. Each body type was assumed to have a distinguishing personality. Endomorphs were short, small-boned, and fat. They were also thought to be easygoing, to crave affection, and to favor comfortable life-styles. Mesomorphs were muscular, athletic, and heavy-chested with a large torso, hands, and wrists. They were described as aggressive, excitement loving, and very active. Ectomorphs were thin, frail, and had rounded shoulders. Their dispositions were marked by shyness, unstable attitudes, and an inclination to be withdrawn. Sheldon applied his theory to a study of institutionalized delinquents. He found a large portion of the sample (200 boys) to be mesomorphic. Some were endomorphic. Very few were ectomorphic.

Sheldon and Eleanor Glueck also found delinquent boys to be predominately mesomorphic in body structure. The Gluecks stressed, however, that body build is not a direct cause of delinquency. Rather, a person's physical appearance may simply just affect his behavior. For example, muscular boys who are looked up to by friends may commit aggressive acts to maintain their respect and admiration. Some of these acts may be defined as delinquent by the authorities. The Gluecks noted that many factors may work together to cause delinquency—body build is just one of them.[6]

In a later study, Cortes and Gatti compared the body types of officially labeled delinquents with those of a nondelinquent sample. Their findings generally agreed with the Gluecks' conclusion that delinquents are decidedly more mesomorphic than nondelinquents. Cortes and Gatti also warn, as did the Gluecks, that body type and disposition are not a cause of delinquency. At best, they are indirectly related to crime and delinquency.[7]

All of the body-type theories of crime may be criticized on three general grounds. First, the definition or description of body type lacks precision. Second, the relationship between body type, disposition, and behavior is unclear; that is, why don't all mesomorphs commit offenses or why are not all offenders mesomorphs? Third, research samples of criminals and delinquents have not included the large number of offenders who escape the criminal justice system.

Glandular Dysfunctions and Crime

The glands produce hormones that affect the sex drive, weight, height, excitement, and activity levels. During the 1920s, some criminologists began to associate glandular dysfunction with criminal behavior. In general, these theories maintain that imbalances in the endocrine glandular system (thyroid, pituitary, etc.) produce emotional instability that may lead to criminal acts. Schlapp and Smith claimed that almost one-third of all prison inmates suffer from irregular glandular functioning.[8]

A study by Ellis and Austin found that aggressive behavior among female offenders was more pronounced during premenstrual and menstrual periods. They noted that this is also the time when the amount of progesterone (a hormone) is at a significantly low level for females.[9] In similar fashion, some researchers have found that the male hormone, testosterone, exists at higher levels among violent male offenders.[10] Allen and his research associates observed that inmates diagnosed as "sociopathic" (impulsive, lacking a conscience, repeat offenses, etc.) were deficient in the secretion of adrenaline.[11]

Glandular dysfunction orientations are subject to much of the same criticisms as are body-type approaches. Thus, most people who have glandular disorders do not commit crime. Furthermore, many criminals appear to have no glandular abnormalities.[12] Finally, there is the issue of faulty sampling techniques. More controlled research which includes random sampling from the general, uninstitutionalized population is necessary.

Chromosome Irregularities

Normal individuals have two sex chromosomes. Females possess two Xs, whereas males have one X and one Y. Researchers in the 1960s began to study male offenders who possessed an extra male, or Y, chromosome. Among institutionalized criminals, Jacobs and her associates found a much higher proportion of XYY males than the proportion expected to exist in the general population.[13] Though many of the chromosome studies have linked XYY males with added aggressiveness, an equal number have found no substantial relationship to exist. Any added criminality of XYY males appears to be more a function of their lower intelligence.[14]

Despite some suggestion of a relationship between the XYY karyotype and crime, it should be remembered that most XYY males appear to function normally. Second, only a very small percentage of all male criminals possess an XYY karyotype. Finally, most chromosome studies have been plagued by very small samples.

Abnormal Brain or Nervous System Activity

The brain affects emotions. When its functioning is impaired due to disease, accident, or birth defects, one may overreact to normal stimulation. Situations that usually produce no problems for most people may become explosive for the brain-damaged individual. Some of this behavior is clearly criminal in nature.

Early studies of the brain's relationship to aggression were conducted with animals. Cats and monkeys appear to become more aggressive when certain parts of the brain are stimulated or surgically altered. Regarding humans, one technique for locating brain disorder is the use of the electroencephalograph (EEG). The EEG measures brain wave activity and is capable of recording unusual or abnormal patterns. Studies have demonstrated that some violent offenders reveal abnormal brain wave patterns.[15] But there is no clear evidence that aggressive criminal behavior is the direct result of brain damage or disease. The results of EEG measurements should be cautiously considered.

Eysenck believes that individuals have inherited different degrees of sensitivity to pain or punishment. According to his theory, all voluntary acts concentrate on obtaining pleasure. One must be conditioned, through punishment, to avoid pleasure that is unlawful. Eysenck claims that mesomorphs, who are extroverts (outgoing, active, etc.), have nervous systems that are less sensitive to pain then are those of others. It is, therefore, more difficult to condition mesomorphs to act in socially approved ways. Eysenck feels that this is one reason for their increased involvement in crime and delinquency.[16]

Lykken's early research on sociopathic individuals—those characterized as manipulators, seemingly likable but ruthless, very verbal and lacking a sense of guilt for wrongdoing—reflects much of Eysenck's key ideas. Accordingly, sociopaths are believed to suffer from a nervous system deficiency that causes them to be abnormally insensitive to pain.[17] Other researchers have found that injections of adrenaline (a hormone, known as epinephrine, that increases sensitivity and excitement) produces increased pain awareness for some inmates diagnosed as sociopathic.[18] Presumably, increased sensitivity may enhance the probability of inducing approved behavior among sociopaths through conditioning techniques.

In a recent and widely critiqued book, James Q. Wilson and Richard Herrnstein argue that people choose to commit crime but that those who have inherited an impulsive and aggressive personality, coupled with low intelligence, are more likely to choose such actions. Their book, *Crime and Human Nature*, further specifies that criminal predispositions may be somewhat neutralized by family reinforced morality and punishment for misbehavior that counteracts any expected pleasure.[19]

Some criminal behavior may be traced to brain or nervous system defects. But it appears that other factors besides these must operate. Not all brain-damaged or nervous system disordered people commit crimes. Only a small percentage of criminals have identifiable irregularities in this regard. Further, the EEG is not accurate in some respects. For example, it does not measure extensive brain activity or the complicated interrelationship between the brain and the entire nervous system.

PSYCHOLOGICAL THEORIES OF CRIME

Psychological (and psychiatric) theories of crime have much in common with biological explanations. All more or less emphasize factors or defects within the individual that cause crime. Psychological (and psychiatric) theories, like biological ones, also overlook or treat lightly the interplay of economic, social, and political factors with individual behavior. In general, psychological (and psychiatric) theories may be grouped according to whether they concentrate on mental capabilities, personality structures, or personality development in attempting to explain crime and delinquency.

Mental Capabilities

The early explanations of crime as the result of mental defects were closely tied to biology. In particular, the role of heredity in producing feebleminded offspring was considered important. At the time that Lombroso was writing, Richard Dugdale investigated a family known as the Jukes. He determined that one of the illegitimate (born out of wedlock) Juke daughters produced over 1,000 descendants. Most of them were found to be defective. Some were criminals, others were prostitutes, several had venereal disease, and many were ''guilty'' of being poor. Dugdale concluded that inferior intelligence and crime were linked together by the breeding of degenerate people. Although he did credit the environment with having effects on behavior, Dugdale stressed the primary influence of heredity.[20]

Goddard felt that behavior was a consequence of one's degree of intelligence and that low intelligence could combine with an improper environment to produce criminal conduct. Like Dugdale, he also believed that intelligence was inherited and unchangeable. To demonstrate his theory, Goddard did a case study of the families produced by a Revolutionary soldier named Martin Kallikak. Kallikak had an illegitimate son by a degenerate barmaid. Following the war, Kallikak married a ''decent girl'' and fathered several children. Goddard compared the offspring resulting from the barmaid with those from the ''decent girl.'' He noted that the barmaid's descendants included a sizable number of mental defects, sexual deviants, alcoholics, and criminals. The family resulting from the ''good marriage'' contained only a handful of feebleminded or deviant descendants. Goddard concluded that the retarded barmaid had ultimately cost society a great deal of social problems!

Goddard was also a pioneer in the mental testing movement. The first IQ (intelligence quotient) test was devised by French psychologists, Benet and Simon, in 1905. Since then, several varieties of IQ tests have been developed by psychologists. In its fundamental form, the IQ of an individual is obtained when one's mental age is multiplied by 100 and then divided by one's actual age. The mental age is determined by the score one achieves on a standardized test. So, IQ is estimated using the following formula:

$$IQ = \frac{\text{Mental Age}}{\text{Actual Age}} \times 100$$

IQ tests have been administered to criminals and delinquents since World War I. The results have been contradictory. Goddard claimed that about one-half of the criminal population was subnormal in intelligence. Other early leaders of the mental testing approach found criminals to have below average intelligence. However, some researchers began to look closely at the techniques employed by mental testers and found that mental retardation was no more prevalent in criminal than in noncriminal populations.[21] Eventually, studies began to reveal that the entire notion of criminals being a mentally inferior group was questionable. In some of these studies, prisoners were found to have performed better on IQ tests than samples from the general population did.[22]

Studies of feeblemindedness and low intelligence are marked by several shortcomings. First, case studies of "degenerate" families (the Jukes, Kallikaks, etc.) ignored social conditions and were based on hearsay evidence or poorly kept public records. Second, intelligence tests and scores are clearly related to cultural values, individual backgrounds of subjects, and environmental factors. In this sense, they may not actually measure raw intelligence. Third, as research and testing have become more refined, the differences in IQ scores between criminals and noncriminals have been minimized. Few criminologists now feel that there is a significant direct relationship between low intelligence and crime.

Personality Structures

Explanations that concentrate on the influence of personality structure on criminal behavior are referred to as psychodynamic theories. Psychodynamic interpretations see criminal behavior as a symptom of motivations and/or psychological conflicts that may be conscious or subconscious. The psychodynamic approach is usually adopted by clinical psychologists and psychiatrists. Clinical psychologists typically hold advanced degrees (masters or doctorates) in psychology. Psychiatrists are medical doctors who have completed a residency in psychiatry. Psychologists and psychiatrists typically use different techniques to evaluate personality structures.

In addition to IQ tests, psychological instruments are also designed to yield personality profiles. There are several tests which fall into this category. Included among the more widely used are the MMPI (Minnesota Multiphasic Personality Inventory),

Rorschach test, the CPI (California Psychological Inventory), and the TAT (Thematic Apperception Test). Psychological instruments such as these have been administered to criminals and delinquents in order to determine if there exists a pronounced criminal personality structure.

The results of psychological testing have been contradictory. Using Rorschach testing, a method whereby the interpretation of inkblots is assumed to reveal personality profiles, the Gluecks noted differences between delinquents and nondelinquents. The former were found to be more extroverted, impulsive, antiauthority, hostile, and aggressive than the nonoffenders in the study.[23] The developers of the MMPI, Hathaway and Monachesi, have found that it identifies psychological differences between offenders and nonoffenders.[24] More recent assessments of past attempts to establish a criminalistic personality profile have cast doubt on the usefulness and validity of these instruments.[25]

In summary, some psychological tests may be reliable in isolating traits more common among criminals than noncriminals. But no psychological tests have been able to identify a personality structure that is common to most criminals or delinquents. In fact, not one of the tests is capable of determining whether criminal behavior leads to certain personality traits or if a certain personality structure leads to criminal behavior.[26]

Psychiatrists generally view crime in psychodynamic terms. While clinical psychologists rely heavily on testing, psychiatrists have been influenced by a technique known as psychoanalysis. The leading pioneer of psychoanalysis was Sigmund Freud (1856–1939).

Freud believed that the personality is made up of three core elements: the id, ego, and superego. The id is the seat of instinct and basic drives such as sex and aggression. The superego is comparable to the moral term conscience. It consists of the commands that guide us as to what we can and cannot do. That is, rules and values that society and authority figures impress upon a person. The id and the superego often conflict with one another. It is the function of the ego to keep the id and the superego in balance with reality. Freud theorized that the ego supplies defense mechanisms that keep the id in check. One important defense mechanism is repression. It operates to force id drives into the subconscious so that they are not acted out. Freud thought that much antisocial behavior symbolized a search for needs not sufficiently resolved or repressed by the ego.

Psychoanalysis is an attempt to unravel the internal conflicts and repressions that may be at the heart of antisocial (criminal or delinquent) behavior. Regarding crime, psychoanalysis assumes that the causes or motives are subconscious. The offender must be able to understand these subconscious reasons before treatment can be effective. Psychiatrists differ as to the specific causes of an individual's internal conflicts. However, the most often cited general source is family relationships.

The psychoanalytic model emphasizes the case study approach. The individual is presumed to have a unique personality structure (id, superego, and ego interrelationships) and background experiences that must be thoroughly explored. Psychoanalysis developed alongside the psychological testing approach and reached its peak of influence in the 1940s and 1950s. The impact of psychoanalytic theory can be seen in the passage of sexual psychopath laws beginning in the late 1930s.[27] The psychoanalytic model remains but has diminished in importance as an explanation of crime. Social scientists and some psychiatrists [28] have attacked psychoanalysis for its reliance on the concept of mental illness to explain a large assortment of behaviors. Also, the psychoanalytic model is frequently criticized for its use of unclear terminology and narrow scope. Psychoanalysis gives little recognition to broad social factors that contribute to crime, its definition, and control.

Personality Development

Psychological theories that center around personality development picture maturity as a stage-wise progression. As the individual passes from one stage to the next, one becomes more morally responsible and aware of the consequences of one's behavior. Piaget (1896–1980) was closely identified with the study of personality development regarding the ability to understand and appreciate moral judgments. [29]

Sullivan, Grant, and Grant have applied the basic points of development theory to crime and delinquency. [30] They state that full adult maturity is reached by passing through seven levels of personality development. Before a person can move from one level to the next, a critical interpersonal problem must be overcome. Once overcome, the individual properly adjusts, integrates previous experiences, and moves on to the next level. According to this theory of interpersonal maturity levels, criminals and delinquents fail to advance to higher stages of maturity. It is their inability to appreciate social rules and control behavior (immaturity) that increases the probability of unlawful behavior.

The theory was the basis for a massive juvenile rehabilitation program in California. Delinquents were classified according to the level of maturity that they had reached. All were placed in the second, third, or fourth level. Each maturity level contained subtypes, as the following reveals. [31]

MATURITY LEVEL	DELINQUENT SUBTYPE (CODE NAME)
I_2	Asocial, aggressive (Aa)
	Asocial, passive (Ap)
I_3	Conformist, immature (Cfm)
	Conformist, cultural (Cfc)
	Manipulator (Mp)
I_4	Neurotic, acting-out (Na)
	Neurotic, anxious (Nx)
	Situational emotional reaction (Se)
	Cultural identifier (Ci)

Delinquents in the Community Treatment Project were given different types of treatment depending upon their maturity level and sublevel category. Early research reports indicated that the experimental group which received treatment according to their maturity diagnosis was more successful than the control group that received regular probation. However, in a recent evaluation of the Project, Martinson found that the experimentals were handled more favorably than the controls. That is, the success was due

> not so much [to] a change in the behavior of the experimental youths as [to] a change in the behavior of the experimental probation officers, who knew the "special" status of their charges and who had evidently decided to revoke probation status at a lower than normal rate.[32]

Developmental theories assist criminologists by providing some insights into the complications that may occur while growing up. They are weak in that they do not adequately explain why underdeveloped personalities may be especially crime-prone. Regarding moral responsibility or maturity, developmental approaches have largely failed to show a relationship between moral beliefs and moral behavior. People often commit acts which they believe to be immoral.

SUMMARY

The Positivist School of criminology was a response to the legal-philosophical approach of the Classical School. Early Positivists emphasized the scientific study of the offender. They assumed that there were conditions that caused or determined criminal behavior. Eventually, the Positivist approach influenced the development of theories that searched for causes of crime among physical, mental, and social conditions. This chapter examined two categories of Positivism: biological and psychological-psychiatric theories.

Biological theories of crime focus upon the criminal effects of body types, glandular disorders, chromosome irregularities, and abnormal brain or nervous system activity. In general, theories which claim that biological abnormalities may explain crime suffer from three shortcomings.

First, research samples tend to include only institutionalized or officially recognized offenders. The large number of criminals who fail to be caught can never be sampled. Second, the particular biological abnormality under consideration (e.g., chromosome structure, glandular system) usually accounts for only a small portion of offenders. Third, biological explanations usually fail to clearly establish what it is about the defect that leads to criminal behavior.

Psychological-psychiatric theories also see crime as a product of individual defects. They differ from biological explanations by stressing mental abnormalities. These theories may be grouped into three primary areas, depending on whether they concentrate on mental capabilities, on personality structures, or on personality development as related to criminal behavior. The weaknesses of the psychological (psychiatric) theories are similar to those of the biological explanations.

First, samples are often restricted to officially defined groups of criminals. Second, psychological-psychiatric theories treat lightly the relationship between crime and broad social, economic, and political factors. Third, both tend to rely on techniques that have questionable reliability and precision. Psychologists often use tests which vary in their ability to measure intelligence or locate criminal mental traits. Psychiatrists have relied on psychoanalysis which has been criticized for its lack of precision. Fourth, neither approaches have been able to identify traits or developmental stages peculiar to criminals or delinquents as a whole.

At best, it may be said that some criminals and delinquents are indirectly affected by biological or mental abnormalities. As a group, criminals appear to be pretty much like the rest of the population both mentally and physically. In the next chapter we will explore sociological attempts to explain or theorize about crime and criminals.

SUGGESTED ACTIVITIES

- Observe the editorial cartoons in your local newspaper. How do they compare with Lombroso's theories about crime as an expression of biological inferiority? How are criminals portrayed?
- Visit a psychologist at your college or university and discuss the various tests used to measure personality characteristics. In particular, you may wish to ask what the tests measure, how they are scored, and evaluated. If possible, ask to see a copy of one of the tests.
- Visit your local hospital, individually or as a class, and request a demonstration of the electroencephalograph (EEG). Ask the hospital personnel about the EEG's capabilities and its drawbacks. How may it evaluate future behavior possibilities?
- If possible, discuss the principles of psychoanalysis with a psychiatrist. You may wish to write to the American Psychiatric Association or the American Psychoanalytic Association for literature dealing with crime and mental illness. A local physician or medical board will be able to supply you with the correct address.

REVIEW

A. List the major differences between the Classical and Positivist Schools of criminology.

B. List four major biological explanations of crime and briefly discuss their positions.

C. List and briefly discuss three primary psychological (psychiatric) approaches to crime.

D. List the general weaknesses of biological and psychological (psychiatric) theories discussed in this chapter.

E. Multiple Choice. Select the best answer.

1. The early Positivists:
    a. denied free will
    b. rejected the principle of hedonism
    c. replaced legal philosophy with scientific studies of offenders
    d. all of these

2. Who of the following has been called the "father of criminology?"
    a. Ferri
    b. Lombroso
    c. Garofalo
    d. Sheldon

3. The Law of Saturation was proposed by:
    a. Ferri
    b. Lombroso
    c. Garofalo
    d. Goring

4. The body type found to be most common among juvenile delinquents by Sheldon and the Gluecks:
    a. ectomorphs
    b. endomorphs
    c. mesomorphs
    d. octomorphs

5. Dysfunctional glands are thought to be a cause of crime because they:
    a. may affect emotional or sensory stability
    b. excite the id
    c. suppress the superego
    d. produce high fevers

6. A sociopathic condition has been associated with:
    a. endomorphic body types
    b. XYY chromosome structures
    c. abnormal nervous system activity
    d. mesomorphic body types

7. A psychological test that evaluates the interpretation of inkblots to establish personality structures is:
    a. MMPI
    b. CPI
    c. Rorschach
    d. psychoanalysis

8. Relies on unconscious motives, repressed conflicts, and the case study method to explain antisocial behavior:
    a. psychoanalysis
    b. developmental psychology
    c. experimental psychology
    d. chromosomal analysis

9. In general, biological and psychological-psychiatric theories:
    a. explain the vast majority of criminal behavior
    b. tell us nothing about crime
    c. give insights into some possible indirect causes of crime
    d. are no longer found to be held by criminologists

REFERENCES

1. George B. Vold, *Theoretical Criminology*, 2nd ed., Thomas J. Bernard (ed.) (New York: Oxford University Press, 1979), 55.
2. Marvin E. Wolfgang, "Cesare Lombroso," in Herman Mannheim (ed.) *Pioneers in Criminology*, 2nd ed. (Montclair, N.J.: Patterson, Smith, 1973), 235–290.
3. Francis A. Allen, "Raffaele Garofalo," in Mannheim, *ibid.*, 326.
4. Quoted in Sue Titus Reid, *Crime and Criminology*, 4th ed. (New York: Holt, Rinehart and Winston, 1985), 101.
5. Vold, *op. cit.*, 43.
6. Sheldon Glueck and Eleanor Glueck, *Physique and Delinquency* (New York: Harper and Row, 1956), 249.

7. Juan B. Cortes and Florence M. Gatti, *Delinquency and Crime: A Biopsychological Approach* (New York: Seminar Press, 1972).

8. M. G. Schlapp and E. H. Smith, *The New Criminology* (New York: Liveright, 1928).

9. Desmond P. Ellis and Penelope Austin, "Menstruation and Aggressive Behavior in a Correctional Center for Women," *Journal of Criminal Law, Criminology and Police Science*, 62 (1971), 388–395.

10. L. E. Kreuz and R. Rose, "Assessment of Aggressive Behavior and Plasma Testosterone in a Young Criminal Population," *Psychosomatic Medicine*, 34 (1972), 321–332.

11. Harry E. Allen, et al., "The Social and Bio-Medical Correlates of Sociopathy," *Criminologica*, 6 (1969), 68–75.

12. Richard Rada, "Plasma Androgens in Violent and Non-Violent Sex Offenders," *Bulletin of the American Academy of Psychiatry and Law*, 11 (1983), 149–158.

13. Patricia A. Jacobs, et al., "Aggressive Behavior, Mental Subnormality, and the XYY Male," *Nature*, 208 (1965), 1351.

14. Lee Ellis, "Genetics and Criminal Behavior," *Criminology*, 20 (1982), 51.

15. R. D. Hare, *Psychopathy: Theory and Research* (New York: John Wiley, 1970), 47; K. E. Moyer, *The Psychobiology of Aggression* (New York: Harper and Row, 1976); Vicki Pollock, et al., "Crime Causation: Biological Theories," in Sanford Kadish (ed.) *Encyclopedia of Crime and Justice*, Vol. 1 (New York: Macmillan, 1983), 311.

16. H. J. Eysenck, *Crime and Personality* (London: Routledge and Kegan, 1977).

17. David T. Lykken, "A Study of Anxiety in the Sociopathic Personality," *Journal of Abnormal and Social Psychology*, 55 (1957), 6–10.

18. Allen, et. al., *op. cit.*

19. James Q. Wilson and Richard Herrnstein, *Crime and Human Behavior* (New York: Simon and Schuster, 1985).

20. Stephen Schafer, *Theories in Criminology* (New York: Random House, 1969), 205–206.

21. L. D. Zeleny, "Feeblemindedness and Criminal Conduct," *American Journal of Sociology*, 38 (1933), 564–578; A. E. Gregg, "Criminal Behavior of Mentally Retarded Adults," *American Journal of Mental Deficiency*, 52 (1948), 370–375.

22. See Simon H. Tuchlin, *Intelligence and Crime* (Chicago: University of Chicago Press, 1939).

23. Ernest G. Schachter, "Notes on Rorschach Tests of 500 Juvenile Delinquents and a Control Group of 500 Non-Delinquent Adolescents," *Journal of Projective Techniques*, 15 (1951), 144–172.

24. Starke Hathaway and Elio Monachesi, *Analyzing and Predicting Juvenile Delinquency with the MMPI* (Minneapolis: University of Minnesota Press, 1953).

25. Gordon Waldo and Simon Dinitz, "Personality Attributes of the Criminal: An Analysis of Research Studies, 1950–1965," *Journal of Research in Crime and Delinquency*, 4 (1967), 191–195; D. J. Tannenbaum, "Personality and Criminality: A Summary and Implications of the Literature," *Journal of Criminal Justice*, 5 (1977), 225–235.

26. *Ibid.*

27. Edwin H. Sutherland, "The Diffusion of Sexual Psychopath Laws," *American Journal of Sociology*, 56 (1950), 142–148.

28. Thomas S. Szasz, *The Myth of Mental Illness* (New York: Harper and Row, 1961).

29. Jean Piaget, *The Moral Judgment of the Child* (Glencoe, Ill.: Free Press, 1948).

30. C. E. Sullivan, M. Q. Grant, and J. D. Grant, "The Development of Interpersonal Maturity: Applications to Delinquency," *Psychiatry*, 20 (1957), 373–385.

31. Marguerite Q. Warren, "The Community Treatment Project," in N. Johnson, L. Savitz, and M. Wolfgang (eds.) *The Sociology of Punishment and Correction* (New York: John Wiley, 1970), 675.

32. Robert Martinson, "What Works? Questions and Answers about Prison Reform," in Robert G. Leger and John R. Stratton (eds.) *The Sociology of Corrections* (New York: John Wiley, 1977), 514.

8

Sociological Theories

OBJECTIVES

After studying this chapter, the student should be able to:

- Describe two groups of theories that explain crime in environmental terms.
- Discuss two sociological theories that view crime as a consequence of interactional forces.
- Summarize those sociological theories that examine the relationship between crime and internal restraints.

In previous chapters, we have examined the Classical School with its focus on legal reform, deterrence, and free will. In addition, we have noted the Positivist theories of crime that locate the source of criminal behavior either in the individual's body (biological theories) or mind (psychological theories). In this chapter, the student will be exposed to those theories that attempt to explain crime primarily as the result of social factors.

Most sociological theories fall within the Positivist School. They favor an analysis of crime that emphasizes society's impact upon individual behavior. Free will is more or less downplayed and the person's behavior is seen as the outcome of situations or conditions created by society. As we shall see, some of these explanations include psychological factors. But the main thrust of the theories considered here largely center around forces generated by the society in which one lives and interacts.

Since the early 1900s, sociology has contributed more to the theory of crime than, perhaps, has any other academic study. Most of the sociological theories deal specifically with delinquent behavior. It will not be possible to discuss all of the theories that are considered to be sociological in nature. Because this textbook is designed to be a fundamental introduction to criminology, only the more prominent theories will be presented. For purposes of clarity and understanding, those theories that emphasize the role of economics and social class conflict will be treated separately in the following chapter. The sociological theories presented in this chapter may be grouped into three general categories: crime, society, and the environment; crime, society, and interactional forces; and crime, society, and internal restraints.

CRIME, SOCIETY, AND THE ENVIRONMENT

An individual's environment may include several unfavorable variables. First, it entails physical conditions such as slum housing, disease, and malnutrition. Second, it includes psychological factors; for example, hostility, negativism, and despair. Third, the environment also contains or lacks opportunities—both legitimate (employment, education, etc.) and illegitimate (crime and delinquency).

Crime and Ecology

In the early 1920s, Chicago became conscious of its growing problem with urban crime. One journalist described the city as being the "first in violence, deepest in dirt, loud, lawless, unlovely, ill-smelling, irreverent, new, an overgrown gawk of a village, the 'tough' among cities, a spectacle for the nation." [1] In spite of its unflattering reputation, Chicago was really no different than other large cities of the day. Given these conditions and the emergence of scientific criminology, extensive research was begun under the leadership of such men as Ernest Burgess, Clifford Shaw, and Henry McKay at the University of Chicago.

The researchers adopted the view that certain urban environments create more favorable conditions for crime than do others. Thus, cities were divided up into various zones for purposes of identifying environmental factors associated with crime. Burgess and his colleagues drew up five residential areas for the city of Chicago. [2] The resulting map resembled a target, cut in half from north to south, with the bull's eye representing the central business district. Each area or zone had distinguishing characteristics.

Shaw and McKay applied the findings of Burgess to delinquency. They noted that delinquency rates were highest in zone two, the "zone of transition," next to the central business district. Also, delinquency rates decreased as one moved away from zone two toward the suburbs (zone five). Finally, the rates remained high in the zone of transition over time and regardless of the racial or ethnic group that resided there. Zone two, the high delinquency area, was characterized by the presence of "flop houses," congested living quarters, transient residents, pawn shops, and warehouses. In addition to crime and delinquency, socially injurious conditions such as poverty, truancy, and high rates of suicide and mental illness were commonplace. [3]

Since the early work of Shaw and McKay, others have examined the ecology of high delinquency areas in several cities. Their findings have generally agreed with the original and later studies of Shaw and McKay.[4] On the other hand, a study by Lander challenged the ecologist's position that crime and delinquency were closely related to the environment's physical characteristics. Lander studied the relationship between urban zones and delinquency in Baltimore. He concluded that community permanence (home ownership and stable populations) was more related to low delinquency rates than were the physical features of a zone or its nearness to the central business district.[5]

Crime and Subcultures

Social permanence or stability is related to social cohesion. Sociologists have recognized that the glue that holds society together and keeps its members functioning in approved ways is the normative (rules, values, and ethics) system. Emile Durkheim, a famous sociologist, theorized that complicated, industrialized societies promote isolation of the individual. That is, with advanced development, jobs become specialized and people are expected to survive on an individual rather than a group basis. As isolation increases, commonly approved social norms and values become weakened or disappear. This condition of normlessness is termed *anomie*.

Subculture theories are closely tied to the concept of anomie. They basically propose that there is a specific delinquent subculture that exists among lower class adolescents. In this sense, one may assume that this subculture is more likely to be found in certain areas of the city.

According to Cohen, the lower-class child is denied the means of achieving middle-class goals. The child's environment does not prepare him or her to succeed in a society dominated by middle-class definitions of success. To counteract feelings of failure, worthlessness, and frustration, some lower-class adolescents create a subculture. This subculture environment is one which possesses its own set of norms and values that are in opposition to those of the middle class. Cohen terms this psychological process of rejecting middle-class values for delinquent subcultural ones as reaction formation. These subcultural norms encourage behavior that is often illegal or defined as delinquent by the larger society.[6]

Disagreement exists over Cohen's idea about the so-called process of reaction formation. Lower-class adolescents, according to Miller, do not create a set of delinquent values because they are frustrated in their efforts to achieve middle-class goals. Rather, there simply exists a tradition of lower-class "focal concerns" independent of middle-class goals or values. So the lower-class value system operates apart from the norms of the rest of society. Miller lists and describes these subcultural concerns as "trouble," "toughness," "smartness," "excitement," "fate," and "autonomy." Working-class individuals come into conflict with the law because their behavior is based on values or concerns (norms) that are not approved by the influential middle and upper classes.[7]

Cloward and Ohlin developed a subcultural theory known as differential opportunity. They state that individuals differ as to their ability to achieve middle-class goals through both legitimate and illegitimate means. It is assumed that working-class children have limited access to legitimate means. Consequently, the lower-class adolescent may become a member of one of three subcultures depending upon the available illegitimate means. The *criminal subculture* is found in urban areas where adult criminals provide highly visible models and illegitimate means that are available to teenagers. The subculture is a stable element of the neighborhood and draws success-oriented children who lack legitimate opportunities. The *conflict subculture* is likely to be located in unstable, disorganized lower-class areas. Because of the area's instability and lack of legitimate and organized illegitimate opportunities, violence and aggression are a typical feature of this subculture. The *retreatist subculture* is a dumping ground for those who cannot adopt legitimate or illegitimate means to success. This subculture is made up of individuals who do not fit into a criminal or conflict subculture. A large proportion of its members are drug users.[8]

Sociological theories that relate crime to the physical or subcultural environment may be criticized on several points. First, they are deficient because they concentrate on lower-class delinquency and crime. Several self-report studies have revealed that much illegal behavior is committed by middle-class adolescents and adults. Second, environmental theories give little consideration to the effect of criminal justice agencies on high-crime areas. Excessively high delinquency rates may be somewhat a result of increased law enforcement efforts in those areas marked by poverty, unemployment, and street-corner groups. Third, by focusing upon the physical or social structure, these theories do not adequately deal with psychological factors. Finally, the tendency of subcultural theories (especially Cohen's) to assume that lower-class children accept middle-class goals and are frustrated over their failure to achieve them is questionable.

CRIME, SOCIETY, AND INTERACTIONAL FORCES

Social environments may lend themselves to criminal values and opportunities. But social environments do not necessarily create criminals. Some individuals are exposed to poor physical conditions and delinquent subcultures but remain law-abiding. Others grow up in very comfortable, conventional surroundings but turn to crime. For some, it may be the combined influence of values, methods, and norms learned in association with others that makes the difference. The process of becoming a criminal has been theoretically discussed along two primary dimensions. First, the influence of one's association with peers (friends, fellow employees, and so on) and, second, the behavioral effects of contacts with criminal justice agencies.

Differential Association, Reference Groups, and Crime

Edwin Sutherland first proposed his theory of differential association as an attempt to explain career criminal behavior. He assumed that society contains a variety of values and behaviors (some of which are criminal) and then attempted to explain how criminal values are transmitted. According to Sutherland, sustained associations with those guided by antisocial values were likely to lead the individual to accept and learn criminal behavior. Thus, criminal conduct was seen by Sutherland as being neither inherited nor a necessary outcome of socially disorganized environments.

Differential association theory rejects the Positivist approach that has been discussed previously. It does not state that criminals are different (biologically, psychologically, or socially) from noncriminals. Sutherland stressed that crime is learned just as noncriminal behavior is learned. Most important, the theory does not even suggest that criminal behavior is determined. The actor does appear to have some choice regarding his or her conduct. However, the actor's choice will be influenced by associations and situational definitions that favor or disfavor criminal activities.[9]

Sutherland is also noted for his application of differential association theory to white-collar crime. The concept of white-collar crime is more thoroughly discussed in Chapter 14. At this point it should be noted that Sutherland was able to demonstrate the broad meaning of his theory by employing the principles of differential association to explain crime at all levels of society, both in the underworld and in the upperworld.

Reference group theory goes beyond differential association. Sutherland stated that "impersonal agencies of communication, such as movies and newspapers, play a relatively unimportant role in the genesis of criminal behavior."[10] Reference group theory takes into account all groups that the individual identifies with whether or not the individual holds membership in them. The reference group may be positive wherein the actor identifies it as desirable and acts accordingly. The group may be a negative reference serving as an identification to be consciously avoided or actively rejected by appearing as one with an opposite identity. Glaser borrowed from reference group theory and role theory to add the concept of differential identification to Sutherland's theory of differential association. Glaser notes that individuals identify with other characters or groups whether they know them personally or impersonally (movies, television, or novels). Some of these reference groups may be pro-criminal and come to influence actual behavior.[11]

Labeling Theory and Crime

The effects of associations or contacts between individuals and criminal justice personnel have also been studied. Labeling theory holds that society's reaction to some forms of behavior may encourage the development of criminal or delinquent careers. The theory was first introduced by Tannenbaum who noted that criminal behavior is much more than an isolated legal procedure of arrest and prosecution. It is a process of "tagging, defining, identifying . . . stimulating . . . and [generating] the very traits"[12] which are undesirable in the first place. Tannenbaum was suggesting that the law enforcement process itself may produce the very behavior that it is supposed to deter.

Edwin Lemert was the first to specify the theory's details.[13] He states that labeling operates in the following fashion. First, some kinds of behavior are viewed as threatening or undesirable by those who have the power to make or enforce laws. This behavior is then assigned a negative meaning. It may be defined as crime, delinquency, or, simply, deviance. Second, people choose or haphazardly wander into a variety of activities on a daily basis. Third, some of their behavior may fall into negative categories which are then singled out for official action. Fourth, several factors will determine whether or not the behavior is officially labeled as "bad." These factors include (1) the actor's social status in the community, (2) his or her mannerisms toward the police, (3) the visibility of the act, and (4) the degree of community agreement that the act is threatening. At this point, Lemert notes that the individual is at a stage known as primary deviance. As society begins to react more formally to the deviant (arrest, prosecution, probation, incarceration, or parole), the phase of secondary deviance is set into motion. Secondary deviance is the individual's adoption of a deviant identity or role in response to society's reaction to his or her behavior.

Labeling theory interprets social reaction—that is, the law enforcement response—as a cause of deviance rather than as an effect of deviance. The theory disagrees with the Positivist assumption that criminals are somehow different from noncriminals. Labeling theorists point out that there is a lot of crime and delinquency committed within all segments of society (rich and poor, black and white, urban areas and rural areas, etc.). The key question then becomes one of why are some people more likely to be picked out for official handling while others are not. Further, what are the effects of such social reaction?

Sociological theories that stress the influence of associations on behavior have achieved considerable recognition. As sociologists have become less accepting of Positivism, the theories of differential association and labeling have achieved added appeal. But these theories are not without their critics.

Perhaps the dominant criticism of differential association is the difficulty one encounters in trying to test it. The theory contains terms and concepts that are hard to measure. How does one measure the "intensity" of associations? How can a researcher accurately calculate the "amount of definitions favorable to violation of the law" that tips the scales in favor of criminal behavior? Other shortcomings exist. For example, the theory does not account for personality differences that come together in an association. The theory says nothing as to why some acts are defined as crimes. Also, Sutherland failed to explain why criminal associations arise in the first place. Finally, some types of crime are not explainable using the theory of differential association (e.g., crimes of passion).[14]

Labeling theory has also been faulted in several respects. First, it makes no attempt to explain the first (primary) act of deviance that led to a societal reaction. Second, it assumes that the offender has no control over the labelers. That is, once society labels the deviant, the label is assumed to be accepted; and the individual acts according to it. Third, labeling theory offers few realistic alternatives to criminal justice agencies regarding serious offenses. If law enforcement agencies cause further deviance by reacting to initial deviance, then it would appear that little or no response is the best course to take. The theory suggests that, left alone, the delinquent will "grow out" of his or her undesirable behavior patterns. What about serious crimes such as assault, robbery, and burglary? Should these be ignored? One could argue that ignoring such acts positively reinforces the behavior. Finally, labeling theory appears to take the side of the underdog; that is, the low-status individual who is singled out for official treatment. In doing so, it fails to focus on the misdeeds of "respectable" members of society.[15]

CRIME, SOCIETY, AND INTERNAL RESTRAINTS

The sociological theories considered so far have had little to say about psychological factors other than generalized statements about the role of learning. The remaining theories to be discussed in this chapter represent an attempt to merge social and psychological variables. Sometimes called "control theories," they emphasize the importance of mental mechanisms, self-images, and feelings or attachment in influencing our behavior. In order of discussion, we will briefly describe neutralization theory, containment theory, and Hirschi's version of control theory.

Neutralization Theory and Crime

Sykes and Matza proposed neutralization theory as an alternative to subcultural theories (Cohen, Cloward, and Ohlin, etc.).[16] According to the theory, delinquents do not form subcultures that have values contrary to the rest of society. Through the process of socialization (learning society's rules, being exposed to a variety of behavior), children also learn defenses or excuses for behavior. While growing up and interacting in social settings, they may drift between approved and unapproved behavior patterns. It is through techniques of neutralization that the individual is freed from law-abiding commands and allowed to drift. Once in this state of drift, the person may commit delinquent or criminal acts. However, after the act occurs the offender is not, according to Sykes and Matza, committed to delinquent or criminal values. In fact, they state that most delinquents drift out of delinquency in due time. The techniques of neutralization that temporarily free the juvenile to commit delinquencies are: [17]

1. Denial of Responsibility—a technique whereby the offender defends his or her actions by claiming that larger social forces are to blame for his or her behavior.
2. Denial of Injury—a defense which is employed to excuse conduct on the basis that no one is really harmed by the behavior.
3. Denial of the Victim—the technique of claiming that the injured party "got what was coming to him."
4. Condemnation of Condemners—a neutralization that shifts attention from the actor's delinquencies to the presumed misdeeds of authorities.
5. Appeal to Higher Loyalties—the notion that the expectations of friends are more important than those of society.

Neutralization theory also rejects the Positivist argument that criminals and delinquents are different from normal people. The theory assumes that offenders, by and large, hold conventional law-abiding values of the larger society. Sykes and Matza feel that the unique quality of delinquency is drift and the capacity to employ techniques of neutralization to justify undesirable behavior.

Containment Theory and Crime

How does one explain the existence of nondelinquents in a high-delinquency area as well as delinquents in a good neighborhood? Reckless and Dinitz identify the interaction of social and personality factors behind most delinquent acts. They claim that containment theory explains the broad "middle range" of delinquency and "crimes against the person as well as crimes against property." [18]

Containment theory asserts that outer, or social, pulls and pushes (poverty, social inequality, family conflict, etc.) combine with inner, or personality, pushes (hostility, frustration, pleasure seeking, etc.) to promote delinquency. These factors may be overruled by outer, or social, containments (good friends, a supportive family, etc.) and inner, or personality, containments (strong superego, tolerance of frustration, the ability to resolve psychic conflicts, etc.). Inner containment is equated with the term self-concept. Because society today is impersonal and rapidly changing, control must come from within. Therefore, Reckless and Dinitz see a good self-concept as the best insulation against delinquency. [19]

Containment theory stands somewhat in agreement with Positivist principles. It emphasizes the role of self-concept in explaining delinquency. As such, it assumes that the bulk of delinquents differ from others in that their self-concepts are weak. Reckless did not claim to have established the cause of delinquency (poor self-concept). Nevertheless, the theory supports the implication that children with poor self-concepts are predictable ("determinably") candidates for the juvenile court.

Criminological theories that incorporate social and mental set variables have difficulty in meaningfully weaving the two together. It is an extremely complicated process that occurs from the presence of social influences, to mental sets ("drift" or "self-concept"), to actual behavior (delinquency). Research has been unable to establish whether techniques of neutralizations occur before the act (as the theory states) or operate as rationalizations after the act. [20] Containment theory includes many vague notions that defy assessment. In particular, can the self-concept be measured? At what point is a self-concept judged as being "bad" or "weak"? If some delinquents are found to have a good self-concept and some nondelinquents a bad self-concept, then how meaningful is containment theory? Finally, both theories overlook the fact that delinquency (and crime) is conduct that is defined through the political process of lawmaking and law enforcement.

Hirschi's Control Theory and Crime

Hirschi captures the essence of his theory by quoting Durkheim, a central figure in the development of sociology, as follows:

> The more weakened the group to which [the individual] belongs, the less he depends on them, the more he consequently depends only on himself and recognizes no other rules of conduct than what are founded on his private interests. [21]

This expression of control theory stresses the critical effect of proper socialization—the internalization of conventional norms and values—on behavior. Of particular importance is the role played by key institutions, such as the family and school, and peers. Socialization, therefore, is the ''glue'' that bonds the person to society. The elements of the bond specified by Hirschi are attachment, commitment, involvement, and belief.[22]

An adolescent who is attached to significant others, committed to socially approved pursuits and values, and involved in prescribed activities, and who believes in the ideals of law possesses a strong moral bond to society. This is accomplished through parents who elicit love and admiration, schools that inspire creative thought, and an authority structure that breeds respect. When social bonds (attachment, commitment, involvement, and beliefs) are weak because of a faulty connection between the child and key socializing agents, delinquent pursuits are more probable.

Though research has generally found support for Hirschi's theory, there is still much room for refinement and elaboration. For example, the priority and sequence in which the family, school, and peers influence behavior needs additional clarification.[23] Also, to be more complete, Hirschi's theory must account for significant variables, such as the family's social-class background and the youth's inherent abilities, which other researchers have found to be related to delinquent involvement.[24]

SUMMARY

Theories of crime that rest on sociological interpretations may be divided into three general categories. First, there are explanations that tie crime and delinquency to environmental conditions. Second, sociological theories exist which view crime as a function of associations or social contacts. Third, there are those theories that explain crime as a consequence of the presence or absence of certain types of internal restraints.

Environmental theories may be further divided into ecological and subcultural approaches. Ecological orientations emphasize the relationship between crime and environmental characteristics. This position grew out of early research done at the University of Chicago and is evident in the work of Burgess, Shaw, McKay, and others. The subcultural tradition rests upon the concept of anomie (normlessness) and the lack of means to achieve middle-class goals on the part of lower-class adolescents. In response to these conditions, it is theorized that juveniles develop subcultures that have values which are contrary to those of the larger society. The subcultural norms are believed to promote delinquency. This approach may be found in the work of Cohen, Cloward and Ohlin, and Miller. While Miller challenges some aspects of subcultural theory, he still maintains that delinquency is a lower-class, subcultural activity.

Theories that tie criminal and delinquent behavior to associations are based on two levels of analysis. The peer group (friends, employees, etc.) is the focus of differential association theory. Sutherland believed that criminal behavior is learned in association with others. Further, it was an overabundance of these associations that fostered crime. Glaser joined reference group theory with role theory and developed the concept of differential identification. Differential identification emphasizes that both personal and impersonal groups or associates (television, fictional, newspaper, and movie characters) may provide a reference and role for the individual's behavior. Labeling theory examines the impact of social reactions to deviance upon the future behavior of the offender. Proposed by such scholars as Tannenbaum, Lemert, and others, the theory stresses that once society reacts to a deviant act (primary deviance), the individual assumes the label and develops a deviant career pattern (secondary deviance) as a response.

Theories which attempt to merge social and psychological variables, largely through the socialization process, focus upon the dynamics of internal restraints. Neutralization theory holds that delinquents and adult criminals, while generally accepting approved norms and values, commit misdeeds when internal restraints are weakened. This weakening process occurs when a state of psychological drift is induced through techniques of neutralization. Containment theory states that juveniles often struggle with internal and external pressures that promote delinquency. In order to be restrained or dissuaded from violating laws, they must draw upon inner containment (self-concept) resources. Hirschi's control theory stresses the importance of the social bond. As such, juveniles are thought to be restrained from delinquent acts by way of strong attachments, commitments, involvement, and belief in moral precepts. Essential to these bonds are primary institutions, such as the family and the school.

Each of the theoretical categories discussed in this chapter possess serious weaknesses. The shortcomings are either theoretical (something is missing) or methodological (their concepts are difficult to validate through research). Some follow the Positivist tradition by assuming that criminals and delinquents are somehow different from normal individuals. That is, delinquents come from bad environments, or subscribe to subcultural delinquent values, or lack a good self-concept. Other theories (differential association, labeling, and neutralization theory) reject all or some of the key principles of Positivism. The major fault of the theories discussed so far is that they all ignore the basic point that behavior is neither bad, delinquent, nor criminal until it is declared as such by those with the power to do so. The next chapter will examine theories that evaluate the political implications of crime.

SUGGESTED ACTIVITIES

- Contact probation or parole officers and ask them to discuss their ideas about the causes of crime and delinquency. Place these ideas within the theoretical categories presented in this chapter.
- Read your local newspaper and look for articles dealing with juvenile delinquency and crime. What kinds of offenses are discussed? Do the articles hint at any of the theories covered in this chapter?
- Identify any youth advocacy or delinquency prevention programs that exist in your community. Are they based on any of the theories described in this chapter? If so, list and discuss the theories that appear to be guiding these programs.
- Privately list those things that you did as a juvenile that could be classified as delinquent acts. What do you think leads some people to continue law-violating behavior? Relate this to your own experience and discuss in class.

REVIEW

A. Discuss theories that relate the environment to crime and delinquency.

B. Discuss theories that view crime and delinquency as a consequence of associations or social contacts.

C. Discuss theories that explain crime and delinquency in terms of intrapersonal conflict.

D. Multiple Choice. Select the best answer.

 1. The ecological interpretation of crime stresses:
  a. anomie
  b. the physical characteristics of environments
  c. labeling
  d. political factors

 2. Subcultural theories:
  a. explain much middle-class delinquency
  b. focus on lower-class delinquency
  c. have been termed ''middle range'' theories
  d. are not part of the Positivist School

 3. Reaction formation is a concept identified with:
  a. differential association
  b. labeling
  c. mesomorphs
  d. subcultural approaches

 4. Differential association theory emphasizes that crime:
  a. is inherited
  b. is learned in association with others
  c. is primarily lower-class behavior
  d. is associated with different racial groups

 5. The concept of differential identification was developed from:
  a. labeling theory
  b. subcultural and ecological theory
  c. reference group and role theory
  d. neutralization and containment theory

 6. According to labeling theory, when the offender adopts a deviant identity or role after society reacts to him or her, this is termed:
  a. primary deviance
  b. tertiary deviance
  c. displaced deviance
  d. secondary deviance

 7. Which of the following sociological theories rejects Positivist principles?
  a. neutralization theory
  b. subcultural theory
  c. containment theory
  d. ecological theory

 8. Denial of injury is:
  a. a part of containment theory
  b. an example of primary deviance
  c. a technique of neutralization
  d. an example of secondary deviance

 9. The most crucial factor in containment theory is:
  a. drift
  b. conflict subculture

c. self-concept
d. retreatist subculture
10. Hirschi's control theory stresses that:
a. delinquency is learned
b. delinquents lack self-control
c. delinquents have weak social bonds
d. delinquency is a function of social class

REFERENCES

1. John Kobler, *Capone* (Greenwich, Conn.: Fawcett Publications, 1972), 45.
2. Donald J. Shoemaker, *Theories of Delinquency* (New York: Oxford University Press, 1984), 74–76.
3. *Ibid.*, 78–80.
4. See, for example, Harold Finestone, *Victims of Change* (Westport, Conn.: Greenwood Press, 1976); Donald R. Taft and Ralph W. England, Jr., *Criminology* (New York: Macmillan, 1964), 153–154.
5. Bernard Lander, *Toward an Understanding of Juvenile Delinquency* (New York: Columbia University Press, 1954), 88–89; R. A. Gordon, "Issues in the Ecological Study of Delinquency," *American Sociological Review*, 32 (1967), 924–944.
6. Shoemaker, *op. cit.*, 102–105; Albert K. Cohen, *Delinquent Boys: The Culture of the Gang* (Glencoe, Ill.: Free Press, 1955), 124–137.
7. Walter B. Miller, "Lower Class Culture as a Generating Milieu of Gang Delinquency," *Journal of Social Issues*, 14 (1958), 5–19. See also the work of Edward Banfield, *The Unheavenly City* (Boston: Little, Brown, 1968).
8. Richard A. Cloward and Lloyd E. Ohlin, *Delinquency and Opportunity: A Theory of Delinquent Gangs* (Glencoe, Ill.: Free Press, 1960), Chap. 6.
9. Edwin H. Sutherland and Donald R. Cressey, *Criminology*, 10th ed. (Philadelphia: J. B. Lippincott, 1978), 80–82.
10. *Ibid.*, 80–81. See also the work of Gary F. Jensen and Dean G. Rojek, *Delinquency* (Lexington, Mass.: D. C. Heath, 1980) critiquing the importance of peer associations.
11. Daniel Glaser, "Criminality Theories and Behavior Images," *American Journal of Sociology*, 61 (1956), 433–444.
12. Frank Tannenbaum, *Crime and the Community* (Boston: Ginn, 1938), 19–20.
13. Edwin Lemert, *Social Pathology* (New York: McGraw-Hill, 1951).
14. Jensen and Rojek, *op. cit.* A summary of the theory's vulnerable propositions may be found in Sutherland and Cressey, *op. cit.*, 87–92. Also see, Gwynn Nettler, *Explaining Crime* (New York: McGraw-Hill, 1978), 266–267.
15. Edwin Schur, *Labeling Deviant Behavior* (New York: Harper and Row, 1972), 21; Alexander Liazos, "The Poverty of the Sociology of Deviance: Nuts, Sluts and Perverts," *Social Problems*, 20 (1972), 103–119.
16. Gresham Sykes and David Matza, "Techniques of Neutralization: A Theory of Delinquency," *American Sociological Review*, 22 (1957), 664–670.
17. *Ibid.*
18. Walter C. Reckless and Simon Dinitz, "Pioneering with Self-Concept as a Vulnerability Factor in Delinquency," *Journal of Criminal Law, Criminology and Police Science*, 58 (1967), 515–523.
19. *Ibid.*; Edward Wells, "Theories of Deviance and the Self-Concept," *Social Psychology*, 41 (1978), 189–204.
20. Henry W. Mannle and Peter W. Lewis, "Control Theory Re-Examined: Race and the Use of Neutralizations among Institutionalized Delinquents," *Criminology*, 17 (1979), 58–74.
21. Emile Durkheim, *Suicide*, John A. Spaulding and George Simpson (trans.) (New York: Free Press, 1951), 209.
22. Travis Hirschi, *Causes of Delinquency* (Berkeley, Calif.: University of California Press, 1969).
23. LaMar T. Empey, *American Delinquency*, 2nd ed. (Homewood, Ill.: Dorsey Press, 1982), 292–296.
24. Michael Wiatrowski, et al., "Social Control Theory and Delinquency," *American Sociological Review*, 46 (1981), 525–541.

9

Political
Explanations

OBJECTIVES

After studying this chapter, the student should be able to:

- Discuss some of the major ideas of Karl Marx regarding the structure of capitalist societies.
- Describe Bonger's application of Marxist theory to the problem of crime.
- Critique the "new criminology" and list some of its contributions to the study of crime.

Two views of the nature of society were presented previously in this book (Chapter 3). One view holds that the vast majority of people agree on basic values learned in the socialization process. These values include legal commands regarding what is forbidden by society. For a number of reasons (biological, mental, or social deficiencies), a small minority of individuals break society's rules (the law). This is the consensus view of society.

Another image of society maintains that the socialization process is not uniform. That is, society is believed to be composed of people who possess different, and often conflicting, values. This perspective further assumes that people differ concerning their political power to influence legal values as they are both written and applied. This is the conflict view of society. It is the basis for a theory of crime.

The fundamental, primary distinction between criminals and noncriminals is the violation and prosecution of behavior that is declared illegal. All of the theories considered so far have more or less assumed a consensus view of society. Except for the labeling approach, they have offered little in the way of explaining the role of political power in deciding what is a crime and who is a criminal. This chapter sketches politically oriented explanations of crime that have contributed to what is now referred to as "the new criminology."

CRIME, ECONOMICS, AND CLASS CONFLICT

Political explanations of crime typically take economic conditions as their starting point. Some, however, emphasize the role of economics more than others do. A very influential social analyst of all time was Karl Marx (1813–1883). His philosophical and economic interpretation of society provides the official foundation for a large portion of today's world governments.

In actuality, Marx made few direct statements that would qualify as a specific theory of crime. But his belief that economic conditions determine behavior is certainly relevant to the subject of criminal behavior. Marxist theory has undergone considerable interpretation and revision since it was first put forth in the nineteenth century. A thorough discussion of Marxist principles is beyond the purposes of this book. Only the more essential points of Marxism will be presented.

Marx's most fundamental point is that the economic system of a society determines the entire nature of that society. Every aspect of life, social relationships, psychological attitudes, religious beliefs, international politics, living conditions, and the law, are viewed as a reflection of the society's economic structure. Capitalism is the target of Marxist theory. Societies where the means of production (industry and agriculture) are privately owned and the distribution of goods and services are based on a free enterprise system have capitalistic economies.

According to Marxism, a capitalist state is made up of two major classes: the ruling (bourgeois) class and the working (proletariat) class. The ruling class owns the means of production and controls the daily lives of the people. Marx argued that the proletariat is abused by the bourgeois. Both the capitalist state and its laws are seen by Marxists as tools that the ruling class use to keep the workers "in their place." The ultimate solution to this situation is revolution. The workers must unite and struggle to free themselves of capitalist domination. The final goal is the establishment of a working-class state wherein the law would "serve the people." The state would thus become one in which the means of production would be held in common. The community (made up of the working class) would control property, goods, and services. The state would be communist in nature.[1]

Friedrich Engels, Marx's co-author for several books and pamphlets, related the class conflict between the bourgeois and proletariat to crime. He maintained that the negative conditions imposed on the working class by capitalism left them with few opportunities for improvement. One opportunity that remains is criminal behavior.[2] As stated previously, Marx made few systematic statements about the causes of crime. He did, however, tie crime to capitalism by noting its usefulness for the ruling class. The crime problem that is supposedly created by capitalism also helps to further the system by providing jobs. Marx thus commented that:

> The criminal produces not only crime but also the criminal law; he produces the professor who delivers lectures on this criminal law, and even the inevitable textbook in which the professor presents his lectures as a commodity for sale in the market. . . . Further-more, the criminal produces the whole apparatus of the police and criminal justice, detectives, judges, executioners, juries, etc. . . . The criminal, therefore, appears as one of those ''equilibrating forces'' which establish a just balance and open up a whole perspective of useful occupations.[3]

Bonger (1876–1940) applied the writings of Marx and Engels specifically to the crime problem.[4] He attempted to show that there is a direct relationship between poverty and crime. His underlying theory was that criminal motives and values result from self-centered attitudes promoted by capitalism. As individuals become greedier under capitalistic economies, criminal motives are further encouraged. Capitalism also fosters crime because it does not include ''moral training'' which is seen as unnecessary for industrial growth by the ruling class. For Bonger, the solution is to replace capitalism with socialism. Under a socialist state, man would be encouraged to follow his natural instinct toward group preservation (''one for all, all for one'') rather than selfish interests created by capitalism. Unlike Marx, Bonger favored an orderly change from capitalism to socialism rather than a violent revolution to communism.[5]

Both Marx and Bonger viewed crime as a reaction to the conditions created by capitalism. They also stressed the necessity of social change as a prerequisite to reducing crime. Both men accepted the notion that the law is the instrument of the ruling class. However, Marx did not say a great deal about crime and Bonger did not fully apply Marxism to crime. Much remained to be said about the role of political power in shaping the law, enforcing it, and creating criminal identities.[6]

CRIME AND POLITICAL CONFLICT

George Vold has pointed out that an understanding of crime involves two lines of questioning. First, why do some people commit crime? Several theories have been presented which attempt to answer this question. Second, and more fundamental to our study, why are some behaviors defined as crime in the first place?[7] Vold speaks to this question in the following manner:

> As one political group lines up against another, both seek the assistance of the organized state to help them defend their rights and protect their interests. Thus the familiar cry, ''there ought to be a law'' (to suppress the undesirable) is understandable as the natural recourse of one side or the other in a conflict situation.[8]

He then gives examples of crime that express group conflict; for example, crimes commit-ted in the name of social reform and crimes arising out of labor-management disputes.[9] In each of these instances, Vold underscores the notion that, for the groups involved, crime is a means to an end.

It has been observed that Vold was incomplete in his analysis of interest group activity as it influences the content and application of criminal law.[10] Quinney concludes that:

> The conflict model is incomplete if it stops here. If a critical perspective is to be developed, and if a theory of crime in American society is to be built from the model, we must recognize the economic structure of the society and its class conflict. In other words, then, what began as a conflict analysis must be turned into a class analysis. That America is a capitalist society is a crucial fact in analyzing its crime and criminal behavior.[11]

Thus, modern Marxists would claim that Vold was shortsighted in two respects. First, he did not adequately emphasize the unequal distribution of power (based on an unequal distribution of wealth) that places certain groups at a basic disadvantage. Second, Vold did not consider that the state (dominated by capitalist values) itself acts as an interest group.

Marxism of one variety or another is the basis for what is referred to as the "new criminology." The new criminology is also termed "critical" or "radical" criminology. The writings of Quinney,[12] Krisberg,[13] Chambliss and Seidman,[14] and others represent attempts to systematically (more or less) apply Marxism to an interpretation of crime in American society today. The new criminology starts with the assumption that the United States, as a capitalist society, is controlled by a ruling class. This ruling class is composed of industrial conglomerates, high-ranking bureaucrats, and their representatives. They control the state and the content and application of the criminal law. They create the conditions that spawn the crime problem. Only when capitalism is replaced by socialism will crime be reduced. The perspective of the new criminology proceeds in the following fashion.[15]

The ruling class shapes the content of the law to serve its purposes or interests. Cited as examples are drug laws that criminalize some narcotics but make addictive, potentially dangerous (and highly profitable) pharmaceuticals "freely" available. Also noted are laws written to protect and further the interests of the ruling class. Included in this area are the existing legal tax loopholes, draft laws in time of war (wars are seen as economic stimulators), and the legal principle of eminent domain. Eminent domain allows the state to acquire (with some compensation) any private property considered to be in the "public interest." In addition, laws which are geared to the direct control of the lower classes (e.g., welfare laws) are cited by Marxist criminologists as examples of ruling class influence. Ordinary ("street") crimes committed by the lower class (robbery, burglary, etc.) are seen by some Marxists as protests against an unjust society. In summary, so the argument goes, much of the law is the work of those who "either (1) own or control the resources [economic or political] of the society or (2) occupy positions of authority in the state bureaucracies."[16]

Crime is found at all levels of a capitalist society. Its characteristics result from one's class position. Lower-class people commit crimes of violence and ordinary theft because of deprivation and a lack of "refined" criminal opportunities. Members of the ruling class commit crimes that are a function of their class positions (e.g., corporate crime and government-related illegalities). Because the ruling class controls the law enforcement process, it is able to impose criminal definitions on the lower class and evade prosecution for its own crimes. Even when the ruling class commits "ordinary" crimes, they have the power and influence to receive favorable treatment. Therefore, official crime appears to be concentrated among the lower classes.

Defining the crime problem in terms of the lower class serves the purpose of the state's ruling class. First, it allows them greater control over the lower class. Second, the issue of crime is used to take attention away from the exploiting conditions created by capitalism. Third, crime is a means of convincing the noncriminal lower classes that they have fears and values in common with the ruling class.[17]

Supporters of the new criminology do not uniformly accept the Marxist position as stated here. Some of the "new" criminologists are less radical ("soft-core Marxist") than others. The less radical approach stresses that criminal definitions arise from conflicting interests, lack of opportunity, and differentials in social and political power. The notion of a ruling class that pulls the strings for the rest of society is downplayed.

The new criminology, as presented from a strong Marxist position, has stirred up considerable controversy. It contains some glaring weaknesses as an explanation of crime. The new criminology also has some rich insights to offer criminologists in their study of a complicated social problem.

Both the cause and solution to crime as stated by the new criminology is in need of clarification. If capitalism causes crime, why aren't more members of the lower class criminals? To solve crime, exactly what kind of a society must replace capitalism? Quinney's answer to this question is simply that "the society and its own forms of regulation will be worked out in the struggle of building a socialist society."[18] According to the new criminology, the only true criminals are those who have power; that is, the ruling class. One might ask: (1) why does power lead to crime? and (2) in the "new" socialist society, whose power will enforce the "forms of regulation" that Quinney speaks of? Also, what is meant by the term "ruling class"? How many of "them" exist and, specifically, how do they control society? Further, is the concept of a class struggle between the rulers and the lower class relevant today? What about the growing ranks of the middle class that do not appear to be awaiting a socialist revolution? Finally, is it accurate to state that crime, *per se*, is defined by the ruling class? It would seem that society as a whole defines robbery, murder, rape, and the like as criminal conduct. These are socially injurious acts regardless of the offender's class position in a capitalist or any other kind of society. As Gibbons notes:

> Although rape may be a form of symbolic revenge conducted by persons who feel the sting of racial discrimination, the fact remains that innocent persons are victimized by rapists. . . . Rape is rape, whatever the motives of the rapist.[19]

The new criminology has challenged some of the long-held beliefs about the nature of society. By placing the attention on power, it has introduced the idea that the force of the law rather than social agreement plays a part in holding society together. The new criminology also encourages a broader look at crime; that is, crime committed by the powerful and by the criminal justice system, as well as ordinary street crime. It supplies a humanistic tone to the study of crime. Traditional criminology has concerned itself with behavior that is forbidden by law. The new criminology suggests that criminologists concern themselves with behavior that should be declared criminal—any behavior that violates human rights (e.g., racism, sexism).[20] Criminologists disagree over whether they should mix professional objectives (studying crime) with social reform (combating racism, sexism, and the like). However, many of those criminologists who argue against political involvement agree that a denial of opportunities on the basis of race or social class contributes to the crime problem.

SUMMARY

This chapter examined those views of crime that are based on a political conflict model. Political explanations of crime generally begin with an analysis of society's economic structure. The works of Karl Marx (and Friedrich Engels) have served as the basis for much of modern political conflict explanations of crime.

Marx noted that a society's economic structure determines its nature. Every aspect of life is influenced by the ownership and distribution of goods and services. In capitalist societies the means of production (industry and agriculture) are privately owned. The goods and services are distributed on a free enterprise basis. The ruling class controls the means of production and abuses the workers. The workers are kept under control through the law. The solution rests with an overthrow of the ruling class by the workers and the establishment of a communist state.

Bonger attempted to apply Marxist principles to crime. He emphasized that poverty created by capitalism led to crime. Capitalism was seen as promoting selfish attitudes and greed that resulted in criminal motives. According to Bonger, societies based on capitalism did not support moral training because the ruling class saw this as unrelated to industrial growth and economic profits. He based the solution to crime on the development of socialism.

The question of why some behaviors are defined as crime was raised by Vold. He recognized that legal development and administration was influenced by the political process. But Vold did not adequately (according to modern Marxists) emphasize the unequal distribution of power in society nor the state itself acting as an interest group.

What has been termed the "new criminology" represents an effort to apply Marxist theory to an interpretation of crime in American society today. It proposes that a ruling class of industrialists and bureaucrats controls society, including the development and administration of the criminal law. Crime is found in all levels of society, but it is defined by those who rule as a problem of the lower class. This definition allows the ruling class greater control over the working class and helps to ensure the ruler's privileged position.

The new criminology has raised some interesting issues but falls short of offering a clear and logical explanation of crime. It neither adequately explains cause nor offers specific alternatives to the existing society. As an explanation, its terms (ruling class, class struggle, etc.) are vague, and its statements ("the ruling class defines crime") superficial.

SUGGESTED ACTIVITIES

- How do economic conditions affect your life? Would your life be different in terms of personal values, attitudes, political beliefs, and friendships had you been raised in an agricultural society, a small fishing village, or a large industrial city? Discuss in class.

- Suppose that the impossible happened: crime as we know it disappeared. How would this affect the economy? Discuss in class.

- Discuss public attitudes regarding "Robin Hood" crimes in which the rich are victims of theft. Are people as upset when, for example, an automobile manufacturing company is "ripped off" by employees as they are when the same company illegally tries to influence legislation? Both activities are illegal. Why the difference in public reaction, if any?

- In some countries the government claims that there should be no crime where socialism provides that each contributes according to one's means (ability) and receives according to one's needs. In the Soviet Union, common criminals are often declared to be mentally ill. Why is this the case?

REVIEW

A. Briefly discuss the views of Karl Marx regarding the structure of capitalist societies.

B. What is the significance of George Vold's notion of conflict theory?

C. Discuss the "new criminology" in terms of its major points and weaknesses.

D. Multiple Choice. Select the best answer.

1. Political explanations of crime usually begin with a consideration of:
    - a. economics
    - b. religion
    - c. war
    - d. psychology

2. A leading nineteenth-century communist was:
    - a. Bonger
    - b. Quinney
    - c. Marx
    - d. Vold

3. Marx primarily criticized countries founded upon:
    - a. kings or czars
    - b. capitalism
    - c. communism
    - d. socialism

4. A key concept of the "new criminology" is:
    - a. anomie
    - b. ruling class
    - c. welfare
    - d. none of these

5. According to the "new criminology," crime is:
    - a. actually found throughout society
    - b. officially identified as lower-class activity
    - c. defined by the ruling class
    - d. all of these

6. A major shortcoming of the new criminology is that it:
   a. ignores political considerations
   b. does not adequately consider crimes of the powerful
   c. does not adequately define "ruling class" and explain precisely how that group operates
   d. is too conservative

REFERENCES

1. Karl Marx and Friedrich Engels, *The Communist Manifesto* (New York: International Publishers, 1930).
2. Friedrich Engels, *The Condition of the Working Class in England in 1844* (London: Allen and Unwin, 1950).
3. T. B. Bottomore (ed.), *Karl Marx: Selected Writings in Sociology and Social Philosophy* (New York: McGraw-Hill, 1956), 229–230.
4. Willem Bonger, *Criminality and Economic Conditions* (Boston: Little, Brown, 1916).
5. Ian Taylor, Paul Walton, and Jock Young, *The New Criminology* (New York: Harper and Row, 1973), 222–234.
6. *Ibid.*
7. George B. Vold, *Theoretical Criminology*, 2nd ed., Thomas J. Bernard (ed.) (New York: Oxford University Press, 1979), 282–297.
8. *Ibid.*, 287.
9. *Ibid.*, 290–296.
10. Taylor, Walton, and Young, *op. cit.*, 238.
11. Richard Quinney, *Criminology* (Boston: Little, Brown, 1975), 95. See also, Richard Quinney, *Criminology*, 2nd ed. (Boston: Little, Brown, 1979), 26–28.
12. Richard Quinney, *Class, State and Crime* (New York: David McKay, 1977); Richard Quinney, *Social Existence: Metaphysics, Marxism, and the Social Sciences* (Beverly Hills, Calif.: Sage Publications, Inc., 1982).
13. Barry Krisberg, *Crime and Privilege* (Englewood Cliffs, N.J.: Prentice-Hall, 1975).
14. William J. Chambliss and Robert B. Seidman, *Law, Order, and Power* (Reading, Mass.: Addison-Wesley, 1982).
15. For a survey of the development of Marxist criminology during the past decade, see Ronald Hinch, "Marxist Criminology in the 1970s: Clarifying the Clutter," *Crime and Social Justice*, 19 (1983), 65–74.
16. William J. Chambliss, "Functional and Conflict Theories of Crime," *MSS Module*, 17 (1973), 11.
17. *Ibid.*, 8–9.
18. Richard Quinney, *Critique of the Legal Order* (Boston: Little, Brown, 1974), 190.
19. Don C. Gibbons, "Emerging Perspectives in Criminology," mimeograph, 15. See also, Gresham Sykes, "The Rise of Critical Criminology," *Journal of Criminal Law and Criminology*, 65 (1974), 210–216.
20. Herman and Julia Schwendinger, "Social Class and the Definition of Crime," *Crime and Social Justice*, 7 (1977), 9–10.

10

Violent Crime

OBJECTIVES

After studying this chapter, the student should be able to:

- Summarize the general patterns and features of criminal homicide, aggravated assault, forcible rape, and robbery.
- Compare and contrast the offenses of criminal homicide, aggravated assault, and forcible rape.

The FBI designates certain crimes which are frequently committed and are serious in nature as Index offenses. These eight offenses (Chapter 2) are often referred to as "street crimes." They are further divided into two categories: personal and property crimes. This chapter focuses upon the four predatory personal crimes of criminal homicide, assault, rape, and robbery.

HOMICIDE

Homicide simply means the killing of a person by another person. It is always unpleasant but not always illegal. The law recognizes special conditions when a homicide is not illegal. Excusable homicides refer to some accidental killings where no intent to injure exists. Justifiable homicide involves killings which may include intent but are considered to be necessary (e.g., police officer who kills a fleeing felon, or a citizen who kills in self-defense). Criminal (felonious) homicide is the unlawful killing of one person by another. It typically includes first- and second-degree murder as well as voluntary and involuntary manslaughter. The following are broad definitions of the types of criminal homicide: [1]

> *First-degree murder*: all killings with malice aforethought, which are willful, deliberate, and premeditated. Includes other specific types of murder such as those committed in the act of another violent felony (felony-murder).
>
> *Second-degree murder*: all killings with malice aforethought, other than those classified as first-degree murder.
>
> *Voluntary manslaughter*: an intentional killing without premeditation or malice aforethought and done in the heat of passion caused by reasonable provocation.
>
> *Involuntary manslaughter*: unintentional killing while engaged in the commission of either an unlawfully dangerous act that is not a felony or criminally negligent conduct. Sometimes referred to as negligent manslaughter.

More has been written about criminal homicide than about any other single kind of crime. We find examples of material having homicide as a central theme in academic books, newspapers, magazines, and novels. The subject produces much public interest because murder represents, perhaps, the most serious violation of orderly social life. In addition, criminal homicide is associated with other emotional issues such as capital punishment and abortion. People who are opposed to the death penalty in general often waver when faced with specific types of killings (e.g., that of a police officer or child) that appear to justify capital punishment. Those opposed to abortion often equate it with murder; that is, the "killing of the unborn." For these and other reasons, the public is very sensitive to the topic of criminal homicide.

Although widely feared, criminal homicides make up a very small portion of all Index crimes known to the police. UCR figures indicate that usually less than 1 percent of all reported Index offenses are criminal homicides,[2] and only about 2 percent of all predatory crimes are criminal homicides. In general, cities have the highest rates, though some rural areas often have rates which are well above the national average. By region, the southern states continue to have the highest number of criminal homicides annually. In terms of raw numbers, over 16,000 people are victims of a criminal homicide in a given year.[3]

FBI statistics reveal that criminal homicide disproportionately affects young, nonwhite, male individuals both as offenders and as victims. Of those arrested in a typical year, over 40 percent are under the age of twenty-five, 45 percent are nonwhite (mostly black), and about 85 percent are males. In similar fashion, over 40 percent of the victims are under the age of thirty and are nonwhite. Three out of four victims are males.[4] National-level data also indicate that homicide situations fall into two categories. First, there are those situations in which the victim and the offender have a prior close or casual relationship. Second, there are many circumstances wherein the victim, a stranger, is killed during the course of another related felony (typically a robbery). As strongly suggested by Table 10-1, criminal homicide is a "friendly" sort of crime.

Table 10-1 Murder Circumstances by Relationship (Percent Distribution)

VICTIM*	TOTAL	FELONY TYPE	SUSPECTED FELONY TYPE	ROMANTIC TRIANGLE	ARGUMENT OVER MONEY OR PROPERTY	OTHER ARGUMENTS	MISCELLANEOUS NONFELONY TYPE	UNABLE TO DETERMINE
Total*	100.0	100.0	100.0	100.0	100.0	100.0	100.0	100.0
Husband	3.2	0.4	—	3.9	1.3	6.9	3.1	0.5
Wife	5.2	0.8	—	7.4	2.4	9.0	7.4	1.8
Mother	0.8	0.3	—	—	0.7	0.9	1.8	0.4
Father	1.2	0.3	0.2	—	1.1	2.3	1.4	0.2
Daughter	1.3	1.0	—	—	0.4	0.5	4.3	0.8
Son	1.6	1.2	0.2	—	0.7	1.3	4.7	0.5
Brother	1.3	0.1	—	0.2	2.4	2.5	1.7	0.2
Sister	0.3	0.2	—	0.5	0.4	0.5	0.5	0.1
Other family	2.6	1.2	0.2	0.2	4.6	4.3	3.3	1.1
Acquaintances	29.8	23.8	9.3	57.6	56.9	39.3	37.8	9.7
Friend	3.9	1.7	0.9	4.4	12.8	6.1	4.6	1.2
Boyfriend	1.6	0.2	—	3.7	1.3	3.3	1.2	0.4
Girlfriend	2.4	0.5	—	7.4	1.3	4.7	2.0	0.7
Neighbor	1.3	1.2	—	1.0	1.8	1.9	1.3	0.5
Stranger	17.6	40.5	66.4	11.3	8.8	11.3	13.9	7.5
Unknown relationship	25.8	26.7	22.8	2.5	2.9	5.3	11.1	74.5

* Because of rounding, percentages may not add to total.

Source: Federal Bureau of Investigation, *Uniform Crime Reports—1984* (Washington, D.C.: U.S. Government Printing Office, 1985), 11.

That is, about two-thirds of the yearly unlawful killings involve people who know one another (spouses, parents, lovers, etc.) long enough to generate a homicidal drive or incident.

Several extensive studies of homicide by criminologists have supported the data and implications of the *Uniform Crime Reports*. One of the first such studies was carried out by Wolfgang. Between 1948 and 1952, he examined homicide patterns in Philadelphia as they related to age, race, sex, and contacts between victims and offenders. He also noted time periods, weapons used, and the surroundings in which homicides were most likely to occur.[5] Following Wolfgang's early work, criminologists have conducted intensive studies of homicide in other major cities.[6] Barlow has summarized their findings by noting that:

1. young, black, adult males are most likely to be identified as offenders and victims;
2. offenders and victims tend to be of low socioeconomic status [of the same race] and to reside in inner-city slums;
3. homicides usually occur during the late evening and early morning hours of the weekend;
4. around half of the known homicides occur in either the offender's or the victim's home;
5. homicides do not follow consistent seasonal patterns; they do not, as prevalent myth would have it, occur more often during the hot months of the year;
6. offenders and victims are usually acquainted and often live in the same immediate neighborhood;
7. strangers are killed most often during the commission of another felony, such as robbery or burglary.[7]

The motives for homicide vary considerably from one case to the next. People kill each other out of frustration, greed, jealousy, or simple anger. Whatever motivates individuals to kill, there does exist a relationship between criminal homicide and three social variables. These factors do not necessarily cause criminal homicide. They do appear, however, to facilitate the commission of the crime. The three variables are access to weapons, the presence of mind-altering drugs (alcohol), and the availability of medical services.

In a typical year, less than 10 percent of the known criminal homicides result from beatings, poisoning, strangulations, and so on. Thus, over 90 percent occur when the offender is armed with a lethal weapon. About two-thirds of the year's criminal homicides are committed with a firearm. More specifically, a handgun is the weapon used in over 50 percent of the nation's unlawful killings.

Certainly, there is some common-sense truth in the saying that "Guns don't kill, people do." But, it should also be kept in mind that some weapons are more deadly than others. Newton and Zimring observe that the fatality rate in intrafamily murders is five times higher when a handgun is used instead of any other weapon. [8] More handguns are privately owned in the United States, per capita, than in any other country of the world. It has been estimated that there may now be more than 30 million privately owned handguns in the United States.[9] Gun control is a hotly debated issue. It would be difficult to prove that gun control would reduce murder, and, even if one could, to arrive at a universally agreeable policy.

There is reliable evidence that easy access to handguns affects the amount of criminal homicide in an area. In a careful statistical study of homicide in Detroit, Fisher concluded that the availability of handguns definitely contributed to the city's rather high homicide rate.[10] In another study, researchers concluded that most privately owned guns are unrelated to criminal or accidental deaths.[11] The National Advisory Commission on Criminal Justice Standards and Goals has adopted a strong position on gun control. In particular, the Commission has recommended that: (1) the private possession of handguns should be prohibited for all persons other than law enforcement and military personnel, (2) the manufacture and sale of handguns should be terminated, (3) existing handguns should be acquired by the states, and (4) handguns held by private citizens as collectors' items should be modified and rendered inoperative.[12] While many would be against some or all of the Commission's proposals, one study surprisingly revealed that a sizable number of gun owners favor such action.[13]

Alcohol is present in many homicide situations. Wolfgang found alcohol to have been consumed by the victim or offender in about two-thirds of the cases that he studied.[14] The National Commission has also suggested that alcohol "is an important catalyst in homicides, assaults, and to a lesser extent, rapes."[15] Alcohol obviously does not cause homicide. It does appear to reduce sober inhibitions (e.g., fear of the consequences) and to make killing easier.

Finally, available medical services affect the homicide rate. When a person is injured as the result of a crime, speedy and efficient medical attention may make the difference between life and death for the victim. This, perhaps, is one reason why rural homicide rates surpass those of small cities. Remoteness in terms of sophisticated medical facilities can transform an aggravated assault into a criminal homicide when valuable time is lost between the offense and medical services. It may also be the case that the homicide rate would be much higher if it were not for improved medical delivery services and techniques in our urban areas.

Law enforcement officials are able to clear more homicides than any other street crime (somewhere between 70% and 80%). This is due to the high visibility of the crime, availability of evidence, and prior victim-offender relationships. Of those eventually charged with homicide, about one-half are convicted as charged. The remainder are either convicted of lesser charges, have their charges dropped, or are acquitted.

ASSAULT

Assault is of two general kinds: simple and aggravated. Simple assault is a misdemeanor and is generally interpreted to mean an intentional show of force that results or could result in a minor injury to the victim. Aggravated assault, a felony, involves an intentional show of force that results or could result in more serious harm than a simple assault. Some jurisdictions have separate assault categories that are treated as felonies; for example, assault with a deadly weapon or with intent to kill, rape, or do great bodily harm.[16]

Aggravated assault and criminal homicide share many features. As with homicide, aggravated assault constitutes a small (about 5%) portion of the known Index offenses. However, it comprises about 50 percent of all predatory crimes. Assaults, like homicide, occur with greater frequency in cities and are more prevalent in the South than in any other region. Over half a million aggravated assaults are reported annually throughout the nation.[17]

Government statistics indicate that aggravated assault is disproportionately committed by young, nonwhite, male offenders. Of those arrested, about 50 percent are under the age of twenty-five, 40 percent are nonwhite, and 87 percent are males.[18] The relationship between offenders and victims is not as clearly established as it is in the case of murder. Some studies report that almost two-thirds of the assaults involve people who are at least known to one another.[19] Others note instead that two-thirds of these incidents involve strangers.[20] Like homicide, aggravated assault appears to be primarily an intraracial event. Further, both parties tend to be disproportionately nonwhite;[21] when the event is interracial, the victim is typically white and the offender nonwhite.[22]

A study by Dunn indicated that the race, weapon used, place of attack, and participant's age varied with the social characteristics of the area where the crime occurred. Regarding race, nonwhites assaulted nonwhites in low-income areas characterized by predominantly nonwhite populations and multiple social problems (substandard housing, broken homes, etc.). In predominantly white areas, the assaultive situation usually involved a white offender and a nonwhite victim.

Type of weapon and place of attack also varied according to the area's social features. For example, assaults committed with knives, and on the street, were likely to have occurred in areas having multiple social problems, high assault rates, and a large nonwhite population. Similarly, knife attacks involving nonwhite females against nonwhite males also took place primarily in these areas. However, assaults committed with personal weapons (fists, feet, etc.), in private dwellings, most frequently occurred in areas having moderate assault rates, apartment houses, and a substantial white population.

Dunn also discovered that the ages of victims and offenders varied with an area's social characteristics. Offenders and victims tended to be adolescents somewhat more often in areas having low and moderate assault rates. On the other hand, older offenders and victims were likely to be found where social problems and high assault rates existed.[23]

Aggravated assault seems to differ from criminal homicide in the three major aspects of motives, weapons, and the proportion of stranger-to-stranger encounters. The motive given for an aggravated assault was more likely to be either "to escape arrest" or "unknown" than in cases of criminal homicide.[24] While firearms (particularly handguns) are most often found in criminal homicides, aggravated assaults usually involve personal weapons or knives.[25] The large percentage of unknown motives suggests that many aggravated assaults "are apparently random, unprovoked, unexplainable attacks."[26]

About two-thirds of all reported aggravated assaults are cleared by an arrest. Police typically arrive on the scene during or immediately after a disturbance when the suspect is still present. Because of the frequency of close relationships between victims and offenders, few arrests result in convictions as charged. In many instances, charges are dropped by the victim.

RAPE

Common law traditionally restricted rape to the carnal knowledge (sexual intercourse) of a female, without her consent, by a male other than her husband. Beginning in the 1970s, many states established new sexual assault laws permitting husbands to be charged with the rape of their wives. Some states distinguish between rape and aggravated rape, the latter including physical abuse (e.g., serious beating) beyond the rape and typically involving a harsher penalty upon conviction. There are, in addition, statutory rape laws which criminalize sexual intercourse involving a female below a statutorily defined age (e.g., sixteen or seventeen years old).[27] The key elements in successfully prosecuting a forcible rape charge are proof that a sexual act (intercourse) occurred, that force was used, and that the act was done "without consent" and "against the will." [28]

Rape is a crime that invites much public indignation and anger. This is especially the case when the victim is very vulnerable (e.g., young, pregnant, or the target of a gang rape). The public response to rape also varies with the offender. For example, a disproportionate number of nonwhites have been executed for raping white females. The reverse situation (nonwhite victim, white offender) has not had the same effect on the public.

Forcible rape constitutes only about 1 percent of the reported Index offenses each year and less than 10 percent of the known serious violent crimes. The largest number (36% in 1984) of rapes have been reported in the South, though the West continues to have the highest rates (rapes per 100,000 people). Rape is similar to homicide and assault in that it, too, is most prevalent in cities. Almost 85,000 forcible rapes were reported in one recent year.[29]

Male suspects arrested for forcible rape tend to be young (about 50% are under the age of twenty-five) and are evenly split on racial lines.[30] Victim characteristics tend to vary widely in terms of age, marital status, socioeconomic status, and so on. But research indicates that rape victims are concentrated in a younger age range (sixteen to twenty-four years old) and are disproportionately nonwhite.[31] For example, a Philadelphia study found that black females were victimized at a rate four times greater than their portion of the general population.[32]

Several clinical studies of the various types of rape situations exist, such as paired rapes (two offenders, one victim) and gang rapes.[33] These studies focus on psychological aspects of offenders. Amir's leading sociological study of the crime has revealed the following portrayal of victim-offender relationships as well as the nature of forcible rape.[34]

1. Reported rapes are more likely to involve victims and offenders who are young and nonwhite.
2. Rape is an intraracial crime. Nonwhites tend to rape nonwhites; whites are likely to rape other whites.
3. Offenders tend to be of low socioeconomic status, regardless of race, and live in close proximity to the victims.
4. Rapes occur more often on weekends during the late evening and early morning hours.

5. In about one-half of the rapes, the victim was first encountered in either her own home, that of the offender, or in a place of entertainment (party or bar). Further, most of the actual rapes took place (56%) at either the home of the victim or the offender. Thus, rapes do not appear to be overwhelmingly committed, as many people think, on dark streets or in deserted parks.

6. There is no consistent seasonal pattern for rape. The crime does not occur with unusual frequency during hot months of the year.

In these respects, forcible rape is similar to criminal homicide and, to some extent, aggravated assault. But Amir's research shows that it may differ from these offenses in three primary ways. First, the use of alcohol was absent in most rapes while it was found to be present in a large portion of homicides (and assaults). In two-thirds of Amir's cases, neither the victim nor the offender had consumed alcohol. Second, unlike homicide and aggravated assault, forcible rape does not appear to be an "explosive" event. Amir found that most offenders (71%) planned the crime in advance. Third, although physical force was used in most instances, the victim was beaten in less than one-half of the forcible rapes.[35]

While it is not necessary that the victim prove resistance, a minority of states require some corroborative evidence (something more than the victim's accusation) to obtain a rape conviction. This requirement may cause problems. Many rape victims experience a pseudoadjustment period shortly after the crime.[36] They try to act as if nothing has happened; that is, they deny the traumatic reality. To create the appearance of normalcy, victims often thoroughly cleanse themselves and destroy clothing that was worn at the time of the attack. The destruction of corroborative evidence that force was used can damage the prosecution's case in those states requiring such additional proof. Even in states (the majority) which do not require corroborative evidence, the police may be less likely to believe a victim who has gone through the pseudoadjustment phase and appears at the police station nicely dressed and well groomed claiming that she has been forcibly raped.

Many victims of rape never file a police report. Because of fear of further harassment by the offender or the consequences of a public trial or out of embarrassment, many victims do not report their rapes. It has been estimated that there are almost four times as many actual rapes as are reported each year.[37] One explanation for the high amount of reported rapes involving nonwhite victims is that women of the lower socioeconomic class (a large percentage of nonwhites) have fewer unofficial (physicians, counselors, etc.) outlets than do middle-class victims. That is, their only alternative is the police.

The feminist movement has done much to bring the subject of rape out into the open and create a climate of understanding for the victim. Much attention has been devoted to destroying the myth that women who are raped actually desire it. Women are being encouraged to shun embarrassment and to report and prosecute offenders.[38]

Slightly more than one-half of the reported rapes are cleared by an arrest. Almost one-half of those prosecuted for the crime are acquitted or have their cases dismissed. Around 40 percent are found to be guilty as charged.

ROBBERY

Of the Index offenses, robbery is one of the better general indicators of the nature, extent, and trends of street crime.[39] It combines theft with actual or potential violence wherein the offender is a predator and usually is a stranger to the victim. Robbery and its several forms (e.g., muggings) generate great fear because the acts are unprovoked, often occur randomly, and are committed by an unknown offender "out of the blue."

Robbery is defined as the taking of another's property by force or threat of force.[40] Many jurisdictions specify degrees of robbery according to the amount of violence used by the offender. First-degree robbery, for example, typically refers to those instances in which the victim's life is endangered or the victim suffers or faces serious bodily harm. In such jurisdictions, all other robberies generally fall into the category of second-degree felonies. In some states, first degree is labeled "armed robbery," whereas second degree is referred to as "simple robbery."[41]

Robbery occurs with about as much frequency as aggravated assault. Over one-third of all predatory crimes and about 5 percent of all Index offenses are robberies. The crime appears to be closely associated with population density. Robbery rates are the highest in cities with a population of 1 million or more residents and decrease as city size grows smaller. Thus, rural areas continue to have the lowest robbery rates. The heavily populated states of the Northeast have the highest rates for robbery. Almost half a million robberies are reported annually throughout the nation.[42]

Those arrested for robbery are primarily young, nonwhite, and male. About two-thirds of the suspects are under twenty-five years of age, 60 percent are nonwhite (primarily black), and over 90 percent are males.[43] According to research, victims also tend to be young, nonwhite, and male.[44] Young offenders dominate arrest statistics because they are more likely to act in groups and thus account for multiple apprehensions involving one incident.

Nationwide statistics and academic research restricted to specific cities have provided the following profile of robbery.[45]

1. The majority of robberies involve a weapon, typically a handgun but also including knives and blunt objects. However, this aspect varies with the situation.
    a. Firearms are used predominantly when residents of private dwellings, vehicles, or commercial establishments are robbed.
    b. Knives are the favored weapon in street robberies that occur in invisible places (alleys, hallways, etc.).
    c. For the most part, other street robberies involve the use of physical force rather than weapons. But, when a visible street robbery takes place against a choice victim (one known to carry large sums of money or valuables), a weapon is typically employed by the offender.
2. The average amount taken in a robbery (all situations collectively averaged) exceeds $600. However, this varies with the nature of the incident.
    a. Street robberies have been estimated to average over $400.
    b. Robberies of banks average over $2,500.
3. In general, offenders tend to be young, nonwhite (primarily black) males. However, the nature of the offender varies with the situation.
    a. Street robberies are frequently committed by young, black, unprepared groups

(no planning). The same features apply to robberies in "invisible" places except that the offenders are more likely to operate in pairs and be armed.

 b. In residential robberies, offenders usually intended to burglarize but robbed when confronted by owner. They tend to be more "professional" and have a more extensive criminal record.

 c. Robberies of vehicles (cabs, delivery vans, etc.) usually involve young offenders who have planned the crime.

 d. Robbers of commercial establishments are predominantly young and black, and they usually plan the crime and operate in pairs. If committed by a white offender, the robbery is usually executed by one individual.

4. Overall, the victims of robbery tend to be nonwhite and relatively young. However, there are also situational differences in this regard.

 a. The victims of street robberies are typically women and older men. But, in less visible situations, the women tend to be young or middle aged while the men remain older.

 b. The victims of residential robberies are more likely (than in other situations) to have had at least a casual acquaintance with the offender. No clear age, racial, or sexual patterns have been established.

 c. The victims of vehicle robberies are more likely to be determined on the basis of occupation. That is, cab drivers, delivery van drivers, especially those who operate in the inner city, are likely targets.

 d. Commercial establishments, like street robbery victims, are chosen for their vulnerability. The most likely selected sites are isolated stores operated by one person.

5. Overall, robbery victims are not physically injured by the offender. However, injuries to victims are most likely to occur in one of two situations.

 a. When the robber is unarmed.

 b. When the robbery is a street offense committed by young, inexperienced offenders who are unarmed and are resisted by the victim.

6. The volume of robberies varies by situation.

 a. Over one-half of reported robberies occur on the street; the fewest number are committed against banks.

Robbery is a very complicated crime. It involves several factors and patterns which may be difficult to establish in terms of long-range trends. Criminologists are now devoting more effort to the analysis of specific offenses. Offense analysis is the first step toward establishing procedures for dealing with the problem of predatory crime.

SUMMARY

This chapter discussed the four types of predatory crimes: criminal homicide, aggravated assault, forcible rape, and robbery. It was noted that each of the crimes comprise a small portion of the total number of Index offenses. Of the predatory Index offenses, the most frequent are aggravated assault and robbery.

While these crimes are complex, some patterns and general traits do appear. Criminal homicide, aggravated assault, and forcible rape have many similarities. The crimes are primarily intraracial and involve a disproportionate number of nonwhites as offenders and victims. Offenders and victims tend to live close to one another. The crimes are more likely to occur on weekends, and there are no consistent seasonal patterns. Aggravated assault is unlike criminal homicide in that firearms are less likely to be used, motives are often different, and the crime is more likely to be random or unprovoked. Rape differs from homicide and assault primarily in that alcohol is not present, the offender plans the attack, and the victim is unlikely to be seriously injured (beyond the sexual assault).

Robbery is unique. It involves both the elements of theft and violence or potential violence. However, certain patterns or traits have been established for this offense. In general, offenders and victims tend to be young and nonwhite. Most robberies involve the presence of some weapon but the victim is, statistically speaking, unlikely to be injured. The likelihood of injury increases, however, when the robbery is committed on the street by a young, unarmed, inexperienced offender who encounters resistance from the victim.

Crimes of passion (criminal homicide and aggravated assault) that involve friends and relatives are almost beyond the control of the criminal justice system. Other predatory crimes (rape and robbery) may be subject to better preventive measures through offense analysis and the education of potential victims.

SUGGESTED ACTIVITIES

- Compare the features of homicide as discussed in this chapter with those which are portrayed in the media (e.g., television and the movies). Discuss any similarities or differences in class.
- Develop a speech to be given to a group of women regarding ways to prevent rape and what steps to take in the event of being victimized. Hint: the National Organization for Women provides a list of rape counseling services located throughout the country.
- Wolfgang states that robbery arises out of a ''subculture of violence,'' whereas Normandeau emphasizes that robbery arises more from a ''subculture of theft.'' Based upon our discussion of the crime of robbery, whose statement is more accurate? Discuss in class.

REVIEW

A. List the basic characteristics of criminal homicide.

B. Summarize the essential features of aggravated assault.

C. List the important elements of forcible rape.

D. Briefly summarize the characteristics of robbery.

E. Multiple Choice. Select the best answer.

1. A victim is more likely to be seriously injured during a(n):
  a. forcible rape
  b. armed robbery
  c. simple assault
  d. unarmed robbery

2. Offenders and victims are most likely to be strangers when the criminal homicide is:
  a. second-degree murder
  b. first-degree murder

      c. related to another felony

      d. voluntary manslaughter

3. The most frequently used weapon in a criminal homicide is:

      a. knife

      b. handgun

      c. blunt object

      d. personal weapon (e.g., fist)

4. Which of the following is not related to the majority of criminal homicides?

      a. alcohol

      b. firearms

      c. premeditation

      d. days of the week

5. Aggravated assault is most similar to:

      a. criminal homicide

      b. robbery

      c. forcible rape

      d. negligent manslaughter

6. Forcible rape differs from criminal homicide in which of the following respects?

      a. offenders and victims are disproportionately nonwhite

      b. planning on the part of the offender

      c. the crime is intraracial

      d. the crime is likely to occur during the late evening and early morning hours of a weekend

7. Which of the following crimes is the best general indication of the extent and trends of street crimes in general?

      a. aggravated assault

      b. forcible rape

      c. robbery

      d. criminal homicide

8. Which of the following traits is common to each of the predatory crimes discussed in this chapter?

      a. offenders generally tend to be disproportionately young, nonwhite, and male

      b. victims tend to be young, white, and male

      c. all of these crimes tend to have high rates of convictions as charged

      d. all tend to be explosive events with little or no planning

9. Police are most likely to clear, with an arrest, the crime of:

      a. forcible rape

      b. criminal homicide

      c. aggravated assault

      d. robbery

REFERENCES

1. Jay A. Sigler, *Understanding Criminal Law* (Boston: Little, Brown, 1981), 84–87.
2. Federal Bureau of Investigation, *Uniform Crime Reports, 1984* (Washington, D.C.: U.S. Government Printing Office, 1985), 44. UCR statistics for criminal homicide do not include deaths caused by negligence. They do include deaths attributed to first- and second-degree murder and nonnegligent manslaughter.
3. *Ibid.*, 7–12.
4. *Ibid.*
5. Marvin E. Wolfgang, "A Sociological Analysis of Criminal Homicide," in Marvin E. Wolfgang (ed.) *Studies in Homicide* (New York: Harper and Row, 1967), 15–28.
6. Recent research includes Richard Block and Frank E. Zimring, "Homicide in Chicago: 1965–1970," *Journal of Research in Crime and Delinquency*, 10 (1973), 1–12; Joseph C. Fisher, "Homicide in Detroit:

The Role of Firearms,'' *Criminology*, 14 (1976), 387–400; Robert S. Munford, et al., ''Homicide Trends in Atlanta,'' *Criminology*, 14 (1976), 213–232; Paul and Patricia Brantingham, *Patterns in Crime* (New York: Macmillan, 1984), 5.

7. Hugh D. Barlow, *Introduction to Criminology*, 3rd ed. (Boston: Little, Brown, 1984), 139.
8. George Newton and Franklin Zimring, *Firearms and Violence in American Life: Report to the National Commission on the Causes and Prevention of Violence* (Washington, D.C.: U.S. Government Printing Office, 1969), 44.
9. *Ibid.*, 6.
10. Fisher, *op. cit.*, 399.
11. James D. Wright and Linda L. Marston, ''The Ownership of the Means of Destruction: Weapons in the United States,'' *Social Problems,* 23 (1975), 106.
12. National Advisory Commission on Criminal Justice Standards and Goals, *A National Strategy to Reduce Crime* (Washington, D.C.: U.S. Government Printing Office, 1973), 140.
13. Wright and Marston, *op. cit.*
14. Wolfgang, *op. cit.*
15. National Advisory Commission, *op. cit.*, 23.
16. Sigler, *op. cit.*, 88–89.
17. FBI, *op. cit.*, 22–23.
18. *Ibid.*
19. President's Commission on Law Enforcement and the Administration of Justice, *The Challenge of Crime in a Free Society* (Washington, D.C.: U.S. Government Printing Office, 1966), 78; D. J. Mulvihill, M. M. Tumin, and L. A. Curtis, *Crimes of Violence: A Staff Report to the National Commission on the Causes and Prevention of Violence*, Vol. II (Washington, D.C.: U.S. Government Printing Office, 1969), 287.
20. A. L. Paez and R. W. Dodge, *Criminal Victimization in the U.S.* (Washington, D.C.: U.S. Department of Justice, 1982).
21. D. J. Pittman and W. Handy, ''Patterns in Criminal Aggravated Assault,'' *Journal of Criminal Law, Criminology and Police Science*, 55 (1964), 468.
22. *Ibid.*; Mulvihill, et al., *op. cit.*
23. Christopher Dunn, *Assault Incident Characteristics: Utilization of Criminal Justice Statistics Project, Analytic Report 14* (Washington, D.C.: U.S. Government Printing Office, 1976), 25.
24. *Ibid.*, 10.
25. Pittman and Handy, *op. cit.*, 465; Mulvihill, et al., *op. cit.*, 345; FBI, *op. cit.*, 22.
26. Dunn, *op. cit.*
27. Sigler, *op. cit.*, 89–90.
28. Thomas J. Gardner, *Criminal Law: Principles and Cases* (St. Paul: West, 1985), 354.
29. FBI, *op. cit.*, 14–15.
30. *Ibid.*
31. Paez and Dodge, *op. cit.*
32. Menachem Amir, *Patterns in Forcible Rape* (Chicago: University of Chicago Press, 1971).
33. See J. M. MacDonald, *Rape Offenders and Their Victims* (Springfield, Ill.: Chas. C Thomas, 1971); D. Chappell and S. Singer, ''Rape in New York City: A Study of Material in the Police Files and Its Meaning,'' mimeograph (Albany, N.Y.: State University of New York, 1973).
34. Amir, *op. cit.*
35. *Ibid.*
36. Ann Burgess and Lynda L. Holmstrom, ''Rape Trauma Syndrome,'' *American Journal of Psychiatry*, 131 (1974), 981.
37. Mulvihill, et al., *op. cit.*, 59.
38. L. Brodyaga, et al., *Rape and Its Victims: A Report for Citizens, Health Facilities and Criminal Justice Agencies* (Washington, D.C.: U.S. Government Printing Office, 1975), 241.
39. John E. Conklin, *Robbery* (Philadelphia: J. B. Lippincott, 1972), viii.
40. Sigler, *op. cit.*, 95.
41. Gardner, *op. cit.*, 307–309.
42. FBI, *op. cit.*, 17–20.
43. *Ibid.*, 167–182.
44. Bureau of Justice Statistics, *The Risk of Violent Crime* (Washington, D.C.: U.S. Government Printing Office, 1985).
45. *Ibid.*; FBI, *op. cit.*; J. MacDonald, *Armed Robbery: Offenders and Their Victims* (Springfield, Ill.: Chas. C Thomas, 1975); Paul and Patricia Brantingham, *op. cit.*, 124–127.

11

Property Crime

After studying this chapter, the student should be able to:

- Describe the general features and patterns of burglary, larceny, motor vehicle theft, and arson.
- Compare and contrast the offenses of burglary, larceny, motor vehicle theft, and arson.
- Make comparisons, using Chapter 10 for reference, between predatory and property Index crimes.

As a group, the Index crimes that are most feared (predatory offenses) are committed the least. This chapter focuses upon four of the more frequently committed Index crimes. They are the property offenses of burglary, larceny, motor vehicle theft, and arson. About 90 percent of all known Index crimes are property offenses.

BURGLARY

The old English common law required that a burglary include the "breaking and entering of a dwelling during the nighttime with the intent to commit a felony." [1] Many modern statutes have dropped the dual requirement of "breaking and entering," expanding the meaning of "dwelling," and omitted the specific period of "nighttime." As a consequence, there are several different definitions of burglary among the various states.[2] For purposes of consistent reporting, the FBI defines burglary as "the unlawful entry of a structure to commit a felony or theft."[3]

Burglary is particularly upsetting because it often underscores the fact that one's home or business is vulnerable to unwanted outsiders. It is one thing to have something stolen from a yard or garage; it is quite another if the target has been the bedroom or family den! The matter of a stranger having gained access to one's home is at least as disturbing as the actual theft of belongings. One indication of the public's anxiety about this crime is the increasing amount of residential and commercial security devices and systems being purchased.

Compared with predatory, violent crime, burglary occurs with relatively greater frequency. Each year about 25 percent of all Index crimes and 30 percent of the serious property crimes represent some form of burglary. Although this Index crime is not as markedly urban in nature as robbery is, the highest rates exist in cities. By region, the southern states report the largest volume. Nationwide, 3 million burglaries are recorded each year.[4]

The UCR data indicate that offenders tend to be young, white, and male; approximately 75 percent of those arrested are under the age of twenty-five, 70 percent are white, and over 90 percent are male.[5] While there is a career burglar pattern, quite a few of the offenders are amateurs.[6] Two-thirds of the places victimized are residential in nature.

Criminologists have devoted less attention to property offenses than to other forms of crime. Nonetheless, there are sufficient studies available to provide us with some insight into the characteristics of burglary.[7] For purposes of clarity, the general traits of burglary are summarized as follows.

1. There appears to be little relationship between the characteristics of burglary and the characteristics of burglars. That is, certain types of burglars do not commit specific types of burglaries.
2. There are, however, some traits associated between the offense and the offender:
    a. Female and juvenile offenders are more likely to work in groups when committing a burglary.
    b. Juveniles are more likely to burglarize a target that is near their own neighborhood.
    c. Females are more likely to burglarize a place that is outside of their neighborhoods.
    d. Younger offenders are more likely to burglarize during the daylight hours (3:00 P.M.–6:00 P.M.).
    e. Female burglars are more likely to operate during weekday, daylight hours.
3. Burglary is unlikely to include a personal confrontation between the offender and the victim.
4. Residential burglaries (the majority) are more likely to occur during a weekday and during daylight hours. Nonresidential burglaries are more likely to occur at night during weekends.
5. There is no apparent seasonal pattern for burglary, either residential or nonresidential.
6. While most burglaries involve the use of force, this factor is associated with the target and the offender's sex and race.
    a. In general, nonresidential burglaries are more likely to include forcible entry than residential burglaries.

b. Males and nonwhite offenders are more likely to use force than are females and whites, in general.

7. The losses attributed to single burglary incidents tend to be moderate and to include goods that are easily liquidated into cash. Considering all burglaries, the annual losses are substantial given the volume of the crime. The UCR data reveal that in a recent year (1984): [8]

a. Total losses due to burglary amounted to almost $3 billion.

b. The average dollar loss per burglary approached $1,000.

Burglary is a crime of opportunity. Many attempted burglaries are unreported simply because the victims are unaware of their occurrence. Few burglaries are cleared by an arrest. Only about 15 percent of the reported burglaries result in the arrest of a suspect. Time is a major factor in clearances. Generally, the longer the time period between the crime's occurrence and reporting, the less the likelihood of apprehension. In the research previously summarized, it was found that most arrests occurred on the premises, while the offender was fleeing, or as the result of a citizen apprehension. In other words, arrests were more likely while the scene was "hot." Once eventually charged, approximately 60 percent of the suspects are convicted as charged.

LARCENY

Larceny is the taking of another's property with the intention of permanently depriving the owner of it.[9] Most jurisdictions divide larceny into the two categories of petty and grand theft. Petty larceny, a misdemeanor, involves the theft of money or goods of lesser value. Grand larceny, a felony, refers to the theft of money or goods of greater intrinsic value. The value of the property stolen is determined by the court or jury.[10] The chief distinction between larceny and burglary is that burglary includes illegal entry and larceny does not. Unlike robbery, larceny does not include violence or the threat of harm to the victim.

Stealing may take many forms such as shoplifting, employee theft, vending-machine pilfering, "car clouting" (stealing of automobile accessories and parts). Some larcenies are committed by professional rings but most are the work of unorganized amateurs, many of whom are juveniles.

The most frequently reported street crime is larceny. Over 50 percent of all known Index crimes and about 60 percent of all such property crimes are larcenies. Larceny rates are highest in cities and, regionally speaking, the South reports the largest percentage of thefts annually. Almost 7 million larcenies were reported in a recent year.[11]

Those arrested for larceny are typically young and white. In contrast to other street crimes, a sizable number of females are arrested each year for stealing—more than for any other Index offense—amounting to almost one-third of the total arrests for this crime. Approximately three-fourths of those arrested are under the age of twenty-five years (one-third are under eighteen), and 70 percent are both male and white.[12]

Larceny involves such a variety of offenders (young, old, male, female, professional, amateur, etc.) and objects stolen that it is difficult to generalize about the crime. Victims are chosen at random for the desirability of their goods and the opportunity for theft. For some years, the "hottest" items have been automobile parts and accessories (about 35 percent of yearly thefts), articles from buildings (15%), and bicycles (10%). Shoplifting (by customers and employees) has become increasingly costly in recent times.

Between 1980 and 1984 most forms of larceny experienced a decline. Shoplifting, on the other hand, increased by almost 15 percent.[13] The value of the "take" is difficult to estimate because merchants often lump all merchandise losses (employee theft, customer shoplifting, misplacement, burglary, etc.) into the category of "inventory shrinkage."[14] One estimate placed shoplifting losses at $3.5 billion annually.[15]

Shoplifting is difficult to control. One research team observed that a New York store was victimized (shoplifting) each day by 10 percent of its customers.[16] Security personnel must be extremely cautious in handling suspected shoplifters. False arrest can amount to bad store publicity and, more important, costly lawsuits. For these and other reasons (the desire not to "get involved"), law-abiding customers are reluctant to report observed shoplifting.[17]

Shoplifting by employees (usually termed "employee theft") is, perhaps, more costly than customer theft. Because they are overlooked, at least initially, employees may repeatedly steal over a long period of time before they are caught. Coupled with available time, employees also have access to large inventories. Cameron recounts the following typical incident:[18]

> The stolen merchandise recovered from the apartment of a teenage boy who had worked in the camera section of a department store for six months included twenty suits, racks of neckties, forty-two cameras, and closets full of sheets, blankets, towels, shoes, underwear, cooking utensils, women's wear, etc.

Some estimates have concluded that employee theft amounts to 75 percent of all shoplifting.[19]

In a study of five large American cities, larcenies committed against private individuals and households were examined in order to determine any exisiting patterns. The following general characteristics were found to be associated with these two types of larcenies:[20]

1. Most personal larcenies:
    a. took place during the daytime hours (two-thirds) between 6 A.M. and 6 P.M.
    b. occurred on streets, in parks, playgrounds, school grounds or parking lots (two-thirds).
    c. involved victims who were white (split evenly among males and females).
2. Most household larcenies:
    a. took place during the late evening hours.
    b. increased in volume with the number of residents in the home, when the home was owned (not rented), and with the family's income level.

This same study placed losses as moderate; that is, usually less than $50. However, the *Uniform Crime Reports* data have estimated the average value of losses (due to various kinds of larcenies) to be almost $400.[21]

Few larcenies are reported to the police. Of those reported, only a small portion (one out of five) are cleared with the arrest of a suspect. Given the volume of larceny committed, more people are charged with this crime than with any other Index offense.

MOTOR VEHICLE THEFT

A special category of larceny is motor vehicle theft. It involves the theft of a high-value, usually insured, and easily accounted-for item. Motor vehicle theft is defined by the *Uniform Crime Reports* data as "the theft or attempted theft of a motor vehicle." [22] This does not include incidences wherein a person having lawful access temporarily uses a vehicle.

Auto thefts amount to about 9 percent of all reported Index crimes and 10 percent of the property Index offenses. [23] Similar to robbery, motor vehicle theft is highly associated with city size. The rates are highest in large cities and markedly decline as cities or areas become less populated. Though the overall volume is evenly spread among the nation's major regions, the Northeast continues to have the highest auto theft rates. Over 1 million auto thefts are reported each year. [24]

Known offenders are concentrated among young, white, male individuals. Over 50 percent of those arrested are under the age of twenty-one (one-third of the total are under eighteen), 70 percent are white, and 90 percent are males. [25] Most stolen vehicles are automobiles with trucks and busses accounting for less than 15 percent. The average value of each vehicle stolen (1984) stands at $4,500. This figure is based on the vehicle's worth at the time of its theft. [26]

There has been little research dealing specifically with the offense of motor vehicle theft. It is usually characterized as a crime committed by either joyriding juveniles or professionally organized auto theft rings. More will be noted about offenders in Section 5. Based upon an analysis of the few existing studies, motor vehicle theft has the following general profile: [27]

1. Unlike other property street crimes, the victim usually recovers his goods. The majority of stolen vehicles are recovered although they have frequently been abused or damaged by the offender.
2. Victims often, although unintentionally, contribute to the crime through carelessness; for example, keys left in ignition, doors unlocked.
3. Unless the automobile is stolen for resale, it is rather common for it to be abandoned near the residence of the offender(s).
4. Automobiles tend to be stolen for one of five purposes:
    a. joyriding
    b. temporary transportation
    c. permanent transportation
    d. resale or profit from stolen accessories
    e. use in another crime
5. Stolen autos are least likely to be recovered as damaged or with items missing when the theft had the purpose of providing temporary or permanent transportation for the offender.
6. Auto theft, regardless of its purpose, tends to involve more than one offender per incident.

Most motor vehicle thefts are reported because of insurance considerations. While a majority of the stolen vehicles are recovered, most offenses are not cleared by the arrest of a suspect. Only 15 percent of the reports of stolen vehicles result in an arrest of an alleged thief, and many of those arrested are referred to the juvenile court (a higher proportion than for any other Index crime are so referred).

ARSON

The *Uniform Crime Reports* data defines arson as "any willful or malicious burning or attempt to burn, with or without intent to defraud, a dwelling house, public building, motor vehicle or aircraft, personal property of another, etc." [28] It was the costly nature of arson, plus its frequency, which contributed to the offense's recognition as an Index crime in 1979. Some analysts have estimated that arson costs amount to more, in terms of direct and indirect costs (e.g., insurance premiums), than do the total expenses of all Index crimes in a given year.[29] Although the techniques of arson investigation have become increasingly sophisticated and precise, detection of actual arson cases remains a problem. For this reason, the FBI does not tabulate fires of suspicious origin as arson until an investigation has determined that such is the cause.

Because nationwide data collection on arson is relatively new and spotty, it is difficult to present reliable longitudinal trends and patterns of the crime. However, available data indicate that permanent structures are the most common target, with more than one-third being residential buildings. Overall, the crime annually destroys property valued at close to $1 billion. The highest average losses in a recent year (1984) were recorded for industrial and manufacturing structures ($82,000 per incident).[30]

Since arson was formally classified as a Part II offense, "crimes known" data for years prior to 1979 are unavailable. Comparative regional statistics are also lacking. Nonetheless, data analysis indicates that rates are highest in large cities and diminish rather dramatically as population density decreases. Arrest figures reveal that two-thirds of the suspects are under the age of twenty-five years (over 40 percent are under eighteen). Approximately 80 percent are white and 90 percent are males. Thus, like other property Index offenses, arson arrests reflect it to be a crime favored by young, white males. Slightly over 100,000 arson offenses were reported in 1984.[31]

SUMMARY

The property offenses of burglary, larceny, motor vehicle theft, and arson make up approximately 90 percent of all known Index crimes. Burglary is a crime that threatens one's feeling of security. It occurs with considerable frequency and known offenders are concentrated among young, white males. In general, most burglaries are of residential places and do not include a confrontation between the owner and the intruder. Losses attributable to a single burglary tend to be moderate. The crime exhibits patterns based on offender and target characteristics. Few burglaries are cleared by the arrest of a suspect.

Larceny is the most common of all Index crimes. It differs from burglary in that there is no illegal entry of a dwelling. Unlike robbery, larceny does not involve violence or potential violence against a victim. Known offenders are mostly young and white. While the majority arrested are males, more females are apprehended for larceny than for any other Index crime. Much larceny takes the form of shoplifting and employee theft. Patterns of larceny have been established wherein the target has been a person or private household. As with burglary, only a small percentage of larcenies are cleared with the arrest of a suspect.

Motor vehicle theft is a type of larceny that, for recording purposes, is restricted primarily to automobiles. The crime is highly associated with population size. Much like robbery, motor vehicle theft rates decrease proportionately with reductions in city size. Known offenders are typically young. A higher proportion of suspects are referred to juvenile court than for any other Index crime. In addition, those arrested are typically white males who operate in pairs or groups. The crime differs from other property offenses in that the owner is likely to recover his or her property. However, few motor vehicle thefts are cleared with the arrest of a suspect.

Arson is a property offense which has recently been classified as an Index crime. Its cost and relative frequency have made it a significant concern of law enforcement officials, insurance companies, and property owners. What little systematic information we have seems to indicate that it is a crime committed by young, white males. As such, arson has similarities with other property Index offenses in this regard.

SUGGESTED ACTIVITIES

- Contact your local police department and inquire whether or not they sponsor a community burglary prevention program. If so, obtain information about it for class discussion. You may also find out more about a nationally sponsored program by writing to:

    National Neighborhood Watch Program
    c/o National Sheriffs' Association
    Suite 320
    1250 Connecticut Avenue
    Washington, D.C. 20036

- As a class project, invite a representative from a local law enforcement agency to speak to your group about property crimes in your community.
- Talk with a local department store manager about shoplifting and employee theft. Inquire about the extent of this problem and the measures used to deter it.
- What measures have automobile manufacturers taken to reduce theft and improve chances of tracing stolen vehicles? Local law enforcement officials will be able to provide you with specific information.

REVIEW

A. List some basic features of burglary.

B. Briefly discuss some important characteristics of larceny.

C. Discuss motor vehicle theft in general terms.

D. Multiple Choice. Select the best answer.

1. The most commonly reported street crime is:
   - a. automobile theft
   - b. burglary
   - c. larceny
   - d. motor vehicle theft

2. Which of the following property offenses is most highly associated with city size?
   - a. motor vehicle theft
   - b. larceny
   - c. residential burglary
   - d. nonresidential burglary

3. Females are more likely to be arrested for the crime of:
   - a. burglary
   - b. larceny
   - c. motor vehicle theft
   - d. unarmed robbery

4. The highest proportion of juveniles who are arrested are charged with the crime of:
   - a. larceny
   - b. residential burglaries
   - c. motor vehicle thefts
   - d. personal larcenies

5. It has been estimated that most shoplifting is committed by:
   - a. customers
   - b. employees
   - c. young black males
   - d. young white females

6. Which of the following is estimated to be the most costly of all Index offenses?
   - a. burglary
   - b. robbery
   - c. rape
   - d. arson

7. Most personal larcenies:
   - a. occur in public places
   - b. take place during the daytime
   - c. specifically occur between 6 A.M. and 6 P.M.
   - d. all of these

8. Regarding burglaries:
   - a. female offenders are more likely to operate on weekends
   - b. female offenders are more likely to burglarize a target outside of their neighborhood
   - c. residential burglaries typically occur on weekends
   - d. forcible entry rarely occurs

9. Most likely to result in the recovery of stolen item(s):
   - a. household larceny
   - b. residential burglary
   - c. motor vehicle theft
   - d. personal larceny

10. Property offenses comprise approximately this percentage of all street crimes:
    a. 90 percent
    b. 95 percent
    c. 80 percent
    d. 75 percent

REFERENCES

1. See Thomas J. Gardner, *Criminal Law: Principles and Cases* (St. Paul: West, 1985), 314.
2. Paul E. Dow, *Criminal Law* (Monterey, Calif.: Brooks/Cole, 1985), 148–150.
3. Federal Bureau of Investigation, *Uniform Crime Reports, 1984* (Washington, D.C.: U.S. Government Printing Office, 1985), 24.
4. *Ibid.*, 25.
5. *Ibid.*, 27.
6. Thomas A. Reppeto, *Residential Crime* (Cambridge, Mass.: Ballinger, 1974).
7. James Inciardi, *Careers in Crime* (Skokie, Ill.: Rand McNally, 1975); Reppeto, *ibid.*; Carl E. Pope, *Crime Specific Analysis: The Characteristics of Burglary Incidents*, Analytic Report 12 (Washington, D.C.: U.S. Government Printing Office, 1977), 41–46.
8. FBI, *op. cit.*, 25.
9. Jay A. Sigler, *Understanding Criminal Law* (Boston: Little, Brown, 1981), 98.
10. Gardner, *op. cit.*, 304.
11. FBI, *op. cit.*, 29.
12. *Ibid.*, 32.
13. *Ibid.*, 30.
14. Mary Owen Cameron, "An Interpretation of Shoplifting," in Freda Adler and Rita James Simon (eds.) *The Criminology of Deviant Women* (Boston: Houghton Mifflin, 1979), 159–166.
15. C. Swanson, N. Chamelin, and L. Territo, *Criminal Investigation* (New York: Random House, 1984).
16. See Harold J. Vetter and Ira J. Silverman, *The Nature of Crime* (Philadelphia: W. B. Saunders, 1978), 150.
17. Donald P. Hartman, et al., "Rates of Bystander Observation and Reporting of Contrived Shoplifting Incidents," *Criminology*, 10 (1972), 247–267.
18. Cited in Mary Owen Cameron, "The Five Finger Discount," in E. O. Smigel and H. C. Ross (eds.) *Crimes Against Bureaucracy* (New York: Van Nostrand Reinhold, 1970), 99.
19. *Ibid.*
20. U.S. Department of Justice, *Criminal Victimization Surveys in the Nation's Five Largest Cities* (Washington, D.C.: U.S. Government Printing Office, 1975), 15–36.
21. FBI, *op. cit.*, 29.
22. *Ibid.*, 33.
23. *Ibid.*, 34.
24. *Ibid.*, 33.
25. *Ibid.*, 35.
26. *Ibid.*, 34.
27. See Charles H. McCaghy, Peggy C. Giordano, and Trudy Knicely Henson, "Auto Theft," *Criminology*, 15 (1977), 367–383.
28. FBI, *op. cit.*, 36.
29. John F. Bourdreau, et al., *Arson and Arson Investigation: Survey and Assessment* (Washington, D.C.: U.S. Government Printing Office, 1977), 1.
30. FBI, *op. cit.*, 37–38.
31. *Ibid.*, 37, 39.

12

Victimless Crime

OBJECTIVES

After studying this chapter, the student should be able to:

- Define the term victimless crime and list three general types of behavior that are often classified as such.
- Describe some general notions about gambling.
- Discuss homosexuality and prostitution as they relate to the notion of victimless crime.
- Explain drug usage as it relates to the concept of victimless or consensual crime.

Victimless crimes are sometimes referred to as consensual crimes. The central feature of this offense category is that the participants consent to an exchange of money for, or mutually agree upon, certain goods or services. The crimes are victimless in the sense that no one else is harmed, and there is no desire by the purchaser to arrest or prosecute the supplier. The customer may feel victimized if the expected merchandise or actual transaction turns out to be undesirable. But, the initial arrangement (that which is officially labeled a crime) does not include an expectation of victimization just as the decision to purchase a new automobile is not based upon an expectation to be victimized. In the case of consensual crimes, so-called victims rarely seek prosecution because of direct involvement in an activity that is officially illegal and, perhaps, embarrassing (e.g., prostitution).

The criminal justice system spends vast amounts of time and money attempting to control behavior that results from the decisions of two or more willing parties. The deployment of personnel, the expenses of prosecution, and the seemingly ineffectiveness of it all raises serious questions. Should the law concern itself with the enforcement of morals in the first place? Is the cost of enforcement really worth it? Several kinds of illegal behavior may fall within the category of victimless crimes. This chapter is restricted to a discussion of three behaviors commonly identified as victimless or consensual crimes: gambling, voluntary sexual practices, and drug usage.

GAMBLING

Games of chance have deep historical roots that go back to the times of the ancient Greeks and Romans. The Puritans of New England imposed some restrictions on gambling, but virtually all of the colonies permitted lotteries as a means of creating public revenue. In spite of the restrictions, most other types of gambling (cards, dice, etc.) were more or less tolerated.[1] A majority of states now license some form of gambling, be it horse racing, dog racing, jai alai, or bingo. Though only a few states (e.g., Nevada and New Jersey) license casino gambling, approximately 20 jurisdictions now have state lotteries with more legislatures currently considering the question.

Even in states that permit gambling, there are several laws and regulations aimed at control and at prevention of invasion by syndicated crime. The public, however, appears to be more concerned about having the opportunity to gamble than about who controls gambling or whether it is legal. Gambling laws are among the more commonly violated statutes. Over a decade ago, one racing commission in a southeastern state estimated that illegal betting exceeded legal betting by a ratio of $4:1$.[2] Because of illegal gambling's diversity and clandestine nature, it is next to impossible to approximate the amount of money involved in it. Figures from the late 1970s place annual illegal sports wagering at $700 million in the New York City area alone.[3]

The profits from illegal gambling are enormous. They are a major source of revenue for organized crime. Authorities in one midwestern state estimated organized crime's profits for illegal sports betting and the numbers game to be between $500 and $700 million annually.[4]

A central figure in many illegal gambling ventures is the "bookie," or bookmaker. A bookie operates as an intermediary, usually between a gambling syndicate and individual bettors. Even where off-track betting is legal (e.g., New York), bookies do a thriving business. Bookies use a variety of techniques. Some take bets from permanently located "fronts" (e.g., tobacco stores, pool halls, newsstands), others travel to bettors' hangouts (e.g., taverns, gyms), and still others use public telephone booths or rent motel rooms.[5]

Bookmakers do not confine their business to horse racing. They also take bets on football, baseball, basketball games, soccer matches, boxing matches, and so on. Perhaps the most widespread and well-paying illegal game is "policy" or "numbers." Policy (called "Bolita" in the South) is a game of chance that requires no skills and a minimal wage. Because of these factors, it is commonly found in the inner city among the poor or working class. In one form of policy, the player simply picks a three-digit number and bets a small amount (50 cents to a few dollars) that it will match an independently determined figure. That figure may be the last three digits of the combined bets placed at a designated racetrack on a particular day. For example, if a bettor selects the number "472" and the total daily amount bet at a given track is, say, $632,472, then the bettor wins. Even though the payoff is high (typically 500 times the original bet), the odds of winning are extremely low. The "numbers man" always has the advantage.

Thus, the combination of illegal bookmaking, policy, floating card and crap games, and slot machines adds up to a considerable amount of so-called crime. It is illegal activity that is pursued by customers desiring to gamble. Obviously, no one can force people to gamble. The crime, in this sense, is victimless. Apparently there is significant public support for this kind of activity. Arguments supporting the legalization of gambling may also be found among some law enforcement officials. One commentator has noted that:

> Frustrated law enforcement officials, too, are calling for legalization. They say their efforts are hopelessly compromised by judges—and a public—who do not take gambling laws seriously. Plea bargains are common; fines are low; and jail sentences are very rare.[6]

VOLUNTARY SEXUAL PRACTICES

Though the American Law Institute has called for the abandonment of laws forbidding homosexual practices between consenting adults, over two dozen states still restrict such behavior.[7] The remaining half of the states have decriminalized consensual "sodomy." In some of the restrictive states (e.g., Georgia), conviction of violating such sodomy laws may result in up to twenty years in prison. It seems curious, indeed, that society may punish homosexuals by placing them in the one-sex environment of a prison.

In actual practice, the enforcement of homosexual statutes is infrequent. Further, only a small percentage of the homosexual population are convicted of having committed "unnatural sexual acts." Of those arrested, the charge is likely to be one of "soliciting," "loitering," or "lewd behavior" (misdemeanors) and results from occasional police surveillance of suspected or known homosexual meeting places (public lavatories, bathhouses, gay bars, parks, etc.). Consequently, the gay (homosexual) community has charged that much police activity amounts to harassment.

Because of the nature of law enforcement practices, arrest statistics are unreliable as to the extent of homosexuality and the number of homosexuals. One of the most widely cited studies, the *Kinsey Report*, suggests that about 40 percent of the male population experiences a homosexual contact resulting in orgasm between the time of adolescence and old age.[8] Yet, the same research observed that less than 5 percent of the white male population is exclusively homosexual over the life span.[9] The central issue is not the extent of homosexuality nor what should be done to control the "problem." The chief argument is that no one should ever be subject to criminal penalties because of voluntary sexual preferences.

Public attitudes toward homosexuality are difficult to evaluate. On one hand, it does appear that the public in some sections of the country is becoming more tolerant of adult homosexuality. The press, television, and other media channels have recently done a great deal to educate the public regarding the realities of homosexual life-styles. Many of the negative images and stereotypes surrounding homosexuality have been attacked by the gay liberation movement, religious leaders, social scientists, and the medical profession. For example, in 1973, the American Psychiatric Association dropped "homosexuality" from its list of mental diseases.[10] As homosexuals have gained political power in some places, they have succeeded in electing political candidates sympathetic to their cause.[11]

On the other hand, homosexuality is highly stigmatized behavior in society. Changes favorable to homosexuals in some communities have been matched by setbacks elsewhere. The recent AIDS (acquired immune deficiency syndrome) epidemic, no doubt, has done a great deal to increase the public's fears and to ignite hostilities toward gays. One of the more recent, publicized antihomosexual campaigns was carried out by entertainer and former Miss America, Anita Bryant. Based largely on her efforts, homosexuals in the Miami area lost the protection of that city's gay rights' ordinances. Other communities have followed suit.[12] Toleration of homosexuality is one thing; acceptance of it is quite another matter. As one writer has expressed his feelings:

> I find I can accept it [homosexuality] least of all when I look at my children. There is much my four sons can do in their lives that might cause me anguish, that might outrage me, that might make me ashamed of them and of myself as their father. But nothing they could ever do would make me sadder than if they were to become homosexual.[13]

Prostitution represents another pattern of voluntary sexual practices that is illegal in all but one state. As noted previously, Nevada provides for legalized prostitution on a county-option basis. Before World War II, the primary source of commercialized sex was the brothel. One area of New Orleans, known as "Storyville," was the location of over 200 brothels. The "red light" districts functioned as centers of prostitution until waves of public protest led to their closing by the late thirties.[14] Today, prostitution outlets are more diverse and include a wide variety of participants and settings.

Streetwalkers tend to cluster in commercial or central business districts of major cities. They may frequent certain lounges, bus stations, or convention centers. Quite often, they reside in cheap hotels where they bring their clients. Customers ("johns" or "tricks") may also be serviced in their own cars, in alleys, or in vacant buildings. The street prostitute ("hooker") leads a hazardous and brief career. She is very vulnerable to police activity and has little control over the clients that she accommodates. Depending upon the age at which she begins her trade, a hooker's life on the street may span only a few years. Exposure to disease and the general effects of a harsh existence takes its toll at a relatively early age.

The streetwalker is the most commonly visible type of prostitute. Other styles of prostitution flourish. The degree of their visibility varies with the experience and imagination of the observer. Some hookers confine their business to bars. The casual setting of a bar offers comfort, some protection, and the opportunity to screen potential customers. So-called b-girls may use the bar as a base of operation for prostitution. B-girls may also be planted by the establishment simply to solicit drinks (at inflated prices) in return for the possibility of a sexual encounter. Thus, some b-girls are prostitutes; others are mere con artists who earn a commission on the number of drinks that they can get customers to buy for them. Massage parlors also act as a front for prostitution. Few men enter a gaudy parlor advertising ''topless' or ''bottomless'' massages solely for the purpose of a conventional massage. The prostitute working in a massage parlor is therefore guaranteed a source of business that is much more stable than she would find on the street. More important, the customer often must do the soliciting for ''extras.'' This, in effect, somewhat protects the prostitute from arrests. In many jurisdictions, a vice officer's arrest based on the acts of a prostitute he solicits is void. This technique to obtain an arrest is termed ''entrapment.'' It is usually the basis for dismissing a charge.

In the world of prostitution, the call girl is accorded the most status. Call girls may operate alone with relative independence or in a ring that is centrally controlled. Customers are typically obtained by referral from other customers or call girls. It is not uncommon for a so-called dating service to be the front for a call girl operation. Some of the more elegant call girls are college educated, of middle-class background, and stunning in appearance.[15] They may cater to corporate executives, professionals, and politicians—those who can afford their expensive fees.

Recent examinations of prostitution have focused on male prostitutes and on child prostitutes of both sexes. Male prostitutes (children and adults) cater to homosexual clients. Their places of operation vary from gay bars to parks, public transportation centers, and rest-room facilities. Boy prostitutes, referred to as ''chickens,'' offer their services to older males termed ''chicken hawks.'' Young male prostitutes may work the streets and gay bars or be part of a referral service. As is the case with some call girls, ''chickens'' may even be advertised through magazines that promote commercialized sex (e.g., movies, photos, ''sexual aids,'' and ''swinger'' contacts). Neglected or runaway girls may turn to prostitution as a method of survival. Recognizing this problem, many urban areas have established residential centers where these children of the streets may find shelter, counseling, and an escape from a life of exploitation. While offering temporary relief, the counseling centers have not been very successful in returning girls to their home environments. As noted in one recent study, a surprisingly large number of current teenage hookers come from middle-class backgrounds.[16]

All sorts of explanations have been proposed as to why individuals become prostitutes. A commonly cited cause rests on the notion of force or compulsion. That is, it is believed that unsuspecting women are enticed into prostitution on the pretext of successful careers in, for example, modeling or the entertainment world. Once under the control of an enforcer or ''manager,'' they are then forced through threats, violence, or drugs into submission. The ''manager,'' also known as a ''pimp,'' may hang around areas where runaways are likely to concentrate (e.g., bus terminals). After offering a bewildered and confused juvenile "friendship" and a place to stay, pressure is placed on her to work the streets. Regarding how runaway girls are pressured into the business, one pimp has stated that:

> You've got to stomp her ass a few times to let her know where you're coming from. You've got to set the rules, make her show respect. . . . If she makes it through tomorrow, the process will take three days. We'll get her a wig, some clothes, then put $10 in her pocket and see if she tries to run. You watch her close, maybe send another girl out with her. If she turns her first trick and comes back smiling, you've got her.[17]

No doubt, some individuals do find their way into prostitution through deceit and force. At this point, then, prostitution is not a victimless crime—especially when children are the victims. However, it seems reasonable to believe that a large proportion of women or men prostitutes choose to offer their bodies in return for payment. Because of limited legitimate opportunities and the prospect of relatively high pay, prostitution becomes an acceptable livelihood for many people. Even with apparent legitimate opportunities, prostitution is an appealing life-style for some women. When asked about her chosen occupation, one prostitute remarked:

> What can I say? Where else could I make as much money? How could I ever go back to being a typist after having what I have now? How could I afford this apartment? or the clothes? I don't know . . . one day you wake up and realize that you can't get out of it. The money and everything has you surrounded and maybe, deep down you really don't want to get out of it, because part of you really likes it.[18]

The voluntary nature of much prostitution is underscored by the attempts of prostitutes to organize. In 1974, a national "hookers convention" was sponsored by an organization known as COYOTE. COYOTE's goals continue to center around decriminalizing prostitution and promoting the right of women to solicit sex for pay if they choose to do so. For years, men have been legally selling their bodies as athletes. For an even longer period, men have been soliciting sex if the price was right. The fact that criminologists and the police know more about prostitutes than their customers is, in itself, evidence of society's double standard. Although it appears that the pimp often supplies necessary psychological support for hookers, legalized prostitution would reduce the importance of his role as a supplier of police protection, bail money, and the like. Nevertheless, some exploitation would likely continue, as it does in all walks of life. But declaring voluntary behavior (i.e., prostitution) a crime eliminates neither the exploitation nor the activity.

DRUG USAGE

Drugs include a broad range of substances. Just about anything that affects behavior may be classified as a drug. Some drugs are quite legal, widespread, and freely available (e.g., aspirin and liquor). Other drugs are legal and widespread but subject to control (e.g., barbiturates and amphetamines). Still other drugs carry a criminal penalty and are a major concern of criminal justice agencies but are frequently consumed (e.g., heroin and marijuana).

A drug's designation as illegal may be more dependent upon the political process than the harmful properties of the drug itself. Although we do not have all of the facts, it now appears that tobacco is probably at least as harmful as marijuana. Yet, the selling (and advertising) of cigarettes is perfectly legal while the sale of marijuana "joints" is a crime. Most drugs (legal and illegal) have the potential to harm the user. The primary points to keep in mind regarding drug usage as victimless crimes are the following: (1) the voluntary nature of the activity, (2) the individual's right to do something that is potentially self-destructive, (3) the effects of criminalizing certain drugs, and (4) the advisability of having public health agencies, not the criminal justice system, deal with drug abuse. The following discussion includes four drugs which are highly restricted or illegal (opiates, psychedelics, marijuana, and cocaine) and one drug which is relatively unrestricted and legal (alcohol).

Restricted or Illegal Drugs

Opium comes from the seed pods of the poppy plant. It has been used as a painkilling medicine for centuries. In the early 1800s, morphine was derived from opium and became widely used at midcentury when the hypodermic needle and syringe were invented. During the Civil War, morphine was freely administered to the wounded of both armies. Those who survived their wounds were often addicted to the drug. Morphine addiction was thus known as the "soldier's disease." Around the turn of the century, heroin was extracted from morphine as a substitute that was mistakenly thought to be less addictive and more effective as a painkiller than morphine.

Heroin is a powerful drug that produces a euphoric effect or state of intense pleasure. It may also cause nausea. Over a period of time, the user must take increased dosages to maintain the desired effect. This pattern of required increased dosage is known as tolerance. Once tolerance (physical addiction) develops, attempts to withdraw from the drug usually produce extreme physical reactions such as vomiting, cramps, and chills. After withdrawal, remembrances of the intense pleasurable effects of heroin may signify psychological addiction leading to renewed use.

Prior to 1914, opium addiction occurred across a broad base of the public. Chinese immigrants smoked the drug in opium dens which were visited by a growing number of white, middle-class people. Opium could also be purchased through the mail, in dry goods stores, or found as a prime ingredient in such home remedies as "Mrs. Winslow's Soothing Syrup." [19]

In 1914, the Harrison Act was passed in order to honor international drug control agreements. The Act required that the sale and distribution of opium be recorded and a small tax placed on such transactions. Many of the more "respectable" opiate users (white, middle-class, middle-aged women) discontinued their habit or switched to drugs more easily obtainable (e.g., barbiturates). Beginning in the 1920s, stronger controls were placed on the opiates. Eventually heroin became outlawed even for use as a medicine.

The placing of tight controls on opium and its byproducts did not cause the drug scene to disappear. It simply changed in appearance. With the removal of opiates from purely medical to legal controls, addicts sought supplies from sources other than physicians. Older "respectable" addicts could often get their morphine from cooperative family physicians. For those less fortunate, a secret network developed into an illegal drug subculture. Because of its superior "high," the difficulty of getting morphine, and the development of markets in Europe and the Middle East, heroin eventually became the preferred opiate among addicts.[20] Since the end of World War II, the opiate (i.e., heroin) addict population has shifted to that of young, male minority group members living in the inner city. The urban ghetto is also a place where plenty of potential customers could care less about avoiding a new thrill because it is against the law.[21]

Various psychedelic substances have been known for some time prior to the lysergic acid diethylamide (LSD) "craze" of the early 1960s. Indian tribes of Mexico and the United States have continuously used mescaline which they obtain from the peyote cactus. Wild mushrooms have also been sought after for the psilocybin which is found in them. In 1934, LSD was manufactured and used primarily by the medical community in isolated experiments involving mental patients. In 1963, LSD became a public issue when a Harvard University psychologist (Dr. Timothy Leary) was fired for dispensing LSD to students while advocating the drug's universal benefits.

LSD was then adopted in the "hippie" subculture and on some college campuses due to its acclaimed power to produce extraordinary insights into nature, the universe, and oneself. The drug does produce strong hallucinations and increase sensitivity to sight and sound. However, it is not physically addictive nor unusually habit forming. LSD became increasingly controversial in the 1960s. The drug was linked to sudden suicides, brain damage, and birth defects. By 1965, LSD was no longer manufactured legitimately and several states passed laws prohibiting its usage. Federal legislation followed in 1970.

Because of highly publicized "bad trips," overdoses, suicides, and accidents related to the drug, LSD declined in popularity. Evidence exists that disputes the health hazard claims made against LSD.[22] Some people have suggested that the publicity itself caused many users to experience exactly what they had been told to expect from an LSD trip.[23] LSD is not receiving the attention that it did two decades ago. Other psychedelics, such as PCP (phencyclidine hydrochloride) or "angel dust," more recently caused alarm as a suspected favorite among juveniles.

In fear of the consequences, many users turned off LSD and tuned in to marijuana after the early 1960s. Prior to that time, marijuana was used primarily in minority communities. In the 1950s, it became identified as a drug commonly used by "beatniks" (poets, artists, and musicians) that congregated in such places as New York's Greenwich Village.

Marijuana ("pot" or "grass") is derived from the female hemp plant which grows wild or is cultivated in many parts of the world. Its use in one form or another is centuries old. The Chinese and Hindus of India used hashish (resin from the plant) for medicine and religious purposes. During colonial times many Americans grew hemp in order to make rope, while physicians prescribed marijuana for several of the day's illnesses. The drug produces some mild hallucinations and no physical dependence, and may be less harmful than an equal dosage of alcohol.[24] Further, marijuana ingestion does not appear to be as habit forming as conventional cigarette smoking is.

Serious efforts to criminalize marijuana began in 1937 with the passage of the Marijuana Tax Act. Later legislation (Boggs Act of 1951 and the Narcotics Control Act of 1956) grouped marijuana with the opiates and specified equally serious penalties for violations. In the 1960s, pot became a symbol of middle-class youth's protest over the "establishment" and existing social conditions (e.g., Vietnam War, civil unrest). Usage spread rapidly. By the end of the 1970s, over 50 percent of the high school students surveyed admitted to having smoked pot.[25] As the children of the influential middle and upper classes openly violated the law in increasing numbers, harsh marijuana penalties tended to go unenforced. Eventually several states began to drastically reduce penalties for possession of small amounts of the substance. Alaska now permits marijuana cultivation for personal consumption.

We are all familiar with the advertising slogan proclaiming that "Things go better with Coke," or "Coke adds life." But many are unaware of the fact that the popular soft drink, Coca Cola, contained cocaine in its original formula. Long before Coca Cola became an international trademark, cocaine was (and is) used by South American Indians. The leaves of the coca shrub are chewed as a stimulant. They increase endurance for strenuous work that the Indians perform in the high altitudes of the Andes mountains.

Cocaine has also had medical uses. Hundreds of years ago, it was administered as an anesthetic for "skull surgery" performed by primitive tribes. Until recently, physicians and dentists used cocaine for some of their surgical procedures. Today's commonly prescribed dental anesthetic, Novocain (procaine hydrochloride) has the pain-relieving properties of cocaine but does not have cocaine's stimulating qualities.[26]

Acting as a stimulant, cocaine ("coke," "snort," or "snow") excites the user, counters feelings of tiredness, and is often accompanied by mood changes. Under the influence of cocaine, people tend to feel more self-confident, alert, and, on occasion, sexually aroused.[27] This latter characteristic, which may or may not result from cocaine, caused early reformers to fear its use among blacks. Groups calling for the criminalizing of cocaine stated that it was a major factor in the rapes of white women by "dope crazed" blacks. There is no evidence that the drug was used more often by blacks than by whites.[28] Formerly, cocaine was thought not to be physically addictive; recent upsurges in its use and abuse, however, have dramatized the dangerously addictive qualities, both physical and psychological, of cocaine.[29] Unlike users of heroin, users of cocaine come from all social backgrounds and are not predominantly found among lower-class, inner-city residents. "Crack," a cheap version of cocaine, came to be feared as a leading substance of abuse during the 1980s.

Obviously, the criminalizing of certain drugs has affected supply and demand. Where an illegal commodity is in short supply and consumers will pay anything for it, a distribution network will develop. Further, the excessive costs of some drugs (e.g., heroin) are directly related to their illegal status. This has an impact on other crimes. Given heroin's strong addictive qualities, crimes such as robbery and burglary are often impulsive acts of the addict looking for another "hit." The personal ill effects of drugs (including heroin) appear to be related more to the user's self-denial of food, sanitation, and general health care in order to buy drugs than they are to the drug itself. Thus, much of the crime and personal misery associated with heroin may be attributed to its having been criminalized. For other, less compulsive drugs (e.g., psychedelics and marijuana), the relationship to crime may be no more direct than that of alcohol. Perhaps the major criminogenic distinction is that the former are declared illegal (and thus using or possessing them is a crime by definition), whereas liquor is not.

Alcohol: An Unrestricted and Legal Drug

It is estimated that alcohol has been in use (and abuse) since as early as 8000 B.C. Efforts to control or regulate drinking date back to Egyptian society and the year 3000 B.C. In 1100 B.C., China enacted regulatory laws concerning alcohol. The American colonies permitted drinking but imposed fines or relatively light penalties for drunkenness.[30]

Except for regulations on the purchaser's age and local prohibitions or ordinances, ethyl alcohol (beer, whiskey, and wine) is basically an unrestricted or legal drug today. This has not always been the case. Much of the violence, inflated costs, and underworld control now associated with illegal drugs was present when liquor was illegal in the United States. The Volstead Act of 1919 brought in the era of Prohibition. Some fourteen years later (1933), it was repealed after almost everyone agreed that it had been a failure.

Few would seriously argue that nationalized prohibition of alcohol should be attempted again. However, alcohol is related to many social and personal problems that are identified with hard drugs. As noted in previous chapters of this text, alcohol (drinking) is associated with a high proportion of homicides and assaultive behavior. It disrupts people's lives and has costly effects. For example, business estimates that companies lose $10 billion each year due to alcoholism.[31] Alcoholism can lead to self-destruction through liver damage or accidental death. For many, alcohol is psychologically habit forming. For a growing number of Americans, it is physically addictive in that withdrawal is followed by serious side effects such as delirium tremens (the DTs).

At one time, public drunkenness constituted the largest percentage of arrests for any single crime recorded by the *Uniform Crime Reports*. In 1965, almost one-third of all arrests were for drunkenness (not counting disorderly conduct or driving while intoxicated). Since then, this figure has decreased to about 10 percent.[32] But where jurisdictions have decriminalized public drunkenness, intoxicated individuals are sometimes arrested on charges of loitering or vagrancy.

Recognizing the consensual nature of alcoholism, over twenty years ago the President's Commission recommended that, "Drunkenness should not itself be a criminal offense." [33] State and local agencies have responded to this recommendation by establishing detoxification and treatment centers for alcoholics who would formerly have been processed at the local jail. In those jurisdictions which have not adopted such practices, the arrested offender continues to be the victim of society's inaction.

Of greater concern, however, is the problem of driving while intoxicated (DWI). In 1984, over 1 million individuals were arrested for this offense,[34] and many of them had multiple prior arrests. The carnage left on the highways due to alcohol-related accidents has led to the formation of such groups as Mothers Against Drunk Drivers (MADD) and Students Against Driving Drunk (SADD). These and other interest groups have pioneered volunteer programs for transporting intoxicated would-be drivers, as well as organizing lobbying efforts for tough legislation against those who drive while drunk. Over one-half of the states have passed strict laws that include mandatory jail sentences, fines, and, in some states, the confiscation of cars involved in felonies committed by intoxicated drivers.[35]

THE PROS AND CONS OF VICTIMLESS CRIME

The area known as victimless crime is controversial. Numerous interested parties have entered the debate. It is beyond the scope of this book to discuss fully all of the many arguments for or against decriminalizing the behaviors examined in this chapter. A brief survey of the pros and cons regarding the victimless crime issue follows.[36]

PRO	CON
1. It is not the proper function of government or the criminal justice system to regulate private morality or behavior through criminal laws; that is the role of nonlegal institutions.	1. Because morality affects the viability of a nation, it is a proper function of government to regulate morality by the use of criminal laws.
2. The laws are ineffective. They do not deter involvement in the proscribed activities, either by organized crime or the public. Neither fines nor jail rehabilitate or alter the behavior of offenders.	2. The laws do not serve as deterrents because they are not strictly enforced and the sanctions are not strong enough.
3. The laws are unenforceable. The volume of activity is too great, public support is lacking, and criminal justice system resources are inadequate.	3. The fact that a law seems unenforceable is no reason to abolish it. For example, murder and theft laws are not 100 percent enforceable but are nevertheless needed. A preferable alternative to abolishing the victimless crime laws is providing more resources to implement them.
4. There is no evidence that legalization or decriminalization will lead to a harmful increase in immoral behavior. The activities are already easily accessible to anyone who wants them.	4. Modification of the sanctions against these activities will result in a disastrous increase in their occurrence. This in turn will lead to a moral decline of society. The nation will become a second-class power. Both the Greek and Roman civilizations were destroyed by the decadence of their citizenry.
5. The rights of individuals to live as they want, so long as they do not harm others, is a fundamental principle on which this nation was founded.	5. The activities known as victimless crimes are antithetical to Christian beliefs and to the principles on which this nation was founded.

SUMMARY

Victimless crimes are those acts in which adult participants consent to an exchange of money for certain goods or services. They are crimes in which no one is harmed except, perhaps, the willing consumer. Commonly cited victimless crimes include gambling, voluntary sexual practices, and drug usage. All of these behaviors have been around for centuries. There is no evidence that declaring them to be criminal acts has reduced their occurrence. In fact, it appears that criminalizing some activities has multiplied the problems. Much victimless crime (e.g., gambling, prostitution, and marijuana smoking) has considerable unofficial public support or tolerance. Other forms of consensual crime are less condoned (e.g., homosexuality and ''heavy'' drug usage) but relatively frequent in occurrence.

Crimes categorized as victimless do have harmful or negative aspects. Gambling may become compulsive and lead to abuses. The same is true for drug usage (including alcohol) and certain sexual practices. A major issue, then, is whether the individual or the government should decide if someone has the right to behave in a possibly self-destructive manner.

These behaviors also have harmful consequences when others are involuntarily exploited. The use of children in prostitution is most definitely not victimless crime. In these instances, the voluntary or consensual adult factor is removed. The debate concerning the decriminalizing of victimless crimes is surrounded by many points and counterpoints. This chapter has presented some fundamental information about certain victimless crimes. One should consider this information as well as opposing arguments in making a decision concerning the notion of victimless crime.

SUGGESTED ACTIVITIES

- Determine to what extent legalized gambling is permitted in your state (e.g., horse racing, state lottery, bingo). What are the duties of the state agency (e.g., Gaming Commission, Gambling Control Board) that controls or regulates this activity?
- Visit with a representative of your city's police department. Discuss the nature and extent of prostitution and illegal drug usage in your community.
- Write to your U.S. congressional representative or senator and request a copy of the Comprehensive Drug Abuse Prevention and Control Act of 1970. Compare it with your state's drug control legislation. Note any similarities and/or differences.
- As a class project, debate the issue of decriminalization of the victimless crimes discussed in this chapter.
- If possible, invite a representative of an alcohol or drug treatment program to your class to discuss the program and its relationship, if any, to the criminal justice system.

REVIEW

    A. Give a brief definition of the term victimless crime.
    B. List three general types of victimless crimes.
    C. State three reasons why victimless crimes should be decriminalized.

D. State three reasons why victimless crimes should not be decriminalized.

E. Multiple Choice. Select the best answer.

1. Which of the following types of illegal gambling is most common?
- a. horse racing
- b. policy
- c. bingo
- d. lotteries

2. In general, gambling is:
- a. illegal in all states except Nevada
- b. legal in all states except South Carolina and New Mexico
- c. restricted to certain types or forms of games in most states
- d. an activity of lower-class people

3. Homosexuality practiced by consenting adults is:
- a. legal in some states
- b. usually behavior resulting in an arrest on the charge of committing "unnatural sexual acts"
- c. defined as a mental disease by the American Psychiatric Association
- d. acceptable to a vast majority of Americans, based on Gallop Polls

4. The most visible type of prostitute is:
- a. b-girl
- b. call girl
- c. john boy
- d. street hooker

5. A slang term for a juvenile male prostitute is:
- a. chicken
- b. john boy
- c. cookie
- d. lollipop

6. An arrest made on the basis of an illegal act solicited by a law enforcement officer may be held by the court to constitute:
- a. double jeopardy
- b. contempt
- c. entrapment
- d. transactional immunity

7. The male "manager" of a prostitute is known as a:
- a. bookie
- b. D.I.
- c. bouncer
- d. pimp

8. Which of the following drugs is physically addictive in the sense that severe withdrawal symptoms occur?
- a. cocaine
- b. marijuana
- c. LSD
- d. none of these

9. The first major drug legislation passed at the federal level was the:
- a. Marijuana Tax Act
- b. Harrison Act
- c. Narcotics Control Act
- d. Boggs Act

10. The criminalizing of certain drugs has resulted in:
- a. their disuse

b. an underground distribution network

c. fewer social problems

d. fewer related crimes

11. It has been established that psychedelic drugs are:

a. physically addictive

b. difficult to obtain

c. now less popular than marijuana

d. a major cause of suicide

12. Cocaine:

a. was originally thought not to be physically addictive

b. is a powerful depressant

c. is a recent discovery

d. was first discovered in China

13. Which of the following is not an opiate drug?

a. heroin

b. "angel dust"

c. morphine

d. all of these are opiates

14. Alcohol is:

a. potentially addictive

b. potentially habit forming

c. related to crime, personal and social problems

d. all of these

15. Drugs are declared illegal as the result of:

a. their being dangerous to health as opposed to legal drugs

b. politics and public policy

c. their being related to crime

d. their cost to the consumer

REFERENCES

1. Howard Abadinsky, *Organized Crime* (Boston, Mass.: Allyn and Bacon, 1981), 130.
2. National Advisory Commission on Criminal Justice Standards and Goals, *Task Force Report on Organized Crime* (Washington, D.C.: U.S. Government Printing Office, 1976), 12.
3. Peter Reuter, *Disorganized Crime* (Cambridge, Mass.: MIT Press, 1983), 33.
4. National Advisory Commission, *op. cit.*, 13.
5. Denny F. Pace and Jimmy C. Styles, *Organized Crime: Concepts and Control* (Englewood Cliffs, N.J.: Prentice-Hall, 1975), 114–115.
6. *Ibid.*, 233.
7. American Law Institute, *Model Penal Code*, Section 207.5; "A Government in the Bedroom," *Newsweek*, July 14, 1986, 36–38.
8. Alfred C. Kinsey, et al., *Sexual Behavior in the Human Male* (Philadelphia: W. B. Saunders, 1948), 650.
9. *Ibid.*, 651.
10. Barry M. Dank, "The Homosexual," in Don Spiegel and Patricia Keith-Spiegel (eds.) *Outsiders USA* (San Francisco: Rinehart Press, 1973), 283.
11. See John H. Gagnon and Bruce Henderson, "Human Sexuality: An Age of Ambiguity," *Social Issues Series* (Boston: Little, Brown, 1975).
12. Houston, Texas recently (1985) voted to retain laws permitting descrimination against homosexuals in the hiring, termination, and promotion of city employees.
13. Charles H. McCaghy, *Deviant Behavior* (New York: Macmillan, 1976), 349.
14. Abadinsky, *op. cit.*, 138.

15. Harold J. Vetter and Ira J. Silverman, *Criminology and Crime* (New York: Harper and Row, 1986), 196.
16. See Dorothy Heid Bracey, *Baby-Pros*, *Criminal Justice Monograph*, No. 12 (New York: John Jay Press, 1978).
17. "White Slavery, 1972," *Time*, June 5, 1972, 24, as cited in McCaghy, *op. cit.*, 354.
18. Freda Adler, *Sisters in Crime* (New York: McGraw-Hill, 1975), 71.
19. Oakley Ray, *Drugs, Society, and Human Behavior* (St. Louis, Mo.: C. V. Mosby, 1983), 332. Also see Edward M. Brecher, *Licit and Illicit Drugs* (Boston: Little, Brown, 1972).
20. Erich Goode, *Drugs in American Society* (New York: Knopf, 1972), 193.
21. Daniel Glaser, et al., "Opiate Addicted and Nonaddicted Siblings in a Slum Area," *Social Problems*, 18 (1971), 510–521. Also see Ray, *op. cit.*, 358, in which the author notes some shifts in the characteristics of users based upon admissions to treatment programs.
22. Brecher, *op. cit.*, Chap. 52; Ray, *op. cit.*, 394.
23. *Ibid.*
24. Ray, *op. cit.*, 71; A. T. Weil, et al., "Clinical and Psychological Effects of Marijuana in Man," *Science*, 162 (1968), 1234–1242.
25. Ray, *op. cit.*, 439.
26. *Ibid.*, 296–299.
27. Robert J. Wicks and Jerome J. Platt, *Drug Abuse: A Criminal Justice Primer* (Beverly Hills: Glencoe Press, 1977), 87.
28. David F. Musto, *The American Disease: Origins of Narcotic Control* (New Haven, Conn.: Yale University Press, 1973), 6.
29. Ray, *op. cit.*, 299–303.
30. *Ibid.*, 148–149.
31. Wicks and Platt, *op. cit.*, 18.
32. Federal Bureau of Investigation, *Uniform Crime Reports, 1984* (Washington, D.C.: U.S. Government Printing Office, 1985), 166.
33. President's Commission, *The Challenge of Crime in a Free Society* (Washington, D.C.: U.S. Government Printing Office, 1967), 236.
34. FBI, *op. cit.*
35. See Larry J. Siegel, *Criminology*, 2nd ed. (St. Paul: West, 1986), 429.
36. National Advisory Commission, *op. cit.*, 230–231.

13

Organized Crime [1]

OBJECTIVES

After studying this chapter, the student should be able to:

- Cite weaknesses of the President's Task Force definition of organized crime.
- State another definition of organized crime that accounts for a broad coverage of the problem.
- Discuss three major concepts necessary for an understanding of organized crime.
- Describe briefly the development of crime societies or "families" in this country.
- List three examples of criminal alliances including at least one example of the corporate criminal alliance.

The subject of organized crime usually creates images of gun-toting gangsters who belong to a secret criminal society commonly called the "Mafia." Other forms of criminal behavior have similar structures, motivations, and economic origins. Upon examination, it becomes clear that organized crime is a lot more than secret criminal societies. This chapter attempts to enlarge the image of organized crime. It includes a definition of the activity and a discussion of its nature.

DEFINITION OF ORGANIZED CRIME

One of the most influential definitions of organized crime was presented by the President's Task Force Report. It stated that:

Organized crime is a society that seeks to operate outside the control of the American people and their governments. It involves thousands of criminals, working within structures as complex as those of any large corporation, subject to laws more rigidly enforced than those of legitimate governments. Its actions are not impulsive but rather the result of intricate conspiracies, carried on over many years and aimed at gaining control over whole fields of activity in order to amass huge profits.[2]

This definition emphasizes that organized crime is: (1) a secret society, (2) tightly controlled, (3) opposed to the public's values and interests, and (4) similar to (but does not include) corporate structures and behavior.[3] The public is strongly inclined to accept these notions about organized crime. They are also widely shared by social scientists, journalists, other writers, and law enforcement agents. The Task Force's statements about organized crime actually represent a set of conclusions rather than a definition.

Is organized crime a society? If one agrees that "intricate conspiracies . . . aimed at gaining control over . . . huge [illegal] profits" is the major objective of organized crime, then the activity goes far beyond the concept of a society. A decade ago, Gulf Oil Company agreed to pay $42.2 million to the Treasury Department for allegedly overcharging consumers. According to Federal Energy Administration officials, Gulf had based the "illegal" charges on a $79.1 million overstatement of their foreign crude oil costs.[4] This certainly appears to be a case of conspiring to amass a sizable illegal profit. This is crime which is highly organized. But, is Gulf Oil Company a society? Is it the Mafia in disguise? It may be more accurate to state that organized crime includes, but is not limited to, criminal societies.

Is organized crime tightly controlled? To be organized, any activity must involve the element of control. Crime societies do attempt to control members through the use of enforcers, threats, and occasional violence. However, there are indications that this control is not as powerful as is often believed. Continuous friction between groups and increasing numbers of members willing to testify in return for government protection suggest a decline of centralized control. Secrecy is also important to any type of criminal conspiracy. It is present, to some degree, among crime societies. But, it is also important for organized crime to exist at other levels. Corporations that conspire to fix prices and presidential aides that plan the "bugging" of another party's headquarters (Watergate) all depend on secrecy. In other words, control and secrecy are not the chief distinction between crime societies and other groups that commit organized crime.

Is organized crime opposed to the public's values and interests? In one sense it is, and in another sense it is not. Official social values condemn such things as extortion, bribery, and price rigging. On the other hand, the public unofficially condones these forms of deviance. It is not uncommon for speeders to offer a traffic officer the fine in advance so as to avoid the hassles of a ticket or DWI (driving while intoxicated) charge. The selling of athletic tickets at highly inflated prices ("scalping") often occurs when demand outstrips supply. Also, while the public may outwardly oppose gambling, or prostitution, organized crime would not be in these businesses if there were no demand. Prohibition (discussed in the previous chapter) is a glaring example of how the public and crime societies supported one another: one as consumers, the other as producers. Finally, there is even evidence that the services of crime societies have been used by the government. During World War II, the Navy worked closely with Lucky Luciano (a notorious crime society figure in New York) to prevent the sabotage of shipping by German spies on the east coast.[5] Several years later, Sam Giancana (a Chicago crime family boss in Chicago) was linked with the CIA in a conspiracy to assassinate Fidel Castro of Cuba.[6]

What are the similarities between organized crime and some corporate structures and activities? Organized crime requires some structure, whether it is committed by crime societies or others. The Task Force identified organized crime and crime societies as being one and the same. Further, it stated that organized crime is the work of twenty-four crime families having the structure shown in Figure 13-1.[7]

A close examination of Figure 13-1 reveals that the structure of crime families is strikingly similar to that of a corporation. Positions within a "family" parallel those of a legitimate corporation. Thus, a boss ("capo") corresponds to a corporation president, underboss ("sottocapo") to a vice-president, lieutenants ("caporegima") to company managers, and soldiers ("soldati") to sales representatives. But the similarity goes further than the Task Force indicated. Figure 13-1 reveals that crime families are involved in both legal and illegal activities. Some corporations are involved in both legal and illegal activities. Their illegitimate activities often amount to highly organized crime.

To illustrate the more complete picture of organized crime, another definition with additional concepts is appropriate. This chapter's description of organized crime is based upon the following definition and concepts.

> Organized crime consists of illegal acts, executed by five or more "producers" with varying degrees of participation, to directly or indirectly secure a system of recurring financial rewards through the provision of goods and services for consumer groups differing in size and knowledge of involvement.[8]

For the sake of discussion, five was chosen as the number of participants because of its legal specification in the Organized Crime Control Act of 1970.[9] The student should note that this definition says nothing of a society. This is intended. As this chapter has emphasized, the use of the term "society" tends to result in a very narrow image of organized crime. To understand organized crime, three fundamental concepts must be recognized and defined. These concepts are: criminogenic (crime-producing) market structures, criminal societies, and criminal alliances.

A criminogenic market structure may arise when certain goods or services are declared illegal or become scarce and the demand for them exceeds the supply. These market structures are strengthened by weakly enforced or ineffective laws. Further, the market is such that organization is necessary to protect suppliers or producers from law enforcement and competitors. Criminal societies refer to those groups of individuals, united by a bond of ethnic identity, personal loyalty, or other shared experiences that are in addition to economic concerns. The financial ventures of criminal societies are varied and may entail both legal and illegal activities. Criminal alliances include persons for whom the attachment to others is based mainly upon specific and primarily illegal economic pursuits. These pursuits may be directly related to legitimate occupations. One major example of this form of organized crime is the corporate criminal alliance.

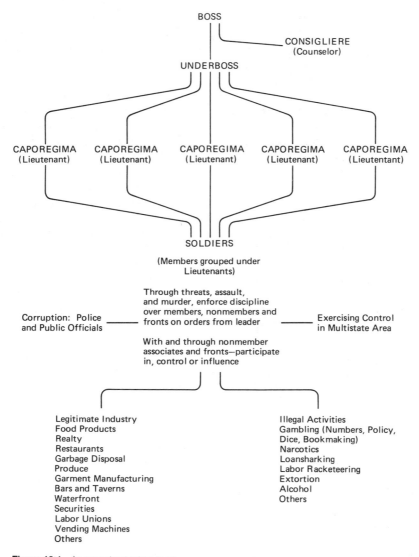

Figure 13-1 An organized crime family

Source: President's Commission on Law Enforcement and the Administration of Justice, *Task Force Report*: *Organized Crime* (Washington, D.C.: U.S. Government Printing Office, 1967), 9.

THE NATURE OF ORGANIZED CRIME

Much crime is strongly related to economic factors. This is especially true in economies where the profit motive freely operates as a driving force. When certain goods or services become illegal, or simply become scarce for this or other reasons, the continued demand leads to a criminogenic market structure. That is, an organized, illegal system of supply and distribution tends to arise. The resulting organized crime is carried on by criminal societies and/or criminal alliances.

Criminal Societies

Sicily is an island that lies off the west coast of southern Italy. A secret criminal society known as the Mafia has existed in Sicily since the 1800s. By 1900, hundreds of thousands of southern Italian immigrants poured into the United States each year. Most tended to settle in the urban slums of the industrial northeastern or midwestern states. The vast majority were simple, law-abiding peasants who wanted to escape the harsh existence of the old country. A few, however, had criminal backgrounds and were being sought by the Italian police. Some probably had minor Mafia connections. But it is very unlikely that they were leading figures who had come to this country to establish an American organization. At this time, there was little reason for Mafia leaders to face the uncertainty of a foreign land. There was little cause for giving up their positions of power in Sicily.

Crime in the Italian ghettos was largely internal and localized. That is, Italians victimized other Italians. The offenses centered around blackmail, extortion, fraud, kidnapping, and the common street crimes of burglary and robbery. The usual technique was to send a threatening letter to the victim and to sign it with a black hand. There was never a formal organization known as the ''Black Hand.'' It was simply a crude method of creating fear on the part of intended victims.

Thus, the Mafia did not exist in America during the first part of this century. The criminal element of the Italian population committed mostly petty, unorganized crime. They lacked the political connections that existed in Sicily between Mafia leaders (''dons'') and officials. Many could barely speak English.

It was some children of immigrants who would eventually form the predominantly Italian criminal syndicates. Most had come to this country as small children; others were born in the United States. Many of the future syndicate leaders dropped out of school at an early age. They joined local delinquent gangs and began committing small-time crimes. As had been the case with other minority group children, crime was a way of getting the luxuries that would otherwise be unavailable.

The passage of the Volstead Act (Eighteenth Amendment) resulted in the prohibition of liquor. Booze became illegal, but the demand did not disappear. A criminogenic market structure was created. The kids who had grown up on the streets saw these events in terms of economic opportunity. They had become Americanized. The old world values of respect for tradition, obedience to elders, and the primary importance of personal honor were shunned. More significant to them were the new world values. Making fast money and establishing a business enterprise became important goals. In this sense, they did not establish organizations copied after the Sicilian Mafia.

The organizations built by such men as Al Capone and Lucky Luciano were, first and foremost, business machines. They included non-Sicilians. Al Capone, for instance, was not a Sicilian. Some of the most powerful men in organized crime societies were not even of Italian descent. Some were Jewish (Meyer Lansky), Welsh (Murray Humphreys), Polish (Joe Saltis), or Irish (Dion O'Banion). The syndicates made their initial capital and thrived through bootlegging and prostitution. Following Prohibition, their ventures turned primarily to gambling and racketeering.

Today's crime societies have a sizable, but not total, Italian membership. They exist in several parts of the country and are referred to as "families." The President's Commission has estimated that there are now twenty-four such families. The most influential families are reputed to reside in the New York City area. It has also been stated that these families dominate the "Commission." [10] The "Commission" serves as a "board of directors" that attempts to solve conflicts within and between families. While some claim that the "Commission" directs the activities of crime societies throughout the country,[11] others disagree.[12] There are a number of reasons to suspect that the "Commission" is not as powerful as some would believe.

Crime families have grown in number, location, and membership. They have taken on a wide variety of activities, both legal and illegal. Therefore, it is difficult to imagine that a "Commission" centered in New York can directly control complicated activities in, say, Chicago, Arizona, Miami, and Los Angeles. At best, crime families are now joined together in a loose confederation. Gambling is, perhaps, the single greatest source of illegal funds for crime societies. Unlike hard narcotics, illegal wagering (e.g., numbers, cards, dice, and slot machines) cuts across a broad section of the public.

Another sizable source of illegal revenue is loansharking. Loansharking is the lending of money at rates higher than are permitted by state law. These illegal rates (called "vigorish") have been estimated to run somewhere between 5 percent and 20 percent on a weekly or monthly basis. There is always the threat of violence for nonpayment of the principal or interest. People from a variety of circumstances may seek out a loan shark. The need for cash can arise from gambling debts or business deals that require "seed" money to get started. Loansharking is also known as the "juice racket."

Criminal societies are involved in other illegal businesses such as black marketing and extortion. In addition, "scam" operations are apparently increasing. A "scam" involves gaining control over an established business. Through the use of the company's good credit, merchandise is overpurchased and sold in volume at very low prices. Bankruptcy is eventually declared. Crime families are involved in many legitimate concerns such as real estate, restaurants, laundries, resorts, and so on. According to one recent article, legal ventures are becoming a major activity of groups that have been labeled as "La Cosa Nostra" or the "Mafia." [13] In the course of their legal and illegal pursuits, crime families interact with others who operate as "free agents" (e.g., independent "hit men" who kill for hire) or criminal alliances.

Criminal Alliances

Criminal alliances are held together primarily by their common involvement in a central illegal activity. Sometimes criminal alliances work with crime societies (families). At other times they operate independently.

The illegal drug market is an example of cooperation between criminal societies and criminal alliances. The process of harvesting, manufacturing, selling, and distributing controlled substances is complex. It requires cooperation on the part of many factions. It represents an illegal enterprise of international dimensions. Actually, American crime families play a relatively minor role in this trade when the total operation is considered.

Books such as *The Heroin Trail* [14] reveal the intricate arrangements among many groups. Heroin (opium) is harvested by Turks or Mexicans; refined by Corsicans; transported by Cuban exiles, Frenchmen, and Americans; distributed by crime families and alliances of blacks, Puerto Ricans, and so on. It is peddled on the street by "free agents" and lower level members of criminal alliances. Much of the illegal drug traffic is being increasingly handled by criminal alliances as they grow less dependent upon crime families for national-level distribution. Some forms of gambling (e.g., "policy" or "numbers") are also being taken over by criminal alliances made up of various minority factions living in the inner city. [15]

Criminal societies have always depended upon the cooperation of authorities to achieve success. Unfortunately, our cities have had their share of corrupt politicians, police officers on the "pad," and the "best judges that money can buy." Corruption and organized crime go hand in hand. Victimless crimes such as gambling and prostitution are at least unofficially condoned by the public. Police officers have traditionally received low pay. At the same time, they have a great deal of street-level discretion. They may choose to arrest or not arrest violators. Given their relatively low pay, much discretion, public tolerance of victimless crimes, and significant payoffs, police officers may find it easy to ignore some forms of organized crime.

Corruption, however, begins at the top. When several politicians and police officers are organized to receive regular bribes for not enforcing the law, they form a criminal alliance. These corrupt authorities are, most definitely, a part of organized crime. If gambling, for example, were legalized in some places, many corrupt officials would have to look to other resources for their "extra spending money."

Corporate Criminal Alliances

Edwin Sutherland defined white-collar crime as "a crime committed by a person of respectability and high social status in the course of his occupation." [16] Some have criticized Sutherland's definition as focusing too much on corporate-level crime and too little on small business crimes and confidence games. [17] Small business crimes (e.g., home and appliance repair swindles) and confidence games (e.g., correspondence school "rip-offs") are costly crimes. They often involve several participants who operate over a long period of time. However, the real threat of white-collar crime comes from those who are highly organized, big, and powerful. Corporate criminals are more costly to the public and have a greater affect on daily lives than other white-collar criminals. They are more likely to avoid criminal prosecution. Because of these factors, this chapter adopts Sutherland's emphasis on corporate-level white-collar crime. Other forms of white-collar crime will be covered in Chapter 14.

The world of big business is influenced by extreme competition. The pressure to produce profits for the company and stockholders often encourages illegal shortcuts.

These illegal shortcuts are carried out by criminal alliances within and among corporations. Criminogenic market structures are encouraged when: (1) existing laws are weakly enforced, (2) loopholes in existing laws foster corporate crime, or (3) new laws are proposed that will promote organized crime. The following examples illustrate the relationship between organized corporate crime and the situations just mentioned.

The Sherman Act of 1890 was passed to prevent corporations from agreeing to fix the prices of their products. The fixing of prices reduces competition among companies. It is likely to result in a few corporations controlling an entire industry. Criminal violations have traditionally been classified as misdemeanors with the punishment ranging from fines to jail sentences or both. It is, therefore, a crime to restrain trade by conspiring to fix prices.

In 1961, forty-five executives became defendants to the criminal charge of price-fixing in the electrical industry. These men had carried out their illegal business over an eight-year period. They had rigged the prices of electrical goods valued at $1.75 billion annually. Seven executives received prison terms of less than one year and twenty-three others obtained a suspended sentence and/or fine. General Electric (GE), the apparent ring leader of the conspiracy (which included Westinghouse, the Carrier Corporation, and others), received the largest corporate fine ($437,500). But GE was able to weaken further civil suits by being allowed to plead *nolo contendere* (no contest) on thirteen of the original indictments.

Following the verdict, several of the defendants returned to their old jobs. Some were convinced that they had been scapegoats for doing what "everyone" knew was necessary to succeed in the corporate world. When asked if he had learned anything from the experience, one defendant remarked: "One thing I've learned out of all this, is to talk to only one other person, not to go to meetings where there are lots of other people." [18] The prosecution of the electrical company conspirators represented an effort to strike back at the "big guys." However, as a practical matter it demonstrated that crime does pay if one goes about it properly. Recall that GE received only a fine of $437,500. It directed a criminal alliance that amounted to crimes involving $1.75 billion a year for eight years. How effective are laws that send people to prison for three or more years for petty burglaries but only fine criminals who cost the public billions of dollars annually?

Some laws which are meant to regulate business actually encourage organized crime by leaving large loopholes. These loopholes are exploited by some industries. Patent laws are designed to protect inventors against the theft of their ideas or discoveries over a certain period of time. This, in turn, is intended to promote the advancement of science and technology. Many countries do not allow patents on drugs because they consider the lack of patents to be in the public interest. That is, people need pharmaceuticals at any price. They cannot voluntarily stop buying them as they would a second car or TV set. But drugs may be patented in the United States. The laws are written so that many patent abuses are encouraged on products that much of the public must have.

There is evidence that a substantial number of drug companies slightly change the chemical structure of pharmaceuticals so as to obtain a new patent. This procedure has been termed molecular manipulation. It allows the parent company to obtain a large share of the market on a related drug grouping. In the United States, 7 percent of the drug companies capture 80 percent of the sales annually.[19]

There have been attempts to control the monopolistic practices of the legitimate drug industry. These efforts have met with heavy resistance largely at the hands of the Pharmaceutical Manufacturers Association and the American Medical Association. Contrary to medical ethics, some physicians invest heavily in certain drug company stocks. They tend to prescribe medicines that are marketed by the company in which they have an interest. Before being passed, reform laws have largely been rewritten in a form acceptable to both medical and pharmaceutical interests. Certainly one way to reduce drug company monopolies is to prohibit or to restrict severely patent laws that apply to pharmaceuticals.

On occasion, new laws are proposed which have the effect of creating behavior that we label as organized crime. During the inflationary 1970s, some states passed bills which eliminated set legal interest rates on conventional home loans. This allowed banks and savings-and-loan associations to charge any interest rate that the borrower was willing to pay. The sponsors of such bills argued that the elimination of interest rates would draw investment money from other states. That is, their state would get lending money because of the higher return on investments.

The end result is that borrowers are no longer protected from having to pay excessively high interest rates. Because of ignorance or having nowhere else to go, they have to pay whatever the banks want to ask. This, by definition, appears to be no different than loansharking. It is legal because the law provides for it. In this case, banking interests and not the Mafia are behind such legislation.

Organized crime is a complex problem. It is much more than gangsters in pin-striped suits shooting at each other with machine guns. Whether it be the workings of a crime family, a criminal alliance, or, in particular, a corporate criminal alliance, the content and objectives are the same. Regardless of who does it, organized crime refers to:

> illegal acts designed to directly or indirectly secure a system of financial rewards through the provision of goods and services for consumer groups differing in size and knowledge of involvement.[20]

SUMMARY

Organized crime is a much broader problem than the images created by the mass media imply. It is a great deal more than the notion of a criminal society. This chapter presented a discussion of organized crime that questioned the image presented by the President's Task Force. In particular, it questioned the idea that organized crime is: (1) a secret society, (2) tightly controlled, (3) opposed to public interests and values, and (4) similar in structure but not the behavior of corporate crime.

In addition to a new definition of the problem, three key concepts were presented and defined. Criminogenic market structures may arise when certain goods or services become illegal or scarce and the demand exceeds supply. Criminal societies refer to those groups of individuals, united by a bond of ethnic identity, personal loyalty or other shared experiences beyond economic concerns. Criminal alliances include persons for whom the attachment to others is based mainly upon specific and primarily illegal economic pursuits. This concept includes the corporate criminal alliance.

Secret criminal societies developed in southern Italy during the 1800s. The Mafia originated in Sicily, an island that lies off the west coast of southern Italy. Around the turn of the century many immigrants from southern Italy came to the United States. The vast majority were law-abiding peasants looking for a better life. The few who had criminal backgrounds committed mostly conventional crimes against their fellow immigrants. There is no evidence that they transplanted the Mafia to this country. Schemes involving extortion, kidnapping, or fraud usually included threatening notes signed with a black hand. However, the black hand represented a technique, not an organization or society as some people have claimed.

Some of the children of immigrants eventually formed the predominantly Italian crime syndicates. The children who grew up on the streets as members of delinquent gangs viewed Prohibition in terms of economic opportunity. Their organizations were business machines. They included non-Sicilians as well as non-Italians. Although the Italian-dominated crime syndicates have some elements of the old world Mafia, they are essentially different. Those who established them placed greater emphasis on new world Yankee values of business economics than on old world Sicilian values of respect for tradition and loyalty to elders. Also, America was urban and industrial. Sicily was rural and agricultural. Each setting required different approaches.

Today's crime societies ("families") have grown in number, location, and membership. They are joined in a loose confederation. Crime family activities include many illegal (e.g., gambling, loansharking, racketeering, "scams") and legal (e.g., real estate, resorts, restaurants) operations. The families interact with free agents and criminal alliances in the course of their illegal and legal ventures.

Criminal alliances contain people of various backgrounds who are held together primarily for specific illegal activities. The illegal drug market is an example of an international level crime alliance. Gambling is often the result of combined criminal society and alliance efforts. When authorities become part of a bribery network, they form a criminal alliance. Organized crime is also found in the legitimate business world. Corporate criminal alliances are a response to the pressures of competition and the absence of effective or proper legal controls. This chapter cited examples of corporate criminal alliances in the electrical and legitimate drug industry as well as the banking establishment.

SUGGESTED ACTIVITIES

- Obtain a copy of the *Task Force Report: Organized Crime* prepared by the President's Commission on Law Enforcement and the Administration of Justice by writing to your U.S. congressional representative or to:

Superintendent of Documents
U.S. Government Printing Office
Washington, D.C. 20402

What does this document say about: (1) criminal alliances, and (2) corporate crime?

● Using the new definition presented in this chapter, determine if organized crime exists in your community, city, or state. If so, is it the work of criminal societies, criminal alliances, corporate criminal alliances, or some combination? Compare the information that you obtain from newspapers, television, and law enforcement officials. How broad a picture do they create?

● Has the recent energy crisis produced organized crime? If you feel that it has, explain why and how this has happened. Discuss in class.

● Write to your state attorney general's office and determine if there is an Organized Crime Strike Force. If so, contact this organization's director for information or to request a guest speaker for the class. In what terms does the Strike Force view organized crime?

REVIEW

A. Give a definition of organized crime that is not restricted to crime societies or the Mafia stereotype.

B. List and define the concepts of criminogenic market structure, criminal society, and criminal alliance.

C. Discuss the basic nature of today's crime families.

D. Give one example of a corporate criminal alliance.

E. Multiple Choice. Select the best answer.

1. The Task Force Report definition emphasizes that organized crime:
    a. is a criminal society
    b. is supported by the public
    c. includes high-level corporate crime
    d. all of these

2. According to the Task Force, the boss of a crime family is known as:
    a. caporegima
    b. soldati
    c. capo
    d. sottocapo

3. Crime groups held together mainly by economic goals are termed:
    a. families
    b. alliances
    c. societies
    d. Mafia

4. The "black hand" was a:
    a. secret criminal society
    b. forerunner of the Mafia
    c. ritual performed by criminal societies
    d. method of carrying out crimes

5. Crime families (societies):
    a. contain only Sicilians
    b. contain only Italians
    c. have members who share common identities and backgrounds but are business oriented
    d. are involved in only illegal activities

6. Loansharking is:
   a. the "juice racket"
   b. no longer widely practiced
   c. the same thing as extortion
   d. the lending of counterfeit money
7. Which of the following is an example of organized crime?
   a. illegal gambling operated by crime societies
   b. law enforcement officers accepting bribes over a long period of time
   c. price-fixing by corporations
   d. all of these
8. Legitimate drug companies create monopolies on certain pharmaceuticals through:
   a. molecular manipulation
   b. extortion
   c. "scams"
   d. shylocking
9. Organized crime, at all levels, is basically a product of:
   a. evil people
   b. criminogenic market structures
   c. Italian gangsters
   d. slum conditions
10. Crime societies:
   a. are held together in a loose confederation
   b. respond to public desires
   c. are involved in legal businesses
   d. all of these

REFERENCES

1. Much of this chapter is adapted from Henry W. Mannle, "Organized Crime: Business as Usual," in Jack Wright, Jr. and Peter W. Lewis, *Modern Criminal Justice* (New York: McGraw-Hill, 1977), 53–79. Permission to edit has been obtained from McGraw-Hill, Inc.
2. President's Commission on Law Enforcement and the Administration of Justice, *Task Force Report: Organized Crime* (Washington, D.C.: U.S. Government Printing Office, 1967), 14–15.
3. See especially, Frederick D. Homer, *Guns and Garlic* (West Lafayette, Ind.: Purdue University Studies, 1974), 1–20.
4. *New York Times*, July 28, 1978, D1, D12.
5. Martin A. Gosch and Richard Hammer, *The Last Testament of Lucky Luciano* (Boston: Little, Brown, 1975), 261–262.
6. William Brashler, *The Don* (New York: Ballantine Books, 1977), 218–229.
7. President's Commission, *op. cit.*, 9.
8. This definition was developed through a combination of concepts and related terms found in the minutes of the Oyster Bay Conference as cited in Dwight C. Smith, Jr., *The Mafia Mystique* (New York: Basic Books, 1975), 70–71, and Homer, *op. cit.*, 12–20.
9. See Organized Crime Control Act of 1970, Public Law 91–452; § 1955(c).
10. President's Commission, *op. cit.*, 8.
11. *Ibid.*
12. Gordon Hawkins, "Organized Crime: Is There a Summit?" in Leon Radzinowicz and Marvin E. Wolfgang (eds.) *The Criminal Society* (New York: Basic Books, 1971), 235–240.
13. Francis A. J. Ianni and Elizabeth Reuss-Ianni, "The Godfather Is Going Out of Business," *Psychology Today*, 9 (1975), 86–92.
14. *Newsday*, "The Heroin Trail" (New York: New American Library, 1974).
15. See Francis A. J. Ianni, *Black Mafia* (New York: Simon and Schuster, 1974).
16. Edwin Sutherland, *White Collar Crime* (New York: Holt, Rinehart and Winston, 1949), 9.

17. Herbert Edlehertz, *The Nature, Impact and Prosecution of White Collar Crime* (Washington, D.C.: U.S. Government Printing Office, 1970), 3–4.
18. Richard Austin Smith, ''The Incredible Electrical Conspiracy,'' in Donald R. Cressey and David A. Ward (eds.), *Delinquency, Crime and Social Process* (New York: Harper and Row, 1969), 911.
19. Philip Shaw, ''The Privileges of Monopoly Capitalism: Market Power in the Ethical Drug Industry,'' *The Review of Radical Political Economics*, 2 (1970), 9.
20. Mannle, *op. cit.*, 57.

14

Occupational and Career-Oriented Crime

OBJECTIVES

After studying this chapter, the student should be able to:

- Define occupational crime and career-oriented crime.
- Give examples of crimes in business, commerce, and the professions.
- Describe confidence games and give examples.
- Discuss conventional crime as a profession and give examples.

' The successful commission of crime requires opportunity and often some degree of expertise. The business world and the professions provide many opportunities for crime. In addition, crime careers tend to develop around certain offenses. Through experience, knowledge, and acquired skills, career criminals achieve a high degree of success. This chapter presents a discussion of those crimes which are related to occupations or criminal careers.

OCCUPATIONAL CRIMES

The opportunity to commit criminal or deviant acts by virtue of one's job, vocation, or profession is referred to as occupational crime. The offenses may occur frequently, occasionally, or just once. The criminal conduct is usually a pattern. It is made possible because of one's occupation.

Crimes in Business and Commerce

Consumers may be cheated in several ways.[1] One estimate places the number of different schemes at well over 800.[2] These crimes often victimize those who can least afford the costs. Shady home repairs and improvement businesses account for millions of dollars in yearly losses. The central feature of these frauds is misrepresentation. Trusting poor and elderly consumers are given misleading information as to the job's cost, specific details, and financing arrangements. Victims are promised work that is never completed or is inferior. The cost is usually inflated through monthly payment plans with large interest charges. Toward the end of the credit period, the victim receives an unmanageable bill (the "balloon") covering remaining interest and most of the principle.[3] The householder must then obtain another loan, and the cycle continues.

Similar approaches are used by some businesses in the sale of furniture and appliances. One technique which has aided the dishonest businessman is the holder-in-due-course doctrine. Thus, a dishonest repair firm or merchant will promise services when the consumer signs a credit contract. The contract is then sold to a finance company. The shady dealer profits from this sale before any goods or services are delivered. The finance company has the right to collect the installments whether or not the service or product is satisfactory. Consumers are told to take all complaints to the business that made the promises. It is often necessary to take legal action which costs more time and money. At best, some partial settlement is reached when legal action is taken. Few even bother to go through this process. The end result is that the dishonest businessperson has been paid for a fraud by the installment company which then proceeds to collect from a victimized consumer.[4] New laws ("truth-in-lending") are now in effect which are intended to cut down on such abuses.

Consumer fraud in the auto repair business is another common example of occupational crime. According to Leonard and Weber, complaints regarding auto repair and warranty irregularities have swamped the Federal Trade Commission's office.[5] Today, the Office of Consumer Affairs handles many of these problems. The usual methods of cheating customers are (1) charging for more labor than the job requires, (2) doing unnecessary repairs, (3) charging for repairs not made, and (4) replacing perfectly good parts.[6] These violations may be committed by franchised dealers as well as independent garages or service stations. They cost as much as $12 billion a year.[7]

Dishonest business practices not only hurt consumers but often cause the public to transfer their feelings of distrust to the entire business community. As a result, the respectable business person or merchant is injured.

Crimes are also committed against businesses. Positions of trust, the availability of opportunities, and special knowledge allow some employees to cheat their employers. Embezzlement occurs whenever an employee fraudulently obtains money or goods that have been entrusted to him or her by the company. Embezzlement is carried out in a variety of ways. A few of the examples are (1) placing fake employees on the payroll and collecting their checks, (2) giving unauthorized discounts and pocketing the change, (3) expense account inflating, and (4) tampering with supply invoices.

Employee theft or pilferage is one of the leading causes of stock shrinkage. The availability of valuable goods combines with employer trust to make theft an easy task for the dishonest employee. Both employee embezzlement and ordinary theft are easier and are more likely to occur in larger businesses. The methods of stealing vary with the imagination and opportunities of the employee. Typical techniques include: (1) taking merchandise and then altering the inventory sheet, (2) having incoming merchandise sent to a "drop" address, (3) short-loading a shipment and keeping the leftovers for personal use or sale, and (4) simply stealing goods that can be easily carried off and attributing it to shoplifters.

"Rip-offs" by employees develop when the individual feels under pressure to pay debts or keep up a certain front or life-style.[8] Upon being caught, embezzlers frequently claim that the money was just being "borrowed" and that they had planned to repay the company or bank. Sometimes the stealing begins when employees feel that they are underpaid. Pilferage or embezzlement is then rationalized as "justifiable" supplements to their incomes.[9] In a study of factory workers, Horning noted that employees had unwritten "rules" regarding what could be taken. Property labeled as being of "uncertain ownership" was fair game for pilferage. In actuality, all such property (such as scrap and byproducts) was company-owned. Pilfering of this property had unofficial restrictions. These limits were (1) take only what can be personally used, and (2) don't arouse company suspicion by extensive and frequent stealing.[10]

The computer has incredibly streamlined the operation of industry and commerce. It has also provided abundant criminal opportunities for those who have the skill and motivation to steal. In the wrong hands, the computer can become the instrument for stealing millions of dollars. Unlike using a gun, using a computer involves no risk of violence and far less likelihood of detection. The computer has infinite criminal potential. It can be used to embezzle, steal confidential marketing data, and pirate technical information. The costs are enormous.

Single episodes of computer crime run as high as $5 million.[11] These crimes may be carried out by one or a handful of participants. If detected at all, the discovery usually comes long after the crime has been set in motion. Soble and Dallos have described a $2-billion computer fraud that survived for years before being noticed.[12] Such sophisticated, long-term crimes fit neatly into the category of a criminal alliance as discussed in Chapter 13.

Crimes Committed in the Professions

Human health care is dependent upon a pyramid of professional roles. At the top stands the physician or medical doctor. Physicians generally receive much recognition and status from the public. As the public has become more educated and less trusting, the physician is being viewed with increasing contempt. Most physicians appear to be ethical practitioners of the healing art. However, an alarming number of them seem to be guided by the profit motive.

Disreputable physicians violate ethics, medical ideals, or the criminal law in their pursuit of money. As stated in a recent book on the subject, medical offenses are widespread:

> unnecessary medical procedures are not only costly but may pose a serious threat to health and even the life of the patient. There is, moreover, ample evidence of large-scale ''overdoctoring'' of American patients . . . a House subcommittee investigating the medical profession calculated that there were 2.4 million unnecessary surgical procedures a year, which cost the public $4 billion and resulted in the loss of 11,900 lives.[13]

Drug company abuses of federal patent laws, leading to monopolies, were noted in Chapter 13. Profiteering physicians abuse the drug laws of some states at the expense of patients. All prescription drugs have both a generic name and a brand name. Generic names refer to the basic chemical structure of similar or identical drugs. Brand names are the commercial titles that pharmaceutical companies give to drugs which are derived from a generic grouping. Brand names are usually more simplified and shorter in length than are generic names. For example, the drug ''Peritrate'' (brand name) has a generic name of ''pentaerythrtoltetranitrate.'' Physicians will frequently prescribe a drug by its brand name simply because it is easier to recall than the more technical generic designation. But other physicians prescribe by brand name for a different reason.

Some states have antisubstitution laws. These laws prohibit a pharmacist from dispensing a cheaper, equally effective drug when a specific brand name is prescribed. Contrary to medical ethics, there are physicians who have large stock holdings in certain drug companies. In addition, drug companies reward physicians who prescribe their brand names with gifts, free vacations, and so on. Thus, some medical doctors are unable to resist the temptation to prescribe, by brand name, drugs marketed by a particular company. The consumer must then buy the brand name drug even though there may be a cheaper, equally effective drug available. This behavior on the part of physicians helps to further the monopolies of some drug companies. Several states have reacted to this practice by striking down existing antisubstitution laws.

Some medical practitioners will treat health problems that are clearly beyond their capabilities. The result is often negligence. Most negligence cases are handled through the civil procedure of a malpractice suit. Civil suits are attempts by patients (or their survivors) to recover a financial award for damages. However, physicians commit outright felonies (criminal offenses) when they are grossly negligent in their practices. In cases of criminal negligence resulting in a patient's death, the physician may be convicted of manslaughter. Usually some combination of greed, ignorance, and lack of professional concern leads to negligence. The growing number and size of malpractice suits have acted as some deterrent to medical abuses. Upon being asked if he still did all of his own diagnosing, a physician charged with a ''serious misdiagnosis'' replied: ''No, . . . I send a lot of patients fifty miles to the medical center.'' Whereupon, the court asked: ''When did you start doing that?'' His reply: ''The day that I got this subpoena.''[14]

Because of their professional privileges, physicians are in positions to commit numerous profitable crimes. Loosely policed health care programs provide abundant criminal opportunities for unethical medical doctors. Through inflated fees, surgery not performed, services for nonexistent patients, and unnecessary therapy, large sums of money are swindled each year from private and public health care programs. Medicine is not the only profession that provides deviant and criminal opportunities.

The practice of law is considered to be a profession. It has also been described as a confidence game. As such, defense attorneys advance their careers and the court's bureaucratic goals by conning clients.[15] Questionable behavior on the part of attorneys (and physicians) is often unethical but not technically criminal. One area subject to abuse by unethical attorneys is the contingent fee system. This fee typically amounts to one-third of the settlement in a civil suit. If one man sues another and wins a settlement of, say, $99,000, the attorney receives $33,000.

In some areas, the fee varies a great deal and is relatively uncontrolled by local or state legal associations. It may run as high as 50 percent or 60 percent. Such a high fee "ceases to be a measure of due compensation for professional services and makes a lawyer a partner . . . in the lawsuit."[16] Even if the fee is one-third, the client is often not informed that the lawyer's percentage is paid before expenses (costs of investigation, expert witnesses, referral payments, etc.) are deducted. In one instance, a man won a suit of $52,000. His lawyer immediately claimed one-third ($17,000). After all other expenses were paid, the man received little more than $3,000 (only about one-fifth of what the attorney received).[17] It has been argued that attorneys should receive their one-third after all or part of the expenses have been covered.

Some attorneys charge a referral fee to other lawyers. The lawyer receiving the referral is expected to pay the first lawyer a fee if the case is won. This referral fee usually comes out of the second lawyer's fee (one-third) for winning the case. Such fees are unethical but not illegal. However, in some cases it is disguised as an additional expense to be paid by the client. In these cases, it is fraudulent behavior and can be criminally prosecuted.

Because they occupy positions of trust, attorneys have several opportunities to commit crimes. Money can be easily stolen from estates in complicated settlements. As legal guardians of elderly or incompetent persons, dishonest attorneys have opportunities to help themselves to trust funds. The theft can occur through excessive fraudulent fees or outright embezzlement. In the practice of criminal law, some attorneys routinely commit crimes until they are discovered. Where judges are elected, a disreputable lawyer knows that by contributing to the judge's campaign fund, his or her client can be helped. More direct "fixes" can be arranged by paying off the judge through a "bagman." A bagman is the person who collects the bribes from cooperative lawyers. Attorneys have also been convicted of destroying the evidence of a crime and of planning crimes for their clients.[18]

In the business and professional world, the opportunities to commit unethical or criminal acts are plentiful. Fortunately, most businesspeople and professionals are honest individuals. Those who are not cripple the public as well as their more legitimate associates.

CAREER-ORIENTED CRIMES

Career-oriented crimes are committed by those who look upon a specific offense as a central focus of livelihood. Confidence games and conventional kinds of crime (e.g., robbery, burglary, and theft) become careers for some individuals. The remainder of this chapter is devoted to examples of career-oriented crimes. The characteristics of career criminals will be discussed in the next section.

Confidence Games

Some years ago, over 100 kinds of confidence games were identified.[19] Schemes which are simple and require little time to execute are known as the short con. More complicated swindles involving equipment and time are referred to as the big con. All successful con games are dependent upon quick-witted, convincing schemers and upon gullible victims looking for fast money. The games tend to progress through ten stages, as outlined by Maurer: [20]

1. Discovery of a suitable victim or "putting up the mark";
2. Winning the victim's (mark's) trust or "playing the con";
3. Introducing the mark to another "inside" con artist or "roping the mark";
4. Informing the mark about a get-rich-quick scheme or "telling the tale";
5. Permitting the mark to earn a small profit (especially in big cons) or "the convincer";
6. Establishing how much the mark can put up or "the breakdown";
7. Getting the mark to put up his money or "putting him on the send";
8. Taking possession of his money or "the touch";
9. Losing him after he is ripped-off or "the blowoff";
10. Avoiding law enforcement action or "putting in the fix."

One of the more elaborate con games was portayed in the popular movie, "The Sting." It was a form of the big con known as "The Wire." It has since disappeared. In its peak years, it operated in the following manner and serves to illustrate how con games progress.

First, a wealthy victim was located (putting up the mark). A friendly con artist would engage him in conversation or in some way be helpful (playing the con). The mark would then be introduced to another friendly con artist (roping the mark). This third person would pose as a telegraph operator. The two con artists proceed to tell the mark how they are able to obtain the results of races before they are called at a local betting parlor. The telegrapher supposedly taps the wire and telephones the name of the winning horse to the other, who is waiting by a public telephone in the betting parlor. They thus have the potential to make a fortune but do not have the necessary funds. The mark is told that if he will put up the money, they will give him the majority of the winnings. It's a sure thing (telling the tale)!

The mark is then taken to an elaborate (phony) betting parlor. There are cashiers, odds boards, and loudspeakers for calling races as they come in over the wire. The mark is encouraged to place a few small bets to test the system. Sure enough, he wins (the convincer). The amount of money that the mark can place on one big bet is determined (the breakdown). Convinced of the foolproof nature of the scheme, the mark returns home to get his money (putting him on the send).

Shortly thereafter, the mark and the roper go to the parlor and await the telephone call from the "telegrapher." The telegrapher telephones and says: "Here's the winner. The bet should be *placed* on 'Little Lady.' "The mark then bets his money [e.g., $50,000 on "Little Lady" to win (the touch)]. The race is excitedly called for a period of one or two minutes. Unfortunately, "Little Lady" comes in second ("places") rather than first ("wins"). The mark is sadly informed that he was told to bet his money on "Little Lady" to *place*, not to win. How could he possibly have gotten it confused! The mark is made to feel that his stupidity was at fault (the blowoff). At this point, a phony police raid is staged and the mark is hustled through a back door. Upset, yet thankful that he has avoided an arrest, the mark does not go to the police (putting in the fix).[21]

The short con requires less planning and time to carry out. Participants are fewer in number and needed equipment ("props") is minimal. Many short cons have disappeared along with "The Wire" game. But some are still being successfully operated. The "pigeon drop" is an example of a short con that continues to pay off. It works in this fashion.

A mark (victim) is encountered by someone who needs directions or the name of a particular store. While the victim and the first con artist are talking, an excited third party (another con artist) approaches. He or she produces an envelope purportedly containing a large sum of money that was just found. What should be done? They all decide not to go to the police. Instead, it is agreed that one will keep the envelope for a few weeks to see if it has been reported lost or stolen. If the money's appearance is unexplained, they will split it three ways. But the other two (victim and first con artist) must put up "good faith" money.

The mark puts up the money and gives it to the "finder." The two swindlers agree that the mark can hold the envelope for a few weeks. They agree to separate and meet later to divide up the contents of the envelope. When the mark gets home and eventually opens up the envelope, he finds it to be stuffed with paper. In the meantime, the two swindlers have since divided the mark's "good faith" money and moved to another location.

Many other short cons and big cons are to be found. The themes are different but the plots are the same. Easy money or pleasure is available after the victim makes an investment. As always, the easy money winds up in the hands of the swindlers.

Conventional Crime as a Profession

Some conventional (street) crimes (i.e., robbery, burglary, and theft) are routinely committed as a regular source of income. Most of these crimes are not the work of "professionals." Those that are, however, do have distinguishing features.

Robberies by true professionals involve extensive planning. Partners are chosen for their needed skills. Backup services are arranged such as bail, legal, and medical sources if needed. The target (e.g., a bank) is scouted or cased as to its interior design, parking facilities, and exit routes. A car is stolen and license plates switched shortly in advance of the job. On a "dry run" to the bank, employees are evaluated. The ages and sexes of bank personnel serve as a good indication of their anticipated behavior during a robbery.

Professional robberies are less likely than are amateur robberies to result in injuries to victims. Those who commit them are prepared to manage the victims. A strong show of force and authority is maintained by displaying weapons, giving loud orders, and threatening violence. If the robbery is successful, little actual violence is necessary.[22] Robberies committed by professionals result in higher amounts of cash than those committed by others less skilled. In one study, a professional robbery ring operated for over six months, netting $5,000 to $10,000 per crime.[23]

Various forms of burglary attract professionals. Bank burglary and safecracking are appropriate examples of careers in burglary. The safecracker, in particular, has been accorded a great deal of prestige in the underworld. The ability to open a safe distinguishes the safecracker from the burglar who specializes in business establishments, homes, or banks. For the burglar, getting into the structure is the major task. The safecracker must not only gain entry but also must be able to penetrate a large metal container. Safecrackers specialize in types of safes and techniques for opening them. Most jobs rarely involve more than two participants. Similar to professional robbers, safecrackers prepare their crimes well in advance. However, with improved security systems, safecracking and bank (business) burglary are declining. Some claim that this has led to an increase in bank robberies.[24]

The professionalization of theft is most often illustrated by the career activities of pickpockets and accomplished shoplifters. A top-notch pickpocket is known in the trade as a "cannon." A good cannon is capable of matching sleight-of-hand tricks with any conventional magician. Some current nightclub acts are based on the routine of a cannon. These acts center around a performer who randomly selects a member of the audience. While engaged in rapid conversation, the magician removes practically all but the patron's socks in a matter of seconds.

Pickpockets usually operate in teams of two or three. Places where there are large crowds or special seasons (e.g., Christmas shoppers) attract pickpockets. The basic pattern is simple. A mark is selected on the basis of appearing to have enough money to make the job worthwhile. One of the cannons (the "stall") jostles or shoves (termed "pratting") the mark around. While being pratted, the mark's pockets are felt (called "fanning") for the wallet. Once located, another cannon (the "hook" or "tool") removes the wallet. The wallet is then passed to a third cannon. This removes the evidence should the stall or hook be stopped. The technique requires considerable training and manual skills. Maurer has noted that few professional pickpockets remain today.[25] This is due primarily to a short supply of apprentices wishing to learn the "profession." According to one cannon, "The kids are just not interested in it as a profession. Probably 'cause there's no money in it. And they're right." [26]

Professional shoplifters ("boosters") use techniques similar to those of pickpockets. Operating as teams, one acts as a "stall" by distracting store personnel. This is carried out by creating some scene such as starting an argument or falling down. During the distraction, others from the team steal. Pros often employ special equipment or clothing. The "bobo box" is a large package (resembling something to be mailed or a gift) with a trap door. Display merchandise may be slipped into the box while clerks are detained by legitimate customers or a member of the team. There are also male and female booster clothes. These are coats, pants, or blouses that have paneled linings. Merchandise may be channeled into the linings through enlarged pockets or openings. Other techniques include using duplicate fake jewelry to switch with genuine items (termed "pennyweighting").

Shoplifting is one of the faster growing property Index offenses reported by the FBI. Most shoplifters are amateurs. Quite a few are females. One study of shoplifting revealed that 10 percent of those apprehended in a store were professionals—other studies have cut this figure in half.[27] This should not be interpreted as meaning that only 5 to 10 percent of all shoplifters are professionals. Professional shoplifters rarely get caught.

SUMMARY

Crime is related to opportunity and skill. Several outwardly legitimate businesses and professions provide criminal opportunities for disreputable individuals. Consumer fraud is commonly found in home repair, auto maintenance, and general merchandising schemes. The key to these swindles is misrepresentation. Legitimate businesses are often injured by the offenders. Employees also victimize honest business enterprises. This usually occurs through embezzlement or pilferage. More complicated crimes involve the misuse of the computer.

In addition, the professions provide ample occasions for crime and deviant behavior. Physicians may abuse state drug laws at the expense of patients. Health care programs often become pork barrels for fraud-minded medical doctors. Life-threatening offenses occur as the result of medical negligence. Most negligence cases are handled through civil (malpractice) suits. Gross negligence cases may be criminally prosecuted as manslaughter if death occurs. The practice of law presents opportunities for crime and deviance. Clients may be charged excessive fees and receive second-rate services. Because of positions of trust, dishonest attorneys may embezzle from estates or trust funds. In the practice of criminal law, bribery, obstruction of justice, and direct involvement in street-type crime occur all too often.

Career-oriented crime refers to offenses that provide a livelihood for participants. Various confidence games and conventional crimes become careers for some individuals. Confidence games are of two types: the short con and the big con. Short cons are relatively simple and require little time and equipment. Big cons are complicated and necessitate time and equipment. All con games depend upon clever schemers and upon gullible victims in search of fast money.

Some conventional crimes tend to attract career-minded offenders. The participants are sometimes called "professional criminals." Robbery, specific kinds of burglary (safecracking and bank burglary), and theft (pickpocketing and shoplifting) have become professions for a select few. Technological advancements and changing socioeconomic conditions have reduced the ranks of certain professional criminals.

SUGGESTED ACTIVITIES

- Ask your local Chamber of Commerce or Better Business Bureau for information regarding the avoidance of consumer fraud.
- Visit a large department store or industrial plant. Discuss their procedures regarding computer crimes and how they are prevented or detected.
- Write to your state legislator and inquire about the existence of drug antisubstitution laws. What is their current status? If amended, how have they been changed? How do they affect prescriptions?
- Write to your state's medical and legal (bar) associations requesting copies of their respective code or cannon of ethics. As a project, determine the steps that may be taken against an alleged occupational crime committed by a physician or attorney.
- Discuss the nature and extent of confidence games in your community with the local law enforcement authorities.

REVIEW

A. Define occupational crime and give examples.

B. Define career-oriented crime and give examples.

C. List four common techniques of employee pilferage.

D. List, using appropriate slang, the ten stages of a confidence game.

E. Multiple Choice. Select the best answer.

1. An "unpayable" bill given to a consumer at the end of a credit cycle is called a:
   a. booster
   b. balloon
   c. hood
   d. cannon

2. A package of laws designed to protect the consumer in credit arrangements is known as:
   a. antitrust
   b. holder-in-due-course
   c. fair trade
   d. truth-in-lending

3. Laws that permit some physicians to monopolize certain brand name drugs for personal gain are termed:
   a. antisubstitution laws
   b. malpractice laws
   c. fair trade laws
   d. prosubstitution laws

4. In general, referral fees are:
   a. illegal
   b. rarely requested
   c. unethical
   d. all of these

5. The stage of a con game in which the victim's trust is secured is known as:
   a. the touch
   b. the convincer

          c. roping the mark

          d. playing the con

6. Which of the following is an example of the big con?

          a. The Wire

          b. Bank Examiner Game

          c. pigeon drop

          d. none of these

7. A professional pickpocket is referred to as a:

          a. booster

          b. cannon

          c. prat

          d. snitch

8. Professional robberies tend to be:

          a. more violent than amateur robberies

          b. less profitable than amateur robberies

          c. less violent than amateur robberies

          d. none of these

9. Distracting a pickpocketing victim by shoving is termed:

          a. fanning

          b. stalling

          c. hooking

          d. pratting

10. Shoplifting jewelry by substituting fake items for genuine ones is called:

          a. boosting

          b. pennyweighting

          c. bobo boxing

          d. fanning

REFERENCES

1. Sheila Balkan, et al., *Crime and Deviance in America* (Belmont, Calif.: Wadsworth, 1980), 109.
2. Chamber of Commerce of the U.S., *White Collar Crime* (Washington, D.C., 1984), 26.
3. *Ibid.*, 10.
4. *Ibid.*, 9.
5. William N. Leonard and Marvin Glenn Weber, "Automakers and Dealers: A Study of Criminogenic Market Forces," in Geis and Meier (eds.) *White Collar Crime* (New York: Free Press, 1977), 140.
6. *Ibid.*
7. Gerald F. Seib, "Dallas Ordinance Against Car Repair Frauds," in J. M. Johnson and J. D. Douglas (eds.) *Crime at the Top* (Philadelphia: J. B. Lippincott, 1978), 319.
8. Charles McGaghy, *Deviant Behavior* (New York: Macmillan, 1976), 178.
9. John Clark and Richard Hollinger, *Theft by Employees in Work Organizations* (Washington, D.C.: U.S. Government Printing Office, 1983), 2–3.
10. Donald N. M. Horning, "Blue-Collar Theft: Conceptions of Property, Attitudes toward Pilfering, and Group Norms in a Modern Industrial Plant," in Smigel and Ross (eds.) *Crimes Against Bureaucracy* (New York: Van Nostrand Reinhold, 1970), 63–64.
11. Donald Parker, "Computer-Related White-Collar Crime," in Geis and Stotland (eds.) *White Collar Crime: Theory and Research* (Beverly Hills: Sage Publications, Inc., 1980); Chamber of Commerce of the U.S., *op. cit.*, 20.
12. See Ronald L. Soble and Robert E. Dallos, *The Impossible Dream: The Equity Funding Story, Fraud of the Century* (New York: Putnam, 1975).
13. Cited in James W. Coleman, *The Criminal Elite* (New York: St. Martin's Press, 1985), 113.
14. Howard R. Lewis and Martha E. Lewis, *The Medical Offenders* (New York: Simon and Schuster, 1970), 14.

15. Coleman, *op. cit.*, 115; Abraham S. Blumberg, "Practice of Law as a Confidence Game: Organizational Cooptation of a Profession," *Law and Society Review*, 1 (1967), 15–39.

16. Murray Teigh Bloom, *The Trouble with Lawyers* (New York: Simon and Schuster, 1968), 150.

17. *Ibid.*, 154.

18. *Ibid.*, 161.

19. J. C. R. MacDonald, *Crime Is a Business: Bunco, Confidence Schemes* (Stanford, Calif.: Stanford University Press, 1939).

20. Adapted from David W. Maurer, *The Big Con* (Indianapolis, Ind.: Bobbs-Merrill, 1940), 15–16.

21. For a description of modern betting procedures, see Howard Abadinsky, *Organized Crime* (Boston: Allyn and Bacon, 1981), 120–126.

22. Peter Letkemann, *Crime As Work* (Englewood Cliffs, N.J.: Prentice-Hall, 1973), 90–116.

23. John E. Conklin, *Robbery* (Philadelphia: J. B. Lippincott, 1972), 67.

24. Letkemann, *op. cit.*, 89.

25. David Dressler, "Maxie the Goniff," in David M. Petersen and Marcello Truzzi (eds.) *Criminal Life* (Englewood Cliffs, N.J.: Prentice-Hall, 1972), 38–41.

26. As cited in James A. Inciardi, *Careers in Crime* (Skokie, Ill.: Rand McNally, 1975), 21.

27. Mary O. Cameron, *The Booster and the Snitch*: *Department Store Shoplifting* (Glencoe, Ill.: Free Press, 1964), 58; S. Curtis, *Modern Retail Security* (Springfield, Ill.: Chas. C Thomas, 1972).

15

Political Crime

OBJECTIVES

After studying this chapter, the student should be able to:

- Define political crime.
- Give examples of political crime committed against the government and by the government.
- Describe terrorism.

Political crime is a difficult concept. Many types of crimes are committed for political motives. Some are serious. Hijacking a plane in order to bargain for the release of imprisoned members of a particular movement is deplored by most of society. Other politically motivated crimes are minor infractions. Demonstrating a point of view by having a parade without a permit is usually no more than a city ordinance violation. Nevertheless, it is a politically motivated offense. Except for acts that have obvious political meanings (e.g., treason, espionage, sabotage), the law does not specify crimes of a political nature.

All crimes are defined through the political process of legislation. Therefore, all violations of the law, broadly speaking, are basically political. Strictly speaking, however, the apparent motive of an act may qualify it as a political crime. Specifically, a political crime is an attack directed toward a society's total value system or its basic institutions.[1] Political crimes may be committed against the government or by the government.[2]

ATTACKS AGAINST GOVERNMENT

The formation of a government is followed by the enactment of laws intended to protect it from internal threats. This creates a dilemma for democratic societies. How far can the government go in the name of self-protection without denying individual freedoms? When do government actions to prevent a revolution actually become political repression? When does free speech become sedition? When do defiant acts of protest become treason?

When the American colonies began to resist the economic policies of Britain, the crown brought charges of treason. The famous Boston Tea Party (1773) was interpreted as an act of war against the Crown. The English government soon reasoned that public trials and executions for treason would end the civil unrest. There was even talk of bringing leading colonial insurrectionists to England for trial. Such attempts only inflamed the colonists further. What began as a movement for colonial rights became a war for independence.[3]

Upon gaining independence, the American states considered the law of treason as essential to the new government's security. However, efforts were made to prevent governmental abuses. Strictly defined rules of evidence and procedural safeguards for the accused were adopted. Interestingly, the founding fathers used the law of an early English king (Edward III) as a model.[4]

During the course of American history, relatively few people have been tried for treason. Other laws have been used to reduce perceived threats to the government. They include statutes which forbid inciting a rebellion, obstructing military operations during wartime, conspiring to overthrow the government, committing espionage (spying), and sabotage (destroying war or defense material). In times of political or social crises, these statutes are increasingly used, and new ones are created.[5] The Smith Act of 1940 was drafted when Europe was at war, and America's eventual involvement was all but certain. Concern over domestic enemies (pro-Nazi and procommunist) led to its passage. According to the Act, it is a crime to:

> knowingly or willfully . . . advocate the violent overthrow or destruction of the government of the United States, or of any government therein, or to organize any group for this purpose, or to become a member thereof with knowledge of its objective.[6]

Public hysteria followed President Truman's announcement that the Soviet Union had exploded an atomic device in 1949. The early 1950s was a period when people built bomb shelters in their backyards. School children were drilled in air-raid exercises. The cold war with Russia had begun. A Wisconsin senator made headlines by charging that communists held key positions in the United States. Senator McCarthy even asserted that the Department of State had been seriously infiltrated by ''Reds.'' The McCarran Act of 1950 required the registration of communist organizations and their fronts. It was followed by the McCarran-Walter Act (1952) which allowed for the deportation of aliens suspected of disloyalty. These acts and other legislation were responses to the intense communist scare period that developed after World War II had ended.[7]

Treason, espionage, sabotage, and the like are clearly political crimes. They are illegal acts involving some degree of allegiance to a foreign power. Other crimes may be equally political even though they do not rest on giving "aid and/or comfort" to an enemy government. On the surface the acts appear to be no different from other crimes. However, they become political when the intention is to challenge basic values or institutions of a society.

Antiwar (Vietnam) rallies, urban riots, and peace marches marked the 1960s. Having grown impatient with present circumstances, most of those involved were calling for social change rather than revolution. However, radical groups (e.g., Students for a Democratic Society, Weathermen) operated on the fringes or adopted the issues of the peace and civil rights movements. In a sense, they contributed to a revolutionary image of the movements themselves. This was particularly true toward the end of the decade. Those in disagreement with government policies at home and abroad were charged with a variety of crimes. City ordinance violations, disturbing the peace, resisting arrest, and conspiracy to cross state lines to commit an illegal act constituted many criminal charges. Because basic values (e.g., the draft, patriotism, limits on free speech) and institutions (e.g., the government, economic system, etc.) were being challenged, the crimes (burning of draft cards, sit-ins) were political.

The most threatening form of political crime today is terrorism. It has reached international proportions. Like political crime in general, terrorism is hard to specifically define. Violent acts may be committed by one or a group of dedicated followers. It can take the form of a skyjacking, assassination, bombing, or kidnapping. Terrorism may be one isolated incident or part of a series in a long-term struggle. One definition defines terrorism simply as:

> criminal acts and/or threats by individuals or groups designed to achieve political or economic objectives by fear, intimidation, coercion or violence.[8]

Accordingly, there are at least nine characteristics that appear to be common to most acts of terrorism. They are:

1. The use of violence as a method of systematic persuasion
2. The selection of targets and victims with maximum propaganda values
3. The use of unprovoked attacks
4. The selection of acts that gain maximum publicity with minimum risk to the terrorists
5. The use of surprise to overcome countermeasures
6. The use of threats, harassment, and violence to create an atmosphere of fear
7. The lack of recognition of civilians or women and children as "noncombatants"
8. The use of propaganda to maximize the effect of violence and to achieve political or economic goals
9. The perpetration of terroristic acts by groups whose only loyalty is to one another [9]

Political terrorism is usually aimed at the governmental process. The terrorism is sometimes directed toward a government's representatives (e.g., the police). With few exceptions, urban terrorist groups rarely survive longer than a few years.[10] The

United States experienced its most recent episode of terrorism during the late 1960s and early 1970s. The Black Panthers, the Black Liberation Army, the Weathermen, and the Symbionese Liberation Army have all appeared and mostly disappeared. Lack of popular support, internal fighting, money problems, and law enforcement countermeasures took their toll.

Groups in Ireland (Irish Republican Army), the Mideast (Palestine Liberation Organization), Europe (Red Army Faction), the African states (various liberation organizations) continue political warfare today.[11] Unlike their American counterparts, many of these groups have had dramatic international impact. Their objective is largely one of discrediting a government's ability to deal with disorder. The operations involve careful, long-range planning but allow for flexibility. Broad strategies are mapped out by the central leadership while local units are allowed to improvise. Specialized terrorist units are usually a small faction within the total guerilla operation.[12] Weapons and tactics vary from assassination, kidnapping, robbery, and extortion to ambush shootouts. Advancements in nuclear energy have not been universally applauded, even though there is a serious energy crisis. Besides possible accidents, there is a widely held fear of potential holocaust should terrorist groups seize such installations.

CRIMES BY THE GOVERNMENT

Governments are also capable of political crime when they violate basic social or institutional values. Political corruption is a violation of the public trust. In this sense, the Watergate scandal unveiled a wide assortment of political crimes. The extent of this episode was such that several government officials went to prison. In addition, an American president was forced to resign from office. The Koreagate affair, involving congressional bribes in return for legislation favorable to South Korea, appears to be organized political crime. More recently, the so-called "Irangate" incident, wherein arms were allegedly supplied to Iran in exchange for funds to be diverted to Nicaraguan rebels, has generated talk of political crime linked to another American president.

In attempting to subdue real or imagined security threats, the government may violate basic values of due process and fundamental fairness. These acts often occur during periods of national emergency. A principal constitutional guarantee forbids the indefinite detention of an individual without due process.

At the outbreak of World War II, over 100,000 Japanese-Americans were involuntarily removed from their west coast homes. Through an Executive Order signed by President Roosevelt, they were shipped to relocation camps that stretched from eastern California to Arkansas. There were no trials or hearings to determine who was a security risk. Men, women, and children of Japanese descent were simply ordered to depart on sealed trains, with only their simplest belongings, for destinations unknown. Many prominent politicians supported this internment policy. Earl Warren, who would become a champion of civil rights as Supreme Court chief justice, "testified that the American-born Japanese were even more dangerous to the security of the United States than the alien Japanese."[13] J. Edgar Hoover, however, indicated that it was nothing less than government-sponsored kidnapping. During the internment period, the camp residents displayed exemplary behavior. In addition, a Japanese-American army unit (the 442nd Regimental Combat Team) won an extraordinary number of medals and citations. Following the war, the Japanese-Americans sought, and won, redress from Congress.

Trials that take place in a charged political climate often leave lingering doubts. Was justice served? Did the defendants really receive a fair and impartial trial? Were they victims of emotions and scapegoating? It is difficult to prove (after the fact) a prosecution frame-up. However, a conviction based on a so-called frame-up is political crime. The offender is the state.

As previously noted, the 1950s was an era of communist witch-hunting. Accusations of being "Red" or "pink" were flying in all directions. Much of this hysteria was spurred on by the Soviet Union's first atomic bomb explosion. It was assumed that the Russians did not have the scientific capability to develop their own atomic weapons. Did someone pass our secrets on to them? In 1950, a prominent English spy (Dr. Klaus Fuchs) was arrested. He had traveled extensively in the United States during the war. Although he did not implicate Julius and Ethel Rosenberg, they were arrested on charges of wartime espionage for the Soviet Union.

Many believe that the Rosenbergs were scapegoats for the political atmosphere of the McCarthy (Senator Joseph McCarthy) period. First, throughout the trial, the judge consistently acted in a biased manner against the defendants. Second, the government's chief witnesses gave very questionable testimony linking the Rosenbergs to the crime. Third, the evidence was very circumstantial. Fourth, wartime espionage is interpreted to apply to enemies, not allies. At the time of the alleged espionage, the Soviet Union was an ally of the United States. The Rosenbergs were executed in 1953.[14]

Political crime occurs when the government uses illegal means to apprehend or frighten opposition. Unlawful wiretapping and illegal searches are examples of government crimes. They are political in that they attack fundamental values expressed in the Constitution. During the turmoil of the 1960s, the government vigorously pursued those thought, correctly or incorrectly, to be challenging its existence.

Legitimate governments have a duty to defend themselves against violent overthrow. The dangers lie in the suspension of civil liberties in the name of "law and order." The old question "Do the ends justify the means?" applies in this case. There must be safeguards against the possibility of a police state. The United States Supreme Court is acutely aware of this dilemma; that is, of the problem of balancing national security with the principle of due process.

Shortly after President Nixon was elected (1968), he announced that those suspected of being threats to national security were subject to wiretapping without prior court approval. This meant that, in practice, anyone on some sort of subversive list could have his or her telephone tapped or home bugged without a court showing of probable cause. The Supreme Court recognized the dangers in this policy. In 1972, the Justices voted overwhelmingly (including Nixon's appointees) that such "taps" were illegal.[15] Ironically, the Administration was linked to the bugging of the Democratic Party's national headquarters a short time later. Had the Supreme Court not acted a few years earlier, it still would have been difficult to claim that the Democratic Party was a national security risk.

A more recent example of serious crime committed by elected government officials was revealed by an FBI "sting" operation known as ABSCAM. In this case, federal agents represented themselves as "fronts" for a fictitious important Arab seeking special favors from Washington. Several government officials, including U.S. senators, accepted bribes in return for sponsoring special interest legislation and securing government contracts for the "Mideast power broker." Many were convicted on a variety of charges and received fines or imprisonment, or both.[16]

SUMMARY

Except for offenses that have clear political meanings (e.g., treason), the law does not specifically label political crimes. Political crimes may be distinct (e.g., espionage) or they may be similar to ordinary crimes (e.g., kidnapping). The key factor is motive. A political crime is an attack directed toward a society's total value system or its institutions.

Crimes of a political nature may be committed against the government or by the government. All governments establish laws designed to protect themselves from threats. In times of crisis, these laws are more frequently applied. Some perceived internal threats are dealt with through conventional criminal laws (e.g., peace disturbance and ordinance violations). The most feared political crime today is terrorism. It has international implications.

According to one definition, terrorism refers to "criminal acts and/or threats by individuals or groups designed to achieve political or economic objectives by fear, intimidation, coercion, or violence." Political terrorism is usually aimed at the governmental process. Specially trained terrorist units are typically a small faction within the total guerilla operation.

Political crimes by governments include the violation of public trust and the perversion of laws or the concept of due process. Governments violate basic social values when they become corrupt, suspend civil liberties in the name of "law and order," or ignore due process in times of national hysteria. The Watergate scandal, illegal wiretaps, unlawful searches, and political "show trials" are examples of government crimes.

SUGGESTED ACTIVITIES

- Read the First Amendment of the United States Constitution. Should it be interpreted differently in times of war than in times of peace? Debate this as a class project.
- How do nondemocratic countries deal with political crime? What are the policies of the Soviet Union? Note the recent dissident trials in the Soviet Union and discuss in class.
- Can you think of reasons, other than "national security," why Japanese-Americans were interned and not German or Italian-Americans? Discuss in class.
- Read your local newspaper as well as national news magazines and check for political crimes as discussed in this chapter. Categorize them as either crimes committed against the government or crimes committed by the government.

REVIEW

A. Give a definition of political crime.

B. Present examples of political crime committed against the government.

C. Give examples of political crime committed by the government.

D. List nine characteristics of terrorism.

E. Multiple Choice. Select the best answer.

 1. An example of political crime is:
    a. extortion
    b. kidnapping
    c. sabotage
    d. all of these may be political, depending upon the motive of the offender(s)

 2. Which of the following is not a characteristic of terrorism?
    a. use of surprise
    b. use of unprovoked attacks
    c. careful avoidance of women and children as victims
    d. publicity seeking

 3. Which of the following did not support the policy of Japanese-American internment during World War II?
    a. J. Edgar Hoover
    b. General DeWitt
    c. Earl Warren
    d. President Roosevelt

 4. Governments tend to commit political crimes when:
    a. there is social and political calm
    b. there is a sense of public distrust of government
    c. there are real or imagined threats to those in power
    d. all of these

 5. The so-called McCarthy period occurred in the:
    a. 1940s
    b. 1950s
    c. 1960s
    d. 1970s

 6. Which of the following cases best demonstrates the possible dangers to civil liberties during times of public hysteria over internal threats?
    a. Watergate case
    b. Koreagate case
    c. Rosenberg case
    d. none of these

 7. Which of the following is an example of government-sponsored terrorism?
    a. policies of Nazi Germany
    b. executions of convicted criminals
    c. the draft
    d. Symbionese Liberation Army

REFERENCES

1. Edwin Schur, *The Politics of Deviance* (Englewood Cliffs, N.J.: Prentice-Hall, Inc., 1980); Stephen Schafer, ''The Relativity of Political Crimes,'' in Stephen Schafer (ed.) *Readings in Contemporary Criminology* (Reston, Va.: Reston, 1976), 77.

2. See J. Roebuck and S. Weber, *Political Crime in the United States: Analyzing Crime by and against Government* (New York: Praeger, 1978).
3. Bradley Chapin, *The American Law of Treason* (Seattle, Wash.: University of Washington Press, 1964), 10–28. See also Jay A. Sigler, *Understanding Criminal Law* (Boston: Little, Brown, 1981), 167.
4. Chapin, *op. cit.*, 116.
5. U.S. Select Committee to Study Government Operations, ''Intelligence Activities and the Rights of Americans,'' in Jerome Skolnick and Elliott Currie (eds.) *Crisis in American Institutions*, 4th ed. (Boston: Little, Brown, 1979).
6. 18 U.S.C.A. §2385.
7. See John Wexley, *The Judgement of Julius and Ethel Rosenberg* (New York: Ballantine Books, 1977), 164–165.
8. Private Security Advisory Council, *Prevention of Terroristic Crimes: Security Guidelines for Business, Industry and Other Organizations* (Washington, D.C.: U.S. Government Printing Office, 1976), 3.
9. *Ibid.*, 3–4.
10. Walter Laqueur, *Terrorism* (Boston: Little, Brown, 1977), 86.
11. For a discussion of these groups, their history, organization, and techniques, see Albery Parry, *Terrorism* (New York: Vanguard Press, 1976).
12. Laqueur, *op. cit.*, 79–86.
13. Ronald O. Haak, ''Co-Opting the Oppressors: The Case of the Japanese-Americans,'' *Society*, 7 (1970), 23.
14. See Wexley, *op. cit.*, and Brandt Aymar and Edward Sagarin, *World's Great Trials* (New York: Bonanza Books, 1967), 327–329.
15. United States v. United States District Court, 407 U.S. 297 (1972).
16. ''Abscam's Toll,'' *Time*, August 24, 1981, 20.

16

Violent Criminals

OBJECTIVES

After studying this chapter, the student should be able to:

- Describe the characteristics of those who commit murder and assault and those who commit robbery.
- Explain the crime of rape and the psychological motivations of the rapist.
- Discuss the role of the victim in violent crimes.

Violent offenders commit crimes that have physical force or the threat of it as a central feature. In the case of criminal homicide, the force obviously is maximal and results in the victim's death. This chapter considers those violent offenders who commit murder and assault, forcible rape, and robbery. In addition, a discussion of the victim's role in crime is presented.

MURDERERS AND ASSAULTERS

Criminal homicide takes several forms. It springs from a variety of circumstances and motives. Criminals who kill may be divided into four general categories. They include individuals who (1) are subcultural assaulter/homicide offenders, (2) exhibit a deliberate antisocial life-style, (3) are one-time offenders, and (4) are mentally ill or deranged.[1]

A large proportion of murders are committed by the subcultural assaulter/homicide offenders. Wolfgang coined the term "subculture of violence" three decades ago.[2] The subculture consists of people who accept or expect violence as a problem-solving technique. They carry weapons in anticipation of violence. Situations are defined in which violent physical responses are condoned and even expected. In the subculture of violence, assault and homicide rates are high.

The results of Wolfgang's homicide study in Philadelphia were explained through the concept of a subculture of violence. In that study, he noted that most murders were crimes of passion. They were neither premeditated nor committed by mentally ill persons. The murders occurred when social interaction was intense—that is, on a weekend—when alcohol had been consumed and weapons were easily available. Both offenders and victims tended to have past police records of violent conduct. As summarized by Wolfgang:

> Quick resort to physical combat as a measure of daring, courage, or defense of status appears to be a [subcultural] expectation, especially for lower socioeconomic class males of both races. When such a cultural norm response is elicited from an individual engaged in social interplay with others who harbor the same response mechanism, physical assaults, altercations, and violent domestic quarrels that result in homicide are likely to be relatively common.[3]

Thus, the bulk of homicides are a product of cultural and subcultural values that support acts of violence when certain circumstances arise. Typical circumstances include threats to a man's masculinity, arguments over past debts, or disputes regarding female companions. The unplanned murder involves a victim and an offender who are at least casually acquainted.

Offenders who have a history of assaultive behavior appear to be products of the subculture of violence. Several studies of assault reveal it to have patterns quite similar to subcultural homicide.[4] Both assaults and a sizable number of homicides are committed by offenders caught in the same web of social and psychological circumstances. The chief distinction between the two crimes is the type of weapon. Firearms are much more pronounced in homicides. Many contend that it is the presence of a gun that transforms assault into a homicide.[5]

At times, a subculturally related murder is premeditated against a victim who is a stranger to the killer. During the violent days of the civil rights movement, subcultural norms held by some southerners dictated that overly ambitious blacks or outside agitators be dealt with by violent means. The circumstances were such that the subculture condoned the violence. In this sense, killings sponsored by the Ku Klux Klan reflected subcultural homicides. Except for an inclination toward violence, subcultural killers/assaulters are neither psychologically abnormal nor committed to a criminal value system.

Homicide offenders who exhibit an antisocial life-style usually have a lengthy criminal history. This is particularly true of the individual who kills in the act of committing a felony. Unlike subcultural killers, antisocial murderers are strangers to their victims in an overwhelming number of cases. The killings are likely to occur during the course of a robbery, burglary, or other conventional crime. Although all murders are felonies, this situation is termed a "felony-murder" because it is committed as part of another related felony. Even though the killing just happens as a byproduct (unpremeditated) of another crime, most states equate it with first-degree (premeditated) murder in terms of seriousness. Those jurisdictions which have capital punishment statutes subject felony-murderers to the possibility of a death sentence.

As individuals, antisocial murderers lack community ties, have extensive interpersonal problems, and come from disrupted families. Few suffer severe psychological abnormalities. Many are clinically diagnosed as being sociopaths. So-called hit men who are hired by crime syndicates to kill on contract fit this pattern. Sociopaths are:

> chronically antisocial individuals who are always in trouble, profiting neither from experience nor punishment, and maintaining no real loyalties to any person, group or code. They are frequently callous and hedonistic, showing marked emotional immaturity, with lack of sense of responsibility, lack of judgement and an ability to rationalize their behavior so that it appears warranted, reasonable, and justified.[6]

One-time homicide offenders refer to those who lead an apparently uneventful life. They do not belong to a subculture of violence nor are they remarkably antisocial. A set of circumstances occur in which they simply snap and commit homicide. In a novel by Malcolm Braly, the author characterizes the one-time circumstantial killer:

> Formerly a mild-mannered and mother-smothered high school teacher, [Watson] had killed his two small sons, attempted to kill his wife, cut his own throat, then poisoned himself, all because his wife had refused a reconciliation with the remark, "John, the truth is you bore me."[7]

Other one-time homicide offenders are convicted of manslaughter. That is, the victim's death is due to criminal negligence; for example, driving recklessly or carelessly handling a revolver while intoxicated. As indicated, such offenders lack a commitment to crime, are nonviolence-oriented and have normal personality structures. A small portion of the total numbers of murders are committed by this type.

A minority of homicides are committed by mentally ill or deranged offenders. These individuals suffer from severe psychiatric disorders. Their crimes are unpredictable and their motives are irrational. It is not uncommon for such offenders to murder several people over a period of time. Because the crimes are unpatterned and lack a rational motive, they are difficult to solve. Psychologically or psychiatrically the killers are frequently diagnosed as having a psychotic (serious mental) condition. Psychosis includes hallucinations, delusions, and outlandish behavior which, for some, becomes homicidal and is expressed in killings which are sadistic and often sexual in nature. Recent examples include the so-called Hillside Stranglers in California and the as yet (as of this writing) unapprehended Green River Killer in Seattle who preys on young prostitutes.

RAPISTS

Most of those arrested for rape have prior records, are young, and come from lower-class, minority groups. Victims tend to share the same background characteristics. This has led some to interpret rape as primarily a result of the subculture of violence.[8]

Others adopt a broader view by noting that society, in general, fosters the idea of the "naturalness" of male conquest over "female submissiveness." It is also pointed out that official arrest statistics are biased against lower-class victims and offenders. Rapes attributed to middle-class offenders and victims frequently escape official police records.[9]

Unreported rapes may result from misunderstanding during the dating game. Women are typically caught in the dilemma of wanting to be sexually attractive but not necessarily sexually available. Men, on the other hand, are expected (by society and their peers) to be aggressive. Petting is one technique of promoting sexual attractiveness. It may also be interpreted as a "come-on" by the male. A female's resistance to go beyond petting may be understood by the male as a challenge to his masculinity or as the female's manner of wanting not to appear as being "too easy." If the male's response is to "go all the way," the female clearly feels that she has been raped. The male, however, perceives her charge as a "bum rap." Many accused rapists rationalize their acts by claiming that the victim actually wanted to be raped.[10]

Given all the varieties of rape situations—for example, dating, encounters in public places or parties, or the occasional "dark alley" episodes—the majority of rapists are not mentally ill. In fact, most studies of convicted rapists agree that the offenders do not suffer from severe psychiatric disorders.[11] However, rapists have been categorized on the basis of psychological motivations which are not expressed by the majority of the male population.[12]

For some males, a rape may be motivated by a desire for aggression. In this instance, the offender's objective is to overpower the female and assert control or dominance. The sexual consequences of the act are secondary to the aggressive drive. Physical brutality (threatened or acted out) becomes the major source of stimulation. Other offenders are motivated by purely sexual drives. The act is characterized by caresses while force is kept to a minimum. Quite often the rapist who operates with this motive retreats when the victim resists. The most violent (and infrequent) rapes occur when the drive results from a sexual-aggressive diffusion (combination). Rapists motivated by this drive mix sadism with conventional sexual arousal. In an extreme form, the victim's death follows or occurs simultaneously with the act of intercourse. The fourth type of rapist is the offender who acts out of impulse. The rape experience overlaps with other predatory behavior. During the commission of a nonsexual crime (burglary or robbery, for example), the offender impulsively rapes the female victim. Distinct sexual and/or aggressive conquest of a female are not the prime motives of the act. Nonetheless, rape is coming to be increasingly understood as an act of violence rather than of sexual release.

TYPES OF ROBBERS

Robbers are difficult to type because the crime has elements of both personal and property offenses. The object of robbery is to acquire a quick source of cash. However, unlike the perpetrator of other property crimes, the robber expresses a willingness to use force or violence to make a "score." The most widely cited typology of robbers has been developed by Conklin. Three factors were considered in constructing the typology: (1)

motivations for the crime, (2) methods of carrying it out, and (3) degree of commitment to crime as a life-style.[13] The four types of offenders that Conklin has identified are the professional, opportunist, addict, and alcoholic robber.

Professional robbers commit their crimes for purposes of maintaining a pleasure-seeking existence. Robbery is viewed as a quick method of obtaining a large sum of money for high living which includes many pleasures but rarely hard drugs. Following a score, the offender frequently leaves the area for a distant vacation spot. Funds are set aside for necessities (e.g., legal and medical fees). Other than this, the life-style is largely one of "easy come, easy go." When the supply of cash is exhausted, another job is planned.

The actual crime requires little skill. But success depends upon careful planning and preparation. Favored targets (e.g., banks, loan companies, businesses with large payrolls) require special attention. An unnoticed parking spot for the getaway car, exit routes, and the establishment security measures must be considered. Some career robbers pull a "selective raid" or an "ambush" if time and the necessity for fast money do not permit a planned job.[14] Professionals usually work with a few partners who collectively reach agreement on the heist's potential before it is executed. The partnerships are unlikely to be permanent and often vary from one robbery to the next.

The commitment to crime as an occupation is firm and justified in the eyes of the professional. However, professionals vary in their degree of commitment to the specific crime of robbery. Some limit their offenses to robbery. Others combine it with different forms of criminal enterprises (e.g., burglary, forgery, etc.). A small percentage of all robbers are professionals.[15]

Opportunist robbers are motivated to commit crime by immediate felt needs. Unlike professionals, the money does not represent a source of funds for sustained luxurious living. It is seen as useful for purchasing a car, fancy clothes, appliances, or as extra cash. While professionals tend to be relatively old, white, and criminally experienced, opportunists are likely to be young, black, and inexperienced.

Targets are selected because they seem to be easy scores—not because of their large cash reserves. Opportunists are likely to focus upon individuals or small commercial establishments. The operations are typically ambushes or selected raids rather than highly planned crimes. The average score is considerably smaller than that of the professional. There is little commitment to robbery. Other forms of small-time theft are favored along with an occasional armed or strong-arm robbery. The largest portion of robbers falls into the opportunist category.[16]

Drugs provide the motive for the addict robber. Money obtained from robbery is of secondary importance. The crime's chief purpose is not to support a high-level (the professional) or improved (opportunist) life-style. Robbery is one method of maintaining a drug supply. While several addictive drugs are potential sources of motivation, Conklin focused upon users of heroin and amphetamines.

Addict robbers organize their crimes more than opportunists do, but less than professionals do. Victims are chosen for their vulnerability and low likelihood of risk. The object is not a big score but just enough money for more drugs. Thus, difficult targets where the chances of apprehension are greatest (places with large amounts of money) are avoided. Commitment to drug usage is stronger than commitment to a particular form of crime or crime life-style. Because addicts prefer to avoid problems, less dangerous forms of theft (e.g., shoplifting, auto larceny, and burglary) are preferred to robbery. If the thief is caught, these crimes tend to draw less harsh penalties and thus shorter periods of abstinence from drugs. When robbery is selected, firearms are shunned or are often unloaded for the same reasons.[17]

Alcohol is recognized as having the power to drastically alter behavior. For some, it may be a primary factor in the commission of a robbery. Alcoholic robbers usually lack a clear motive for their crime. There is rarely any planning or consideration of a likely victim. Conklin noted that a few in his sample robbed to obtain money for alcohol. Most, however, blundered into a robbery after an assault or argument while intoxicated.

There is little evidence of a commitment to crime as a life-style for the alcoholic robber. Few in Conklin's study had extensive adult criminal records. Many did have petty theft arrests as juveniles. Because of the careless, random nature of the offense, apprehension rates for alcoholic robbers are higher than those for other types.[18]

THE VICTIM'S ROLE IN VIOLENT CRIME

The study of the victim's role in the commission of crime is known as victimology. It is most often discussed in relation to violent crimes. The topic was first strongly proposed in this country by Hans von Hentig.[19] Others have since explored its dimensions.[20] According to those who have studied the subject, crime may directly or indirectly result from the victim's behavior or personal characteristics.

A victim's behavior may directly cause a crime when the victim provokes an attacker. In instances of subcultural homicide, the murder victim may have been the one who started the argument or physical fight. As noted by Wolfgang,

> In many cases the victim has most of the major characteristics of an offender; in some cases two potential offenders come together in a homicide situation and it is probably often only chance which results in one becoming a victim and the other an offender.[21]

Crime may indirectly result from the victim's behavior. People who display large amounts of money or drunkenly stagger through a high-crime area invite robbery. The same may be true of the service station owner who operates in an isolated area, keeps late hours, and deals in cash rather than credit cards. In all of these cases, there is some degree of victim responsibility for the crime. The degree varies from outright provocation to stupidity regarding the harsh realities of crime.

Most innocent are those who become victims because of their personal characteristics. Being elderly, female, a resident of the inner city, or mentally handicapped can increase the odds of becoming a crime victim. Regarding these kinds of victims, several state and local governments have established victim compensation or victim restitution programs. Compensation refers to the state's correction for damages or injuries caused the victim. It is an admission of the state's responsibility to protect the citizen from criminals or, in this case, correct damages that it obviously did not prevent. Restitution places the responsibility on the offender to repay the victim for his or her suffering. As summarized by Schafer, "Compensation calls for action by society; restitution calls for a decision by a criminal court and payment by the offender."[22]

Victims, through behavior or personal characteristics, may also play a role in the commission of property offenses, confidence games, and business-related swindles. People who leave town without canceling the paper tempt burglars. The individual looking for a fast buck is also being sought after by the con artist. Elderly poor people may be easy marks for financing schemes. Every crime requires a victim. Unfortunately, criminals often find this requirement easy to meet.

SUMMARY

Murderers may be divided into four types: subcultural assaulter/homicide offenders, antisocial offenders, one-time offenders, and mentally ill offenders. Many murders are committed by subcultural offender types. The murders are unplanned, crimes of passion and involve offenders and victims who share expectations of violence in response to certain situations. The environment in which these individuals are raised is termed the subculture of violence. Many assaults are committed by people socialized in this same subculture. The chief distinction between homicide and assault offenders is the presence or lack of a gun.

Antisocial offenders are also responsible for many homicides. Unlike subcultural murderers, their crimes typically are committed against strangers—usually during the course of another felony (e.g., robbery, burglary). Like the subcultural homicide, the offense of murder is often unpremeditated. While few murderers suffer from severe mental illness, many are diagnosed as sociopaths.

One-time murderers lack a commitment to crime, are not prone to violence, and are psychologically normal. Under a specific set of circumstances, they "snap" and commit murder. The crimes are typically unpremeditated and the possibility of their murdering a second time is remote.

The most unusual kinds of murder are carried out by the mentally ill offender. The homicides are unpatterned and lack a rational motive. Several people may become victims over a long period of time. Psychologically, the offenders are usually diagnosed as "psychotic."

Rape has been interpreted as a product of the subculture of violence. However, a broader view notes that much rape is unreported so that official statistics are biased against lower-class offenders and victims who are more likely to be handled officially. Further, it is argued that society, in general, promotes the values of "male aggression" and "female submissiveness." A sizable number of unreported rapes result from these values expressed in dating rituals. Given the diverse nature of rape, most rapists do not appear to be mentally ill individuals. But psychological studies of rapists reveal that motives may center around aggression, sexual drives, sexual-aggression diffusion, or impulsive behavior.

Robbers are classified in terms of motives, methods, and criminal values. On this basis, Conklin identified four types: professional, opportunist, addict, and alcoholic robbers. Professionals are motivated by the desire to maintain a pleasure-seeking life-style. Methods involve much planning, and robbery is seen as a career. Some professionals concentrate on robbery while others combine it with different forms of crime.

Unlike professionals, opportunists are motivated by immediate felt needs. Planning is kept to a minimum, and robbery is not viewed as a career pattern. Both addict and alcoholic robbers commit their crimes in response to the usage of these substances. Addict robbers use planning more often than opportunists and alcoholics but less often than professionals. Neither addicts nor alcoholics are committed to robbery as a career. Addicts prefer less risky forms of theft. Alcoholics often blunder into a robbery after an assault or argument while intoxicated. Because alcoholic robbers commit careless and random robberies, they are more likely to be apprehended. Of all types of robbers, opportunists are the most abundant while professionals are the least common.

Every crime requires a victim. Individuals frequently play a direct or indirect role in their victimization. Through behavior or personal characteristics, some people are more likely than others to be victims of crime. Those whose behavior directly or indirectly prompts crime share some degree of responsibility for the act with the offender. Those whose personal characteristics (age, sex, residence, etc.) render them vulnerable to crime are more correctly labeled as innocent victims. Various compensation and restitution programs are available with these victims primarily in mind.

SUGGESTED ACTIVITIES

- Watch several television crime shows and classify the homicide offenders using the typology presented in this chapter. If most of the portrayed homicides are premeditated, why is this relatively uncommon form of murder a favorite of television writers?
- Develop a list of robberies that have recently occurred in your community. On the basis of the targets, predict the type of offender(s) involved.
- Based on the psychological motives of rapists, develop some suggestions regarding the treatment of convicted rapists.
- As a class project, discuss the pros and cons of victim compensation and restitution programs. What would be the advantages and disadvantages of implementing each of these programs?

REVIEW

A. List the four types of murderers and discuss the two most common types.

B. List four psychological motivations of rapists.

C. List four types of robbers and discuss the most common type.

D. Define victimology, victim compensation, and victim restitution.

E. Multiple Choice. Select the best answer.

1. In the subculture of violence:
    a. physical aggression is condoned and expected in some situations
    b. blacks are the primary participants
    c. homicides are committed by older offenders
    d. most murders are premeditated

2. Antisocial murderers are commonly diagnosed as:
    a. completely normal
    b. schizophrenic
    c. insane
    d. sociopathic

3. Homicide resulting from negligence is likely to be committed by:
    a. subcultural murderers
    b. one-time murderers
    c. antisocial murderers
    d. mentally ill murderers

4. The least number of homicides are committed by:
    a. subcultural murderers
    b. sociopathic murderers
    c. antisocial murderers
    d. mentally ill murderers

5. Most known rapists are:
    a. middle class and middle aged
    b. severely psychotic
    c. not severely psychotic
    d. also child abusers

6. Which of the following views robbery in terms of a career commitment?
    a. opportunist
    b. professional
    c. adult
    d. a and b of these

7. Which of the following are select targets because of easy access?
    a. professionals
    b. opportunists
    c. alcoholics
    d. none of these

8. Robbery itself is rarely premeditated by which of the following?
    a. a professional
    b. an opportunist
    c. an addict
    d. an alcoholic

9. When a victim is repaid by the state, this is:
    a. restitution
    b. compensation
    c. destitution
    d. none of these

10. The most common type of robber is:
    a. professional
    b. opportunist
    c. addict
    d. alcoholic

REFERENCES

1. William A. Morrison, "General Homicide and the Death Penalty in Canada: Time for Reassessment and New Directions: Toward a Typology," *Canadian Journal of Criminology and Corrections*, 15 (1973), 367–396. See also, Daniel Glaser, Donald Kenefick, and Vincent O'Leary, "The Violent Offender," in Stephen Schafer (ed.) *Readings in Contemporary Criminology* (Reston, Va.: Reston Publishing, 1976), 192–205.

2. Marvin E. Wolfgang, *Patterns in Criminal Homicide* (Philadelphia: University of Pennsylvania Press, 1958). Also see D. Luckenbill, "Criminal Homicide as Situated Transaction," *Social Problems*, 25 (1977), 176–186.

3. Wolfgang, *op. cit.*, 188–189.

4. See David J. Pittman and William J. Handy, "Patterns in Criminal Aggravated Assault," *Journal of Criminal Law, Criminology and Police Science*, 55 (1964), 362–470; Alex D. Pokorny, "Human Violence: A Comparison of Homicide, Aggravated Assault, Suicide, and Attempted Homicide," in Bernard Cohen (ed.) *Crime in America* (Itasca, Ill.: Peacock Publishers, 1970), 109–110.

5. Franklin E. Zimring, "Getting Serious About Guns," *The Nation*, April 10, 1972, 457; Joseph F. Sheley, *America's Crime Problem* (Belmont, Calif.: Wadsworth, 1985), 103.

6. American Psychiatric Association, *Diagnostic and Statistical Manual* (Washington, D.C.: American Psychiatric Association, 1952), 38, as cited by Harold Goldman, Simon Dinitz, Lewis Linder, Thomas Foster and Harry Allen, *A Designed Treatment Program of Sociopathy by Means of Drugs: A Summary Report, Monograph No. 29* (Columbus, Ohio: Ohio State University, Program for the Study of Crime and Delinquency, 1974), 1.

7. Malcolm Braly, *On the Yard* (Boston: Little, Brown and Company, 1967), 106, as cited in John Irwin, *The Felon* (Englewood Cliffs, N.J.: Prentice-Hall, 1970), 73.

8. Menachim Amir, *Patterns of Forcible Rape* (Chicago: University of Chicago Press, 1971), 115. M. Hindelang and B. Davis, "Forcible Rape in the United States: A Statistical Profile," in D. Chappell, et al. (eds.) *Forcible Rape* (New York: Columbia University Press, 1977); D. Chappell and S. Singer, *Rape in New York City: A Study of Material in the Police Files and Its Meaning* (Albany, N.Y.: State University of New York Press, 1973).

9. Amir, *op. cit.*, 319–326.

10. Kurt Weis and Sandra S. Borges, "Victimology and Rape: The Case of the Legitimate Victim," *Issues in Criminology*, 8 (1973), 85–89.

11. James C. Coleman, *Abnormal Psychology and Modern Life* (Glenview, Ill.: Scott, Foresman, 1980); P. Gebhard, et al., *Sex Offenders: An Analysis of Types* (New York: Harper and Row, 1965).

12. A. Groth, *Men Who Rape: The Psychology of the Offender* (New York: Plenum Press, 1979).

13. John E. Conklin, *Robbery and the Criminal Justice System* (Philadelphia: J. B. Lippincott, 1972), 59.

14. Werner J. Einstandter, "The Social Organization of Armed Robbery," *Social Problems*, 17 (1969), 76.

15. Conklin, *op. cit.*, 63–66.

16. *Ibid.*, 68–70.

17. *Ibid.*, 71–74.

18. *Ibid.*, 75–76.

19. Hans von Hentig, *The Criminal and His Victim: Studies in the Sociology of Crime* (New Haven, Ct.: Yale University Press, 1948).

20. See, for example, Andrew Karmen, *Crime Victims: An Introduction to Victimology* (Monterey, Calif.: Brooks/Cole, 1984; I. Drapkin and E. Viano (eds.) *Victimology* (Lexington, Mass.: Lexington Books, 1974); Stephen Schafer, *The Victim and His Criminal* (New York: Random House, 1968).

21. Marvin E. Wolfgang, "Victim-Precipitated Criminal Homicide," in Marvin E. Wolfgang (ed.) *Studies in Homicide* (New York: Harper and Row, 1967), 87.

22. Schafer, *op. cit.*, 112.

17

Property Offenders

OBJECTIVES

After studying this chapter, the student should be able to:

- Describe the nature of burglars as property offenders.
- Discuss the characteristics of larcenists, with special attention to shoplifters.
- Explain the nature of auto thieves, especially the differences between joyriders and professionals.

Property offenders represent a broad category of criminal behavior. Their crimes range from arson to vandalism. The scope of this text does not permit a coverage of each of these types of offenders. Criminologists have devoted little attention to property offender characteristics. Much of what is known about burglars, larcenists, and auto thieves will be presented in this chapter.

BURGLARS

Burglars rarely commit their crimes on impulse. Most burglaries involve some degree of planning. The crime represents rational, economic motives. It is an attempt to acquire cash or convertible goods. Given the fact that few burglaries even result in an arrest, the odds of success are relatively good. As noted by Scarr, burglars may go through nine phases between the decision to commit a burglary and the development of an offense pattern. The cycle proceeds in the following manner:

1. There are real or imagined needs that may be satisfied through burglary.
2. Certain skills of a high or low degree are gained.
3. The opportunity to burglarize exists.
4. The felt need and the possibility to burglarize are joined.
5. Burglary is accepted above other methods as the solution to real or imagined needs.
6. A burglary is committed.
7. The merchandise is converted to cash.
8. Real or imagined needs are met.
9. A behavior pattern is encouraged, reinforced, or established.[1]

The cycle need not result in a career as a professional burglar. In fact, studies indicate that most burglaries are not the work of career criminals.[2] The crime of burglary attracts several different kinds of people. Movies glamorize the highly skilled "cat burglar" who specializes in the theft of jewels or furs. In addition to these select few, there are many more ordinary or amateur types of offenders.

Teenagers occasionally engage in burglary for thrills or easy money. Many grow out of this behavior and lead a straight life as adults. There are also "junkies" who prefer less risky burglaries to robberies as a means of buying drugs. A large portion of offenders concentrate on modest burglary targets between prison terms. Quite a few of these offenders "burn out" with age and withdraw from criminal pursuits.

Pope analyzed burglary arrests in California for a period of one year. It is difficult to generalize from a single study that focused upon a unique area for a short period of time. However, "the characteristics [of burglars] are found to be quite similar regardless of geographical area."[3] Approximately 1,200 burglary offenders were examined. The following profile emerged. It is in agreement with other similar studies.[4]

Burglars were found to be predominately young (often juveniles), male opportunists rather than mature professionals. Most of those arrested were white. A large proportion of the adult offenders had at least one prior arrest. Few, however, had been previously arrested for the specific crime of burglary. The small number of females in the study usually had minor prior records rather than serious criminal backgrounds. Nonwhites were more likely than whites to have had serious records that included past burglary arrests. Official records, although questionable in terms of accuracy, revealed that a minority of arrested burglars had a history of drug involvement. However, males were more likely than females to possess drug records. Nonwhite offenders with drug involvement tended to have been opiate users. The prior criminal behavior and drug involvement records of juveniles were not available to the researchers.[5]

The study also indicated that burglars were, in general, more likely to operate in groups of two or three rather than alone. Nevertheless, the factor of companionship varied with age and sex. Both females and juveniles were more likely than males and adults were to operate in groups. The majority of burglars tended to commit their offenses within 1 mile of their residences. Again, however, age and sex affected this pattern.

Younger offenders and males were more likely to burglarize in their own neighborhoods than were older offenders and females. Race did not appear to affect the likelihood of group involvement or location of the target. That is, sex and age were more related to these factors than the race of the burglar.[6]

As pointed out by the lead researcher, the study is not conclusive but does support some interesting generalizations. In particular, the data do indicate that burglary is primarily the work of opportunists. Pope notes that:

> Although there is no way of knowing the characteristics of burglary offenders who were not arrested, those offenders who were arrested and those who were not, seem to be committing the same types of burglaries. Furthermore, these burglaries do not seem to be the type likely to be committed by persons skilled at their trade. These data, then, lend some measure of support to Shover's (1971) observations about the type of burglary offender emerging today: an occasional, unskilled offender who evidences little sophistication, planning, or specialization.[7]

In addition to this surplus of amateurs, there are professionals.

For a select few, burglary becomes a career in crime. Shover has referred to these professionals as the "good burglar" type. They have the qualities of (1) mastered technical skills, (2) specialized involvement in burglary, (3) established reputations of personal integrity, and (4) proven success as a burglar.[8]

Professional burglars [9] operate over relatively long periods of time and support themselves almost exclusively through criminal activities. They work in crews of at least two, but usually more, partners. Membership in a burglary crew may be gained through reputation. In this instance, a person with a known skill is sought out for a particular score. Membership may also be won through meetings at hang-outs (e.g., bars, lounges) or introductions by fences. Large crews rarely stay together for long periods. Disagreements, arrests, and career changes take their toll. Crews limited to two or three members are more likely to pull off a string of jobs over time. During a typical score, each member has a role based upon a particular skill, preference, or ability. Within crews, degrees of prestige are determined by "age, criminal experience, or skill." It is unlikely for the crew to have a formal leader.

Targets for burglaries are investigated well in advance. They are often far from their residences, sometimes in distant cities. Possible scores are disclosed through tipsters or direct discovery. Once a score is decided upon, the premises are cased. Of particular interest to the crew is the location of the safe, valuable merchandise, exit routes, and break-in points (windows, roof, etc.). Transportation is arranged by stealing a vehicle or purchasing a used one under a phony name. The car is then stored until the heist.

Good burglars, or professionals, are dependent upon outsiders for a successful career. These outsiders include tipsters, fences, bondsmen, attorneys, and sometimes corrupt police officers. Tipsters inform burglars about potentially good scores. They are likely to be fences who need more merchandise, ex-burglars, or other practicing burglars who cannot make the score for one reason or another. The tipster usually gets 10 percent of the take.

Fences convert stolen merchandise into cash for a burglary crew. They buy the goods at a fraction of their value and channel them into prearranged or potential outlets. Bondsmen and criminal lawyers develop daily relationships with the underworld. They depend upon criminals for their livelihood. Criminals depend upon them for their freedom. Unethical bondsmen and attorneys may act as tipsters or fences to assist their clients in meeting legal expenses. Attorneys may be chosen by professional burglars for two purposes: (1) fixing cases through bribes and political manipulation, and (2) winning cases through courtroom skills.

LARCENISTS

Larceny encompasses acts of theft that do not involve violence, illegal entry, or fraud. It includes shoplifting, purse snatching, car clouting (theft of cargo or accessories from autos), pickpocketing, and so on. The crime represents a "grab bag" of property offenses not covered in other specific categories (e.g., burglary, robbery, embezzlement, confidence games). A common form of larceny is shoplifting. It, like most stealing, is primarily the work of amateur larcenists. According to one report, a typical shoplifter in 1972 was a white, married female, was age twenty-one to twenty-five, had one child, and had a husband who made above $10,000 per year.[10] Since customers are drawn from all walks of life, offenders necessarily represent a broad cross-section of the population. While the young, white female is often seen as typical, it should be noted that shoplifting is frequently committed by children, elderly people, middle-aged males, minority group members, and so on. There really is no specific type of amateur shoplifter.

Although their behavior is criminal, amateur shoplifters do not think of themselves as criminals. Because of this, many stores display signs reminding customers that "Shoplifting is a Crime!" When apprehended, the typical shoplifter expresses embarrassment and concern about his or her reputation. The excuses given by apprehended shoplifters reveal their acceptance of traditional values and lack of commitment to a criminal code. One woman snitch (amateur shoplifter), upon being caught, exclaimed:

> I didn't intend to take the dress. I just wanted to see it in the daylight. Oh! what will my husband do! I did intend to pay for it. It's all a mistake. Oh! my God! what will mother say! I'll be glad to pay for it. See, I've got the money with me. Oh! my children! They can't find out I've been arrested! I'd never be able to face them again.[11]

The motives of snitches vary a great deal. Young children find it to be a thrilling game. Homemakers see it as a means of stretching their monthly budget. Other people justify shoplifting as a way to retaliate against "unfair" high prices. Nevertheless, the motives of amateurs differ from those of professionals in one major respect. Snitches steal goods for personal consumption; "boosters" (professionals) and "shadow professionals"[12] (semiprofessionals) steal for resale to fences or friends. There are other differences between amateurs and professionals. Amateurs tend to work alone; professionals operate in groups or gangs. Boosters steal more expensive, resalable items than do snitches. Finally, boosters shoplift systematically and skillfully over periods of time as a primary source of income. Snitches are occasional offenders who steal on impulse when the situation is tempting or looks promising. Shadow professionals occupy a middle ground between snitches and boosters. They have more skill and steal more selectively than do snitches. However, unlike professionals, they do not live off the proceeds of shoplifting.

Purse snatching and car clouting resemble shoplifting in that the offenders are largely amateurs. However, unlike shoplifters, the offenders are concentrated among young males who work in groups and may have an established delinquent career. On occasion, car clouters are organized older offenders who systematically steal favored items (tape decks, CB radios, etc.) for sale to a fencing operation. Pickpocketing requires enough skill that it is confined to professional criminals.[13] But, as noted in Chapter 13, pickpockets are rapidly becoming a rare variety of larcenist.

AUTO THIEVES

Auto theft, perhaps more than any other Index property offense, is a juvenile crime. The offenders also tend to be white, male, and middle class.[14] For most of them, the theft is carried out for excitement and kicks. The stolen cars are kept for a short time and then abandoned, often near the residence of the offender(s). This broad class of auto thieves is known as joyriders. They do not see themselves as criminals and typically redefine the act as one of simply "borrowing" a car.

The few existing studies of auto theft indicate that joyriders are often juveniles with identity problems. For example, Gibbons has profiled a likely offender in the following terms:

> The pimply lads who have communication difficulties with girls and other persons, the boys who are too small to engage in high school athletics, or the ones whose families move frequently within the city, so that the youngsters have difficulties in becoming socially integrated into school life, are the kinds of youths who are candidates for delinquent careers in joyriding.[15]

Joyriders usually belong to a group of boys who share similar identity problems and are looking for fun and excitement. The group is not fixed or rigid; there is no officially recognized leadership. The cars are used purely for pleasure and not for involvement in other crimes (e.g., robbery or burglary). Techniques may vary from simple "hot-wiring" to more sophisticated methods of theft. Occasionally there may be some minor damage or theft of accessories or cargo, but usually not.

Early studies of joyriders indicated that they tended to have more favorable backgrounds than did other delinquents. They were, for example, found to have better relationships with nondelinquent peers and to be better adjusted personally and socially than were other delinquents.[16] A more recent study challenged this image, noting that joyriders, though still young, are more evenly spread throughout the social and economic structure.[17] Additional data are needed in order to clarify this apparent divergence.

Professional auto thieves carry out their crime in groups or rings. They are usually composed of white, young, adult males. Amateur thieves (nonjoyriders) steal cars simply to strip them of valuable parts for sale to a fence. More professional thieves prefer the entire automobile as an item for resale.

Car theft rings avoid arrest by hiring amateurs to steal cars. The amateurs are paid anywhere from $50 to $200 per automobile. The thief delivers the car to a drop location where the professionals apply their talents. The techniques vary with the skills of the thief. If cars are stolen by an amateur, the method is commonly one of hot-wiring. If the cars have been stolen directly by ring members (professionals), more elaborate schemes are used. Dealership cars are test-driven by a phony buyer who copies the key and serial number for a future theft. In other instances, newspaper ads are followed up by ring members. Owners wishing to sell their cars are contacted. On the pretext of test-driving the car, the thief simply takes the automobile without returning. Rental cars are stolen in the same manner.[18]

Cars are prepared for resale by giving them new paint jobs, serial numbers, license plates, and titles. They are then distributed through shady domestic and foreign outlets. In some cases, specific types of popular cars are stolen on an order basis. Customers are often willing to ''ask no questions'' in return for a Trans Am or Corvette at one-fourth of its market value.

Professional car thieves are similar to others who specialize in crime. They take pride in their skills and view their operations as long-term business propositions. Further, the pros distinguish themselves from amateurs and joyriding ''punks.'' While committed to a criminal subculture, professional auto thieves justify or rationalize their activities. Hellman records one professional's opinion about his contribution to the economy as follows:

> First of all, I create work. I hire men to deliver the cars, work on the numbers, paint them, give them paper, maybe drive them out of state, find customers. That's good for the economy. Then I'm helping working people to get what they can never afford otherwise. A fellow wants a Cadillac but he can't afford it; his wife wants it but she knows he can't afford it. So I get this fellow a car at a price he can afford; maybe I save him as much as $2,000. Now he's happy. But so is the guy who lost his car. He gets a nice new Cadillac from the insurance company—without the dents and scratches we had to take out of it. The Cadillac company—they're happy too because they sell another Cadillac.[19]

Regarding insurance companies, the obvious loser, the professional in the previous interview stated: ''They got a budget for this sort of thing anyway.''[20]

SUMMARY

Property crimes span a wide range of activities. The major property offenders are burglars, larcenists, and auto thieves. Most are amateurs.

Burglars operate on economic motives and plan their crimes to some extent. They may go through nine phases between the decision to commit a burglary and the development of an offense pattern. Most burglars are amateurs or ordinary offenders. Few are professionals. Profiles of arrested burglars reveal that they are young, white, male opportunists. Most have at least one prior arrest. A minority have previous burglary records or histories of drug involvement. The offenses are committed by groups and occur relatively close to the offenders' neighborhood.

Professional burglars operate in crews of two or more partners. Within crews, there are usually prestige rankings based on "age, criminal experience, or skill." The crimes are well planned with the potential value of the score of major importance. Outsiders such as tipsters, fences, bondsmen, and attorneys are relied upon throughout the burglar's career. Unlike amateur or ordinary burglars, professionals are technically skilled specialists with reputations of personal integrity and success as burglars.

A common type of larcenist is the shoplifter. Like most forms of stealing, shoplifting is basically a crime of amateurs (snitches). Apprehended shoplifters come from all walks of life. There is really no single, specific profile of a snitch. Most amateurs are law-abiding, work alone, steal on impulse, and personally consume or use the stolen merchandise. Other larcenists (e.g., purse snatchers and car clouters) are also primarily amateurs. However, they tend to be young males who work in groups and have established delinquent careers.

Boosters, or professional shoplifters, steal for resale to fences. Unlike amateurs, boosters work in groups and focus upon expensive and resalable goods. Shadow professionals occupy a middle position between snitches and boosters. They are more skilled and selective than snitches but less skilled than boosters. As opposed to boosters, the shadow professional does not shoplift as a primary source of income.

Auto thieves are divided into two primary categories: joyriders and professionals. There is also a category of amateurs who steal cars for their parts or for a professional ring to distribute. However, these amateurs lack the skills, experience, and connections of the professionals.

Joyriders are typically young males who come from diverse social and economic backgrounds. Though many are white and middle class, recent studies suggest that the offense is more evenly distributed among the youth population. Professional auto thieves steal cars for resale by car theft rings that are often well organized and are based on intricate operations. Amateurs may be used for the actual theft or the ring may rely on its own experts. Distribution networks, with cars on order, are often part of a national or international operation. Professional auto thieves are usually white, young adult males who are committed to a criminal subculture. They usually rationalize their activities by claiming to serve a valuable economic or social concern that differs little from legitimate business.

SUGGESTED ACTIVITIES

- Obtain arrest data from your local police department. Construct a profile of burglary, shoplifting, and auto theft suspects.
- Read newspaper accounts of those arrested for burglary, larceny, and auto theft. Develop a profile of suspects and compare it with those presented in this chapter.

● Talk to a detective or ask one to visit your class for purposes of discussing property offenders. Ask what method is used to determine if a crime is the work of an amateur or a professional burglar, larcenist, or auto thief.

REVIEW

A. List some major features of the typical amateur or ordinary burglar.

B. List nine phases that make up the cycle of burglary involvement as noted by Scarr.

C. List the chief differences between snitches and boosters.

D. List the major characteristics of joyriders.

E. Multiple Choice. Select the best answer.

1. According to Pope's study, most arrested burglars were:
   a. nonwhites
   b. free of previous arrests
   c. heavy drug users
   d. group offenders

2. Career or "good burglar" offenders:
   a. operate alone
   b. primarily commit offenses close to their residence
   c. depend upon outsiders more than amateurs do
   d. are usually nonwhite

3. A fence:
   a. is a barrier that prevents burglary
   b. is a person who buys and sells stolen goods
   c. is used to "fix" burglary arrests
   d. is a burglar who acts as the lookout during a heist

4. A group of professional burglars is known as a:
   a. crew
   b. troupe
   c. cadre
   d. platoon

5. Larcenists commit property offenses that do not involve:
   a. violence
   b. illegal entry
   c. fraud
   d. all of these

6. Amateur shoplifters are known as:
   a. shadow professionals
   b. boosters
   c. snitches
   d. cannons

7. Professional shoplifters differ from amateurs in that they:
   a. are mostly females
   b. steal more often
   c. work alone
   d. steal for resale

8. In general, purse snatchers differ from shoplifters, as a group, in that they:
   a. are mostly amateurs
   b. are older
   c. have delinquent careers
   d. are more likely to be apprehended

9. Most of those arrested for auto theft are:
   a. joyriders
   b. professionals
   c. nonwhite
   d. lower class
10. Professional auto thieves:
   a. operate in organized rings
   b. operate alone
   c. rarely steal expensive cars
   d. rarely steal cars on a special-order basis

REFERENCES

1. Harry A. Scarr, *Patterns of Burglary* (Washington, D.C.: U.S. Government Printing Office, 1973).
2. See Thomas A. Reppetto, *Residential Crime* (Cambridge, Mass.: Ballinger, 1974); Neal Shover, "The Social Organization of Burglary," in Anthony L. Guenther (ed.) *Criminal Behavior and Social Systems* (Chicago: Rand McNally, 1976), 282–284; Marshall B. Clinard and Richard Quinney, *Criminal Behavior Systems* (New York: Holt, Rinehart and Winston, 1967), 18; Peter D. Chimbos, "A Study of Breaking and Entering Offenses in 'Northern City,' Ontario," *Canadian Journal of Criminology and Corrections*, 15 (1973), 320.
3. Carl E. Pope, *Crime Specific Analysis: An Empirical Examination of Burglary Offense and Offender Characteristics, Analytic Report No. 12* (Washington, D.C.: U.S. Government Printing Office, 1977), 49.
4. See Reppetto, *op. cit.*; Chimbos, *op. cit.*; and Shover, *op. cit.*
5. Carl E. Pope, *Crime Specific Analysis: An Empirical Examination of Burglary Offender Characteristics, Analytic Report No. 11* (Washington, D.C.: U.S. Government Printing Office, 1977), 16–26.
6. *Ibid.*, 18–22.
7. Pope, *op. cit.*, 50.
8. Shover, *op. cit.*, 269.
9. See *Ibid.*, 269–282; C. Swanson, N. Chamelin, and L. Territo, *Criminal Investigation* (New York: Random House, 1984); Harry King and William Chambliss, *Harry King: A Professional Thief's Journey* (New York: John Wiley, 1984).
10. Robert Wright, "Nation's Retail Merchants Mobilize Security Systems to Combat Fast-Growing Shoplifting Trends," *New York Times*, May 21, 1972, C59.
11. Mary Owen Cameron, *The Booster and the Snitch* (New York: Free Press, 1964), 164.
12. Peter Hellman, "One in Ten Shoppers Is a Shoplifter," *New York Times Magazine*, March 15, 1970, 34.
13. James A. Inciardi, *Reflections on Crime* (New York: Holt, Rinehart and Winston, 1978), 140.
14. FBI, *Uniform Crime Reports, 1984* (Washington, D.C.: U.S. Government Printing Office, 1985); Don C. Gibbons, *Society, Crime and Criminal Careers* (Englewood Cliffs, N.J.: Prentice-Hall, 1978), 312–320.
15. Gibbons, *op. cit.*, 314.
16. W. W. Wattenberg and J. Balistrieri, "Automobile Theft: A 'Favored-Group' Delinquency," *American Journal of Sociology*, 57 (1952), 577–578; Erwin Schepses, "Boys Who Steal Cars," *Federal Probation*, 25 (1961), 56–62.
17. C. H. McCaghy, P. Giordano, and T. Henson, "Auto Theft: Offender and Offense Characteristics," *Criminology*, 15 (1977), 367–385.
18. Federal Bureau of Investigation, "Auto Theft Rings," *FBI Law Enforcement Journal* (Washington, D.C.: U.S. Government Printing Office, 1975), 7.
19. Peter Hellman, "Stealing Cars Is a Growth Industry," *New York Times Magazine*, June 20, 1971, 45.
20. *Ibid.*

18

Offenders
of Public Morality

OBJECTIVES

After studying this chapter, the student should be able to:

- List the characteristics associated with pedophiliacs, exhibitionists, and voyeurs.
- Describe some features of the homosexual life-style.
- State the background characteristics associated with entry into prostitution.
- Compare heroin and marijuana users.
- Explain the major characteristics of alcoholics or problem drinkers.

Those who offend public morals come from a broad cross section of the general population. In many instances, the offenses may be labeled as victimless crimes. That is, the behavior is voluntary for the parties concerned (e.g., homosexuality, prostitution). In other cases, the offenses clearly involve victims who are preyed upon or who lack the capacity for mature judgment (e.g., child molestation). For purposes of discussion, this chapter will deal with sex offenders (excluding rapists) and substance abusers.

SEX OFFENDERS

The law forbids a wide variety of sexual behavior. Some have charged that the law has attempted to control too much activity that is really a private matter. The criminal statutes of some states prohibit "everything but solitary and joyless masturbation and 'normal coitus' inside wedlock.''[1] There are laws which forbid homosexuality, oral intercourse, anal intercourse, premarital sex, and so on. A large portion of the public morality laws regarding sex between consenting adults is not enforced. To do so would be difficult. It would also involve the arrest of many people. Four types of sex offenders to be discussed are child molesters, exhibitionists, homosexuals, and prostitutes.

Child Molesters

The sexual abuse of a child by an adult ranges from indecent exposure of the genitals to sexual intercourse. Offenders who victimize children are termed pedophiliacs. Regardless of the nature of the act, the preferred sex object of the pedophiliac is a child.

Pedophiliacs are overwhelmingly male,[2] and come from the ranks of three age groups: teenagers, those in their middle to late thirties, and middle to late fifties. There are cases of female pedophilia. But women are less likely to be discovered and officially dealt with because of their socially endorsed roles as child caretakers. In addition, males (especially older men) are viewed as more threatening than females are. Thus, the small percentage of known child molesters who are female is partly due to these factors. Nevertheless, there is reason to believe that pedophilia, known and unknown cases, is predominantly a male offense. The victims are most likely to be girls.

In a lengthy study by one research team, sexual abusers of children were divided into two categories on the basis of the victim's age. The research focused upon adult, male, child molesters who had had sexual contact with girls (1) under the age of twelve years and (2) between the ages of twelve and fifteen years.[3] The first category involved offenders who tended (1) to come from broken homes, (2) to have poor parental relationships, (3) to demonstrate prior sexual development little different than nonoffenders, (4) to be unmarried, (5) if married, to have been married more than once, (6) to have minor criminal records of a sexual nature, and (7) to exhibit a greater degree of psychiatric disturbances than other sex offenders. The second group differed from the first in a few respects. They were characterized as having (1) better parental relationships, (2) poorer peer group relationships, and (3) more stable marital histories.

There is little about these characteristics that explains child molestation. Evidence does indicate that feelings of sexual inferiority operate as a motivating factor among pedophiliacs. According to Reinhardt, many offenders turn to children only after they have failed with adult partners.[4] Groth and associates, however, have concluded that most molesters are not sexually frustrated.[5] Evidence does support the thesis that, contrary to popular images of the aggressive sex fiend, pedophiliacs are generally nonviolent offenders.[6]

When young children are the victims, the offense usually consists of fondling and rarely includes attempted intercourse. The episodes often continue over a period of time until the relationship is reported by the child. Unfortunately, children are reluctant to reveal the activities out of a sense of shame or personal guilt. When told, adults may not believe the story because the offender is frequently someone who is known to and unsuspected by the family. Another problem is that adults overreact when they are told of a believable incident.[7]

Exhibitionists and Voyeurs

Those who indecently expose themselves solely to children may be termed pedophiliacs. In general, however, one who publicly exposes his or her genitals for sexual pleasure is termed an exhibitionist. Most are males and young adults who choose unknown juvenile victims. The acts are compulsive and difficult to avoid. Relief comes only after the exhibition occurs and is usually followed by masturbation. They rarely victimize the same person more than once. According to one major study, offenders have (1) better relationships with their mothers than their fathers, (2) poor peer group associations, (3) a sexual need for prostitutes, (4) low incidence of marriage, and (5) generally law-abiding records.[8]

Past research has classified exhibitionists into three categories: patterned, alcoholic, and mentally retarded offenders.[9] More recent studies have categorized exhibitionists as individuals who inappropriately respond to either emotional immaturity or personal stress.[10] A large proportion of exhibitionists are immature regarding interpersonal skills with females. They lack self-confidence and the necessary social abilities for relating to women. These inadequacies often foster feelings of sexual inferiority. Exposing the erect penis becomes a way of asserting masculinity without having to prove it through intercourse. The remaining exhibitionists are individuals who react to interpersonal problems by exposing themselves. The act serves to reduce tension or symbolize rebellion against failure. The following case is typical of this group of exhibitionists:

> The compulsive urge to expose himself generally appeared when he was under emotional stress, as when after he had had an argument with his wife or employer. This combination of insecurity, real or imagined emotional deprivation, and sense of failure is common . . . and the exposure may be a simultaneous expression of retaliation, declaration of masculinity, and sexual solicitation.[11]

Voyeurism is the opposite of exhibitionism. The voyeur ("Peeping Tom") spies on women who are changing clothes or undressing. These offenders share many characteristics that are common among exhibitionists. They are almost always male, often single, and young to middle age adults. In addition, they compulsively seek out female strangers as their victims and (as adults) operate alone. Unlike exhibitionists, voyeurs are selective regarding their victims. That is, they choose physically desirable women and patiently await the opportunity to view a personally erotic scene. Unlike many exhibitionists, Peeping Toms share the pedophiliac's tendency to victimize one individual or area repeatedly.

Research which has investigated the background characteristics of voyeurs provides differing conclusions. However, one study indicates that a voyeur is likely (1) to be the only or the youngest child in the family, (2) to have good parental relationships, (3) to experience poor peer association, (4) to have comparatively extensive homosexual experiences, and (5) to possess serious delinquency records. The same study divided "peepers" into four major types: (1) sociosexually immature, (2) alcoholic, (3) mentally retarded, and (4) situational (opportunist) offenders.[12] In summary, the various sex offenders discussed above tend to be (1) nonviolent; (2) sexually passive; (3) repeaters, but often at a lower rate than nonsexual offenders; and (4) possessed by feelings of sexual inferiority.

Homosexuals

Sexual exchanges between two individuals of the same sex is known as homosexuality. It is treated as a crime in many jurisdictions. Early views of the behavior held that the participants were products of psychological disorders or of deprived parental relationships. More recent findings do not agree with this concept. That is, homosexuality is not significantly related to psychosis, neurosis, or exposure to a dominant mother and a rejecting father.[13] Attempts to demonstrate a connection between biology and homosexuality have largely failed. There appear to be no significant differences between homosexuals and heterosexuals in terms of chromosomes or hormones.[14]

Homosexuals may be young or old, male or female. They come from all social classes and races. They also differ in their degree of commitment to homosexuality. Some identify themselves as totally homosexual. Others claim to be partly homosexual (bisexual). Still others admit to situational or temporary homosexuality as young boys, prison inmates, and so on. For example, Kinsey found that a sizable number of white males in his sample had had at least one intense homosexual encounter.[15]

For fear of embarrassment, loss of jobs, or social rejection, many homosexuals attempt to lead a double life. On the outside, the individual displays a conventional life-style. Inside, the homosexual drive either is suppressed or is expressed in a most cautious manner. An outward commitment to homosexuality (''coming out'') represents a serious break with straight society. It is the acceptance of a homosexual identity.

Males are more likely than females to identify themselves formally as homosexuals. This is due, in part, to the ability of females to shield their sexual inclinations. While two adult males living together may raise eyebrows, women may openly display affection and live together without much public disapproval. Therefore, confirmed male homosexuals are more apt to live in gay communities, frequent gay bars, and openly adopt a homosexual life-style.

There are several myths about the relationship between homosexuality and other forms of sexual deviance. Many believe that homosexuals and pedophiliacs are identical or similar in motives, behavior, and characteristics. In fact, most cases of pedophilia involve adult males and female children. This is not to suggest that homosexuals always avoid children. Rather, homosexuality, like heterosexuality, is usually a consensual relationship that excludes other forms of deviance such as child molestation, exhibitionism, and voyeurism.

Prostitutes

Prostitutes are members of the ''oldest profession.'' They agree to sexual favors in return for money. Most are women but males also contribute to this behavior primarily serving homosexual clients. The variation among prostitutes is greater than it was in the past. Some are addicts who prostitute themselves in order to maintain a drug supply. Others are fashionable call girls who cater to prosperous clients. Recent investigations have identified married female homemakers who work at prostitution on a part-time basis. "Massage parlors" may hire students who work their way through college as prostitutes.

Historically, women worked for madams in established houses located in "red light" districts of large cities. Today, they may work for a massage parlor, be under the control of a pimp, or operate independently or in a loose confederation with other hookers. By and large, the motive for entering prostitution is simply money. The "profession" represents the only opportunity for a high income to women lacking approved salable skills. For others, it is a good alternative or source of additional funds. Prostitutes are similar to con artists in that they often pretend to get sexual satisfaction (some claim that they actually do) from the act, thus playing to the customer's pride.

Most women enter prostitution at an early age when they are attractive and physically fit for the activity. In spite of the numerous attempts to determine what causes women to become prostitutes, few conclusions have been reached. McCaghy has summarized some common background features that facilitate the decision to become a prostitute. First, early adolescent years are marked by frequent and careless sexual relations which include intercourse. Second, rationalizations and justifications of prostitution are learned and accepted through associations. Third, there is a realization that prostitution provides a relatively high financial reward otherwise unavailable.[16]

SUBSTANCE ABUSERS

The public tends to associate substance abuse, or drug abuse, with criminal behavior. There is often a fine line between substance use and substance abuse. Because some substances are legal, they may be consistently abused without intervention by law enforcement officials (e.g., alcohol and nicotine). Other substances may be used in moderation but be subject to criminal penalties (e.g., marijuana). The law selects certain substances for their perceived abusive features or their potential for abuse. Either the drug itself is illegal regardless of how it is used, or the individual is criminalized when the drug is abused. The following discussion considers those who use or abuse certain narcotics or dangerous drugs and alcohol.

Narcotics and Dangerous Drug Users

Today, heroin usage is concentrated among minority groups in urban slum areas. More specifically, the users are likely to be young, male, and have a delinquent or criminal record prior to using heroin.[17] In one drug treatment program in New York City, 44 percent of the clients had criminal arrests before they began using drugs.[18] The reasons for using heroin are complicated. Given the fact that it is largely a lower-class minority-group drug, poverty and lack of legitimate opportunities encourage heroin usage. Heroin becomes a means of escape from a depressing situation. But the fact that heroin is used by those with criminal backgrounds also suggests that it may symbolize a rebellion against straight society; that is, something that is "cool." This is particularly the case with black, adolescent users.

Heroin addicts frequently use other drugs such as amphetamines, barbiturates, or cocaine. Some of these drugs are used before heroin and continue to be taken after the onset of heroin addiction. While it is true that many heroin users once smoked marijuana, many more marijuana users never use heroin. That is, there is no direct causal relationship between smoking marijuana and using heroin.

Unlike narcotic addicts, marijuana (classified as a dangerous drug) users may be found throughout society. Some have claimed that it is "second only to alcohol in global usage."[19] Surveys indicate that marijuana has been used at least once by over half of the population aged eighteen.[20] Thus, a relatively large number of users exist. A significant number are juveniles or young adults, middle class, white, and college educated.

Most marijuana users smoke the substance on a moderate basis (i.e., less than once a month). Only a very small percentage use it on a weekly basis. Unlike heroin, marijuana is mostly used in a group situation rather than in an individual setting. The reasons for "turning on" to marijuana vary with time. The drug was originally used by minority groups in the Southeast and Southwest. Early attempts to curb importation focused upon Mexicans and Mexican-Americans believed to be the prime source of the drug. For these people, marijuana was an economical, easily accessible source of pleasurable relief.

By the mid-1960s, marijuana was widely used among young, white, middle-class people as a "protest" drug. It symbolized a challenge to existing norms and values. The 1970s has witnessed marijuana usage passing from "hippies" or "radicals" to more conventional segments of the population. As a drug that has come to symbolize sophistication or "hipness" for many, penalties for possession and use have dropped in severity and application. Respectability has brought acceptance and a rather vocal movement calling for outright legalization of marijuana.

Although classified as a dangerous drug, there is inconsistent evidence that marijuana is particularly dangerous to the user or closely related to criminal behavior. Studies of the drug's effect have yielded conflicting results. Whenever a damaging claim is made on the basis of one investigation, another research finding tends to discredit that claim. Regarding crime, marijuana's relatively low cost, wide availability, and lack of addictive qualities do not encourage criminal behavior as does heroin. For these reasons, too, it is being increasingly argued that marijuana should not be classified as dangerous.

Alcoholics or Problem Drinkers

The most common type of substance abuser is the alcoholic or problem drinker. Alcohol itself is not illegal. However, those who repeatedly abuse it are likely to come into contact with the criminal justice system. Their crimes vary from public drunkenness or driving while intoxicated to manslaughter or homicide.

The condition commonly referred to as alcoholism lacks a clear, widely accepted definition. Even more difficult to define is the person who is labeled as being a "problem drinker." According to the Cooperative Commission on the Study of Alcoholism, an alcoholic is one who "has lost control over his [or her] alcohol intake in the sense that he [or she] is consistently unable to refrain from drinking or to stop drinking before becoming intoxicated.'' [21] Problem drinkers, a much broader category, includes those whose ''repetitive use of beverage alcohol cause[s] physical, psychological, or social harm to [themselves] or to others.'' [22] Alcoholics thus differ from problem drinkers in the degree of their commitment to alcohol. While both groups harm themselves and/or others, the alcoholic has considerably more difficulty in controlling his or her drinking than does the problem drinker.

Alcohol abuse, then, is more a matter of degree than of kind. It covers a broad territory of individuals. There are skid row derelicts who isolate themselves in a world of booze. There are also middle-class men and women who attempt to lead responsible lives but excessively use (abuse) alcohol as a crutch. For this reason, many prefer the term ''problem drinker'' to that of ''alcoholic.'' [23]

A profile of the known alcohol abuser, either an alcoholic or problem drinker, reveals one who is (1) a young to middle-age male, (2) lower or working class, (3) a minority group member, and (4) a city dweller. This, however, is a very narrow image of the alcohol abuser. Profiles such as this one are based on data gathered from public treatment programs, arrests for drunkenness or driving while intoxicated, and hospital admissions. Juveniles, middle-class males and females, white suburban and rural residents are less likely to receive official attention for alcohol abuse. These individuals typically seek necessary treatment from private physicians or counselors. Further, law enforcement agencies are more likely to allow them to handle their own problems or take them home upon detection rather than refer them to a public program or take them to jail for sobering up purposes.

Given the wide backgrounds of alcohol abusers, the broad range of ages (especially the growing number of juvenile abusers) and the circumstances of abusive drinking patterns, there is no distinct profile of the alcoholic or problem drinker. They may be young, old, black, white, rich, poor, male, female, and so on. Many speak of a so-called addiction-prone personality. However, several of the traits associated with this personality may be found in those who do not abuse alcohol. The only common characteristic among alcohol abusers is the existence of a personal problem for which alcohol is used as a source of relief.

Attempts have been made to define progressive stages in the development of alcoholism or problem drinking.[24] Nevertheless, all alcohol abusers do not go through these stages nor do they all go through them in the same order. While alcoholism has sometimes been thought of as a disease that is inherited or caused by biological factors, the evidence is neither consistent nor convincing.[25] The most that one can say about alcohol abuse (and other substances as well) is that it results from some combination of psychological and sociological conditions. The significance attached to one or more of the following factors may vary on the basis of the individual's age, race, and sex. These factors are:

1. Attitudes which promote drinking as a positive experience
2. Friends, relatives, or associates who share a favorable attitude toward drinking and do so excessively
3. A feeling of isolation, helplessness, or rejection regarding the rest of society

4. Acceptance of nonconforming and impulsive behavior
5. Feelings of doom, failure, or the impossibility of improvement
6. A lack of primary group sources (family, spouse, and friends) of behavior control [26]

SUMMARY

Offenses against public morality cover many types of behavior. Among these are sex offenders and substance abusers. This chapter discussed such sex offenders as pedophiliacs, exhibitionists and voyeurs, homosexuals, and prostitutes. Those involved in the use or abuse of heroin, marijuana, and alcohol were considered as substance abusers.

Sex offenders with victims (pedophiliacs, exhibitionists, and voyeurs) differ according to some attributes. However, they have similarities in that they are likely to be (1) nonviolent, (2) sexually passive, (3) repeaters, and (4) possessed by feelings of sexual inferiority. Homosexuality and prostitution (victimless sex offenses) are diverse categories. The people in these groups do not lend themselves to the development of a profile or typology. Efforts to establish causes of homosexuality and prostitution have not been successful. However, the decision to enter prostitution does appear to be related to certain experiences and attitudes.

Substance abuse tends to result from a combination of psychological and sociological factors. There is little in the way of conclusive evidence that this behavior is caused by biological conditions. Substances commonly abused include marijuana and alcohol. Although marijuana is usually smoked in moderation, it is considered as an abused drug because, by definition, it is illegal. Heroin abuse is not widespread. Heroin abusers or addicts fall within a narrow range, being lower class, urban, male, and members of minority groups. On the other hand, marijuana usage is spread throughout the population. Likewise, alcohol abusers come from a variety of backgrounds and social circumstances.

SUGGESTED ACTIVITIES

- By referring to your state's criminal code, list all offenses of a sexual nature (excluding rape) and the prescribed penalties.
- Discover if your state has a treatment program for sex offenders. If so, find out the particulars of the program. You may receive information about such programs by requesting a copy of *Treatment Programs for Sex Offenders* from:

  National Criminal Justice Reference Service
  Box 6000
  Rockville, Maryland 20850

- What kinds of narcotic and dangerous drug treatment programs exist in your community? Visit one and gather information about the program and the characteristics of its clients.
- If your community has an Alcoholics Anonymous chapter, contact it and request permission to attend a meeting. Ask the director about the nature of alcoholism and problem

drinking, the means used for their treatment, and the kinds of people who are alcohol abusers.

REVIEW

A. Define pedophiliac, exhibitionist, and voyeur; and list characteristics which are common to these three categories of sex offenders.

B. List three background features that facilitate a decision to enter prostitution.

C. Compare heroin abusers with marijuana smokers.

D. List six psychological or sociological factors that contribute to alcoholic and problem drinker behavior.

E. Multiple Choice. Select the best answer.

1. Pedophiliacs usually:
   a. rape their victims
   b. select girls as victims
   c. select boys as victims
   d. are eventually caught and prosecuted

2. Exhibitionists differ from pedophiliacs in that they:
   a. are predominantly male
   b. operate alone
   c. often victimize one person for a long period of time
   d. rarely victimize the same person more than once

3. Voyeurs differ from exhibitionists in that they:
   a. are more selective about victims
   b. usually choose female victims
   c. operate alone as adult offenders
   d. are usually older (i.e., above age 60 years)

4. Homosexuals:
   a. vary in their degree of commitment to homosexuality
   b. are usually child molesters
   c. are more likely to adopt an open homosexual life-style if they are female
   d. are usually exhibitionists

5. Most prostitutes:
   a. are females
   b. enter the "profession" while young
   c. operate on the basis of an economic motive
   d. all of these

6. Heroin abusers are typically:
   a. young, ghetto males with a prior criminal record
   b. young, ghetto males with no crime record prior to heroin usage
   c. older, ghetto males with a prior criminal record
   d. older, ghetto males with no prior criminal record

7. Marijuana users usually:
   a. smoke the substance on a weekly basis
   b. smoke the substance alone
   c. commit crimes to buy the drug
   d. use the drug moderately and rarely commit crimes in order to buy it

8. Alcoholics and problem drinkers:
   a. come from a broad background
   b. suffer from a personal problem for which alcohol provides a relief

      c. are motivated to drink by psychological and sociological conditions

      d. all of these

9. Which of the following is least likely to be found in the background of an alcoholic or problem drinker?

      a. feelings of isolation or helplessness

      b. negative attitudes toward drinking

      c. acceptance of nonconforming behavior patterns

      d. friends and family members who drink excessively

10. Pedophiliacs are generally:

      a. nonviolent offenders

      b. sexually aggressive individuals

      c. violent offenders

      d. one-time offenders

REFERENCES

1. Norval Morris and Gordon Hawkins, *The Honest Politician's Guide to Crime Control* (Chicago: University of Chicago Press, 1970), 15.
2. James D. Page, *Psychopathology* (New York: Aldine-Atherton, 1971), 378; See also Susan Brownmiller, *Against Our Will: Men, Women and Rape* (New York: Simon and Schuster, 1975), 278.
3. Paul H. Gebhard, et al., *Sex Offenders: An Analysis of Types* (New York: Harper and Row, 1965), 54–105.
4. James M. Reinhardt, *Sex Perversions and Sex Crimes* (Springfield, Ill.: Chas. C Thomas, 1957).
5. A. N. Groth, et al., "A Study of the Child Molester: Myths and Realities," *LAE Journal of the American Criminal Justice Association*, 41 (1978), 17–22.
6. Gebhard, et al., *op. cit.*, 81–82.
7. H. J. Vetter and I. J. Silverman, *Criminology and Crime* (New York: Harper and Row, 1986), 107; "Sexually Abused Children: Victims of a Horrifying Hidden Crime," *LEAA Newsletter*, August, 1978, 6–7.
8. Gebhard, et al., *op. cit.*, 380–399.
9. Sheldon B. Kopp, "The Character Structure of Sex Offenders," *American Journal of Psychotherapy*, 16 (1962), 64–65.
10. James C. Coleman, *Abnormal Psychology and Modern Life* (Glenview, Ill.: Scott, Foresman, 1980).
11. Gebhard, et al., *op. cit.*, 397.
12. *Ibid.*, 358–378.
13. Marvin Siegelman, "Parental Background of Male Homosexuals and Heterosexuals," *Archives of Sexual Behavior*, 3 (1974), 3–18.
14. See Charles H. McCaghy, *Deviant Behavior: Crime, Conflict and Interest Groups* (New York: Macmillan, 1976), 374.
15. Alfred C. Kinsey, et al., *Sexual Behavior in the Human Male* (Philadelphia: W. B. Saunders, 1948), 259.
16. McCaghy, *op. cit.*, 355–357.
17. National Institute of Drug Abuse, *Demographic Trends and Drug Abuse, 1980–1995* (Washington, D.C.: U.S. Government Printing Office, 1981); J. D. Miller and Associates, *National Survey on Drug Abuse, Main Findings, 1982* (Washington, D.C.: U.S. Government Printing Office, 1983).
18. James Vorenberg and Irvin Lukoff, "Addiction, Crime and the Criminal Justice System" (Paper presented to the Fifth National Methadone Conference, March 17–19, 1973), 2.
19. Sidney Cohen, *The Drug Dilemma* (New York: McGraw-Hill, 1969), 49.
20. Lloyd Johnston, et al., *Student Drug Use, Attitudes, and Beliefs* (Rockville, Md.: National Institute of Drug Abuse, 1982), 16.
21. Thomas F. A. Plaut, *Alcohol Problems: A Report to the Nation by the Cooperative Commission of the Study of Alcoholism* (New York: Oxford University Press, 1967), 39.
22. *Ibid.*, 38.

23. See McCaghy, *op. cit.*, 272.
24. See E. M. Jellinek, "Phases of Alcohol Addiction," in David J. Pittman and Charles R. Snyder (eds.) *Society, Culture and Drinking Patterns* (New York: John Wiley, 1962), 356–368; Robert J. Wicks and Jerome J. Platt, *Drug Abuse: A Criminal Justice Primer* (Beverly Hills: Glencoe Press, 1977), 18–19.
25. Julian B. Roebuck and Raymond G. Kessler, *The Etiology of Alcoholism: Constitutional, Psychological and Sociological Approaches* (Springfield, Ill.: Chas. C Thomas, 1972). Early studies also challenge the notion of inherited alcoholism; for example, Anne Roe, "The Adult Adjustment of Children of Alcoholic Parents Raised in Foster Homes," *Quarterly Journal of Studies on Alcohol*, 5 (1944), 380–382.
26. Don Cahalan, Ira H. Cisin, and Helen M. Crossley, *American Drinking Practices: A National Survey of Behavior and Attitudes* (New Brunswick: Rutgers Center of Alcohol Studies, 1969), 81–85.

19

Career and Occupational Criminals

OBJECTIVES

After studying this chapter, the student should be able to:

- Define career criminal and give examples.
- Trace the changes regarding career criminals and crime.
- Describe the occupational criminal and give examples.
- Provide actual cases of occupational criminal pursuits.

Career and occupational criminals routinely and systematically violate the law. Crime is a primary or major source of income. The behavior is long term and may even continue throughout a lifetime. Overall, the criminals in this group are most costly to society. There are two categories of criminals for which illegal acts are a significant source of income. First, there are those for whom crime is a central activity. These individuals are commonly called ''career criminals.'' Second, there are those for whom crime is a spin-off of an otherwise legitimate business or profession. These offenders are usually referred to as ''occupational criminals.''

CRIME AS A CENTRAL ACTIVITY: CAREER CRIMINALS

Crime is a central activity for professional offenders and members of criminal syndicates. Today, professional offenders make up a relatively small group of highly skilled criminals. With some exceptions, they are mature males who have limited criminal records, and with relatively few periods of imprisonment. Occasionally, they may commit different kinds of crime but there is a tendency to concentrate on one offense area, such as robbery, burglary, larceny, pickpocketing, or confidence games.

A professional class of criminals began to emerge in the late 1400s. The decline of feudalism led to the creation of roving groups of homeless and jobless men. These vagabonds or vagrants eventually spread throughout the countryside seeking shelter in the forests. Many were thieves, robbers, and swindlers. As towns increased in size and opportunities, many vagrant criminals settled in certain areas of the city. By the 1700s, there was a distinct class of professional criminals in England and other European countries. Upon being apprehended, many such men were deported to the colonies of the mother country. America was a favorite dumping ground for England's undesirables.[1] The transporting of convicts to such places as Virginia and Georgia did not end until the outbreak of the Revolutionary War.

During the early 1800s, a professional criminal subculture took root in the United States. It continued to flourish until the mid 1900s.[2] For this period of 150 years, professional criminals maintained the following characteristics: [3]

1. Commitment to crime as a livelihood.
2. Extensive planning of crimes and preparation for setbacks (arrests, prosecution, etc.).
3. Development of technical skills learned in association with other professionals. The skills were gained primarily through selective recruitment and became a source of great personal pride.
4. A sense of belonging to a distinct, high status criminal group which had its own:
   a. rules, code of behavior, or value system;
   b. philosophy toward life and the straight world;
   c. terminology and shared understandings.

As noted by Clinard and Quinney, professional criminals traditionally devoted themselves to a life of nonviolent offenses. The ability to score successfully without the use of force was a mark of skill. Violence or victim confrontation symbolized the work of an amateur. Thus, verbal skills and the ability to manipulate the victim were often more essential than manual skills. Recruitment and the teaching of technical skills were related to an intricate network of contacts, recommendations, and apprenticeships. The entire behavior system was held together by a sense of brotherhood or "we feeling." [4]

The characteristics of the professional criminal today have undergone considerable change.[5] To begin with, as a group they are fewer in number than in past decades. The subculture that fostered recruitment, skill development, and apprenticeships has largely disappeared. Technological changes in society (e.g., credit cards, improved safes and security systems) have reduced both profits and opportunities. The con games of days gone by are less easily executed as the public becomes more informed. Most swindlers today focus upon the opportunities available in what appears to be a legitimate business (e.g., finance companies, home repairs). Younger offenders are less inclined to specialize or to commit themselves solely to crime as a livelihood. Instead of the confident, patient professional, many of today's career criminals are more likely to be devil-may-care rounders or hustlers. According to the President's Commission, the hustler's life is one of:

moving around bars and being seen; it means asking "what's up." It means "connecting" in the morning with two others who have a burglary set up for the evening, calling a man you know to see if he wants to buy 10 stolen alpaca sweaters at $5 each, and scouting the streets for an easy victim. It means being versatile; passing bad checks, burglarizing a store. It's a planless kind of existence, but with a purpose—to make as much money as can be made each day, no holds barred.[6]

Nevertheless, there are still those people for whom crime is a central activity or primary business. Criminals who belong to crime societies or alliances make illegal behavior pay handsomely over the long run. Organized criminals existed in American cities following the Revolutionary War. In New York City these early gangs were mostly made up of young males of Irish heritage with such names as the O'Connell Guards, Bowery Boys, and Chichesters. Their activities focused upon extortion, vandalism, and intergang feuds.[7] Other large cities (e.g., Chicago) also had roving gangs of street hoodlums. They, too, were dominated by the children of Irish immigrants. Toward the end of the nineteenth century, urban gangs began to include Jewish, Slavic, and Italian youngsters.

Between 1890 and 1914, immigrants from Southern Italy and Sicily poured into the United States.[8] Their sons soon found excitement and opportunities in the crowded streets of tenement districts. They formed juvenile gangs, dropped out of school as soon as legally possible, and devoted themselves to delinquent pursuits. One account of a leading crime society figure reveals the early development pattern for syndicate members.

Frank Costello went to school at P.S. 172, a red-brick building that has since been demolished. He evidently didn't profit from the experience, for he left when he was in the fifth grade to work in his father's grocery store. He learned what he needed to know in the streets. . . . He learned that there were other ways to make a buck than selling tomato paste to fat ladies. . . . He . . . absorbed the lesson[s]—don't be a sucker, get tough, make a buck, get out of the ghetto and get some respect for yourself.[9]

One of the best known groups to be led by an Italian (Paola Vaccarelli) was the Five Points Gang in New York City. The gang's chief concerns were heavy street crime (e.g., robbery and extortion) and prostitution. Many future syndicate men got their start as Five Pointers (e.g., Lucky Luciano and Al Capone).[10] With the coming of Prohibition, young Italian gang members moved into the lucrative bootlegging business. To ensure the maximization of profits, the gangs were structured and organized along the lines of a business concern. By 1930, Italians had become the dominant ethnic group involved in organized crime. These new crime syndicates (known as "families") included non-Italians as well. After Prohibition, other sources of income were developed, such as gambling, loansharking, labor racketeering, and drugs.[11]

Members of crime families gain admission through recruitment and proven worth to the organization. At the lower levels, candidates tend to work their way into the family through successful careers as conventional criminals. Many begin as members of local juvenile gangs. The sons of ranking members may qualify by virtue of needed skills (accounting) or professional training (law) in addition to family connections. Regardless of the method of entry and the position within the organization, membership is typically maintained throughout life.

Organization members more or less share a code of values that serves to protect the criminal operation. Secrecy is a major concern that is occasionally violated. Members are impressed with the notion that the organization is above the individual and that its needs come first. A man's personal family is largely insulated from criminal activities as well as internal and external threats. This means that wives and small children are told very little about the "business." Further, a member's family is to be shielded from violence and harassment whether it comes from organizational feuds or law enforcement activities.[12] The code represents an ideal set of rules. To be sure, the rules are broken or altered. But they are outwardly emphasized and supported.

The behavioral code of crime societies and alliances serves to isolate members from the rest of society. The wives and children of crime society figures tend to associate with those of organized crime families. Marriages are promoted between the sons and daughters of syndicate members. The code also provides a set of jurisdictions for the life-style of crime society members. The government and authority figures are looked upon with contempt. The public is thought of as being hypocritical. It is recognized that people often support or demand laws against some goods and services but, nevertheless, are willing purchasers of these illegal goods and services.

The nature of the crime family is changing. Many of the grandchildren and great grandchildren of syndicate founders are marrying "outsiders," choosing legitimate careers and abandoning the old values. As noted by the Iannis:

> The fourth generation . . . is even more dispersed geographically and socially than the third generation . . . they have far more friends outside the clan, even outside the Italian-American community, than their parents ever had. . . . Most of the sons have entered professions, and most of the daughters have married professional businessmen.[13]

The changing character of the syndicate criminal is due in large part to the changing character of syndicate crime. Much of the "dirty" business (drugs, prostitution, numbers, etc.) is being shared with blacks, Cubans, and Puerto Ricans. New ventures into legitimate markets (real estate, resorts, etc.) require different perspectives and skills. However, crime is still the central feature of the society although it is becoming increasingly diluted by legitimate concerns.

CRIME AS A SPIN-OFF OF LEGITIMATE BUSINESS OR PROFESSIONS: OCCUPATIONAL CRIMINALS

White-collar criminals are offenders whose main concern is legitimate business but who, "in the course of his [her] occupation,"[14] may occasionally or repeatedly commit crimes. When several white-collar (corporate officials) offenders join together for purposes of crime, a corporate criminal alliance is formed. It shares many of the features found among organized crime societies.[15]

The white-collar criminal may be a businessperson, professional (lawyer or physician), or political official. The crimes may be against the person's own corporation through embezzlement or the theft of company goods. The public may also be the victim through dishonest advertising, consumer fraud, or the misappropriation of public funds. Offenders are likely to be male and white, and are often, but not necessarily, middle class.[16] It should be noted, however, that as increasing numbers of women and minorities enter the business, professional, and political worlds, the profile of the white-collar criminal is expected to change. But, since female and minority inroads into positions of substantial corporate and professional power remain minimal,[17] changes in the occupational crime picture are not likely to be significant.

Whether the crime is committed by corporate officials, lower-level employees, professionals, or political figures, the white-collar criminal has the following objectives: [18]

1. An intent to commit a wrongful act or to achieve a purpose inconsistent with law or public policy.
2. An effort to disguise purpose or intent.
3. Concealment of the crime by
    a. preventing the victim from realizing that he has been victimized, or
    b. relying on the fact that only a small percentage of victims will react to what has happened, and making provisions for restitution to or other handling of the disgruntled victim, or
    c. creation of a deceptive paper, organizational, or transactional facade to disguise the true nature of what has occurred.

The following cases provide some insights into the background characteristics of white-collar criminals and their crimes.

The Engineering of a Corporate Fraud

The B. F. Goodrich Company once received a contract to supply brake assemblies for a new Air Force plane. The contract was awarded primarily because the company proposed brake units that weighed less and were less expensive to manufacture than those of competing firms. Unfortunately, preliminary tests indicated that the brake system was faulty and unquestionably dangerous. What had made the brake system appealing (light and economical) also contributed to its inefficiency. The brakes were simply too small to stop safely a rapidly moving jet plane. Examinations following laboratory tests designed to simulate routine aircraft landings revealed that the brakes "glowed a bright cherry-red and threw off incandescent particles of metal [while] . . . the linings were found to be almost completely disintegrated." [19]

Several officials of Goodrich's development and testing section purposely concealed the faulty brake design. Certain test results were altered, fabricated, or omitted in order to preserve the contract. Those involved in the conspiracy were middle class, college educated, and in other ways, respectable men. Using all sorts of justifications, they furthered the fraud for the sake of personal security.

> An expert engineer, Gretzinger had been responsible for several innovations in brake design. It was he who had invented the unique brake system used on the famous XB70.

A graduate of Georgia Tech, he was a stickler for detail and he had some very firm ideas about honesty and ethics. . . .

"You know," he went on uncertainly, looking down at his desk, "I've been an engineer for a long time, and I've always believed that ethics and integrity were every bit as important as theorems and formulas, and never once has anything happened to change my beliefs. Now this. . . . Hell, I've got two sons I've got to put through school and I just . . . ." His voice trailed off. . . .

. . . "Well, it looks like we're licked. The way it stands now, we're to go ahead and prepare the data and other things for the graphic presentation in the report, and when we're finished, someone upstairs will actually write the report."

"After all," he continued, "we're just drawing some curves, and what happens to them after they leave here, well, we're not responsible for that." [20]

Shortly after this, a test pilot skidded his plane over a quarter of a mile before finally stopping.[21] Eventually, there were hearings before a Senate subcommittee chaired by Senator Proxmire. As a result, the Defense Department revised its requirements for testing procedures and Goodrich redesigned the brake. However, the Goodrich executives primarily involved in the fraud either maintained their jobs or were promoted.

Diseased Practices and Health Insurance

Patients who possess health insurance are often desirable targets for physician-thieves. Medical doctors have generally been able to charge whatever they choose without the likelihood of being challenged by insurance companies. Only recently have the companies begun systematically to balk at excessive fees. The guilty physicians usually rationalize their behavior as harmless, and very few ever consider themselves to be criminals. There are several techniques whereby unethical physicians steal from health care insurance programs. One method involves providing unnecessary treatment in order to drive up the bill. In a reported case, a physician:

snowballed the costs of treating an insured case after a policyholder wanted a small wart removed from the back of his hand. The doctor arranged to have the procedure done in a hospital, thereby, raising the insurance payment to him from $15 to $37.50. This simple operation required only Novocain, which the doctor himself administered by injection. But the hospital's anesthetist billed the insurance company for $25, and the hospital charged for a day's room and board even though the patient was never in a hospital bed. The bills for the removal of a wart measuring less than a quarter of an inch totaled about $200, all so the doctor could collect the higher insurance payment.[22]

The greatest source of abuse arises from overcharging or fee inflation. Greedy physicians sometimes up their fees once they learn that a patient is a health policyholder. In one California case,

a surgeon operated on an eleven-year-old boy for a hernia and undescended testicle. Believing the family carried insurance, he submitted a bill for $3,500. Although the policy had not yet gone into effect, the insurance company protested in behalf of the boy's parents. Ultimately they got a revised billing of $500.[23]

A major problem with physicians who cheat is that they operate under a cloak of public trust. The public is frequently not in a position to judge either the quality or the quantity of a physician's required services. Further, when a third party (insurance company) is paying the fee, the incentive for challenging the charges is to some degree removed. Far too often, the medical profession is reluctant to censure the undesirable members within its ranks. However, unless the medical profession makes a serious effort to "clean up its act," greater federal control should be expected.[24]

POLITICIANS FOR PROFIT

Political corruption typically takes three forms: misfeasance, malfeasance, and nonfeasance. Misfeasance is the wrongful carrying out of an otherwise legal act. Malfeasance is the commission of an illegal act. Nonfeasance is the failure to commit or carry out a required act.

In 1971, the Knapp Commission of New York City uncovered established practices smacking of misfeasance, malfeasance, and nonfeasance. Large payoffs were given to the police, inspectors, and permit agency personnel in return for nonenforcement of construction codes. In addition, builders and contractors were able to avoid harassment by paying bribes demanded by the police and their superiors. According to the Knapp Commission Report:

> In a small job like the renovation of a brownstone, the general contractor was likely to pay the police between $50 and $150 a month, and the fee ascended sharply for larger jobs. An excavator on a small job paid $50 to $100 a week for the duration of excavation to avoid summonses for dirt, spillage, flying dust, double-parked dump trucks, or for running vehicles over the sidewalk without a permit. A concrete company pouring a foundation paid another $50 to $100 a week to avoid summonses for double-parking its trucks or for running them across a sidewalk without a curb cut.[25]

So-called machine politics contribute greatly to political corruption. Large cities are divided into precincts and wards. Each unit has a leader, often called a "precinct captain" or "ward boss." In return for delivering votes on election day, these bosses are given control over various numbers of patronage jobs. The patronage jobs (from sewer inspector to assistant state's attorney) are then doled out to the party faithful. The recipients are expected to contribute votes in future elections. In addition, they are expected to perform favors for their sponsors or secure future votes by doing favors for the "right people." Favors may be "free" or may come only after a bribe has been paid.

Corruption has been a visible part of American politics for some time. Its roots go deep and far beyond the Watergate affair. There are no simple solutions. Corruption sometimes arises because political machines are able to meet needs otherwise unavailable through legitimate government channels. Corruption may also spring from misplaced values that, unless redirected, will continue to erode legitimate government.

> As long as we countenance violence, consider personal gain to be more important than equity, are . . . willing to bend the law for ourselves in the pursuit of wealth, power, and personal gratification and to persuade government officials, through corrupt dealings, to cooperate in that process—to that extent we will have a society receptive to illicit enterprise generally.[26]

SUMMARY

Crime is a primary source of income for both career criminals and occupational offenders. For career criminals, illegal acts form a central activity. Examples would include professional offenders and members of criminal syndicates. The nature of career crime and criminals has changed in recent times. They are fewer in number. The subculture that provided recruitment, training, and apprenticeships is nearly extinct. Technological changes in society have also taken their toll. Instead of the confident, smooth professional, many of today's career criminals are opportunistic hustlers.

However, crime is still a central activity for the career criminal belonging to a crime syndicate. American crime syndicates can be traced to the street gangs that developed in the late 1800s. Children of various ethnic stock dropped out of school and devoted themselves to delinquent pursuits. With the coming of Prohibition, young Italian gang members moved into the lucrative bootlegging business. After Prohibition, other sources of income were developed such as gambling, loansharking, labor racketeering, and drugs. The activities of crime families now entail a large portion of otherwise legitimate ventures. Membership is based on needed skills, the "right attitude," and connections. An operating behavioral code serves to isolate syndicate members from the rest of society. The nature of the crime family is changing as are the characteristics of the descendants of syndicate founders.

Crime is a spin-off for many occupations. It becomes a major money-making enterprise for some businessmen, professionals, and politicians. So-called white-collar criminals steal billions from the public each year. These offenders differ from career criminals in that they are typically respectable, solid middle-class, college-educated individuals. Their illegal pursuits are based upon long-range deviance and contempt for the public good. Actual cases of corporate, professional, and political crime are presented in this chapter. They provide some insights into the background characteristics of white-collar criminals and their crimes.

SUGGESTED ACTIVITIES

- List some common forms of hustling that have replaced traditional career criminal activities. Talk with a local law enforcement official.
- Review your city newspapers or those of another large city for stories on crime family members. Do these stories tell you anything about that "family's" life-style?

REVIEW

A. Define a career criminal and give two examples.

B. Define an occupational criminal and give three examples.

C. List four characteristics commonly found among career criminals.

D. List three major objectives of white-collar (occupational) criminals.

E. Multiple Choice. Select the best answer.

1. A professional class of criminals first appeared in Europe following the:
   - a. decline of feudalism
   - b. Norman Conquest
   - c. Protestant Reformation
   - d. French Revolution

2. A professional (career) criminal subculture first arose in the United States after:
   - a. the Civil War
   - b. 1950
   - c. the late 1700s
   - d. World War I

3. Traditional career criminals avoid:
   - a. con games
   - b. street crimes
   - c. big scores
   - d. violence

4. Career criminals have largely been replaced by:
   - a. hustlers
   - b. females
   - c. better-trained experts
   - d. square johns

5. Organized criminals:
   - a. no longer exist
   - b. are found primarily in western states
   - c. have channeled their concerns into legitimate areas
   - d. have always been Italians

6. The behavior code of crime syndicates:
   - a. is always obeyed
   - b. is never obeyed
   - c. isolates members from the rest of society
   - d. stresses charity toward other members

7. Which of the following is not an example of an occupational criminal?
   - a. a corporate executive who conspires to fix prices
   - b. a con artist
   - c. a physician who defrauds a health insurance company
   - d. a politician who takes bribes

8. Occupational criminals differ from career criminals in that occupational criminals:
   - a. have more money
   - b. are less criminal
   - c. are more organized
   - d. have greater public acceptance and respectability

9. Which of the following is the greatest source of physician fraud regarding health insurance policies?
   - a. fee splitting
   - b. fee inflation or overcharging
   - c. embezzlement
   - d. narcotics sales

REFERENCES

1. James A. Inciardi, *Careers in Crime* (Chicago: Rand McNally, 1975), 7–11.
2. *Ibid.*, 75–76.
3. Edwin H. Sutherland, *The Professional Thief* (Chicago: University of Chicago Press, 1937), 2–42. Sutherland's use of the term "theft" applies to a general category of crimes wherein the wrongful taking of money or property is the object.
4. Marshall B. Clinard and Richard Quinney, *Criminal Behavior Systems* (New York: Holt, Rinehart and Winston, 1973), 249–258.
5. *Ibid.*, 260.
6. President's Commission on Law Enforcement and the Administration of Justice, *Task Force Report: Assessment of Crime* (Washington, D.C.: U.S. Government Printing Office, 1967), 97. See also, Michael H. Agar, *Ripping and Running* (New York: Academic Press, 1973).
7. Herbert Asbury, "The Gangs of New York," in Gus Tyler (ed.) *Organized Crime in America* (Ann Arbor: University of Michigan Press, 1971), 96.
8. Humbert S. Nelli, *The Business of Crime* (New York: Oxford University Press, 1976), 103.
9. Henry A. Zeiger, *Frank Costello* (New York: Berkley Publishing Corp., 1974), 6.
10. Nelli, *op. cit.*, 107.
11. Francis A. J. Ianni, *A Family Business* (New York: Russell Sage, 1972), 58–59.
12. Ralph Salerno and John Tompkins, "Rules to Live By," in Nicholas Gage (ed.) *Mafia, U.S.A.* (Chicago: Playboy Press, 1972), 194–200.
13. Francis A. J. Ianni and Elizabeth Reuss-Ianni, "The Godfather Is Going Out of Business," *Psychology Today*, 9 (1975), 92.
14. See James W. Coleman, *The Criminal Elite* (New York: St. Martin's Press, 1985), 2–5.
15. See Section 4, Chapter 13 of this text.
16. Edwin H. Sutherland, "White-Collar Criminality," *American Sociological Review*, 5 (1940), 11.
17. Eileen B. Leonard, *Women, Crime and Society* (New York: Longman, 1982), 20–24.
18. Herbert Edelhertz, *The Nature, Impact and Prosecution of White-Collar Crime* (Washington, D.C.: U.S. Government Printing Office, 1970), 12.
19. Kermit Vandiver, "Why Should My Conscience Bother Me?" in M. David Ermann and Richard J. Lundman (eds.) *Corporate and Governmental Deviance* (New York: Oxford University Press, 1978), 83.
20. *Ibid.*, 88, 90.
21. *Ibid.*, 96.
22. Howard R. Lewis and Martha E. Lewis, *The Medical Offenders* (New York: Simon and Schuster, 1970), 128.
23. *Ibid.*, 130.
24. "Weeding Out the Incompetents," *Time*, May 26, 1986, 57–58.
25. Knapp Commission, "Official Corruption and the Construction Industry," in Jack D. Douglas and John M. Johnson (eds.) *Official Deviance* (Philadelphia: J. B. Lippincott Co., 1977), 229.
26. Dwight C. Smith, Jr., *The Mafia Mystique* (New York: Basic Books, 1975), 335.

20

Nature and Purpose of Law

OBJECTIVES

After studying this chapter, the student should be able to:

- Discuss the purpose of law and define and describe its constituent elements.
- Distinguish between natural and positive law.
- Describe the nature and function of statute and case law.
- Explain the nature and effect of constitutional requirements.
- Distinguish between substantive and procedural law.
- Delineate the process by which law is created in the United States and the mechanisms used for enforcing the law.

In our discussions of criminology and criminal justice, the term "law" is one to which we often refer. "Law" is a term that is frequently used without any deep consideration of exactly what it is and how it comes into existence. In this chapter, the nature and purpose of law and the process by which it is created are examined.

THE MEANING AND PURPOSE OF LAW

As defined by Funk and Wagnalls, law is "a rule of conduct, recognized by custom or decreed by formal enactment, considered by a community, nation or other authoritatively constituted group as binding upon its members." [1] It is a formal system of rules according to which people are expected to conduct their lives.

Consider the following situation:

Smith owns a construction company. He agrees to build a house for Jones. Six months after the house has been built and Jones and his family have moved in, it suddenly collapses. No one is hurt, but the Jones' lose all of their possessions. Jones is furious. He purchases a gun and shoots Smith.

In the situation described above, Jones is said to have ''taken the law into his own hands.'' He has had a misfortune befall him; he has decided that Smith is to blame; and he has decided upon the appropriate remedy—shooting Smith. In most countries, however, Jones will have acted against the law; for there are rules and regulations stating what he should do if someone appears to have wronged him. Shooting that person is not usually one of the options. Indeed, such an act by Jones will generally result in legal action being taken against him.

Law may be considered to be a formal mechanism for regulating conduct. It describes ways in which people should behave and transact their business. It describes what should happen to those individuals who do not act in an appropriate manner. Law is also a means of promoting peace and order in a complex society. It is a method of social control in much the same way religion was, and still is, for many segments of the population.

THE ELEMENTS OF LAW

Thus far our discussion has focused on the purpose of law. But what exactly does law consist of? Theorists have debated for centuries about the meaning and nature of law. For our purposes, the following is offered as a working definition of law:

Explicit rules of conduct, created and enforced by a sovereign state, with planned use of sanctions to support the rules and designated officials to interpret and enforce those rules.[2]

This definition contains four distinctive elements:

1. Explicit rules of conduct
2. Planned use of sanctions to support the rules
3. Designated officials to interpret and enforce those rules
4. The body of rules must be created and enforced by a sovereign state.

As stated previously, one of the purposes of law is to provide a set of instructions for conduct, both personal and business. The first element of law previously cited (the existence of specific rules of conduct) would appear, therefore, to be essential. In order for people to know what is considered appropriate, the rules must exist. Since these rules are to act as a guide, they need to be reasonably specific, understandable, and known by those to whom they apply.

That law consists of a series of instructions, rather than commands, may seem surprising at first. Most of us are familiar with the fact that the law tells us how to go about buying a house, making a will, obtaining a driver's license, and doing innumerable other things. In this area of law we are dealing with positive acts (things we can do) and appropriate ways of doing them. When we turn to acts we should not do, we may expect them to appear as they do in the Bible, as a set of commands, such as: "Thou shalt not kill." [3] This, however, is not reality. Few, if any, legal codes will contain such a provision. It is far more likely that something along the following lines will exist:

> A murder which shall be perpetrated by means of poison, lying in wait, imprisonment, starving, torture, or by any other kind of willful, deliberate, and premeditated killing, or which shall be committed in the perpetration or attempted perpetration of any arson, rape, robbery, kidnapping, burglary, or other felony committed or attempted with the use of a deadly weapon, shall be deemed to be murder in the first degree, and any person who commits such murder shall be punished with death or imprisonment in the State's prison for life as the court shall determine pursuant to G.S. 15A-2000. [4]

What we have here is a definition of the prohibited behavior and a set of instructions as to what can be done to an individual who indulges in such behavior. Thus the law states what people should not do, and what should happen to those who nonetheless act in the prohibited manner. This leads us to the second element of our definition of law—the planned use of sanctions to support the rules.

It is unreasonable to expect everybody to abide by all of the rules of conduct all of the time. Thus there must be some inducement to encourage compliance with the rules. This may occasionally take the form of a positive inducement, such as the promise of a reward for turning in a criminal. More regularly it will consist of a threat of adverse action in the case of noncompliance. Since noncompliance is always a possibility, there must be some prearranged plan of action for that situation, should it arise.

If Smith, in our earlier example, was negligent in the way he built Jones' home, he would probably have to pay Jones damages. If Jones, as appears likely, shot Smith without a legally justifiable reason, he too might have to pay a penalty for his action. For Jones, this might well be imprisonment. The point here is that a breach of the law might be followed by adverse action being taken against the offending party. Without the existence of planned use of sanctions, the law, it is believed, would have "no teeth." It would be disregarded and would become ineffective since there would be no incentive to abide by it.

The existence of specific rules of conduct and planned use of sanctions to support those rules are necessary elements of law. They are not by themselves, however, sufficient to establish an orderly and workable system of law; for however well phrased and specific a law may be, its meaning and applicability may not be totally self-evident. A definition of murder was given previously. Though its meaning may appear clear at first, a more thorough examination of the provision may raise some questions. Does the provision, for example, cover the situation where Adams pulls a gun on Banks and Banks shoots and kills Adams in self-defense? How about if Banks shoots and kills

Adams while Adams is advancing at him with a knife? How about if Adams is advancing on Banks unarmed, but with his hands raised, ready for action? Obviously, there is a need for a third party who will examine the rules of law, decide whether they apply in the particular situation, and if they do apply, enforce them accordingly. This gives rise to the third element of law, cited in our working definition, the existence of designated officials to interpret and enforce the rules.

Even with the addition of this element, our definition of law is not complete; for these three elements could apply just as well to an administrative body or an organization such as a corporation, a university, or a local rape crisis center. Each may well have its own rules and regulations, with planned use of sanctions to support the rules and designated officials to interpret and enforce the rules. What is needed is that

> the body of rules (be) created and enforced by a sovereign state. The state is seen as a political community which governs a territory and all the inhabitants within it.[5]

This would include, for example, the State of California and the country France, but not a corporation or a university.

NATURAL AND POSITIVE LAW

Now that both the nature and purpose of law have been discussed, it is important to examine the process by which law is created. A distinction that has long been made, and has been discussed in Section 1, is that between natural and positive (human-made) law. The term positive law, or *ius positum*, refers to the law actually created by the appropriate authority in a sovereign state. It is human-made law and as such is tied to a particular time and place. Positive law is the duly created law of the land, the law to be found in the law books. Laws prohibiting taking certain drugs, gambling, working as a prostitute, or driving faster than 55 miles per hour would all constitute examples of positive law.

Natural law, or *ius naturale*, on the other hand, is law believed to come from a higher source, law which exists whatever the enactments of humans. It is:

> A system of rules and principles for the guidance of human conduct which, independently of enacted law or of the systems peculiar to any one people, might be discovered by the rational intelligence of man.[6]

Thus while positive law is human-made, changeable, and temporary, natural law is abstract, everlasting, and everywhere. It is, however, not easily found. It decrees, for example, that it is wrong to take another's life except in certain circumstances. The nature of those circumstances is, however, subject to debate and has to be interpreted by humans, generally in the form of positive law. Thus, for our purposes, we will focus on positive, rather than natural, law. We will now begin to examine the procedures by which humans create law.

STATUTE AND CASE LAW

Generally there are two sources from which positive law is derived. These are (1) statute, and (2) case law. Statute refers to an act of the legislative branch of government, which declares, commands, or prohibits something.[7] The legislative branch of government refers to that part of the government entrusted with law-making powers. With regard to the United States federal government, for example, a statute would be an act of Congress approved by the president (or if vetoed by the president, passed with a two-thirds majority of each house). It might be an act that, for example, prohibited the importation of marijuana or an act that required citizens to register with the Draft Board. Statutes are general in nature and are aimed at the citizenry, or a particular defined segment of the citizenry. Statutes do, however, need to be interpreted and applied in particular cases. This a function which is left largely to the courts and case law.

Case law is judge-made law. It emanates from the decision in a particular case, but has impact beyond the facts of that particular case. It may involve the interpretation of a statute, endow a custom with the stamp of law, or establish a new principle of law.

A fundamental purpose of law is to maintain a well-ordered and peaceful society. While a decision has to be made in a particular case, it is an accepted maxim that "like cases should be treated alike." Thus it is that a decision in one case may have an important bearing on a later case.

Suppose, for example, that Judge Sweet has decided that Ms. Smith is entitled to keep her engagement ring after her fiancé broke their engagement. It seems only fair that Judge Sour, faced with the same situation in Ms. Brown's case, should make a similar decision. Judge Sweet would have established a precedent, which would have provided an authoritative guide for Judge Sour to follow.

This following of precedents is part of the legal doctrine of *stare decisis*, which literally means let the decision stand. It embodies the notion that judges should abide by the rulings in earlier cases.

The extent to which Judge Sweet's decision is binding upon Judge Sour would depend upon how the judges were related to each other in the court hierarchy. The higher judge would possess the greater authority. If Judge Sour was at the same level as Judge Sweet and rendered a verdict against Ms. Brown, then Ms. Brown would in all probability be entitled to appeal to a higher court. Court structure and judges' powers are matters which will be investigated in greater detail in Section 8.

GOVERNMENT CONSTITUTIONS

It is legislatures and courts that play significant roles in the creation and development of law. Their activities are not, however, given totally free reign; for they are usually constrained by the dictates of government constitutions. These constitutions contain fundamental principles to which acts of the legislature must conform and which the courts must take into account when rendering their decisions.

The federal and the state governments have their own constitutions. The federal Constitution is binding upon all of the states in the union. Each state constitution is binding upon only its own state.

THE BILL OF RIGHTS

The first ten amendments to the federal Constitution, known as the Bill of Rights, were enacted in 1791 solely as limitations upon the federal government. In 1868 the Fourteenth Amendment was passed. It placed federal constitutional restrictions upon the states' treatment of their subjects. Among other provisions the Fourteenth Amendment declares that no state shall "deprive any person of life, liberty or property without due process of the law." [8] Interpretation of this "due process" clause by the United States Supreme Court has over the years resulted on a case by case basis in nearly all of the criminal law provisions contained in the Bill of Rights being held applicable to the states. Thus the Fourth Amendment freedom against unreasonable search and seizure,[9] the Fifth Amendment provisions against self-incrimination [10] and double jeopardy,[11] and the Sixth Amendment rights to assistance of counsel,[12] speedy trial,[13] trial by jury,[14] and confrontation of witnesses [15] have all been held to apply to the states. Indeed, the only provision which definitely still does not apply to the states is the Fifth Amendment requirement that prosecution of infamous crimes be by grand jury indictment.[16]

LEGISLATIVE FUNCTIONS WITHIN THE UNITED STATES

In the United States, laws are passed at different levels—federal, state, and local. Each level has its own formally constituted method of enacting law. At the federal level, it is the Senate and House of Representatives which are jointly responsible for making laws. At the state level, it is the state legislature. At the local level, it is the duly constituted city or county body.

Each of these units of government can pass laws relating to its own legitimate areas of concern. The federal government can pass laws concerning matters of federal interest, such as issues relating to the operation of the U.S. Postal Service or interstate crimes (crimes committed in more than one state). The states, meanwhile, can enact laws regulating the lives of people situated within their respective state boundaries. This would include such matters as setting the minimum ages for driving, marriage, and drinking alcohol within that state, the types of activities that would constitute state crimes and the punishments therefor, and the amount of state income tax to be paid. The local communities, finally, are able to pass local laws (ordinances) which would apply to persons living within their boundaries. This might involve such matters as driving speed limits and opening hours for shops and bars.

The laws passed by these different governmental units, of course, must comply with the provisions of the federal Constitution. Suppose, for example, that a state, on January 1, 1987, made it illegal to have sung in the bathtub in 1986. Richards is prosecuted for singing in his bathtub on February 20, 1986. Is it fundamentally fair for him to be prosecuted for an act which was not an offense when he committed it? Fortunately for Richards, under Article 1 Section 10 of the United States Constitution, the States are forbidden to pass "any *ex post facto* law." They are not allowed to pass any law which retroactively changes the legal consequences of an act in such an adverse fashion. Thus the law passed by that state would be unconstitutional, and Richards could not be punished for having sung in his bathtub in 1986.

In addition to complying with the dictates of the federal Constitution, state and local legislative bodies are also bound by the provisions of their respective state constitutions.

SUBSTANTIVE AND PROCEDURAL LAW

The types of law passed by the respective governmental legislative units may be classified as either substantive or procedural law. Substantive law is that part of law that outlines duties, rights, and obligations. It would include, for example, the criminal code which contains the various criminal offenses. Procedural law, on the other hand, is that part of the law that defines the way in which rights are to be enforced, legal redress is to be obtained, and law violators are to be prosecuted. In the criminal justice area, for example, procedural law would outline the methods to be employed for apprehending, charging, trying, convicting, and sentencing offenders.

THE ENFORCEMENT OF LAW

While substantive law provides a listing of the rules and regulations that should be followed, procedural law describes the mechanisms to be employed in enforcing them. In the case of noncompliance, procedural law describes the processes for providing redress and imposing penalties. Essential to the functioning of this system is the existence of personnel who will be responsible for seeing that the laws are enforced. Thus, there are internal revenue agents, health inspectors, housing inspectors, and law enforcement officials. Each is responsible, within his or her own area of concern, for seeing that there is compliance with legal requirements, and for initiating action in the case of noncompliance. In many areas, private citizens may of their own accord initiate actions against alleged wrongdoers. Allegations of wrongdoing, complaints, and disputes will be referred through the appropriate channels for resolution. Everything proceeds according to a prearranged plan. This is, after all, to be expected from our insistence that for the existence of law there be "planned use of sanctions to support the rules and designated officials to interpret and enforce those rules." [17] A detailed examination of the means of enforcing the criminal law is to be found in the following sections of this book.

SUMMARY

In this chapter, the nature and purpose of law have been discussed. Law is considered to be a formal mechanism for regulating conduct, a measure of social control, and a means of promoting peace and order in a complex society.

Law consists of four elements, and all four are considered essential for the existence of law. There must be explicit rules of conduct. There must be planned use of sanctions to support the rules. There must be designated officials to interpret and enforce those rules. And, in order to distinguish the rules and regulations of a corporation or university from the laws of a politically organized society, the body of rules must be created and enforced by a sovereign state.

A distinction was made between positive and natural law. Positive law is human-made law, the law created by the appropriate authority in a sovereign state; natural law, on the other hand, comes from a higher source, involves universally correct values, and exists regardless of the enactments of humans.

The two major sources of positive law are statute and case law. Statutory law is the enactments of the legislative branch of government; case law is judge-made law. While statutes are general in nature, case law is law that emanates from the decision in a particular case, but which has impact beyond the facts of that case. Of importance in case law is the judicial concept of precedent, the proposition that like cases should be decided alike.

Legislative enactments and judicial decisions usually have to comply with the dictates of government constitutions. In the United States, the legislative pronouncements of federal, state, and local authorities must comply with the provisions of federal and state constitutions.

A distinction was made between substantive and procedural law. While substantive law provides a listing of the rules and regulations that should be followed, procedural law describes the mechanisms to be employed in enforcing them.

Finally, in order for a system of law to function effectively, there must be a body of officials entrusted with overseeing the enforcement of the law, and prearranged procedures established for processing complaints, hearing disputes, punishing wrongdoers, and compensating the wronged.

SUGGESTED ACTIVITIES

- Write down what you believe to be the minimum legal age for drinking, driving, or getting married in your state. Locate the appropriate statute to verify or refute what you thought.

- Locate any criminal statute from your state and compare it to the North Carolina law against murder as given in this chapter. Describe in simple terms (1) the prohibited behavior or behaviors, and (2) the sanction for indulging in the prohibited behavior.

- Obtain a copy of the United States Constitution and list at least two requirements that any legislation enacted in the United States must meet. Consult the *United States Supreme Court Reports* and explain how these requirements have been applied in cases.

- Obtain a copy of your state constitution and list at least two requirements that any legislation enacted in your state must fulfill. Consult the appropriate court reports and explain how these requirements have been applied in cases.

- Give an example of natural law and explain why you feel it fits in this category. Do you think everyone would agree with you?

REVIEW

A. Briefly explain the purpose of law.

B. State the four elements necessary for law to exist.

C. Distinguish statute law from case law.

D. Describe constitutional requirements and give an example of one.

E. Distinguish between substantive and procedural law.

F. Multiple Choice. Select the best answer.

1. Which of the following is not necessary for law to exist?
   - a. explicit rules of conduct
   - b. planned use of sanctions
   - c. designated officials to interpret and enforce the rules
   - d. a prison system

2. The use of precedent is a component of
   - a. natural law
   - b. positive law
   - c. statute law
   - d. case law

3. The minimum ages for driving, drinking alcohol, and getting married in the United States are set by
   - a. the Constitution
   - b. the federal government
   - c. state legislation
   - d. local ordinances

4. A law regulating the postal service would most appropriately be enacted by
   - a. the federal government
   - b. the state legislature
   - c. the local council
   - d. none of these

5. The judicial principle that judges should give similar decisions in similar cases is known as
   - a. judicial legislation
   - b. precedent
   - c. constitutional lawmaking
   - d. case law

6. Constitutional requirements contain fundamental principles to be observed by
   - a. legislatures
   - b. judges
   - c. police officers
   - d. all of these

7. Law which involves universally correct values and which comes from a higher source is referred to as
   - a. supernatural law
   - b. natural law
   - c. positive law
   - d. none of these

8. The branch of the law which specifies the methods to be used in enforcing the law is known as
   - a. procedural law
   - b. case law
   - c. substantive law
   - d. natural law

9. Which of the following is the purpose of law?
   a. promote peace and order
   b. act as a social control
   c. regulate conduct
   d. all of these

10. Which of the following provisions of the federal Bill of Rights does not presently apply to the states?
   a. the privilege against self-incrimination
   b. the right to trial by jury
   c. the right to a speedy trial
   d. all of these apply to the states

REFERENCES

1. Funk and Wagnalls, *Standard College Dictionary* (New York: Harcourt, Brace, 1968), 766.
2. This is a definition derived from the elements of law discussed by Richard Quinney in his book, *The Problem of Crime* (New York: Dodd, Mead, 1970), 8–14. This, in turn, is based on the earlier work by F. James Davis et al., in F. James Davis, Henry H. Foster, Jr., C. Ray Jeffery, and E. Eugene Davis, *Society and the Law* (New York: Free Press, 1962), p. 43.
3. Exodus XX:13.
4. N.C. Gen. Stat. Sec. 14–17.
5. Quinney, *op. cit.*, 9.
6. Henry Campbell Black, *Black's Law Dictionary*, 4th ed. (St. Paul: West, 1975), 1177.
7. *Ibid.*, 1581.
8. *U.S. Constitution*, Amendment XIV.
9. Mapp v. Ohio 367 U.S. 643 (1961) and Ker v. California 374 U.S. 23 (1963).
10. Malloy v. Hogan 378 U.S. 1 (1964).
11. Benton v. Maryland 395 U.S. 784 (1969).
12. Gideon v. Wainwright 372 U.S. 335 (1963).
13. Klopfer v. North Carolina 386 U.S. 213 (1967).
14. Duncan v. Louisiana 391 U.S. 145 (1968).
15. Pointer v. Texas 380 U.S. 400 (1965).
16. Hurtado v. California 110 U.S. 516 (1884).
17. See footnote 2.

21

Origins and Features of Criminal Law

OBJECTIVES

After studying this chapter, the student should be able to:

- Trace the origins of criminal law.
- Discuss the rationale for the emergence of criminal law.
- Describe the major features of criminal law.
- Distinguish criminal law from civil law.
- Distinguish between crimes which are *mala in se* and *mala prohibita*, and between felonies and misdemeanors.

It may be recalled from the previous chapter that the existence of law is tied inextricably to the existence of the state. It is the state (a politically organized society) that creates and enforces the law. Without the existence of the state, there is no law.

> Law, sanctioned by coercive force, can be distinguished from custom, which has the sanction of group disapproval, from religion, which has a supernatural sanction, and from morality, where the sanction is the superego or conscience.[1]

In this chapter, the origins of law will be examined and criminal law will be distinguished from civil law.

THE EMERGENCE OF CRIMINAL LAW

The emergence of law, and from it the criminal law, has been described in various ways by many authors. Differences of approach and interpretation can largely be ascribed to whether the author took a consensus or conflict view of the origins and functions of law. In the consensus view the law, and especially the criminal law, is seen as the embodiment of the will or spirit of a group or a society. In the conflict view, the focus is on the existence of competing interests within a group or a society, and the ability of one group to become dominant and promote its own interests and subjugate the interests of others, through legislation.

Originally, humans lived in close-knit groups of herdspeople and hunters. Decisions were made through group consensus and custom prevailed. "The disputes that arose in primitive societies [were] generally resolved informally and the aim [was] in effect a reconciliation between conflicting parties." [2] When wrongs were committed against an individual in the group, it was up to the individual and his or her family to exact revenge. This is most notably exemplified in the concept of the "blood feud." This was the situation that occurred when, for example, a member of the Green family killed a member of the Brown family. The Brown family retaliated by killing a member of the Green family, and the Green family responded by killing a member of the Brown family, and so on.

With the exacting of retribution left in the hands of the wronged individual and his or her family, and with the existence of the state of affairs described, it is not surprising that societies began to place limits on the nature and extent of retaliation that was permissible. One of the first limitations that took place was to demand that the retaliation sought did not exceed the amount of the initial injury. Thus in the Bible it is stated: "thou shalt give life for life, eye for eye, tooth for tooth, hand for hand, foot for foot, burning for burning, wound for wound, stripe for stripe." [3] Likewise in the Twelve Tables of Rome, allegedly enacted in 450 B.C., it is stated that "*Si membrum rupit, ni cum eo pacit, talio esto.*" [4] Translated, this provision states that if someone has broken another's limb, and has not made his peace with that individual, then he should be reduced to the same condition. Noteworthy is the fact that the first recourse should be an attempt to make peace. If this is unsuccessful, then retaliation is allowed. The retaliation should, however, be limited to the extent of the initial injury.

As groups and societies grew larger and more complex in organization, decision-making powers moved from the group as a whole to acknowledged and recognized leaders within the group. The customs became more formalized and were often reduced to writing. Thus the Code of Hammurabi was developed in about 2000 B.C., the Laws of Moses somewhere between 1500 and 900 B.C., the Laws of Dracon and Solon around 600 B.C., and the Twelve Tables of Rome around 450 B.C.

With the establishment of formalized codes, and with specific bodies entrusted with legislative and dispute-settling powers, societies had begun to take a more active interest in regulating relationships between individuals. One of the first actions was to change a system of retaliation into a system of regulated retaliation. Wrongs were still essentially considered private injuries, but society as a whole had begun to recognize its interest in promoting peace and order by supervising the revenge exacted by the wronged individual. The loss of a limb might be compensated by the loss of one of the offender's limbs, the loss of an ox by receiving one of the offender's oxen. Gradually, instead of the wronged individual exacting revenge, the offender was to pay monetary compensation for the loss or injury. This was a logical means of making amends; for it saved the wrongdoer from incurring injury and covered the situation where the wrong-doer had no ox to present to the injured party.

As societies became still more organized and their members more diversified in nature and function, the state, through its recognized leaders, began to play a far more active role in protecting and promoting its own interests. The existence of the state depended upon peace and order. A wrong against an individual constituted a breach of the peace and was therefore a wrong against the state. Wrongs against individuals thus became threats against the society as a whole. The offense of treason was born. The state itself could be the victim of wrongful acts.

Often religion provided a justification for state intervention. The wrongdoer had by the wrongful act angered the gods. It was up to the state to see that the gods were appeased. This was evident as late as the Middle Ages when the system of trial by ordeal prevailed. The guilt of the alleged wrongdoer was determined by the outcome of the ordeal. The wrongdoer might, for example, be thrown into a pool of water (trial by water). Drowning indicated guilt; survival, innocence. The determination of guilt or innocence had been made by God. It is interesting to note that the early criminal codes in America still reflected similar religious influence. "The Laws punished religious offenses, such as idolatry, blasphemy and witchcraft. Infractions against persons or property were declared to be offenses against God." [5]

In Anglo-Saxon England the rulers of the different kingdoms were responsible for maintaining peace and order within their own realms. The machinery of justice was entirely local in nature. As was true in other societies in that stage of development, one of the main aims of the lawgivers was "to force the injured man or the slain man's kinsfolk to accept a money composition instead of resorting to reprisals." [6] It had been a small but important step from limiting the nature and extent of revenge allowed the wronged party, to permitting the wrongdoer to pay monetary compensation for the injury suffered.

Around this time the concept of breach of the peace evolved with added significance. Since the ruler was responsible for maintaining peace and order within his kingdom, any disturbance in his kingdom was a breach of his peace. Any breach of his peace had to be compensated. Thus, along with the wergild (compensation) paid to the wronged individual, an additional payment, the wite, had to be made to the ruler for the disturbance of his peace. This provided the ruler with a pragmatic reason for taking on the responsibility for law enforcement. For the wite, or fine, could provide an important source of revenue. This was an advantage that did not go unnoticed by subsequent rulers.

As England became unified after the Norman Conquest, a common system of law and law administration developed throughout the land. The major responsibility for this at first lay in the hands of itinerant judges, then in the courts in existence at different places throughout the kingdom. The state, through the Crown and its officials, played an active role in the administration of justice. Of particular concern were wrongs considered to be wrongs against the state (crimes). The responsibility for taking action in such cases gradually moved from the individual to the state itself. The development of state machinery for the investigation and prosecution of crimes is discussed in later chapters.

MAJOR FEATURES OF CRIMINAL LAW

One major feature of criminal law is that the acts prohibited in the criminal code are considered wrongs against the state, rather than wrongs against individuals. While there may be a particular victim or complainant, the wrong is considered serious enough to be pursued by the state in the interests of the people generally. Thus in England a criminal case instituted against Jones will appear as *Regina (the Queen)* v. *Jones*. In the United States it might appear, for example, as *U.S.* v. *Jones* or *The People of the State of New York* v. *Jones*.

A second major feature of the criminal law is that the sanction for the commission of a crime is not the payment of compensation to the wronged party, but punishment of the wrongdoer. The punishment may take the form of a fine, imprisonment, or in some cases, even death. This prompted the statement by Sutherland that:

> The essential characteristic of crime is that it is behavior which is prohibited by the state as an injury to the state and against which the state may react, at least as a last resort, by punishment.[7]

A third major feature of the criminal law, which many feel exists, arises essentially out of the first two. This is the social stigma that is attached to a criminal charge, and the public condemnation that accompanies conviction and the imposition of a criminal sanction. Indeed, for Henry M. Hart, Jr., the distinguishing factor between criminal and noncriminal sanctions lies in "the judgment of community condemnation which accompanies and justifies its [the criminal sanction's] imposition."[8]

THE DISTINCTION BETWEEN CRIMINAL AND CIVIL LAW

Many acts that occur can give rise to actions both in criminal and in civil law. Suppose, for example, that Ash is looking for a parking space on a crowded downtown street. He sees an empty parking meter, pulls up in front of the empty space, and prepares to back into it. While he is doing this, Beech pulls into the space with his small sports car. Ash gets out of his car and politely tells Beech that since he (Ash) was there first, he believes he is entitled to the space. Beech, a much larger man than Ash, responds with expletives and begins to beat Ash up savagely. The police are called, and Beech is arrested for assault. Ash is hospitalized for two weeks and is off work for six weeks. The expensive suit he had been wearing at the time of the assault is ruined, and there is a dent in the side of his car where Beech had placed a kick for good measure. The cost of repairing the dent is not covered by insurance.

What we have here is a private interaction between two individuals which becomes a matter of public concern. Had Ash and Beech settled their problem verbally, there would have, in all likelihood, been no state involvement in the matter. Beech's savage, and rather unprovoked, attack on Ash, however, constituted a very definite breach of the peace. It was clearly within the category of behavior that the state, through its penal code, discourages in its citizens. Beech's arrest by the police is the start of state action being taken against Beech for a wrong committed against the state, *viz.* a violation of the criminal code. The primary purpose of this action is to punish Beech for the way he has acted. He is to pay penance for his wrongful act, and this hopefully will deter him from behaving in a similar fashion in the future. Ash will, in all probability, derive little from the criminal action being taken against Beech, except perhaps for the psychological satisfaction of seeing an offender brought to justice. The criminal law is geared at taking action against a person who violates the criminal code, not at providing compensation for the injured party.[9]

Should Ash wish to obtain compensation from Beech for his hospital expenses, his pain and suffering, his loss of wages, and the damage to his clothes and car, he will have to initiate a civil action against Beech. The primary purpose of such action is to provide Ash with compensation for his losses, not to punish Beech. The action will be an action in tort, a civil action designed to provide redress for private injuries and losses.

The primary aim of the criminal law is to protect the peace and security of the state and to take action against a wrongdoer on behalf of the people of the state in general. The primary purpose of the civil law is to protect and enforce the rights of private individuals. The law of tort is just one branch of civil law, but perhaps the branch that is most similar to the criminal law.

CRIMES *MALA IN SE* AND *MALA PROHIBITA*

Crimes have long been classified in terms of their perceived seriousness. Two classifications, mentioned in Section 1, merit repetition. The first is the classification of crimes as either *mala in se* (wrong of their own accord) or *mala prohibita* (wrong because they are prohibited). Crimes *mala in se* are those believed to be inherently wrong in themselves. They are, in essence, violations of natural law. They might include such crimes as murder, rape, and robbery. *Mala prohibita*, on the other hand, are offenses only because they are contained in the penal code of a particular state or nation. They might include such offenses as driving in excess of the speed limit, trafficking in illegal drugs, or prostitution.

FELONIES AND MISDEMEANORS

A second, and in modern times, far more important categorization of crimes according to their seriousness is the division of crimes into felonies and misdemeanors. Felonies constitute the more serious category of crime. Originally, conviction of a felony resulted in the loss of the convicted felon's property. In present times, the greater seriousness of felonies is reflected in the harsher sentences that can be imposed upon conviction. Generally only conviction of a felony can result in a sentence of imprisonment for more than one year, or, in the case of murder, the death penalty. Conviction for a misdemeanor, on the other hand, generally carries a maximum sentence of one year's imprisonment. In most states, police powers and the nature of the judicial proceedings will vary depending upon whether a felony or a misdemeanor has been committed. Finally, certain civil disabilities, such as loss of the vote, or the right to enter certain trades or professions, may face the convicted felon, but not the convicted misdemeanant. Examples of felonies include murder, manslaughter, rape, robbery, and burglary. Examples of misdemeanors include petty or simple assault, petty larceny, and prostitution.

SUMMARY

This section of the text has examined how the emergence of criminal law and the state are inextricably bound to one another. Law originally evolved as a system for regulating and resolving private affairs. As the state developed, it became concerned with the maintenance of peace and security. Many offenses against individuals constituted breaches of the peace, and hence were offenses against the state. Gradually, the state itself took on the responsibility for taking action in such cases, and this led to the development of criminal law.

The major features of criminal law are that violations of the criminal code are considered wrongs against the state, that the sanction for the commission of a crime is punishment of the wrongdoer, and that public condemnation accompanies the imposition of the criminal sanction. The primary aim of the criminal law is to protect the peace and security of the state and to take action against a wrongdoer on behalf of the people of the state in general. The primary purpose of the civil law, on the other hand, is to protect and enforce the rights of private individuals and to compensate individuals for their injuries or losses. Whereas the unsuccessful defendant in a civil case would generally have to pay monetary compensation, the unsuccessful defendant in a criminal action would be punished for his or her wrongdoing.

SUGGESTED ACTIVITIES

- Show how the expression "an eye for an eye, a tooth for a tooth" could be used either as a justification to limit the amount of punishment, or as an argument to increase the punishment being imposed.
- Locate a history of criminal law and briefly describe the author's theory of the origins of criminal law. Classify the author as a consensus or conflict theorist.
- What is the distinction made in your state between a felony and a misdemeanor? Locate the definitions in the statute books.
- Obtain a copy of the most recent *Annual Court Reports* available in your state. Compare the number and types of criminal cases with the number and types of civil cases.

- Interview a police officer and ask how police powers differ depending upon whether the offense committed is a misdemeanor or a felony.
- Thumb through a daily newspaper for a two-week period and keep a record of the number of civil cases and the number of criminal cases that are reported. Note also the types of cases reported. From your record, state whether civil or criminal cases are given more press coverage. Which types of criminal cases receive the most coverage? Is what you have found representative of the actual numbers and types of cases passing through the system?

REVIEW

A. Briefly explain how something that was originally viewed as a wrong against an individual came to be seen as a crime.

B. Explain the rationale behind "trial by ordeal."

C. List three major features of criminal law.

D. Distinguish criminal law from civil law.

E. Name and briefly describe two different ways crimes can be categorized according to seriousness.

F. Multiple Choice. Select the best answer.

1. One of the early uses of law was to limit the extent of revenge to:
    a. one-third of the offender's property
    b. the death of the party responsible
    c. the extent of the injury
    d. none of these

2. The "blood feud" was
    a. a cycle of exacting revenge
    b. a conflict over the family name
    c. a trial by ordeal
    d. none of these

3. The wite in Anglo-Saxon England was a precursor of modern day
    a. fines
    b. speed limits
    c. courts
    d. none of these

4. An important feature of civil law is that it
    a. is a wrong against the state
    b. provides compensation for the victim
    c. provides punishment of the offender
    d. all of these

5. In the case of *North Carolina* v. *Johnson*,
    a. Johnson is the defendant
    b. Johnson is the complainant
    c. the federal government is the defendant
    d. the federal government is the complainant

6. If Brown assaulted Green, and Green sued him successfully, Brown would probably have to
    a. go to prison for less than one year
    b. go to prison for more than one year
    c. pay a fine
    d. pay compensation

7. A shoots B. This situation could give rise to:
   a. a criminal action
   b. a civil action
   c. both a criminal action and a civil action
   d. neither a criminal action nor a civil action

8. Premeditated murder is a
   a. felony and a *malum prohibitum*
   b. felony and a *malum in se*
   c. misdemeanor and a *malum prohibitum*
   d. misdemeanor and a *malum in se*

9. The Twelve Tables of Rome were
   a. an early formal legal code
   b. a location in the Roman Forum where trials were held
   c. part of the Bible
   d. all of these

10. Tort is
   a. a criminal offense
   b. a civil action
   c. a constitutional requirement
   d. a punishment

REFERENCES

1. F. James Davis, Henry H. Foster, Jr., C. Ray Jeffery, and E. Eugene Davis, *Society and the Law* (New York: Free Press, 1962), 264.
2. James T. Carey, *Introduction to Criminology* (Englewood Cliffs, N.J.: Prentice-Hall, 1978), 18.
3. Exodus XXI:23–25.
4. See, for example, R. W. Lee, *The Elements of Roman Law* (London, England: Sweet and Maxwell Ltd., 1956), 389.
5. Richard Quinney, *Criminology* (Boston: Little, Brown, 1970), 69.
6. F. W. Maitland, *The Constitutional History of England* (Cambridge, England: Cambridge University Press, 1965), 4.
7. Edwin H. Sutherland, *White Collar Crime* (New York: Holt, Rinehart and Winston, 1949), 31.
8. Henry M. Hart, Jr., ''The Aims of the Criminal Law,'' *Law and Contemporary Problems*, 23 (1958), 404.
9. Most state codes do, in fact, provide for the possibility of an offender being ordered to pay restitution to a victim. This is, however, very much of a secondary function performed by the criminal law.

22

Law
and Social Control

OBJECTIVES

After studying this chapter, the student should be able to:

- Define the meaning of social control and describe different methods of social control.
- Describe the relationship between law and morality.
- Delineate the usage of criminal law as a method of social control, with special focus upon such social problems as consensual sex, alcoholism, and drug abuse.
- Discuss the usage of civil law as a mechanism for the control of such social problems as alcoholism and drug abuse.

An issue of fundamental importance to societies is their own self-preservation. In order to ensure their continuity, societies tend to identify, label, and attempt to control behaviors which they consider threatening to their very existence. They are, therefore, highly concerned with exercising social control over their members.

SOCIAL CONTROL

In any society, there are people whose behavior differs markedly from most of the other members of that society. These individuals are what may be termed deviants, individuals who diverge from the accepted social norms of their society. Which behaviors are labeled deviant depends upon the philosophies and beliefs held by those individuals who are empowered with the ability to decide what behavior is deviant. Thus, in one society, a person who smokes marijuana (or drinks alcohol) may be considered a deviant, while in another society a person who does not smoke marijuana (or drink alcohol) may be the deviant.

In our complex society there are many methods of social control or ways of promoting the likelihood that people conform their behavior to the expectations of society as a whole. As Davis and colleagues have stated, social control may be regarded as: "The process by which subgroups and persons are influenced to conduct themselves in conformity with group expectations." [1]

Methods of social control may be either formal or informal. They may range from a nod of approval or a shake of the head to imprisonment, or even death. Major agents of social control include the family, religion, and the law. Many people feel that as the family and religion have lost their influence as agents of social control, the law has been increasingly used to denote appropriate and desired ways of behaving. A prime example of such usage of the law is desegregation legislation, which attempts to discourage racial bias and to encourage the integration of people of different racial backgrounds.

LAW AND MORALITY

Law may be said to reflect the values of a society and the problem areas within a society. A society that is greatly concerned with property will have many laws regarding property. This will involve such matters as the acquisition and transference of property and offenses against property. A society that is concerned with social conformity will have laws regulating freedom of expression. A society that is concerned with religious conformity will regulate religious thought and practice. Thus it is that the Puritans of New England had many laws regulating religious practice, the Soviet Union limits freedom of expression, and the capitalist societies of the modern world have many laws defining and protecting property rights.

Law is a body of rules of conduct, created and enforced by a sovereign state. The sovereign state is not just an abstract entity. Rather it is comprised of those individuals who have the power and authority to run the state. These individuals may, or may not, be representative of the majority of the people in that state.

It has been alleged that: "The criminologist in his research usually proceeds on the premise that the criminal law embodies important social norms and that these norms are held by most persons in society." [2] However, while criminal law is the embodiment of someone's moral values, it does not necessarily reflect the values of everyone or even of a majority of people. Thus, depending upon the nature of the society, and upon the particular law in question, every individual within a society may not regard it as an embodiment of his or her own values and norms. Many people in the United States, for example, question the desirability of laws regulating various sexual practices (such as fornication, prostitution, and homosexual acts committed by consenting adults) and laws controlling gambling and the usage of drugs and alcohol. Thus while the laws of a society tend to reflect the values of that society as a whole, every law is not necessarily an accurate representation of every individual's morality.

What is morality and how does it differ from law? Morality, like law, comprises a set of rules distinguishing appropriate behavior from inappropriate behavior. However, law is a formal set of rules created by the state for all to follow. Morality, on the other hand, is an informal, personal guide for conduct. Since individuals within a society establish their own moral codes, these codes may well differ in content.

How can we state that the laws of a society reflect the values of that society if individual members each retain distinct moral values? The answer lies in the fact that while individuals differ on specifics, the general moral code of any society is common. As Devlin has argued:

> If men and women try to create a society in which there is no fundamental agreement about good and evil they will fail; if, having based it on common agreement, the agreement goes, the society will disintegrate. For society is not something that is kept together physically; it is held by the invisible bonds of common thought. If the bonds were too far relaxed the members would drift apart. A common morality is part of the bondage. The bondage is the price of society; and mankind, which needs society, must pay its price.[3]

> Law and morality to a large extent cover common ground.

> For both are concerned to impose certain standards of conduct without which human society would hardly survive and, in many of these fundamental standards, law and morality reinforce and supplement each other as part of the fabric of social life.[4]

There are, however, areas where law operates on issues that are not considered moral, except in the sense that it might be considered immoral to violate the law. These would generally include acts described as *mala prohibita*, such as driving faster than the posted speed limit or selling goods half an hour after the store should have been closed.

There are also areas which are included in moral codes but which are outside the scope of the law. To understand this it is helpful to examine the distinction made by Fuller between the "morality of duty" and the "morality of aspiration." The morality of duty "lays down the basic rules without which an ordered society is impossible, or without which an ordered society directed toward certain specific goals must fail of its mark." [5] On the other hand,

> the principles of a morality of aspiration . . . are "loose, vague, and indeterminate, and present us rather with a general idea of the perfection we ought to aim at, than afford us any certain and infallible directions of acquiring it." [6]

The morality of duty would, undoubtedly, cover much the same territory as would be covered by law. However, it is evident that what for one person may constitute a morality of aspiration is to another a morality of duty. Thus, for one person, looking after one's parents in old age may merely constitute part of the morality of aspiration;

for another it may be part of the morality of duty. The issue of whether morality should become law is aided to a great extent by deciding whether a particular behavior should be part of the morality of aspiration or the morality of duty.

When viewing any behavior, each of us can decide whether, in our own mind, that behavior is right or wrong. When we do this, we are passing moral judgment on that behavior. Any moral judgment we make may be in accord, or in discord, with the legal provisions regarding the act. There are two levels at which we may be at discord. First, we may disagree about the behavior being inherently right or wrong, and hence moral or immoral. Second, we may disagree about whether the behavior belongs to the realm of the morality of duty or the morality of aspiration. If it belongs to the morality of duty, it is a basic rule essential for the functioning of society and presumably, therefore, should be clothed with the added force of law. The supposition is that most behaviors considered to constitute part of the morality of duty will become legal requirements.

When a person violates a rule of society, there is often an accompanying sanction. When the act is a breach of morality but not illegal, the person may find that he or she is censured verbally or even ostracized by other members of society. Legal wrongdoing, however, may bring about financial sanctions, imprisonment, or even death. Obviously a person who has committed both moral and legal wrongdoing may face both types of sanctions. While in some cases law and morality overlap, in general the standards the law seeks to safeguard are far more concrete and specific than those protected by morality. In this regard the criminal law "defines the minimum conditions of man's responsibility to his fellows and holds him to that responsibility." [7]

An age-old debate that ensues is whether, as Devlin suggests,[8] the law ought to promote and uphold moral positions, or whether:

> the only purpose for which power can rightfully be exercised over any member of a civilized community against his will is to prevent harm to others. . . . His own good either physical or moral is not a sufficient warrant. He cannot rightfully be compelled to do or forbear because it will be better for him to do so, because it will make him happier, because in the opinion of others, to do so would be wise, or even right.[9]

A basic problem with this philosophy relates to whether it is possible for a man to harm himself without also harming society at large. Whatever the merits of either philosophical stance, it cannot be denied that the law has been used to uphold what many consider to be moral positions.

USE OF CRIMINAL LAW AS A MECHANISM OF SOCIAL CONTROL

Few would argue about whether most of the serious crimes, the crimes which are *mala in se*, should be prohibited by law. Society has, for its own sake, a major interest in trying to prevent its members from murdering, raping, assaulting, and robbing each other. The need for order and self-preservation would also appear to justify such laws as those regulating which side of the road we should drive on, minimum building safety requirements, and the like. More questionable is society's interest in trying to stop such activities as gambling, alcohol and drug use, and various consensual sexual activities.

In each of these cases, the law may be said to be upholding a moral position. The extent to which individual members of society advocate legal involvement in each of these areas may depend upon the extent to which the legislation reflects their own positions on these issues. The law, it should be stressed, may aid in enforcing a society's general sense of morality by punishing those who transgress its provisions. Law and morality are, however, not necessarily the same. Thus an important issue relates to whose sense of morality is used as the basis for legislation, and who has the power to define morality as law. Discussion of the politics of lawmaking, however, will be left until the next chapter.

SEX, ALCOHOL, AND DRUGS

The laws regulating consensual sex, alcohol, and drugs arguably involve matters which are issues of personal concern and conscience. If anyone is harmed, it is only those who participate in these activities. Others might argue, however, that laws regulating these activities embody important social norms which ought to be followed by all. Failure to abide by these legal proscriptions threatens the basic fabric of society. The behaviors in question, they might state, are part of the morality of duty, not the morality of aspiration. As such, they should be given the force of law.

Background information on these topics was presented in Section 4 under the discussion of victimless crimes. In this chapter further exploration will be undertaken of the usage of law as a mechanism of social control with regard to these activities.

It has been stated that:

> The criminal laws have been shaped within the religious, economical, and social foundations of the United States. The result is a code of criminal laws with the purpose of preserving and controlling the American social order.[10]

A major part of the American social order is derived from the Puritan heritage with its emphasis on hard work, delay of gratification, and moral righteousness. These attitudes provide part of the basis of, and justification for, the legislation under discussion.

Consensual Sex

In the area of consensual sexual activity, legislation has aimed at discouraging casual sexual relationships and at promoting and upholding the sanctity of the institution of marriage. Forbidden activities have included: fornication (consensual intercourse between persons of the opposite sex, at least one of whom is unmarried); adultery (consensual sexual intercourse between persons of the opposite sex, at least one of whom is married); homosexuality (consensual sexual activity between persons of the same sex); and prostitution (consensual sexual activity with payment for services rendered). Even within marriage certain sexual activities have been prohibited.[11] All this has prompted two commentators to suggest that the purpose of all of this legislation is to:

> provide an enormous legislative chastity belt encompassing the whole population and proscribing everything but solitary and joyless masturbation and "normal coitus" inside wedlock.[12]

The existence of these laws does not mean that they are enforced with any regularity. Indeed, ambiguity in our society about the desirability of such laws has led in some instances to selective enforcement, in other instances to nonenforcement, and yet in other instances to repeal.

In the past, homosexuals in particular have suffered the pains of selective enforcement. Those singled out for attention by the law had to face the added trauma of unwelcome publicity that attends such an arrest. Those as yet undetected by law enforcement had their fear of exposure heightened, and as a consequence perhaps found themselves more open to blackmail from people who knew of their sexual orientation. Although homosexuals have more recently striven hard to advance their civil rights, the link between homosexuality and the dreaded AIDS has caused some people to question the advisability of tolerating homosexuality.

Those people involved in offenses of fornication and adultery, on the other hand, have perhaps been the greatest beneficiaries of policies of nonenforcement. Although many people have indulged in such proscribed behaviors, criminal prosecutions have been rare. Were fornication statutes to be enforced, the criminal justice system would be even more seriously overloaded than it is today. Lack of enforcement of adultery criminal provisions is exemplified by the large number of divorces that have been granted on the grounds of adultery, and the exceedingly small number of corresponding criminal prosecutions.

Most people would agree that society should protect the young from being sexually exploited by adults and that both young and old should be protected against forced sexual relations. Objections might be raised about prostitutes soliciting customers, and homosexuals openly seeking partners in public. The involvement of the criminal law in attempting to regulate consensual sexual activity conducted by adults in private is, however, quite another matter. The underlying issue is the standard of sexual morality society wishes to impose upon its members as law. Are these sexual activities purely matters of personal conscience? Are they part of the morality of aspiration, or are they part of the morality of duty? Is this an area of overreach by the criminal law, an area where a person should enjoy "an inalienable right to go to hell in his own fashion, provided he does not directly injure the person or property of another on the way,"[13] or is it, as Devlin might perhaps suggest, part of the bondage of common morality which is essential for the functioning of society?[14] Reasonable individuals may well differ in their opinions.

In the area of consensual sexual activity, we are dealing very much with the question of morality and whether it should, through legislation, be clothed with the binding authority of law. There is little to suggest that persons other than the participants are injured in any specific manner. Even the participants themselves, if they are injured in any way, suffer harm only because of their allegedly lessened moral standards. If they are able to contribute less effectively to society, it is usually because of society's reaction to them (e.g., by prohibiting professed homosexuals from teaching in a school system). The threat to society is a general threat to the moral fabric of society.

Alcohol and Drugs

In the area of alcohol and drug use, on the other hand, there is not only the moral issue. There is also very possible direct danger to society and to the addict or alcoholic. The participant may be unable to function effectively while under the influence of the mind-altering substance. Few of us wish to encounter a drunk driver on the road. Addiction to a particular substance may, in addition, prevent an individual from being master over his or her own destiny, and render the individual a burden to society. Whatever our opinions about the legal status of a drug, few of us would probably like to let an alcoholic or an addict freeze to death on the sidewalk.

Thus, it is clear that factors, other than just the properties of the drug itself, determine its legal classification. There are generally three legal classifications of drugs. A legal drug is one which is freely available. A controlled drug is available only under certain circumstances, such as with a doctor's prescription. An illegal drug is not legally available at all. Thus, while smoking tobacco is generally legal or controlled (by age), smoking marijuana (which some would claim is a far less harmful substance) is generally illegal. With regard to alcohol, Prohibition and the Repeal of Prohibition were by no means predicated on scientific research findings about the harmful properties of the substance.

There are, in fact, two different issues that need to be addressed here. The first relates to whether a particular substance should be classified as legal, controlled, or illegal. The decision is likely to be affected by moral, political, and law enforcement concerns as well as medical and social considerations. Second, since, regardless of the classification of the substance, the potential for abuse exists, there is the issue of what should be done to, or for, the drug abuser, the drug addict, and the alcoholic. A fundamental issue concerns whether society should ever substitute its own judgment for that of the individuals who have apparently lost control over their own decision-making powers. This is a controversial issue. Even in the example previously mentioned, it is by no means clear that all of us would agree that alcoholics or addicts should be taken to warmer surroundings, let alone that they should be punished or forcibly given treatment for their conditions.

The criminal law is used in this area as an attempt at social control. We are told by the law what substances we can use and under what conditions. Some of the laws concerning drug use are manifestly aimed at protecting society and preventing direct harm to others. The prohibition of driving while under the influence of drugs or alcohol is one such example. The crime of being intoxicated and disruptive in public is another. Laws prohibiting the smoking of marijuana and the prescription of Laetrile to cancer patients, on the other hand, present a different issue. In the case of marijuana, the law has taken away the individual's right to determine whether to indulge in an activity which may be potentially self-destructive. In the case of Laetrile, the law has denied both the physician and the patient the opportunity to use a form of medical treatment which may well not be beneficial. In both cases, the law is attempting to protect the individual from himself or herself. With regard to marijuana, the law, some people would argue, is also aimed at protecting other members of society from being encouraged by the marijuana smoker to take up the disapproved behavior. What this argument does, in essence, is to deny the potential marijuana smoker the freedom of choice.

As in the area of consensual sexual activity, probably few of us would like to see the young exploited. We have observed how legislation has been drawn up to prohibit the use of any drug in the wrong circumstances. Legislation could also be phrased in such a way as to prevent exploitation of the young without restricting the freedom of adults. Consider, for example, the following provision of New York State Law:

> A person is guilty of endangering the welfare of a child when: 1. He knowingly acts in a manner likely to be injurious to the physical, mental or moral welfare of a male child less than sixteen years old or a female child less than seventeen years old.[15]

This type of provision could certainly include endangering the welfare of a child by giving him or her a dangerous or potentially dangerous substance. Such legislation may, indeed, provide a better approach than the blanket proscription of a substance; for as noted in a previous section,[16] making a substance illegal may be costly in certain respects. It may, for example, bring the law into disrepute, stigmatize otherwise lawful citizens, overburden law enforcement and the rest of the criminal justice system, and provide a market for organized crime.

The criminal law provides punishment for an individual who indulges in prohibited behavior. Anyone who possesses, uses, buys, or sells an illegal substance is breaking the law. Likewise, anyone who possesses a controlled substance, without having the legal right to possess it, is breaking the law. Thus, if a certain state, for example, prohibits the possession of heroin and marijuana, and a person is found in possession of either of these substances, arrest, prosecution, and punishment may follow. Each person is held responsible for his or her actions.

With regard to individuals who have become totally dependent on a substance, however, the law often acts in a rather different manner. These individuals are no longer in control of their lives. They are addicts. They have, in the general meaning of the term, developed "an extremely compulsive craving for and habitual use of a substance."[17] They are, perhaps, no longer healthy and responsible individuals. Rather, they are sick persons who need, for their psychological, and sometimes physical, functioning the very drugs that society has prohibited. Sick people, the argument runs, should not be punished merely for being sick.

Both the drug addict and the alcoholic are generally treated in the United States as sick people. The law does not, however, exempt them to any great extent from criminal responsibility for offenses arising out of their sickness.

In the United States Supreme Court case of *Robinson* v. *California* it was held that it is unconstitutional for a state to legislate that drug addiction constitutes a criminal offense:

> we deal with a statute which makes the ''status'' of narcotic addiction a criminal offense. . . . It is unlikely that any State at this moment in history would attempt to make it a criminal offense for a person to be mentally ill, or a leper, or to be afflicted with a venereal disease. A State might determine that the general health and welfare require that the victims of these and other human afflictions be dealt with by compulsory treatment, involving quarantine, confinement, or sequestration. But, in the light of contemporary human knowledge, a law which made a criminal offense of such a disease would doubtless be universally thought to be an infliction of cruel and unusual punishment in violation of the Eighth and Fourteenth Amendments.[18]

A drug addict can, therefore, no longer be criminally prosecuted merely for being an addict. Addicts can, however, still be prosecuted for possessing, using, buying, or selling the substances to which they are addicted.

While alcoholism has been held by several lower courts [19] to constitute a defense to a charge of public intoxication, the Supreme Court in *Powell* v. *Texas* did not hold that it constituted cruel and unusual punishment to convict an alcoholic of that crime.[20] The Court felt that the case was going one step beyond the *Robinson* doctrine. Powell was not being punished solely for the status of being an alcoholic. He had also committed an act, the act of being in public. Despite the decision in *Powell*, some states have enacted provisions that allow a defense of alcoholism. In North Carolina, for example, no person may be prosecuted solely for being intoxicated in a public place.[21] There may be a prosecution for being intoxicated and disruptive in public.[22] To this charge, however, the defendant may raise the defense of alcoholism.[23]

USE OF CIVIL LAW AS A MECHANISM OF SOCIAL CONTROL

Like the criminal law, the civil law is used to a great extent as a mechanism of social control. Unlike the criminal law which sets out a person's duties to society as a whole, the civil law focuses on people's relationships with others. People are regulated, for example, in the agreements they make, the way they conduct business, and the standard of care they owe other people. Should they conduct themselves inappropriately, they may be held liable by the civil law to make amends to any injured parties.

While the civil law does, for the most part, function in the aforementioned manner, it has been, and continues to be, put to another use. In the discussion of alcoholism and drug addiction, it was noted that both the drug addict and the alcoholic tend to be viewed as sick people suffering from a disease. Since they are sick, they should be treated rather than punished. Since the focus has changed from punishment to treatment, handling of these individuals moves from the criminal law to the civil law and its civil commitment procedure. The purpose of the civil commitment procedure is to treat individuals for their conditions, not punish them for their wrongful acts. Thus the aim of civil commitment of addicts or alcoholics is cure, not punishment.

The switch from criminal to civil proceedings, the change of focus from punishment to treatment, does not mean a lessening of the usage of law as a mechanism of social control. On the contrary, civil commitment proceedings can be, and very often are, instituted against the individual's will. Many states, such as North Carolina,[24] provide for the civil commitment of drug addicts and alcoholics under the same provisions as for the commitment of the mentally ill. Others, such as California[25] and New York,[26] have had separate provisions for addicts, often tied to the initiation of the criminal justice process. Provision may often be made for transference from the criminal to the civil system. A defendant who, under the North Carolina statute previously cited, successfully raises the defense of alcoholism to the charge of being intoxicated and disruptive in public, may not necessarily walk away free. The court retains jurisdiction over the defendant for fifteen days to decide whether civil action should be taken.[27]

With the lower standard of proof required in civil as opposed to criminal cases, and with lesser procedural safeguards generally available,[28] society can utilize these proceedings to impose conformity upon its deviants. Indeed, since the avowed purpose of these proceedings is treatment and cure, extended control over the addict or the alcoholic can be justified. It is not a question of the addict or the alcoholic making amends for a wrongful act. It is a question of society treating the addict or the alcoholic and helping the individual to conform with the prescribed morality of society.

SUMMARY

The law is used to a great extent as a method of social control. While there may be great overlap between law and morality, they are not one and the same. Law is a formal set of rules created by the state for all to follow. Morality, on the other hand, is an informal personal guide for conduct. For a society to be viable, there must be a certain degree of common shared morality. However, since morality is a matter of personal decision and conscience, there may be disagreement as to when morality should be clothed with the added force of law. The social control of such matters as consensual sexual activities and alcohol and drug usage represent such an area of disagreement.

With regard to the various consensual sexual activities discussed, the issue is whether participation in such activities should be solely a matter of personal choice, or whether the state, through the law, should attempt to promote and enforce a common standard of morality. With regard to drug and alcohol use, the issue is much the same. Society does, however, appear to need some protection from the acts of those under the influence of drugs or alcohol. In addition, there is the question of what should be done for, or to, the drug addict or the alcoholic who has lost the ability to function effectively in society.

The criminal law defines a minimum standard of responsibility and holds people to that standard. Since the drug addict and the alcoholic are generally viewed as sick individuals who are not necessarily responsible for their acts, it seems harsh to punish them for their dependence. What they need is help and treatment, not punishment. This is provided by the civil law through its civil commitment procedure, rather than by the criminal law. With its focus on treatment and cure, rather than punishment, this branch of the civil law may be even more forceful than criminal law as a method of social control.

SUGGESTED ACTIVITIES

- Examine the use of criminal law as a method of social control in your state. Select either consensual sexual behavior or drug use, and locate the statutes that prohibit or restrict these activities. List the behaviors that are illegal and controlled, and the corresponding punishments for violation. Note whether the offenses are misdemeanors or felonies. Find out how many prosecutions there have been for each in your area during the past year.

- Decide if the law you researched accurately represents the moral views of the citizens in your area. Survey a varied group of people and explain the law to them. Then ask them whether (1) they agree with the moral position taken by the law, and (2) they feel that it is an appropriate area for the law to operate. Report your findings.

- Find out the status of public intoxication in your state. Locate the statute, if there is one, that prohibits either public intoxication or public intoxication and disruption. Is alcoholism a defense? Is there a provision for transference to the civil arena?

- What are the civil commitment procedures for drug abuse in your state? Locate the statutes and briefly describe the procedures.

- Is there a drug treatment or alcoholism program in your community to which addicts or alcoholics are committed? If so, visit the facility and arrange an interview with a staff member. Find out how the program receives most of its clients, how long they remain, and what procedures are used for their release. To what extent do the drug addicts or alcoholics benefit from their participation in the program?

- Is adultery illegal in your state? Is adultery grounds for divorce? Find out how many divorces were granted on those grounds last year, and how many people were criminally prosecuted for adultery.

REVIEW

A. What is social control and why is it used?

B. Distinguish between law and morality.

C. Give an example of how the criminal law has been used to uphold a moral position.

D. Briefly describe how civil law has been used as a means of social control.

E. Multiple Choice. Select the best answer.

1. The mechanisms used to encourage people to conform their behavior to social norms are called
   a. normalization
   b. social control
   c. deviance
   d. none of these

2. Which of the following would be most likely to be part of the morality of aspiration?
   a. not stealing from others
   b. telling the truth

       c. not hitting others

       d. all of these

3. In some states amphetamines may be prescribed under certain conditions for medicinal purposes. In those states amphetamines are

       a. legal

       b. illegal

       c. controlled

       d. none of these

4. According to the Supreme Court decision in *Robinson* v. *California*, an addict cannot be criminally prosecuted for

       a. being an addict

       b. possessing the drugs one needs to feed one's habit

       c. buying the drugs one needs to feed one's habit

       d. all of these

5. In the decision in *Powell* v. *Texas*, the Supreme Court held that it was

       a. unconstitutional to convict an alcoholic of public intoxication

       b. not unconstitutional to convict an alcoholic of public intoxication

       c. unconstitutional to convict an alcoholic of being intoxicated and disruptive in public

       d. none of these

6. An adverse effect of making a substance illegal is that

       a. a potential market is provided for organized crime

       b. it may bring the law into disrepute

       c. it may overburden the criminal justice system

       d. all of these

7. The civil law uses civil commitment

       a. to treat a condition

       b. to punish a person for a wrongful act

       c. to force a person to make amends

       d. all of these

8. Which of the following does not act as a social control?

       a. religion

       b. civil law

       c. criminal law

       d. none of these

9. Consensual sexual intercourse between persons of the opposite sex, at least one of whom is unmarried, is a definition of the crime of

       a. adultery

       b. fornication

       c. homosexuality

       d. prostitution

10. Law has been used as a method of controlling

       a. sexual activity

       b. business transactions

       c. acts of violence

       d. all of these

REFERENCES

1. F. James Davis, Henry H. Foster, Jr., C. Ray Jeffery, and E. Eugene Davis, *Society and the Law* (New York: Free Press, 1962), 39.

2. Richard Quinney, *The Problem of Crime* (New York: Dodd, Mead, 1970), 27.

3. Patrick Devlin, *The Enforcement of Morals* (New York: Oxford University Press, 1965), 10.
4. Dennis Lloyd, *The Idea of Law* (Baltimore, Md.: Penguin Books, 1964), 57.
5. Lon L. Fuller, *The Morality of Law*, 2nd ed. (New Haven, Conn.: Yale University Press, 1969), 5–6.
6. *Ibid.*, 6 (citing Adam Smith, *The Theory of Moral Sentiments*).
7. Henry M. Hart, Jr., "The Aims of the Criminal Law," *Law and Contemporary Problems*, 23 (1958), 410.
8. Devlin, *op. cit.*
9. John Stuart Mill, *On Liberty* (London, England: Watts, 1930), 11.
10. Richard Quinney, *Criminology* (Boston: Little, Brown, 1975), 67.
11. Fellatio and cunnilingus for example. See, for example, Smith v. State 150 Ark. 265, 234 S.W. 32 (1921); Honselman v. People 168 Ill. 172, 48 N.E. 304, 305 (1897); State v. Nelson 199 Minn. 86, 94, 271 N.W. 114, 118 (1937); State v. Schmit 273 Minn. 78, 139 N.W. 2d 800 (1965).
12. Norval Morris and Gordon Hawkins, *The Honest Politician's Guide to Crime Control* (Chicago: University of Chicago Press, 1970), 15.
13. *Ibid.*, 2.
14. Devlin, *op. cit.*, 10.
15. N.Y. Pen. L. Section 260.10.
16. Chapter 12 in Section 4.
17. Daniel Glaser, *Crime in Our Changing Society* (New York: Holt, Rinehart and Winston, 1978), 272.
18. 370 U.S. 660, 666–67 (1960).
19. See, for example, Driver v. Hinnant 356 F.2d 764 (4th Cir. 1966) and Easter v. District of Columbia 361 F.2d 50 (D.C. Cir. 1966).
20. 392 U.S. 514 (1968).
21. N.C. Gen. Stat. Sec. 14.447.
22. N.C. Gen. Stat. Sec. 14.444.
23. N.C. Gen. Stat. Sec. 14.445.
24. N.C. Gen. Stat. Sec. 122.56 ff.
25. Cal. Wel. & Inst. Code Sec. 3050 ff.
26. N.Y. Mental Hygiene Law Sec. 205 ff.
27. N.C. Gen. Stat. Sec. 14.446.
28. For a detailed discussion of these issues see, for example, Fred Cohen, *The Law of Deprivation of Liberty* (St. Paul: West, 1980); Nicholas N. Kittrie, *The Right To Be Different* (Baltimore, Md.: Penguin Books, 1971).

23

Law
and Interest Groups

OBJECTIVES

After studying this chapter, the student should be able to:

- Define what an interest group is.
- Distinguish between direct and indirect interests.
- Describe the way in which interest groups have contributed to, and affected the outcome of, alcohol and drug legislation.
- Summarize the way in which interest groups affect the enforcement of the criminal law.

An important issue raised in our discussion of the relationship between morality and law was: whose sense of morality becomes law? Apparent in our formulation of this question is the recognition that within a particular society different individuals and different groups of individuals may have different standards of morality. Also implicit in our question is the idea that the proponents of the different standards of morality may be unequal in their ability to influence legislation. Thus, if there is a clash of interests, the more powerful prevail. According to Quinney: "Crime as a legal definition of human conduct is created by agents of the dominant class in a politically organized society." [1] He also asserts that: "Definitions of crime are composed of behaviors that conflict with the interests of the dominant class." [2]

In these statements there is recognition of the inequality of individuals and classes of individuals in the lawmaking process. Also acknowledged is the fact that those whose interests prevail may not be responsible themselves either for the formulation or for the application of the law. These activities may well be carried out by other people; for the agents referred to are such people as legislators, police, prosecutors, and judges.[3] The question for consideration here becomes: who are the members of that dominant class whose interests shape the formulation and application of law?

INTEREST GROUPS

In a complex and heterogeneous society such as exists in the United States, it may be fair to say that there is no single dominant class. Different groups of individuals have different interests, which are often at variance with one another. At various times different combinations of these interest groups prevail. Support for or against a particular piece of legislation may be prompted by economic, social, moral, or political considerations. As Carey has remarked, "The statement that law comes into existence as a result of the activities of various more or less organized interest groups is not particularly controversial." [4]

When the history of various legislative acts is examined, the effect of these interest groups at work is apparent. The involvement of interest groups in legislation has centered on acts which are *mala prohibita* rather than on acts which are *mala in se*. The general opposition of the National Rifle Association to gun control legislation is well publicized. Religious interests in the maintenance of the Sunday Blue Laws (laws limiting business and pleasure activities on Sundays) are likewise self-evident. Sutherland has pointed out that psychiatrists were the major motivating group behind the enactment of sexual psychopathy laws.[5] They were the group whose expertise was to be used in determining whether an individual was or was not a sexual psychopath.

DIRECT AND INDIRECT INTERESTS

Often the interest of a group in legislation may relate to some definitive advantage or disadvantage that would accrue to them as a result of the passage of the legislation. As Quinney has noted, the "frozen custard lobby" actively promoted a 1957 amendment to the Massachusetts Sunday law, which allowed frozen custard stands to operate on Sunday. Likewise, the National Automobile Dealers Association has persuaded several states to allow the sale of automobiles on Sunday.[6]

At times interest in legislation may involve less direct personal gain for the group. It may relate to promoting or maintaining a certain way of life, or encouraging a certain mode of behavior. Thus, religious groups seeking to promote Sunday Blue Laws may well feel they are trying to maintain, for the good of society as a whole, the sanctity of the Sabbath. They themselves do not benefit directly from the legislation they support. Likewise, Right to Life groups who oppose abortion are promoting a basic value they cherish dearly—the sanctity of the life of the unborn. Many individuals who advocate restricted availability of drugs and alcohol are attempting to impose the norm of limited use, or even abstinence, on the rest of society. This is, in their view, for the moral good of society as a whole.

Different individuals are likely to advocate legislation that either benefits them directly or promotes a value they consider essential to the proper functioning of society. It is not surprising that individuals who have similar interests and concerns are likely to band together and form what we have called interest groups. These interest groups naturally differ in their ability to affect legislation. The extent of their power involves such factors as their status in the political hierarchy, the support they can muster from the community, and their relationships with key legislative figures. Groups such as the American Federation of Labor and Congress of Industrial Organization (AFL-CIO) and the National Rifle Association are able to exert tremendous pressure on their own accord. Other groups, such as the Right to Lifers and groups seeking the preservation of various animal species, depend to a great extent upon public support for their positions. The mainly successful campaign for tougher legislation against drunk drivers was largely a result of a grassroots movement set in motion by such groups as MADD (Mothers Against Drunk Drivers) and SADD (Students Against Drunk Drivers). Each group is aided by access to and support from the influential political leaders of the day.

An interesting element of this process is that very different interest groups may join together to work for or against a particular piece of legislation. Thus it was in the interest of both gun control advocates and domestic gun manufacturers to restrict the importation of foreign guns. These two diverse (and often conflicting) groups joined together to overcome the resistance of the National Rifle Association. Together they managed to gain passage of the 1968 Federal Gun Control Act which limited the importation of foreign guns.[7] Likewise, opposition to governmental restrictions on the availability of tobacco may well stem from varied sources. One group might include, for example, representatives of the tobacco industry with their well-defined self-interest. Another group might consist of civil libertarians who support the right of an individual to engage in self-destructive activities.

ALCOHOL AND DRUGS

The drinking of alcohol and the use of drugs represent activities that elicit moral stances by members of society. They are activities which have long been subject to the control of criminal legislation. Such legislation has been influenced both by interest groups of certain moral persuasions and by groups with a more tangible interest in the outcome of legislation. The composition of the target population of such legislation may also have contributed to the nature of the legislation. Thus, for example, passage of more severe narcotics laws in the 1950s [8] was undoubtedly aided by the fact that at that time most addicts were from the lower classes. Likewise, the recent relaxation of marijuana penalties has almost certainly been influenced by the involvement of many middle and upper class persons in such drug use.

Restrictions on the use of alcohol have not operated in a political vacuum either. Thus, while temperance societies argued their case on the evils of alcohol, there was also a political motivation behind the Prohibition campaign. In many ways, the national Prohibition experiment was a last ditch attempt by rural Protestant America to enforce its way of life on the rather different immigrant members of a new industrialized society. The ban on alcohol was ''a final assertion of the rural Protestant mind against the urban and polyglot culture that had emerged at the end of the nineteenth century and the beginning of the twentieth.'' [9]

Prohibition lasted from 1920 to 1933. It did not succeed, and perhaps never could have. It was not possible for one interest group to impose, through legislation, its morality upon a heterogeneous society, a large percentage of whom did not subscribe to the norm of abstinence. The enactment of the National Prohibition (Volstead) Act was followed by widespread disregard of it. Illegal manufacture, transportation, and sale of liquor was common. Speakeasies (saloons where illegal liquor was sold) sprung up. Organized crime was provided with a very valuable source of business. The whole experiment of Prohibition was a dismal failure. ''An outdated morality could not be enforced by criminal law.'' [10]

In the drug area, moral and political interests have also played their part in shaping legislation. To many, the opiate addict evokes the image of the ultimate dope fiend, an individual enslaved by drugs who preys on the rest of society. The public image of the drug addict has, indeed, changed drastically since the turn of the century. As Duster has remarked,

> There was once a time when anyone could go to his corner druggist and buy grams of morphine or heroin for just a few pennies. There was no need to have a prescription from a physician. The middle and upper classes purchased more than the lower and working classes, and there was no moral stigma attached to such narcotics use. The year was 1900, and the country was the United States.
>
> Suddenly, there came the enlightenment of the twentieth century, full with moral insight and moral indignation, a smattering of knowledge of physiology, and the force of law. By 1920, the purchase of narcotics was not only criminal (that happened overnight in 1914), but some men had become assured that the purchase was immoral. [11]

To an extent the public attitude toward the opiate addict was influenced by the puritanical mood that swept the country just after the turn of the century and brought about the National Prohibition Act. To a large extent, however, the Federal Bureau of Narcotics and its predecessors were responsible for the change in the legal status of opiate addicts.

There was little or no control of the narcotics trade at the beginning of the twentieth century. In 1909 a ban was imposed on the importation of raw opium, but not on opiates (the chemicals derived from opium). [12] In 1914, as a result of a number of international conventions, including the 1912 Hague Convention on International Narcotics Control, a federal law was passed regulating the distribution of narcotics within the United States. This law, the Harrison Act of 1914, required that a tax of 1 cent per ounce be paid on each sale of opiates, that anyone involved in the production or distribution of opiates register with the federal government and maintain records of all drug transactions, and that registered physicians prescribe opiates only for legitimate medical purposes.[13]

> The Act did not make addiction illegal and it neither authorized nor forbade doctors to prescribe drugs regularly for addicts. All that it clearly and unequivocally did require was that whatever drugs addicts obtained were to be secured from physicians registered under the act and that the fact of securing drugs be made a matter of record. While some drug users had obtained supplies from physicians before 1914, it was not necessary for them to do so since drugs were available for purchase in pharmacies and even from mail-order houses.[14]

The Harrison Act in itself did not completely change the status of the opiate addict. Subsequent Supreme Court rulings and interpretative guidelines issued by the Narcotics Division of the Department of the Treasury (the agency initially responsible for enforcing the provisions of the Harrison Act) were, however, to have a major impact.

It has, indeed, been suggested by some writers that public and medical opinion had little to do with the establishment of our present system of drug control.

> It is a program which, to all intents and purposes, was established by the decisions of administrative officials of the Treasury Department of the United States. After the crucial decisions had been made, public and medical support was sought and in large measure obtained for what was already an accomplished fact.[15]

According to Dickson, the change in public opinion about the opiate addict was greatly influenced by the propaganda of the Narcotics Division of the Department of the Treasury, which was interested in expanding its sphere of operations.[16]

> At this point, the public's attitude toward narcotics use could be characterized as only slightly opposed. Faced with a situation where adaptation to the existing legislation was bureaucratically unfeasible, where expansion was desirable, and where environmental support—from both Congress and the public—was necessary for continued existence, the Division launched a two-pronged campaign: 1) a barrage of reports and newspaper articles which generated a substantial public outcry against narcotics use, and 2) a series of Division-sponsored test cases in the courts which resulted in a reinterpretation of the Harrison Act and substantially broadened powers for the Narcotics Division.[17]

In its early decisions involving the Harrison Act, the United States Supreme Court greatly limited the physician's ability to prescribe opiates. A physician could no longer prescribe opiates merely to keep an addict comfortable.[18] A physician could not prescribe opiates "to cater to the appetite or satisfy the craving of one addicted to the use of the drug."[19] In 1921, in the *Behrman* case (in which there was serious overprescribing) it appeared that opiates could not be prescribed even if the purpose were to treat and cure the addict.[20] In the *Linder* case in 1924, the court held that a physician could legally prescribe small amounts of opiates for the relief of conditions incident to addiction.[21] The Narcotics Division, however, prevented this from occurring

> by refusing to recognize *Linder* in its regulations, thus creating a situation where few would accept the risks involved in testing the doctrine, and by launching an all-out campaign against doctors, and publicizing records and convictions of physician addicts.[22]

It was a powerful interest group, the Narcotics Division of the Department of the Treasury, that was responsible largely in its own interests of expansion, for bringing about a change in the status of the opiate addict. The growing moral concerns over the status of the addict were encouraged by the Division and used to its advantage. The change in the composition of the addict population must likewise have helped.

> Whereas in 1900 the addict population was spread relatively evenly over the social classes (with the higher classes having slightly more), by 1920, medical journals could speak of the "overwhelming" majority from the "unrespectable" parts of society.[23]

The subsequent history of narcotics legislation was indeed one of tighter controls and harsher penalties.

INTEREST GROUPS AND THE ENFORCEMENT OF LAWS

The description of the Division of Narcotics' involvement in drug legislation is just one example of an interest group exerting great influence over the shape of the law. Countless others exist. Arguably the Federal Bureau of Narcotics was largely responsible for enactment of the Marijuana Tax Act of 1937. Self-interest was again a factor. For

> the Narcotics Bureau, faced with a nonsupportive environment and a decreasing budgetary appropriation that threatened its survival, generated a crusade against marijuana use which resulted in the passage of the act and the alteration of a societal value.[24]

Another example was cited earlier in this book, when it was discussed how the drug industry influenced legislation concerning both amphetamines and the commonly used tranquillizers, Valium and Librium.[25]

It is, however, not solely at the national level that interest groups exert influence on lawmaking. As we have seen in our example of the Massachusetts frozen custard lobby, state legislation is also shaped by interest groups. Though little legislation is carried out at the local level, many law enforcement decisions are of a local nature. Thus at the local level, interest groups may play more of a role in the enforcement as opposed to the enactment of law. It was mentioned earlier how there is often selective enforcement of laws concerning the activities of, for example, homosexuals and prostitutes. Frequently, bursts of law enforcement activity are generated by pressure from influential groups within the community. The issue of police and law enforcement is, however, a matter that will be addressed in a later section.

SUMMARY

This chapter has examined how law is often the product of influences exerted by interest groups. Different individuals and different groups of individuals vary in their desires for legislation. Their concerns may involve economic, social, moral, or political considerations. Their interest in legislation may be either direct or indirect. Sometimes groups who usually oppose each other may join together to fight for or against a particular piece of legislation.

The struggle over national Prohibition provided us with an example of strong moral and political interests competing against each other. The change in the legal status of the opiate addict was influenced by the work of the federal agencies who stood to gain from such a change. Often when the history of legislation and law enforcement in a particular branch of the law is examined, the effect of different interest groups at work can be seen.

SUGGESTED ACTIVITIES

- Find out which interest groups are powerful in your community. Check the newspapers and television news and list five organizations which could be termed interest groups. Mention the legislation they support or oppose.
- Contact a local interest group and find out what it does to try to influence legislation. How successful is it?
- Write to an elected official in your community and ask what influence interest groups have in formulating legislation.
- Find out what changes have been made in the drinking and driving laws in your state in the past ten years. Contact a local chapter of MADD or SADD, and inquire about their efforts to influence legislation.

REVIEW

A. Define interest group.

B. Distinguish between direct and indirect interests.

C. Briefly describe the role of interest groups in Prohibition.

D. Briefly describe the role of interest groups in drug legislation.

E. Multiple Choice. Select the best answer.

1. According to Quinney, crime as a legal definition of human conduct is created by agents of
- a. the upper class
- b. the middle class
- c. the lower class
- d. the dominant class

2. Who are the agents referred to by Quinney?
- a. the legislators
- b. the police
- c. the judges
- d. all of these

3. Which of the following was an interest group whose interest was in promoting a way of life rather than benefit for themselves?
- a. the National Rifle Association
- b. the frozen custard lobby
- c. the Right to Life group
- d. the National Automobile Dealers Association

4. In order to be classified as an interest group, which of the following interests must be sought?
- a. moral
- b. political

       c. financial

       d. any of these

5. Prohibition was brought about by an interest group with more than one motivation. These were:

       a. moral and political

       b. moral and financial

       c. political and financial

       d. none of these

6. The view presented in this chapter indicates our system of drug control was heavily influenced in the first part of the twentieth century by

       a. the AMA

       b. the FBI

       c. the Department of the Treasury

       d. none of these

7. The interest of the Narcotics Division in formulating our system of drug control was primarily:

       a. the moral good of society

       b. the medical health of society

       c. its own expansion

       d. none of these

8. The frozen custard lobby of Massachusetts argued for

       a. the right to sell frozen custard to the legislature

       b. the right to sell frozen custard on Sunday

       c. restriction of imported Italian ices

       d. all of these

9. The limitation of foreign guns was lobbied for by

       a. the National Rifle Association

       b. gun control advocates and gun manufacturers

       c. the National Rifle Association and gun manufacturers

       d. all of these

10. Interest groups influence

       a. legislation

       b. law enforcement

       c. public opinion

       d. all of these

REFERENCES

1. Richard Quinney, *Criminology* (Boston: Little, Brown, 1975), 37.
2. *Ibid.*, 38.
3. *Ibid.*, 37.
4. James T. Carey, *Introduction to Criminology* (Englewood Cliffs, N.J.: Prentice-Hall, 1978), 8.
5. Edwin H. Sutherland, "The Sexual Psychopath Laws," *Journal of Criminal Law, Criminology and Police Science*, 40 (1950), 543–554.
6. Quinney, *op. cit.*, 80.
7. Daniel Glaser, *Crime in Our Changing Society* (New York: Holt, Rinehart and Winston, 1978), 262.
8. See, for example, the 1951 Boggs Act (65 Stat. 767 (1951)) and the 1956 Narcotics Control Act (70 Stat. 567 (1956)).
9. Andrew Sinclair, *Prohibition: The Era of Excess* (Boston: Little, Brown, 1962), vii (Preface by Richard Hofstadter).
10. Quinney, *op. cit.*, 86.
11. Troy Duster, *The Legislation of Morality* (New York: Free Press, 1970), 3.
12. 35 Stat. 614 (1909).

13. 38 Stat. 785 (1914).
14. Alfred R. Lindesmith, *The Addict and the Law* (New York: Vintage, 1965), 5.
15. *Ibid.*, 3.
16. Donald T. Dickson, ''Bureaucracy and Morality: An Organizational Perspective on a Moral Crusade,'' *Social Problems*, 16 (1968), 143–156.
17. *Ibid.*, 149.
18. Webb v. U.S. 249 U.S. 96 (1918).
19. Jim Fuey Moy v. U.S. 254 U.S. 189 (1920).
20. U.S. v. Behrman 258 U.S. 280 (1921).
21. Linder v. U.S. 268 U.S. 5 (1924).
22. Dickson, *op. cit.*, 151.
23. Duster, *op. cit.*, 11.
24. Dickson, *op. cit.*, 143.
25. See *ante*, Section 1, Chapter 3.

24

Criminal Responsibility

OBJECTIVES

After studying this chapter, the student should be able to:

- List the elements necessary for criminal responsibility.
- Distinguish between *actus reus* and *mens rea* and discuss the need for each in criminal cases.
- Give examples of classes of people who are exempted from the provisions of criminal law because of lack of criminal capacity.
- Discuss the defense of insanity and the different legal tests of insanity.
- Describe traditional defenses to criminal charges, such as mistake of fact, duress, self-defense, and entrapment.

The criminal law defines an individual's personal responsibility to society, and holds each individual to that responsibility. The criminal law focuses on overt acts. It seeks to take action against individuals for what they do or do not do, not for what they feel or think. In this chapter, the elements of criminal responsibility are examined, and the grounds on which specific individuals and classes of individuals are exempted from that criminal responsibility are investigated.

ACTUS REUS AND *MENS REA*

Criminal responsibility consists of two elements. These are:

1. The need for an overt criminal act: [which may be an act of commission (doing) or omission (not doing something),]
2. Personal responsibility for that act.

These two elements of criminal responsibility are often referred to as *actus reus* (a guilty act) and *mens rea* (a guilty mind). In order for a person to be convicted of committing a crime, it must generally be proved that the person committed an *actus reus*, and that the *actus reus* was committed with the *mens rea* required by law.

In order for an act to constitute an *actus reus* it must be forbidden by the criminal law. If, for example, a state has not made it a crime for two unmarried adults to engage in consensual sexual intercourse, then two people who have participated in such activity cannot be arrested and prosecuted for doing so; for what they have done is not a violation of the criminal law. There is no provision in the criminal law of their state that forbids the activity in which they have indulged. This state of affairs is what is referred to by the Latin maxim, *nulla poena sine lege* (no punishment without law).

In order for a particular individual to be convicted of a crime it must be proved that the conduct in question is a violation of the criminal law. It must, of course, also be proved that the alleged conduct actually occurred. This is a question to be resolved by the police officer who investigates the case, the prosecutor who decides whether to bring charges, and the judge or jury who ultimately decides the case. If, for example, Mr. Jones complains that Mr. Smith criminally assaulted him, the responding police officer will have to decide whether the alleged act actually occurred and, if it did, whether it was a violation of the criminal code.

An *actus reus* may, as previously mentioned, be either an act of commission or an act of omission. The vast majority of crimes are, in fact, acts of commission. Killing, raping, robbing, and assaulting are, for example, all acts of commission. Failing to respond to a reasonable request for assistance by a police officer would, on the other hand, constitute an act of omission.

In order to impose criminal liability upon an individual, it is not sufficient to prove that he or she committed an *actus reus*. The individual must also have possessed the requisite *mens rea*.

> It is a principle of natural justice, and of our law, that "*actus non facit reum nisi mens sit rea.*" (The act itself does not make a man guilty, unless the mind is guilty.) The intent and the act must both concur to constitute the crime.[1]

The type of *mens rea* required will vary from crime to crime. For conviction of some crimes it is necessary to prove that the accused acted intentionally, that the accused intended the natural consequences of his or her action. The accused pointed the gun at Mr. Blue and intended to shoot him. In other crimes it must be proved that the accused was reckless. An individual is reckless when he or she unjustifiably engages in behavior that is very likely to be harmful. Thus an individual who discharges a firearm in a public place may not intend to injure anyone. The person may not even know that he or she is likely to injure anyone. The person, however, may be grossly indifferent to the consequences of his or her actions and be engaging in behavior which is highly likely to be injurious. Thus, the person could be said to be acting recklessly.

For the conviction of other crimes, it may be required that the accused acted knowingly, that the accused knew what he or she was doing, and that the accused was aware of the facts that made this act a crime. For instance, an unmarried woman may be convicted of bigamy when she goes through a marriage ceremony with a person she knows is married. Other crimes may require proof of negligence. Negligence occurs when an individual does not exercise the proper standard of care that a reasonable person would be expected to exercise in the circumstances. A charge of negligent driving would, for example, suggest that the accused was not driving as carefully as he or she should have been. The individual was careless, however, not reckless. A charge of reckless driving would have suggested that the individual had been grossly indifferent to the danger he or she was posing.

Some crimes appear to require no *mens rea*. It is, for example, generally no defense to a charge of statutory rape that the accused thought that the woman was over the relevant age. Likewise the fact that an individual broke the speed limit is usually of itself sufficient to sustain a conviction for speeding. There is no need to prove intent, recklessness, knowledge, or even negligence. These offenses are known as offenses of strict liability. It is sufficient to prove that the accused committed the *actus reus*. If the accused voluntarily committed the *actus reus* (the accused was not, for example, acting under duress), then he or she is presumed to possess the requisite *mens rea*. Here the *actus reus* itself indicates the necessary standard of responsibility.

The concept of *mens rea* should not be confused with that of motive. Motive refers to the reason for engaging or not engaging in a particular act. For example, Mr. Orange may state that he struck Mr. Black because Mr. Black insulted his wife, because he hit his son, or simply because he (Mr. Orange) hates Mr. Black. Mr. Orange is stating why he struck Mr. Black. He is describing his motive. He is not referring to the mental state required for conviction of a crime.

LACK OF CRIMINAL CAPACITY

The possession of *mens rea* is generally required for conviction of a crime. The basic reason for this is that it is a fundamental principle of our system of criminal law that we should only take criminal action against individuals who are responsible for their behavior. If people are not responsible for their actions, then it appears unfair to punish them for what they have done.

A number of classes of people are exempted from the provisions of criminal law precisely because it is felt that they should not be held responsible for their actions. Infants and the insane constitute two such classes.

Infancy

At common law there was an irrebuttable presumption that a person under seven could not possess *mens rea*. Thus, if an individual who committed an otherwise criminal act was under the age of seven, the individual could not be criminally prosecuted for the act. Between the ages of seven and fourteen there was a rebuttable presumption that the child did not possess *mens rea*. This means that if the state could prove that the child knew what he or she was doing and that it was wrong, then the child might be held criminally responsible for the wrongful act. Once he or she reached the age of fourteen, the individual was treated as an adult.

Different states have set different minimum ages at which individuals may be held criminally liable for their actions. In general, a person under the age of sixteen will be processed and treated by the juvenile justice system. The person will not be held responsible for his or her acts by the adult criminal justice system. However, in cases involving serious felonies, such as murder or forcible rape, many states allow for a juvenile to be transferred to the adult system at an earlier age.

Insanity

The insane, like the very young, are also exempted from criminal responsibility. The initial premise is, however, that a person is presumed sane until proven otherwise. Two terms that must be distinguished here are incompetence and insanity. Incompetence refers to a defendant's state of mind at the time that the criminal proceedings are taking place. A defendant is incompetent when that person does not understand the nature of the proceedings instituted against him or her, and cannot assist the lawyer in a defense. If a person is judged to be incompetent, the criminal proceedings are suspended until the person regains the capacity to stand trial.

Insanity, on the other hand, refers to the defendant's state of mind at the time that the crime was committed. It is a defense to a criminal charge. The plea of insanity argues that the defendant was not capable of possessing *mens rea*. The issue of insanity is one that must be raised by the defense. The burden of proof required varies from jurisdiction to jurisdiction. Though insanity is a defense that can generally be raised with regard to any criminal charge, it is usually invoked in only the most serious cases, such as murder. The reason for this is that an individual who is acquitted by reason of insanity will not ordinarily go free. Generally, civil commitment proceedings will be instituted against this person. The result of these proceedings may well be that the individual is deprived of personal liberty for a very long period of time, confined in a mental institution rather than a prison.

Evaluating a person's mental state of being is a difficult process at best. Deciding what a person's mental state was like at some time in the past further complicates the issue. It is not surprising, therefore, that the insanity defense has been a matter of considerable controversy.

A number of legal tests of insanity have been accepted in the United States. Four will be discussed here. Each has been criticized for being vague and difficult to apply.

The M'Naghten rule [2] is the oldest and, until recently, the most commonly used of these four tests. Laid down in 1843 in a decision of the English House of Lords, the rule states that:

> to establish a defence on the ground of insanity, it must be clearly proved that, at the time of the committing of the act, the party accused was labouring under such a defect of reason, from disease of the mind, as not to know the nature and quality of the act he was doing; or, if he did know it, that he did not know he was doing what was wrong. [3]

To present a successful defense of insanity the accused must prove two things:

1. At the time the crime was committed, the accused was suffering from some "defect of reason, from disease of the mind."
2. The result of this was that the accused did not know what he or she was doing; or, if so, did not know that it was wrong.

Considerable problems have ensued with regard to interpreting such terms as "disease of the mind," "know," and "wrong." What types of abnormality, for instance, are diseases of the mind? The problem here is twofold. First, there is no unanimity among the medical profession as to what constitutes a disease of the mind. Second, although medical testimony offered at trial may be expert opinion, the courts are not bound to follow it. Thus, there may be a clash between legal and medical definitions of mental disease. This is, indeed, all the more likely to occur in view of the differences of opinion that exist among the medical experts themselves.

The three other tests of insanity are by no means unambiguous and easy to apply either.

The "irresistible impulse" test, which is employed in a number of jurisdictions in the United States, is used in addition to the M'Naghten rule. Thus in these jurisdictions, if an individual qualifies under the M'Naghten rule, that person is judged insane. If, however, for example, the person does know the difference between right and wrong, he or she may still be judged insane. This is so if it can be proved that the criminal act was committed because of an "irresistible impulse," an impulse the person was unable to control.

A criticism that psychiatrists have raised with regard to this rule is that

> a person's behavior may be calculated and planned, rather than sudden and explosive, but still be impulsive. Conduct that is committed as the result of excessive brooding and melancholy is not considered to be impulsive under the irresistible impulse test. [4]

In addition, it may be difficult to distinguish between behavior that is uncontrollable, and that which is uncontrolled. [5]

Similar in some ways to the irresistible impulse test is the defense of diminished capacity or partial insanity. The issue here is whether an abnormal state of mind, insufficient to require acquittal in a case on the grounds of insanity, nonetheless calls for conviction of a lesser offense. Suppose, for example, that Fred, believing his wife to be having an affair with his best friend, kills her in a moment of blind rage. He is placed on trial for first-degree murder. To obtain Fred's conviction, the prosecution must prove that the killing was premeditated and deliberate. Fred's defense attorney is unable to raise the defense of insanity successfully, because he is unable to prove that Fred did not know right from wrong or that he was suffering from an irresistible impulse to kill his wife. He might, however, be able to prove that Fred was suffering from such a state of mind that he was incapable of forming a premeditated and deliberate intent to kill his wife. Such a defense, if successfully raised, might reduce the charge from first-degree murder to a lesser degree of criminal homicide.

A third test of insanity, which was established in 1954, was the Durham rule.[6] Under this test the defendant had to prove that the act committed was the product of a mental disease or defect. A seemingly simple test, its undoing has been the lack of clarity of its key concepts, "mental disease," "defect," and "product." Not only has this test found little favor in other jurisdictions, but it has also been abandoned by the very jurisdiction that established it.[7]

A fourth test, which has recently been adopted by many states, is that created by the American Law Institute in its Model Penal Code. It states that:

> A person is not responsible for criminal conduct if at the time of such conduct as a result of mental disease or defect he lacks substantial capacity either to appreciate the criminality (wrongfulness) of his conduct or to conform his conduct to the requirements of law.[8]

It has been remarked that this test differs greatly from the others:

> Other tests divide the human mind into at least three artificial compartments—the intellect, the will, and the emotions—and then concentrate on only one compartment. Hence, the M'Naghten rule concentrates on the intellect (ability to distinguish right from wrong). The irresistible impulse test concentrates on the will (powerlessness to control an impulse). The Durham rule concentrates on emotions (brooding, reflecting, melancholy). On the contrary, the Model Penal Code test views the human mind as a unified entity and recognizes that mental disease or defect may impair its functioning in more than one way.[9]

Whether the broad nature of this provision is a desirable feature is a matter for debate. As the history of the other tests has shown, problems of interpretation and application will probably continue to exist. With this test new questions arise concerning, for instance, the meaning of "substantial" and "appreciate."

Dissatisfaction with the traditional "not guilty by reason of insanity" verdict has, in fact, caused a number of states to add a new "guilty but mentally ill" verdict.[10] This new verdict applies to defendants who are mentally ill, but are not actually legally insane, at the time they commit criminal acts. Under this verdict, juries have a choice other than that of convicting a person who was suffering from mental problems at the time of committing the criminal act, or acquitting a person whom they believe to be factually guilty of the crime charged.

The defendant who is found guilty but mentally ill is given a specific sentence. After sentencing, the convicted defendant is sent to a mental unit for treatment. If cured prior to the expiration of the sentence, the convict is transferred to a penal facility. If still mentally ill when the sentence expires, the convict must be subject to civil commitment proceedings if confinement in the mental unit is to continue.

The aim of this new verdict is twofold: to provide treatment for the mentally ill defendant, and to protect society from the early release of a dangerous person. Some people believe, however, that this new verdict undermines our traditional notions of criminal responsibility by allowing the conviction of defendants who because of mental problems were not totally responsible for their criminal conduct. Others are cynical about the quality of the treatment these convicted offenders are likely to receive.

LACK OF CRIMINAL CULPABILITY

Infancy and insanity relate to criminal capacity. They focus on the inability of two classes of persons to possess *mens rea*; infants, because of their age, and the insane, because of their mental state at the time of committing the criminal act. The law does, in addition, recognize other situations in which a defendant is not held to be criminally responsible for his or her actions. Here, however, the issue is not whether the defendant had the capacity to possess *mens rea*; rather the question is whether the defendant's actions should be excused. Is there a reason why the defendant should not be held criminally culpable (blameworthy)? Four defenses will be discussed here: (1) mistake of fact, (2) duress, (3) self-defense, and (4) entrapment. Successful establishment of any of these defenses results in acquittal of the defendant.

Mistake of Fact

A defendant may generally be excused from criminal liability if he or she has acted under an honest and reasonable mistake of fact which relates to the offense which is being charged.

> Since ignorance or mistake of fact in the commission of an act which, but for such mistake, would be a crime results in the absence of the malice or criminal intention which is generally an essential element of crime, the general rule is that such ignorance or mistake of fact will exempt one from criminal responsibility, unless the mistake arises from a want of proper care on the part of accused.[11]

Consider, for instance, the following example. Tom Brown lends John Green an automobile. Green is driving the automobile, which he believes belongs to Brown, when he is stopped by the police. He is charged with unauthorized use of a motor vehicle. Unknown to Green, the car had been stolen by Brown. Since lack of consent by the owner is a crucial element of the offense charged, John Green may well have a valid defense. He must prove that his mistake in believing that Brown was the owner of the automobile was an honest and reasonable mistake. In determining the reasonableness of the mistake, all the facts of the case would be considered from the viewpoint of a reasonably prudent person standing in the defendant's position.

An honest and reasonable mistake of fact may constitute a valid defense to a criminal charge. Ignorance of the law, however, does not generally provide any defense.

> It is a rule which is deep in our law that ignorance of the law or mistake of law is no excuse, furnishes no exemption from criminal responsibility, and is ordinarily no defense to a criminal prosecution, since . . . everyone is presumed to know the law of the land, both common and statutory.[12]

Duress

A second defense to be considered here is the defense of duress or compulsion. In this case a defendant is in essence alleging that his or her *actus reus* was not voluntary; that the defendant was forced to commit the act. Not surprisingly, the law requires strict criteria for the successful establishment of the defense of duress. Thus the duress must be

> present, imminent, and impending, and of such a nature as to induce a well grounded apprehension of death or serious bodily harm if the act is not done. It must be continuous, and there must be no reasonable opportunity to escape the compulsion without committing the crime.[13]

In most states, duress cannot be used as a defense to a charge of homicide. The difficulties of establishing the existence of duress over a long period of time are well illustrated by the case of Patty Hearst. After being kidnapped by a radical group, this young heiress partook in a series of bank robberies. At trial the defense of duress was unsuccessful because she did not take advantage of the opportunities to escape that arose during the months she remained with her captors.

Self-Defense

It is a fundamental principle of our law that one may use reasonable force to protect oneself from the attack of another. Again the issue revolves around the key concept "reasonable." Suppose, for instance, that Mr. Glum, an insurance agent, keeps a gun in his desk drawer. One day while he is working quietly at his desk an irate client bursts in. The man is waving a gun and threatens Mr. Glum. Just as the client is about to fire at him, Mr. Glum reaches into his drawer and takes out his gun. He shoots and wounds the client before the client fires a shot.

In this case Mr. Glum would probably have a valid defense to any criminal charge of wounding the client; for the force he used was probably reasonable in the circumstances. Indeed had he not shot the client, Mr. Glum himself might well have been wounded or killed. Had Mr. Glum shot an unarmed client who was merely verbally abusing him or threatening him with his fists, he would in all likelihood have been held criminally responsible for his act.

Entrapment

Another commonly recognized defense to a criminal charge, which will be discussed briefly here, is the defense of entrapment. A defendant who raises this defense is in essence alleging that he or she would not have committed the crime if someone working for the government had not raised the idea and encouraged the act. In order to establish a successful defense of entrapment, it must generally be proved that:

> the criminal design originates with the officials of the government and they implant in the mind of an innocent person the disposition to commit the alleged offense and induce its commission in order that they may prosecute.[14]

The rationale for this defense is that the government should not benefit from its own wrongdoing. Law enforcement is entrusted with the prevention and detection of crime, not with its instigation.

SUMMARY

In this chapter we have examined the issue of criminal responsibility. In order to be held criminally liable for an act, a defendant must have committed an *actus reus*. The *actus reus* must also have been committed with the requisite *mens rea*. In order to establish an *actus reus*, the prosecution must prove that the alleged act actually occurred and that it was a violation of the criminal law. The *mens rea* required for conviction will depend on the crime in question. It may be, for instance, intent, recklessness, knowledge, or negligence.

A number of classes of individuals are considered incapable of possessing *mens rea*. Infants and the insane constitute two such classes. Infants are exempted from criminal responsibility because of their age. The insane are exempted because of their mental state at the time they committed the criminal act. There are, however, many difficulties in interpreting and applying the different legal tests of insanity.

While some defendants may lack criminal capacity, others may lack criminal culpability. Four defenses that may be raised with regard to a criminal charge are mistake of fact, duress, self-defense, and entrapment. The rationale for these defenses is, for the most part, a lack of blameworthiness on the part of the defendant. This relates back to the need to establish that in addition to committing a guilty act, the defendant must also have a guilty mind.

SUGGESTED ACTIVITIES

- Locate two crimes in your state's statutes that require different types of *mens rea* for conviction.
- Find out the minimum age for criminal responsibility in your state. What happens to cases when the act is committed by someone under the minimum age?

- Examine court records in your state to see if you can find out how many pleas of insanity there were in the last year, and for which offenses.
- Is there a mental health facility in your area to which the insane may be committed? Find out what percentage of the population is there after acquittal of a criminal charge on the grounds of insanity. What is the average length of stay for such individuals?
- Contact a local judge, district attorney, or defense attorney and ask how many criminal cases he or she has handled in the last year. How many of the defendants pleaded mistake of fact, duress, self-defense, or entrapment? How many of these were successful?

REVIEW

A. List the components of criminal responsibility and describe each.

B. List four different types of *mens rea* that may be required for conviction.

C. List two classes of people who are not held criminally responsible for their actions because they lack criminal capacity.

D. Distinguish between incompetence and insanity.

E. List and briefly describe four legal tests of insanity.

F. Briefly describe the following defenses:
1. mistake of fact
2. duress
3. self-defense
4. entrapment

G. Multiple Choice. Select the best answer.

1. *Mens rea* refers to the defendant's
   a. motive
   b. overt act
   c. state of mind
   d. all of these

2. In crimes of strict liability, it is necessary to prove that the defendant acted
   a. intentionally
   b. knowingly
   c. recklessly
   d. none of these

3. What was the age at common law below which a child could not be held criminally responsible?
   a. seven years
   b. fourteen years
   c. sixteen years
   d. eighteen years

4. Which of the following can generally constitute a valid defense to a criminal charge?
   a. lack of knowledge of the law
   b. mistake of fact
   c. incompetence
   d. all of these

5. Which test of insanity requires that the defendant ''lacks substantial capacity either to appreciate the criminality (wrongfulness) of his conduct or to conform his conduct with the requirements of law''?
   a. M'Naghten rule
   b. Durham rule
   c. ''irresistible impulse'' test
   d. American Law Institute's test

6. Which of the following is alleged to undermine our traditional notions of criminal responsibility?

    a. Durham rule

    b. "irresistible impulse" test

    c. American Law Institute's test

    d. Guilty but mentally ill verdict

7. To constitute a valid defense, a mistake of fact must be:

    a. honest

    b. reasonable

    c. both of these

    d. neither of these

8. When a person is judged incompetent, what is the result of the criminal charge?

    a. conviction

    b. acquittal

    c. the proceedings are suspended until the person is fit to stand trial

    d. none of these

9. When a defendant successfully pleads insanity, he or she usually will then be

    a. acquitted of the charge

    b. civilly committed

    c. confined in a mental institution

    d. all of these

10. To constitute a valid defense of self-defense, the force used must

    a. not result in injury

    b. not result in death

    c. be reasonable

    d. all of these

REFERENCES

1. Fowler v. Padget 7.T.R. 509 (1798), per Lord Kenyon C.J. See also, 22 C.J.S. *Criminal Law,* 329 (Brooklyn, N.Y.: American Book, 1961).
2. R. v. Daniel M'Naghten 10 Cl. and F. 200 (1843).
3. *Ibid.*
4. David A. Jones, *Crime and Criminal Responsibility* (Chicago: Nelson-Hall, 1978), 48.
5. Gwynn Nettler, *Explaining Crime* (New York: McGraw-Hill, 1974), 26.
6. Durham v. United States 214 F. 2d 862 (D.C. Cir. 1954).
7. United States v. Brawner 471 F. 2d 969 (D.C. Cir. 1972).
8. American Law Institute, *Model Penal Code: Proposed Official Draft* (Philadelphia: A.L.I., 1962), section 4.01.
9. Jones, *op. cit.,* 49–50.
10. Such states include Alaska, Delaware, Georgia, Illinois, Indiana, Kentucky, Michigan, New Mexico, and South Carolina. For a thorough discussion of the guilty but mentally ill verdict, see, for example, Bradley D. McGraw, Daina Farthing-Capowich, and Ingo Keilitz, "The 'Guilty but Mentally Ill' Plea and Verdict: Current State of the Knowledge," *Villanova Law Review*, 30 (1985), 117–191.
11. 22 C.J.S. Criminal Law, section 47 (Brooklyn, N.Y.: American Book, 1961).
12. *Ibid.,* section 48.
13. *Ibid.,* section 44.
14. Sorrells v. U.S. 287 U.S. 435, 442 (1932).

25

History
of the Police

OBJECTIVES

After studying this chapter, the student should be able to:

- Give reasons for the existence of law enforcement agencies.
- Distinguish between private and public law enforcement.
- Trace the development of public law enforcement.
- Discuss the scope of operations of federal, state, and local law enforcement agencies.

In the previous section, the emergence of criminal law was discussed and its major features were outlined. It was also said that states enunciate rules of conduct for their citizens to follow. The need for the state to designate officials to interpret and enforce these rules was also noted. It is the police who are, in essence, the front-line agency entrusted with the enforcement and, to a degree, the interpretation of the criminal law.

> In a broad sense, the term police connotes the maintenance of public order and the protection of persons and property from the hazards of public accidents and the commission of unlawful acts; specifically, it applies to the body of civil officers charged with maintaining the public order and safety and enforcement of the law, including the detection and suppression of crime.[1]

In order to function properly, a state must maintain a certain degree of peace and security within its borders. The police role includes both the preservation of peace and order and the detection and apprehension of criminals. It is with reason that the police are referred to as "civil officers;" for this distinguishes them from military personnel, a distinction that was considered important both in England and in the United States.

The police, with their general peacekeeping powers and duties, are also to be distinguished from other more specialized law enforcement officials. These other officials have the task of seeing that there is compliance with the provisions of certain laws, detecting breaches of those laws, and apprehending alleged violators. As we shall see, general police powers are exercised by the states, mainly through local police departments. All levels of government, federal, state, and local, have established law enforcement agencies with specific regulatory duties.

PUBLIC VERSUS PRIVATE LAW ENFORCEMENT

Law enforcement is today perhaps thought of primarily in terms of a public function. The different units of government each maintain their own law enforcement agencies. There are law enforcement forces at the federal, state, and local levels. The officers of these forces serve the public at the public's expense. They are agents of the state, employed to preserve and enforce the law without favor or discrimination.

Not all law enforcement is, however, of such a public nature. Businesses and private individuals hire security guards to provide added protection against the criminal element. Private security firms such as Wells Fargo, Pinkerton's, and Brink's have long specialized in such work. In addition, there are private detective agencies who will obtain, for a fee, information for private individuals. Because of the contractual nature of the services rendered, these firms, unlike their public counterparts, owe their duty of service to specific individuals, and not to the public in general. They are, nonetheless, bound to uphold the law in the performance of their duties.

THE DEVELOPMENT OF PUBLIC LAW ENFORCEMENT

The system of public law enforcement in the United States has its antecedents in other countries. Some important highlights in the history of its development follow.

In the early days of civilization, retribution for wrongs suffered was essentially a matter of private concern. Indeed, since in a strict sense there was no law in existence, there could be no machinery of law enforcement. Revenge was left largely in the hands of the wronged individual and his or her family. At that time the state did not pursue wrongdoers in its own interests of peace and security.

With the emergence of the state as a strong central force, laws were enacted; and there developed a need for the state to establish a means of enforcing the laws. In early times, the maintenance of law and order was largely the responsibility of the military. The ruler was the chief lawmaker and his power depended to a great extent upon his control of the armed forces. They in turn were responsible for preserving peace and security within the kingdom.

Ancient Rome

The Roman emperor Augustus is generally credited with the establishment of the first large-scale civilian police force. In the early part of his reign (which began in essence in 31 B.C. after the Battle of Actium), the city of Rome was guarded by three cohorts. A cohort was a military unit of some 600 men. In addition, forces of slaves under the command of appointed officials were utilized to help fight fires and quell internal civil disorders.

When this system proved inadequate, Augustus established (in about 6 A.D.) the Vigiles of Rome. The men in this unit were not military personnel and were for the most part freed slaves. They were responsible for "policing and for security from riot or fire." [2] An interesting feature of the Augustan system was the division of the city of Rome into wards, and the assignment of groups of Vigiles to the various wards, thus giving rise to the "police administrative concept, division by area." [3]

England

Both the Anglo-Saxon and later medieval systems of law enforcement in England relied heavily upon the community. During the ninth century most of the Anglo-Saxon towns were divided into tithings, groups of ten families. Each tithing was responsible for the conduct of all of its members and for seeing that any of its offending members were brought to justice (the mutual pledge system). Each tithing in turn took on the overall responsibility for maintaining law and order within the town. The tithings also served as basic military units, and were organized into groups of ten which were called hundreds. The hundreds' courts were the main judicial forums for the administration of justice and the settling of private disputes. The hundreds were in turn organized into larger geographical areas called shires.

> The military and police systems were closely allied; the national militia was organised in tythings and hundreds, and had a place to fill in the complete design of peace maintenance; its embodiment was not only resorted to in time of war, it was also liable to be called out by "summons of the array" if disturbances were feared, or even for the pursuit of a single fugitive from justice, but its members could not be called upon to serve beyond the limits of their respective shires except to repel invasion.[4]

The shire-reeve, who was the precursor of the modern-day sheriff, was "responsible for the conservancy of the peace in the hundreds" [5] and was

> enabled to muster the *posse comitatus*, or whole available police force of the shire, in case of emergency. All men went armed in those days, and since the members of a tything were obliged on the summons of a headborough to join in the pursuit, the cry of "Stop thief" was a formidable weapon in the hands of the local executive.[6]

In addition to law enforcement duties, the shire-reeve, as the direct representative of the Crown, was also responsible for collecting taxes and overseeing government affairs.

After the Norman Conquest of 1066, there was a general strengthening of the central government. There was still primary emphasis on local administration of justice, but with greater involvement of the Crown. Itinerant justices began to travel throughout the country, hearing and deciding cases.

In 1285 King Edward I introduced, through the Statute of Winchester, some important developments in the system of law enforcement. Communal responsibility for crime was strengthened and watches were required to be established in every town. Every man under the age of sixty was to arm himself according to his means so that he could help maintain order and defend the kingdom. Constables in every hundred were to conduct regular arms inspections and draw up lists of those liable to serve. In London, for example, "The city was divided into twenty-four wards, and in each ward there were six watchmen." [7] The "watch and ward" system was thus firmly established.

During the next century, the offices of justice of the peace and constable took on much of the form that they have today. The justice of the peace was the main local judicial official. The constable was the main law enforcement official, under whose supervision the watch and ward system operated. The authority and power of the sheriff waned considerably.

Both the constables and the members of the watch were civilians who were for the most part unpaid for performing what were considered public duties. In time, as might be expected, men began to buy their way out of their duties and pay substitutes to perform their work. "These paid substitutes were generally regarded by more generous historians as men of low ability and questionable character." [8] Thus, important functions were being carried out by men who were ill equipped to perform them properly.

With the Industrial Revolution of the late 1700s, the crime situation within the cities worsened considerably. People flocked to the cities. Unemployment rose. Savage criminal penalties did little to stem the rising tide of crime.

> Eventually, many forms of private police came into existence. *Merchant police* were employed by merchants to protect their places of business. *Parish police* consisted of church members serving in rotation to protect members of the congregation. *Dock police* or police employed by shipping companies concerned themselves with protecting goods on the docks. Needless to say, none of these proved capable of handling the problem, and, in fact, their inefficiency and disorganization probably contributed to the problem. [9]

The late eighteenth century saw the emergence of paid public police forces. The Fielding brothers, both in turn London magistrates, formed the Bow Street Runners in about 1750. These officers responded to reports of crime and attempted to apprehend the wrongdoers. Though distrusted at first, they began to win the confidence of the public. Interestingly, they were entitled to receive any rewards offered for the detection and apprehension of criminals.

England in the early 1800s was a country of growing political unrest. The Bow Street Runners had proved to be somewhat of a success, as had the state-run Marine Police, established in 1798 to help render the London docks and waterways more secure from the attacks of thieves and robbers. The establishment of a large-scale public police force was a controversial issue. Most people desired to see London made a safer and more orderly city. Many, however, feared that the establishment of a central police force might pave the way for a police state.

A strong proponent of a central police force was the politician, Robert Peel, who became home secretary in 1822. In 1829, a Police Bill was passed by Parliament and later that year the first organized English metropolitan police force came into existence. The 3,000-man force was originally led by two magistrates called commissioners. Their jurisdiction encompassed all of the large urban area of London except for the ancient City of London, which received its own public police force in 1839. Other police forces were established throughout the country, and a parliamentary act of 1856 required every borough and county to have a police force. The debt owed to Sir Robert Peel for his part in establishing the modern police force is still recognized today by the fact that English police officers are often referred to as "bobbies." Though this term was originally used in a contemptuous manner, today it is a mark of the respect that has been earned.

The United States

The colonists brought their systems of law enforcement over to America with them. Two main systems were transplanted: the sheriff from rural England and the constable and watch and ward system from the urban areas. As a generalization, the sheriff was the more common law enforcement official in the open agricultural areas of the South. The watch and ward system, on the other hand, was more likely to be established in the more urban areas of the North.

> The transfer of the officers of constable and sheriff to rural American areas—which included most colonial territory—was accomplished with little change in structure of the offices. Drawing upon the pattern of the mutual pledge system, the constable was made responsible for law enforcement in towns, while the sheriff took charge of policing the counties.[10]

The lack of apparent outward difference between the law enforcement systems of the new and old world should not, however, detract attention from the differing underlying philosophy of the law enforcement system of the new world. For dissatisfaction with the ways of the old world led the colonists to establish, almost from the start, a system that focused more on civil rights and liberties and saw law enforcement officers more as "proxies for other citizens" than as representatives of the monarch or some powerful elite.[11]

In the early days of colonization, great use was made of the military to help maintain peace and security. The first city to establish a civilian night watch to supplement the military guard was Boston. This occurred in 1636, and other cities, such as New York and Philadelphia, followed suit.

> As in England, the early night watches were anything but effective. They had the appearance of vigilantes and were often lazy. Usually, members of the watch were citizens who had to rotate the responsibility among themselves. Like their counterparts in England,

these citizens frequently hired substitutes who often were less than respectable citizens. It was also not uncommon for a court to sentence a minor misdemeanor to be a watchman as a form of punishment.[12]

As the American towns and cities grew larger, the crime problem increased; and the system of law enforcement became less and less capable of dealing with the situation.

In 1833, the city of Philadelphia established a day watch. Other cities followed this lead. The existence of what were separate day and night watches was, however, by no means satisfactory. The watches came under the administration and supervision of different authorities. Rivalries existed among the men in the different watches, and this led to a lack of coordination of efforts and sharing of information.

To remedy this situation, New York established in 1844 the first combined day and night police force. By the early 1900s "there were few cities of consequence without such unified forces."[13]

FEDERAL, STATE, AND LOCAL LAW ENFORCEMENT AGENCIES

The development of public law enforcement in the United States occurred primarily at the local level. The colonists were fearful of establishing a strong central government. As a result they entrusted the federal government with only such powers as were deemed necessary. Consequently, general police powers were exercised by the States, which left the task of policing to the local units of government. The focus on local policing was reinforced by the small size of many of the communities and by difficulties in travel and communication between them. The federal government itself did not have any general police force. Rather, it established specialized law enforcement agencies to enforce particular laws. Though there has been considerable growth in the number and size of such federal agencies, the picture today is not very different.

Though the numbers are open to debate, it may be estimated that there are close to 25,000 law enforcement agencies operating within the United States.[14] Well over 90 percent of them are local police agencies. Many of them are very small in size. A survey of employment and expenditure in the criminal justice system[15] noted that in October, 1982, there were at all levels of government about 724,000 full-time and full-time-equivalent employees engaged in police and law enforcement functions. Of these, about 590,000 were employed on the local level and 78,000 on the state level.

The vast number of police agencies has to a large extent helped prevent the realization of the fear that establishment of a public police force would lead to the development of a police state. The large number of agencies has also, however, presented somewhat of a barrier against effective law enforcement. For while crime is no respecter of geographical boundaries, lack of cooperation and coordination between different police departments has hampered, and indeed still hampers, law enforcement efforts.

Largely in response to these types of concerns, in the nineteenth century some of the states began to set up their own state police forces. These original state police forces were, however, generally small in size and limited in purpose. In 1835, the then Republic of Texas formed the Texas Rangers, who, operating as a military unit, were responsible for patrolling the border and investigating crimes within the republic. In 1865, in an effort to control the vice problem within the state, Massachusetts established a small state police force.

In 1905, the state of Pennsylvania set up what is considered to be the first full-scale state police force. This was largely in response to growing unrest, particularly in the state's coal fields. Other states followed suit and by the outbreak of World War II such forces were to be found in virtually every state in the Union. The jurisdiction of these state police agencies is varied, however. Some, such as California and Ohio, are responsible only for enforcing traffic laws and protecting life and property on the highways. Others, such as New York and Michigan, possess a general authority to investigate criminal matters throughout the state. Many of the state police agencies retain a riot control function. Many of them provide the local agencies with technical assistance and support services such as crime laboratories and training facilities. Whatever the jurisdiction of the state police force, it has merely supplemented, and not supplanted, the existing local machinery of law enforcement.

Not to be forgotten, too, are the large number of specialized law enforcement agencies that exist on both the state and local levels. Thus there are public agencies with limited police authority such as campus and park police. There are also persons with limited law enforcement responsibilities such as officials entrusted with enforcing alcoholic beverage control, health, and housing laws.

The establishment of federal law enforcement agencies has occurred in somewhat of a piecemeal fashion. Reliance for law enforcement has rested primarily on the local police agencies. The federal agencies have, for the most part, been created to oversee the enforcement of particular federal legislative measures.

In 1789, the federal Revenue Cutter Service was established in an attempt to control the smuggling problem. In 1836, the postmaster general was authorized to employ salaried postal agents to investigate infringements of the postal laws. In 1865, the U.S. Secret Service was formed within the Department of the Treasury. Its main original objective was to deal with the serious counterfeiting problem that then existed.

In addition to these agencies, many other federal law enforcement units came into existence, including the U.S. Border Patrol and the Federal Bureau of Narcotics, which is now part of the Drug Enforcement Administration.

In many ways the U.S. marshal was the original federal law enforcement official. The position was established in 1789, and the image is often given of a gallant official striving to maintain law and order in the frontier days of the wild west. Today the U.S. marshal is essentially an officer of the court. General federal law enforcement responsibilities are carried out by the Federal Bureau of Investigation.

The FBI was established in 1908 and was reorganized in 1924 with the appointment of J. Edgar Hoover as its director. It is the investigative arm of the U.S. Department of Justice, the federal agency with the major responsibility for law enforcement activity. The FBI is responsible for the investigation of all violations of federal law that do not come under the jurisdiction of another federal agency. This includes the investigation of violations of federal criminal law, such as tampering with the U.S. mail and interstate crimes.

Over the years, the Bureau has grown greatly in size and jurisdiction. Under the careful guidance of J. Edgar Hoover, who directed the Bureau from the time of his appointment in 1924 until his death in 1972, the FBI grew from "441 special agents in 1924 to 8,000 special agents and more than 1,100 civilian employees in 59 field offices located throughout the United States and Puerto Rico." [16] In addition to investigating federal criminal matters, the FBI provides centralized criminal laboratories, and crime reporting and identification systems.

SUMMARY

This chapter has discussed the need for some system of law enforcement and examined the development of public law enforcement agencies.

In early times, revenge was left largely in the hands of the wronged individual and his or her family. There was no public machinery of law enforcement. With the emergence of the state as a central force, law enforcement became far more of a public concern. At first, the maintenance of law and order was mainly the responsibility of the military. It was the Roman emperor Augustus who is generally credited with the establishment of the first large-scale civilian police force.

In both Anglo-Saxon and later medieval England there was heavy emphasis upon community responsibility for law enforcement. This system, and in particular the watch and ward, proved ineffective. Private law enforcement agencies emerged and there developed a desire for a paid public police force. Though there was much opposition to the creation of such a force, Sir Robert Peel managed in 1829 to bring about the establishment of a London metropolitan police force. Support for such forces spread, and an act of 1858 required every borough and county in England to have a police force.

The colonists of the United States brought their law enforcement systems with them. As in England, they did not prove to be highly effective. In time, paid civilian night watches were established. To these were added separate day watches. In 1844, New York established the first combined day and night watch. The modern-day United States local police force was born.

While most public law enforcement in the United States is still of a local nature today, there are also in existence state and federal law enforcement agencies. Problems of cooperation and coordination between local law enforcement units led largely to the formation of state police forces. Federal law enforcement agencies have been created in somewhat of a piecemeal fashion, for the most part to oversee the enforcement of particular federal legislative measures. Foremost among the present-day federal law enforcement agencies is the Federal Bureau of Investigation. Formed in 1908, the FBI is responsible for investigating federal criminal matters. In addition, it provides centralized criminal laboratories, and crime reporting and identification systems.

SUGGESTED ACTIVITIES

- What is the history of your local police? Consult the police department to find out how long it has existed, what changes have evolved, and what existed before it was established. Go as far back as you can.
- What is the history of your state police force: when and why was it formed?
- Find out what powers your state police have, and what functions they perform. In what ways does your state police force work with your local police force?
- Where is the nearest branch office of the FBI? To what extent and in what manner does the FBI work with your local and state police forces?

REVIEW

A. List three reasons for the existence of police.

B. State the main difference between public and private law enforcement.

C. Trace the history of public law enforcement in England and in the United States.

D. What is the jurisdiction of the state police?

E. What does the FBI do?

F. Multiple Choice. Select the best answer.

1. Private security firms
   a. provide additional protection
   b. are not bound to uphold the law
   c. owe their duty to the public
   d. all of these

2. Without law there can be no
   a. law enforcement
   b. order
   c. punishment
   d. all of these

3. The earliest law enforcers were
   a. judges
   b. soldiers
   c. sheriffs
   d. none of these

4. A tithing was
   a. a group of ten families in ninth-century England
   b. the precursor of the modern-day sheriff
   c. a military unit that guarded Rome
   d. none of these

5. The shire-reeve was
   a. the king's representative in the community
   b. the precursor of the modern-day sheriff
   c. the tax collector
   d. all of these

6. The "watch and ward" system was strengthened by
   a. the Battle of Actium
   b. the Statute of Winchester
   c. the Norman Conquest of 1066
   d. all of these

7. The Fielding brothers formed the
   a. merchant police
   b. Bow Street Runners
   c. marine police
   d. parish police
8. The large number of police agencies has
   a. helped prevent emergence of a police state
   b. hindered effective law enforcement
   c. both of these
   d. neither of these
9. Most police agencies in the United States are
   a. local
   b. state
   c. federal
   d. none of these
10. The federal law enforcement agencies were set up
    a. to enforce local, state, and federal statutes
    b. to oversee particular federal legislation
    c. to regulate local police agencies
    d. all of these

REFERENCES

1. *Encyclopedia Britannica*, Vol. 18 (Chicago: Encyclopedia Britannica Ltd., 1960), 158.
2. Ronald Syme, *The Roman Revolution* (London: Oxford University Press, 1960), 357.
3. Vern L. Folley, *American Law Enforcement*, 3rd ed. (Boston: Allyn and Bacon, 1980), 40.
4. W. L. Melville Lee, *A History of Police in England* (Montclair, N.J.: Patterson Smith, 1971), 7.
5. *Ibid.*
6. *Ibid.*, 7–8.
7. *Ibid.*, 31. The Statute of Winchester did not, in fact, apply to London, which was governed by a special act which was enacted that same year.
8. Harry Caldwell, *Basic Law Enforcement* (Pacific Palisades, Calif.: Goodyear, Inc., 1972), 16.
9. Folley, *op. cit.*, 59.
10. The President's Commission on Law Enforcement and Administration of Justice, *Task Force Report: The Police* (Washington, D.C.: U.S. Government Printing Office, 1967), 5.
11. Victor G. Strecher, *The Environment of Law Enforcement: A Community Relations Guide* (Englewood Cliffs, N.J.: Prentice-Hall, 1971), 15.
12. Folley, *op. cit.*, 70.
13. The President's Commission on Law Enforcement and Administration of Justice, *op. cit.*, 5.
14. The exact number is not known. Though the President's Commission on Law Enforcement and Justice cited the existence of some 40,000 law enforcement agencies—50 at the federal, 200 at the state and 39,750 at the local levels—[The President's Commission on Law Enforcement and Administration of Justice, *Task Force Report: The Police* (Washington, D.C.: U.S. Government Printing Office, 1967), 7.], this estimate has been revised downwards. Thus, The National Advisory Commission on Criminal Justice Standards and Goals refers to the "25,000 police chief executives in America." [National Advisory Commission on Criminal Justice Standards and Goals, *The Police* (Washington, D.C.: U.S. Government Printing Office, 1973), 4.] Meanwhile, a 1975 directory of criminal justice agencies listed 20,158 state and local law enforcement agencies. [U.S. Department of Justice, *Criminal Justice Agencies* (Washington, D.C.: U.S. Government Printing Office, 1975), 1.]
15. U.S. Department of Justice, *Bureau of Justice Statistics Bulletin: Justice Expenditure and Employment, 1982* (Washington, D.C.: U.S. Government Printing Office, 1985).
16. Folley, *op. cit.*, 100.

26

Role
of the Police

OBJECTIVES

After studying this chapter, the student should be able to:

- Enumerate the different demands placed on the police by society.
- Distinguish between the law enforcement, order maintenance, and service functions performed by the police.
- Explain the concept of police discretion.
- Discuss the issue of police-community relations.

To many individuals the word "police" typically conjures up the image of officers arresting criminals or following up leads on reported crimes. However, the solving of crimes and the apprehension of suspects are only two of a great many tasks performed by the police. This chapter examines these various functions and duties entrusted to the police.

THE DIVERSITY OF POLICE AGENCIES

The large number of law enforcement agencies that exist in the United States was discussed in the preceding chapter. Reference also was made to distinctions between the powers and duties of federal, state, and local police agencies. While federal agencies are responsible for dealing with matters affecting federal interests (such as the commission of federal crimes), state and local police departments are responsible for preserving and enforcing state laws. The local police departments comprise over 90 percent of the 25,000 or so police agencies operating within the United States. They indeed possess the prime responsibility for carrying out police functions. The size and nature of these departments vary considerably, ranging from one-officer police forces in some rural areas to departments of thousands of officers in some of the larger cities (New York City, for example, currently employs some 25,044 police officers).[1] The roles and functions of these local police departments naturally vary as a result of both their own composition and that of the community they serve. Thus the following discussion of the functions of the police will certainly not apply in a like manner to all local police forces. Their powers, their structure and organization, their problems, and their approaches to tasks and problems will all differ.

LAW ENFORCEMENT, ORDER MAINTENANCE, AND SERVICE FUNCTIONS

The general functions performed by the police can be divided into three main categories: law enforcement, order maintenance, and service. Law enforcement is the police mission of seeing that there is compliance with the provisions of the law, detecting breaches of the law, and apprehending alleged violators. Order maintenance, on the other hand, is the task of preserving peace and security. Service functions consist of such tasks as escorting funerals, ambulances, or oversize vehicles; guarding dignitaries; rescuing cats; locating missing persons; and providing emergency assistance for the injured or sick. It should be noted that a particular activity may involve more than one of these categories. For example, directing traffic may be viewed as both a service and an order maintenance function.

Law Enforcement

The law enforcement function—that is, the task of crime control—is what is generally thought of as the police role. Police efficiency is often measured by arrest or clearance rates, and sometimes, and far more unfairly, by the fluctuations in crime rates. The majority of a police department's time is, however, by no means directed toward law enforcement activities. Some officers may spend virtually all of their time on law enforcement tasks. Detectives, for example, are responsible for the investigation of criminal cases. Other officers, however, may be assigned to what are essentially order maintenance or service duties.

Primary responsibility for law enforcement in many ways rests upon the shoulders of the patrol officer (who may also be the detective in some of the very small departments). This officer is ever present in the community, seeking to prevent breaches of the law and attempting to take appropriate action when breaches do in fact occur. The objectives of the patrol unit have been stated to include the following:

1. deny the criminal the opportunity to commit crime;
2. control conditions, within the patrol unit's sphere of influence, that are conducive to crime;
3. provide instant response to requests for police services;
4. protect lives and property;
5. maintain the peace and tranquillity of the community;
6. seek voluntary compliance with the law;
7. enforce the law and arrest offenders.[2]

The law enforcement demands placed upon the patrol officer are diverse and comprehensive. The patrol officer's presence is believed to have a deterrent effect on criminal activity. Indeed, with the advent of computer technology, some police departments calculate the number of officers who are to work on each shift, and the deployment of those officers, in the light of current crime patterns.[3]

Whenever a crime is reported to the police department, the patrol officer is the officer responsible for responding immediately to the scene. On occasion, the patrol officer may witness a crime in progress. At the crime scene, the patrol officer is responsible for discovering exactly what has happened; determining whether a crime has been committed; attempting, if at all possible, to obtain the immediate apprehension of the alleged suspect; seeing to the immediate medical needs of the crime victim; locating witnesses and obtaining statements from them; and securing the crime scene—seeing that there is no tampering with objects that may serve as physical evidence in the case.

After leaving the crime scene, the patrol officer may have to transport the crime victim to a hospital, give the victim advice on precautionary measures that can be taken in the future, carry evidence to the crime lab, locate witnesses, and attempt to arrest the alleged violator. In some police departments—particularly the very small ones—the same officer may be responsible for carrying out the complete investigation of the case up to its conclusion. In most departments, however, the follow-up investigative functions are carried out by detectives.

The primary emphasis of the patrol officer's function is on law enforcement. This does not, however, mean that all, or even most, of the officer's time is taken up with law enforcement activities. Indeed, it has been estimated that:

> An ordinary patrol officer in a metropolitan police agency probably devotes no more than 10 to 15 percent of available time to activities directly related to criminal law enforcement. And even here, "crime fighting" most often entails intervention in minor crime situations involving misdemeanors and public order offenses.[4]

Order Maintenance

A second important function performed by the police department is that of order maintenance. The emphasis with respect to the law enforcement function is on promoting compliance with the dictates of the law. With regard to order maintenance the emphasis is on the preservation of peace and security. Though we often speak of "law and order," the interests of law and those of order are by no means always the same. The interests of law require that if a violation of the law occurs, the violator should be pursued and made to pay the appropriate penalty. The interests of order maintenance, on the other hand, may suggest that the full force of the law not be applied and that, in some cases, violations of the law actually be overlooked. Thus if, for example, a police officer comes upon two young men busily engaged in a fistfight, the officer may arrest them for disturbing the peace, or for assault or some other similar offense. On the other hand, the officer may simply tell them to stop fighting, investigate the cause of the dispute, attempt to settle it, and let them go after issuing an appropriate warning or some advice. What the officer has done is restore peace and order, rather than enforce the law. Indeed, to enforce the law may in some situations make matters worse rather than better. An arrest for a minor offense in a racially inflamed neighborhood may give rise to a major disturbance. The better course of action here may be to deal with the matter in a less formal fashion. Indeed, it must be recognized that:

> To the patrolman, the law is one resource among many that he may use to deal with disorder, but it is not the only one or even the most important. . . . Thus he approaches incidents that threaten order not in terms of enforcing the law but in terms of "handling the situation." [5]

The officer on the street enjoys a certain amount of discretion in handling situations. Often departmental policy will dictate a certain type of approach. Sometimes the approach to a particular type of problem will change over the years. Such has happened with spouse abuse cases. For many years, police employed an order maintenance approach through use of crisis intervention and mediation techniques. Now, however, as a result of pressure from women's groups and research studies that indicate that arrest may be a more effective response,[6] the police are moving toward more regular use of a law enforcement approach.

To some people, the answer may be simple. The law should always be enforced. An additional point that must be made here, however, is that the criminal justice system is ill equipped to handle full enforcement of the law. The system is overcrowded and backlogged as it is. The problems faced by courts, prosecutors, and the correctional system would become overwhelming if anything approaching full enforcement of the laws were ever attempted by the police.

Service

A third function performed by police agencies is the service function. Service functions include the multitude of duties entrusted to the police that often have little to do with law enforcement. The police are responsible for the performance of these tasks partly as a result of their historical development as the agency responsible for the peace and general well-being of the community and partly as a result of the fact that they are for the most part the only government agency that continuously provides service twenty-four hours a day, seven days a week. As the National Advisory Commission on Criminal Justice Standards and Goals has pointed out,

The role of the police has expanded greatly as society has become more complex. Many and varied demands have been made upon the police because of their unique authority. Dealing with alcoholics and the mentally ill, providing ambulance service, handling stray animals, and controlling vehicular and pedestrian traffic are but a few examples.

Because police are usually the only government representatives available around-the-clock, and because they have investigative resources and the authority to use force, the police are frequently called upon to perform municipal services that could more appropriately be performed by another agency of government.[7]

There has, indeed, been considerable debate about whether the police should continue to perform these service functions. Some people think that carrying out such tasks has several negative consequences. These include the inflation of the police budget and the distortion of the apparent cost of crime control; prevention of professionalism in the police career group; dilution of police attention to their primary assignment of combating violation of traditional criminal laws; and, finally, prevention of more satisfactory performance of the service functions by an especially constituted agency.[8]

Pitted against these beliefs about police involvement in service tasks are the counterarguments that such use of the police might well help generate goodwill toward them; help obtain information which is of value in combating traditional crimes; and provide governmental economy by entrusting these functions to an already existing government agency.[9]

Police agencies vary greatly with regard to the extent that they carry out service functions. Faced with the allegation that their performance in this area is less than totally adequate, some agencies have responded by instituting special training programs or establishing specialized units. Some police departments have established Family Crisis Intervention Units which in many ways perform more of a social service than either order maintenance or law enforcement. Other police departments have begun to work far more closely with social service agencies. Still other police agencies have handed over prime responsibility for this type of work to social service agencies and private organizations. The crucial question to be faced by police departments is whether they wish to continue to perform these service functions or have other agencies assume prime responsibility for them. If a police department does decide to continue to perform these various service functions, then a second issue to be addressed is whether sworn police officers should be utilized to carry out these duties. Civilian employees currently perform many of the clerical duties. Other duties might be entrusted to them as well. Traffic control might be one such example. Some foreign countries have an agency other than the police perform this task. Even if this model were not adopted in the United States, traffic regulation might be undertaken by civilian employees rather than sworn police officers; for, as has been remarked,

Traffic direction is a necessary, but boring, unstimulating, unchallenging activity requiring little education and only a minimum of training. Its primary requirements are a pair of high arches and a marked imperviousness to inclement weather. It demands none of the skills needed for combatting violations of the traditional criminal law.[10]

Each police department decides upon the emphasis it will give to its service role. It also decides what balance is to be struck between the functions of law enforcement and order maintenance.

THE POLICE AND THE COMMUNITY

It is ironic that police functions were originally performed by members of the community, and thus the police and the community were essentially one and the same. In many instances nowadays a sharp distinction seems to exist between the police and the community. There is sometimes an "us" versus "them" type of mentality on both sides. As the community's agents of social control, it may be argued that the police should, within the framework of the law, represent and enforce that community's interests. A number of factors, however, may serve to increase the distance between the police and the community.

First, a community is rarely homogeneous. It is generally composed of different ethnic, social, religious, and economic groups. Just as different interest groups may favor or oppose a particular piece of legislation, so they may disagree about the desirability of enforcing a particular law. It is both impractical and socially undesirable to attempt to achieve full enforcement of the laws. Thus a decision must be made, at some level, as to the extent to which the law will be enforced. With regard to the serious felonies such as murder, rape, and robbery this may not pose much of a problem, as few would argue against full enforcement. With regard to other laws, however, such as laws concerning gambling, drugs, alcohol, and consensual sexual activity (the so-called victimless crimes), there may be bitter debate about both the desirability of such legislation and the need to enforce it.

As the governmental agency entrusted with enforcing the law, the police may encounter difficulties no matter what action they take. If they enforce the law, some segment of the community may feel that they are being harassed and discriminated against. If, on the other hand, they fail to enforce the law, another segment of the community may feel that they are shirking their duty to uphold the law.

Integral to this issue is the concept of police discretion, the idea that the police enjoy a certain amount of freedom in their decision making. As Kenneth Culp Davis has stated: "A public officer has discretion whenever the effective limits of his power leave him free to make a choice among possible courses of action or inaction."[11]

Though the mandatory nature of the law appears to leave them with little discretion, the police do have to decide to what extent they will enforce laws and whether they will apply them in particular situations. Administrative guidelines may be issued at the police executive level. Whether or not such guidelines are issued, a great deal of discretion remains with the individual police officer. When confronting a particular situation, each officer must decide upon the appropriate course of action. Often a legalistic approach to law enforcement will serve to alienate the community.

Indeed, it is here that the police often face conflicting demands placed on them by the public. As the English attorney, Ben Whitaker, has remarked:

The public uses the police as a scapegoat for its neurotic attitude towards crime. Janus-like we have always turned two faces toward a policeman. We expect him to be human and yet inhuman. We employ him to administer the law, and yet ask him to waive it. We resent him when he enforces the law in our own case, yet demand his dismissal when he does not elsewhere. We offer him bribes, yet denounce his corruption. We expect him to be a member of society, yet not to share its values. We admire violence, even against society itself, but condemn force by the police on our behalf. We tell the police that they are entitled to information from the public, yet we ostracize informers. We ask for crime to be eradicated, but only by the use of "sporting" methods.[12]

There is at best a difficult relationship between the police and the public they serve. The police are, however, dependent upon public support and cooperation for the proper performance of their tasks. As Louis Radelet has stated:

Paid police officers, even under conditions of intensive specialization and extensive training, cannot possibly perform their duties effectively without abundant self-policing by the citizen. This custom is not merely a matter of cooperation or good relations between police and community. Ideally, it is a matter of organic union, with the police as part of, rather than apart from, the community they serve.[13]

SUMMARY

This chapter has examined the different tasks performed by the police. The police role was described as encompassing law enforcement, order maintenance, and service functions. Some people consider law enforcement to be the main police responsibility. It is, however, in a sense only one of the approaches that the police may utilize in their task of order maintenance. Each department and, to a greater or lesser extent, each police officer must decide upon the emphasis that is to be given to law enforcement and order maintenance respectively. Indeed, a police department which is overly legalistic in its approach may only serve to alienate members of the community and promote disorder rather than peace in the community.

The police have been entrusted with a wide diversity of service tasks. Some people feel that performance of these duties detracts from the primary police functions and that they should be carried out by other agencies or organizations. Again, the decision concerning the police role is one that is made at the local level. Regardless of the decision that is made, it is important that the service functions be satisfactorily carried out by some agency.

The police exist to protect and serve their respective communities. Yet often a deep division exists between the police and various segments of the community. This may be fostered by differences in ethnic, social, religious, or economic background; by police enforcement (or nonenforcement) of particular laws; or by perceptions of unfair exercise of police discretion. Whatever the nature or cause of this rift between the police and the community, it serves no useful purpose when it succeeds in setting up two bitterly opposed camps. In order to function effectively, the police must be "part of, rather than apart from, the community they serve."[14]

SUGGESTED ACTIVITIES

- Scan your local newspaper for two weeks and make a note of any reference to police officers. Keep a tally of whether each reference is positive, negative, or neutral, and whether the officer is engaged in essentially a law enforcement, order maintenance, or service function. Can you draw any conclusions from your results?

- Interview a police officer and ask what portion of time is spent on law enforcement, order maintenance, and service. What percentage of the department's time is spent on each of these three functions? Does the officer agree with these priorities?

- Conduct an informal survey among your friends to find out how many of them feel the police are the appropriate people to handle a number of the service functions (e.g., locating missing persons, rescuing cats, escorting funerals). If they feel the police are not appropriate, ask them who should handle these functions. Report your results. Do you agree with them?

REVIEW

A. Distinguish between the law enforcement, order maintenance, and service functions performed by the police.

B. What are some factors that cause tension in police-community relations?

C. What is meant by police discretion?

D. Multiple Choice. Select the best answer.

1. Which of the following constitute most of the police agencies in the United States?
   a. state police departments
   b. local police departments
   c. federal police departments
   d. none of these

2. Approximately how many police agencies are there in the United States?
   a. 225
   b. 750
   c. 1,250
   d. 25,000

3. Locating a missing person is essentially a
   a. service function
   b. law enforcement function
   c. order maintenance function
   d. none of these

4. Law enforcement accounts for how much of a police department's time?
   a. 100 percent
   b. 90 percent
   c. 75 percent
   d. none of these

5. The officer who is present in the community seeking to prevent breaches of the law is called the
   a. patrol officer
   b. detective
   c. informant
   d. none of these

6. Law enforcement and order maintenance
    a. are distinctly different functions
    b. are the same function
    c. are separate functions which sometimes overlap
    d. none of these

7. A detective spends the most time on
    a. law enforcement
    b. order maintenance
    c. service
    d. none of these

8. Why have the police been entrusted with the service function?
    a. it is related to law enforcement
    b. they are one of few agencies that provide continuous twenty-four-hour service
    c. they have special training for it
    d. none of these

9. Which of the following could be carried out by civilian employees of police departments?
    a. clerical work
    b. service functions
    c. directing traffic
    d. all of these

10. Which of the following is not an objective of the patrol unit?
    a. to seek voluntary compliance with the law
    b. to enforce the law and arrest offenders
    c. to provide instant response to requests for police services
    d. all of these are objectives

REFERENCES

1. Federal Bureau of Investigation, *Uniform Crime Reports, 1984* (Washington, D.C.: U.S. Government Printing Office, 1985), 281.
2. Harry Caldwell, *Basic Law Enforcement* (Pacific Palisades, Calif.: Goodyear, 1972), 33.
3. For a more detailed discussion of such issues, see, for example, Margaret J. Levine and J. Thomas McEwen, *Patrol Deployment* (Washington, D.C.: U.S. Department of Justice, 1985).
4. Donald J. Newman, *Introduction to Criminal Justice*, 3rd ed. (New York: Random House, 1986), 111.
5. James Q. Wilson, *Varieties of Police Behavior* (New York: Atheneum, 1972), 31.
6. See, for example, Lawrence W. Sherman and Richard A. Berk, ''The Specific Deterrent Effects of Arrest for Domestic Assault,'' *American Sociological Review*, 49 (1984), 261–272.
7. National Advisory Commission on Criminal Justice Standards and Goals, *Police* (Washington, D.C.: U.S. Government Printing Office, 1973), 14.
8. Richard A. Myren, ''The Role of the Police,'' in Harry M. More, Jr. (ed.) *Critical Issues in Law Enforcement* (Cincinnati: Anderson, 1975), 29.
9. *Ibid.*
10. *Ibid.*, 42.
11. Kenneth Culp Davis, *Discretionary Justice* (Baton Rouge, La.: Louisiana State University Press, 1969), 4.
12. Ben Whitaker, cited in Norval Morris and Gordon Hawkins, *The Honest Politician's Guide to Crime Control* (Chicago: University of Chicago Press, 1970), 89–90.
13. Louis A. Radelet, *The Police and the Community*, 2nd ed. (Encino, Calif.: Glencoe Press, 1977), 6.
14. *Ibid.*

27

Police
Professionalism

OBJECTIVES

After studying this chapter, the student should be able to:

- Define the concept of professionalism and relate it to police work.
- State and justify the type of minimum standards that should be required for employment as a police officer.
- Describe the nature and content of police training programs.
- Outline procedures relating to the appointment and removal of police chiefs.
- Describe police organizations.
- Explain the concept of police accountability.

Now that we have reviewed the different functions performed by the police, we will examine the concept of professionalism and how it relates to police work. This chapter discusses the minimum standards required for employment as a police officer, the procedures for appointing and removing police chiefs, police training, police organizations, and police accountability.

PROFESSIONALISM

Police professionalism is a concept that has been discussed and debated for decades. To label a particular occupation as a profession is a sign of high esteem. Some occupations, such as those of lawyers and doctors, have long been recognized as professions.

Other occupations have sought and received professional recognition. Still others, including the police, are in the process of attempting to acquire that status.

What is a profession, and what criteria must be met for an occupation to qualify as a profession? According to Funk and Wagnalls, a profession may be defined as "An occupation that properly involves a liberal, scientific or artistic education or its equivalent, and usually mental rather than physical labor." [1]

Two major components of a profession are presented here: the need for education, and an emphasis on "brain" rather than "brawn" in carrying out occupational tasks. In the 1930s, a committee on the professionalization of police service set up by the International Association of Chiefs of Police stated that a profession consists of the following elements:

1. An organized body of knowledge, constantly augmented and refined, with special techniques based thereon.
2. Facilities for formal training in this body of knowledge and procedure.
3. Recognized qualifications for membership in, and identification with the profession.
4. An organization which includes a substantial number of the members qualified to practice the profession and to exercise an influence on the maintenance of professional standards.
5. A code of ethics which, in general, defines the relations of the members of the profession to the public and to other practitioners within the group and normally recognizes an obligation to render services on other than exclusively economic considerations. [2]

Attention is drawn here to the need for the existence of a specific body of knowledge relating to the occupation, formal training in that body of knowledge, establishment of certain minimum standards for entrance into the occupation, a code of ethics followed by members of the occupation, a certain degree of self-regulation with regard to occupational standards, and a general sense of service to the public in the performance of occupational tasks. To this might be added the exercise of discretion and judgment in the performance of these occupational tasks.

The issue of whether or not policing is or should be considered a profession is complicated by several factors. One such factor is the diversity of police functions. Thus, policing entails many varied tasks which differ in the level of knowledge, expertise, training, and discretion required for their proper performance. Directing traffic, for example, does not require the same level of expertise and sensitivity as handling a touchy domestic situation.

Another factor to bear in mind is that professionalism is a relative concept rather than an absolute. Pavalko has pointed out that an occupation can be assessed on a number of dimensions related to professionalism and placed on a continuum. On some of the dimensions a particular occupation may appear to merit professional standing. On others it may not. Thus we must consider the issue of police professionalism from the standpoint of the extent to which it is or should be regarded as a profession. [3]

Another factor which complicates the issue of police professionalism is a lack of clarity as to what is meant by professional police. To some, professional police may merely mean highly efficient police. Thus it may be argued that a police department that focuses on bureaucratic efficiency, technological sophistication, and strong authoritarian leadership typifies one kind of professional police department. It may not, however, afford its officers the same opportunity for individual professionalism as a police department that highlights the officers' legitimate use of discretion and participation in management of the police force. In essence, there may be a conflict between what is meant by a professional police department and what is expected of a professional police officer.

Many people would argue that as yet policing cannot properly be regarded as a true profession. Reasons advanced for this conclusion include the allegations that there does not yet exist a sufficient shared body of knowledge or expertise peculiar to the occupation, and that there is not sufficient freedom to make discretionary judgments.[4]

But what are the implications of according or not according professional standing to the police? The benefits associated with professionalism, such as greater public esteem and perhaps higher salaries, will not automatically ensue once the police are labeled professionals. Police professionalism is rather an evolutionary process which, it is to be hoped, will continue to occur as the quality of policing is improved. Developments in a number of areas have served to upgrade the quality of policing and advance the cause of police professionalism.

MINIMUM ENTRANCE REQUIREMENTS

One aspect of police professionalization is the establishment of minimum requirements for entrance into the occupation. It has been stated that:

> Nineteenth-century policemen could not claim professional status, nor is there much evidence that they were interested in it. In most cities, entry into the department demanded political connections, not education.[5]

Minimum entrance requirements in the police occupation have traditionally focused on the physical attributes of applicants as opposed to their intellectual or educational backgrounds. The President's Commission on Law Enforcement and Administration of Justice reported in 1967 that "Existing selection requirements and procedures in the majority of departments, aside from physical requirements, do not screen out the unfit."[6] The Commission acknowledged that the complexities of policing require that police officers "possess a high degree of intelligence, education, tact, sound judgment, physical courage, emotional stability, impartiality, and honesty."[7] They concluded that "modern professional policing must place a priority on education, intelligence, and emotional stability, and provide greater flexibility in physical requirements."[8]

In a similar vein, the National Advisory Commission on Criminal Justice Standards and Goals recommended in 1973 that each state establish a state commission to develop and enforce minimum entrance requirements. Such minimum requirements were

> to incorporate compensating factors such as education, language skills, or experience in excess of that required if such factors can overcome minor deficiencies in physical requirements such as age, height, or weight.[9]

The National Advisory Commission did, however, warn that: "Physical strength standards cannot be abandoned: cops still have to slug it out in back alleys, chase fleet-footed burglars, and physically disarm dangerous persons."[10]

The thrust of these recommendations has, perhaps, been toward establishing minimum entrance requirements which will supply police departments with better qualified personnel. They do also allow for wider recruitment of females and of members of certain minority groups. This has been a matter of general concern both in view of the desire to have such representation in police departments in order to enhance police-community relations, and because of certain governmental affirmative action programs.

Language skills and experience, as well as education, are advocated as compensating factors for minor deficiencies in physical requirements. The relevance of a college education as a minimum entrance requirement has long been a matter of controversy. Many people fear that it would hamper effective minority recruitment. In addition, it is debatable whether a college-educated officer is necessarily a better officer. The National Manpower Survey of the Criminal Justice System included a task analysis study.[11] It was noted that there were several tasks performed by supervisors and managers for which a college education was either necessary or desirable. However, no line patrol task that required a college education for successful completion was found. Despite these concerns, the federal government, through financial assistance, and local police departments, through salary incentives, have encouraged officers to participate in education programs.[12]

To a large extent standardized civil service requirements have been imposed on police departments. This has, indeed, helped lessen the level of political interference in the selection and promotion of police officers.

However, there is still considerable controversy as to what background qualities comprise a good police officer, and how those qualities should be assessed and weighed in relation to one another. In addition, many police entrance requirements have been challenged in the courts. Some have been modified as a result of lack of proof of their job-relatedness.

TRAINING

Reference has been made to the allegation that policing does not possess a sufficient shared body of required knowledge to merit designation as a profession. Some people have felt that this allegation is supported by the fact that for a long time little formal training was given to police recruits. With the officers receiving their training in the field, policing had more the appearance of a craft than a profession. Indeed, to some people policing did not even attain the status of a craft; for a craft generally required a fairly lengthy period of training in a supervised setting.

Though many police departments (especially the larger ones) had already instituted basic training programs, until 1959 no state in the Union actually required as a matter of law that such training be given. By 1970, thirty-three states had instituted such a requirement. However, as the National Advisory Commission on Criminal Justice Standards and Goals pointed out in 1973, only one state demanded a minimum of 400 hours training as recommended by the Presidential Commission in 1967.[13] The National Advisory Commission itself recommended that basic training be mandatory, that it be at least 400 hours, and that it be given prior to the officer exercising police authority in the community. Basic training would include instruction in law, the criminal justice system, patrol and investigation, human values and problems, police proficiency, and administration. This would be followed by at least four months of structured field training.[14]

In addition to basic training, the National Advisory Commission recommended that each police officer of the rank of captain or below receive at least forty hours of formal in-service training per year. This training would be "designed to maintain, update, and improve necessary knowledge and skills."[15] Training would also be given prior to assignment to any specialized function which required additional training and prior to promotion.[16]

Under this scheme, police officers would receive formal training prior to their entrance to the occupation and at regular and appropriate intervals during their policing careers. An attempt would be made to ensure quality instruction. Consolidated regional or state training centers would be established where such a need existed.

Such centers have turned out to be of vital importance to the many small police departments which are ill equipped to conduct their own formal training programs. Indeed, there appears to have been at least some improvement in the overall police training situation. A 1975 survey of police chiefs in 400 cities with a population of at least 10,000 revealed that 44.8 percent of the agencies required at least 400 hours of training for their recruits. Of these departments, 55.2 percent required one week of annual in-service training.[17] A 1978 survey showed that at least 400 hours of entry training were provided by 91 percent of all agencies with 400 or more employees. "However, only 56% of the agencies with between 75 and 399 employees and 26% of the agencies with fewer than 75 employees (met) this standard."[18]

POLICE CHIEFS

It is important that highly qualified personnel be recruited as police officers and that they receive suitable training. It is just as vital, if not more so, that police departments be led by top-quality administrators. The political connection between the office of the chief of police and city hall has long been a matter of grave concern. It has been stated that

> Most, if not all, early police departments were traditionally impregnated with political appointees who were often corrupt and who were not necessarily concerned with individual rights. Even today, there are departments so ingrained with such traditionalism that appointments and promotions are still politically made.[19]

There is great variety in the way that police chiefs are selected. At the local level, county sheriffs are generally elected directly by the people. City, town, and village police chiefs are generally appointed by the mayor, the city council, the city manager, the town or village board, and the like, depending upon the structure of the local government. At the state level the police executive is often appointed by the state attorney general or the governor. At the federal level the director of the FBI is appointed by the president, subject to congressional approval. In most systems there has been great room for political interference. It is important that police chiefs be selected on the basis of professional expertise and not as a result of political affiliation. It is equally important that police chiefs not be removed from office simply as a result of a change in the office holder.

A report published in 1977 by the Police Chief Executive Committee of the International Association of Chiefs of Police contains proposed standards to be used for the selection and retention of police chief executives.[20] Through the establishment of objective and relevant evaluation criteria and of impartial selection procedures, the hiring of a police chief is to be carried out on the basis of merit. While in office the police chief is to be fully accountable, and is also to be subject to punitive action, but only for ''substantiated charges of misconduct as opposed to rumor, supposition, political expediency or the impetuous or indiscreet unilateral action of one person.''[21]

POLICE ORGANIZATIONS

Professional bodies have generally established formal organizations that cater to their professional interests and concerns. Thus in the United States the lawyers, for example, have the American Bar Association, and the physicians the American Medical Association. The police are not without their own formal organizations. Perhaps the most prestigious of these is the International Association of Chiefs of Police (IACP). Formed in 1893, the IACP has been extremely active in promoting occupational standards, developing training materials, and disseminating information. Its membership, however, is limited to chiefs of police and other law enforcement executive officials.

The lower ranks within the police departments have had their interests represented in differing ways by a variety of organizations. The Fraternal Order of Police and the Police Benevolent Association each have chapters in different areas in the United States. Their activities have been mixed. They have been involved in advocating major changes in police policy. Thus the actions of the Police Benevolent Association in New York City and the Fraternal Order of Police in Philadelphia were largely responsible for the dissolution of the civilian review boards in those two cities. These organizations have also been involved in airing police officers' concerns about pay and working conditions.

These organizations have been concerned with obtaining better working conditions for their members. Though not termed unions, they have functioned to an extent as such. In recent years the growth of more formal unionization of police officers and greater usage of collective bargaining strategies have taken place. It is now estimated that 75 percent of all police officers are members of unions.[22] The concern has been voiced that unions, with their primary focus on the basic needs of their members and not on the advancement of the occupation, detract from the cause of police professionalization.

There are, however, other organizations that exist with the avowed purpose of upgrading policing. *Lambda Alpha Epsilon*, a national association that requires its members to have some college education, is one such organization.

POLICE ACCOUNTABILITY

Two further features of police professionalization relate to the ability of an occupational group to exercise discretion in the performance of occupational tasks and to set, regulate, and enforce required standards of performance. Embedded here are the twin issues of autonomy and accountability. "Autonomy" refers to the ability of police departments, and members of police departments, to make their own decisions and be responsible for, and to, themselves. "Accountability," on the other hand, refers to the extent to which police departments, and their members, are responsible and answerable to other persons and other bodies. As has been remarked,

> Accountability, in its broadest sense, includes much more than responsibility for determining policies in discretionary areas. It covers every aspect of administration of an agency, including, for example, its operating efficiency, its hiring and promotion practices, and its financial management. Accountability encompasses as well responsibility for the conduct of individual employees—for the use which they make of their authority and for their integrity.[23]

Police chiefs, within the confines of the agency structure, are responsible for setting the tone and quality of their administrations. They are also ultimately responsible for the rules and regulations within the department and for determining the amount of discretion each officer employs in the performance of his or her duties. Complaints and matters of discipline are generally handled by an internal police review board. Thus there is a fair amount of autonomy exercised by police departments.

The police are, on the other hand, subject to a considerable amount of external constraints and accountability, both formal and informal. The legislature defines the nature of both substantive and procedural criminal law. It sets, perhaps with other governmental units, the amount of money that will be available for police departments to spend. The courts are responsible for hearing actions taken against police departments and their members and for defining the constitutional standards that must be observed by the police in the performance of their duties. The community itself, finally, may exert great influence over the police department, for, as has been remarked,

> The police chief executive usually is held much more accountable by the public for the activities of his personnel than most other public agency officials. As the "top cop," he is in the constant view of the public. He is expected to recognize and respond to the problems of the community more than any other local department head.[24]

An overabundance of police accountability, however, is not desirable. Undue outside interference in matters of professional judgment may undermine the status and quality of policing. Entrusting undue discretion, on the other hand, may lead to abuse. The ultimate objective is to find the correct mesh between police autonomy and police accountability.

SUMMARY

In this chapter an examination has been conducted of a number of issues concerning the designation of an occupation as a profession. The acquisition of professional status is undoubtedly a sign of high regard for the members of the occupation. Whether or not an occupation is designated as a profession may not, however, be as important as whether the occupation is carrying out its tasks in a professional manner. Of particular concern with regard to policing are such issues as the minimum standards required for employment as a police officer, procedures for appointing and removing police chiefs, police training, and police accountability. It is important that standards be established in each of these areas that will promote efficient, responsible, and effective policing.

SUGGESTED ACTIVITIES

- Conduct an informal survey of people in your community and ask whether they feel policing should be regarded as a profession. What do they understand a profession to be? Include a few police officers in your survey. Report your results.
- Contact your local police department and find out what the minimum entrance requirements are for becoming a police officer. Consult your state police department and find out their minimum requirements. Compare the two criteria. How do you feel about these requirements?
- Find out if your state has mandated training for police officers. If so, what is the nature and content of the required training?
- Research the issue of civilian review boards. How do you feel about the desirability of instituting a civilian review board in your area?

REVIEW

A. List some of the components of a profession.

B. Can policing be regarded as a profession?

C. State and justify the characteristics that police recruits should be required to have.

D. Describe the nature and content of police training programs recommended by national committees.

E. On what basis should police chiefs be selected and removed?

F. What types of police organizations exist?

G. Multiple Choice. Select the best answer.

1. The police are not universally acknowledged as professionals because of
   a. the allegation that they lack an organized body of specialized knowledge
   b. the diversity of their functions
   c. the lack of enforced standardized minimum entrance requirements
   d. all of these

2. The National Advisory Commission recommended modifying minimum physical entrance requirements by
   a. dropping them
   b. allowing compensating factors to overcome minor deficiencies in them

  c. raising them
  d. none of these

3. Police training requirements are
  a. 400 hours of basic training
  b. 400 hours of basic training and forty hours per year of in-service training
  c. variable
  d. none of these

4. Which of the following has been undertaken by the International Association of Chiefs of Police?
  a. unionization of patrol officers
  b. development of training materials
  c. collective bargaining
  d. all of these

5. The ability of police departments to be responsible to and for themselves is called
  a. autonomy
  b. accountability
  c. accessibility
  d. all of these

6. The decision to appoint and remove police chiefs has traditionally been
  a. made on the basis of merit
  b. politically motivated
  c. made by the rank and file
  d. all of these

7. The trend in policing is toward
  a. more educational prerequisites
  b. more basic training
  c. more in-service training
  d. all of these

8. Which of these is important for a police officer to have to perform his or her duties well?
  a. political connections
  b. a college education
  c. sound judgment
  d. all of these

9. Are police officers required by law to undergo basic training prior to exercising police authority?
  a. yes
  b. no
  c. yes, in a few states
  d. yes, in most states

10. To whom are the police accountable?
  a. the courts
  b. public officials
  c. the community
  d. all of these

REFERENCES

1. Funk and Wagnalls, *Standard College Dictionary* (New York: Harcourt, Brace, 1968), 1075.
2. Harry W. More, Jr., *Critical Issues in Law Enforcement* (Cincinnati: Anderson, 1975), 438 citing J. A. Greening, "Report of the Committee on Professionalization of Police Service," *Yearbook of the I.A.C.P.*, 1938–39, 20.

3. Ronald M. Pavalko, *Sociology of Occupations and Professions* (Itasca, Ill.: F. E. Peacock, 1971), 16. See also, Richard H. Hall, *Occupations and the Social Structure* (Englewood Cliffs, N.J.: Prentice-Hall, 1969).

4. See, for example, Barbara Raffel Price, *Police Professionalism* (Lexington, Mass.: D. C. Heath, 1977), 11.

5. James F. Richardson, *Urban Police in the United States* (Port Washington, N.Y.: Kennikat Press Corp., 1974), 132.

6. The President's Commission on Law Enforcement and Administration of Justice, *Task Force Report: The Police* (Washington, D.C.: U.S. Government Printing Office, 1967), 125.

7. *Ibid.*

8. *Ibid.*, 133.

9. National Advisory Commission on Criminal Justice Standards and Goals, *The Police* (Washington, D.C.: U.S. Government Printing Office, 1973), 334.

10. *Ibid.*, 335.

11. U.S. Department of Justice, *The National Manpower Survey of the Criminal Justice System*, Vol. 2, *Law Enforcement* (Washington, D.C.: U.S. Government Printing Office, 1978), 18.

12. See, for example, "Education Update: The Value of Incentive Pay," *Police Chief*, 53 (1986), 36.

13. National Advisory Commission on Criminal Justice Standards and Goals, *op. cit.*, 380.

14. *Ibid.*, 380–381.

15. *Ibid.*, 404.

16. *Ibid.*, 392.

17. Erik Beckman, "Police Education and Training: Where are we? Where are we going?" *Journal of Criminal Justice*, 4 (1976), 320.

18. U.S. Department of Justice, *op. cit.*, 27–28.

19. Vern L. Folley, *American Law Enforcement*, 3rd ed. (Boston: Allyn and Bacon, 1980), 107.

20. National Advisory Committee on Criminal Justice Standards and Goals, *Report of the Police Chief Executive Committee of the International Association of Chiefs of Police* (Washington, D.C.: U.S. Government Printing Office, 1977).

21. *Ibid.*, 75.

22. Samuel Walker, *The Police in America* (New York: McGraw-Hill, 1983), 285.

23. Herman Goldstein, *Policing in a Free Society* (Cambridge, Mass.: Ballinger, 1977), 131.

24. National Advisory Commission on Criminal Justice Standards and Goals, *op. cit.*, 442.

28

The Police
and Suspects

OBJECTIVES

After studying this chapter, the student should be able to:

- Describe Packer's Due Process and Crime Control models of the criminal justice system.
- Detail the major constitutional restrictions on police powers to stop and question, frisk, arrest, and search suspects.
- Discuss the major U.S. Supreme Court cases limiting police powers in these areas.
- State when evidence is excluded, and explain the rationale behind the exclusion of evidence.

A major function performed by a police force is generally considered to consist of the solving of crimes and the apprehension of suspects. Since these tasks are so important, many people feel that the police should be entrusted with the broadest of powers to accomplish them. The police are not, however, given unrestricted freedom to conduct investigations and pursue suspects. Constitutional provisions, legislative and departmental mandates, and judicial decisions all dictate the manner in which the police may perform their duties. The police powers to stop and question a person, to frisk a person, to search a person and that person's property, to arrest a person, and to interrogate a person are all limited to some extent. In this chapter, an examination of the police powers in each of these areas will be undertaken.

PACKER'S CRIME CONTROL AND DUE PROCESS MODELS
OF THE CRIMINAL PROCESS

The American system of criminal justice is often viewed as being much the same as a sporting contest. It is an adversary system, with two sides pitted against each other, and prescribed rules to follow. On one side is the law enforcement machinery of the criminal justice system, the police, and the prosecutors. On the other is the defendant, generally accompanied by a lawyer in the formal stages of the process.

The system is for the most part weighted toward the defendant. It is presumed that a person is innocent until proven guilty. The supposition is that it is better to let ten guilty people go free than to convict one innocent person. This slant of the scales toward the defendant is seen most clearly at the trial stage where there is need for proof "beyond a reasonable doubt" in order for the defendant to be convicted of the crime charged. It is, however, evident at the other stages too, including those stages in which the police are involved.

Herbert Packer has suggested that two models may be seen to underlie the criminal justice process. They are called the Crime Control model and the Due Process model. The Crime Control model is "based on the proposition that the repression of criminal conduct is by far the most important function to be performed by the criminal process." [1] It

> requires that primary attention be paid to the efficiency with which the criminal process operates to screen suspects, determine guilt, and secure appropriate dispositions of persons convicted of crime. [2]

It is this model of the system that would give the police the greater latitude in carrying out their duties. It stresses informal processes over formal processes and extrajudicial processes over judicial processes. It seeks the avoidance of "ceremonious rituals that do not advance the progress of a case," [3] and advocates the uniform handling of cases. It is a system that:

> throws off at an early stage those cases in which it appears unlikely that the person apprehended is an offender and then secures, as expeditiously as possible, the conviction of the rest, with the minimum of occasions for challenge, let alone post-audit. [4]

The Due Process model, on the other hand, focuses on the rights of the defendant and guards against errors in the fact-finding process.

> If the Crime Control Model resembles an assembly line, the Due Process Model looks very much like an obstacle course. Each of its successive stages is designed to present formidable impediments to carrying the accused any further along in the process. [5]

Traces of each model are to be seen operating in our current criminal justice system. Individuals who support the extension of defendants' rights tend quite naturally to be advocates of the Due Process model. Those who, on the other hand, complain about undue legal restrictions being placed on the police generally tend to be proponents of the Crime Control model. The system itself, primarily through the legislative and judicial processes, attempts to strike a balance between the power it entrusts to the police and the rights it grants to private individuals.

THE UNITED STATES CONSTITUTION

The United States Constitution, as interpreted by the courts, lays down the basic minimum requirements that must be followed in dealing with a suspect. Each individual state must grant suspects rights which are equal to or greater than these constitutional rights. Thus, the rights afforded suspects by the states cannot be less than those granted by the Constitution. As the highest court in the land, the United States Supreme Court is the authoritative source of interpretation of these rights.

Four amendments to the U.S. Constitution are of significant importance in the area of suspects' rights. The Fourth Amendment provides protection against unreasonable searches and seizures. The Fifth Amendment grants the privilege against self-incrimination. The Sixth Amendment affords the right to counsel. The Fourteenth Amendment, finally, guarantees due process and equal protection of the laws to the citizens of each state, and declares that: "No state shall abridge the privileges or immunities of citizens of the United States." [6] It has, indeed, been the Fourteenth Amendment that has been largely used to extend federal constitutional rights to the inhabitants of the individual states.

CONSENT AND THE POLICE PROCESS

In their tasks of detecting crime and apprehending suspects, the police must obtain information from the general public, including the suspects themselves; they must secure evidence that proves both the commission of the crime and the identity of the suspect; they must protect both themselves and others from incurring harm. All this must be accomplished without violating constitutional rights.

To a large extent the police task is simplified by the cooperation of individuals whose assistance the police seek. The more individuals who come forward to report crimes, who of their own accord make incriminating statements about themselves or others, and who help the police obtain tangible evidence of the crimes committed, the easier the police task becomes.

Many people do, in fact, cooperate with the police. Some confess to committing crimes. Some voluntarily allow the police to search their persons and property. Some present the police with the crime weapon, such as the gun used in the murder. Others present them with the fruits of the crime, such as the stolen bank notes. Embodied in the fabric of the criminal justice process, however, is the individual's right to defend himself or herself against criminal accusations. One cannot be forced to incriminate oneself. One is not bound to subject oneself or one's property to unreasonable searches and seizures. An individual may obtain the assistance of counsel in conducting his or her defense.

ARREST AND SEARCH AND SEIZURE

The Fourth Amendment of the U.S. Constitution provides that:

> The right of the people to be secure in their persons, houses, papers and effects, against unreasonable searches and seizures, shall not be violated and no warrants shall issue, but upon probable cause, supported by oath or affirmation, and particularly describing the place to be searched, and the persons or things to be seized.[7]

Both arrests and searches may be made either with or without a warrant. A warrant is a written order issued and signed by a magistrate which commands that a specified person be arrested or some specified property be searched. The standard for issuance of a warrant is establishment of probable cause. Probable cause may be found to exist

> where "the facts and circumstances within (the officers') knowledge and of which they had reasonably trustworthy information (are) sufficient in themselves to warrant a man of reasonable caution in the belief" an offense has been or is being committed.[8]

The standard of proof required for an arrest without a warrant is also probable cause. Generally, a law enforcement officer has the legal authority to make an arrest when he or she has probable cause to believe that a crime has been (or is being) committed and that the person the officer suspects has perpetrated it. Less stringent evidentiary criteria are generally required when the suspected crime is a felony. If the suspected crime is a misdemeanor, an arrest may not generally be made unless the offense was committed in the police officer's presence; otherwise, the officer must first obtain a warrant. An arrest may be considered to take place when an individual is restrained of his or her liberty for the purpose of instituting criminal charges against him or her.

The Supreme Court has generally stated a strong preference for searches conducted with a warrant.[9] Nonetheless, most searches are in fact conducted without a warrant. The search incident to a lawful arrest is one such example.[10] To be "reasonable" (the standard required by the Fourth Amendment) and hence valid, such a search must be limited to the arrestee's person and areas within his or her immediate reach or control.[11] Thus, for example, if the police arrest a person at work, they will not usually have the legal authority to conduct a warrantless search of the person's home. An arrest for a traffic violation has been held to justify a full search of the arrestee's person for contraband unrelated to the traffic offense.[12] To effect an arrest, a police officer may use only as much force as is reasonable and necessary in the circumstances. Deadly force may be used only to prevent the escape of a fleeing felon whom the officer "has probable cause to believe . . . poses a significant threat of death or serious physical injury to the officer or others." [13]

STOP AND FRISK AND OTHER LIMITED INTRUSIONS

The police may make arrests and conduct searches if they possess the requisite standard of proof, probable cause. Often, however, it is desirable for them, as they patrol the neighborhood or conduct investigations, to stop citizens and make inquiries of them. This general type of questioning is for the most part permissible. If, however, the citizen does not wish to cooperate, the police may not be able to proceed further unless they possess the evidentiary standard required. Thus the Supreme Court has held that the police cannot stop a person and ask for identification simply because he or she looks suspicious. They must have a reasonable suspicion that the person is involved in criminal activity before they demand identification.[14]

If, after stopping an individual, a police officer has reasonable grounds to believe that the person is armed and that the officer or other people may be in physical danger, the individual may be frisked. A frisk is a patdown of a person's outer clothing for the purpose of discovering the existence of weapons. It is justified because

> there must be a narrowly drawn authority to permit a reasonable search for weapons for the protection of the police officer, where he has reason to believe that he is dealing with an armed and dangerous individual, regardless of whether he has probable cause to arrest the individual for a crime.[15]

CONFESSIONS AND OTHER INCRIMINATING STATEMENTS

Confessions and other incriminating statements made by suspects are of great help to the police in their investigations and may well provide an easy path to conviction. Two fundamental issues must, however, be addressed here. First, in order for any such statement to be legally valid, it must have been made voluntarily. Second, by virtue of the Fifth Amendment, made applicable to the states through the Fourteenth Amendment,[16] no person "shall be compelled in any criminal case to be a witness against himself." [17] Thus, every person enjoys the privilege against self-incrimination.

A confession is generally not considered voluntary if it was obtained by force or threat of force. In one 1936 case the defendants had been whipped in order to obtain confessions. The deputy who supervised the beatings conceded that one of the defendants had been whipped but "not as much as I would have done if it were left to me." [18] The Supreme Court did not allow the confessions to be used in court. The rationale for the decision related to the inherent untrustworthiness of evidence that had been obtained in such a manner.

Over the years the Supreme Court gradually shifted in its rationale for disallowing certain confessions and other incriminating statements from being used as evidence. The focus became not so much the inherent unreliability of the evidence as concern with the voluntary nature of the confession and a show of disapproval of undesirable police methods.[19]

In 1966 in the case of *Miranda* v. *Arizona*[20] the Supreme Court did, in fact, lay out the procedures to be followed in the interrogation of suspects. The court held that:

> the prosecution may not use statements, whether exculpatory or inculpatory, stemming from custodial interrogation of the defendant unless it demonstrates the use of procedural safeguards effective to secure the privilege against self-incrimination. By custodial interrogation, we mean questioning initiated by law enforcement officers after a person has been taken into custody or otherwise deprived of his freedom of action in any significant way. As for the procedural safeguards to be employed, unless other fully effective means are devised to inform accused persons of their right to silence and to assure a continuous opportunity to exercise it, the following measures are required. Prior to any questioning, the person must be warned that he has a right to remain silent, that any statement he does make may be used as evidence against him, and that he has a right to the presence of an attorney, either retained or appointed. The defendant may waive effectuation of these rights, provided the waiver is made voluntarily, knowingly and intelligently. If, however, he indicates in any manner and at any stage of the process that he wishes to consult with an attorney before speaking there can be no questioning. Likewise, if the individual is alone and indicates in any manner that he does not wish to be interrogated, the police may not question him. The mere fact that he may have answered some questions or volunteered some statements on his own does not deprive him of the right to refrain from answering any further inquiries until he has consulted with an attorney and thereafter consents to be questioned.[21]

When the *Miranda* decision was handed down, cries were heard of how it would seriously hamper the law enforcement process. This has, however, not turned out to be the situation, though some cases have been lost by law enforcement because of a violation of *Miranda* rights.[22] Subsequent Supreme Court decisions have, in fact, clarified the meaning of the *Miranda* ruling,[23] and have narrowed the scope of its operation to some extent.[24]

RIGHT TO COUNSEL

One of the rights enumerated in the *Miranda* decision was the right to counsel. The assistance of counsel is, indeed, one of the fundamental rights that an accused is considered to possess. The Sixth Amendment of the U.S. Constitution does, in fact, provide that: ''In all criminal prosecutions, the accused shall enjoy the right to . . . have the Assistance of Counsel for his defence.'' [25] This right most obviously pertains to the criminal court process, but it has been held to apply to every ''critical stage'' of the proceedings against an accused. Thus far these critical stages have included in-custody interrogation [26] and participation in a lineup after the initiation of adversary judicial proceedings.[27]

THE EXCLUSION OF ILLEGALLY OBTAINED EVIDENCE

From the suspect's standpoint, perhaps the major consequence of police violation of his or her Fourth, Fifth, or Sixth Amendment rights is the exclusion of the illegally obtained evidence at trial. Thus, a confession obtained in violation of a suspect's Fifth

Amendment privilege against self-incrimination will generally not be admissible in court.[28] The same holds true for physical evidence obtained in violation of the suspect's Fourth Amendment right against unreasonable searches and seizures,[29] and a lineup identification obtained in violation of the suspect's Sixth Amendment right to counsel.[30] In order for evidence to be declared inadmissible, a suppression hearing is held. At that time the judge rules on whether the evidence is to be suppressed.

There are a number of rationales for the exclusion of such evidence. The inherent untrustworthiness of coerced confessions has already been discussed. Improper lineups may also be said to be subject to the same charge. Indeed, the presence of counsel at lineups was felt to be warranted on the grounds that it might help lessen the "high incidence of miscarriage of justice from mistaken identification." [31]

The exclusion of illegally seized physical evidence, however, has been felt by many people to be unwarranted on these grounds, for such evidence is "no less reliable when illegally obtained." [32] The result is simply that "the criminal is to go free because the constable has blundered." [33]

Two other rationales are, in fact, considered to come into play here. They are what are termed the normative and deterrent rationales. The normative rationale supports the idea that the agents of government should not benefit from their own wrongdoing and that the courts should not participate in illegal behavior by using evidence obtained by it. The deterrent rationale presents the idea that the exclusion of illegally obtained evidence will serve to deter the police from indulging in such behavior. Debate about the merits of these rationales, and about the overall desirability of excluding illegally obtained physical evidence, has been fierce.[34] Opponents of the exclusionary rule were heartened by a 1984 U.S. Supreme Court decision which limited the scope of the rule. Evidence obtained in good faith by police officers relying on a search warrant which was later ruled to be defective was held to be admissible in court.[35] Whether this is, in fact, the beginning of the end of the exclusionary rule remains to be seen.

SUMMARY

In this chapter, police powers with regard to suspects were examined. The criminal justice process contains traces of what Packer has termed the Crime Control model and Due Process model. The Crime Control model is primarily concerned with the repression of criminal conduct and the efficient processing of criminal cases. The Due Process model, on the other hand, focuses on the rights of the defendant and guards against errors in the fact-finding process.

The U.S. Constitution, as interpreted by the courts, lays down the minimum standards that must be afforded suspects by the police.

The Fourth Amendment provides individuals with protection against unreasonable searches and seizures. In general, probable cause is required before a police officer can either make an arrest or conduct a search. On occasion, however, more limited intrusion on lesser evidentiary standards is permissible. One such occasion is the frisk for weapons.

The Fifth Amendment provides a suspect with the privilege against self-incrimination. The police are not entitled to force a confession or other incriminating statement out of a suspect. The *Miranda* decision outlines procedures to be followed in conducting in-custody interrogations.

The Sixth Amendment provides a suspect with the right to the assistance of counsel. In addition to in-custody interrogations, this right has been held to apply to lineups conducted after the initiation of adversary judicial proceedings.

Any evidence obtained in violation of these constitutional rights will generally be inadmissible at trial. In addition to concerns about the trustworthiness of illegally obtained evidence, arguments for exclusion are advanced on the basis of the normative and deterrent rationales.

In its basic structure, the criminal justice process is an adversary system. To a large extent, however, its ability to function depends upon the cooperation of the general public and of the criminal suspects themselves. Both consent and the waiver of constitutional rights greatly facilitate the task of law enforcement.

SUGGESTED ACTIVITIES

- Which do you think should be the higher priority in our criminal justice system, solving crime or protecting an individual against being wrongly accused? State why, and under what conditions, if any, these priorities would change.
- Find out if you can attend, or look at the record of, a suppression hearing. State the reasons the defense felt evidence should be suppressed. Which of the defendant's rights were allegedly violated? What was the judge's ruling? Do you agree? Do you feel the exclusion of evidence will serve as a deterrent against future police violations?
- Can you think of a way to protect a suspect's constitutional rights without suppressing evidence?
- What happens if a person is searched in a way that violates his or her Fourth Amendment rights, and the officer does not find any incriminating evidence?

REVIEW

A. Contrast Packer's Crime Control model and his Due Process model of the criminal justice system and state how the system incorporates these models.

B. List the four amendments to the U.S. Constitution that provide for suspects' rights and state which rights they protect.

C. State the legal requirement necessary for a police officer to do each of the following: stop and question, frisk, arrest, and search.

D. What rights of suspects did the *Miranda* decision uphold?

E. Under what conditions is evidence excluded at trial?

F. Multiple Choice. Select the best answer.

1. Police activity is regulated by
   a. departmental mandates
   b. the U.S. Constitution
   c. judicial decisions
   d. all of these

2. Packer's Due Process model of the criminal justice system embodies the principle that:
   a. efficiency in solving crime is of primary importance
   b. police should be given great latitude in carrying out their duties
   c. errors in the fact-finding process must be safeguarded against
   d. all of these

3. Individual states must afford citizens rights which are
   a. equal to or less than
   b. less than
   c. greater than
   d. equal to or greater than

those provided by the U.S. Constitution as interpreted by the U.S. Supreme Court.

4. Which Amendment to the U.S. Constitution provides citizens the right to a lawyer?
   a. Fourth
   b. Fifth
   c. Sixth
   d. Eighth

5. Which Amendment guarantees equal protection of the law to the citizens of each state?
   a. Sixth
   b. Fourth
   c. Fifth
   d. Fourteenth

6. The standard of proof for issuance of a warrant is
   a. preponderance of evidence
   b. probable cause
   c. balance of probabilities
   d. none of these

7. A rationale for the exclusion of illegally obtained evidence is that
   a. such evidence may be inherently untrustworthy
   b. it would be wrong for the courts to condone unlawful behavior
   c. excluding it will deter police from such action in the future
   d. all of these

8. To be constitutional, searches conducted by the police must
   a. be conducted with a warrant
   b. be reasonable
   c. both of these
   d. neither of these

9. Which of the following rights was granted by the *Miranda* decision?
   a. the right to remain silent
   b. the right to resist an unreasonable search and seizure
   c. the right to bail
   d. all of these

10. A defendant enjoys the right to counsel
   a. at every stage of the proceedings
   b. at every critical stage of the proceedings
   c. only at trial
   d. only at trial and at suppression hearings

REFERENCES

1. Herbert T. Packer, *The Limits of the Criminal Sanction* (Stanford, Calif.: Stanford University Press, 1968), 158.
2. *Ibid.*

3. *Ibid.*, 159.

4. *Ibid.*, 160.

5. *Ibid.*, 163.

6. *U.S. Constitution*, Amendment XIV.

7. *U.S. Constitution*, Amendment IV.

8. Draper v. U.S. 358 U.S. 307, 313 (1958) citing Carroll v. U.S. 267 U.S. 132, 161 (1925).

9. See, for example, Camara v. Municipal Court 387 U.S. 523, 528–529 (1967); McDonald v. U.S. 335 U.S. 451, 453 (1948); Johnson v. U.S. 333 U.S. 10, 14 (1948).

10. Others include searches conducted with the consent of the suspect and searches made in exigent circumstances. [See, for example, Schmerber v. California 384 U.S. 757 (1966) (blood sample for intoxication allowed to be taken without a search warrant because of probable loss of evidence), or in hot pursuit of a suspect, see, for example, Warden v. Hayden 387 U.S. 294 (1967).]

11. Chimel v. California 395 U.S. 752 (1969).

12. U.S. v. Robinson 414 U.S. 218 (1973).

13. Tennessee v. Garner 471 U.S. 1, 3 (1985).

14. Brown v. Texas 443 U.S. 47 (1979).

15. Terry v. Ohio 392 U.S. 1, 27 (1968).

16. Malloy v. Hogan 378 U.S. 1 (1964).

17. *U.S. Constitution*, Amendment V.

18. Brown v. Mississippi 297 U.S. 278, 284 (1936).

19. See, for example, Ashcraft v. Tennessee 322 U.S. 143 (1944); Watts v. Indiana 338 U.S. 49 (1949).

20. 384 U.S. 436 (1966).

21. *Ibid.*, 444–445.

22. See, for example, Fred E. Inbau, "Commentary: Overreaction—The Mischief of Miranda v. Arizona," *Journal of Criminal Law and Criminology*, 73 (1982), 797; "Interrogations in New Haven: The Impact of Miranda," *Yale Law Journal*, 76 (1967), 1519; Seeburger and Wettick, "Miranda in Pittsburgh: A Statistical Study," *University of Pittsburgh Law Review*, 29 (1967), 1; "The Impact of Miranda in Colorado," *Denver Law Journal*, 47 (1969), 1.

23. See, for example, North Carolina v. Butler 441 U.S. 369 (1979). An explicit statement of waiver is not always necessary to support a finding that the defendant waived the right to counsel guaranteed by the Miranda decision.

24. See, for example, Harris v. N.Y. 401 U.S. 222 (1971). Statements which are inadmissible in the prosecution's case-in-chief because they were obtained in violation of Miranda may, if trustworthy, be used to attack the credibility of a defendant who takes the stand; N.Y. v. Quarles 467 U.S. 649 (1984). In the interests of public safety there may be a short delay before reading a suspect the Miranda warnings. In this case the defendant, who was arrested in a supermarket, was asked about the location of a firearm before he was read his rights.

25. *U.S. Constitution*, Amendment VI.

26. Miranda v. Arizona 384 U.S. 436 (1966).

27. U.S. v. Wade 388 U.S. 218 (1967); Kirby v. Illinois 406 U.S. 682 (1972).

28. Malloy v. Hogan 378 U.S. 1 (1964); Miranda v. Arizona 384 U.S. 436 (1966).

29. Mapp v. Ohio 367 U.S. 643 (1961); Ker v. California 374 U.S. 23 (1963).

30. U.S. v. Wade 388 U.S. 218 (1967).

31. U.S. v. Wade 388 U.S. 218, 223 (1967).

32. Dallin H. Oaks, "Studying the Exclusionary Rule in Search and Seizure," *University of Chicago Law Review*, 37 (1970), 737.

33. People v. Defore 242 N.Y. 13, 21 (1926); (Per Cardozo, J.).

34. For a more thorough examination of the issues involved, see, for example, J. David Hirschel, *Fourth Amendment Rights* (Lexington, Mass.: D. C. Heath, 1979); Pierre J. Schlag, "Assaults on the Exclusionary Rule: Good Faith Limitations and Damage Remedies," *Journal of Criminal Law and Criminology*, 73 (1982), 875; Steven H. Schlesinger, "The Exclusionary Rule: Have Proponents Proven that it is a Deterrent to Police?" *Judicature*, 62 (1979), 404.

35. U.S. v. Leon 468 U.S. 897 (1984). See also, Massachussetts v. Sheppard 468 U.S. 981 (1984).

29

The Criminal Courts

OBJECTIVES

After studying this chapter, the student should be able to:

- Describe the characteristics of a court.
- Define the concept of jurisdiction.
- Compare trial and appellate courts.
- Distinguish between the federal and state court systems.
- Outline the jurisdiction of the United States Supreme Court in criminal cases.

In our earlier discussion of the nature of law, it was stated that law could be considered to consist of: "Explicit rules of conduct, created and enforced by a sovereign state, with planned use of sanctions to support the rules and designated officials to interpret and enforce those rules." [1]

In the last section it was stated that one of the most important functions performed by the police is the detection and apprehension of lawbreakers. The police constitute the front-line agency entrusted with the enforcement of the rules of law. They are also obliged, to an extent, to interpret those rules of law as they deal with the specific situations they encounter in the course of their work. They are not, however, responsible for the formal, legally binding interpretation and enforcement of the rules of law that have been enacted by the appropriate legislative bodies. That is a function that has been entrusted to the courts. In this chapter, the nature of the court process and the major features of the criminal court systems currently operating in the United States will be examined.

THE COURTS

The word "court" is defined by Funk and Wagnalls as "a place where justice is judicially administered." [2] Embodied in the concept is the idea that a just resolution to an issue is to be sought. Furthermore, this resolution is to be obtained by an impartial third party in accordance with fair and standardized rules of procedure. The major characteristics of courts have been stated to include the following:

1. Courts apply known rules to facts presented by litigants (the parties to a dispute).
2. They follow an established procedure in the process of resolving disputes.
3. The outcome sought is a "just" one.
4. Decisions are made by one or several judges who enjoy a special legal status.
5. Decisions by courts are binding upon the parties; and
6. Courts usually seek independence from outside pressures. [3]

The courts, after hearing arguments on both sides, are responsible for deciding what the facts are in a given case. After resolving the questions of fact, they apply the relevant legal rules to the facts; that is, they decide upon matters of law. All this is done, in theory, in an impartial manner according to established rules of procedure, and without outside interference. The court's decision is binding upon the parties; however, a party dissatisfied with the decision in the case can generally make an appeal to a higher court. An appeal is a request to a higher court to review the case or certain aspects of the case. It should be noted that in criminal cases the state has a very limited right of appeal.

CIVIL AND CRIMINAL COURTS

In the United States the legislative branch of government is, for the most part, responsible for enacting laws. The legislative branch of the government also has the prime responsibility for defining the powers of the various courts. Of course these legislative provisions must comply with constitutional requirements.

The term "jurisdiction" refers to a court's legal authority to hear and decide cases. A court's jurisdiction is limited both by the geographic area over which it has authority and the types of cases it can hear. A court with civil jurisdiction has the power to hear and decide cases concerning matters of civil law. A court with criminal jurisdiction has the power to try cases involving breaches of the criminal law. Many courts have the power to hear both civil and criminal cases. However, the concern here is solely with the criminal jurisdiction of the courts.

In a criminal case, the state is seeking to take action against an individual who is accused of committing a wrong against the people of that state by violating one of the provisions of the criminal code. The court here is responsible for determining first, whether the individual is guilty of the violation of the criminal law with which he or she is charged; and second, if guilty, what type of sanction, or punishment, the individual should receive.

A further limitation on the types of cases a court may hear depends upon whether the court is a trial or an appellate court, or both. A trial court, or court of original jurisdiction, is the court that initially hears and decides the case. It is the court that is presented with all the evidence in the case. It hears first hand the arguments of the attorneys and the testimony of witnesses. An appellate court, on the other hand, is a court that reviews cases that have already been tried in a trial court. Its review is usually confined to matters of law (e.g., whether the trial court was correct in deciding that Jane was legally searched and that the heroin found on her person should be admitted as evidence in court). It cannot usually concern itself with matters of fact (e.g., whether Jane had heroin on her person).

A court of record is a court that maintains a record of its proceedings, including, for example, the rulings of the judge and the testimony of witnesses. A trial court is usually a court of record. Should an appeal be made to an appellate court from a trial court which is a court of record, the appellate court will be able to review the transcript (written record) of the proceedings. The attorneys may present oral arguments to the higher court. The witnesses, however, will not have to appear before the court in person. However, should the trial court not have been a court of record, the appellate court would have to try the case again. In this case, the witnesses would have to present their testimony a second time.

FEDERAL AND STATE COURTS

The United States possesses what is known as a "dual court system;" for there are, in fact, two court systems operating side by side. There is, first, the federal court system, and second, what is referred to as the state court system.

Basically, the federal courts are responsible for hearing cases that involve violations of federal criminal law (crimes such as stealing from the U.S. mail or transporting a stolen automobile across state lines). The state courts, on the other hand, are responsible for trying cases that involve violations of state criminal law. Though the two court systems have their own separate spheres of jurisdiction, it is possible for one crime to involve both federal and state offenses. Thus suppose that Shifty steals an automobile in Nevada and brings it into California, where he is arrested. He may be charged in the Nevada State Courts with the crime of auto theft. In addition, Shifty may be charged in the federal courts with the crime of transporting a stolen motor vehicle across state lines. Most crimes, however, involve either a state or a federal criminal offense, but not both. The vast majority of criminal cases (estimated at over 85% [4]) are cases which are tried in state courts.

THE FEDERAL CRIMINAL COURTS

The federal criminal court system consists of three levels of courts: the United States District Courts, the United States Courts of Appeals, and the United States Supreme Court.

The U.S. Supreme Court, the highest court in the federal court system, is located in Washington, D.C. The U.S. Courts of Appeals are spread over the United States, with one Court of Appeals to each federal judicial circuit. The United States is divided into thirteen judicial circuits with at least three states in each of the first eleven circuits, and the District of Columbia and the Federal Circuit constituting the last two. There are District Courts in each state in the Union, with at least one District Court in each state. While the U.S. Supreme Court was established by the Federal Constitution,[5] the Courts of Appeals and the District Courts were established by Acts of Congress.[6]

The District Courts are the federal trial courts. They are responsible for trying cases involving federal offenses. Thus, if Shifty were tried for the federal offense of transporting a stolen motor vehicle across state lines, his case would be heard in the federal District Court. The attorneys would present their arguments; the witnesses would give their testimony; and the court would rule on matters of fact and law.

The U.S. Courts of Appeals are the intermediate appellate courts in the federal criminal court system. They are the courts which generally hear the appeals from decisions made in the District Courts. Thus, if Shifty had been convicted in District Court, and now wished to appeal his conviction, his appeal would be to the U.S. Court of Appeals, which would review his case. The Court of Appeals might either affirm or reverse the lower court ruling. In some circumstances, it might order that a new trial be held in District Court.

The U.S. Supreme Court is the highest court in the federal court system. While essentially an appellate court, the Supreme Court also possesses, under the Constitution, original jurisdiction to hear cases "affecting Ambassadors, other public Ministers and Consuls, and those in which a State shall be a party."[7] Most of these cases, however, can be and are heard in the lower federal courts.[8]

The appellate jurisdiction of the Supreme Court is also set out in the federal Constitution; however, it is to be "with such Exceptions, and under such Regulations as the Congress shall make."[9] Basically, in criminal cases, the most important function of the Supreme Court relates to the interpretation and application of the provisions of the federal Constitution. In carrying out this task, the Supreme Court is often asked to decide upon the constitutionality of federal and state statutory provisions. As the highest court in the federal court system, it performs the significant function of interpreting the meaning of federal statutes.

Cases can reach the U.S. Supreme Court either through the federal court system or from the state courts. If the case comes from a state court, it must involve a federal question (usually an issue concerning the federal Constitution), and come from the state court of last resort, the highest court in the state that has the jurisdiction to rule upon the matter at issue. This will usually be the highest court in the state system.

The Supreme Court enjoys substantial discretion in deciding which cases it will hear. Motions for review of a case by the Supreme Court are generally through the petitions for the issuance of either a *writ of appeal* or, far more common, a *writ of certiorari*. A *writ of certiorari* is an order directing the lower court to send up the record for review. The issuance of this writ is a matter of judicial discretion, and it requires a vote of at least four of the nine Supreme Court Justices for it to be granted. According to the Court's own rules the *writ of certiorari* will be granted "only where there are special and important reasons therefor." [10]

Unlike the *writ of certiorari*, the *writ of appeal* is to be granted as a matter of right. It is to be granted in a number of specified circumstances. One such circumstance is when a state statute has been unsuccessfully challenged in a state court of last resort as being unconstitutional. [11]

Although the Supreme Court is theoretically bound to accept a valid appeal, "since 1928 the high tribunal has had the very considerable discretionary power to reject such an appeal on the ground that the federal question, otherwise validly raised, is 'insubstantial.' " [12] The result is that very few such cases (generally less than 10% [13]) are, in fact, heard by the Supreme Court. The desired outcome is that the Supreme Court hears only those cases involving substantial federal issues that have great significance for far more than just the parties involved in the case.

As the highest court in the land, the Supreme Court is the final arbiter for both the federal and state court systems on matters involving federal constitutional law. As has been stated earlier, the U.S. Constitution, as interpreted at the most authoritative level by the U.S. Supreme Court, lays down the basic minimum constitutional requirements with which both the federal and state governments must comply as they seek to regulate their citizenry. The U.S. Supreme Court thus fulfills the highly significant role of establishing minimum standards of conduct that must be employed by governmental units throughout the United States. Thus, for example, all police agencies in the United States are required to read suspects their *Miranda* rights prior to in-custody questioning and to allow them to have the assistance of counsel during a lineup conducted after the initiation of adversary judicial proceedings. [14] States are obliged to follow these minimum federal constitutional requirements. There is, however, nothing to prevent a state from providing rights in excess of these minimum requirements, and a number of state constitutions do precisely that.

THE STATE CRIMINAL COURTS

Reference has been made to the state criminal court system as if there were a single unified network of courts operating throughout the different states. In actuality, there is no such state criminal court system. Each state has its own network of criminal courts. The jurisdictions, names, and number of levels of criminal courts vary from state to state. In general, however, there are a number of different types of criminal courts to be found in each state. There are, in essence, the trial courts, which may be of limited or general jurisdiction. Then there are the appellate courts, which serve to review the decisions of the trial courts. There are often, in fact, two levels of both trial and appellate courts.

The first level of trial courts that is usually found in the different states is what is generally known as either the justice of the peace, the magistrates', the city, or the police courts. These are usually courts with limited criminal jurisdiction. They may, for example, try violations of city or county ordinances and try misdemeanors for which the maximum penalty is no more than a certain specified sentence (e.g., six months imprisonment). They are frequently not courts of record, and thus any appeal from their decisions will result in a total rehearing of the case in a superior court. Often they have jurisdiction to hear the first stages in a felony case, though the trial of the felony case itself must be in a superior court.

The second level of trial courts consists of trial courts of general criminal jurisdiction. These courts usually try criminal cases that involve felonies or serious misdemeanors. They are courts of record, and thus any appeal from their decisions will not result in a total rehearing of the case in the superior court.

At the next level are the appellate courts. In most states (e.g., California, New York, Florida, and Illinois), there are two levels of appellate courts: intermediate appellate courts, often called the state courts of appeals, and a final appellate court, often called the state supreme court. In some states (e.g., Vermont, Mississippi, and Nevada), however, there are no intermediate appellate courts.

A ruling by a state appellate court is, of course, binding upon all lower courts within that state. Thus suppose that the highest appellate court in a state were to rule that a person is not constitutionally entitled to the presence of an attorney during a search of his or her residence. This ruling would apply to all similar cases tried in all courts in that state. If, however, the case were appealed to the U.S. Supreme Court and that court were to rule that such a constitutional right did exist, then that ruling would apply not only to all cases in the state from which the appeal came, but to all cases tried in all of the states.

SUMMARY

This chapter has examined the structure of the criminal court system of the United States. It has been explained that the United States possesses a dual court system consisting of federal and state courts. While the federal courts are basically concerned with cases involving violations of federal law, the state courts try cases involving violations of state law.

The federal court system has three levels of courts that deal with criminal cases: the District Courts, the Courts of Appeals, and the Supreme Court. In addition to being the highest court in the federal court system, the U.S. Supreme Court also hears cases from the state courts of last resort, provided that those cases involve substantial federal questions. Through its decisions on constitutional issues, the Supreme Court sets out basic minimum standards that must be adhered to throughout the nation.

The state court system does not consist of a single unified network of courts. Rather, each state has its own criminal court system, with the jurisdictions, names, and number of levels of criminal courts varying from state to state. Basically, however, each state court system tends to have two levels of trial courts, consisting of courts of limited and general criminal jurisdiction, and one or two levels of appellate courts.

SUGGESTED ACTIVITIES

● Report on your state court system. How many levels of trial courts are there? What are the trial courts called, and what are their jurisdictions? How many levels of appellate courts are there, and what are they called?

● Leaf through your local newspaper over a two-week period, and keep a record of reports on criminal cases. How many cases are federal cases, and how many are state cases? How many involve trials, and how many are about appeals?

● Find out about the federal court system in your area. Which judicial circuit are you in? What states compose that circuit? Where is the U.S. Court of Appeals in your circuit? Where is the District Court which has jurisdiction over your area?

REVIEW

A. What are the general characteristics of a court?

B. What does "jurisdiction" mean, and how is it limited?

C. What is the difference between a trial court and an appellate court?

D. What is a court of record, and of what importance is that fact?

E. Explain what is meant by the "dual court system" of the United States; distinguish between the two systems.

F. What are the levels of courts in the federal system?

G. What is the jurisdiction of the U.S. Supreme Court in criminal cases?

H. Multiple Choice. Select the best answer.

1. A court of original jurisdiction must be
    a. a trial court
    b. an appellate court
    c. a district court
    d. a court of record

2. The appellate court is usually concerned with
    a. matters of fact
    b. matters of law
    c. both of these
    d. neither of these

3. Which of the following is part of the federal criminal court system?
    a. the District Courts
    b. the Courts of Appeals
    c. the Supreme Court
    d. all of these

4. How many U.S. Courts of Appeals are there?
    a. one
    b. ten
    c. thirteen
    d. fifty

5. How many levels of federal criminal courts are there?
    a. one
    b. two
    c. three
    d. four

6. The U.S. Supreme Court is
    a. an appellate court for federal cases
    b. an appellate court for state cases
    c. a trial court
    d. all of these

7. The U.S. Supreme Court hears
    a. all appeals from state courts of last resort
    b. all appeals from federal Courts of Appeals
    c. cases involving substantial federal issues
    d. all of these

8. The state court system
    a. is a unified network of courts throughout the United States
    b. varies from state to state
    c. does not allow for appeals
    d. none of these

9. A court's legal authority to hear and decide cases is referred to as its
    a. jurisdiction
    b. transcript
    c. district
    d. none of these

10. A request to a higher court to review a case or certain aspects of it is called
    a. a trial
    b. an appeal
    c. a plea bargain
    d. none of these

REFERENCES

1. See *ante*, Section 6, Chapter 20.
2. Funk and Wagnalls, *Standard College Dictionary* (New York: Harcourt, Brace, 1968), 310.
3. John P. Richert, "Courts: A Comparative Perspective," in Fannie J. Klein, *Federal and State Court Systems—A Guide* (Cambridge, Mass.: Ballinger, 1977), 255.
4. Hazel B. Kerper, *Introduction to the Criminal Justice System* (St. Paul: West, 1972), 215.
5. *U.S. Constitution*, Article III.
6. The District Courts in 1780, the Courts of Appeals (known until 1948 as the Circuit Courts of Appeals) in 1891.
7. *U.S. Constitution*, Article III (2). It should, however, be noted that the Eleventh Amendment of the United States Constitution provides that: "The Judicial power of the United States shall not be construed to extend to any suit in law or equity, commenced or prosecuted against one of the United States by citizens of another state, or by citizens or subjects of any Foreign State."
8. 28 U.S.C. Sec. 1251 sets out the jurisdiction of the Court. Available data show that very few of the cases that come before the Supreme Court involve the Court's original jurisdiction. In 1983, for example,

there were 5,079 cases on the Court's docket. Only 17 were cases where the Court had original jurisdiction [Robert A. Carp and Ronald Stidham, *The Federal Courts* (Washington, D.C.: Congressional Quarterly, 1985), 43].

9. *U.S. Constitution*, Article III (2).
10. Rule 19, 1970 Revised Rules of the Supreme Court.
11. 28 U.S.C. Sec. 1257.
12. Henry J. Abraham, *The Judicial Process*, 5th ed. (New York: Oxford University Press, 1986), 181.
13. *Ibid*.
14. See *ante*, Section 7, Chapter 28.

30

Judges and Lawyers

OBJECTIVES

After studying this chapter, the student should be able to:

- List the qualifications necessary to become a judge and the criteria and procedures used for the selection, continued service, and removal of judges.
- List the powers, duties, and functions of judges.
- Outline the procedures used for the appointment of public prosecutors and describe their duties and functions
- Describe the role of the defense attorney and distinguish between the different types of defense attorneys: privately retained, court appointed, and public defenders.

The previous chapter examined the structure of the United States court system. This chapter discusses the officials who are most actively and regularly involved in the criminal court process—the judges and the lawyers, both for the prosecution and for the defense.

THE JUDGES

When one thinks of a court of law, the central figure that almost invariably comes to mind is that of a judge wearing a black flowing robe and administering justice. The term ''judge'' is, in fact, a wide one, encompassing any ''public officer, appointed to preside and to administer the law in a court of justice." [1] Thus any such officer, from a justice of the peace in a justice of the peace court to an associate justice of the U.S. Supreme Court, is a judge who is entrusted with the administration of the laws.

The jurisdictions of the different courts vary greatly. The judges presiding in the many criminal courts in the United States differ in terms of their qualifications and training, the criteria and procedures for their appointment and removal, their powers and duties, their functions, and the prestige they are accorded. As is the case with most aspects of the criminal justice system in the United States, any generalization is subject to exceptions.

Powers, Duties, and Functions of Judges

The judge is the primary officer of the court, regardless of the nature of the court. The judge is responsible for seeing that the business of the court, which is the resolution of cases, is carried out. This may well involve administrative as well as judicial duties.

A trial court judge may be involved in the processing of criminal offenders from a time prior to arrest until after the offender has been convicted and sentenced. Trial court judges in different courts are responsible for issuing search and arrest warrants, granting bail, holding preliminary hearings, hearing pretrial motions (e.g., a motion to suppress evidence), trying cases, sentencing convicted offenders, and conducting probation revocation hearings. The judge of a particular court is the final arbiter on all matters of law, and may also be the decision maker on matters of fact, for example when a defendant stands trial without a jury. Finally, the judge is responsible, within statutory limits, for imposing sentences on convicted offenders.

The duties of a trial court judge are highly important. It is up to this judge to ensure that an accused person is processed fairly through the criminal justice system and, if convicted, sentenced fairly. The appellate court judges, on the other hand, have the responsibility of reviewing cases that have been appealed from the trial courts. In this manner, in essence, they set judicial policy for the lower courts through the establishment of legal precedents. In dealing with cases involving the police or corrections, the judges also set guidelines for these segments of the criminal justice system.

In addition to their judicial duties, judges often have administrative functions to fulfill. A judge may be responsible for seeing that the court is fully staffed, for example filling such positions as clerk of the court or court reporter. It may be the judge's job to make certain that the court budget is in order and that resources are suitably allocated. All this, along with maintaining a reasonably swift flow of cases through the system, requires a different type of expertise on the part of the judge. The current trend in the larger court systems is to have such functions taken over by trained professional court administrators.

Background Qualifications and Training of Judges

Judges play a significant role in the administration of criminal justice. Thus it might be expected that candidates for judicial office would be required to have certain detailed background qualifications and undergo formal training prior to assuming duties on the bench. However, unlike some other countries, this is not so in the United States. Even a law degree may not be required either in theory or practice.[2] The philosophy is that an understanding personality and a discerning mind may be more important than formal legal education. In practice, though, most judges are lawyers; many judges in the lower courts, however, do not possess law degrees.[3] Even in the higher courts, a law degree may not be theoretically required. In the federal court system, for example, a law degree "is neither a constitutional nor a statutory requirement for appointment, yet custom would automatically exclude from consideration anyone who did not have it."[4]

It is perhaps the general esteem accorded to judges that results in their rarely being required to undergo any formal training prior to assuming their duties. It may appear presumptuous to demand that a newly elected or appointed judge return to school. Yet is is possible "for a judge who the day before had made his living drafting corporate indentures to be called upon to rule on the validity of a search or to charge a jury on the law of entrapment."[5] Judges in the higher courts are not necessarily required to have prior judicial experience. It is of interest to note that:

> Among the 102 individual Justices who served on the Supreme Court between 1789 and the middle of 1984, only twenty-two had ten or more years of previous judicial experience on any lower level, federal or state, at the time of their appointment, and forty-two had no judicial experience whatsoever.[6]

Selection of Judges

The method of selecting judges has for a long time been tied in with the philosophy that the people should have the right to choose public officials. Even today, among the three principal methods of selecting judges (election, appointment, and merit selection), election by popular vote is still the most common. Indeed, about one-half of the states currently elect at least some of their judicial officers by popular vote. About one-half of these states select their judges through partisan elections, and the rest through nonpartisan elections. In the partisan elections, candidates run with party affiliations (e.g., Democrat or Republican). In the nonpartisan elections, candidates do not have any such official party affiliations.

Numerous concerns have been voiced about selecting judges through popular elections. It has been suggested, for example, that the most qualified candidates for judicial posts may be unwilling to become involved in the unfamiliar and risky process of running for office; that the general electorate is not well equipped for the task of selecting judicial officers; that in general elections, judicial candidates maintain a low profile, appear at the end of a long list of candidates for public office, and are unknown and unrecognized by an uninformed electorate; that in special elections, voter turnout is very low; and, above all, that political party involvement is undesirable in the process of selecting judges who are expected to administer the law without prejudice or favor. Although nonpartisan elections were intended to reduce the undesirable political element in the election of judges, this has not always been the result.

A few states provide for the appointment of judicial officials. Usually the appointments are made by the governor, with the consent of the legislature. As with selection by election, selection by appointment can be highly political in nature, with the governor of a state sometimes seeking to reward people for their support.

In the federal court system, all judges are appointed by the president and confirmed by the Senate. Since 1846 this process has received input from the American Bar Association's Committee on the Federal Judiciary which has rated each of the candidates selected by the president.

It was with a view to diminishing the influence of politics on the selection of judges that the ''merit selection'' procedure of choosing judges was formulated. Also known as the Missouri Plan (after the first state to establish such procedures), merit selection involves a combination of appointment and election. Basically, a nominating commission of lawyers and laypeople scrutinizes the qualifications of potential candidates and submits to the governor a list of three nominees. The governor then chooses one of these nominees who is appointed to serve for one year. After one year the newly appointed judge faces the electorate. However, the judge does not run against another candidate but, rather, runs against his or her own record; for the sole question facing the electorate is ''Shall Judge _____ be retained in office?'' If a majority of the electorate votes yes, then the judge remains in office until the end of the term. At that time, the judge can again face the electorate, who determine whether the judge should be retained for a second term.

Merit selection received the endorsement of many groups, including the American Bar Association and the American Judicature Society. It was, in essence, recommended by the National Advisory Commission on Criminal Justice Standards and Goals as the most desirable method of selecting judges.[7] As of 1983, about one-third of the States had adopted the Missouri Plan or a modified version of that plan.[8] To an extent this system would appear to have diminished the influence of political parties in the process of selecting judges. On the other hand, it greatly enhances the role played by the legal profession. Though the electorate retains a highly significant role in that it can turn a judge out of office, it appears to have rarely exercised that right. Thus, for example, ''from 1940 through 1970, 179 judicial elections under the plan were held in Missouri: only one of these saw a judge rejected by the vote of the people—and he received 46.4 percent affirmative votes.''[9] Nationwide in 1978 only ''13 of 486(!) judges in retention ballots were rejected.''[10] Whether a popular judge is necessarily a good judge is, of course, open to debate.

Tenure and Removal of Judges

Politics thus plays a significant role in the selection of judges. It is important, however, that regardless of the procedure utilized, once selected, the judges be able to exercise their judicial powers without prejudice or favor. To an extent, selecting judges for long terms of service fulfills the function of promoting an independent judiciary. Generally the higher the court, the longer the period of tenure a judge has. In the federal system, all judges ''hold their offices during good behavior,''[11] a phrase which translates into a possible lifetime tenure. Even when elected for a term of years, an incumbent judge usually finds it relatively easy to win reelection. Thus,

In Wisconsin, for instance, only four incumbent supreme court justices were defeated between 1853 and 1949. In Minnesota only one supreme court justice was defeated for reelection between 1912 and 1941, and only four of eighty-four district judges were defeated in their reelection bids during that time.[12]

In Ohio, forty-two (6.5%) of the 644 judges in the courts of common pleas who ran for reelection between 1962 and 1980 were defeated either in the primary or the general election.[13]

While it is important that the judiciary be able to maintain its independence, it is just as important that incompetent or corrupt judges be removed from office. Traditional methods for seeking the removal of judges have included impeachment, legislative address, and recall. Impeachment involves indictment by one house of a legislature and trial by the other. Legislative address involves a vote by the legislature on a resolution to remove a judge from office. Recall involves a special election in which the electorate is asked to vote on whether a judge should be recalled, that is, removed from office. All have been stated to be "cumbersome and political and . . . rarely used."[14]

As a consequence, most states have established judicial disciplinary commissions which are responsible for investigating complaints against judges. In California, for example, a nine-person commission consisting of five judges, two lawyers, and two laypeople investigates complaints and makes recommendations to the State Supreme Court, which can take appropriate action. The model recommended by the National Advisory Commission on Criminal Justice Standards and Goals is a judicial conduct commission. No more than one-third of the members of the commission are to be judges, and the commission itself is to be empowered to take the appropriate action.[15] Important as it is to improve procedures for removing unfit judges, "it would seem obvious that concentrating efforts on perfecting a removal system is far less productive than emphasizing stricter qualifications for becoming a judge in the first place."[16]

PUBLIC PROSECUTORS

The judge is often thought of in a criminal case as an arbiter between two opposing sides: the public prosecutor, on the one side, and the defendant, usually represented by a lawyer, on the other.

The public prosecutor (often known as the district attorney) has jurisdiction over a certain geographical area, and represents the interests of the people in that area. This jurisdiction usually extends over a county, sometimes over a judicial district. In all but a handful of states, the public prosecutor is elected by the people and is answerable to them through the electoral process. The most common term of service is, in fact, four years. A lawyer by profession, the public prosecutor may see the public prosecutor's office as a possible permanent position or as one stage in a long political career. In the federal system both the U.S. district attorneys and the attorney general are appointed by the president. The U.S. district attorneys are the trial court prosecutors. The U.S.

attorney general, like the state attorneys general, is responsible for conducting the appeals in the higher appellate courts.

In all but the smallest prosecutors' offices, the public prosecutor has a staff of assistants. These assistants, also qualified lawyers, process most, if not all, cases. Indeed, in the large prosecutors' offices, the task of the public prosecutor is that of an administrator, setting office policy, and supervising the staff's performance. Unfortunately, the salaries in a public prosecutor's office are generally rather low compared to those that can be obtained as a private attorney. In addition, the chances for advancement are limited. Hence, public prosecutors' offices tend to attract young, recent law school graduates who spend a few years in the public prosecutor's office and then move on, often to private practice.

The prime function of the public prosecutor is the prosecution of violations of the criminal law committed within the area of jurisdiction. Occasionally the public prosecutor may initiate investigations into alleged criminal conduct. Far more commonly dealt with, however, are cases where a suspect has already been arrested. In this situation, the public prosecutor has, in essence, two initial decisions to make. The first is whether or not to prosecute a suspect. Then, if a suspect is to be prosecuted, it must be decided with what offense or offenses the suspect is to be charged.

In making these decisions, the prosecutor may be influenced by several factors. These include the seriousness of the alleged offense; the strength of the evidence available against the suspect; the background characteristics of the suspect; the prosecutor's own organizational needs of seeing cases move through the office; the characteristics and attitudes of the complainant or victim; possible public reaction to the decision; and the prosecutor's ongoing relationship with other criminal justice personnel, such as the police and the defense attorneys. In recognition of the fact that a few offenders account for a great percentage of serious crime,[17] a number of prosecutors' offices have instituted career criminal programs to ensure that prosecution of these offenders receives the added attention and resources it deserves.[18]

There is, in fact, little formal control over the prosecutor's decision of whether or not to charge a suspect. If the prosecutor decides not to charge a suspect, there is no formal avenue of appeal for a victim or complainant. If it is decided to prosecute, then the case will proceed through the court system. Even later in the process, however, the prosecutor may still decide to have the charges dismissed.

It has been stated that "the Prosecutor's primary function should be to represent the State in court."[19] The public image of the public prosecutor is probably that of an attorney vehemently arguing the state's case against an accused in court. Not to be forgotten, however, is the fact that the vast majority of criminal cases are settled through a plea bargain, thus avoiding the necessity of taking the case to trial. The public prosecutor has an important role in the plea bargaining process, a topic which will be discussed in far greater detail in a later section. Though assuming an adversarial role against an accused, the public prosecutor is obliged to act in the best interests of the people within the area of jurisdiction. Of concern also is the conviction record of the prosecutor's office. Thus, the certainty of a guilty plea to a reduced charge may be preferable to the lengthy, costly, and risky prospects of going to trial.

DEFENSE ATTORNEYS

The defense attorney is the defendant's legal representative during, and in some situations prior to, the court process. Each individual suspected of committing a crime is entitled to handle his or her own case. However, it is generally recognized that because of the legal complexities of our society a private individual, unversed in either the law or the legal process, may be ill equipped to handle an adequate self-defense.

The Sixth Amendment of the U.S. Constitution provides that, ''In all criminal prosecutions, the accused shall enjoy the right to . . . have the assistance of counsel for his defence.'' [20] Two questions need to be addressed. First, at what stage of the process is an accused entitled to have the assistance of counsel? Second, what situation develops if an accused desires to have the assistance of counsel but cannot afford to hire one?

With regard to the court proceedings, the U.S. Supreme Court has held that an accused must at the very latest be allowed to have the assistance of counsel when he or she is arraigned (formally charged) [21] or at the preliminary hearing (where the state must provide sufficient evidence for an accused to be held for arraignment on a felony charge at superior court).[22] The Supreme Court has also held that a suspect has the right to counsel during an in-custody interrogation,[23] and when participating in a lineup conducted after the initiation of adversary judicial proceedings.[24] All of these situations have been felt to be critical stages of the proceedings against an accused which require the assistance of counsel.

With regard to the issue of an accused unable to afford counsel, it has been stated by the U.S. Supreme Court that: ''There can be no equal justice where the kind of trial a man gets depends on the amount of money he has.'' [25] Provisions have therefore been made to provide indigents with attorneys without charge. All the aforementioned stages are ones in which it has been held that an indigent should have the right to a state-appointed attorney. With regard to the types of cases to which such a right applies, it has been held that, without a knowing and intelligent waiver, no person can be imprisoned for any offense unless he or she was represented by counsel.[26] This provides for legal representation in all felony and most misdemeanor cases. The National Advisory Commission on Criminal Justice Standards and Goals has recommended that this right to counsel be extended to defendants in all nonmotor criminal cases.[27]

The defense counsel is a lawyer who undertakes criminal defense work as a privately retained attorney, as an assigned counsel, or as a staff member of a public defender's office. A privately retained attorney is a lawyer who is hired by a client for a fee, and thus tends to represent the more affluent type of client. Assigned counsel and public defenders, on the other hand, represent clients who are indigent. Both types of legal representation for the indigent are to be found throughout the United States. The assigned counsel is a lawyer who is appointed by the judge from a list of attorneys who are available to represent indigent defendants. The assigned counsel is appointed on a case-by-case basis and is paid by local or state funds. An assigned counsel may devote all, or only part, of his or her practice to criminal work. A public defender, on the other hand, is a lawyer who works for a public defender's office, a public agency with salaried staff. Often underpaid, understaffed, and overworked, the public defender's office is solely involved in providing legal representation for indigent defendants.

Criminal law work has not been notoriously attractive to members of the legal profession. The types of clients they generally have to deal with, their working environment (such as jails and police stations), the lower pay, and lower status than that accorded civil lawyers, all contribute to this state of affairs. A few lawyers have become noted for handling criminal work, but these are the exceptions.

The primary function of the defense counsel is to represent a client's interests in the best possible manner. This includes, of course, attempting to prevent the conviction of the innocent. It also includes the protection of the constitutional rights of all defendants, both innocent and guilty. Thus if an attorney is defending a client who has been charged with illegal possession of heroin and the attorney believes that the heroin was illegally seized, it is the attorney's duty to attempt to prevent the heroin from being admitted as evidence in court, even if (or perhaps especially if) the suppression of that evidence will result in setting the client free. While pursuing the client's interests in an aggressive manner, the defense attorney is, of course, duty-bound not to defraud the court.

The adversary model of the criminal court process depicts the defense lawyer as continuously fighting for a client's rights. It perhaps overlooks the role of the defense attorney as a negotiator, as an individual trying to obtain from the prosecutor the best possible deal for a client. It may be true that a quick and not entirely satisfactory deal is occasionally struck by an assigned counsel who is eager to dispose of cases quickly or by a public defender because of a heavy case load. However, the fact remains that an accused who is represented by an attorney who knows the system and the personnel within the system is probably better off than an accused who is unrepresented by counsel and tries to take on the system alone.

Indeed, concern has been raised that the kind of justice people receive may depend upon the nature of their legal representation. Those without legal representation may not fare as well as those who have a lawyer acting for them. Additionally, those who are represented by a privately retained attorney may fare better than those who have a public defender or a state-appointed attorney.

In a nationwide study of state grand larceny cases processed in 1962, Nagel found that defendants who had legal representation were more likely to be released on bail and have their cases result in dismissal or acquittal than those who did not have attorneys. When found guilty, those with legal representation were more likely to receive suspended sentences or probation. Finally, when prison sentences were given, they were far more likely to receive shorter terms than those who had not had legal representation.[28]

With regard to having a hired attorney, as opposed to a court-provided one (either a public defender or an assigned counsel), Nagel found that having a hired counsel was related to a greater likelihood of being released on bail and receiving a suspended sentence or probation if found guilty.

In a survey of criminal defendants in three cities, Casper found that defendants do not trust public defenders as much as they do private defense attorneys.[29] While 81 percent of the defendants who had a private lawyer felt that their lawyer was on their side and 6 percent felt that the lawyer was on the state's side, only 58 percent of defendants represented by a public defender thought that the lawyer was on their side, and 25 percent felt that the lawyer was on the state's side.[30] Private attorneys were consistently rated more highly than were public defenders.

SUMMARY

This chapter has examined the duties and functions of the officials most actively and regularly involved in the criminal court process, the judges and the prosecution and defense attorneys.

The methods by which judges are selected and removed from office were discussed. The kind of background qualifications and training judges need prior to assuming office was noted. It was said that judges may perform administrative as well as judicial duties and that their judicial duties are not confined to presiding over trials.

The public prosecutor has been depicted as a public official who represents the people's interests in seeing that violations of the criminal law committed within his or her jurisdiction are prosecuted. The prosecutor decides whether to charge a suspect; and if so, what charges to bring. Often the prosecutor may prefer to accept the certainty of a guilty plea to a lesser charge than to undertake the lengthy, costly, and risky process of going to trial.

The defense attorney is the defendant's legal representative. Whether a privately retained attorney, an assigned counsel, or a public defender, a defense attorney's duty is to act in the best interest of the client. At times this may mean defending a client at trial; it may mean attempting to enforce a client's constitutional and procedural rights; and it may mean acting as a negotiator and obtaining the best possible deal for a client.

SUGGESTED ACTIVITIES

- Arrange an interview with a judge or a prosecuting attorney in order to ask about the person's education, experience, and opinion regarding the qualifications which should be necessary for that position.
- How is the public prosecutor selected in your area? How long is the term of office? What qualifications are required? How many assistants work in the prosecutor's office, and what qualifications and training are required of them?
- How are the different judges in your area selected? How long are their terms of office? What qualifications are required? What procedures are available for removing them from office?
- What type of defense counsel is provided in your area for indigents?
- Arrange an interview at the public defender's office, if there is one in your area. Find out how many lawyers work there, and what their case loads are like. Ask what percentage of clients are acquitted, and what percentage of convicted clients receive active sentences. Then ask the same questions of a private defense attorney and compare the answers. Are the two offices handling different types of cases or different types of clients?

REVIEW

A. What are the minimum qualifications for becoming a judge?

B. What are the powers, duties, and functions of judges?

C. List and briefly describe the three methods of selecting and retaining judges.

D. What procedures are used in the appointment of a public prosecutor?

E. Briefly describe the duties of the public prosecutor.

F. Briefly describe the duties of the defense attorney.

G. Distinguish between a public defender, an assigned counsel, and a privately retained attorney.

H. Multiple Choice. Select the best answer.

1. In order to become a judge, a person must
  a. be a lawyer
  b. have courtroom experience as a lawyer
  c. undergo formal training
  d. none of these

2. The final arbiter on matters of law in a court is
  a. the judge
  b. the clerk of the court
  c. the defense attorney
  d. the prosecutor

3. Which of the following is a method currently used for selecting judges?
  a. appointment
  b. election
  c. merit selection
  d. all of these

4. Impeachment, legislative address, and recall are all
  a. types of appeals
  b. pretrial motions
  c. methods of removing judges
  d. none of these

5. The decision of whether or not to charge a suspect is made by
  a. the judge
  b. the prosecutor
  c. the clerk of the court
  d. none of these

6. An accused has the right to the assistance of counsel
  a. at his or her arraignment in superior court
  b. at the preliminary hearing
  c. during an in-custody interrogation
  d. all of these

7. A private attorney who is appointed by the judge to represent an indigent defendant is called
  a. a public defender
  b. an assigned counsel
  c. a privately retained attorney
  d. all of these

8. The duty of a defense attorney is to
  a. represent a client's best interests
  b. not defraud the court

    c. protect a guilty client's constitutional rights

    d. all of these

9. It is the function of the prosecutor to

    a. present the state's case in court

    b. participate in plea bargaining

    c. act in the best interests of the people in his or her jurisdiction

    d. all of these

10. Research has shown that defendants represented by private attorneys rather than by court-provided attorneys tend to

    a. be released on bail more often

    b. have more confidence in their attorneys

    c. receive lighter sentences

    d. all of these

REFERENCES

1. Henry Campbell Black, *Black's Law Dictionary*, 4th ed. (St. Paul: West, 1975), 976.

2. North v. Russell 427 U.S. 328 (1976).

3. This is the case, for example, with many of the justice of the peace or general sessions (TN) courts.

4. Henry J. Abraham, *The Judicial Process*, 5th ed. (New York: Oxford University Press, 1986), 53.

5. The President's Commission on Law Enforcement and Administration of Justice, *Task Force Report: The Courts* (Washington, D.C.: U.S. Government Printing Office, 1967), 68.

6. Abraham, *op. cit.*, 55.

7. National Advisory Commission on Criminal Justice Standards and Goals, *The Courts* (Washington, D.C.: U.S. Government Printing Office, 1973), 147–149.

8. Edmund F. McGarrell and Timothy J. Flanagan (eds.) *Sourcebook of Criminal Justice Statistics—1984* (Washington, D.C.: U.S. Government Printing Office, 1985), 85–89.

9. Abraham, *op. cit.*, 40. As of 1984 no additional judge had been defeated.

10. Abraham, *op. cit.*, 40.

11. *U.S. Constitution*, Article III, Section 1.

12. Herbert Jacob, *Justice in America*, 4th ed. (Boston: Little, Brown, 1984), 124. [Both Wisconsin and Minnesota are states that select judges through nonpartisan elections; with regard to judges selected through partisan elections, Jacob states that "very few incumbent judges are defeated" (*op. cit.*, 123).]

13. Lawrence Baum, "The Electoral Fates of Incumbent Judges in the Ohio Court of Common Pleas," *Judicature*, 66 (1983), 420, 424.

14. Fannie J. Klein, *Federal and State Court Systems—A Guide* (Cambridge, Mass.: Ballinger, 1977), 27.

15. National Advisory Commission on Criminal Justice Standards and Goals, *op. cit.*, 153–155.

16. Merlin Lewis, Warren Bundy, and James L. Hague, *An Introduction to the Courts and Judicial Process* (Englewood Cliffs, N.J.: Prentice-Hall, 1978), 284.

17. See, for example, Peter W. Greenwood, *Selective Incapacitation* (Santa Monica, Calif.: Rand Corp., 1982).

18. The Bronx Major Offense Bureau is probably the best known of these programs. See, for example, U.S. Department of Justice, *The Major Offense Bureau* (Washington, D.C.: U.S. Government Printing Office, 1976).

19. National Advisory Commission on Criminal Justice Standards and Goals, *op. cit.*, 244.

20. *U.S. Constitution*, Amendment VI.

21. Hamilton v. Alabama 368 U.S. 52 (1961).

22. White v. Maryland 373 U.S. 59 (1963); Coleman v. Alabama 399 U.S. 1 (1970).

23. Escobedo v. Illinois 378 U.S. 478 (1964); Miranda v. Arizona 384 U.S. 436 (1966).

24. Kirby v. Illinois 406 U.S. 682 (1972).

25. Griffin v. Illinois 351 U.S. 12, 19 (1956). (The case involved an indigent defendant's right to be furnished with a transcript for appeal.)

26. Argersinger v. Hamlin 407 U.S. 25 (1972). This extended the requirement imposed on states by the

landmark case of *Gideon* v. *Wainwright* (372 U.S. 335 (1963)) that indigent defendants in felony cases be provided with counsel.

27. National Advisory Commission on Criminal Justice Standards and Goals, *op. cit.*, 253.
28. Stuart S. Nagel, *Improving the Legal Process* (Lexington, Mass.: D. C. Heath, 1975), 57–80.
29. Jonathan D. Casper, *Criminal Courts: The Defendant's Perspective* (Washington, D.C.: U.S. Government Printing Office, 1978).
30. *Ibid.*, 31.

31

Initial Stages
of the Court Process

OBJECTIVES

After studying this chapter, the student should be able to:

- Describe the stages of a criminal case and distinguish between the procedures for processing a felony and a misdemeanor case.
- Delineate the functions and characteristics of the initial appearance, preliminary hearing, grand jury hearing, and trial.
- Explain the provision against double jeopardy.
- Discuss the bail process and contrast it with release on recognizance.
- Outline the characteristics and functions of jail.

In the previous chapters, the criminal court system and the personnel most actively involved in its operation—the judges and the attorneys for the prosecution and the defense—were examined. In this chapter, the criminal court process itself will be discussed.

THE CRIMINAL COURT PROCESS

The criminal court process may begin either before or after a suspect has been arrested. In some cases an arrest warrant will have been issued by a court, and a suspect will be arrested by the police as a result of the issuance of that warrant. In most cases, however, the police will arrest a suspect without the prior issuance of a warrant. Once arrested, the suspect will usually be taken to the police station and booked. This means that detailed information is obtained on the suspect and the crime, including perhaps a "mug-shot" (photograph) and fingerprints. If the suspect has committed a minor offense, instead of being taken to the police station, he or she may simply be issued a summons (an order directing the suspect to appear in court). If taken to the police station, the suspect may be either released or held in a cell pending the initial appearance in court.

The initial appearance is the first of the postarrest court proceedings in which an accused will be involved. Most state laws require that the initial appearance be held a very short time after the arrest has taken place (usually within twenty-four or forty-eight hours). It is generally held in one of the lower trial courts. Its purpose is to notify the accused of the charges, to advise the accused of his or her right to be represented by a lawyer, and to consider pretrial release of the accused. If the offense charged is a felony, the accused will also be informed of his or her right to a preliminary hearing, if such a right is provided by that state.

Misdemeanor Cases

If the offense charged is a misdemeanor, the next stage of the criminal court process will generally be the trial. Prior to trial, however, any one of a number of pretrial motions may be brought by a defendant, such as a motion to suppress evidence that is alleged to have been illegally seized. The prosecution, it should be noted, is constitutionally required to meet a request by the defense for any evidence that is "material either to guilt or to punishment." [1]

Instead of going to trial, the prosecutor may decide to drop charges or to agree to a plea bargain. A plea bargain is an agreement made between the prosecutor and the defendant (usually through the defendant's attorney) whereby the defendant agrees to plead guilty to a lesser charge, to one of a number of charges (the others being dropped), or to the offense charged in return for the prosecutor's recommendation to the judge that the defendant receive a lighter sentence than might otherwise be imposed. If a plea bargain is made, then there is no trial; for the purpose of the trial is to determine the guilt or innocence of the defendant.

At trial, the prosecution must prove beyond a reasonable doubt all of the elements of the offense charged. To achieve a verdict of not guilty, the defendant must raise a reasonable doubt as to his or her guilt. In a misdemeanor trial it will nearly always be the judge who will determine the guilt or innocence of the defendant. There is a constitutional right to jury trial when conviction of an offense may result in imprisonment for more than six months. [2] In practice, however, this right may often be waived.

If the defendant has either pleaded guilty or been found guilty at trial, the next stage will be for the judge to sentence the defendant. In sentencing the defendant, the judge chooses which of a number of sanctions to impose (e.g., fine, imprisonment, or probation). After sentencing, the defendant may still choose to appeal to a higher court.

Double Jeopardy

It is a well-established principle of law that a person not be tried more than once for the same offense. This principle, known as the provision against double jeopardy, is contained in the Fifth Amendment of the United States Constitution, which states that: ''nor shall any person be subject for the same offense to be twice put in jeopardy of life or limb.'' [3] In *Benton* v. *Maryland* this provision was held to apply to the States. [4]

The provision against double jeopardy applies at the trial stage when the jury has been impaneled, or, in a nonjury trial, the first witness sworn. [5] It is an absolute bar against retrial for the same offense in the same jurisdiction. However, it does not apply if there is a mistrial, or if the defendant wins an appeal against conviction. In addition, it may not necessarily bar the defendant from being tried in another jurisdiction for the same offense. Thus, if a person has been acquitted of a crime in a state court, the acquittal may not bar that person from being tried in federal court.

Felony Cases

If the offense charged is a felony, the next stage in the court process after the initial appearance will usually be the preliminary hearing. Since felonies must generally be tried in a higher court than that which holds the initial appearances and preliminary hearings, the preliminary hearing is, in essence, the formal court proceeding at which the prosecution must show that there is sufficient evidence to hold the defendant for trial in superior court. In fact, the prosecution must prove that there are reasonable grounds to believe both that a crime was committed and that the defendant was the person who committed it. This decision is made by the judge after hearing the evidence and witnesses presented by the prosecution.

The preliminary hearing can serve as a useful discovery device for the defendant, who can see and challenge parts of the prosecution's case. The evidentiary standard required of the prosecution at this stage (generally ''reasonable grounds to believe'' or ''probable cause'') is, however, a far lower standard than the standard of proof of ''beyond a reasonable doubt'' required for conviction at trial. Hence, only some of the evidence the prosecutor has against the defendant will have to be offered. The defendant has no federal constitutional right to a preliminary hearing, and it is sometimes bypassed by the prosecutor. When such a right is provided by a state, a defendant may still decide to waive it.

The next stage in a felony case may well be a grand jury hearing. Although a grand jury hearing is constitutionally required in federal felony cases,[6] there is no such constitutional requirement in state cases. Some states require that a grand jury hearing be conducted. Others do not.[7] The result is that in a state felony case either a preliminary hearing or a grand jury hearing or both may be held. To a great extent the grand jury hearing fulfills the same functions as the preliminary hearing; for its purpose is to test the sufficiency of the prosecutor's case and to determine whether there is probable cause to believe that the accused has committed a crime. Unlike the preliminary hearing, the grand jury hearing is conducted in secret and is nonadversarial in nature. Neither the defendant nor the defendant's attorney usually participate in the proceedings. The prosecutor simply presents his or her case (including the testimony of witnesses) to the citizen members of the grand jury. The grand jury, which varies in size from state to state, is responsible, upon a finding of probable cause, for bringing the formal charges (a Bill of Indictment) against the accused. Since the prosecutor has brought the Bill of Indictment before the grand jury, the grand jury is said to be returning "a true bill." The grand jury, it should be noted, hears only the prosecutor's case and thus nearly always finds a true bill.[8] As a consequence, the grand jury hearing has been felt by many to be merely a rubber stamp for the prosecutor. This is a far cry from one of its original purposes, which was "to act as a buffer between the state and its citizens by weighing accusations of criminal activity made by the state to see if a trial should be held." [9]

After the prosecutor has successfully brought the case through the preliminary hearing or grand jury hearing or both,[10] the case is ready to proceed to superior court. The first stage of the proceedings at superior court is the arraignment. At the arraignment, the accused is formally charged and enters a plea of guilty or not guilty. If the accused enters a plea of guilty, the next stage of the proceedings will be the sentencing. If the accused pleads not guilty, the case will proceed to trial. Before trial, any of a number of pretrial motions may be brought; also, of course, a plea bargain may still be struck between the accused and the prosecutor. If the case does go to trial, the accused is entitled to a trial by jury,[11] though this right can usually be waived. If found guilty, the accused is then sentenced accordingly. If the accused feels the trial court has made an error, an appeal may be lodged.

BAIL OR JAIL?

The nature of the final resolution of a criminal case is of great significance for the accused. However, his or her status prior to the ultimate disposition of the case is also of importance. After being arrested, the accused may in some circumstances be issued with a summons to appear in court. Often, however, the accused is detained until the initial appearance, at which time the decision is made on whether he or she should be released on bail.

Bail

Bail is the process whereby an accused is released from custody after some security has been given that he or she will appear for the scheduled court hearings. Usually the security given is cash; occasionally it may take the form of property. The understanding is that the defendant will forfeit the cash or property if he or she does not turn up for court. The threat of forfeiture is considered to be likely to guarantee the presence of the accused at court. Very often the accused is unable to raise the bail money alone. In this case the accused may persuade a relative or friend, or, most commonly, a professional bail bondsman to put up the bail money. A fee is charged for the bail bondsman's services (usually about 10% of the amount of bail that has been set), and the bail bondsman has the authority to pursue persons who jump bail.

The Eighth Amendment of the federal Constitution states that "Excessive bail shall not be required." [12] Though this would not appear to provide a federal constitutional right to bail, many states provide such a right in the case of all crimes except capital offenses (those which carry the death penalty). The supposition in capital cases is that the defendant has so much at stake that a financial loss, however severe, may not ensure his or her presence at court.

In setting the amount of bail, the judge usually considers just the offense charged and the accused's prior record. Although these factors may not be highly related to the accused's likelihood of turning up at court, they may be all the judge has to go on. Very little time has passed since the accused's arrest; and there usually will not be much information available on other factors that might in fact be more relevant, such as the accused's ties to the community, the accused's family situation, and the accused's employment record.

Although the sole avowed purpose of bail is to secure an accused's presence at court, it may serve other purposes as well. Foremost among these purposes is the protection of society by seeing that potentially dangerous individuals are not released before trial. This may be achieved by setting a higher bail than the accused can hope to meet. Although the Eighth Amendment does prohibit the imposition of "excessive bail," this provision has not prevented what has amounted to the tacit preventive detention of potentially dangerous individuals. Indeed, it is not uncommon for a judge to increase, at the request of the prosecutor or the police, the amount of bail required from an accused. A number of states have recognized the need to detain potentially dangerous defendants, and have enacted legislation that permits the pretrial detention of defendants whose release would pose a significant threat to the community. [13]

The major complaint about the bail system is, however, that it discriminates against the poor. As a defense attorney once stated:

> Those defendants who have the money to afford bail are also the most able to absorb the financial loss as well as have the financial capabilities to flee the jurisdiction. On the other hand, impoverished defendants who could not even afford a bus ticket out of town are the very ones who cannot make bail and are detained awaiting trial. [14]

Nationally, about 5 percent of those released on bail fail to turn up for court. [15] Arguably, many of those currently detained could be released without greatly increasing this failure rate.

Jail

The prospects facing an accused who has not been able to meet bail are, in fact, not very inviting. First of all, the accused is deprived of his or her liberty. If employed, the accused loses income and possibly his or her job. Family relationships are disrupted. Even though still legally innocent, the accused's detention provides additional stigma. The accused has less freedom to prepare a defense. The accused's jail appearance and attire may have a negative impact at court.

The facilities used to house persons awaiting trial are hardly the most attractive. As the President's Commission on Law Enforcement and Administration of Justice pointed out:

> It is probably true that persons who have not yet been convicted of a crime are subjected to the worst aspects of the American correctional system. Unconvicted persons, as yet legally innocent, are almost inevitably subjected to the highest security and receive the least attention of any group in jails.[16]

In addition to the pretrial detainees, the jail is likely to house convicted offenders who are awaiting sentencing or transfer to a state institution and convicted misdemeanants who are serving their sentences there. The institution is likely to be locally financed and run by the county sheriff. Lacking adequate funding and understaffed, the jail acts as a holding center for pretrial detainees, providing little or no recreational or vocational programs for them. Such staff as do exist are often law enforcement officers who have had no correctional training. The buildings themselves are often old and decayed.[17]

There are many horror stories about jail conditions. Beatings, rapes, and murders have all taken place in jails. Each year, over 500 persons die in jails, mainly as a result of suicide.[18] Courts have declared that certain jails (such as the Manhattan House of Detention in New York City, which was popularly known as the Tombs) impose inhumane conditions on those who are kept there. Though improvements are being made, even in the newly built jails "the concepts of repression and human degradation are remarkably intact."[19]

Release on Recognizance

With concerns being voiced about the conditions in jails, about the bail system discriminating against the poor, and about the pretrial detention of persons who might be safely released into the community, alternatives to bail have been instituted. Foremost among these is release on recognizance (ROR). Patterned after the Vera Institute's Manhattan Bail Project, which was instituted in 1961, ROR programs have been set up in many areas of the country. Instead of being required to give some financial security to obtain release, the accused is released, after a detailed background investigation, upon the accused's own promise to turn up for court hearings. Factors favorable to release on recognizance include strong community and family ties, and current employment. Persons accused of certain crimes (e.g., rape and armed robbery) may automatically be ineligible for ROR. Research, however, has shown that such exceptions may not be warranted.[20]

Those released on recognizance may perform slightly better than those released on bail in terms of turning up for court appearance.[21] In a national bail study, it was noted that there was an increase between 1962 and 1971 in the percentage of defendants released before trial and that the use of nonfinancial releases accounted for most of the change.[22] This is a trend that has continued.[23] However, it has been suggested that,

> By stressing a stable family, residential, and economic lifestyle, as well as penalizing defendants for past experiences with the law, these projects are unable to help the indigent, transient, or youth who fill our nation's pretrial detention facilities.[24]

To help deal with this problem, other innovations have been implemented. Increased usage of the summons in misdemeanor cases has taken place. The Federal Bail Reform Act of 1966 requires federal judges to give first consideration to release on recognizance or an unsecured bond and allows judges to place conditions on those released. In the state court systems, release on unsecured bond and conditional releases are granted more frequently. Pretrial services agencies have been established to help administer the process. Illinois, followed by a number of other states, has instituted what has been called the "10 percent plan." Anxious to cut out the involvement of the professional bail bondsman, the state allows the judge to release a defendant upon his or her posting 10 percent of the amount of bail that has been set. If the defendant appears for trial, the court, unlike the professional bail bondsman, returns 90 percent of the money the defendant has posted. The remaining 10 percent is kept for administrative costs. Though this system is an improvement, the defendant may still have some trouble raising the initial 10 percent.

SUMMARY

This chapter has examined the stages a criminal case may pass through in court, and has distinguished between the processing of a felony and a misdemeanor case.

Of personal importance to the accused is his or her status prior to the final disposition of the case. Although legally innocent, the accused may be detained during this time. The traditional method of pretrial release is bail. The Eighth Amendment prohibits the imposition of excessive bail. Even with the availability of the professional bail bondsman, the poor may be unable to raise sufficient money to obtain release. New programs, such as release on recognizance, though an improvement, may not as yet adequately remedy this situation.

The prospects facing a person who is detained prior to trial are bleak. Deprived of liberty, the normal routine of the accused is totally disrupted; the accused is housed in oppressive surroundings; and the ability of the accused to conduct a successful defense may be impaired. The next chapter examines the procedures through which criminal court cases are actually resolved.

SUGGESTED ACTIVITIES

- Find out whether your state provides for either a preliminary hearing or a grand jury hearing, or both. What is the common practice? Interview a prosecuting attorney and ask which stages are the most challenging and why. Does the attorney favor abolition of the grand jury hearing?

- Where are defendants held prior to trial in your area? What are the conditions like? Are convicted criminals held there also?
- Do suspects have a right to bail? Interview a bail bondsman and ask about the charges, and if there is a going rate for various crimes.
- Are there any alternatives to bail, such as release on recognizance, in operation in your area? If so, prepare a brief report on how the system works, together with the results obtained. If not, have there ever been any alternatives used in the past? What were the results?

REVIEW

A. List the stages in the court process of a criminal case, distinguishing between felonies and misdemeanors.

B. Describe the functions and characteristics of each of the following procedures:
1. initial appearance
2. preliminary hearing
3. grand jury hearing
4. trial

C. What is the provision against double jeopardy?

D. What is the difference between bail and release on recognizance?

E. Describe the functions and characteristics of jails.

F. What disadvantages face a person who is incarcerated while awaiting trial?

G. Multiple Choice. Select the best answer.

1. When a defendant is formally charged in superior court with a felony, it is called being
   a. arrested
   b. arraigned
   c. booked
   d. none of these

2. A defendant has a constitutional right to trial by jury
   a. in all cases
   b. in all nonmotor offenses
   c. in any case when conviction may result in imprisonment for more than six months
   d. under no circumstances

3. A plea bargain will generally result in
   a. a shorter trial
   b. a longer trial
   c. no trial
   d. none of these

4. Which of the following is usually held in secret?
   a. preliminary hearing
   b. grand jury hearing
   c. sentencing
   d. none of these

5. The standard of proof required to convict a defendant at trial is
   a. proof beyond a reasonable doubt
   b. probable cause
   c. reasonable grounds to believe
   d. none of these

6. Smith is acquitted of a criminal charge in state court. He may be retried for the same offense in
    a. state court
    b. federal court
    c. either of these
    d. neither of these

7. If unable to raise bail through his or her own means, the accused may seek the help of
    a. a friend
    b. a bail bondsman
    c. a relative
    d. all of these

8. The amount of bail is usually
    a. set by statute
    b. based on the charge and previous record of the suspect
    c. based on the suspect's income
    d. none of these

9. Which of the following are alternatives to the bail system?
    a. release on recognizance
    b. the "10 percent plan"
    c. jail
    d. all of these

10. One of the advantages of release on recognizance is
    a. most of the suspect's money is returned
    b. it helps the poor obtain pretrial release
    c. there are no absconders
    d. all of these

REFERENCES

1. Brady v. Maryland 373 U.S. 83, 87 (1963).
2. Baldwin v. New York 399 U.S. 66 (1968).
3. *U.S. Constitution*, Amendment V.
4. Benton v. Maryland 395 U.S. 784 (1969).
5. Press Enterprise Co. v. Superior Court 104 S. Ct. 819, 824 (1984).
6. *U.S. Constitution*, Amendment V.
7. For a listing of state requirements, see: Edmund F. McGarrell and Timothy J. Flanagan (eds.) *Sourcebook of Criminal Justice Statistics—1984* (Washington, D.C.: U.S. Goverment Printing Office, 1985), 92–95.
8. A study of grand jury behavior in Houston, Texas, for example, revealed that the grand jury followed the prosecutor's recommendation about 94 percent of the time. Robert A. Carp, "The Behavior of Grand Juries," in Robert G. Culbertson and Mark R. Tezak (eds.) *Order under Law* (Prospect Heights, Ill.: Waveland Press, 1981), 115–133.
9. National Advisory Commission on Criminal Justice Standards and Goals, *The Courts* (Washington, D.C.: U.S. Government Printing Office, 1973), 74.
10. If the judge finds that the prosecutor has not presented sufficient evidence at the preliminary hearing to warrant the case proceeding further, then the prosecutor may generally still take the case to the grand jury although the prosecutor will not ordinarily do so. If the grand jury finds no true bill, then the prosecutor cannot proceed any further with the case, although the prosecutor is not pre vented from bringing the case to the grand jury again since double jeopardy does not attach until the time of trial.
11. *U.S. Constitution*, Amendment VI.
12. *U.S. Constitution*, Amendment VIII.

13. See, for example, 23 D.C. Code secs. 1321–22. For a more thorough discussion of this issue, see, for example, John Goldkamp, "Danger and Detention: A Second Generation of Bail Reform," *Journal of Criminal Law and Criminology*, 76 (1985), 1–74.

14. Paul B. Wice, *Freedom for Sale* (Lexington, Mass.: D. C. Heath, 1974), 5.

15. See, for example, Wice, *op. cit.,* 67; Wayne H. Thomas, Jr., *Bail Reform in America* (Berkeley, Calif.: University of California Press, 1976), 103; David W. Neubauer, *America's Courts and the Criminal Justice System*, 2nd. ed. (Monterey, Calif.: Brooks/Cole, 1984), 228.

16. The President's Commission on Law Enforcement and Administration of Justice, *Task Force Report: Corrections* (Washington, D.C.: U.S. Government Printing Office, 1967), 24.

17. Law Enforcement Assistance Administration, *National Jail Census 1970* (Washington, D.C.: U.S. Government Printing Office, 1971).

18. U.S. Department of Justice, *Bureau of Justice Statistics Bulletin: The 1983 Jail Census* (Washington, D.C.: Author, 1984), 7.

19. William B. Nagel, *The New Red Barn: A Critical Look at the Modern American Prison* (New York: Walker, 1973), 20.

20. Wice, *op. cit.*, 157–158.

21. *Ibid.*, 67–68. However, in a more recent survey no appreciable difference was noted in court appearance rates for those released on nonfinancial as opposed to financial conditions (Mary A. Toborg, *Pretrial Release: A National Evaluation of Practices and Outcomes* (Washington, D.C.: Department of Justice, 1981), 16.

22. Thomas, *op. cit.*, 252.

23. Toborg, *op. cit.*, 6–7.

24. Wice, *op. cit.*, 157.

32

Case Resolution

OBJECTIVES

After studying this chapter, the student should be able to:

- Discuss the reasons for plea bargaining and describe the process and the types of plea bargain that may be made.
- Summarize concerns that have been raised about the plea bargaining process.
- Describe the court trial process.
- List the steps used for selecting jurors, including *voir dire*, and the jury's role in the trial process.

The previous chapter discussed an accused's status prior to the disposition of his or her case. This chapter examines the ways in which a case can be resolved. Two primary methods of case resolution will be investigated. The first, which minimizes the involvement of the court process, is through the guilty plea. About 90 percent of criminal cases are disposed of in this manner.[1] Although some defendants may simply plead guilty to the offense charged, many guilty pleas are undoubtedly the result of a plea bargain. This occurs when an accused agrees to plead guilty in exchange for some concession that is made by the prosecutor.

The second mode of case disposition is through the trial process. This occurs when an accused proclaims innocence of the charge and the prosecutor is compelled to prove the case. The decision as to the accused's guilt or innocence may be made by a jury. Whether the accused pleads guilty or is found guilty at trial, he or she will have to be sentenced for the offense. Plea bargaining, trials, and juries are all topics that will be investigated in this chapter.

PLEA BARGAINING

A fair amount of bargaining may take place in the court process. Delay is a common feature of the criminal court system. It is, to a greater or lesser extent, in the interests of all those involved in the criminal court process to see that the courts operate in a smooth and efficient manner. The adversarial image of the criminal court process may be popular, but it is by no means a totally accurate one. To a great extent the personnel who appear in criminal court are dependent upon each other's cooperation. The most vivid outward manifestation of this is to be observed in the plea bargain.

The plea bargain, or plea negotiation, as it is often called, refers to an agreement made between the prosecutor and the defendant (usually through the defendant's attorney). The defendant agrees to plead guilty to a lesser charge, to one of a number of charges (the others being dropped), or to the offense charged in return for the prosecutor's recommendation to the judge that the defendant receive a lighter sentence than might otherwise be imposed. The judge is not bound by the agreement, but will usually abide by it, since the judge is aware of the importance of the plea bargaining system. The role played by the judge does, in fact, vary from jurisdiction to jurisdiction. Some judges actively participate in the process.

The prime reason advanced for the existence of plea bargaining is court congestion. This refers to the large number of criminal cases and the insufficient supply of courts, judges, prosecutors, and defense attorneys to process them through the adversarial trial model. Even with only 10 percent of the cases going to court, there is great delay in the court system. Even a small increase in this percentage might cause an already overextended system to explode. Such an outlook undoubtedly contains a great deal of truth. It is, however, not the only explanation.

Many of the cases that come to court involve no dispute of fact. They do not require resolution through the adversary system. Plea bargaining allows for routinely disposing of these cases with the prior involvement of the prosecution and defense, and without the expense of a time-consuming trial. Their agreement to a resolution that is acceptable to both sides allows the system to operate more smoothly.

In addition, plea bargaining may have a humanizing effect, better enabling the penalty to fit the criminal. This is especially so when an accused faces a charge which, upon conviction, will result in a mandatory sentence. Thus suppose that Jones, a college student with no prior record, is arrested for possessing a certain amount of marijuana. Let us further suppose that possession of that amount carries a mandatory five-year sentence. If Jones is allowed to plead guilty to possession of a lesser amount, however, he may be given a shorter prison sentence or even placed on probation. For an accused, plea bargaining may have further beneficial effects. It may enable the accused to avoid conviction of a repugnant charge, such as rape of a child, and to escape the added publicity that naturally attends a trial.

Plea bargaining is felt by many to be a process that fosters the routine disposal of cases, mitigates the unfair application of harsh statutory provisions, and, above all, enables the court system to function more efficiently. It is not, strictly speaking, plea bargaining that keeps the court system from becoming completely clogged up. It is the entering of guilty pleas by defendants. Undoubtedly some defendants plead guilty without the inducement of a plea bargain. Others might also do so even if plea bargaining were abolished. However, even a small increase in the percentage of cases that go to trial would cause serious problems for an already overworked court system.

When conducting plea bargains, both the prosecution and defense have an eye on what might happen if the case were to go to trial. For the defendant and the defendant's attorney, the threat of invoking the right to trial may be a useful weapon in negotiating a deal with the prosecutor. In reality, however, the defense attorney may be as eager as the prosecutor to avoid taking the case to trial.

A number of concerns may be raised about the plea bargaining process. Foremost among these concerns is the notion that in some cases the general public, and in other cases the defendant, may be shortchanged by the process. For the general public it may be a case of an offender receiving a very light sentence for the commission of what was in actuality a very serious offense. The belief that this is a common occurrence fosters cynical attitudes toward the criminal justice system.

For an innocent defendant, it might be a case of pleading guilty to a lesser offense for fear of being wrongfully convicted of a more serious offense. Although it is vital that a guilty plea be based on fact and be entered knowingly and voluntarily by a defendant, [2] this is by no means always the case. For many years, a courtroom ritual was followed whereby the defendant denied that the guilty plea had been induced by any threat or promise, even though it had in fact been obtained as the result of a plea bargain.[3]

The prosecutor's plea bargaining position may be strengthened by overcharging the defendant; that is, charging the defendant with a more serious offense than the prosecutor can hope to prove, or charging the defendant with a number of different offenses arising out of the same incident. Afraid of receiving a harsher sentence if the case goes to trial, the defendant may agree to plead guilty to the offense with which he or she originally should have been charged. Indeed, there is a strong likelihood that a defendant who invokes the right to trial and is found guilty after a trial will receive a more serious sentence than what would have been received had he or she pleaded guilty to the same offense.[4] There is thus, in essence, a penalty imposed for invoking the right to trial.

In some prosecutors' offices the plea bargaining process may be fairly visible, with one assistant district attorney responsible for handling the plea negotiations. In addition, the prosecutor's office may have formulated some policies, such as generally accepting a guilty plea to an offense which is one degree below that originally charged. Thus, a guilty plea to attempted robbery (a class C felony) would be acceptable to an original charge of robbery (a class B felony).

In many prosecutors' offices, however, the plea bargaining process may be less standardized and subject to agreements reached with individual prosecutors. The type of plea bargain reached this way may be more dependent upon the individual whim of the prosecutor or the ongoing relationship between the prosecutor and the defense attorney than the particular facts of the case. The secretive nature of the process adds fuel to the belief that defendants are not being accorded equal justice.

The National Advisory Commission on Criminal Justice Standards and Goals has gone so far as to suggest that plea bargaining should be abolished. [5] A few jurisdictions have sought to ban plea bargaining. Although such experiments have met with a certain amount of success,[6] they are perhaps ultimately doomed to failure because of the human desire to deal. Consequently, other prestigious associations, such as the American Bar Association, the American Law Institute, and the President's Commission on Law Enforcement and Administration of Justice, have suggested, in perhaps a far more realistic vein, that improvements be made in the present system. These types of improvements, which the National Advisory Commission has recommended should be adopted as interim measures, are generally aimed at making plea bargaining a far more standardized and visible process. Thus, it has been recommended that each prosecutor's office should establish written statements of plea negotiation policies and practices; that a written record should be made of a plea bargain and presented to the judge for acceptance or rejection, along with the reasons for the decision; and that the sentence given a convicted offender should not be affected by whether or not a plea of guilty has been entered.[7]

THE TRIAL PROCESS

The vast majority of cases are resolved through the guilty plea process. A great many of these may be settled through a plea bargain. An important minority of cases, however, is resolved through a determination of guilt or innocence at trial. At trial, the prosecution must prove that the defendant is guilty beyond a reasonable doubt of the offense charged. To obtain acquittal the defendant must establish a reasonable doubt as to his or her guilt. Matters of law are determined by the judge. Matters of fact are decided by the jury, if there is one. If it is a nonjury trial, then they are decided by the judge.

Trials

The trial is a highly visible stage of the criminal justice process. It shows the system at its most adversarial, as each side attempts to prove its case. Among the constitutional rights enjoyed by a defendant in a criminal trial are the right to a speedy [8] and public trial,[9] the right to assistance of counsel,[10] the right to subpoena,[11] and confront and cross-examine witnesses,[12] the right to trial by jury,[13] and the privilege against self-incrimination.[14] All of these rights are intended to place limits on the power of the state, and to enable the defendant to present a meaningful defense.

The trial begins with an opening statement by the prosecutor. This is followed by an opening statement by the defense, though this right to an opening statement is often waived. After the opening statements have been made, the prosecutor presents the case against the defendant. The prosecutor may present physical evidence (such as the gun that was allegedly used in the robbery), and witnesses who testify about what they saw or know. After each of the witnesses has given their testimony, they are usually cross-examined by the defense. The defense will be attempting to show that either the evidence or the witness, or both, are not reliable or trustworthy. If the witness is an expert witness—that is, someone who is called upon to testify because of professional expertise (such as a chemist in a crime laboratory)—then the background qualifications of the witness may be challenged. This right to confront witnesses is provided to a defendant by the Sixth Amendment of the U.S. Constitution.

After the case has been presented by the prosecutor, it is up to the defendant to present a defense. Before bringing forward the defendant's own evidence and witnesses, the defendant will generally ask the judge for a directed verdict. This is a dismissal on the grounds that the prosecution has failed to prove its case. Unless the judge does give a directed verdict (and this is rarely done), the defense will proceed with its case. All witnesses called by the defense are subject to cross-examination by the prosecutor. Very often the defendant will not take the stand; for, unless the defendant has taken the stand on his or her own behalf, the defendant is not subject to examination by the prosecutor. The Fifth Amendment of the U.S. Constitution provides that no person "shall be compelled in any criminal case to be a witness against himself." [15]

After the defense has presented its case, the prosecution may bring forward rebuttal witnesses who will provide evidence that contradicts some aspect of the defense's case. After the prosecution has presented its rebuttal witnesses, the defense may present further witnesses. After all the witnesses and evidence have been presented, the prosecution and defense give their closing arguments. In their closing arguments, each highlights the strengths of his or her case and the weaknesses of the opponent's case, and asks for a favorable verdict. If the trial is being conducted with a jury, the judge will give the jury instructions on how it is to conduct its deliberations.

Juries

The defendant enjoys a federal constitutional right to trial by jury in all cases where the sentence could be six months or more.[16] This covers all felonies and a number of misdemeanors. In some states there is a more extensive right to trial by jury. In all states the defendant can usually waive the right to trial by jury and elect to be tried by a judge sitting alone.

The trial jury is known as the petit jury to distinguish it from the grand jury which hands down indictments and conducts investigations into alleged wrongdoings. Composed of lay citizen members, it acts as an impartial decision maker on the facts. In a murder trial, for example, it will decide whether the defendant killed the deceased; and if the defendant did, whether he or she possessed the *mens rea* necessary for conviction of the charge of murder. It will decide whether the prosecution has proved that the defendant is guilty beyond a reasonable doubt. In reaching its decision, the jury will be instructed by the judge on all matters of law; for example, whether the prosecution must prove intent, or merely recklessness, in order to sustain a conviction of murder in the first degree.

The Supreme Court of the United States has stated that "a right to jury trial is granted to criminal defendants in order to prevent oppression by the government." [17] The theory is that the jury acts as a buffer between the accused and the government, providing the accused with "an inestimable safeguard against the corrupt or overzealous prosecutor and against the compliant, biased, or eccentric judge." [18]

In order for the jury to perform this function, it is important that it be composed of persons who can decide the facts without prejudice or favor. The Sixth Amendment of the United States Constitution provides that the accused shall have the right to trial by "an impartial jury." [19] The petit jury has traditionally been composed of twelve persons, and unanimity has been required for a verdict of guilty. However, the U.S. Supreme Court has held that neither the number of twelve jurors [20] nor unanimity for verdicts of guilty [21] are constitutionally required.

In order to obtain an impartial jury, it is important that fair selection procedures be used. A juror must be a U.S. citizen, above the age of majority, a resident of the area, and able to speak English. Voter registration lists (sometimes supplemented by other available relevant listings, such as licensed drivers) are generally used to provide a listing of potentially eligible jurors. Members of certain occupations may be automatically exempt or claim exemption from jury service. Some occupations are exempt because their members are professionally employed in the criminal justice system (e.g., police officers and lawyers) and thus might unduly influence jury deliberations. Others are exempt because of the high premium placed on the services they provide (e.g., doctors). From the listing of eligible persons, a large group of jurors (a jury pool) is randomly selected. From the jury pool smaller groups of jurors (jury panels) are chosen. It is from the jury panel that the jurors for a specific trial are selected. The number of jurors on the jury panel is always greater than that required for the trial jury because some of the jurors will be eliminated from serving through the process of *voir dire*.

Voir dire is a courtroom procedure that is used in an attempt to ensure that an impartial jury is selected. Defense and prosecution are entitled to challenge the impanelling of prospective jury members. The challenges may be peremptory or for cause. A peremptory challenge is a challenge for which no reason need be given. The defense or prosecution simply objects to the impanelling of a particular juror, and the juror is excused from service. Prosecutors must, however, be able to justify peremptory challenges that appear to be based solely on racial grounds.[22] The number of peremptory challenges to which each side is entitled is fixed by statute and varies from state to state.

In order to sustain a challenge for cause, a valid reason must be given for excusing the juror from service. It must be shown that the juror is likely to be biased because, for example, the juror has already formed an opinion about the case or is related to the defendant. It is the judge who decides whether to accept a challenge for cause.

There has developed among defense lawyers an elaborate approach to jury selection which involves conducting research on potential jurors, discovering what types of jurors are most likely to be sympathetic or antagonistic, and then attempting to include or to exclude those jurors from service. Such an approach is highly expensive and rarely used. It should be kept in mind, however, that the defendant has a right to trial by an impartial jury, not a sympathetic one.

Through the process of *voir dire* prospective jurors are examined until a trial jury of the requisite size is obtained. Usually a few alternate jurors are also selected. These alternates sit through the trial and are ready to take the place of one of the trial jury members should that juror no longer be able to serve because of, for example, illness. Once the jury has begun its deliberations, there can be no replacement of a jury member.

The jury is responsible for determining all issues of fact. Its prime responsibility is, of course, the determination of the guilt or innocence of the accused. Once all the evidence has been presented, and the judge has given the jury instructions, the members of the jury retire to the jury room to conduct their deliberations. The deliberations are conducted in private and are secret. No outside interference is allowed. In certain circumstances the judge may even order that when not in court the jury be sequestered, that is, be kept in seclusion in a designated place away from the influence of the outside world. On occasion, the jury may ask the judge for further instructions on matters of law. Once the jury has agreed upon a verdict, they return to the courtroom, and the verdict is presented in open court. A verdict of not guilty will result in the defendant's release. A verdict of guilty will lead to the defendant being sentenced. Although most states require unanimity for a guilty verdict, this is not constitutionally required.[23] Some states do allow, for example, an 11-1 or 10-2 vote. There is no time limit in which the jury must reach a decision. However, should the jury be deadlocked and there be no apparent likelihood of a decision, the judge may decide to dismiss the jury. In these circumstances where there is a hung jury, a second trial may be held.

In a few states the jury is also involved in sentencing the defendant. Such involvement is, however, generally considered undesirable. Jurors take part in the court process for a very limited time, are generally unfamiliar with sentencing policies and procedures, and thus may hand down disparate, and perhaps highly unfair, sentences.

SUMMARY

This chapter has examined the two primary methods of case resolution. The first, which minimizes the involvement of the court system, is through the guilty plea. The second, which calls into play the full adversarial model of the court system, is through the trial process.

The vast majority of cases are resolved through defendants entering guilty pleas. Very often the defendant has agreed to plead guilty in exchange for some concession that has been made by the prosecutor. This is the process of plea bargaining.

Plea bargaining is supported on the grounds that it helps reduce court congestion, aids in the routine disposition of cases, and mitigates the unfair application of harsh statutory provisions. On the other hand, there are concerns that innocent defendants may be induced to plead guilty, and that guilty offenders may receive lighter sentences than they deserve. In some prosecutors' offices, the plea bargaining process may be secretive and individualized, adding fuel to the belief that different defendants are not being accorded equal justice. As a consequence, it has been recommended that prosecutors' offices establish written statements of plea negotiation policies and practices; that a written record be made of each plea bargain and presented to the judge for acceptance or rejection; and that the sentence given a convicted offender should not be affected by whether or not the offender has entered a plea of guilty.

When a defendant does not plead guilty and is contesting a charge, the case goes to trial. The trial is a highly visible stage of the criminal justice process, and it highlights the adversarial model of the system. The prosecution, through its evidence and witnesses, attempts to prove that the defendant is guilty beyond a reasonable doubt. The defense attempts to raise a reasonable doubt as to that guilt. Matters of law are determined by the judge. Matters of fact, including the issue of the defendant's guilt, are decided by the jury if there is one. If there is no jury, they are decided by the judge.

The defendant enjoys a federal constitutional right to trial by jury in all cases where the sentence could be six months of imprisonment or more. The process of *voir dire* is a procedure which is used to obtain an impartial jury. Although the trial jury has traditionally been composed of twelve persons and unanimity has been required for a verdict of guilty, neither the number of twelve jurors nor unanimity are constitutionally required. Jury deliberations are conducted in private and are secret. Once the jury has agreed upon a verdict, it will return to the courtroom where the verdict will be delivered in open court. A verdict of not guilty will result in the defendant's release. A verdict of guilty will lead to the defendant being sentenced. If there is a hung jury, a new trial may be held.

After either pleading guilty or being found guilty at trial, the defendant must be sentenced for the crime committed. A number of different rationales affect the sentencing decision. These are discussed in detail in the next section.

SUGGESTED ACTIVITIES

- Interview either a prosecutor or a defense attorney, and find out how plea bargaining is conducted in your area. Prepare a brief description of the nature and style of the plea bargaining process. Whom do you think gains more from the plea bargaining system, the prosecutor or the defendant?

- How do you feel about plea bargaining? Prepare a brief paper defending one side of the issue, bearing in mind the realities of the court situation.

- Find out how many peremptory challenges are allowed in your state for the prosecution and the defense. Ask a prosecutor or a defense attorney how often these challenges are fully used.

- Try to arrange an interview with someone who has been a juror. Find out about the selection process, what questions were asked at the *voir dire*, what the trial was like, and what the judge's instructions were. Find out what the judge thinks of the jury system. Would the judge waive a right to trial by jury if he or she were a defendant?

REVIEW

A. What is a plea bargain? What types of plea bargain may be made?

B. What are the advantages of the plea bargaining system?

C. What are the disadvantages of the plea bargaining system, and what suggestions have been made to improve it?

D. Briefly describe the procedures involved in a trial.

E. What does a jury do in a criminal case?

F. How is a jury selected?

G. Multiple Choice. Select the best answer.

1. Approximately how many criminal cases go to trial?
    a. 100 percent
    b. 90 percent
    c. 50 percent
    d. 10 percent

2. The purpose of the trial is to
    a. punish the offender
    b. determine the guilt or innocence of the accused
    c. inform the suspect of the charges
    d. all of these

3. A challenge to a juror which must be accepted by the judge before the prospective juror may be excused is a
    a. peremptory challenge
    b. challenge for cause
    c. petit challenge
    d. all of these

4. A reason advanced in favor of plea bargaining is that
    a. the prosecutor tends to overcharge the defendant
    b. offenders may receive light sentences for serious crimes
    c. it keeps the system from being overcongested
    d. all of these

5. One reason a defendant may accept a plea bargain is that
    a. it may avoid publicity
    b. it may result in a lighter sentence
    c. it may avoid conviction of a more serious charge
    d. all of these

6. A plea bargain results in
    a. a plea of guilty
    b. a plea of not guilty
    c. an acquittal
    d. none of these

7. One of the complaints about plea bargaining is that
    a. innocent defendants may plead guilty
    b. serious offenders may get off lightly
    c. justice may be unequal
    d. all of these

8. A defendant may be examined by the prosecution
    a. in any case
    b. only when called as a witness for the defense
    c. only when called as a witness for the prosecution
    d. in no case

9. A directed verdict is
    a. a dismissal by the judge
    b. when the judge directs the jury to convict
    c. when the prosecutor asks for conviction
    d. none of these

10. *Voir dire* is
    a. a set of instructions to the jury
    b. a procedure used to insure an impartial jury
    c. a type of plea bargain
    d. none of these

REFERENCES

1. Donald J. Newman, *Conviction: The Determination of Guilt or Innocence Without Trial* (Boston: Little, Brown, 1966), 3; The President's Commission on Law Enforcement and Administration of Justice, *Task Force Report: The Courts* (Washington, D.C.: U.S. Government Printing Office, 1967), 9; National Advisory Commission on Criminal Justice Standards and Goals, *The Courts* (Washington, D.C.: U.S. Government Printing Office, 1973), 42; U.S. Department of Justice, *Special Report: The Prevalence of Guilty Pleas* (Washington, D.C.: Author, 1984), 1.
2. Boykin v. Alabama 395 U.S. 238 (1969) held that the judge must ascertain that a guilty plea is made intelligently and voluntarily. *Bordenkircher* v. *Hayes* 434 U.S. 357 (1978) held that a prosecutor could threaten use of a habitual offender statute to induce a guilty plea as long as the defendant was free to accept or reject the offer.
3. The President's Commission on Law Enforcement and Administration of Justice, *op. cit.*, 9.
4. See, for example, U.S. Department of Justice, *Special Report: Felony Sentencing in 18 Local Jurisdictions* (Washington, D.C.: Author, 1985), 9.
5. National Advisory Commission on Criminal Justice Standards and Goals, *op. cit.*, 46.
6. See, for example, Michael L. Rubinstein, Stevens H. Clarke, and Teresa J. White, *Alaska Bans Plea Bargaining* (Washington, D.C.: U.S. Government Printing Office, 1980).
7. The President's Commission on Law Enforcement and Administration of Justice, *op. cit.*, 50–65.
8. *U.S. Constitution*, Amendment VI. Applied to the states in Klopfer v. North Carolina 386 U.S. 213 (1967).
9. *U.S. Constitution*, Amendment VI. Applied to the states in In Re Oliver 330 U.S. 257 (1948).
10. *U.S. Constitution*, Amendment VI. Applied to the states in Gideon v. Wainwright 372 U.S. 335 (1963).
11. *U.S. Constitution*, Amendment VI. Applied to the states in Washington v. Texas 388 U.S. 14 (1967).
12. *U.S. Constitution*, Amendment VI. Applied to the states in Pointer v. Texas 380 U.S. 400 (1965).
13. *U.S. Constitution*, Amendment VI. Applied to the states in Duncan v. Louisiana 391 U.S. 145 (1968).
14. *U.S. Constitution*, Amendment V. Applied to the states in Malloy v. Hogan 378 U.S. 1 (1964).
15. *U.S. Constitution*, Amendment V.
16. Baldwin v. New York 399 U.S. 66 (1970). Three provisions in the United States Constitution refer to the right to trial by jury: Article III Section 2 (3), the Sixth Amendment, and the Seventh Amendment.
17. Duncan v. Louisiana 391 U.S. 145, 155 (1968).
18. *Ibid.*, 156.
19. *U.S. Constitution*, Amendment VI.
20. Williams v. Florida 399 U.S. 78 (1970).
21. Apodaca v. Oregon [406 U.S. 404 (1972)] held that a verdict of 10-2, and Johnson v. Louisiana [406 U.S. 356 (1972)] held that a verdict of 9-3, was constitutionally permissible in a noncapital case.
22. Batson v. Kentucky 39 CrL 3061 (1986).
23. Williams v. Florida 399 U.S. 78 (1970). It should be noted that while the Supreme Court has held that unanimity is not constitutionally required with regard to twelve-person juries, unanimity may be required for smaller juries. Thus in Burch v. Louisiana [441 U.S. 130 (1979] the Supreme Court held that a vote of 5-1 was not constitutional.

33

Sentencing the Convicted Offender

OBJECTIVES

After studying this chapter, the student should be able to:

- Analyze the different rationales that affect the sentencing decision: retribution, rehabilitation, incapacitation, and deterrence.
- Define general and specific deterrence.
- Distinguish between determinate and indeterminate sentences.
- Discuss the legal status and use of the death penalty as a criminal sanction.
- Describe the sentencing process and sentencing disparity and measures being taken to lessen sentencing disparity.

After either pleading guilty or being found guilty at trial, the newly convicted defendant will have to be sentenced for his or her crime. Sentencing is the process whereby a sanction is imposed upon a person convicted of illegal conduct. The sanction, or punishment, as it is more commonly called, is normally imposed by a judge. It may consist of, for example, a fine, probation, imprisonment, or even, in certain limited cases, the death penalty. A number of different rationales affect the sentencing decision and the subsequent imposition of punishment.

RETRIBUTION, REHABILITATION, INCAPACITATION, AND DETERRENCE

Four different, and often conflicting, rationales affect the nature of the sentence a convicted person may receive: retribution, rehabilitation, incapacitation, and deterrence.

The rationale of retribution embodies the idea of imposing "just deserts" for the harm inflicted, of forcing the wrongdoer to pay the appropriate penalty for the wrong done. It finds outward expression in the Biblical phrases "an eye for an eye, a tooth for a tooth." [1] Though it has come back into favor again recently, retribution has not been strongly advocated for most of this century. Perhaps this is because it is too much like vengeance, and vengeance has an uncivilized ring about it. It should be remembered that one of the reasons for the emergence of criminal law was the need to limit the amount of vengeance exacted by a wronged individual and/or family. This idea of proportionality between the harm suffered and the penalty imposed is basic to the concept of retribution. As the term "just deserts" suggests, the punishment must fit the crime. Imposing the death penalty for a parking offense would seem outrageous, precisely because the commission of such a minor offense would not appear to warrant the imposition of such a serious punishment. Retribution suggests that parking offenders be punished in a way that befits their criminal conduct, and that all those who commit parking offenses be punished in a similar fashion.

It was with the notion that the punishment should not necessarily fit the crime that the rationale of rehabilitation was born. Rehabilitation does not stress the fact that an offender should be punished for an illegal act. Rather it focuses on the fact that the offender has done something wrong and needs to be reformed so that the illegal behavior is not repeated. The emphasis is thus on treatment. Since people differ in their potential for successful treatment, it follows that all persons convicted of a particular crime should not necessarily receive the same or even similar sentences. The punishment should fit the criminal, rather than the crime. Though the unequal treatment of offenders may be justified in this way, the argument rests on the assumption that the treatment will be successful. Such an assumption is, however, by no means totally warranted. Indeed, concern about the success of treatment programs has greatly contributed to a lack of faith in the rationale of rehabilitation.

The rationale of rehabilitation does concern itself with protecting society from possible future criminal activity on the part of the convicted offender. By turning an offender into a law-abiding citizen, through treatment and reform, the future protection of society is sought. While such an outcome may reflect both a secondary and a perhaps somewhat illusory aim of the rehabilitative rationale, it is the avowed purpose of the rationale of incapacitation; for the stark aim of the rationale of incapacitation is the protection of society through the removal of the offender from society. Imprisonment is perhaps the most common mode of incapacitation. Exile and the death penalty are two other modes of incapacitation.

A problem with the rationale of incapacitation is that it relies heavily on predictions as to the future dangerousness of offenders. The task of predicting whether an offender will commit another crime is a tricky process at best. [2] Two types of mistakes may be made: releasing an offender who then commits another crime, and unnecessarily incapacitating an offender who would not have committed another crime if released. The former mistake is the more visible of the two and may result in a public outcry. The latter results in excessive state intervention into the life of the offender and may raise concerns about the suppression of civil liberties. In addition to problems with the process of prediction, the rationale of incapacitation poses difficult questions with regard to the issue of proportionality. Predicting the commission of what type of crime warrants utilization of the rationale of incapacitation—commission of a serious felony, any felony or misdemeanor, a crime similar to the one of which the offender was convicted? In addition, the seriousness of the crime committed may bear no relationship to the likelihood of the criminal offending again. Thus, a person who smokes marijuana may be far more likely than a murderer to repeat the crime.

The rationale of deterrence also seeks to protect society from suffering further harm at the hands of the offender. However, it does not necessarily attempt to achieve that objective through removing the offender from society. Rather, by teaching the offender a lesson and inflicting him with unpleasant consequences for the wrongful act, it seeks to discourage the offender from participating in future illegal activity. This attempt to deter the offender from engaging in further illegal activity is known as specific deterrence.

The aim behind the imposition of punishment may be a broader aim than just discouraging the convicted offender from engaging in further criminal activity. It may be geared at discouraging others from committing crime by making the offender an example. This attempt to deter others from indulging in criminal activity through punishing an offender is known as general deterrence. In essence, the mere existence of criminal penalties is intended to exert a general deterrent effect. The fact that one may receive five years in prison for unlawfully entering another's house is expected to exert sufficient influence to prevent the occurrence of such activity. However, that is manifestly not always the case. Some people would suggest that the criminal penalties deter only those who would be deterred anyway as a result of built-in moral inhibitions. Others would suggest that for punishment to act as a deterrent, it must be swift and sure; for even if the threatened punishment is severe, if its imposition is uncertain, then a potential wrongdoer might well feel that he or she is not going to be either so stupid or so unlucky as to be caught. It should be noted that some crimes, such as crimes of passion, may not be deterrable at all.

The different rationales may complement each other; often, however, they present different interests and suggest a different sentencing disposition for a particular offender. Suppose, for instance, that a man is convicted of the cool and deliberate murder of his wife. A long sentence may well suit the needs of retribution. It will certainly result in the offender's incapacitation. It may well serve as both a specific and general deterrent. Its rehabilitative effect may, however, be highly questionable. A short prison term may well have a more positive influence on the offender than a long one; for a long prison term may simply serve to demoralize and alienate the offender and make him incapable of functioning effectively on his return to the community. A short prison term may, in fact, even fit the needs of specific deterrence. Many people might suggest, however, that a short prison term for killing one's spouse would ill serve the concerns of general deterrence; for the penalty is not severe enough to discourage others from indulging in similar behavior. In addition, with regard to the rationale of retribution, a short prison term might not appear to constitute "just deserts." This would especially appear to be the case if persons convicted of crimes that are generally considered to be less serious (e.g., burglary or assault) were receiving similar or even harsher sentences.

THE SENTENCING STRUCTURE

The legislature is responsible for determining the types of sentencing dispositions that are available upon conviction of the various crimes. The legislature strives to establish a rational and logical system of sentencing alternatives with the more serious options available for the more serious crimes. At times, however, the piecemeal process by which criminal provisions are generally enacted has resulted in inconsistencies. Thus, at one time in California, an offender who broke into an automobile and stole the contents of the glove compartment could receive up to fifteen years' imprisonment. If, however, the car itself was stolen, the offender could receive a maximum sentence of only ten years.[3]

The laws enacted by the legislature generally state that a person convicted of a particular offense may receive any of a number of sentences. In some circumstances the law may specify a mandatory sentence for the commission of a particular offense. This means that anyone convicted of that crime must receive a fixed penalty laid down by the law. An example of a mandatory sentence would be a ten-year prison term for selling heroin.

Prison sentences may be either determinate or indeterminate. A determinate sentence specifies a definite period of time for which a person is to be sent to prison. A five-year prison sentence for burglary would constitute a determinate sentence. The offender is to be imprisoned for a fixed period of five years. Determinate sentences well suit the rationale of retribution. They give the sentencing authority, nearly always a judge, discretion in deciding, within statutory limits, the amount of time to be served. Even with determinate sentences, however, the amount of time actually served in prison is reduced by "good time" (the time allowed off for good behavior) and by the granting of parole. In some states there is provision for what are known as "flat terms." With a flat term, the offender must serve the full time in prison. Thus, a flat term of five years means five years in prison.

The indeterminate sentence is one in which a maximum time of imprisonment is set, and in many cases a minimum period of time is set, too. Thus a sentence of one to seven years would mean that the offender would be imprisoned anywhere from one to seven years. The date of release would depend upon the progress the offender was making. The indeterminate sentence thus well suits the needs of the rationale of rehabilitation. The decision as to the offender's release is generally made by the prison staff and/or the parole board.

Either the imposition or the execution of a prison sentence may be suspended. If the imposition of a prison sentence is suspended, it means that an offender is allowed to remain at liberty. If, however, the offender commits another offense (generally within a certain period of time) and is convicted, he or she may still be imprisoned for the original offense. The amount of time the offender is to serve in prison will be determined at the time of the second conviction. If the execution of the prison sentence is suspended, it means that the term of imprisonment imposed at the time of the original sentencing must be served if the offender is convicted of a subsequent offense. In some cases part of a prison sentence may be suspended. A sentence such as three years' imprisonment with two years suspended would result in the offender serving a maximum of one year in prison. After being released, however, and if convicted of a subsequent offense, the offender might have to serve the other two years of the sentence. This might well be in addition to any sentence the offender might receive for the new crime.

When convicted of more than one crime, an offender may receive either concurrent or consecutive sentences. If the offender receives concurrent sentences, they are served at the same time. If they are consecutive, then one sentence must be served before the next is begun. Suppose, for instance, that Drifter is convicted of two charges of burglary. He receives a five-year prison sentence for each. If the sentences are concurrent, he must serve only one five-year prison term. If, however, they are consecutive, he must serve one five-year term and then begin the second five-year term.

The habitual, professional, or dangerous criminal has generally been considered to pose a particularly dangerous threat to society. As a consequence, many legislatures have provided extended prison terms for such offenders. Thus, an individual convicted of his or her third burglary offense may suddenly be faced with the prospect of serving a maximum of twenty, as opposed to ten, years in prison.

The legislature does in all cases set the maximum penalty that can be imposed upon the conviction of an offense. In general, however, it leaves the sentencing authority a fair amount of discretion to choose among sentencing alternatives. These might range from a fine or probation to a number of years imprisonment. The person responsible for handing down the actual sentence is generally the judge. In a few states, however, the jury does participate in the sentencing decision.

The amount of choice a judge may have in selecting a sentencing disposition varies considerably. The legislature may in some cases set out a mandatory sentence. In this case the judge has no choice. The existence of the mandatory sentence may, however, have led to the defendant obtaining a plea bargain and consequently pleading guilty to a lesser offense. With a determinate prison sentence, the judge sets the amount of time the offender is to serve. With an indeterminate sentence the judge sets the outside limit, and perhaps also the minimum. The judge may suspend imposition or execution of the sentence. In cases where the offender has been convicted of multiple offenses, the judge may hand down concurrent or consecutive sentences.

THE DEATH PENALTY

A penal sanction that has existed since the very earliest of times is the death penalty. Stated simply, it is the state-sanctioned taking of a person's life, ordered as a consequence of his or her conviction of a criminal offense. The crimes for which this punishment could be ordered have varied over time. Generally, it has been the most serious crimes that have carried this penalty. Foremost among these have been murder and rape. In eighteenth-century England, the death penalty could be imposed upon conviction of some 200 crimes. Today, the death penalty is no longer used as a criminal sanction in England, and can, in fact, be ordered in only three circumstances: when a person has been convicted of treason, of piracy on the high seas, or of setting fire to Her Majesty's Docks.

In the United States, the death penalty was imposed fairly commonly for a long period of time. Between 1930 and 1967, 3,859 persons were executed in this country.[4] About 86 percent of those who were executed had committed murder. Twelve percent had committed rape. All but thirty-two (0.8%) were male. Blacks were greatly overrepresented among those who were put to death, especially for the crime of rape.[5] Some 60 percent of the executions took place in the South, with five states (Georgia, New York, California, North Carolina, and Texas) each carrying out more than 200 executions in the time period under consideration.[6]

As can be seen from Figure 33-1, the number of executions taking place dropped steadily through the 1950s and 1960s, and not one execution occurred between 1967 and 1977. The 1960s, in fact, saw the beginning of a series of serious legal challenges to the constitutionality of the death penalty. In the 1970s, the U.S. Supreme Court handed down a number of decisions that have shaped the nature of death penalty provisions. Many prisoners found themselves moved off death row because state statutory provisions under which they were sentenced to die were declared unconstitutional.

In 1972, in the case of *Furman* v. *Georgia*, the U.S. Supreme Court held that

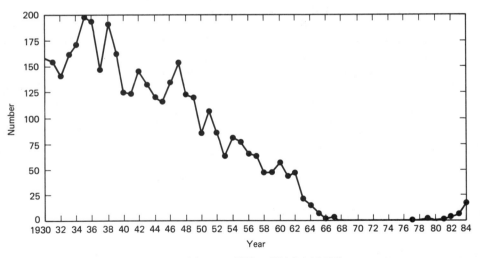

Figure 33-1 Number of persons executed, by year: 1930 to 1984 (total 3,891)

Sources: U.S. Department of Justice, *Capital Punishment 1978* (Washington, D.C.: U.S. Government Printing Office, 1979), 7; U.S. Department of Justice, *Capital Punishment 1984* (Washington, D.C.: U.S. Government Printing Office, 1985), 7.

the imposition and carrying out of the death penalty in this case constituted cruel and unusual punishment. The reason given was that the death penalty was being applied in an arbitrary and capricious manner.[7] The problem was that

> the death penalty is exacted with great infrequency even for the most atrocious crimes and that there is no meaningful basis for distinguishing the few cases in which it is imposed from the many cases in which it is not.[8]

The result of the case was to invalidate the death penalty statutory provisions of most states.

The majority of the states responded to the *Furman* decision by rewriting their laws. The form of the response came in two general types of approach. A number of states enacted statutes that made the death penalty mandatory for certain crimes. Thus, Louisiana and North Carolina, for example, passed laws that required imposition of the death penalty whenever a person was convicted of first-degree murder. A number of other states, such as Florida and Georgia, responded to the *Furman* decision by enacting provisions that required the sentencing authority to apply certain guidelines in its determination of whether or not to impose the death penalty. In 1976, the U.S. Supreme Court ruled on the constitutionality of both types of provisions. It held that the mandatory death penalty provisions were unconstitutional.[9] As the court stated in *Woodson* v. *North Carolina*,

> we believe that in capital cases the fundamental respect for humanity underlying the Eighth Amendment . . . requires consideration of the character and record of the individual offender and the circumstances of the particular offense as a constitutionally indispensable part of the process of inflicting the penalty of death.[10]

The provision of guidelines for the sentencing authority to apply in its consideration of the death penalty was, however, a satisfactory approach.[11] As the court stated in *Proffit* v. *Florida*,

> the requirements of *Furman* are satisfied when the sentencing authority's discretion is guided and channeled by requiring examination of specific factors that argue in favor of or against imposition of the death penalty, thus eliminating total arbitrariness and capriciousness in its imposition.[12]

In 1978, the Supreme Court further elaborated upon the manner in which the sentencing authority's discretion could be guided. It held in *Lockett* v. *Ohio* that it was unconstitutional, in a capital case, for a state to prevent the sentencing authority from considering as a mitigating factor ''any aspect of the defendant's character or record and any of the circumstances of the offense that the defendant proffers as a basis for a sentence less than death.'' [13]

The U.S. Supreme Court has thus provided guidelines that the states must follow in applying the death penalty. In 1977, the court virtually limited imposition of the death penalty to the crime of murder; for in *Coker* v. *Georgia*, the court ruled that the sentence of death for the crime of rape of an adult woman was unconstitutional. It constituted a grossly disporportionate and excessive punishment and was therefore forbidden by the Eighth Amendment as cruel and unusual punishment.[14]

Because of the Supreme Court's rulings, the 1970s were an active period for the rewriting of state laws and for changing offenders' sentences and moving many of them away from death row. In the late 1970s, we witnessed once again the more routine imposition of the death penalty. Starting with the execution of Gary Gilmore in 1977, executions of convicted criminals once again began to be carried out. There has been considerable discrepancy, however, between the frequency with which the death penalty has been imposed and the number of times it has actually been carried out. Each year, far more people are given the death penalty than are executed, with the result that there has been a yearly increase in the death row population. Recently, the pace of executions has been stepped up. Between 1977 and the end of 1982, only six persons were executed; in 1983, five persons were put to death; in 1984, a total of twenty-one were executed.[15] In 1983, however, 252 persons, and in 1984 an additional 280, were *sentenced* to death, with the result that at the end of 1984 there were 1,405 persons on death row awaiting execution in thirty-two states.[16]

The debate on the appropriateness of the death penalty as a criminal sanction remains loud in many circles. Some people feel that the rationale of retribution demands that certain offenders pay for their crimes with their lives. Others believe that the state-ordered taking of life is barbaric and inhumane. The death penalty certainly acts as a specific deterrent and protects society from further injury at the hands of the offender. Whether or not it acts as a general deterrent is a matter of great controversy. As yet no firm proof has been provided for either side of the issue.[17]

THE SENTENCING PROCESS

Sentencing takes place after the offender has either pleaded guilty or been found guilty at trial. The sentencing hearing may occur immediately after the determination of guilt or at a later date.

The offender has a constitutional right to be represented by counsel at the sentencing hearing.[18] At the hearing the prosecutor may recommend one sentence disposition, while the defense attorney, referring to factors favorable to his or her client, may recommend a second, perhaps more lenient, disposition. Often, however, the prosecutor may be recommending a sentence disposition which the defendant has already agreed to through the plea bargaining process.

The judge usually has a fair number of choices among sentencing dispositions. Within a specific mode of disposition the judge also may enjoy a great deal of discretion. In selecting a particular disposition, the judge may be influenced by the different pulls of the rationales of retribution, rehabilitation, incapacitation, and deterrence. In making a decision, it would appear desirable for the judge to have all the necessary background information on the offender and the offense. The judge may, in fact, be aided in making a decision by the presentation of a presentence report. A presentence report is a report compiled for the judge, usually by a probation officer. It contains information about the crime, including perhaps the offender's version of the incident. This may well provide a new perspective since the offender may not have spoken on his or her own behalf at trial. The report will also contain detailed information about the offender. This might include such items as details of the offender's family background, educational and employment histories, prior criminal record, and any special problems the offender may have, such as drug or alcohol abuse. Often the presentence report contains a specific sentence recommendation. When such a recommendation is given, it is generally followed by the judge.[19]

The situations in which presentence reports are given vary from jurisdiction to jurisdiction. Some states require that they be given when the offender has been convicted of certain types of crime. Usually they may be requested by the judge in any case. In general, they are used in felony cases.

Presentence reports are not regularly used in all cases because of the time and money entailed in the preparation of such reports. Yet the information in these reports, which may be of great help in arriving at a sentencing disposition, will not usually have been obtained in the earlier stages of the court process. A suggestion that has been made is that there be two types of presentence reports: a long report containing detailed information which would be desirable in certain specified types of cases, and a short report containing certain basic items which would be used in all other cases.[20]

It has been stated that at the sentencing hearing, the

> Defense counsel's primary duty is to ensure that the court and his client are aware of the available sentencing alternatives and that the sentencing decision is based on complete and accurate information.[21]

The defense attorney's ability to represent a client's interests in the best possible manner is affected by whether the defendant has the right to see the presentence report and to challenge the information contained in it. This issue has raised considerable controversy. Some people feel that to deny the defense the right to examine and challenge the presentence report amounts to a denial of fundamental fairness. In addition, it increases the likelihood that a sentencing disposition may be given on the basis of erroneous information. Others argue, however, that to make the presentence report an open document would lead to an unwillingness on the part of resource persons to furnish valuable information, would result in additional unhelpful legal wranglings in the sentencing process, and might have harmful effects on efforts to rehabilitate the offender. The U.S. Supreme Court has ruled that the defendant has no constitutional right to see the presentence report.[22] Some states, however, do provide such a right. A compromise which has been suggested is that the judge advise the defendant of the "factual contents and conclusions" of the report. The sources of confidential information would not, however, have to be disclosed.[23]

SENTENCING DISPARITY

As mentioned before, there are different competing rationales that affect the type of sentence an offender receives. The legislature generally offers a wide range of possible choices. Judges differ in their own personal philosophies. Hence, it is not surprising that judges vary in their sentencing policies and practices. Of concern here is the situation where offenders convicted of the same crime and with similar background characteristics receive somewhat different sentences. This is the issue of sentencing disparity.

Different types of factors are recognized as affecting the sentencing decision. Some, often referred to as legal factors, are considered to exert an appropriate influence over the type of sentencing disposition an offender might receive. Such factors might include the nature of the offense and the offender's prior record. Other factors, however, often referred to as nonlegal factors, are considered inappropriate determinants of sentencing dispositions. Such factors might include the race of the offender or victim or the personal characteristics of the judge.

A number of research studies have examined the factors that influence the sentencing decision.[24] These have differed in the types of variables they have used and the sophistication of their analyses. Despite their differing perspectives and conclusions, there is little doubt that on occasion nonlegal factors do affect the type of sentencing disposition an offender receives. The exact nature and extent of this influence is a matter of controversy.

The fact that sentencing disparity exists causes problems both for the criminal justice system and for the offender. Where sentencing disparity exists, a sense of injustice prevails. Defense attorneys, anxious to obtain the best possible deal for their clients, may engage in "judge shopping." By using legal maneuvers, such as asking for continuances (postponements of the case), they attempt to have their clients appear before the judge whom they believe will act most favorably toward them. This adds to the delay and congestion in the court system. Offenders who believe they have been given harsh sentences may feel they have received a raw deal. Offenders who believe they have received lenient sentences may feel they have beaten the system. Neither of these feelings enhances the prospects for rehabilitation.

A number of suggestions have been made to deal with the problem of sentencing disparity. These have included sentencing institutes, sentencing councils, sentencing review, sentencing guidelines, and presumptive sentencing.

Previously, it was discussed how judges receive little or no training prior to assuming duties on the bench. The aim of sentencing institutes is to provide judges with information about sentencing and possible sentencing dispositions. They may also give judges an opportunity to compare their sentencing philosophies and practices. This may occur informally or during discussion of mock cases. Such institutes are held by a number of states and have been recommended by the National Advisory Commission on Criminal Justice Standards and Goals.[25]

It is hoped that sentencing institutes will help reduce sentencing disparity through making judges more knowledgeable and aware of one another's practices. The way that sentencing councils are to contribute to that purpose is through shared decision making; for the idea behind sentencing councils is that the judges of a particular court should meet to discuss cases prior to handing down sentences. The judges would maintain responsibility for and jurisdiction over their own cases; however, the judges would receive the benefit of input from their colleagues. Through this process of collaboration it would be hoped that at the very least, extremely harsh and extremely lenient sentences would be avoided. However, like sentencing institutes, the pressure on a judge would be informal. In addition, sentencing councils would require additional resources; for a number of judges would be involved in work that previously was completed by a single judge. Such additional resources cost time and money.

Another process that has been suggested to help reduce sentencing disparity is sentencing review. Although many countries allow for the regular review by an appellate court of sentences handed down by lower court judges, such is not generally the case in the United States. Such appellate review would allow for sentencing policy and guidelines to be set by the higher court. Cases would, however, reach the appellate court on an irregular basis, and the right of appeal might not be equally available to prosecution and defense. Thus the establishment of sentencing policy might occur in a slow and uneven fashion.

The creation of sentencing guidelines is another approach to dealing with the problem of sentencing disparity. The idea is that judges need some help in establishing benchmarks against which to compare desirable dispositions in different cases. Lacking such external standards, judges may set their own with the sentence in one case acting as precedent for the next.[26] The scheme advanced by Wilkins and colleagues is one which the authors claim "retains sufficient judicial discretion to ensure that justice can be individualized and humane as well as evenhanded in application." [27] Assigning each offender both an offense and an offender score through predetermined criteria and locating those scores on a sentencing grid would allow appropriate sentences to be handed out. Sentencing guidelines, which are currently used by about a dozen states, may specify both the form (e.g., probation versus prison) and the length (e.g., three versus five years) of the sentence.[28]

A final approach to the problem of sentence disparity is what has been termed "presumptive sentencing." In this sentencing model, which has been adopted by the State of North Carolina,[29] the legislature sets the sentencing range for each crime, and fixes a presumptive (standard) sentence which must be imposed by the judge. However, if the judge finds the existence of either mitigating or aggravating factors surrounding the offender or the offense, the sentence may be made more lenient or more severe. Deviations from the presumptive sentences must be explained.

SUMMARY

This chapter has examined the sentencing of convicted offenders and the subsequent imposition of punishment. Four different, and often conflicting, rationales affect the nature of the sentence a convicted person may receive: retribution, rehabilitation, incapacitation, and deterrence. Retribution focuses on an offender receiving "just deserts" for the harm inflicted. It stresses making the punishment fit the crime. Rehabilitation looks to treating and reforming the offender. The punishment fits the criminal rather than the crime. Incapacitation seeks to protect society, usually through the removal of the offender from society. Deterrence seeks to discourage, through the threat or the actual imposition of punishment, both the offender (specific deterrence) and the general public (general deterrence) from engaging in criminal activity.

The legislature is reponsible for determining the sentencing dispositions that are available upon conviction of the various crimes. The sentencing authority, usually a judge, is reponsible for handing down specific sentences. Generally, the sentencing authority enjoys a fair amount of discretion in carrying out this function. Sanctions available upon the conviction of a particular offense may range from a fine or probation to a number of years of imprisonment. Prison sentences may be determinate or indeterminate. They may be suspended in their imposition or execution. They may be concurrent or consecutive. The habitual, professional, or dangerous criminal may often be given an extended prison term.

The death penalty was once a widely available sentencing disposition. Today its use in the United States is limited. The U.S. Supreme Court has virtually restricted its imposition to the crime of murder, and has mandated that measures be taken to ensure that it is not used in an arbitrary or capricious manner.

The defendant has a constitutional right to be represented by counsel at the sentencing hearing. In some cases, there is a presentence report, which furnishes the judge with useful information for the sentencing decision.

Given the wide range of sentence dispositions that are available, the competing rationales that affect the sentencing decision, and the different background characteristics and personal philosophies of judges, it is not surprising that on occasion offenders convicted of the same crime and with similar background characteristics are given somewhat different sentences. To counteract the problems posed by sentencing disparity it has been suggested that judges attend sentencing institutes, that sentencing councils be utilized, that sentences be subject to appellate review, that sentencing guidelines be developed, and that presumptive sentencing be instituted. The types of sentences a convicted offender may receive are examined in greater detail in later chapters.

SUGGESTED ACTIVITIES

- Find an example of each of the following in the criminal code of your state, if they exist: a mandatory sentence, a determinate sentence, an indeterminate sentence, the death penalty.
- Look through the court records in your locality until you find five instances of convictions of the same offense. State the offense and list the five sentences. What factors do you think influenced the sentencing decisions? Can you draw any conclusions from this about sentencing disparity in your area?
- Interview a court official and find out about the uses of the presentence report in your area. In what types of cases is it used? Who prepares it? What information does it contain?
- What is the current status of capital punishment in your state?

REVIEW

A. Describe and differentiate among retribution, rehabilitation, incapacitation, and deterrence.

B. Distinguish among determinate, indeterminate, and flat sentences.

C. Explain what is meant by a suspended sentence.

D. Distinguish between concurrent and consecutive sentences.

E. Describe the sentencing hearing.

F. What is sentencing disparity, why is it a problem, and what has been suggested to alleviate it?

G. Briefly explain the current status of the death penalty as set down by the U.S. Supreme Court.

H. Multiple Choice. Select the best answer.

1. The Biblical expression, ''an eye for an eye, a tooth for a tooth'' exemplifies the rationale of
   a. retribution
   b. rehabilitation
   c. incapacitation
   d. deterrence

2. An example of incapacitation is
   a. exile
   b. the death penalty
   c. prison
   d. all of these

3. The theory that people will be discouraged from committing crimes if an example is made of the particular offenders who are caught is referred to as
   a. specific deterrence
   b. general deterrence
   c. retribution
   d. all of these

4. A sentence which must be imposed upon conviction of a particular crime is called
   a. a predetermined sentence
   b. a determinate sentence
   c. a mandatory sentence
   d. none of these

5. Under which type of sentence must the offender serve the full term of the sentence in a correctional institution?
   a. a mandatory sentence
   b. a flat sentence
   c. an indeterminate sentence
   d. a determinate sentence

6. The purpose of the presentence report is
   a. to inform the judge of the plea bargain struck
   b. to allow the defense attorney to plead for leniency
   c. to provide the judge with information about the offender and the offense committed prior to sentencing
   d. to allow the prosecution to recommend a sentence

7. In the case of *Furman* v. *Georgia*, the Supreme Court ruled that imposition of the death penalty
   a. constituted cruel and unusual punishment in all cases
   b. constituted cruel and unusual punishment when arbitrarily imposed
   c. must be limited to first degree murder
   d. all of these

8. A dispute that exists with regard to the presentence report concerns
   a. the types of cases in which it should be presented
   b. whether the defendant should be allowed to see it
   c. whether it should be an open document
   d. all of these

9. A nonlegal factor that might affect a sentencing decision is
   a. employment history of the offender
   b. race of the offender
   c. drug history of the offender
   d. none of these
10. Which of the following occurs as a result of sentencing disparity?
    a. court congestion
    b. a sense of equality before the law
    c. enhanced prospects for rehabilitation
    d. none of these

REFERENCES

1. Exodus XXI: 24.
2. See, for example, J. Monahan, "The Prediction of Violent Criminal Behavior: A Methodological Critique and Prospectus in Deterrence and Incapacitation: Estimating the Effects of Criminal Sanctions on Crime Rates," in Fred Cohen (ed.) *The Law of Deprivation of Liberty* (St Paul: West, 1980), 465–70.
3. The President's Commission on Law Enforcement and Administration of Justice, *Task Force Report*: *The Courts* (Washington, D.C.: U.S. Government Printing Office, 1967), 15.
4. United States Department of Justice, *Capital Punishment 1975* (Washington, D.C.: U.S. Government Printing Office, 1976), 4.
5. 405 (89.0%) of the 455 offenders executed for committing rape were in fact black. 1,630 (48.9%) of the 3,334 offenders executed for committing murder were black. *Ibid.*, 18.
6. *Ibid.*, 4.
7. 408 U.S. 238 (1972).
8. *Ibid.*, 313 (per Justice White, concurring).
9. Roberts v. Louisiana 428 U.S. 325 (1976); Woodson v. North Carolina 428 U.S. 280 (1976).
10. 428 U.S. 280, 300 (1976).
11. Gregg v. Georgia 428 U.S. 153 (1976); Jurek v. Texas 428 U.S. 262 (1976); Proffit v. Florida 428 U.S. 242 (1976).
12. 428 U.S. 242, 258 (1976).
13. Lockett v. Ohio 438 U.S. 568, 604 (1978).
14. 433 U.S. 584 (1977).
15. U.S. Department of Justice, *Capital Punishment 1984* (Washington, D.C.: U.S. Government Printing Office, 1985). All thirty-two had committed murder. All but one were male, and all but three were executed in the South. Ten were black. The average amount of time spent awaiting execution was six years.
16. *Ibid.* Of the 1,405 inmates, 1,388 (98.8%) were male, and 585 (41.6%) were black. A total of 882 (62.8%) were under sentence in the South. Of the 2,233 offenders sentenced to death since 1977, 796 (35.6%) had been removed from death row for reasons other than execution.
17. Arnold Barnett, "Crime and Capital Punishment: Some Recent Studies," *Journal of Criminal Justice*, 6 (1978), 291–303. For an overview of capital punishment, its usage and issues, see Peter W. Lewis, Henry W. Mannle, Harry E. Allen, and Harold J. Vetter, "A Post-Furman Profile of Florida's Condemned—A Question of Discrimination in Terms of the Race of the Victim and a Comment on *Spinkellink* v. *Wainwright*," *Stetson Law Review*, 9 (1979), 1–45.
18. Mempha v. Rhay 389 U.S. 128 (1967); Gardner v. Florida 430 U.S. 349 (1977).
19. See, for example, Robert M. Carter and Leslie T. Wilkins, "Some Factors in Sentencing Policy," *Journal of Criminal Law, Criminology and Police Science*, 58 (1967), 503.
20. National Advisory Commission on Criminal Justice Standards and Goals, *Corrections* (Washington, D.C.: U.S. Government Printing Office, 1973), 184.
21. The President's Commission on Law Enforcement and Administration of Justice, *op. cit.*, 19.
22. Williams v. New York 337 U.S. 241 (1967). But see Gardner v. Florida 430 U.S. 349 (1977) with regard to the right to see the presentence report in a capital case.
23. American Law Institute, *Model Penal Code*: *Proposed Official Draft* (Philadelphia: Author, 1962), Section 7.07 (s).

24. See, for example, Edward Green, *Judicial Attitudes Towards Sentencing* (New York: St. Martins Press, 1961); John Hogarth, *Sentencing as a Human Process* (Toronto: University of Toronto Press, 1971); Cassia Spohn, John Gruhl and Susan Welch, "The Effect of Race on Sentencing: A Re-Examination of an Unsettled Question," *Law and Society Review*, 16 (1981–2), 71–88. For a summary of previous research studies, see John Hagan, "Extralegal Attributes and Criminal Sentencing: An Assessment of a Sociological Viewpoint," *Law and Society Review*, 8 (1974), 357–383.

25. National Advisory Commission on Criminal Justice Standards and Goals, *op. cit.*, 180.

26. Edward Green, "The Effect of Stimulus Arrangements on Normative Judgement in the Award of Penal Sanctions," *Sociometry*, 31 (1968), 125–137.

27. Leslie T. Wilkins, Jack M. Kress, Don M. Gottfredson, Joseph C. Calpin, and Arthur M. Gelman, *Sentencing Guidelines: Structuring Judicial Discretion* (Washington, D.C.: U.S. Government Printing Office, 1976), xiii.

28. For an examination of current sentencing laws and practices, see: U.S. Department of Justice, *Sentencing Reform in the United States: History, Content, and Effect* (Washington, D.C.: U.S. Government Printing Office, 1985).

29. For an evaluation of North Carolina's sentencing reform, see: Stevens H. Clarke, "North Carolina's Determinate Sentencing Legislation," *Judicature*, 68 (1984), 140–152. This entire issue of *Judicature* is devoted to the topic of "Criminal Sentencing in Transition" and contains articles on sentencing guidelines and other sentencing reforms.

34
Noninstitutional Corrections

OBJECTIVES

After studying this chapter, the student should be able to:

- Describe different types of noninstitutional sentences—fines, restitution, community service orders, and probation—a convicted offender may receive.
- Explain the duties and functions of the probation officer.

In the previous chapter the sentencing process was discussed. In this chapter, an examination is conducted of the different types of sentences a convicted offender may receive.

Perhaps the most basic categorization of sentences is between institutional and noninstitutional sentences. With an institutional sentence, the offender is totally deprived of his or her liberty for a period of time. Generally, the offender is sent to a jail or a prison to serve time. The offender is not free to come and go from the institution. With a noninstitutional sentence, the offender is allowed to remain at liberty in society, but must still pay some penalty for his or her criminal conduct. Sometimes, this may involve some restrictions on the offender's freedom. These restrictions, however, fall short of incarceration. In this chapter, the noninstitutional sanctions that can be imposed on an offender will be examined. These include fines, restitution, probation, and community service.

FINES

One of the penalties most frequently imposed upon conviction of a minor offense is a fine. A fine is a sum of money that an offender is ordered to pay to the state as a consequence of the offender's conviction of a criminal offense. The payment may be ordered to be made in one lump sum or in a series of installments over a period of months or years. The fine fulfills two functions. It serves as a punishment for the offender, and it provides revenue for the state.

All states provide for the possibility of imposing a fine upon conviction of certain criminal offenses. These criminal offenses are usually the less serious violations of the criminal code. Thus one would not generally expect a fine to be a sentencing disposition available upon conviction of rape or murder. However, one would expect the fine to be readily available and commonly used for many traffic offenses, such as speeding or disregarding a traffic sign or signal, and for other offenses such as disturbing the peace or petty larcency.

Since offenders come from different economic backgrounds, they may differ in their ability to pay fines. A fine of $100 will not mean the same thing to a rich person as it will to a poor person. Thus it may be argued that the use of fines discriminates against the poor, who cannot absorb the financial loss with the same ease as the rich. This issue is aggravated by the fact that a fine may be an alternative to imprisonment and that nonpayment of a fine may result in imprisonment. It was estimated in 1969 that possibly as many as 40 percent to 60 percent of all offenders confined in county jails were there because they had failed to pay fines.[1] In 1971, the Supreme Court held it unconstitutional to incarcerate an indigent because of the inability to pay a fine. The indigent offender must be given an opportunity to pay the fine over a period of time.[2]

It has been suggested that the court take into account both the seriousness of the offense and the offender's financial resources in assessing the amount an offender should pay.[3] This would allow the penalty to fit the crime. It would also tailor the penalty to fit the economic resources of the offender so that it might have a similar effect on both the rich and poor.

RESTITUTION

Fines involve the payment of money by offenders to the state. Restitution involves the payment of money by offenders to the victims of crime. As with fines, restitution serves a twofold purpose. It serves as a penalty for the offender, and it provides some help to the victim of crime by repaying the victim for at least some of the loss that has been suffered. For the offender, restitution may serve a valuable function. It may help to personalize the crime. It may make the offender aware of the plight of the individual or individuals he or she has harmed; and through allowing the offender to help the victim recoup his or her loss, restitution may help bring about the offender's rehabilitation.

Restitution is generally far more widely available as a sentencing disposition for property crimes as opposed to crimes against the person.[4] The reparation ordered will nearly always be in the form of money and will be related to the amount of the loss suffered. Restitution may be ordered to be paid in one lump sum. It is more common, however, for restitution to be paid in installments. As with fines, there is the danger with restitution that it may operate unfairly against the poor.

For the victim of crime, restitution provides a possible means of receiving redress for a loss wrongfully inflicted. To obtain this redress, the victim is dependent upon a number of factors. First, the offender must be apprehended, convicted, and ordered to pay restitution. Second, when ordered to pay restitution, the offender must follow through and make the payments. The offender's failure to make payments is of concern in the process of restitution.

It should be noted that a great many states have established state-funded compensation programs for the victims of crimes against the person. These programs receive and process applications from victims without offender involvement, though there is generally a requirement that the crime have been reported to the police. From a victim's standpoint, it may be preferable to be covered by a state-operated crime victims' compensation program; for the victim may receive an award even though an offender has not been apprehended. Furthermore, once an award has been made, the victim will be looking toward the state and not an offender for payment of the money.

As with fines, restitution may be ordered by itself or in conjunction with another sentencing disposition. Very often the offender will be placed on probation as well as being ordered to pay restitution. In this case, the probation officer is responsible for overseeing the offender's payments. Some states, such as Georgia and Alabama, have established restitution centers.[5] The offenders who take part in these programs generally work in the community. They live, however, in the restitution center where they are supervised by the center's staff. Very often the center retains control over money received by the offender. In this way, the staff is better able to ensure that the restitution payments are made to the victim.

In general, restitution is of a monetary nature. On occasion, however, an offender may be ordered to perform some direct services for the victim. This direct contact may benefit both the victim and the offender. On the other hand, it may cause fear on the part of the victim or resentment on the part of the offender.

COMMUNITY SERVICE ORDERS

A variation of the process of restitution is the community service order. With restitution, the focus is on providing the victim with reparation. With the community service order, the focus is on making amends to the community as a whole. The offender may be ordered to work a certain number of hours for the community. In some programs, community service is a voluntary alternative to the more traditional sentencing options.

The community service may involve, for example, helping repair government property, providing meals for the needy, or working in some type of health care facility. The type of service ordered can be tailored to fit the background characteristics of the offender. The Pima County, Arizona, community restitution inservice program reports that a Tucson barber who was convicted of stealing from Salvation Army "drop boxes" was required to donate haircuts at the local Salvation Army Men's Social Service Center every Tuesday night. Some young men who were convicted of arson were required to donate service to the Tucson Fire Department.[6]

The Alameda County, California, program, which has been in existence since 1966, has helped provide nonprofit health and welfare agencies with many hours of service.[7] Between July 1, 1976 and June 30, 1977, for example, court-referred volunteers provided over 400,000 hours of service to approximately 600 different agencies.[8] These and similar programs that have continued to spring up throughout the United States [9] benefit the community and the offender. The community benefits through the free services that are provided and through the financial savings that this type of sentencing disposition may bring. The offender gains through avoiding a jail sentence or some judicially imposed financial obligation he or she may be unable to meet. In addition, the offender's prospects of rehabilitation may be enhanced by the sense of well-being and acceptance that involvement in such work may provide. On occasion, the offender may acquire new job skills or better working habits. The organization or the agency may in a few cases hire an offender who has been working for them.

PROBATION

Perhaps the most commonly imposed noninstitutional sentence for nonmotor offenses is probation. Probation is a sentencing disposition which allows an offender to remain free in the community. Certain conditions, however, are placed upon the offender, who remains under the jurisdiction of the sentencing court. If those conditions are violated, the offender may be resentenced by the court. This resentencing may result in the offender's incarceration.

Probation has its origins in the suspended sentence. The suspended sentence was used to keep offenders out of prison. Only if they broke the law a second time would they be liable to be imprisoned. A variant of probation is what is known as "shock probation" or the "split sentence." Under this type of sentence, the offender is placed on probation, but is first sent to jail or prison to serve part of the sentence there (e.g., the first two months of a three-year sentence). This is designed to give the offender a taste of prison and to act as a deterrent to future criminal activity.

For the offender, the process of probation is perhaps at the same time both more burdensome and more helpful than is the suspended sentence. Although additional conditions are placed upon the offender, there is also help and guidance for the offender who is trying to keep those conditions and lead a law-abiding life. This help is provided by the probation officer. The probation officer's role is, however, a confused one; for not only is the officer expected to help the offender, but the officer is also expected to exert control over the offender, to see that he or she does not become involved in trouble again; and if the offender does, to take appropriate action.

John Augustus is generally credited with being the founder of probation. Born in 1785, Augustus was a Boston shoemaker who was concerned by the fact that many minor offenders were being imprisoned because of their inability to pay fines. He persuaded judges to allow him to bail out such offenders and provide them with supervision. This generally occurred after the offender had been convicted but before sentencing. When Augustus reported back to the court that the offender was making very satisfactory progress, the court would tend to impose only a nominal fine and thus avoid imprisoning the offender.

Spurred by the apparent success of this venture, Massachusetts eventually passed the first probation law in 1878. This led to the city of Boston hiring the first salaried probation officer. Gradually the concept of probation spread and by the 1920s nearly all of the states had some type of probation service in operation.

Today it is estimated that over 60 percent of the offenders sentenced to correctional treatment are placed on probation.[10] On December 31, 1984, there were 1,711,190 adults on probation in the United States.[11] The vast majority were male, and nearly one-half were felons.

Probation is a sentence of the court which leaves the offender under the jurisdiction of the court. To an extent, the administrative structure of probation has tended to develop around the court system. Some people have felt, however, that probation should be part of the executive, as opposed to the judicial branch of government, and in a number of states the probation service is housed in the executive branch. This lessens the direct relationship between the courts and probation. It may also focus greater attention on client services and increase interaction with other helping agencies, especially when they themselves are located within the executive branch of government.

Another issue concerns whether probation should be administered by a state or local unit of government. Here the question of statewide coordination and standardization versus retention of local autonomy is faced.

In some states, probation is of a local nature with each court district having its own probation service. In other states there is a single probation agency responsible for the appointment of probation officers and for setting policy and guidelines. Generally, probation services for adults and juveniles are administered by separate agencies.

Whether the probation service is housed in the judicial or executive branch or is administered statewide or locally, the probation officers' functions are essentially the same. They prepare and present presentence reports to the court when required and supervise offenders who are placed on probation.

The presentence report contains information that will be useful to the judge in determining an appropriate sentencing disposition. The situations in which presentence reports are used vary from jurisdiction to jurisdiction. The probation officer is the person who is responsible for gathering the desired information. Often the officer will make a sentencing recommendation to the judge. When such a recommendation is made, it is usually followed. There is some debate as to whether the functions of preparing presentence reports and supervising clients should be entrusted to the same probation officer. Indeed, in those few cases where the judge does not follow the probation officer's recommendation, an awkward situation may occur when a probation officer has to supervise a client who was recommended for incarceration.

Two factors are generally recognzied as most strongly affecting the decision of whether an offender will be placed on probation or given an active prison sentence. These are the seriousness of the offense of which the offender has been convicted and the seriousness of the offender's record.[12] Generally persons convicted of such offenses as murder or rape will not be eligible for probation. Persons with previous felony convictions may similarly be barred from receiving probation; or if eligible for probation, find it difficult to persuade the court to grant probation.

When placed on probation, an offender is given a set of probation conditions with which to comply. These conditions may consist of both general and specific conditions. The general conditions refer to requirements that are imposed on all offenders who are placed on probation in that jurisdiction. Such requirements might include provisions that the offender obey the law, report regularly to the probation officer, remain within the state, and not associate with undesirables. Specific conditions, on the other hand, refer to conditions that are placed on only named individuals. Examples of such conditions might include provisions that the offender: attend a particular alcohol or drug treatment program, participate in a particular type of counseling program, or pay restitution to the victim. It is, of course, desirable that unrealistic conditions not be placed on probationers. Indeed, some specific conditions of probation have been ruled by the courts to be unconstitutional. Sometimes even some of the general conditions may appear unrealistic. Thus the condition that the offender "not associate with undesirables" may seem to be both rather vague and hard to obey, especially in light of the offender's likely living environment. It is perhaps ironic that more is expected of those who have shown themselves unable to abide by society's rules and regulations than of those who have not been convicted of breaking the law.

State and federal statutes specify the maximum term of probation an offender may receive. Within those limits, the judge sets the length of the period of probation. In some states the judge may also set the length of the prison sentence to be served, should probation be revoked. The maximum term of probation that can be imposed in federal cases is five years. The American Bar Association has recommended that the term be two years probation for misdemeanors and five years probation for felonies.[13] The average time served has been stated to be about three years.[14] It is generally recognized that extremely long terms of probation fulfill no useful purpose.

While on probation, the offender is supervised by a probation officer. The probation officer is responsible for helping the offender lead a law-abiding life. The officer is also responsible, however, for taking appropriate action should the offender break the law or violate one of the conditions of probation. Here the probation officer treads on uneasy ground; for the officer has to reconcile the two often opposing functions of helping the offender and providing surveillance over him or her.

The probation officer may seek to help the probationer in a number of ways. The probation officer meets with the probationer and through casework and counseling attempts to aid the probationer in coping with problems he or she may be facing. The frequency with which the probation officer meets with his or her clients may be related to the extent of each of the client's needs. Some probation offices classify their cases as high intensity, medium intensity, or low intensity. The objective is for the probation officers to spend more time on the more difficult cases. Even with this type of system, however, the major determinant of the frequency of client contact is still the actual size of the officer's case load; for the sheer number of clients there are to supervise generally precludes the officer spending as much time with each client as would be desirable. Recommended case loads of thirty-five to fifty clients per officer are rarely met,[15] and average case loads are generally in excess of 100.[16] One hour with each client per month may be all that the officer can spare.

Usually the clients meet with their probation officers in the probation office. Sometimes the probation officer visits the client at home. Indeed, some states require that the probation officer make home visits. The home visit allows the probation officer to see the clients in their home surroundings. This may provide the officer with additional information or insights that may be useful in dealing with the clients. Since home visits are generally unannounced, both the probationer and the probation officer may be in for a surprise.

In addition to providing counseling, the probation officer may act as a resource person, helping to find employment or linking the probationer up with additional treatment services. If the probationer has been ordered to pay a fine or restitution, the probation officer will supervise the payments.

Probation officers differ in the way in which they relate to and supervise their clients. Some stress their desire to work with the probationers. Others may stress their authority and seek compliance through invoking fear. Often the probation officer's approach is modified to meet the perceived characteristics of the client.

The probationer may be terminated from probation either through discharge or revocation. A probationer who is discharged from probation is a person who has successfully completed his or her term of probation. The most common form of discharge is through expiration of the term. Thus if Shifty has been given a sentence of three years' probation and has completed the three-year period without violating the provisions of his probation, he will be discharged. Occasionally a probation officer may request the court to discharge a probationer prior to the expiration of the probationer's term. Such a request might be made when the probationer has complied with all of the conditions of probation, and it is felt that any further period of probation would not be beneficial. Altogether, about 80 percent of all probationers successfully terminate probation.[17]

Unlike discharge from probation, revocation of probation constitutes an unsuccessful termination. Probation revocation may occur either because the probationer has committed another crime or has violated one of the conditions of probation. If the probationer has committed a new crime, a sentence may be imposed for the new crime in addition to revocation of probation. Often, however, the prosecution may just seek to have probation revoked.

If the probationer has not committed a new crime, but has violated one of the conditions of probation, the probation officer may seek revocation for what is commonly referred to as a technical violation. Such a technical violation would occur if, for example, a probationer consistently failed to meet with his or her probation officer. Manifestly, the probation officer retains a great deal of discretion in deciding whether or not to ask for revocation. If it is decided to seek revocation, the probation officer will take the probationer before the court for a revocation hearing. At the hearing the judge must decide whether there has been a violation of the conditions of probation. If it is decided that there has been a violation, the judge may revoke probation and resentence the offender or execute a sentence previously set. Generally, the resentencing will involve imposition of a prison sentence. The offender does in most instances have the right to assistance of counsel at such a probation revocation hearing.[18]

Probation presents many potential benefits for the offender, especially when it is viewed as an alternative to incarceration. The offender is able to remain at liberty, continue to work and support other family members, and avoid the stigma and ill effects of incarceration. The probation officer is available to help the probationer cope with problems and to act as a resource person.

Large case loads may preclude probation officers from working as intensively with clients as they would like. Research on the relationship between the size of probation officers' case loads and client success has not, however, indicated that small case loads are necessarily the key to success.[19] Intensive probation supervision programs for the more serious offenders, however, have recently been coming back into vogue. Under these programs, officers may have case loads of twenty-five or less, meet with clients on almost a daily basis, and have no responsibilities for presentence investigations.[20] Another approach is to use trained volunteers who work with clients on a one-to-one basis under the supervision of the probation officer and help to provide the clients with the added support and attention they may need. Such projects have been developed in a number of areas in the United States and have claimed a certain amount of success.[21] It is important, however, that the volunteers undergo proper selection procedures and be given adequate training and supervision.

SUMMARY

This chapter has examined some of the noninstitutional sentencing dispositions that are available for a convicted offender. Specifically, the general features and uses of fines, restitution, community service orders, and probation have been investigated.

The fine is one of the penalties most frequently imposed upon conviction of a minor offense. The fine provides a sanction for the offender's conduct. In addition, it provides revenue for the state. A concern arises as to potential discrimination against the poor because they are sometimes unable to pay fines levied against them. In assessing the size of a fine, it has been suggested that the court take into account both the seriousness of the offense and the offender's financial resources.

Restitution usually involves the payment of money by the offender to the victim of the crime. It allows the victim to recoup at least part of his or her loss and may serve a valuable rehabilitative function for the offender by personalizing the crime.

On occasion, the offender may be ordered to perform some direct services for the victim of the crime. The offender may, on the other hand, be ordered to perform some direct services for the community as a whole. This type of sentencing disposition is known as the community service order. It benefits the community through the services that are provided and through the financial savings it may bring. It benefits the offender through avoidance of a jail sentence or some judicially imposed financial obligation he or she may be unable to meet.

The sentence of probation allows the offender to remain at liberty in the community, but with certain restrictions placed on that liberty. These restrictions may be either general conditions which are required of all offenders placed on probation or specific in that they are required of only certain named individuals. It is, of course, desirable that unrealistic conditions not be placed on probationers.

The probation officer has two prime responsibilities: to prepare and present presentence reports to the court and to supervise offenders who are placed on probation. In supervising offenders, the probation officer must reconcile what are often two conflicting functions: that of helping and of providing surveillance over the offender. The probation officer may try to help the offender both through counseling and by acting as a resource person. Often the sheer volume of the case load may prevent a probation officer from working as intensely with a client as would be desirable.

The probationer may be successfully discharged from probation. On the other hand, if the probationer has committed a new crime or violated one of the conditions of probation, probation may be revoked. Probation revocation will usually result in the offender's incarceration.

Probation as a sentencing disposition presents many potential benefits for both the offender and for the community. It enables the offender to work out personal problems within the community with the aid of a probation officer and without unduly disrupting his or her life. For the community, probation may present a more economical and more successful sentencing disposition than incarceration. These are, however, issues that will be examined in later chapters.

SUGGESTED ACTIVITIES

- Does your state provide for restitution? Community service orders? Find out for which crimes they are available as sentencing dispositions, and how commonly they are used.
- Find out the general conditions of probation in your jurisdiction. How realistic do you think they are?
- Interview a probation officer and find out the size of the case load, the kinds of crimes of which probationers have been convicted, the frequency with which they are seen, and how often and in what circumstances revocation is requested. What percentage of revocation hearings result in the revocation of probation?
- Find out from the probation office in what types of cases presentence reports are compiled. What information is contained in the presentence report? If a sentencing recommendation is made, how often does the court follow it?

REVIEW

A. Describe each of the following as a sentencing disposition: fines, restitution, and community service orders. Include in your description what the sanction involves, what its advantages and disadvantages are, and when it is used.

B. Briefly describe the major features of the probation sentence.

C. What are the duties of a probation officer, and why do they sometimes conflict?

D. Multiple Choice. Select the best answer.

1. The difference between restitution and state-funded victim compensation programs is that with restitution
   - a. the state will pay only if the victim suffered personal injury
   - b. the state will pay only if the offender is caught
   - c. the offender is responsible for paying
   - d. none of these

2. Conviction of which crime might be most likely to result in a sentence of a fine?
   - a. grand larceny
   - b. disturbing the peace
   - c. rape
   - d. all of these equally

3. A problem with the use of fines is that
   - a. they provide no revenue for the state
   - b. they provide redress for victims
   - c. they discriminate against the poor
   - d. all of these

4. Conviction of which crime might be most likely to result in a sentence of restitution?
   - a. assault
   - b. larceny
   - c. speeding
   - d. rape

5. An advantage of the community service order is that
   - a. it may rehabilitate the offender
   - b. it may help the community
   - c. it may provide new job skills for the offender
   - d. all of these

6. When an offender is ordered to pay monetary compensation to the victim of his or her crime, it is called
   - a. victim compensation
   - b. restitution
   - c. retribution
   - d. a community service order

7. Which of the following is not a function of the probation officer?
   - a. counseling the probationer
   - b. preparing presentence reports
   - c. mandating the conditions of probation
   - d. requesting revocation of probation

8. Which of the following would be a specific condition of probation?
   - a. reporting regularly to the probation officer
   - b. obeying the law
   - c. attending an alcohol treatment program
   - d. all of these

9. Which of the following is a feature of probation but not of the suspended sentence?
   - a. additional conditions attached to the sentence
   - b. a person assigned to help
   - c. the revocation hearing
   - d. all of these

10. Which of the following is an example of a noninstitutional sentence?
    - a. probation

b. community service order
c. restitution
d. all of these

REFERENCES

1. Derek A. Westen, "Fines, Imprisonment and the Poor: Thirty Dollars or Thirty Days," *California Law Review*, 57 (1969), 788.
2. Tate v. Short 401 U.S. 395 (1971).
3. See Anne Newton, "Alternatives to Imprisonment: Day Fines, Community Service Orders, and Restitution," *Crime and Delinquency Literature*, 8 (1976), 109–125.
4. An offender may also be allowed to pay restitution as a pretrial diversion measure. For a more thorough discussion of the use of restitution, see, for example, Burt Galaway, "The Use of Restitution," *Crime and Delinquency*, 23 (1977), 57–67.
5. For a description of these programs, see, for example, Belinda Rodgers McCarthy and Bernard J. McCarthy, *Community Based Corrections* (Monterey, Calif.: Brooks/Cole, 1984), 143–146.
6. Robert Keldgord, "Community Restitution Comes to Arizona," in Burt Galaway and Joe Hudson, *Offender Restitution in Theory and Action* (Lexington, Mass.: D. C. Heath, 1977), 163.
7. Sylvia Sullivan, "Convicted Offenders Become Community Helpers," *Judicature*, 56 (1973), 333–335.
8. James Beha, Kenneth Carlson, and Robert H. Rosenblum, *Sentencing to Community Service* (Washington, D.C.: U.S. Government Printing Office, 1977), 8.
9. See, for example, Kevin Krajick, "Community Service: The Work Ethic Approach to Punishment," *Corrections Magazine*, 8 (1982), 6–19.
10. U.S. Department of Justice, *Probation and Parole 1981* (Washington, D.C.: Author, 1982), 1.
11. U.S. Department of Justice, *Probation and Parole 1984* (Washington, D.C.: Author, 1985), 1.
12. Robert N. Carter, "The Presentence Report and the Decision-making Process," *Journal of Research in Crime and Delinquency*, 4 (1967), 203–211; U.S. Department of Justice, *Sentencing Practices in 13 States* (Washington, D.C.: Author, 1984).
13. American Bar Association, *Standards Relating to Probation* (New York: Author, 1970), 3.
14. Vernon Fox, *Introduction to Corrections* (Englewood Cliffs, N.J.: Prentice-Hall, 1977), 123.
15. See, for example, The President's Commission on Law Enforcement and Administration of Justice, *The Challenge of Crime in a Free Society* (Washington, D.C.: U.S. Government Printing Office, 1967), 167–168.
16. See, for example, Lee H. Bowker, *Corrections: The Science and Art* (New York: Macmillan, 1982), 323.
17. U.S. Department of Justice, *Probation and Parole 1984* (Washington, D.C.: Author, 1985), 1.
18. Mempha v. Rhay 389 U.S. 128 (1967); but see, too, Gagnon v. Scarpelli 411 U.S. 778 (1973).
19. L. Reed Adams and Harold J. Vetter, "Effectiveness of Probation Case Load Sizes: A Review of the Empirical Literature," *Criminology*, 8 (1971), 333–343.
20. See, for example, Stephen Gettinger, "Intensive Supervision: Can It Rehabilitate Probation?" *Corrections Magazine*, 9 (1983), 7–17.
21. See, for example, Richard Ku, *The Volunteer Probation Counselor Program, Lincoln, Nebraska* (Washington, D.C.: U.S. Government Printing Office, 1976); Harry E. Allen, Chris W. Eskridge, Edward J. Latessa, and Gennaro F. Vito, *Probation and Parole in America* (New York: Free Press, 1985), 223–247.

35

Institutional Corrections

After studying this chapter, the student should be able to:

- Discuss the use of incarceration as a sentencing disposition and distinguish among the different types of institutions to which a convicted offender may be sent.
- Describe the conditions generally found in correctional institutions, including the different types of rehabilitative programs.
- Summarize the conflict between the aim of rehabilitation and the concern for maintaining custody and security.
- Identify the problems faced by correctional institutions.
- State the nature and influence of the inmate subculture.

When one thinks of punishment and corrections, the type of penal sanction that perhaps most commonly comes to mind is imprisonment, the deprivation of liberty. To those living in the twentieth century, imprisonment may appear to constitute a logical penal sanction for the commission of the more serious types of crime. It meets the needs of retribution in that deprivation of liberty is an unpleasant consequence that no one can take lightly. Imposed to satisfy society's collective need for vengeance, the period of imprisonment can be tailored to fit the seriousness of the crime committed. Since deprivation of liberty is a situation that most people would strenuously seek to avoid, imprisonment may serve well both as a general and as a specific deterrent.

While confined, the offender is incapable of perpetrating further criminal offenses against those who live outside the prison walls. Thus imprisonment may also fulfill the function of incapacitation. Finally, since the time of imprisonment may be used to provide the offender with training, education, and psychological/psychiatric assistance, the goal of rehabilitation may also be advanced by the sanction of imprisonment.

Though imprisonment may have the potential to achieve all of these somewhat conflicting goals, many people feel that it has little positive effect. It has failed to deter. It has incapacitated offenders only to a limited extent. It has bred rather than rehabilitated criminals. This chapter examines the use and nature of imprisonment as a penal sanction.

HISTORY OF IMPRISONMENT IN THE UNITED STATES

Although imprisonment is commonly used today as a penal sanction, this has not always been the case. Indeed, until the nineteenth century prisons were most commonly used to house offenders awaiting trial or the imposition or execution of a sentence. Men, women, and children were all housed together in these institutions.

In Colonial times, convicted offenders were generally whipped, fined, branded, banished from the area, or put to death. Capital punishment was, in fact, a widely available sentencing option and was used for many crimes that might be considered minor. In the eighteenth century, the rising crime rates, the ineffectiveness of the criminal justice systems that then existed, and the inhumanity of some of the penal sanctions that were utilized led to a search for new solutions for preventing crime and correcting criminals.

In the United States it was felt that the harsh penal codes that had been brought over from Europe were largely responsible for the crime situation. Inhumanity bred inhumanity. Harsh laws were tempered by jury reluctance to convict people who could be sentenced to death for committing minor offenses, such as theft. Lessening the severity of the penal code was thus the first step toward remedying the situation. A second step was the provision of another form of penal sanction that was more humane than many of those currently being used. The prison was such an option.

At first more attention was focused on changing the penal laws than on the prisons themselves in the hope that better laws would decrease or even eradicate criminal behavior. When this state of affairs did not come to pass, the nature of the prison regime became the major concern. The offender was not seen as an inherently evil person, but as an individual who had not been given the right upbringing and training to cope with the evil temptations that abounded in society.

> The duty of the penitentiary was to separate the offender from all contact with corruption, both within and without its walls. There was obviously no sense to removing a criminal from the depravity of his surroundings only to have him mix freely with other convicts within the prison.[1]

American prisons of the early nineteenth century thus stressed the importance of isolating offenders from one another in order to prevent the danger of contamination and promote the likelihood of rehabilitation. They also stressed the need for a disciplined regimen. Just how this was to be done became a matter of bitter dispute. The two major competing philosophies were those espoused by the prison systems of Pennsylvania and of Auburn, New York.

The Pennsylvania system, often referred to as the separate system, demanded the total isolation of the offender. Under this system,

> Inmates remained in solitary cells for eating, sleeping and working, and entered private yards for exercise; they saw and spoke with only carefully selected visitors, and read only morally uplifting literature—the Bible. No precaution against contamination was [considered] excessive. Officials placed hoods over the head of a new prisoner when marching him to a cell so he would not see or be seen by other inmates.[2]

Under the Auburn system, first instituted in about 1820 at Auburn, New York, and often referred to as the "congregate system," the prisoners still lived in individual cells. During the day, however, they worked with the other inmates in the workshops. No conversation or exchange of any kind was allowed between inmates. Infractions were punished by whippings. Group movement was highly regimented.

To the proponents of the Pennsylvania system, the Auburn system was a watered-down version of their own, less equipped to bring rehabilitation. The Pennsylvania system, however, was the more expensive to administer; and total isolation did sometimes cause deterioration in the mental condition of inmates.

MODERN PENAL INSTITUTIONS

Neither the Pennsylvania nor the Auburn system survives in its original state. Of the two, it was the Auburn system that was more widely adopted and that lasted the longer. Both systems to some extent continue to influence the structure and routine of modern maximum security correctional institutions. The congregate working conditions and disciplined regimen of these institutions have their origins in the Auburn system, whereas the use of solitary confinement to discipline inmates can trace its roots back to the Pennsylvania system.

A third system, which focused on rehabilitation through education, gained prominence with the establishment in 1876 in New York State of the Elmira Reformatory for young men. In order to earn release in a system that utilized the indeterminate sentence and the institution of parole, an inmate had to progress through certain grades with sufficient points for release. With its emphasis on education and individual progress toward rehabilitation, this system also exerts its influence on the prisons of today.

The incarcerative institutions that currently exist in the United States vary from one another in many ways. They differ in their architectural designs, the types of inmates they hold, and the nature of the programs they offer.

Both the federal and state governments maintain their own prison systems. Naturally the federal prisons house offenders convicted of federal crimes, while the state prisons hold offenders convicted of state crimes. In addition, most states also have locally administered institutions which are called jails. The state-run prisons typically house convicted felons who are serving sentences of a year or more. The locally run jails, on the other hand, keep convicted misdemeanants, the short-term prisoners. The jails are the institutions that house pretrial detainees. Because of the diversity of their functions, their somewhat rapid turnover, and their dependence on local funding, jails have often presented convicted offenders with the worst of the conditions found in penal institutions.

The objectives of the penal institutions are often somewhat confused. A debate that has long existed centers around the issue of whether a convicted offender is sent to prison "as punishment" or "for punishment." Today most criminologists would probably agree that the deprivation of liberty is the punishment and that the focus in the penal institution should be on rehabilitation of the offender rather than on applying any further punitive measures. Many people would question, however, how well a person, detained in the coercive authoritarian atmosphere of a prison, can be trained to function in the free-flowing atmosphere of the world outside the prison walls.

Each prison system has different types of penal institutions to house different types of offenders. Offenders are categorized according to several factors. The most basic categorization of offenders is by sex and age. Virtually every prison system has separate institutions for its male and female offenders and for its adult and juvenile offenders.

In the adult correctional system, the next most basic classification is by security type. Each offender is classified as a maximum, medium, or minimum security risk, and is generally sent to an institution that holds that particular type of security risk. The security classification of the institution itself is dependent upon the extent to which prison construction is focused upon preventing escape and retaining the offenders securely within the confines of the institution. The maximum security prison tends to look like a fortress, with high walls and armed guards in watchtowers. Inside the institution, the focus is likewise on security, with offenders housed in locked cells and preventive measures taken to minimize the slightest likelihood of trouble.

The outward appearance of the medium security prison is generally less foreboding. The high wall may be replaced by a fence. The armed guards give less of an appearance of being omnipresent. The atmosphere within the institution is less geared toward maintaining security. The minimum security prison may possess no perimeter fence, no watchtower, and no outward manifestation of security measures. Inside, the inmates may be housed in dormitories rather than cells. There is a greater sense of freedom than in either the maximum or the medium security type of institution. Road and forestry camps generally constitute special types of minimum security institutions. A single institution may house in separate wings prisoners with different security classifications.

The prison is typically headed by a warden (or superintendant) who is responsible for the overall functioning of the institution. Under the warden are the deputy wardens who oversee the different operational divisions of the institution, such as custody, treatment programs, and prison industry. The custodial staff, who constitute the majority of the workforce, are organized in military fashion with ranks of captain, lieutenant, and guard (or correctional officer). They often have little in common with the treatment and industry staff, and may well also differ in racial and other characteristics from the inmates they are guarding.

THE PRISON POPULATION

On December 31, 1984, there were 463,866 offenders in state and federal correctional institutions. This represented a 40 percent increase in the prison population from 1980. While 92.7 percent of these prisoners were being held by the states and the District of Columbia, 7.3 percent were in federal institutions. The South, with about 33 percent of the nation's population and 45 percent of the state prisoners, held more than its share of inmates.[3] In addition to the prisoners in state and federal institutions, there were about 100,000 convicted offenders in locally operated jails.[4]

A survey of state prison admissions and releases in 1982 revealed that 94.2 percent of those admitted were male; that 46.3 percent were black; and that 83.7 percent were under thirty-five, with the median age being twenty-five.[5] Thus, males, blacks, and the young are greatly overrepresented in the prison population. Given this fact, it is not surprising that prisoners also tend to have an overrepresentation of the unmarried, the less educated, the poor, and the blue-collar worker.[6] A significant minority also have alcohol or other drug abuse problems.[7]

A total of 37.5 percent of those admitted in 1982 had committed violent crimes. The most common offenses were burglary and robbery, which had been committed by 27.7 percent and 18.3 percent of the offenders, respectively. The median sentence for all offenders was fifty-one months. The median time served by those released in that year was sixteen months.[8]

PRISON PROGRAMS

As mentioned in the previous section, the underprivileged are greatly overrepresented in the prison population. Since most of the inmates are fairly young, one might expect that the emphasis of the prison regime might be on helping them improve themselves so that they are better equipped to function in a productive and law-abiding manner on their return to society. Many treatment programs do in fact operate within the prison walls. Treatment has a broad definition in the context of correctional institutions, referring to all those progams that "bring socializing influences to bear on the inmate population."[9] Such programs include vocational and educational programs, psychological and psychiatric programs, specialized alcohol and drug treatment programs, and prison work. In addition, work or study release, furloughs, and parole may all be considered part of an offender's rehabilitation program.

It has been noted earlier that each prison system has some method of classifying offenders for assignment to the different penal institutions. Sex, age, and security classifications were discussed as criteria for making such assignments. In addition to these factors, the inmate's treatment needs may affect the likelihood of assignment to a particular institution. Thus if the problem is severe drug abuse, the inmate will hopefully be placed in an institution which runs a drug rehabilitation program. Generally, there are separate institutions, or wings of institutions, for the severely disturbed criminal offender.

Within a particular institution, special treatment needs will influence the type of program to which the offender is assigned. The decisions are usually made by a classification committee, consisting of different correctional personnel representing both treatment and custodial concerns.

Educational and Vocational Programs

The foregoing statistics on inmates in state correctional facilities indicate that prison inmates are generally lacking in formal education. Many prisons run some form of educational or vocational program. Some stress the academic type of program with the possibility of earning a high school diploma or in some cases a college degree. Others focus on the more vocational type of program, seeking to equip the participants with practical skills that might be used in the job market. Such programs might provide training in such areas as construction, automobile repairs, or printing.

Both the academic and vocational types of program fulfill an important function. The academic program may provide the offender with the literacy skills and the educational background necessary to compete for many kinds of jobs. The vocational training may equip the inmate with the practical skills needed to acquire a job. Indeed, it has been recommended that "each institution should have a comprehensive, continuous educational program for inmates"; and that "each institution should have prevocational and vocational training programs to enhance the offender's marketable skills." [10] In order to allow maximum flexibility in scheduling, to enable students to proceed at their own pace, and to provide immediate feedback, it has further been recommended that individually programmed instruction be used. [11]

Psychiatric/Psychological, Religious, and Recreational Programs

Both religious and recreational programs are widely available in correctional institutions. The importance of religious guidance was stressed in both the Pennsylvania and Auburn prison systems. Although religious instruction and observation are not required today, all correctional institutions are likely to have members of the clergy attached to their staffs to lead religious services and promote spiritual guidance and leadership for interested inmates. Though only a few inmates may participate, the effect of these services can be quite profound.

Recreational programs are of somewhat more recent origin. As has been stated,

> prior to World War II, with punishment as the predominant function of the institution, prison administrators found it difficult to justify recreation programs. Prisons offered essentially three forms of recreation: the yard, the library, and the auditorium. [12]

Nowadays, however, it is far more widely acknowledged that recreational programs relieve the monotony and boredom of prison life and give room for the ventilation of pent-up emotions. Art and sport may both, in their own different ways, fulfill these functions. Many institutions field their own football, baseball, and basketball teams. Among individual sports, boxing and weight lifting are, rather naturally, quite popular.

The provision of counseling services and psychiatric and psychological help for inmates would appear to be essential. Some institutions do have highly clinical therapeutic programs. Many institutions may, however, have neither the inclination nor the staff to run such programs. The professional staff that they do employ may be more involved in the initial process of evaluating the inmates rather than in treating them.

Prison Work Programs

Correctional institutions differ in the extent to which they provide the types of programs previously discussed. One feature that prisons do have in common is that they require inmates to perform some kind of work during the period of incarceration. Both the Pennsylvania and Auburn prison systems included work as a significant feature of their regimens. Thus prison work always has been, and continues to be, a major aspect of prison life, and an important component in the effort to achieve the offender's rehabilitation.[13]

Prison industry can, in fact, fulfill two diverse objectives. First, it can provide productive work and on-the-job training for inmates. Second, it can enable the state to obtain both goods and services at a lower price than could be obtained elsewhere.

Prison labor can be utilized in a number of different ways. The inmates can be employed in the manufacture of goods. These goods may be sold on the open market, to other state agencies, or simply used in the institution itself. Alternatively, inmate labor may be used for such tasks as the construction and maintenance of buildings and roads. Theoretically, this labor could be used either by the state or by private industry. Finally, the inmates could be employed in performing service functions within the institution itself. Such services might include cleaning, laundering, and cooking.

Until the 1930s, the services of inmates were often either provided under contract or leased to private organizations. The pressure of organized labor, however, helped to stop this utilization of cheap labor. Organized labor was also responsible to a large extent for promoting the passage of federal and state legislation that drastically limited the sale of prison goods on the open market. The result was that virtually the only market open for prison-made goods was provided by other state agencies. Many state agencies, however, have refrained from purchasing prison-made goods; for old machinery and inferior workmanship may often result in an inferior product. In addition, despite the cheap labor, the goods may also be overpriced.

Prison labor could provide the inmate both with industrious work habits and with specific job skills that, upon release, would lead to gainful employment. Often, however, neither of these objectives is achieved within the prison setting. The constant official concern with security, the type of work performed, the lack of adequate work opportunities, and the low pay received are hardly conducive to an industrious atmosphere. The skills provided may not be easily utilized in free society. Among the more common prison industries are the manufacture of signs and auto licenses.[14] Not many companies, however, are seeking to employ an experienced license plate maker! In some cases a released inmate may even be barred from performing a prison trade in the outside world. Thus a prison barber may earnestly wish to obtain employment as a barber only to discover that convicted felons cannot be licensed as barbers in certain states.

One program that has sought to replicate the outside world of work and to use private industry standards in prison work is the Free Venture model.[15] Its initial success, coupled with the general desire to make prisons more self-supportive and to provide inmates with good work habits and transferable job skills, has led to some rethinking about private sector involvement in prison work. Thus, once again we can observe private industry operating in our prisons. Both the final shape and the outcome of this renewed partnership remain to be seen.

PRISON CONDITIONS

There are, indeed, many factors that impede the development of first-rate treatment programs of any nature in correctional institutions. Three factors of ever-present concern deserve special mention: security, overcrowding, and lack of staff and other resources.

Although the emphasis varies from institution to institution, a major concern that faces all correctional institutions is the issue of security. Security entails two aspects: the maintenance of internal order within the institution, and the protection of outside society from the inmates. The security classification of the institution and the nature of its inmates will help determine exactly how much emphasis is placed on security.

With regard to protecting society, the focus is on maintaining custody of the inmates and on preventing their escape. Both architectural and internal security measures may be employed to achieve this objective. The inmates may be securely housed within the institution. Their movements within the institution may be tightly controlled. Their daily activities may be closely monitored. They are frequently counted so that it will be immediately noticed if anyone is missing or out of place.

These measures may also serve the function of helping to maintain internal order. In addition, inmates may be segregated and their persons and cells searched for any signs of weapons, contraband, or escape tools.

Any institution that highlights the need for security may tend to foster distrust rather than trust. This does not appear to be the ideal location to carry out rehabilitative programs. Indeed, it may be suggested that all that correctional institutions may be able to teach inmates is compliance and dependence, qualities that do not aid survival in the outside world.

Overcrowding and lack of staff and other resources are further factors that may contribute to the correctional institution's inability to bring about the rehabilitation of its offenders. Overcrowding can pose a serious problem. It may do more than impede rehabilitative programs in the institution. It may also help foster conditions of unrest and may be a major factor in the occurrence of prison disturbances. Awareness of this fact has helped lessen the extent of the problem. However, a survey of the inmate population on December 31, 1984 revealed that state institutions were operating at about 10 percent above capacity, and federal institutions at about 24 percent above capacity. In addition, some 2.8 percent of state prisoners were in local jails as a result of overcrowding. Many states were releasing prisoners early in order to alleviate overcrowding.[16]

A 1974 survey of the staffing patterns of state correctional institutions revealed that the median ratio of inmates to full-time employees was 3.6:1. Of the 60,604 employees in the institutions, 38,157 (63.0%) were custodial employees, 11,716 (19.3%) were clerical and maintenance employees, and 6,928 (11.4%) were professional specialists (academic and vocational teachers, social workers, and correctional counselors).[17] A 1981 survey of U.S. and Canadian institutions produced a ratio of one psychologist to every 376 inmates, and a ratio of one mental health professional (psychologist, psychiatrist or social worker) to every 150 inmates.[18] Figures such as these appear to indicate that staffing patterns in institutions are geared more toward custody than toward rehabilitation.

PRISON DISCIPLINE

There is considerable concern about maintaining internal order within the institution. However stringent the measures taken, there are inevitably infractions of prison rules and trouble within the institution, occasionally leading to a full-scale riot. Fighting, gambling, homosexual activity, possession of contraband, and refusal to work are typical infractions of prison rules. Official reprimands, withdrawal of privileges, loss of good time, and placement in solitary confinement constitute disciplinary measures that may be taken against an inmate.

The more serious types of disciplinary measures can be imposed only after a disciplinary hearing where the inmate has an opportunity to contest the charges and argue on his or her own behalf.[19] Although the U.S. Supreme Court has not ruled that solitary confinement is of itself unconstitutional, the lower courts have held on occasion that the particular circumstances of solitary confinement have constituted cruel and unusual punishment. Certain basic minimum conditions must be met, such as providing adequate sanitary conditions and sufficient ventilation, heating, and light.

The correctional institution is a setting where the seeds of discontent can erupt into a highly dangerous situation. The riots at Attica in New York State and at the New Mexico prison are vivid examples of correctional tragedies. The provision of inmate grievance procedures is an approach that has been advocated to relieve the tensions and frustrations that exist in correctional institutions. Through providing a formal mechanism for inmate complaints, it is hoped that inmate concerns can be dealt with and prison unrest avoided. Such a mechanism, however, appears ill equipped to combat the conflict created by the emergence of gangs formed on racial lines.

PRISON SUBCULTURE

Thus far this discussion has centered on the role of the institutional staff and institutional procedures in maintaining internal security. The administration has a very firm interest in seeing that the prison functions in a peaceful, orderly, and efficient manner. The inmates, too, have an interest in a stable and safe institution if only for the reason of protecting themselves from harm.

The conviction and subsequent punishment of an offender are manifestations of society's disapproval of the offender's conduct and to a degree of the offender personally. Entry into a correctional institution may constitute for the offender part of a degradation process. Personal identity is considered to be destroyed; the offender is now a number in drab prison uniform, and reduced to a lowly status. The inmate loses a sense of self-worth, and is deprived of autonomy and any control over his or her life. According to Sykes, the pains of imprisonment include the deprivation of five basic needs: liberty, goods and services, heterosexual relations, autonomy, and security.[20] No longer free to come and go at will, to associate freely with friends and relatives, to obtain the goods and services desired, or to have sexual relations with a member of the opposite sex, the inmate finds his or her life heavily regulated by the institutional authorities and perhaps threatened by fellow inmates.

The inmates in a correctional institution have a basic need to restore their sense of self-worth, to lessen their perceptions of loss of autonomy, and to enhance the likelihood of security. To an extent, the inmate subculture enables them to achieve these aims and thus lessen the pains of imprisonment.

> The inmate finds two paths open. On the one hand, he can attempt to bind himself to his fellow captives with ties of mutual aid, loyalty, affection and respect, firmly standing in opposition to the officials. On the other hand, he can enter into a war of all against all in which he seeks his own advantage without reference to the claims or needs of the other prisoners.[21]

The inmate subculture seeks to present a united front against its oppressors, the institutional staff. It has its own vocabulary and its own unwritten code. According to Sykes and Messinger, the inmate code demands the following:[22]

1. That inmates "don't interfere with inmate interest"; in particular, they should "never rat on a con"
2. That inmates should not quarrel or argue unnecessarily with one another; the advice is, "Don't lose your head." "Play it cool and do your own time"
3. That inmates should not exploit other inmates
4. That inmates should maintain their dignity; they should not weaken; they should be tough
5. That they should not give either "prestige or respect to the custodians or the world for which they stand."

The term "prisonization" has been coined by Clemmer to denote the process of "the taking on in greater or less degree of the folkways, mores, customs and general culture of the penitentiary."[23] The extent to which each inmate becomes part of the subculture varies considerably. The inmate's personal characteristics, prior experiences, and associations in prison are factors that affect the degree of prisonization. The type of prison is also likely to influence the extent of the inmate's prisonization. Thus, one might expect prisonization to occur far more readily and permanently in a maximum security institution that stresses custody and security, than in a minimum security institution that focuses on treatment and rehabilitation. According to Wheeler, the extent of prisonization varies according to the phase of the inmate's institutional career. Following along a U-shaped curve, the inmate's adherence to staff expectations is strongest at the beginning and towards the end of the period of institutionalization, and weakest in the middle.[24] The extent to which the inmate subculture is brought in from outside as opposed to being a reaction to conditions inside has long been a matter of debate.[25] The influence of racial and political groupings on the inmate subculture likewise is a subject of ongoing research.[26]

SUMMARY

Until the nineteenth century, prisons were generally used to house offenders awaiting trial or the imposition or execution of a sentence. Today correctional institutions provide a common sentencing disposition for offenders convicted of the more serious types of crime.

Both the federal and state governments maintain their own prison systems. In addition, most states also have locally administered institutions which are called jails. Generally, separate institutions exist for male and female offenders and for adult and juvenile offenders.

A major concern that faces all correctional institutions is the issue of security. Each institution must maintain internal order and protect outside society from suffering any harm at the hands of the inmates. Both the institutions and the inmates have security classifications.

More is expected of correctional institutions than that they simply maintain custody and control over the inmates. They are also expected to exert a positive rehabilitative influence over those whom they hold. A vast array of different rehabilitative programs does in fact exist in correctional institutions. Educational, vocational, recreational, religious, and psychological/psychiatric programs all operate to an extent within the confines of the various institutions. In addition, prisoners are generally required to participate in some form of prison work. In view of the youth and underprivileged backgrounds of many of the prisoners, such programs might appear to have a rich potential. Many factors, however, serve to prevent the realization of this potential. Foremost among these are the ever-present concern with security, the problem of overcrowding, and the lack of staff and other resources. Indeed, some have questioned how well a person, detained in the coercive authoritarian atmosphere of a prison, can be trained to function in the free-flowing atmosphere of the world outside the prison walls. Some might venture to say that all that correctional institutions can teach inmates is compliance and dependence, qualities that do not aid survival in the outside world. The inmate subculture may help inmates to regain a sense of self-worth, to lessen their perception of loss of autonomy, and to enhance their likelihood of security. However, the aims of the inmate subculture and those of the dominant outside culture to which an offender's adherence is sought tend to be very different.

SUGGESTED ACTIVITIES

- On a map, locate and distinguish by security classification the penal institutions in your state.
- Visit two correctional institutions with different security classifications. Contrast their appearances. What types of inmates do they hold? What kinds of programs do they run?
- Has there been a disturbance in a prison in your state? If so, find out from newspaper accounts and other sources what happened, why it happened, how it was resolved, and what precautions have been taken to prevent a recurrence. If there has not been a disturbance in a prison in your state, choose an institution in another state where there has been a disturbance, and answer the same questions.
- Interview a correctional officer and ask him or her to describe the vocational, educational, recreational, and psychological programs in the institution; the disciplinary problems and procedures; and the prison subculture.

REVIEW

A. How are offenders and institutions classified?

B. Distinguish among the three general security classifications of adult penal institutions.

C. Describe the different types of rehabilitation programs that are found in correctional institutions.

D. What factors in prisons impede the process of rehabilitation?

E. What is the inmate subculture, why does it exist, and how does it affect the inmates?

F. Multiple Choice. Select the best answer.

1. A person convicted of a misdemeanor would be most likely to serve a prison sentence
   - a. in a jail
   - b. in a prison
   - c. in a federal penitentiary
   - d. in any of these

2. The main difference between the Auburn system and the Pennsylvania system was that in the Auburn system
   - a. inmates were allowed to talk to one another
   - b. inmates were allowed to see one another
   - c. inmates were allowed to sleep in dormitories
   - d. all of these

3. An institution with a high wall and armed guards in watchtowers is most likely to be a
   - a. minimum security institution
   - b. medium security institution
   - c. maximum security institution
   - d. none of these

4. Which of the following are underrepresented in the prison population?
   a. blue-collar workers
   b. whites
   c. the young
   d. none of these

5. One purpose of vocational programs in prison is to
   a. provide offenders with competitive job skills
   b. help offenders to continue their education
   c. help offenders to earn a high school diploma
   d. all of these

6. One reason that prison industry may not provide inmates with marketable skills is that
   a. private industry may not need the skill developed
   b. a convict may be barred from performing the trade learned
   c. the methods used in prisons are often out of date
   d. all of these

7. Approximately what percentage of full-time employees in state correctional institutions are custodial employees?
   a. 40 percent
   b. 50 percent
   c. 65 percent
   d. 75 percent

8. A prisoner has a right to argue on his or her own behalf
   a. before any disciplinary measure can be taken
   b. before a serious disciplinary measure can be taken
   c. before losing any privileges
   d. under no circumstances

9. The inmate subculture encourages inmates to
   a. respect the guards
   b. respect other inmates
   c. exploit other inmates
   d. none of these

10. Research suggests that inmate adherence to staff expectations is weakest at
   a. the beginning of the period of incarceration
   b. the middle of the period of incarceration
   c. the end of the period of incarceration
   d. all of these equally

REFERENCES

1. David J. Rothman, *The Discovery of the Asylum* (Boston: Little, Brown, 1971), 83.
2. *Ibid.*, 85.
3. U.S. Department of Justice, *Prisoners in 1984* (Washington, D.C.: Author, 1985), 1–2.
4. On June 30, 1983, the latest date for which data were available, there were 107,660 convicted offenders in local jails [U.S. Department of Justice, *The 1983 Jail Census* (Washington, D.C.: Author, 1984), 6].
5. U.S. Department of Justice, *Prison Admissions and Releases, 1982* (Washington, D.C.: Author, 1985), 2.
6. U.S. Department of Justice, *Profile of State Prison Inmates: Sociodemographic Findings from the 1974 Survey of Inmates of State Correctional Facilities* (Washington, D.C.: U.S. Government Printing Office, 1979); U.S. Department of Justice, *Prisons and Prisoners* (Washington, D.C.: Author, 1982).
7. U.S. Department of Justice, *Prisoners and Alcohol* (Washington, D.C.: Author, 1983); U.S. Department of Justice, *Prisoners and Drugs* (Washington, D.C.: Author, 1983).

8. U.S. Department of Justice, *Prison Admissions and Releases, 1982* (Washington, D.C.: Author, 1985), 3–7.

9. Vernon Fox, *Introduction to Corrections*, 2nd ed. (Englewood Cliffs, N.J.: Prentice-Hall, 1977), 205.

10. National Advisory Commission on Criminal Justice Standards and Goals, *Corrections* (Washington, D.C.: U.S. Government Printing Office, 1973), 368–369.

11. *Ibid.*, 369.

12. National Advisory Commission on Criminal Justice Standards and Goals, *op. cit.*, 383.

13. For an overview of the characteristics of state prison industries, see: Edmund F. McGarrell and Timothy J. Flanagan, *Sourcebook of Criminal Justice Statistics—1984* (Washington, D.C.: U.S. Government Printing Office, 1985), 114–117.

14. U.S. Department of Justice, *Prison Industries* (Washington, D.C.: U.S. Government Printing Office, 1978), 30–31.

15. Jack Schaller, "Work and Imprisonment: An Overview of the Changing Role of Prison Labor in American Prisons," *Prison Journal*, 62 (1982), 3–11.

16. U.S. Department of Justice, *Prisoners in 1984* (Washington, D.C.: Author, 1985), 5–6.

17. Nicolette Parisi, Michael R. Gottfredson, Michael J. Hindelang, and Timothy J. Flanagan, *Sourcebook of Criminal Justice Statistics—1978* (Washington, D.C.: U.S. Government Printing Office, 1979), 201–202.

18. Rafael F. Otero, Donna McNally, and Robert Powitzky, "Mental Health Services in Adult Correctional Systems," *Corrections Today*, 43 (1981), 8, 14.

19. Wolff v. MacDonnell 418 U.S. 539 (1974); Baxter v. Palmigiano 425 U.S. 308 (1976).

20. Gresham M. Sykes, *The Society of Captives* (Princeton, N.J.: Princeton University Press, 1958), 63–78.

21. *Ibid.*, 82.

22. Gresham M. Sykes and Sheldon L. Messinger, "The Inmate Social System" in Robert G. Leger and John R. Stratton, *The Sociology of Corrections: A Book of Readings* (New York: John Wiley, 1977), 98–101.

23. Donald Clemmer, *The Prison Community* (New York: Rinehart, 1958), 299.

24. Stanton Wheeler, "Socialization in Correctional Communities," *American Sociological Review*, 26 (1961), 697–712.

25. See, for example, John Irwin and Donald Cressey, "Thieves, Convicts, and the Inmate Culture," *Social Problems*, 10 (1962), 142–155.

26. See, for example, James B. Jacobs, "Race Relations and the Prisoner Subculture," in Norval Morris and Michael Tonry (eds.) *Crime and Justice* (Chicago: University of Chicago Press, 1979), 1–28.

36

Reintegrating the Offender

OBJECTIVES

After studying this chapter, the student should be able to:

- Define the concept of reintegration.
- Discuss the nature and use of furloughs and work and study release.
- Explain the nature and purpose of parole and the way in which the system operates.
- Describe the use of halfway houses to help offenders reintegrate into the community.
- List and evaluate different measures used to assess the effectiveness of penal sanctions.

The previous chapter examined the conditions found within correctional institutions, and the fact that the young and the underprivileged are greatly overrepresented in the prison population. The great diversity of rehabilitation programs that operate within the institutions was discussed. However, it was also said that at best all that an inmate may learn within an institution may be compliance and dependence.

The acid test of the effectiveness of an institutional program does not lie in its ability to enable inmates to function well within the institution itself. Rather, the true measure of a correctional program is to be found in the extent to which it enables offenders to function properly in the outside world; an important fact to be borne in mind is that the vast majority of inmates in correctional institutions are eventually released back into the community. Once released into the community, it is of the utmost concern to society that the offender lead a productive and law-abiding life. This chapter examines some of the measures that are taken to facilitate the offender's reintegration into society. Discussed are some of the programs in which the inmate may participate while still in the correctional institution. These programs include furloughs and work and study release. Also investigated are some of the measures that may aid an offender's return to society, including the process of parole and the use of halfway houses. The different measures used to assess the effectiveness of the various penal sanctions are also discussed.

REINTEGRATION

With regard to a specific offender, the ultimate aim of the correctional process is to obtain that offender's reintegration into the community. The concept, reintegration, refers to the offender's readmission into the community as a fully functioning, wholesome, contributing member. As the President's Commission on Law Enforcement and Administration of Justice pointed out, the task of corrections

> includes building or rebuilding solid ties between offender and community, integrating or reintegrating the offender into community life—restoring family ties, obtaining employment and education, securing in the larger sense a place for the offender in the routine functioning of society.[1]

The offender's stay in a correctional institution represents an abrupt break from a previous existence in the outside world. Ideally, the period of an offender's incarceration may provide the added skills which will enable him or her to function better upon returning to outside society. Life within the institution, however, is totally different from life outside. A sudden return to the outside world without adequate preparation can present the newly released offender with a highly threatening culture shock. The offender, ill equipped to function effectively in a lawful manner prior to being incarcerated, now has some additional burdens to carry. Family relationships must be rebuilt. Reentry into the employment market, with the added stigma attached to a person who has served time, must be faced. The offender must adjust to the customs of a world that has not stood still while he or she has been inside.

While in the institution, offenders may participate in a number of programs that are designed to improve their ability to function properly. Foremost among these are perhaps the various vocational and educational programs that are run in the institutions. In addition, offenders may seek to maintain family and other ties through correspondence and visits by those individuals to the correctional institution. Some states, such as Mississippi and California, allow what are known as conjugal visits. An important aspect of the conjugal visit is that an inmate is allowed to be with a spouse in total privacy for a short period of time. Thus to a very limited extent normal marital relationships may be maintained in what is a highly abnormal marital situation. Though well intentioned, this procedure may be considered highly demeaning to the parties involved since it is obvious why the spouse is there. In addition, objections may be raised to what is in essence the use of sex as a reward for good behavior in prison.

All these types of programs are, of course, programs that are carried out within the confines of the institutions themselves. They may eventually help an offender in his or her attempts at reintegration into the community. They do not, however, have an immediate direct impact on that attempt.

FURLOUGHS AND WORK AND STUDY RELEASE

A different type of approach to the problem of facilitating an offender's reintegration into the community is through working with the offender out in the community itself. Since the ultimate aim of the correctional system is to obtain the offender's reintegration into society, it may be argued that all of the institutional programs should be geared toward meeting that objective. Since the periods immediately before and immediately after release are crucial for an offender's successful adjustment into society, it may further be suggested that these are times when the offender should be given added support and help.

There are in existence a number of programs whose prime purpose is to ease the offender's transition back into the community. Some of these programs, such as furloughs and work and study release, take place while the offender is still an inmate in the correctional institution. They are essentially part of the process of providing an offender with a gradual release from the institution. An offender's freedom is obtained in a series of steps, rather than in one sudden change. Other programs, such as parole and some halfway house projects, are designed to help the offender after actually being released from the institution.

Furloughs

A furlough may be considered to be a period of absence from the correctional institution, granted to the inmate by the authorities for a specific purpose. Long used on an informal basis by many correctional systems, the furlough has now been recognized as fulfilling an important function in the correctional process. Typically, furloughs used to be granted to inmates so that they could visit dying relatives, attend funerals, and the like. Today furloughs are also granted for general home visits, for religious and public holidays, for job interviews, and for other prerelease activities. The aim is to enable the offender to better maintain family ties and to become more adequately prepared for release. The furloughs are generally granted for a specific purpose and are limited to a certain duration—three days, for example. Although the offender is usually entirely responsible for himself or herself, failure to return to the institution at the end of the period of furlough has not been a significant problem.[2] Upon return to the institution, the offender can discuss with staff members any problems encountered while on furlough. Follow-up studies have generally indicated that offenders who have participated in some type of prerelease program have fared more successfully on release than those who have not been involved in such programs.[3]

Work and Study Release

Work and study release are variants of the original type of furlough program. In a work release program, the offender is allowed out into the community to work for pay in free society. After a day's work, the offender must return to the correctional institution where the rest of his or her time is spent. The format of a study release program is basically the same, except that the offender is released to attend some type of study program, rather than to work.

Both types of programs offer the participating offender an opportunity to experience life in the free world and to build community ties. The study release program may help the offender acquire new educational or vocational skills. The work release program allows the offender to become a productive member of society, earning a full day's pay for a full day's work. The money earned may be used for self-support as well as for supporting dependents, thereby reducing the financial burden that would otherwise accrue.

The utility of such programs is widely recognized. As has been suggested,

> When an individual returns from a temporary release to home, work, or school, his experience can be discussed with him by staff, to try to assess his probable adjustment and to note incipient problems. Many difficulties can be anticipated in this way, the inmate's frustration can be relieved by discussion, and help can be given him to develop realistic plans and insights for coping with everyday problems.[4]

Returning to the institution can, however, present the offender with problems. Having had contact with the outside world may make it harder for the offender to cope with life in the institution. There may be pressure from fellow inmates to carry out favors, perhaps to bring in contraband. As a consequence, many correctional institutions have established separate wings where participants in prerelease programs may be housed. In addition, many correctional systems ultilize different facilities to house program participants; for often the correctional institution in which the offender has been kept is far from an urban area where suitable employment or educational opportunities exist.

A number of jurisdictions place offenders in prerelease centers for a month or more prior to their final release. Since 1961, the federal system, for example, has operated a network of prerelease guidance centers. The offenders live in these centers under a regime which systematically removes restrictions on their behavior and allows them to adjust gradually to life in the free world. Under supervision, they prepare for a full return to society.

PAROLE

The focus thus far has been on programs that operate while the offender is still under the full custody of the institutional authorities. Also to be considered are those programs that aid the offender after release from the institution. Many offenders do not participate in the types of prerelease programs under discussion. A large number, however, do receive some form of supervision on their release. In 1984, 191,499 offenders were released from state and federal institutions. Most of these offenders were released on parole, either after a discretionary grant of parole or as a result of the offender fulfilling the conditions for mandatory release.[5]

Parole may be regarded as the

> release of an offender from a penal or correctional institution, after he has served a portion of his sentence, under the continued custody of the State and under conditions that permit his reincarceration in the event of misbehavior.[6]

An offender who is granted parole is released from the correctional institution before serving the full sentence. Typically, an offender is eligible for parole after serving a specified fraction of the sentence, for example, one-third.[7] In these circumstances, if sentenced to twelve years for armed robbery, the offender will be eligible for parole after four years. If, however, the judge has set an indeterminate sentence with a minimum of six years, the offender will be eligible for parole only after having served six years. In addition, the date on which an offender may first be considered for parole may be affected by the amount of "good time" he or she has earned (the time allowed off the original prison sentence as a reward for good behavior).

In some states, certain classes of offenders may be prohibited from being granted parole. Generally an offender has a right to be considered for parole, but no actual right to be granted parole. The decision to grant parole is an administrative decision made by the parole board. Under the indeterminate, but not under the determinate, sentencing structure, the parole board has a great deal of discretion in setting the offender's release date.

The Parole Board

Most commonly the parole board is an independent agency whose members are appointed by the head of the executive branch of government, typically the governor of the state. Most boards have either three or five members, though a few have as many as eleven or twelve. The appointment is nearly always for a fixed period of years. In most states board members serve on a full-time basis. Although a few states require that the parole board members possess certain background qualifications, many states do not have such requirements.[8]

The parole board is responsible for deciding whether or not to grant parole. The supervision of the parolees, the released offenders, is carried out by parole officers. In some states these parole field services are administered by the parole board. Far more commonly, however, they are under the authority of the Department of Corrections. Indeed, in some states the parole board itself is housed within the Department of Corrections. This model provides a clear tie between the institutional and parole authorities and their respective staffs. It is important, however, to ensure that institutional needs, such as releasing offenders to relieve overcrowding, do not take undue precedence over the needs of the offender and the community to which he or she is to be released.

The Parole Process

The parole board acts on the basis of information it receives about the offender. Both the institutional and parole staffs may be involved in supplying the relevant information. Ideally, all of the parties are working toward the goal of releasing the offender at the earliest appropriate time.

> Under ideal conditions, when an offender is first received at the institution he/she is interviewed by the parole staff. The results of the interview, psychiatric and psychological tests, and the information in the presentence report are then used to plan an institutional program for the inmate. The parole staff periodically updates the material with additional information. They discuss tentative release plans with inmates and request the field staff to visit and interview family members and prospective employers. When an inmate is ready to meet the parole board, they provide a report on the inmate that includes an evaluation of changes made since he/she was first interviewed at the prison. The report may also include a recommendation, if this is requested by the board.[9]

The ideal, however, is rarely realized. Lack of sufficient staff generally prevents full preparation of the offender for release or the submission of the aforementioned detailed type of report.

The information on which the parole board will base its decision will include details of the offender's offense(s), performance within the institution, and home environment. Preparations for the offender's release will also be considered, in particular the formal parole plan and the kind of employment opportunities available. The offender will generally appear before the paroling authority. In some states this may be the full parole board, in others a single board member, and in still others a representative of the parole board such as a hearing examiner. In some states the offender has a right to be represented at the hearing.

There are no constitutionally mandated criteria for the granting of parole. Traditionally, the burden of proof has been on the offender to make his or her case for parole. The nature of this burden of proof is far from clear. As the National Advisory Commission on Criminal Justice Standards and Goals has stated:

> Perhaps the most pervasive shortcomings are the undue emphasis in parole hearings on past events and extreme vagueness about the necessary steps to achieve parole. Badly needed are clearly defined objectives for the inmate, attainment of which will result in his parole.[10]

If the offender has appeared in person, he or she may be told of the board's decision immediately after the hearing, or word may be received later on. If parole has been denied, the offender will not generally be given the reasons.

Research has indicated that the factor that most influences a parole board member's decision of whether or not to grant parole is that person's assessment of the likelihood that the offender would commit a serious crime if released.[11] To provide more objective guidelines to what can be a rather subjective process, some jurisdictions have begun to employ what are known as parole prediction tables. By scoring offenders on dimensions that are known to be related to success or failure on parole, a more scientifically based prediction can be made about each offender's future behavior. Use of this information in conjunction with a scale that takes into account the severity of the offender's crime produces a fairer and more uniform approach to the process of granting parole.

The whole parole system itself has by no means been totally free from attack. Concern about the lack of fairness in parole granting procedures, the tension that may arise in prison among inmates who are uncertain when they are to be released, and a feeling among the general public that offenders are not serving as much time as they should, have all contributed to a movement to abolish parole. A number of states have moved to a totally determinate sentencing structure, and eliminated discretionary parole release. The states of Maine and Connecticut have actually abolished parole.[12]

If an offender is granted parole, he or she will be released from the institution under the supervision of a parole officer. Prior to release, the offender will have to sign a parole agreement, which will outline the conditions of parole. Like the conditions of probation, parole conditions may be either general or specific. General conditions might include provisions that the parolee obey all laws, report regularly to the parole officer, and not leave the state without first obtaining permission. Specific conditions, which would apply only to named individuals, might require that the parolee live at a certain halfway house or participate in a particular drug treatment program. A concern that has been raised with regard to parole conditions is that unrealistic expectations not be placed on parolees.

Like the probation officer, the parole officer has a dual function to perform while supervising a client. On the one hand, the parole officer helps an offender attempt to reintegrate into society, acting as the parolee's friend and advisor. In many ways the parole officer acts as a resource manager by helping a client find and maintain suitable employment, training, or treatment, and by guiding a client to lead a law-abiding life. In another function, the parole officer acts as a surveillance agent, watching for any offenses the parolee may commit and taking appropriate action should the parolee break the law or violate one of the conditions of parole.

Parole officers differ in the way they relate to clients and supervise them. Often the parole officer will modify a certain approach to meet the perceived needs of a particular client. The size of the case load may, in fact, prevent the parole officer from spending as much time with each client as might be desirable. In many states the parole officer is also a probation officer and thus supervises a mixed case load of probationers and parolees. The average case load in 1979 was calculated to be seventy-one cases per officer.[13]

The parolee has only been conditionally released from the correctional institution, and remains on parole until the unexpired portion of the sentence has been served. Occasionally, a parolee may be discharged early because the parole officer believes that no useful purpose would be served by having the client remain on parole.

Should a parolee violate one of the conditions of parole, parole may be revoked, and the parolee recommitted to a correctional institution to serve the rest of the sentence there. In some states, credit is given for the time already served on parole; in other states, it is not.

The parolee may have his or her parole revoked either for committing a new crime or for violation of one of the conditions of parole. If the parolee has committed a new offense and been apprehended, he or she may be prosecuted for the new offense, have parole revoked, or both. If the conditions of parole have been violated, it will be up to the parole officer to seek revocation of parole. Unlike the revocation of probation which is a judicial function, parole revocation is an administrative function, handled by an administrative agency, the parole board.

Since the United States Supreme Court decision in *Morrissey* v. *Brewer*,[14] the alleged parole violator must be afforded a two-stage inquiry. First, there must be a reasonably prompt informal inquiry, much like a preliminary hearing, to determine whether there is probable cause to believe that the parolee has violated the conditions of parole. This hearing is to be conducted by an official not directly involved in the case, such as another parole officer. Second, if probable cause is found to exist at this first hearing, then the parolee is to be granted a second, more formal hearing, at which the actual decision with regard to revoking parole is to be made. The requirements of due process were found to include:

> (a) written notice of the claimed violations of parole; (b) disclosure to the parolee of evidence against him; (c) opportunity to be heard in person and to present witnesses and documentary evidence; (d) the right to confront and cross examine adverse witnesses (unless the hearing officer specifically finds good cause for not allowing confrontation); (e) a ''neutral and detached'' hearing body such as a traditional parole board, members of which need not be judicial officers or lawyers; and (f) a written statement by the factfinders as to the evidence relied on and reasons for revoking parole.[15]

In *Gagnon* v. *Scarpelli*[16] the Supreme Court held that a parolee was entitled to assistance of counsel at both stages of the revocation process, certainly when he or she either contests that there has been a violation of parole conditions or where there are ''substantial reasons which justified or mitigated the violation and make revocation inappropriate, and [that] the reasons are complex or otherwise difficult to develop or present.'' [17]

HALFWAY HOUSES

Parole provides the offender with a certain degree of supervision and support when returning to society. The limited amount of contact the parole officer has with each client limits the extent of the help given. To a degree the use of properly selected, well-trained, and adequately supervised volunteers can help alleviate this manpower shortage. An interesting variation of this approach has been the use of ex-offenders as parole officer aides.[18]

Some parolees need a more structured living environment to help them cope with the problems of everyday life. Placement in a halfway house can provide such an environment.

A halfway house has been defined as:

> A nonconfining residential facility for adjudicated adults or juveniles, or those subject to criminal or juvenile proceedings, intended to provide an alternative to confinement

for persons not suitable for probation, or needing a period of readjustment to the community after confinement.[19]

Thus a halfway house may provide a program for offenders prior to, and instead of, incarceration, a "halfway in" type of program. Alternatively, a halfway house may provide a program for offenders on their way back into society after a period of incarceration, a "halfway out" type of program. An interesting new program is electronically monitored home confinement. This involves the use of house imprisonment verified by electronic surveillance during an offender's nonworking hours. This is accomplished by strapping a miniature short-range transmitter to the offender's ankle. The supervising agency is able to make sure that the offender is at home by monitoring a signal sent by the transmitter, via a receiver-dialer plugged into the offender's home telephone circuit, to a central computer.[20]

Reference has already been made to prerelease centers, a type of halfway house to which offenders are sent prior to their release on parole from the correctional institutions in which they have been serving their time. Another type of halfway house program caters to offenders after their release from correctional institutions.[21]

The original halfway house was a facility that provided a place of abode for homeless offenders released from institutions. Today it is seen as a vital part of the reintegrative model of corrections:

> the halfway house is said to offer a gradual reentry, also reintegrative services which assist the resident in getting a meaningful job, raising his educational level, improving his attitude toward himself and others, and increasing his ability to function in the community in a socially acceptable manner.[22]

Under the guidance of the staff at the halfway house, the offender may gradually readjust to life in the free world. The need for such support is underscored by the findings that one of every three prison releasees will return to prison within three years, and that the second half of the first year after release is the time of greatest vulnerability.[23] This second finding has been taken to suggest "the need for maximum correctional support immediately before and during that period." [24]

MEASURING SUCCESS

The basic aim of the programs previously described is to achieve the offender's successful reintegration into society. What are the measures that are used to determine success?

Success is a difficult term to define and an even more difficult one to measure. The success of a penal sanction is generally determined by the success of its clients. Observable factors such as regular employment, stable family relationships, completion of new educational or vocational programs, changes in attitude, successful completion of probation or parole terms, and lack of rearrest or reconviction have all been used as indicators of a client's successful functioning in society.

Even when client success has been defined in an adequate manner, it may be extremely difficult to attribute success to participation in a particular correctional program. For many factors simultaneously affect an individual's behavior. Isolating one of those factors and labeling it as the cause, or even as the main cause, of the behavior is a tricky process. In addition, when comparing the performance of different programs, the types of offenders they receive need to be taken into account. Thus it would be misleading to conclude that probation is more effective than parole simply because 80.9 percent of probationers, but only 63.7 percent of parolees, successfully completed their terms in 1984.[25] Since the more serious offenders are more likely to be sent to prison than to be placed on probation, one might expect the offenders who are on probation to have greater potential for success than the offenders who are sent to prison and then placed on parole. Simply comparing the success rates of the two types of penal sanctions without taking this factor into consideration might well lead to an erroneous conclusion.

Recidivism

Foremost among the measures that are used to indicate success in corrections is the concept of recidivism. Basically, recidivism is the repetition of criminal behavior. It may be measured in a variety of ways; for example, by the offender's rearrest or reconviction of a subsequent offense. Problems arise concerning the stage of the criminal justice process, the type of offense, and the length of the follow-up period that should be considered. Lack of a commonly accepted definition of recidivism often poses a problem in comparing the outcome of different research studies.

As yet the state of the present research methodology is not sufficiently sophisticated to fully answer questions about recidivism. After conducting an exhaustive review of some 231 research studies, Robert Martinson concluded that "With few and isolated exceptions, the rehabilitative efforts that have been reported so far have had no appreciable effect on recidivism." [26] He did, however, add that "It is just possible that some of our treatment programs are working to some extent, but that our research is so bad that it is incapable of telling." [27]

For a period of time in the 1970s, the FBI collected and analyzed data on offenders who had been arrested and had fingerprint cards taken of them. Out of a total of 255,936 offenders arrested between 1970 and 1975, 164,295 (64.2%) had been arrested two or more times before.[28] In addition, a follow-up study was conducted of 78,143 offenders who were released in 1972. Recidivism was measured by any arrest for which a fingerprint card was submitted. Burglary and robbery offenders, with recidivism rates of 81 percent and 77 percent respectively, had the highest rates of recidivism. Embezzlers, with a recidivism rate of 28 percent, had the lowest.

With regard to the type of disposition an offender had received, it was noted that

> Seventy-four percent of the offenders released after serving their prison time were rearrested within four years. Of those persons released on parole, 71 percent repeated and 57 percent of those placed on probation repeated. Of those persons acquitted or who

had their cases dismissed in 1972, 67 percent were rearrested for new offenses within four years.[29]

Numerous methodological concerns have been raised with regard to this study. These have included the use of arrest as the measure of recidivism, the method of selecting the research subjects, and the comparison of different sentencing dispositions without taking into account the different types of offenders with whom they may have been dealing. Other approaches present a different picture. As stated previously, the FBI, defining recidivism as rearrest within four years, showed a recidivism rate of 71 percent for those released on parole. When parole revocation or return to prison has been employed as a measure of recidivism, the recidivism rate has been shown to be about 25 percent.[30] A further point to be made is that a single measure of success is being employed—recidivism, or rather the lack of it. It is possible that an offender may have committed another criminal offense, but yet be showing marked improvement in other ways, such as having a steady job for the first time, refraining from violent outbursts, and the like.

Given the problems that are associated with measuring the success of the various penal sanctions, it is not surprising that other approaches have been suggested. One such approach is the cost-benefit analysis model. The basic argument is that since no particular penal sanction is clearly more effective than any other, those penal sanctions which are less expensive to administer should be preferred to more expensive approaches. Though the basis for making the appropriate calculations is often subject to dispute, this line of reasoning suggests that noninstitutional forms of penal sanctions should in general be preferred to institutional sanctions. Following this type of rationale, some states have instituted what are known as probation subsidy programs. Since probation services are often administered and funded by local units of government, whereas correctional institutions are run by the state, some form of financial incentive for placing offenders on probation was considered desirable. Under probation subsidy programs, local governmental units are paid a certain amount of money for each offender who might have been expected to be incarcerated but was placed on probation instead.

Under this type of cost-benefit approach, the offender may be thought to benefit; for the less restrictive of penal sanctions are likely to be imposed. This type of approach has, however, only been considered in the light of the rehabilitative rationale of sentencing. When the other rationales of retribution, deterrence, and incapacitation are taken into account, there may be no alternative to giving the offender an institutional sentence.

SUMMARY

This chapter has investigated the problem of reintegrating the offender into society. The objective is to achieve the offender's readmission into society as a fully functioning, wholesome, contributing member.

It has been suggested that an offender can learn little within the confines of an institution that will enable him or her to function better upon returning to the free world. A number of programs have been designed to help the offender deal with this problem. Some operate while the offender is still in the correctional institution. Others have been established to aid the offender after release from the institution.

Furloughs and work and study release are programs in which an offender may participate while still in the institution. Furloughs are of limited duration, and are granted for a specific purpose, for example, to attend a funeral, to spend a religious holiday at home, or to go for a job interview. The aim is to enable offenders to better maintain their family ties and to prepare themselves more adequately for their return to society.

Work and study release are variations of the furlough program. In a work release program the offender is allowed to work in the community for pay. In a study release program, the offender is released from the institution to attend some type of study program. The period of freedom, however, is limited to the time the offender is participating in these activities. The rest of the time is spent in the institution. Often program participants may be housed together in a particular wing of the institution. Prior to final release, an offender may be transferred to a separate prerelease center.

These programs allow the offender to reestablish contact with the outside world. Upon returning to the institution, the offender can discuss with staff members any problems encountered while outside. Participating in such programs appears to have a beneficial effect upon performance on release.

Parole is the most common form of release from prison. Parole is a conditional form of release. The offender is released from the institution ". . . after he has served a portion of his sentence, under the custody of the state and under conditions that permit his reincarceration in the event of misbehavior." [31]

The decision to grant parole is an administrative decision made by a parole board. Generally an offender has a right to be considered for parole, but no actual right to parole. The time at which an offender must first be considered for parole will be dictated by the length and nature of the sentence imposed.

The criteria for granting parole are often vague. Traditionally, the burden of proof has been on the offender to make his or her case for parole. Research has indicated that the factor which most influences a parole board member's decision is that person's assessment of the likelihood of the offender committing a serious crime if released. Parole prediction tables have been devised to help with this assessment.

Once released on parole, the offender is supervised by a parole officer. The parole officer, who often carries a mixed case load of probationers and parolees, has a dual function to perform. On the one hand, the parole officer helps an offender attempt to reintegrate into society. On the other hand, the parole officer acts as a surveillance agent, watching for any offenses the parolee may commit and taking appropriate action should the parolee break the law or violate one of the conditions of parole.

Violation of the conditions of parole may lead to an offender's recommitment to an institution. Parole revocation is an administrative function handled by an administrative agency, the parole board. The Supreme Court decision in *Morrissey* v. *Brewer* [32] established a two-stage process for revocation, which involves an initial informal inquiry, much like a preliminary hearing, and a second formal revocation hearing. Should the parole be revoked, the parolee may be recommitted to a correctional institution to serve the rest of the sentence there.

Some parolees need a structured living environment to help them cope with the problems of everyday life. Placement in a halfway house can provide such an environment. Under the guidance of the staff, the offender may gradually readjust to life in the free world.

Measuring the success of penal sanctions and correctional programs is a tricky business. As yet no particular type of approach can be shown to be clearly superior to any other. Recidivism studies have been fraught with methodological problems. The cost-benefit approach has suggested that in general noninstitutional forms of penal sanctions should be preferred to institutional sanctions. The sentencing rationales of retribution, deterrence, and incapacitation may, however, suggest otherwise.

SUGGESTED ACTIVITIES

- Find out about the parole board in your state. How many members does it have? How are they appointed? What qualifications do they have?
- Find out about the parole process in your jurisdiction. Does the offender appear before the entire parole board? How does the parole board decide whether or not to grant parole? How is the offender informed of the board's decision? Are reasons given?
- Interview a parole officer. Find out whether this person is also a probation officer. For what proportion of his or her parolees does this officer request revocation? In what types of situations does this officer request revocation? In what percentage of cases is parole revoked?
- What programs are there in your state to prepare prisoners for their release? What proportion of offenders participate in each type of program?
- Does your state have any halfway houses to which offenders may be sent on their release from prison? If it does, locate one such program. Find out how program participants are chosen and how long they remain in the halfway house. What is it like to live there? Does program participation help with the process of reintegration?

REVIEW

- **A.** What is reintegration?
- **B.** What types of programs attempt to facilitate the offender's future reintegration while still in a custodial institution?
- **C.** What types of programs aid in an offender's reintegration after release?
- **D.** Compare and contrast probation and parole.
- **E.** Describe and criticize some of the measures used to evaluate the effectiveness of the different penal sanctions.
- **F.** Multiple Choice. Select the best answer.

1. A conjugal visit involves
    a. a visit between an inmate and spouse in total privacy
    b. a visit between an inmate and spouse with only a guard present
    c. a visit where an inmate meets with several family members at once
    d. a visit where several inmates meet with a visitor in privacy
2. Furloughs are granted to enable prisoners to
    a. attend funerals
    b. look for jobs
    c. be with their families
    d. all of these
3. In a work release program, the offender generally
    a. works in one wing of the institution but sleeps in another wing
    b. works and sleeps outside the institution
    c. works and sleeps in the same wing of the institution
    d. works outside the institution but sleeps inside the institution
4. Release from a correctional institution after having served a portion of the sentence, under continued supervision and under conditions allowing for reincarceration in case of misbehavior, is called
    a. probation
    b. parole
    c. furlough
    d. all of these
5. Most offenders have a right to
    a. be considered for parole
    b. be granted parole
    c. be informed of the reasons for denial
    d. all of these
6. The authority that decides whether or not an offender is granted parole is usually
    a. the prison warden
    b. a judge
    c. the parole board
    d. the correctional staff
7. The most important factor influencing the paroling authority's decision of whether or not to grant parole has been found to be
    a. the type of crime the offender committed
    b. whether the authority believes the offender will commit a serious crime
    c. the offender's behavior in prison
    d. the offender's family and community ties
8. Which of the following has not been cited as a reason to abolish parole?
    a. unfairness of parole granting procedures
    b. inmate unrest because of uncertainty of release date
    c. general feeling that inmates are being incarcerated too long
    d. all of these have been cited as reasons
9. Most criminologists agree that recidivism can be defined as
    a. rearrest for a similar offense within four years
    b. conviction of a subsequent offense within four years
    c. incarceration for a subsequent offense within four years
    d. none of these
10. It is generally agreed that
    a. institutional penal measures produce lower recidivism rates than noninstitutional measures

b. institutional penal measures are less expensive to administer than noninstitutional measures

c. both of these

d. neither of these

REFERENCES

1. The President's Commission on Law Enforcement and Administration of Justice, *Task Force Report: Corrections* (Washington, D.C.: U.S. Government Printing Office, 1967), 7.

2. Norman Holt, "Temporary Prison Release," *Crime and Delinquency*, 17 (1971), 429. In this research study only two of the 198 furloughees surveyed failed to return.

3. See, for example, Alvin Rudoff and T. C. Esselstyn, "Evaluating Work Furlough: A Followup," *Federal Probation*, 37 (June 1973), 48–53; Daniel Leclair, "Home Furlough Effects on Rates of Recidivism," *Criminal Justice and Behavior*, 5 (1978), 249–258. But see also, Gordon Waldo and Theodore Chiricos, "Work Release and Recidivism: An Empirical Evaluation of a Social Policy," *Evaluation Quarterly*, 1 (1977), 87–108.

4. The President's Commission on Law Enforcement and Administration of Justice, *op cit.*, 57.

5. U.S. Department of Justice, *Probation and Parole 1984* (Washington, D.C.: Author, 1986), 3–4. Generally about 75 percent of prison releases are releases on parole [U.S. Department of Justice, *Parole in the United States, 1980 and 1981* (Washington, D.C.: Author, 1985), 3].

6. U.S. Department of Justice, *The Attorney General's Survey of Release Procedures*, Vol. 4 (Washington, D.C.: U.S. Government Printing Office, 1939), 4.

7. For an overview of state parole eligibility provisions, see: Edward J. Brown, Timothy J. Flanagan, and Maureen McLeod (eds.) *Sourcebook of Criminal Justice Statistics–1983* (Washington, D.C.: U.S. Government Printing Office, 1984), 164–170.

8. For a more detailed discussion of parole systems, see: Vincent O'Leary and Kathleen J. Hanrahan, *Parole Systems in the United States: A Detailed Discussion of their Structure and Procedures*, 3rd ed. (Hackensack, N.J.: National Council on Crime and Delinquency, 1977).

9. Howard Abadinsky, *Probation and Parole: Theory and Practice*, 2nd ed. (Englewood Cliffs, N.J.: Prentice-Hall, 1982), 177.

10. National Advisory Commission on Criminal Justice Standards and Goals, *Corrections* (Washington, D.C.: U.S. Government Printing Office, 1973), 422.

11. Don M. Gottfredson, Peter B. Hoffman, Maurice H. Sigler, and Leslie T. Wilkins, "Making Paroling Policy Explicit," *Crime and Delinquency*, 21 (1975), 34–44.

12. U.S. Department of Justice, *Parole in the United States, 1980 and 1981* (Washington, D.C.: Author, 1985).

13. U.S. Department of Justice, *Parole in the United States, 1979* (Washington, D.C.: U.S. Government Printing Office, 1980), 10.

14. 408 U.S. 471 (1972).

15. *Ibid.*, 489.

16. 411 U.S. 778 (1973).

17. *Ibid.*, 790.

18. See, for example, Ramon R. Priestino and Harry E. Allen, *Parole Officer Aide Program in Ohio—An Exemplary Project* (Columbus, Ohio: Ohio State University, 1975).

19. U.S. Department of Justice, *Dictionary of Criminal Justice Data Terminology* (Washington, D.C.: U.S. Government Printing Office, 1976), 49.

20. Daniel Ford and Annesley Schmidt, "Electronically Monitored Home Confinement," *NIJ Reports*, 194 (November 1985), 2–6.

21. For a more detailed discussion of halfway houses, see, for example, Edward Latessa and Harry E. Allen, "Halfway Houses and Parole: A National Assessment," *Journal of Criminal Justice*, 10 (1982), 153–163.

22. Richard P. Seiter, Eric W. Carlson, Helen H. Bowman, James J. Granfield, and Nancy J. Beran, *Halfway Houses* (Washington, D.C.: U.S. Government Printing Office, 1977), 4.

23. John F. Wallerstedt, *Returning to Prison* (Washington, D.C.: U.S. Department of Justice, 1984).

24. *Ibid.*, 2.
25. U.S. Department of Justice, *Probation and Parole 1984* (Washington, D.C.: Author, 1986), 3–4.
26. Robert Martinson, ''What Works?—Questions and Answers about Prison Reform,'' *Public Interest*, 35 (1974), 25.
27. *Ibid.*, 49.
28. Federal Bureau of Investigation, *Uniform Crime Reports, 1975* (Washington, D.C.: U.S. Government Printing Office, 1976), 42.
29. *Ibid.*, 44.
30. National Council on Crime and Delinquency, *op. cit.*, 8–9.
31. U.S. Department of Justice, the Attorney General's Survey, *op. cit.*, 4.
32. 408 U.S. 471 (1972).

37

Controlling Crime: Outlook for the Future

OBJECTIVES

After studying this chapter, the student should be able to:

- Describe the role of social programs in reducing criminal activity.
- Justify decriminalization as an approach to crime control.
- Discuss the police role in crime prevention.
- Describe the function and purpose of private security arrangements.
- List environmental controls which may reduce criminal activity.
- Outline the types of measures individuals and businesses can take to prevent criminal victimization.
- Describe the use of mechanisms other than the criminal justice system for solving the underlying problems that give rise to criminal activity.

It is clear from our previous discussions that many offenders are not rehabilitated through the correctional process. To cope with the fact that a small number of offenders commit a large percentage of the crimes, career criminal and selective incapacitation programs have been instituted.[1] However, even if these programs were totally successful, the crime problem would not disappear because this is a reactive approach that deals with offenders only after crimes have been committed. What are also needed are proactive approaches that will prevent crimes from being committed in the first place. In this chapter, we will consider both proactive and reactive approaches to controlling crime.

Two proactive approaches to be examined are the institution of social programs to alleviate the social conditions that breed crime, and decriminalization. While the establishment of social programs constitutes an indirect approach, perhaps no approach could be more direct than decriminalization, which makes what was previously illegal no longer illegal. The other proactive approaches to be considered focus on reducing the opportunity to commit crime. The reactive approaches highlight dealing with the underlying problems that give rise to criminal activity, and using processes other than the criminal justice system to resolve those problems.

SOCIAL PROGRAMS

As has already been noted, many theories of crime focus on the inequality among people as an explanation for the greater involvement of the underprivileged in criminal activity. Whether the theory highlights differences in home environment, access to legitimate opportunities, or the ability to perform well according to the standards of the dominant culture, a seemingly obvious solution to the problem of crime control presents itself: improve the lot of the underprivileged. In terms of action, this suggests social programs aimed at improving housing and other living conditions, reducing unemployment and securing better working conditions, and providing more and better educational and vocational training programs.

The assumption has been made that by improving these conditions the amount of crime and delinquency will be reduced. Such an assumption is, however, largely unproven. It has not been shown that improving educational and employment opportunities and providing better living conditions lessen involvement in criminal activity. Easier, quicker, and more satisfying access to wealth may still be provided by illegitimate means. In addition, the concept of relative deprivation must be taken into account. A person earning $10,000 a year may be objectively worse off than a person earning $20,000 a year. The latter, however, may feel subjectively worse off. It depends against whom one compares oneself. If an employee in a store feels deprived of income in relation to what the owners are earning, he or she may decide to appropriate some of the store's money or goods.

DECRIMINALIZATION

The effects of social programs on crime rates are unclear. The results of decriminalization, on the other hand, are beyond dispute; decriminalization means the lifting of legal prohibitions on acts that were formerly illegal. Through the repeal of legislative provisions, acts that were once crimes are crimes no more. As Morris and Hawkins state on the first page of their book, *The Honest Politician's Guide to Crime Control*:

> The first principle of our cure for crime is this: we must strip off the moralistic excrescences on our criminal justice system so that it may concentrate on the essential. The

prime function of the criminal law is to protect our persons and our property; these purposes are now engulfed in a mass of other distracting, inefficiently performed, legislative duties.[2]

Among the acts Morris and Hawkins would decriminalize are public drunkenness; sexual activities between consenting adults in private; the acquisition, purchase, possession, and use of any drugs; and gambling.[3]

What these crimes have in common is that they have all been considered to be victimless crimes. They do not involve involuntary conduct on the part of anyone. No one allegedly is harmed, except perhaps for the participants. The enforcement of the laws, however, requires great expenditure of the resources of the criminal justice system against the wishes of many people and with very limited success. Often it is the underprivileged who bear the brunt of these laws. The lower-class drunk is more likely than is the middle-class drunk to be intoxicated in public and to be subjected to criminal action for this offense. The well-to-do cocaine user is less likely to be arrested and prosecuted than is the street heroin user. The friendly poker game among respectable citizens is far less likely to be subject to police action than is the game that takes place in the ghetto.

Whether these laws were specifically aimed at the underprivileged or are enforced against them in a discriminatory manner, or both, is open to question. Decriminalization would, however, certainly reduce the burden placed on the underprivileged as well as lessen the number of types of activities that come within the purview of the criminal code.

THE POLICE ROLE IN CRIME PREVENTION

The police play a varied role in crime control. They are expected to "deny the criminal the opportunity to commit crime."[4] They have the responsibility for detecting crime and apprehending law violators. They are to preserve the peace and enforce the law in our communities.

There are a number of ways in which the police seek to make it harder for criminals to commit crime. They work with citizens to make them and their property less vulnerable to attack. They try to help the youth steer away from the path of crime. Through the patrol function they try both to deter and to apprehend law violators.

To some people, the answer to the crime problem lies in more police. The available evidence does not suggest, however, that increasing the number of police has any dramatic effect on the crime situation. As previously seen, many factors account for the commission of crime. Having a police officer at one's elbow may certainly act as a deterrent. The police cannot, however, be everywhere at once. At present the police respond to crimes that are reported to them far more frequently than they discover crimes in progress. One research study of police activity in high crime areas of three cities revealed that 87 percent of all patrol mobilizations were citizen initiated.[5]

On the national level it has been noted that, after allowing for population growth, there was a 49 percent increase in per capita police employment from 1960 to 1974. However, during the same time period, the crime rates increased by 157 percent.[6] Some local projects have noted an association between increasing the size of the police patrol force and decreasing crime rates.[7] Others, such as the Kansas City Preventive Patrol Experiment, have not.[8] In a study of crime on New York subways, researchers found that a substantial increase in police patrols in the subways resulted in an initial decrease in serious subway crime. However, after a period of a year or so the crime rate began to rise rapidly and far outstripped the earlier rate. If this result is examined more closely, it may be noted that crime during the night hours, when the additional officers worked, had decreased. Crime during the day, however, after an initial decrease, had increased rather steadily.[9] Two points need to be drawn from the project. First, the concept of crime displacement can be observed in operation. It is possible that increased surveillance during the night hours eventually resulted in increased criminal activity during the day hours. Crime had perhaps not been prevented so much as displaced to another time. For a short period of time, too, it appears that crime was also geographically displaced, with some would-be subway robbers resorting to robbing buses. Second, the cost of each felony deterred at night was calculated to be very high, about $35,000 per felony.[10] If, in fact, increasing the size of our police force does bring about added protection, it is necessary to ask ourselves what price we are willing to pay for that added protection.

Whatever our feelings about the desirability of increasing the size of our present police forces, one way to provide better protection would be to deploy the officers more effectively. Much research is currently being carried out on strategies designed to promote more effective utilization of police personnel. Allocating more officers to the high-crime areas and in the high-crime time periods, prioritizing calls received, and having some routine matters handled by telephone rather than in person, are just a few of the techniques that have been developed to help the police function more effectively.

PRIVATE SECURITY

Demanding more and better protection from public law enforcement agencies has been one approach to the problem of crime control. Another approach has been for businesses, organizations, and even private individuals to employ private security personnel. These private security personnel, unlike public law enforcement officers, owe their duty of service to the specific individuals who employ them and not to the public in general. They are hired to protect "private interests, and their major functions are the prevention and detection of crime on private property and the gathering of information for private purposes."[11] Guards, patrol officers, investigators, and detectives are all employed on a regular basis in the private sector.

There is considerable evidence that certain segments of society are relying heavily on privately employed personnel for added protection and security. The growth of private security in the last two decades has been phenomenal. A 1982 survey indicates that private security personnel now outnumber public law enforcement personnel by nearly two to one.[12] Concern has been raised that there is insufficient screening, training, and supervision of these privately employed personnel. Upgrading of present practice and procedure has been recommended. Despite these concerns, there is little doubt that private security forces help lessen the fear of criminal victimization. At least for those who employ private security personnel, the risk of criminal victimization would appear to be reduced.

SECURITY MEASURES

Thus far this chapter has looked at reducing criminal activity through increasing the numbers of public and private law enforcement personnel. Another approach is to make the targets of criminal victimization less vulnerable. This may be accomplished in a number of different ways. First, the physical targets of criminal activity can be made more secure from criminal attack. Second, the living environment can be structured so as to inhibit the commission of crime. Third, individuals can take additional measures to render themselves and their property less susceptible to criminal victimization.

Target-Hardening

A common approach to the problem of criminal victimization has been to make the targets of criminal attack more secure. This is the process known as target-hardening. Installing strong locks on doors and windows, fitting special alarms in automobiles, limiting the direct contact between bank tellers and customers are all examples of target-hardening. The objective is to make it harder for the potential criminal to carry out a crime. The hope is either to deter the criminal from selecting the particular target; or if the criminal is not deterred, to increase the likelihood of detection and apprehension resulting from the added difficulty attached to the criminal's choice of target. Thus suppose Higgins has installed an alarm on his car. Tom and Mike are looking for a car to take for a joyride. If they notice the alarm on Higgins' car, they may decide not to take it. If they try to take it, the sound of the alarm going off, or the added time it takes to break into the car, may lead to their being apprehended.

Environmental Controls

Target-hardening has been felt by some people to be a reactive approach to crime control that increases the level of fear of crime and results in individuals attempting to build their own fortresses. A more proactive community-planned approach is to structure the environment so as to inhibit the commission of crime. The concept of environmental security has been used to describe this approach. Environmental security has been stated to be "an urban planning and design process which integrates crime prevention with neighborhood design and urban development."[13] Its underlying assumption is that our urban environments can be designed or redesigned to reduce the opportunities for crime to occur—and at the same time the fear of crime—without resorting to the building of fortresses and the resulting deterioration in the quality of urban life.[14]

This approach is in many ways both refreshing and encouraging. It suggests building complexes that encourage greater use of public places and greater interaction among the inhabitants of an area. Research studies have long suggested that improved street lighting may help reduce criminal activity in a given area. The argument is that it deters potential offenders, increases the likelihood of detection and apprehension, and encourages nighttime use of the streets, which is itself an important deterrent to crime.[15] Oscar Newman promotes the concept of defensible space, a term used to describe "a residential environment whose physical characteristics—building layout and site plan— allow inhabitants themselves to become the key agents in ensuring their own safety."[16] Among the architectural guidelines given are making public and semipublic areas such as front entrances, lobbies, stairways, and halls highly visible, and creating small subdivisions in large units so that the members of those subdivisions can act together to assume responsibility for, and maintain control over, the area. As Newman states, when architects plan with environmental security in mind, they

> can create a clear understanding of the function of a space, who its users are and ought to be. This, in turn, can lead residents of all income levels to adopt extremely potent territorial attitudes and policing measures, which act as strong deterrents to potential criminals.[17]

Individual Action

A number of protective measures that both individuals and businesses can take to reduce the risk of criminal victimization have been examined in this chapter. Target-hardening and hiring private security personnel are examples of such measures. In addition, the risk of victimization can be reduced by taking simple precautions in carrying out one's daily activities. Not walking alone at night in a deserted or unsafe area, not allowing strangers into one's home without asking first for identification, driving with the car doors locked, and not parking in deserted areas are all simple protective measures that may help to keep a person safe from attack. Engraving property with personal identification marks may make it less likely to be stolen and more easily recoverable if stolen.

The aforementioned are some of the measures that people can take individually to reduce the risk of criminal victimization. Crime is not, however, just an individual's problem. It is one that faces the whole community. The earlier discussion of the use of environmental controls suggested a community approach to crime control. This community approach has been manifested in other ways, too.

Citizen patrols, block associations, and Neighborhood Watch Programs all require citizen participation in crime prevention. They show a desire on the part of the residents of a given area to assume responsibility for the peace and security of their neighborhood. They evidence a willingness on the part of the residents to work together toward obtaining that objective. Well administered and supervised, and properly coordinated with public law enforcement efforts, these programs can play an important role in the prevention and control of crime.

PROBLEM RESOLUTION

Reducing the opportunity for offenders to commit crime is an important approach to crime control. Given the great amount of crime that is committed by recidivists and the concerns that have been voiced about the ability of the criminal justice system to rehabilitate them, it would appear advisable to explore the use of mechanisms other than the criminal justice system for reducing social conflict and providing solutions for social problems. The following is a discussion of two types of problems, interpersonal disputes and drug abuse, that result in the commission of crime, and alternative solutions for these problems.

Citizen Dispute Settlement Procedures

Many cases that go before the lower criminal courts involve long-term disputes between parties who know each other. Often it is a matter of chance as to who is the complainant and who is the defendant. One problem is that the complainant is often unwilling to follow through with the court case. Another is that the criminal justice process stresses the need to prove the commission of a particular act by a particular individual on a particular day. It also focuses on personal responsibility and hence, blame for that act. This may not be a very helpful approach since the alleged criminal act may be "a symptom of an underlying dispute which cannot be resolved by an adjudication process culminating in a decision that one party is "guilty" and the other blameless." [18]

Less formal approaches to dealing with interpersonal problems have been suggested. Programs have been set up in a number of areas throughout the country. Some, like the Neighborhood Justice Centers established in Atlanta, Kansas City, and Los Angeles, deal with a mixture of civil and criminal matters. Others, like the Columbus, Ohio, Night Prosecutor's Program, focus on minor criminal cases. They all possess less formalized procedures than the court process and utilize third parties to promote settlements between the disputants who are allowed to air their own views.

Advantages of such Citizen Dispute Settlement Programs have been stated to include the rapid and fair dispensation of justice to citizens who become involved in minor criminal conduct; alleviating the burden on the criminal justice system by reducing the number of criminal cases which cause a backlog in the courts; easing community and interpersonal tensions by helping the parties involved arrive at an equitable solution to their problems without resorting to a criminal court case; and removing the stigma of having an arrest record resulting from a minor interpersonal dispute. [19]

Such programs are certainly not without their problems. Questions must be answered concerning the qualifications of third parties and their ability to help disputants find and follow through with solutions to their problems. In addition, the fear has been voiced that:

Support for flexible, informal and individualized disposition of cases without adequate procedures to safeguard the rights of the accused could prove the breeding ground for a "Kangaroo Court," amounting to State sanctioning of vigilantism.[20]

Despite these concerns, however, such programs may still have greater potential than the criminal justice system for helping individuals solve interpersonal disputes.

Treatment Alternatives to Street Crimes Project

Another social problem that the criminal justice system may be ill equipped to handle is drug abuse. Many drug users commit criminal offenses through the possession, use, buying, or selling of drugs. Many drug users commit criminal offenses to obtain the money they need to support their drug habits. Often drug users are prosecuted for and convicted of these offenses. The focus of the criminal sanction is on punishing the offender for his or her criminal act. Rehabilitation may also be a desired objective, but it is not often achieved. Many people have long felt that it would be better for drug abusers to receive treatment for their drug abuse problem rather than be processed through the criminal justice system.

In Section 6, the use of civil commitment proceedings to obtain treatment for addicts was discussed. Though in a few states such proceedings are tied in with the institution of criminal prosecution, in most states they are not. A program which works directly with the criminal justice system and seeks to take drug offenders out of the criminal justice system and refer them to treatment is the Treatment Alternatives to Street Crime (TASC) program.

TASC may be thought of as a program that attempts to intervene in the cycle of drug abuse and arrest. It seeks to identify criminal offenders with drug problems. By referring these individuals for treatment as part of their processing through the criminal justice system, the program attempts to deal directly with their underlying problem of drug abuse and by so doing lessen their future involvement in criminal activity.

The TASC program has been in operation since 1972. Currently it operates in over fifty areas throughout the United States. Some of its clients are referred to treatment early in the criminal justice process, prior to a decision being made on the criminal charge. If these offenders do not perform adequately in treatment, they may be pulled from treatment and continue to be processed through the criminal justice system. Other offenders are referred to TASC late in the criminal justice process. Judges may make it a condition of probation that an offender be admitted to TASC. Probation and parole officers may make direct referrals themselves.

A striking feature of the TASC program is the number of offenders who are receiving treatment for the first time for their drug problems. A 1975 report noted that about 55 percent of TASC clients were receiving treatment for their drug problems for the first time.[21] Concerns have been raised about the effectiveness of drug treatment programs. Referring offenders to treatment and attempting to deal with their underlying problems does, however, appear to be a more positive approach than processing them through the criminal justice system. Moreover, it has been suggested that TASC does save the criminal justice system a great deal of money and does enhance an offender's prospects for rehabilitation.[22]

SUMMARY

In this chapter we have examined some of the measures that can be taken in the struggle to control crime. A simple and direct method of reducing the amount of crime is decriminalization. Another proactive, but indirect, approach is to establish social programs to alleviate the social conditions that breed crime. Other proactive approaches considered focus on reducing the opportunity to commit crime.

There are a number of different ways one may reduce the opportunity to commit crime. Increasing the number of public law enforcement officers, hiring private security personnel, target-hardening, implementing environmental controls, and taking additional individual and collective protective measures are all approaches that have been used to achieve this objective. Some of these approaches, such as target-hardening and hiring private security personnel, essentially involve people working individually to reduce their own likelihood of victimization. Other approaches, such as the implementation of environmental controls and Neighborhood Watch programs, involve far more of a community response. In the battle against crime, the collective approach perhaps holds the greater promise for establishing a healthy, well-functioning society.

Also directly related to this objective are crime control measures that seek to deal with the underlying problems that gave rise to the criminal activity. Two different types of programs were examined: one aimed at solving interpersonal disputes, the other aimed at dealing with the offender whose problems are largely attributable to involvement in drug abuse. In these types of cases, mechanisms other than the criminal justice system may be better suited for solving the underlying problems that these offenders have.

In conclusion, crime is a complex problem. Its roots go deep into the very essence of collective social life. The criminal justice system is just one of many social forces that affect behavior. Acting alone, it is incapable of solving the crime-producing problems that permeate society. Poverty, legal inequality, racial injustice, and a host of other wrongs must be remedied if a well-ordered and tranquil society is to be established. However, this society must not become one in which individual rights are sacrificed in the name of law and order.

SUGGESTED ACTIVITIES

- Find three social service programs in operation in your area. Find out how they are funded, toward whom they are geared, and what they seek to accomplish. How do they measure success? What effect, if any, do you think they have had on crime?
- Has there been any attempt to decriminalize any drugs, gambling, or other victimless crimes in your state? What are the penalties in your state for conviction of social gambling?
- Make up a short questionnaire investigating the issue of whether gambling, possession

of marijuana, or some other victimless crime should be subject to criminal action. Conduct a survey of your friends and relatives to see how they feel about this.

● Arrange for an interview, if possible, with an employee of a private security force. Find out what background qualifications were needed in order to get the job, what training has been received, and what the duties entail. Does the person feel properly qualified for the job? Do you think he or she is?

● Arrange for an interview, if possible, with a member of a firm that hires private security personnel. Find out why the firm finds it necessary to purchase extra protection and whether the person you are interviewing personally agrees with that decision.

● Find out if your local police have a unit or an officer who specializes in crime prevention. If so, try to arrange an interview and find out what crime prevention programs the police are conducting.

● Make a list of five ways you could improve your own personal safety from criminal victimization.

● Locate a community in your area that advertises itself as a crime-conscious community. If possible, interview a resident and find out what collective measures they have taken. Does the person believe that these measures have reduced crime in the neighborhood?

● Try to locate an agency in your area which serves as an alternative to the criminal justice system in trying to solve problems that lead to crime. Describe how it operates and cooperates with the criminal justice system.

REVIEW

A. What role do social programs play in the attempt to control criminal activity?

B. What is decriminalization? How would it help to reduce crime and lessen discrimination against the poor?

C. Compare and contrast the role of the police and private security in crime prevention.

D. Define target-hardening and give an example of it.

E. Describe what is meant by environmental security.

F. Describe individual and group action that can be taken to prevent crime.

G. How can agencies outside the criminal justice system help control crime? Give an example of an agency in such a situation.

H. Multiple Choice. Select the best answer.

1. Which of the following acts would be a likely target for decriminalization?
   a. driving while intoxicated
   b. trespassing
   c. gambling
   d. all of these

2. Installing an alarm on an automobile is an example of
   a. environmental security
   b. target-hardening
   c. providing defensible space
   d. all of these

3. Increasing the number of patrol officers in the New York City subway resulted in
   a. an initial decrease in total serious subway crime
   b. an initial increase in total serious subway crime
   c. a long-term decrease in total serious subway crime
   d. an initial increase followed by a long-term decrease in total serious subway crime

4. Which of the following may be considered a community approach to crime control?
    a. target-hardening
    b. hiring private security personnel
    c. Neighborhood Watch programs
    d. all of these

5. The police role in crime prevention includes
    a. patrolling the streets
    b. helping citizens secure their homes
    c. working with youth
    d. all of these

6. Private security personnel
    a. are rarely used in the United States
    b. unlike public law enforcement officers owe their duty of service to the specific individuals who employ them
    c. are subsidized by the government
    d. none of these

7. Which of the following promotes environmental security?
    a. concealing public areas from public view
    b. decreasing street lighting
    c. creating small subdivisions in large residential units
    d. none of these

8. The solving of long-term interpersonal disputes may be best achieved by a process that
    a. does not allow the parties to the dispute to air their views
    b. attaches personal responsibility for acts
    c. allows the disputants to come to a mutually agreeable settlement
    d. all of these

9. A disadvantage of the Citizen Dispute Settlement Programs has been alleged to be
    a. the criminal record that the defendant in one of these cases receives
    b. the burden placed on the criminal justice system
    c. the lack of enforcement procedures for decisions
    d. all of these

10. TASC may be considered to be essentially
    a. a criminal justice agency
    b. a treatment agency
    c. an agency that provides a link between the criminal justice and treatment systems
    d. none of these

REFERENCES

1. See, for example, Peter W. Greenwood, *Selective Incapacitation* (Santa Monica, Calif.: Rand Corp., 1982).
2. Norval Morris and Gordon Hawkins, *The Honest Politician's Guide to Crime Control* (Chicago: University of Chicago Press, 1970), 1.
3. *Ibid.*, 3.
4. Harry Caldwell, *Basic Law Enforcement* (Pacific Palisades, Calif.: Goodyear, 1972), 33.
5. Albert J. Reiss, Jr., *The Police and the Public* (New Haven, Conn.: Yale University Press, 1971), 11. A later study indicates that the percentage of crimes discovered by the police may, in fact, be lower. An examination of 1983 National Crime Survey data revealed that only 3% of all personal and 2% of all household crimes known to the police were discovered by the police themselves. U.S. Department of Justice, *Reporting Crimes to the Police* (Washington, D.C.: U.S. Government Printing Office, 1985), 5.
6. U.S. Department of Justice, *The National Manpower Survey of the Criminal Justice System—Law Enforcement* (Washington, D.C.: U.S. Government Printing Office, 1978), 1.

7. See, for example, the 1954 and 1966 New York City Police Department Studies described in James Q. Wilson, *Thinking About Crime* (New York: Basic Books, 1975), 82–85.

8. George L. Kelling, Tony Pate, Duane Dieckman, and Charles E. Brown, *The Kansas City Preventive Patrol Experiment: A Summary Report* and *A Technical Report* (Washington, D.C.: Police Foundation, 1974).

9. Jan M. Chaiken, Michael W. Lawless, and Keith A. Stevenson, *The Impact of Police Activity on Crime: Robberies in the New York City Subway System* (New York: Rand Institute, 1974).

10. *Ibid.*, 22.

11. James S. Kakalik and Sorrel Wildhorn, *Private Police in the United States: Findings and Recommendations* (Santa Monica, Calif.: The Rand Corp., 1971), 18.

12. William C. Cunningham and Todd H. Taylor, *The Growing Role of Private Security* (Washington, D.C.: Department of Justice, 1984), 3.

13. Richard A. Gardiner, *Design for Safe Neighborhoods* (Washington, D.C.: U.S. Government Printing Office, 1978), 1.

14. *Ibid.*

15. National Advisory Commission on Criminal Justice Standards and Goals, *A National Strategy to Reduce Crime* (Washington, D.C.: U.S. Government Printing Office, 1973), 64.

16. Oscar Newman, *Design Guidelines for Creating Defensible Space* (Washington, D.C.: U.S. Government Printing Office, 1975), 4.

17. Oscar Newman, *Defensible Space* (New York: Macmillan, 1972), 4.

18. David E. Aaronson, Bert H. Hoff, Peter Jaszi, Nicholas N. Kittrie, and David Saari, *The New Justice: Alternatives to Conventional Criminal Adjudication* (Washington, D.C.: U.S. Government Printing Office, 1977), 34.

19. U.S. Department of Justice, *Citizen Dispute Settlement: The Night Prosecutor Program of Columbus, Ohio* (Washington, D.C.: U.S. Government Printing Office, 1974), 3–5.

20. Aaronson, et al., *op. cit.*, 36.

21. The Lazar Institute, *Treatment Alternatives to Street Crime: An Evaluative Framework and State of the Art Review* (Washington, D.C.: Author, 1975), 9.

22. System Sciences Inc., *Final Report: Evaluation of the Treatment Alternatives to Street Crime Program, Phase II* (Bethesda, Md.: Author, 1978).

Index